How it's really done

D0142224

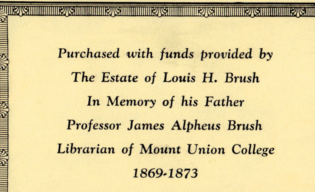

Chemistry Decoded

Leonard W. Fine

State of Connecticut
Housatonic Community College

Chemistry Decoded

New York
Oxford University Press
London 1976 Toronto

To Diane

We see the many faces of chemistry about us all the time. Yet we are often deceived by what we see. A closer look, and new perceptions clear up older deceptions for us. And having learned more, the world of our experience now takes on newer faces. We perceive, edging closer toward true knowledge; yet absolute truth seems to continually recede away from our grasp. Science, beginning in ernest with Galileo and Newton, took on newer dimensions with Einstein. At each level of understanding our picture of the real world expanded and deepened. Newton's laws of motion, unfolding nature's mysteries, left the way open for 200 years of unparalleled development of our understanding; Einstein's theory of relativity, superceding all that, completely restructured 200 years of scientific thought in 50, opening new ways before us.

The study of chemistry is one beginning to knowledge. There is no end . . . only more new beginnings as we continually try our hand at unlocking old mysteries, uncovering new mysteries. The first chapters of **Chemistry Decoded** are devoted to atoms, matter and energy in the universe of our experience, and the techniques, computations, and language of science. It is a mistake to assume that at the lower level of rigor demanded by the non-science student, one need only "talk it through" logically, that number and symbolic statements of that logic ought to be off-limits, or that the technique of doing science be trivial. Also, one should not be afraid to discuss simple concepts of physics and biology in a chemistry course. In any intelligent, reasoned presentation of chemistry, physics and biology are so much a part of the chemistry that detachment is unnatural and uncomfortable, leading to obvious discontinuities which must be smoothed by . . . "well, when you take physics . . . or in your biology course." If a student is to get a natural view of chemistry as science, the student needs to be shown how chemistry fits into the whole framework of human knowledge.

Gases, liquids, solids, and solutions are discussed in subsequent chapters. Water is a topic. The concepts of equilibrium, energy and electricity are discussed from the chemical point of view. Atomic and molecular structure and the nature of the chemical bond are presented. There is a section on the chemistry of the nucleus. Descriptions of the chemical environment, both organic and inorganic, follow in succeeding chapters. The end of course is not the end but hopefully a new beginning, and it is important to note the role of homo sapiens, thinking man . . . and sometimes unthinking man . . . in this scientifically revolutionized world of our experience. Throughout, the theme is *decode.* We perceive and are deceived, and we look again. The house of science is no temple either, and scientists certainly no priesthood. A conscious effort has been made to debunk some of the common mythology that continues to spawn real misconceptions in science.

Each chapter opens with a short series of statements or comments designed to stimulate, provoke, or otherwise subtlely lead the student into the lessons of the chapter . . . in a way which the student will find comfortable, perhaps even fun.

We call these opening statements *Perceptions and Deceptions.* Each chapter ends with a fair number of *Questions to Answer . . . Problems to Solve.* These questions and problems have been pitched at the proper level for these students. One learns subjects such as chemistry better by doing, in addition to reading and studying, and that can be a rewarding and enjoyable experience for the student as well. Doing or working problems and answering questions need not be the ultimate drudgery. It is as important for the nonscience student as for the chemistry majors to try their hand at solving problems. Graphs, tables, photographic materials, and we think some truly creative artwork, illustrate the discussions of the entire text in a meaningful and educational fashion.

It is a pleasure to acknowledge the help and assistance of all those who have made special contributions to the birth of this book. In addition to eight classes of my students, the principal reviewers were William Evans, Norman Juster, Francis Powell, Gus Vlassis, and Dawn Duly. The artistic talents of four special people visually translated many ideas into action with a purpose: my special thanks to Peter Loewer, Jean Loewer, Philip Burke, and the Wizard-maker, Martin Peach. And thanks to Sint Liam Taw for his special attention in setting the manuscript into type. My warm thanks to David Harpp: all those long discussions, stretching into the wee hours at St. Lambert. But most of all, I wish to thank the two women in my life. Nancy Marcus made a one-of-a-kind contribution to this book that no words can begin to adequately describe. And only my long-suffering wife Diane, to whom this book is sincerely dedicated, really knows just how much went into *decoding* chemistry. I thank them all . . . and Dan, Elizabeth, and Josh, too.

L. W. F.
Norwalk, Connecticut
August, 1975

Contents

Excerpt from a talk given by Richard Feynman in 1966, telling of some of his childhood influences. The talk appeared in print in The Physics Teacher, Volume 7, 1969, page 313.

Chemistry Decoded

. . . Mothers were very powerful in those days, as they are now, and they convinced the fathers that they had to take their own sons out for walks in the woods. So all fathers took all sons out for walks in the woods one Sunday afternoon. The next day, Monday, we were playing in the fields and this boy said to me, "See that bird standing on the wheat there? What's the name of it?" I said, "I haven't got the slightest idea." He said, "It's a brown-throated Thrush. Your father doesn't teach you much about science."

I smiled to myself, because my father had already taught me that that doesn't tell me anything about the bird. He taught me "See that bird? It's a brown-throated Thrush, but in Germany, it's called a Halzenflugel, and in Chinese they call it a Chung Ling, and even if you know all those names for it, you still know nothing about the bird. You only know something about people; what they call that bird."

. . . There is a difference between the name of a thing and what goes on.

William Blake's *Ancient of Days*, one of the most splendid and impressive works of the British painter-poet, is one late eighteenth-century view of man. Blake showed his ancient man compelled to live the restrained life of reason as opposed to the free life of imagination. The colossal figure holds the compass down onto the black emptiness below him, perhaps symbolizing the imposition of order on chaos. Blake's work was done at a time when modern science was beginning to take shape in earnest.

A Legacy of Genius

" . . . In his hand
He took the golden Compasses, prepar'd
In Gods Eternal Store, to circumscribe
This Universe, and all created things:
One foot he center'd and the other turn'd
Round through the vast profunditie obscure
And said, thus far extend, thus far thy bounds,
This be thy just Circumferences, O 'World."

Milton, *Paradise Lost,* Book VII

☐ Perceptions and Deceptions

1 The wise and honest scientist-teacher must ". . . pass on the accumulated wisdom and the wisdom that it may not be wisdom."

2 If we were to be allowed only one statement to pass on to the next generation, perhaps the fewest yet most informative collection of words would be the atomic hypothesis, that all things are made of atoms.

3 Science is an achievement, not a method of achieving.

4 "The man of science who cannot formulate an hypothesis is only an accountant of phenomena."

☐ First Words

How do you begin to study and understand a science based on more than two hundred years of highly sophisticated, rigorous, and rapidly expanding research, a science that is intertwined with physics and biology, astronomy and geology, medicine and psychology? In all likelihood, you do not intend to become a chemist. Perhaps all you want is a way to appreciate and take full advantage of today's science and technology. Where do you start?

This tremendous accumulation of knowledge is available and can be useful to you whether you plan to be a chemist or not. Much of our scientific knowledge is summarized in the form of statements called *laws.* Since we won't be able to get four years of scientific sensibility into 400 pages of printed matter, our illustrations and examples will have to be carefully selected. In fact, we are still in the process of uncovering some of the basic laws governing science. As one scientist recently put it, in science we are faced with an "expanding frontier of ignorance." The greater our knowledge, the more clearly we perceive the limits of our understanding.

In order to correctly state the laws and summaries that make up chemistry's defining principles, you will first have to be introduced to some of the less familiar ideas and shown a few new ways of viewing reality as well. Furthermore, you will need to become familiar with a new language made up of chemical symbols that allow us to "talk" chemistry. You'll also have to be shown how a very old language—mathematics—adds strength to our reasoning powers. Each example at best can only be a close approximation of the truth, and then only to the extent that our knowledge permits. Since we don't know all the laws to begin with, everything we do know can be no better than a good approximation. We learn, we correct, we learn anew. All the while, the laws of science are subject to the close and continuing scrutiny of experiment. The scientist's constant query is "How close to the truth are we?" Create a model, test it, then improve it, or if necessary, discard it and create a new model.

□ What Is Real?

Two hundred years ago a Frenchman named Lavoisier carefully conducted a number of experiments involving chemical transformations. He found that matter was never lost (or gained); the total mass of the products was *always* equal to the total mass of the reactants. Lavoisier created a first principle of chemistry called the **Law of Conservation of Matter.** The law stood firm for over a century, a cornerstone of science, until 1905, the year Albert Einstein made the striking prediction that mass *can* be converted into energy. Mass can be and is lost during chemical reactions in the form of energy. The mass lost for a given amount of energy is usually very small; nevertheless, a new and more comprehensive law was now needed. Chemists and physicists reformulated the old law to allow for the new experimental evidence. For ordinary people—that's just about all of us— doing ordinary things such as burning fuel to heat homes and driving automobiles, we can certainly use Lavoisier's law as it was stated in 1777 (Fig. 1-1). But for

Figure 1-1
Modern chemistry is deeply rooted in Lavoisier's work: his discoveries of the composition of air and water and his analysis of the combustion process helped to bury the "phlogiston theory" once and for all. The drawing of Lavoisier in his laboratory was done by Madame Lavoisier and includes the artist herself (right).

more fundamental considerations such as nuclear fission or the mass equivalent of the sun's radiant energy (1 million tons of mass per second radiating into space), it's quite another story. We must use the newer, closer-to-the-truth, more general form of this law which says that *both mass and energy are conserved.* The simpler truth, conservation of matter, has become a special case of mass-energy conservation.

What to do, what to teach? After all, in the year 2005 we might have another Einstein-like revelation as in 1905 and suddenly find we have to start all over again (Fig. 1-2). Should one's first exposure be the kind that shows the more correct but more complicated law, or should one first use slightly less honest lessons which do not require the more difficult ideas? The bigger thrill lies in the perception of the newer reality; but the older theory is easier to get at, easier to understand, and perhaps best opens the road to an understanding of these newer ideas. Many old theories, because of their overwhelming utility and relative simplicity, are happily retained within the basic scientific curriculum—and we do not think any less of them for their limitation. This predicament of pedagogic license and judgment presents itself time and time again. Sometimes we resolve it in favor of the new; sometimes the old comes first, paving the way. Either way, we intend to create a warm and fertile environment in which to view just how accurate any of these approximations of the "truth" seem to be. Perhaps most important of all, we will see how these laws allow the sciences to cohabit— physics and chemistry; biology and chemistry. It would be nice if we could first present the pieces separately and then weld them together into a complete, unified understanding of nature. We will attempt to move in that direction, but all we'll come away with is a progress report. It's not clear that there is *one* complete theory in which all else is a part.

Everything in this book has been based on some assumptions about you: first, you've brought along a certain curiosity about the scientific experience and consciousness of the external world; second, you've acquired a number of misconceptions and uncorrected fixations about science; third, you're aware of the energy crisis, the environmental crisis, and a crisis of confidence with respect to science; fourth, you have consciously or unconsciously gravitated to chemistry because of its broad sweep and interaction with the other two principal sciences, physics and biology. With an honest effort on your part in this course, you can expect to catch on to a great deal of what the science of chemistry is about. However hard or easy it is, our intention at all times has been to be reasonable, stimulating, exciting—and yes, perhaps even fun. Welcome to chemistry.

☐ Where Do We Begin?

You might say that modern science was sired by the time-honored study of natural philosophy, beginning in the classic sense with Aristotle in the 4th century B.C., and in the modern sense with Isaac Newton and the eighteenth

Figure 1-2
"What would the world look like if I rode on a beam of light?" At age 26, Albert Einstein had already published three major papers. The vital experiment confirming his theory of relativity required a total eclipse of the Sun in order to measure the bending of light in the vicinity of its gravitational field. The photo behind Einstein shows that eclipse, observed in 1919.

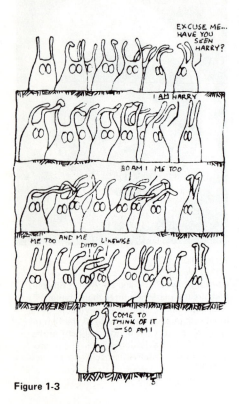

Figure 1-3

century's legacy of genius. While history is not our purpose there are, nevertheless, important threads that run through the fabric of human thought, providing continuity from past to present while offering strength and support for our view toward the future. Perhaps some familiarity with the origins and development of scientific thinking will help you to perceive the natural coherence that exists within the sciences. You will find that our initial description of the universe won't be at all unfamiliar to you. We begin with time and space, and particles called atoms and molecules that have characteristic properties. How many different atom particles are there? About 88 occur in nature, and their unique property is that they are *indivisible*; further, those of the same type are *indistinguishable* (Fig. 1-3). You can't tell one hydrogen atom from another; atomically speaking, old gold and new gold are the same—just gold atoms. Indivisibility has to do with the classical notion of atoms—a limit beyond which matter cannot be further divided. In fact, the Greek word *atomos* means "uncuttable." Besides hydrogen and gold, there are carbon, oxygen, nitrogen, sulfur, mercury, and uranium, to name just a few. What kinds of molecules are formed from chemical combinations of these atoms? Water and methane are small combinations; sugar and wax are larger combinations; nylon and DNA are immense combinations. We shall learn more about atoms and their combinations —molecules—as we progress through the course.

There is apparent stability in nature, yet there is obvious change. The behavior of water suggests apparent stability; the chemistry of uranium is indicative of nature's propensity for change. Consider particles in motion: the motion is perceptible in gases; imperceptible in solids. Heat is a direct result of motion, a random kind of internal behavior that can best be described by the same kinds of rules that govern games of chance—statistical methods and probabilities. With all this motion, how do particles ever stay together at all? When do the particles in a solid become so active that the solid is no longer a solid? What are the forces like that hold particles together or pull them apart? Where does the concept of energy enter into the picture? Why is water H_2O and not HO_2, or just simply HO? All this and more is chemistry. Let's get on with it.

□ Prelude to the Chemist's Atomic Theory

If there is one thing chemists really believe in with evangelical fervor, it is the existence of atoms. We know they exist, despite the fact that even the largest ones (uranium atoms, for example) are enormously tiny, submicroscopic particles of matter. We've known about atoms intuitively for a long time, perhaps 2500 years or longer. But the scientific facts which support their existence are of much more recent vintage. The evolution of the chemist's atomic theory began with Isaac Newton (1687); its most vital contributions emerged from John Dalton more than a century later (1803). That was followed by a flurry of activity leading to two major additions to Dalton's ideas, one by an Italian, Stanislo Cannizzaro (1860), the other by a Russian, Dimitri Mendeleyeff (1869).

General acceptance was not achieved until after 1908, the year one of the giants of modern chemistry, the German chemist, Wilhelm Ostwald, acknowledged the atomic ideal. (See Fig. 1-4.) That was not so long ago, although the Greeks had been talking about atoms some 2500 years earlier. As one famous nineteenth century chemist, Herman von Helmholtz, put it:

> *The originator of a new concept . . . finds, as a rule, that it is much more difficult to find out why other people do not understand him than it was to discover the new truths.*

Ironically, just about the time unanimity among chemists was achieved regarding the Daltonian concept of the atom at the beginning of the twentieth century, the whole idea was almost abandoned. Around 1911 the atom was shown to be *divisible* rather than indivisible, consisting of a positively charged nucleus surrounded by a negatively charged cloud of electrons. That immediately placed us in the midst of a paradox, since Dalton's ideas had really provided compelling support toward belief in "uncuttable" atoms. We know that atoms of a kind are identical. They are also extremely stable, managing to retain their identity no matter what changes are imposed on them. Yet now we suddenly perceive structure within the atom. Atoms can be taken apart. We find them to be composites of still smaller parts. The answer to the paradox goes right to the heart of the matter. Atoms are collections of mass units called **neutrons** and units of electric charge, a plus or positive kind, **protons,** and a minus or negative kind, **electrons.** But the Daltonian atom is still very much with us because of its usefulness. Although no longer *strictly* correct, Dalton's concept has proved to be a harmonious theme for the orchestration of atomic and molecular chemistry.

Theories come and go, although some stay a long time. Even Newton's greatest scientific discoveries were subject to modification by Einstein's theory of relativity and the quantum physics of the twentieth century. But what about the theory of atoms? Doesn't that seem to be a theory almost beyond reproach? It wasn't always, however, as we have noted; Wilhelm Ostwald and many other prominent scientists were not willing believers. Today, the only remaining infidels are a few cranks and mystics. Why so much confidence? Because we have increasingly been able to witness the doings of single atoms, more recently, direct images of single atoms, and under very favorable circumstances, actual single atoms, themselves. Centuries ago, the Roman poet Lucretius wrote about the grains of sand in his poem concerning the nature of things in the universe, *De Rerum Natura*. In that poem, we can find lines relating to the essence of the atomic theory as formulated by the Greeks—Thales, Leucippius, Democritus, and Epicurus—in the sixth, fifth, and fourth centuries B.C. In summary, we might take the atomic theory of Leucippius,

1 Atoms are minute and indivisible particles.

2 Atoms can be neither created not destroyed.

Figure 1-4
For more than a decade, a swirling controversy over the existence of atoms polarized the scientific community into two camps—those that believed in atoms, and those who did not. Ostwald did not until 1908.

Figure 1-5
William Blake's illustrations of the four elements of the Greeks: water, earth, air, and fire. The works were done in 1793.

3 Atoms come in definite sizes, shapes, and masses, but are all composed of the same few common substances.

4 Atoms collect together into aggregates by a variety of entanglements and attachments, and therein lies the source of nature's infinite variety.

5 The space between atoms is just that—space, or emptiness.

6 As the amount of interatomic emptiness increases, the density of a collection of atoms decreases.

7 Atoms are forever in motion.

Too much history? Well, perhaps, but the atomic theory is such a fascinating case study of how modern science has evolved, that taking this route offers a tremendous bonus. Here is one of the clearest illustrations of the use of systematic method and procedures for explaining natural phenomena. Furthermore, the atomic theory has turned out to be so important that if you could only pass one piece of scientific information to the succeeding generation, the atomic theory would be the correct choice.

The Greek View

The atomic theory has been with us since the Golden Age of Pericles, but at that time it was only a philosophical conceptualization. It wasn't until much later that phenomena were actually perceivable in terms of matter and motions. The atomic philosophy of the Greeks first began to move toward scientific theory status with Isaac Newton in the late seventeenth century. Where had the Greeks failed? The fundamental atomic question was unfortunately only an experiment in thought for the Greek philosophers. Imagine a gold ingot continually divided into smaller pieces. Does one ever arrive at the point where the division process cannot continue? Two diametrically opposed points of view developed. Leucippus and Democritus spoke for one view: matter was particulate, or granular—the grains of sand on the beach—and a limit is reached where the granular structure cannot be further divided. These ultimite, indivisible particles are atoms. The other view suggested that matter could be divided *ad infinitum* because matter was continuous; one could subdivide and subdivide matter forever, never coming to an end. The very popular and widely respected Aristotle held this view, and it was the view that most people accepted. For 2000 years this logical but incorrect atomic philosophy misled leading scientific thinkers. Eventually, a new kind of natural philosopher began to emerge, leaning toward an atomic theory that could explain the structure and composition of matter.

It was unfortunate that so many chose to follow Aristotle. The fundamental view of Epicurus that Lucretius had recorded in his poem really struck the correct sense of the matter:

> *. . . the nature of the universe consists then, in its essence, of two things; for there are atoms and there is the void.*

Unfortunately none of the proponents of the two antagonistic points of view relied on experiment. However, in defense of Greek philosophy, two things ought to be noted. There was little experimental tradition to offer much initiative in that direction, and probably not the needed analytical equipment, such as proper balances, anyway. Nevertheless, these Greek concepts and ideas—both right and wrong—were not merely idols of thought. The Greeks were careful observers of nature. If you think about even the most elementary of natural phenomena, for example, "matter cannot be completely destroyed," that seems quite contrary to actual experience. Fire consumes just about completely, or so it seems; so does death, after a while. The Greek atomists were perceptive indeed and not at all deceived by what were apparent annihilations of matter. These early scientists described nature to a degree that is mind-boggling when considered today. The atomic theory of Greek natural philosophy, on the basis of a handful of assumptions, successfully explained most natural phenomena known at that time in a most reasonable fashion. But there were no experiments; and nobody classified or systematized observations. Consequently the classical atomic theory was a sterile conceptualization; it did not take root. Still, Greek atomic theory was the first stage in the development of the modern theory of the atom. Stage two occurred in seventeenth-century England.

☐ 'Let Newton Be!'

In the awakening seventeenth century, the poem of Lucretius became a classic of scientific literature because of its impact on the scientists of the day. Certainly Robert Boyle and Isaac Newton, the two British experimental philosophers, read it. But here was no sterile atomic theory as had been the case 20 centuries earlier. This was the age of experimental science and scientific philosophies based on fact. The atomic theory was resuscitated, and many important people and events contributed to its development at this stage. The Italian, Torricelli, invented the mercury barometer and the technique for creating a vacuum. [Torricelli's vacuum will be a topic of considerable interest in Chap. 3.]

Robert Boyle succeeded in upsetting the Greek notion that all things were composed of combinations of only four elements, namely, air, earth, water, and fire (see Fig. 1-5). By applying the concepts of atomic theory to his experiments, Boyle was able to coherently distinguish between liquids and solids. Liquids could be viewed in terms of atoms in constant motion, but each in contact with the others. Solids could be understood in terms of the ceaseless vibrations of the atoms. He discovered the relationship between the pressure and the volume of a gas at constant temperature. That relationship is called Boyle's law. [A topic for Chap. 6.] Robert Boyle brought new subtleties to analytical chemistry. He noted the characteristic odor of ammonia and the thick white fumes produced by ammonia in contact with hydrochloric acid (muriatic acid). Precipitates, crystal forms, and color tests that were the antecedents of today's indicators were largely his contributions. He also made significant quantitative measurements.

SIR ISAAC NEWTON

Note Boyle's characterization of the element gold:

If you ask a man what gold is and if he cannot show you a piece of gold, and tell you this is gold, he will describe it to you as a body that is extremely ponderous (density), a very malleable and fusible yet fixed in the fire (thermal stability) and of yellowish color; and if you offer to put off to him a piece of brass for a piece of gold, he will presently refuse it and tell you, that though your brass be colored like it, it is not so heavy or so malleable, neither will it like gold resist the utmost brunt of the fire, or resist aqua fortis [nitric acid].

Robert Boyle had truly perceived a great deal of what modern chemistry is all about.

Isaac Newton's major contribution was perhaps this monumental statement that served ultimately to inspire John Dalton to his theory on atoms:

It seems probable to me that God in the beginning formed matter in solid, massy, hard, impenetrable, movable particles, of such sizes and figures, and with such other properties, and in such proportion to space as most conduced to the end for which he formed them; and that these primitive particles being solids, are incomparably harder than any porous bodies compounded of them; even so very hard as never to wear or break in pieces; no ordinary power being able to divide what God Himself made One, in the first creation.

While the particles continue entire they may compose bodies of one and the same nature and texture in all ages; but should they wear away or break in pieces, the nature of things depending on them would be changed. Water and earth, composed of old worn particles and fragments of particles, would not be of the same nature and texture now, with water and earth composed of entire particles in the beginning. And therefore that nature may be lasting, the changes of corporeal things are to be placed only in the various separations and new associations, and motions of these permanent particles, but where those particles are laid together, and only touch in a few points . . .

God is able to create particles of matter of several sizes and figures, and in several proportions to the space they occupy, and perhaps of different densities and forces. . . . At least I see nothing of contradiction in all this.

. . . that the particles of vapors, exhalations and air, do stand at a distance from one another.

. . . particles flying each other with forces that are reciprocally proportional to the distances of their centers, compose an elastic fluid, whose density is as the compression.

With his discovery of carbon dioxide, the Englishman, Joseph Black, recognized that gases were in fact unique chemical species. The experiment was simple.

Your science teacher has probably demonstrated it for you. When Black blew air into lime water producing a milky white precipitate, he was then identifying a chemical property of carbon dioxide. Black's discovery and identification of carbon dioxide was followed by the characterization of a number of other gases.

1 Hydrogen by Henry Cavendish in 1766.

2 Nitrogen, by Daniel Rutherford and Wilhelm Scheele in 1772.

3 Chlorine, by Wilhelm Scheele in 1774.

4 Oxygen by Joseph Priestley and Wilhelm Scheele in 1773-1774.

Of these, the discovery of oxygen was the most important for the progress of chemistry. To Priestley, oxygen was dephlogisticated air. To Lavoisier, a decade later, it was the gaseous element oxygen, and more importantly, the active agent for bringing about oxidations and combustions.

Phlogiston Falls

Since man first began cooking his food and keeping the wolf away from his cave, burning has been a perplexing phenomenon. Through the latter half of the seventeenth century and the better part of the eighteenth century, a deceptively rational theory for combustion [burning] known as the *Phlogiston Theory* had developed. Its origins were metallurgical (Fig. 1-6), and primarily the efforts of George Stahl. Its principal supposition was the existence of something called *phlogiston,* a form of matter presumed present in all combustible substances, the substance's ignitable quality or inflammability principle. Stahl's theory proved to be erroneous, but it had a curious sensibility about it and was accepted by most of the chemists of the day. It is notable today as one of the first chemical theories systematically developed from observation and experiment.

The modern view of **combustion,** the burning of a metal in the presence of oxygen, results in chemical combination, a metal oxide being formed. We can write a chemical equality or equation expressing that event as follows:

metal + oxygen = metal oxide

The metal has been consumed in an atmosphere of oxygen (at the appropriate temperature) and the atomic shuffle (oxidation) that took place produced the new chemical entity, a metal oxide. For Stahl, metals were not elemental substances. Instead, they were compound substances composed of: (1) a *"calx"* or ash formed when a metallic element was burned in air (oxidized) to a metal oxide; and (2) the inflammability principle, phlogiston. Now if you think that's an arbitrary and unjustifiable assumption, follow Stahl's argument. Upon ignition (combustion) the phlogiston is unshackled, freed from the metal; the ash that remains is the oxide. A chemical equation can be written as follows:

metal + combustion = calx + phlogiston

Figure 1-6
Thomas Wyck's seventeenth century (Dutch) depiction of the actual transformation of a base metal into gold. In this weird scene, the senior alchemist says an incantation while the terrified lab assistant kneels within the magic circle: two candles facing East-West, skull, bones, blood, bible. A block of metal is suspended from the ceiling, a skeleton blows a trumpet, lightening illuminates the laboratory, while the sun shines outside.

It is well-known today that the element carbon is an effective agent for freeing metal oxides of their oxygen content, leaving the metallic element behind while producing carbon dioxide. The atomic shuffle in this process is called **reduction**; in a sense it is the opposite process to oxidation. We can write a correct chemical statement for such a reaction as

metal oxide + carbon = metal + carbon dioxide

Now note how Stahl handled the explanation for the same experiment. He reasoned that carbon (charcoal) was a substance rich in phlogiston. If his calx (metal oxide) were heated in the presence of such a substance, phlogiston would be absorbed and the metal regenerated. Hence,

calx + phlogiston = metal
(from charcoal)

Stahl's problem, and the cross which chemical science had to bear for the better part of a century after him, was that metallic elements such as lead, tin, or mercury were regarded as compound substances, combinations of calx plus phlogiston. The metal was considered to be a more complex composition than the calx. Presumably the metallic element was more than its combustion product, the metal oxide.

What progress could be gleaned from such theory? Well, what progress indeed. There were two principle reasons why phlogiston finally fell: first was the rise of quantitative methods for studying chemistry, especially weighing, along with Newton's concept of mass as a means of measuring matter; second was Priestley's discovery of oxygen and Lavoisier's perception of its role in combustion. As a philosophical concept, the phlogiston theory so satisfactorily explained combustion that at least one major difficulty was at first simply brushed aside as a minor nuisance, then rationalized by introducing a concept bearing no support in fact whatsoever. Stahl's metal gained weight on burning; that's as it should be if a metal is combining with oxygen to form a metal oxide; that's *not* as it should be if phlogiston is being given up in forming the metal oxide, or calx. To explain this, the concept of "negative weight" was put forth by the phlogiston theorists. More nonsense!

Priestley's discovery of oxygen gas was drawn from an experiment in which the oxide of mercury was heated in a confined space, freeing the combined oxygen from the metal. Priestley, an ardent phlogistonist who never fully appreciated the significance of his experiment, referred to the trapped oxygen as "dephlogisticated" air (Fig. 1-7). He communicated his results to Lavoisier on a trip to Paris some weeks later. Lavoisier repeated the experiment, perceived the true sense of it, and proceeded to clear the air—in a manner of speaking.

Antoine Lavoisier has come to be known as the father of modern chemistry. His great contributions lay not in the discovery of new substances or the design of

Figure 1-7
Because of his religious beliefs (Unitarian) and his liberal political views (supporting the French and American revolutions), Priestley was attacked and harassed in his native England. The mob scene depicts the rampage and riot that resulted in the decimation of his home, library, and laboratory. Political cartoons of the day taunted him. Priestley eventually settled in the United States outside of Philadelphia where he peacefully lived out the last years of his life.

new or improved experimental methods, but as with Einstein over a century later, in the correct interpretation of factual data already known but improperly understood. Two principal studies placed Lavoisier in this pre-eminent position. The first of these studies struck down the phlogiston theory once and for all. A definite quantity of mercury was placed in a flask and subjected to 12 days of constant heating at a temperature just below the metal's boiling point. When the heating period was completed, the flask was allowed to cool to room temperature. A quantity of the air initially present in the flask had disappeared due to formation of the metal oxide. There had been about a 17% reduction in the volume of the air present. Having carefully and quantitatively burned the mercury metal to mercury oxide, Lavoisier proceeded to perform the reverse experiment, again quantitatively. He place the metal oxide in an apparatus that allowed him to measure the volume of gas produced when heat was applied. As expected, the gas was the same in all ways as Priestley's "dephlogisticated" air, and the volume corresponded to the 17 percent taken up in the experiment done earlier. There are, of course, many more experimental details, but the main theme is clear. The air around us is made up of at least two gases, one of which combines with metals on combustion, bringing about an increase in weight. This component of the air is the active agent, or inflammable principle in combustions. Finally, calxes, or metal oxides, are not simpler element substances, but more complex combinations of metals and oxygen. With that, the phlogiston theory became as dead as the proverbial doornail.

The second study, which had actually been completed first, led Lavoisier to accept the concept of the indestructibility of matter in all his scientific work. Lavoisier repeated and modified some experiments which Robert Boyle had performed nearly a century before. Boyle had noted, as had the phlogiston theorists, that metals gain weight on combustion. But he doubted the explanation that heating caused a component of the metal (phlogiston) to be eliminated, leaving the combustion product (metal oxide, or calx) behind. Boyle did many such experiments and always weighed the calx after opening the sealed reaction container. However, he failed to perceive the meaning of the "hissing" sound as air rushed in. Taking great pains, Lavoisier placed a carefully weighed quantity of tin chips into a glass retort which was then sealed with equal care. After weighing the retort and its contents together, he commenced heating. When it became evident that combustion of the tin chips had ceased, he let the sealed retort and its contents cool back down to room temperature. There was no observable change in weight even though there was obvious evidence of chemical reaction, much of the tin having been oxidized (Fig. 1-8).

Lavoisier proceeded further. He opened the sealed retort, noting a distinct "hissing" as air rushed in. On reweighing retort plus contents there was clearly an increase in weight, and most interestingly, the increase in weight corresponded very well with the increase in weight of the tin and its oxide when compared to

Figure 1-8

the weight of the original tin chips. A chemical reaction had been carried out, and during the course of it, matter was neither created nor destroyed, only transformed. It must therefore be possible to set up a bookkeeping system of mass debits and mass credits, all of which must balance at audit time. The Law of Conservation of Matter led to the modern system of balanced chemical equations for representing chemical reactions: total numbers of atoms reacting in any chemical combination must equal total number of atomic products in any new chemical combination.

Lavoisier set down the principles that became foundation stones for modern chemistry in his textbook *The Elements of Chemistry (Traite Elementaire de Chimie).* In that landmark treatise he clearly explained chemical composition, chemical reactions, quantitative relationships, and set up a reasonable system of nomenclature consistent with these principles. If Helmholtz's perception (see p. 5) suggests deep insight into human nature, Lavoisier spoke of similar difficulties in human understanding a century earlier:

> *I do not expect my ideas to be accepted all at once. The human mind gets creased into a way of seeing things. Those who have envisaged nature from a certain point of view during much of their career, rise only with difficulty to a new idea. It is the passage of time therefore which must confirm or destroy the opinions I have presented. Meanwhile, I observe with great satisfaction that young people are beginning to study the science without prejudice.*

John Dalton Is the Father of the Atomic Theory

John Dalton was born in 1766. By the time he grew to manhood the prelude to modern atomic theory had been completed and the stage was set. The nineteenth century witnessed the first great successes of chemical research for the benefit of mankind, in marked contrast to the groping efforts of the century that lay between Newton and Lavoisier. Dalton's chemical atomic theory was the principal driving force that molded these successes. It is true that Dalton's theories suffered problems of acceptance (as Lavoisier had noted before him, and Helmholtz and an army of successors after him) concerning its ultimate validity. Nevertheless, the chemical atomic theory that John Dalton sired provided the basis for a remarkably successful model for chemical research. One great nineteenth-century chemist wrote of Dalton's theory in retrospect:

> *The characteristic feature of the chemistry of our times is, in a word, the development and elaboration of Dalton's doctrine; for every great advance in chemical knowledge during the last ninety years find its interpretation in this theory.*

That was written in 1902. The scientific community and an innocent world on the threshold of the twentieth century paid homage to the Daltonian atomic model. In the wings and behind the scenes, enormous new atomic events were getting ready to happen. A British scientist by the name of Thomson uncovered the electron; Pierre and Marie Curie, working in France, discovered some strange new radioactive elements; for Germany and the rest of the world, Max Planck's quantum idea was but two years old and the implications little understood; Albert Einstein was 23 and a student in a Swiss university; Ernest Rutherford of New Zealand performed early experiments as a young professor in Canada; Niels Bohr was just a kid growing up in Copenhagen. It was the eve of the birth of the "new chemistry" which revealed the atom's internal structure.

☐ A Guide to the Investigative Method for "Doing" Chemistry

Each new generation has in common with its predecessors an overbearing curiosity about the restless universe. We want to know, and if we don't know, we'd like to find out. What do scientists do? Why, they inquire into the nature of the real world (Fig. 1-9). They scratch, they probe, and in so doing, continually redefine the field of knowledge and understanding. A little of that was revealed in the phlogiston story. The difficulty is that as the field of knowledge grows, the inheritance of succeeding generations becomes ever greater, and few now try to be "Renaissance" scientists. A scientist is a chemist, or one who practices physics, or perhaps biology, geology, astronomy. Others may work at the interfaces, gray areas where chemistry and biology become virtually indistinguishable as biochemistry, or atomic physics, where chemistry and physics mesh, blurring out whatever arbitrary boundaries existed. Science is a rigorously ordered body of knowledge gained through a disciplined method of investigation. In short, science turns out to be very much a practical exercise in curiosity.

There are rules or guidelines for the practicing of science which have come to be known as *the scientific method.* It is a code of action for doing science, a way of looking at and thinking about the real world around us. It has been called "organized common sense." Classically, one begins by collecting information, or data, by observation and experiment. But simply collecting facts is no more than accounting; no science here. The crux of the matter lies in the systematic ordering of information, for only then do apparently unrelated facts show their connectedness, moving us toward understanding. Furthermore, it may then become evident where these related facts fit into the existing field of scientific knowledge. Eventually, one may care to offer an explanation of why the facts have developed as we have noted: a hypothesis. The test of a hypothesis is whether it can successfully predict facts yet to be observed. Let's try it and see. To the laboratory for experimental verification; the test, if successful, proves the hypothesis' prediction. Should many tests of the hypothesis continually produce demonstrations of its predictive power, the hypothesis becomes a law of science, a major structural piece in the house of science.

As things turn out, however, it is never cut and dried. We observe, take note. We look, but as often as not, we fail to see. Perry Mason and Sherlock Holmes always

Figure 1-9
Chemistry is what *chemists* do. Here, a scientist researches the properties of synthetic rubber.

succeeded where the Los Angeles Police Department and Scotland Yard failed because of their special talents for noting what their colleagues failed to observe. Observation, therefore, is no casual business, and perception in a scientific sense is more than just perusal (Fig. 1-10). Training and practice are required. When direct observations become too complex, unreasonable, or simply not possible, we resort to an artificial situation or experiment. Here, one aspect of the universe may be freed of other conflicting and confusing factors and studied alone. In a controlled and reproducible fashion, a carefully designed experiment will allow one access to data not otherwise observable. And don't pooh-pooh that as being "obvious" or "so what else is new," because for thousands of years most learned people felt experiments to be indeed unnecessary and probably dangerously beguiling. The purity of reason and the logical conceptualizations of the mind were believed to be enough to define the aspects of the universe. For those cases where that proved insufficient, why, one could always invoke divine wisdom or appeal to "Mephisto" himself. Unfortunately, we're still not entirely free of such attitudes today.

In a sense, scientists are model builders. Lavoisier's experiments in closed systems suggested mass conservation. Other scientists modeled new experiments to further test the implications of Lavoisier's work, that in a chemical reaction mass is neither created nor destroyed, only transformed. A law was established in this

Figure 1-10
Alexander Fleming's discovery of penicillin began with a chance observation by a pre-pared mind. Discovered in peacetime, this great scientific achievement was truly forged in war (World War II). Penicillin lessened the danger of infection and disease, thereby increasing the chances that a wounded soldier would recover.

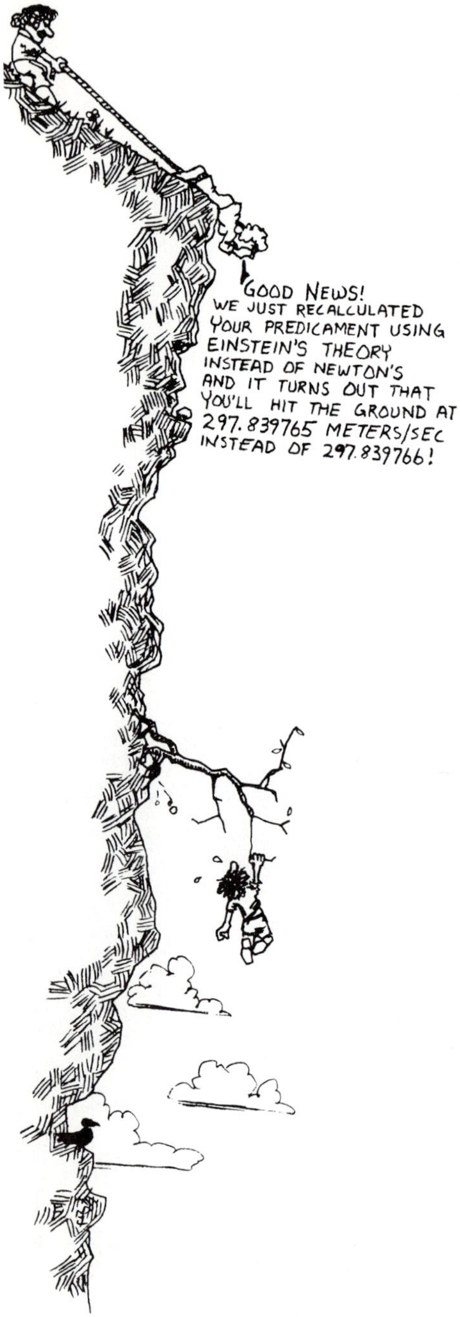

GOOD NEWS!
WE JUST RECALCULATED
YOUR PREDICAMENT USING
EINSTEIN'S THEORY
INSTEAD OF NEWTON'S
AND IT TURNS OUT THAT
YOU'LL HIT THE GROUND AT
297.839765 METERS/SEC
INSTEAD OF 297.839766!

Figure 1-11

case which says that mass is always conserved, a purely experimental law for which no witness to any exception has ever been found. But what if someday there is an exception? After all, haven't we already seen the need to broaden the law to mass-energy conservation? How can one be sure there won't someday be an exception? Well, to be sure one cannot absolutely guarantee against the possibility of an exception. Yet the improbability of exception suggests we can function quite nicely assuming the likelihood of the law. For example, if the sun does not rise tomorrow in the East, it is probably because it is behind a cloud and we simply have not been able to witness the rising that occurred. Our faith in the continuance of the laws describing risings and settings of the sun truly borders on dogma. But be careful. Einstein's ideas on relativity at the beginning of this century brought with it the first modification of Newton's laws in over 200 years (Fig. 1-11). The aftermath required rebuilding the house of science, for Newton's laws were fundamental. When those laws needed redefining, a major section of the foundation for the house of science had to be restructured accordingly. Still, Newton's theories were well-founded and the new physics of the twentieth century was progressive. It has been pointed out that:

> *. . . everything which is true at all in the physics of Aristotle, is contained in classical (Newtonian) physics . . . ; and we should expect the corresponding situation for the relation of our physics to every future one.*

> *The theory of relativity . . . has proved to be the completion and culmination of the structure of classical physics.*

> *With respect to the theory of relativity it is not at all a question of a revolutionary act, but of a natural development . . .*

On the other hand, the phlogiston theory was ill-conceived to begin with. It asserted more than the experiment to prove it could point out; the inferences made were not backed up by the facts and led directly to error and further misconception. Phlogiston was:

> *. . . A hypothetical substance or "principle" . . . supposed to exist in combination in all combustible bodies, and to be engaged in the process of combustion; the matter of fires conceived as fixed in inflammable substances.*

In 1702 Stahl correctly observed that oil of vitriol and charcoal produced sulfur, but then he went on to infer that the sulfur was the product of:

> *. . . the combination of the inflammable principle of the charcoal with the oil of vitriol.*

He had gone beyond what the pure and simple facts of the experiment expressed, and he not only misled himself but led everyone else (just about) down that wrong road for a century.

☐ **Questions to Answer . . . Problems to Solve**

1. Why have learned people spent so much time wondering about atoms and worrying about atomic theories? What is the object of an atomic theory anyway?

2. The famed German scientist-mathematician-philosopher, Leibnitz, rejected Newton's atomic theory because it did not seem possible to him that God would be likely to create two or more atoms, at once identical and indistinguishable. What do you think about that in the year 1700? Today?

3. If "dephlogisticated air" was in fact oxygen, what was nitrogen to these same eighteenth-century scientist-philosophers?

4. What principal chemical technique brought down the phlogiston theory?

5. You are a member of a debate society and you must defend Priestley's position as a phlogistonist. Now take the other position and defend Lavoisier with equal fervor and argument.

6. Make a comparison of the Greek philosophical concept of the atom and the seventeenth-eighteenth century scientific concept of the atom.

7. And having now made a comparison (see Question 6) of a suggestion arrived at scientifically, what do you make of the scientific suggestion that Stahl put forth?

8. Based on your new experience with theories and experiments after the Greek philosophers and Stahl, Priestley and Lavoisier, give a short definition of the word *theory* in the natural sciences.

9. Comment upon this view of Lucretius and atoms:

    "Lucretius with a stork-like fate
    Born and translated in a State
    Comes to proclaim in English verse
    No Monarch rules the Univers.
    But chance and *Atoms* make *this ALL*
    In order Democratical
    Without design, or Fate, or Force."

10. Comment upon Albert Einstein's famous statement that God is subtle, but not malicious.

11. From your worldly experience, list several factors which clearly relate your dependence upon the simplicity, order, and predictability of nature.

In Roy Lichtenstein's *Peace Through Chemistry*, one of the founding fathers of "pop" art has applied his aesthetic sense to chemistry. The overstated dots are a conspicuous and formal part of the work, perhaps recalling the atomic concept of the chemist. This very large oil painting is 8 feet by 15 feet, covering an entire wall.

Chapter 2

Terms, Techniques, and Tools

□ Perceptions and Deceptions

1 Rest isn't what you think it is. In fact, on a microscopic scale, rest simply isn't.

2 I collect my scientific tools: sight, smell, sound, taste, hearing, . . . and intellect.

3 The properties of nature's elemental substances repeat in periodic fashion.

4 Science without mathematics is unthinkable.

5 You say you just bought a meter length of cloth for the price of a yard? And the storekeeper told you it was a bargain!

6 Iron isn't always heavier than wood, but it is always denser.

□ Things Are Made of Matter

Chemistry is the lively science of substances, what they're made of, how they react with each other. To accomodate our study of the observable and measurable characteristics of these substances, it will be helpful to bring certain terms and ideas into sharper focus. For example, the word matter comes from the Latin *materia* meaning building material, hence the stuff of which a thing is made. But that statement still leaves one wondering about the meaning of other words such as *material* or *thing*. Obviously, our meaning isn't sufficiently clear. In this chapter we will try to resolve the language difficulty in dealing with science. Some careful definitions are in order, but definitions alone will not be enough. You must also be shown something of the practice of chemistry applied to real situations, where chemistry fits into everyday life. You need the means to develop the understanding that chemistry is not an isolated or unique experience, but rather a·subject of universal proportions.

Materials are kinds of matter. Wood is a material, so is glass . . . and copper . . . and skin! Materials may be homogeneous or heterogeneous. A **homogeneous** material exhibits continuous or identical properties throughout. **Heterogeneous** materials have portions showing different properties. Glass is homogeneous, wood is heterogeneous. A word of caution; the eye is not the best judge of homogeneity; a magnifying glass is better, a microscope better yet. (See Fig. 2-1.)

Our definition of **substance** shall be a homogeneous form of matter of definite chemical composition. Sodium chloride, or common table salt, is a substance by this definition. Whether prepared synthetically in the laboratory, recovered from sea water, or mined from the earth's crust, sodium chloride's natural chemical composition is always 39.3 percent sodium and 60.7 percent chlorine by mass; it has never been found otherwise because the composition is consistent throughout. On the other hand, ocean water is homogeneous yet not a substance because its composition varies from one sample to another. Dissolve some salt in

Table 2-1

Composition of some common alloys

Alloy	Composition by mass (percent)
Sterling silver	92 silver
	8 copper
Old pewter	20 lead
	80 tin
Common solder	66 lead
	34 tin
Type metal	80 lead
	5 tin
	15 antimony

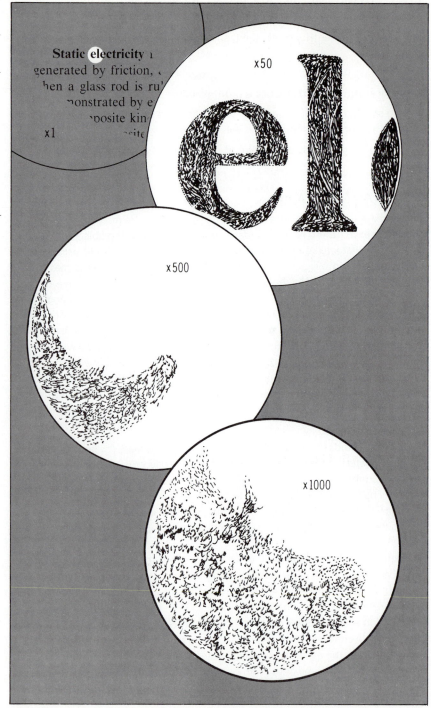

Figure 2-1
The scientists' tools serve to extend the senses, allowing observation of the otherwise unobservable.

water, making a *saline* solution. Although the solution is homogeneous, its composition depends on the amount of salt that was dissolved in the water. Its composition is said to be **variable.** For example at room temperature 100 grams of water may accommodate anywhere from a trace to better than 35 grams of salt. Similarly, **alloy metals** such as sterling silver and pewter, containing several different substances, are homogeneous. Alloys are often referred to as solid solutions (see Table 2-1). Add together and shake oil and water in a container; clearly a mixture. Now mechanically break up the globules of oil until they are very small, in fact, so small you can't see them. The outward appearance may be homogeneous, however, don't be misled; the mixture is still heterogeneous. You can verify this by checking a drop smeared out on a slide under a microscope. Commercial aspirin is another example of a mixture. There are three or four active chemical ingredients in an inert (inactive) substance, suitable for compounding into pill form.

So we have mixtures and solutions, sometimes homogeneous, sometimes heterogeneous, but always separable by reasonably simple physical methods. However, whereas solutions are always homogeneous they are not to be confused with pure substances. We will talk more about solutions in Chapter 6. **System** is a word that chemists use to describe that sample or segment of the universe presently under observation. The system may be large—the solar system; the system may be small—a beaker of water. Our observable (macroscopic) experience tells us that matter comes in three states—solid, liquid, gas—and a system may contain only one, two, or all three states of matter. (See Fig. 2-2.) The **phases** of a system are all of the homogeneous constituents of the system that have identical properties. For example, ice cubes in water in a sealed ampule will have a solid phase (all of the ice), a liquid phase (all of the water), and a gaseous phase (the air plus water vapor present).

Figure 2-2
The three states of matter: solids, liquids, and gases.

☐ Matter Can Be Characterized by Its Physical Properties

Whether what we see is solid, liquid, or gas phase depends to some considerable degree on the heat content of the phase in question. Accordingly, we can bring about phase changes by putting in or taking out thermal energy, in other words, by heating and cooling. Ice melts and we have water; perhaps even steam. Metals such as iron or nickel will melt if we increase the temperature sufficiently. The reverse changes occur as well: steam condenses; molten metals cool and solidify. Such characteristic behavior of pure substances is referred to as the **properties** of the substance; they will be peculiar to the substance, and unchanging if the substance is indeed pure. Here are a few characteristic physical properties.

Freezing Point: The temperature at which freezing normally occurs; almost exactly the same as the **melting point.** Water freezes at $0°C$; grain alcohol at $-117°C$; ethylene glycol at $-15.6°C$.

Boiling Point: The temperature at which vaporization takes place under the

Figure 2-3
Solubility

Figure 2-4
Malleability

normal pressure of the atmosphere; almost exactly the same as the *condensation point.* The boiling point of water is 100°C; grain alcohol boils at 78.5°C; ethylene glycol at 198°C.

Density: The mass per unit of volume. Accounts for misleading statements such as "iron is heavier than wood." If you're talking about a small nail and a large block, it's not true; but if you're referring to two equal volumes, say two identical blocks, one iron and the other wood, then you are correct. It is density you mean.

Solubility: The maximum amount of a pure substance that will normally dissolve in a given amount of a dissolving substance, or **solvent,** at a given temperature. One hundred grams of water dissolves 35.7 grams of sodium chloride at 0°C, and 39.12 grams at 100°C (Fig. 2-3).

Viscosity: The internal resistance of fluids to flow. Water flows more easily than molasses; molasses is more viscous .

Crystal Structure: The orderly arrangement of the atoms into a three-dimensional unit structure or building block out of which a pure crystalline solid is built. Table salt forms in regular cubes; snowflakes have the characteristic structures of ice.

Malleability: The ease with which a substance can be hammered or rolled into sheets. Aluminum is a malleable substance (Fig. 2-4).

Electrical Conductivity: The effectiveness of a substance at transferring electrical current. Copper is a good conductor; ceramic tile is a poor conductor.

Color: The visual appearance of an object due to the nature of light reflected from its surface. Physical form has a lot to do with the color you see; for example, color sometimes lightens as larger particles are ground up into smaller particles.

Thermal Conductivity: The effectiveness of a substance at transferring heat. Steel barbecue tools get very hot, but their wooden or plastic handles remain cool.

Ductility: The ease with which a substance can be drawn into wires or threads. Copper is a ductile substance.

Chemists make use of these physical properties when trying to identify substances and determine their purity. Changes of state (phase transformations) can be put to good use in making not-so-pure substances purer. Note that the word here is *purer*, not pure. *Pure* is, of course, the word we use. But purity is really a matter of degree, limited by our ability to purify. Pure salt is pure because we can't get it any purer in any reasonable fashion. However, those impurities that remain are present in such small amount that they no longer affect the measured physical properties. That's a circular argument perhaps, because our standards for measuring physical properties are based on measuring pure substances. We'll have more to say about this later.

☐ Physical Methods Can Be Used to Separate and Purify Substances

Where were we? Physical properties, changes of state, purification—let's look briefly at five processes, each of special importance to the separation and purification aspects of chemistry: (1) filtration, (2) extraction, (3) distillation and condensation, (4) crystallization, and (5) chromatography.

Filtration: Consider a mixture of sand and water. Complete separation of the two phases, solid sand and liquid water, can be neatly done by **filtration.** The mixture is allowed to pass through a **semipermeable membrane** such as a piece of filter paper or a tea bag that lets the liquid through while retaining the solid. It is much the same as a screen of appropriate mesh size. Now let's complicate our example a bit: Consider a mixture of two solid phases, sand and table salt. We can effect complete separation of the two by making use of a combination of their physical properties, namely salt's solubility in water and sand's insolubility, together with the technique of filtration. Simply place the sand-salt mixture in enough water to dissolve the salt; stir to ensure complete solution. Filter. (See Fig. 2-5.) Wash the sand on the filter with a little additional water to remove any residual salt water wetting the sand, and separation is complete. If you want to remove the salt from solution, simply let the water evaporate, or boil it away if you're in a hurry.

What we have just described is a technique for removal of solid particles from a fluid (gas or liquid) by passing the fluid through a porous filter medium on which the solid collects. The simplest examples of filtration might be described as "straining." A colander separates water from spaghetti; dusty air can be cleaned by removing the solid particles from a gas; filter cigarettes contain plugs of fibrous materials that trap small tar particles; and household vacuum cleaners make use of a variety of filters. Our sand-water discussion described a convenient laboratory-sized demonstration. Many difficult separations, however, require very complicated industrial equipment (Fig. 2-6). Filtration for removing solids from liquids is a technique used in many situations ranging from food processing to water pollution. In some cases gravity can be used to draw the liquid through while other filtrations require pumps to force liquid slurries across appropriate filter barriers.

Extraction: Tea leaves can be extracted by repeatedly dunking a tea bag in hot water; the common coffee percolator allows hot water extraction of crushed coffee beans. In both examples, a solid-liquid extraction procedure has succeeded in removing solid substances from complex mixtures of solids (tea, coffee) by dissolving with a liquid which is then removed.

In its elementary form the liquid-liquid extraction technique involves bringing a solution into contact with a second liquid. Both liquids (which must not

Coffee grounds retained by filter paper

Filtrate of coffee

Figure 2-5
Filtration is a technique commonly practised in the kitchen as well as the laboratory. Here filtration is used in making coffee.

Figure 2-6
High pressure reactor used in the preparation of a prophylactic pharmaceutical agent added to preserved blood to prevent the transmission of syphilis.

mix themselves) are poured into a separatory funnel which is then stoppered, shaken gently, then vigorously (Fig. 2-7). After that, the two liquid layers are allowed to separate, and finally, the denser of the two liquid layers is removed. Such a procedure succeeds in transferring much of the dissolved substance from the solution to the extracting liquid. The entire extraction process can be repeated with a fresh batch of the extracting liquid.

A successful extraction depends on the fact that a given substance will generally exhibit different solubilities in different solvents, and the respective solubilities will differ for the contaminating impurities as well. Simple, convenient, and rapid separations can be carried out with a wide variety of substances. Butyric acid, the organic molecule responsible for the characteristic odor of rancid butter, can be effectively removed from aqueous solution by extraction with ether, a nonaqueous solvent (better known for its anesthetic properties) in which the acid is much more soluble. Bromine dissolved in water can be removed by extraction with chloroform; again, because bromine is far more soluble in chloroform than in water. Applications of liquid-liquid extraction procedures range from large-scale separations of fissionable materials needed for atomic energy to complex separations of petroleum components.

Distillation and Condensation: Seawater is a mixture of a volatile (low-boiling) liquid, along with a number of nonvolatile components. Effectively separating seawater into pure water and dissolved matter (mostly salts) can be done by combining two techniques, distillation and condensation. Distillation requires sufficient heat to bring about boiling and vaporization of the volatile liquid; condensation requires cooling to change the vapor back to liquid again. Dissolved solid matter, being nonvolatile at relatively low temperature such as the boiling point of water, stays behind in the distillation flask; pure water condenses and collects in the receiver (see Fig. 2-8). In similar fashion, but with closer control of temperature, the distillation-condensation technique can be used to separate complex mixtures of volatile components. The several liquid components of the solution commonly referred to as gasoline range hydrocarbons can be so separated. Next time you drive on the New Jersey Turnpike, the Los Angeles freeways, or some of the Texas state highways south of Houston you'll see the large distilling towers for separating crude petroleum into boiling ranges such as the gasoline range (about 40° to 205°C). (See Table 2-2.) Furthermore, most of the oxygen used in industry or for medical purposes is produced by liquification of air, followed by distillation-condensation. The specific technique is called fractional distillation and is so effective that highly purified nitrogen and other trace components of air, the rare gas elements helium, neon, argon, krypton, and xeonon are separated by this method.

Crystallization: This is a commonly used physical method for purifying solids. For example, the residue of salts and other solid impurities recovered from the distillation of seawater may be crystallized to give marketable by-products.

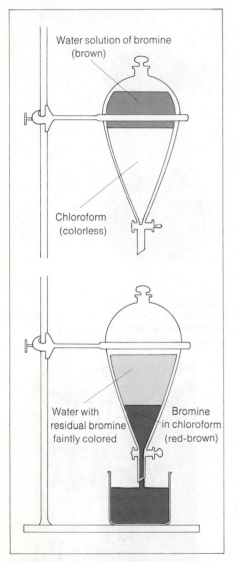

Figure 2-7
Liquid-liquid extraction makes use of the separatory funnel and a pair of liquids (chloroform and water) that will not dissolve in each other, but in which a third substance (bromine) is mutually soluble to different degrees.

The procedure involves dissolution of the crude (impure) residue in hot water and then allowing the resulting solution to cool. Table salt, whose solubility in water is somewhat greater if the solvent is hot than if it is cold, can be purified by crystallization.

Aspirin and sugar are much more soluble in hot water than in cold water; as the solvent cools, the sugar or aspirin crystallizes; solid crystals separate from the solvent as the limits of solubility are exceeded. Some of the impurities in the original solid sample may not be completely soluble and can be removed by simply filtering the hot solution before crystallization begins. Other impurities, being more soluble, or present in much lower concentrations, will stay behind, dissolved in the cold solution, when the newly formed crystals of pure substance are removed by filtration (see Fig. 2-9). The entire drug industry depends upon

Table 2-2

Petroleum refining involves separation according to boiling point

Principal fractions	Boiling point ranges
Petroleum ethers	20-60°C
Ligroin, or light naptha	60-120°C
Gasoline	40-205°C
Kerosene	175-325°C
Gas oil	Beyond 275°C
Lube oils and greases	Vacuum distillation
Asphalt and tars	Vacuum distillation residues

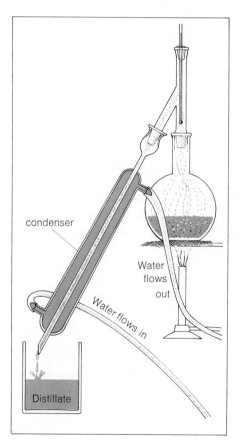

Figure 2-8
Here is a typical set up for laboratory distillation. There are many variations depending on the type of materials being distilled.

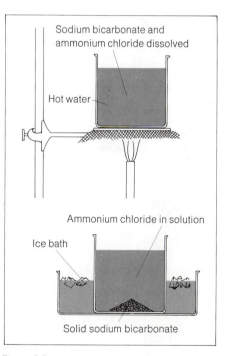

Figure 2-9
Pure sodium bicarbonate crystals collected on the bottom when the solution was cooled. They crystallized selectively because of the much greater solubility of ammonium chloride in hot water.

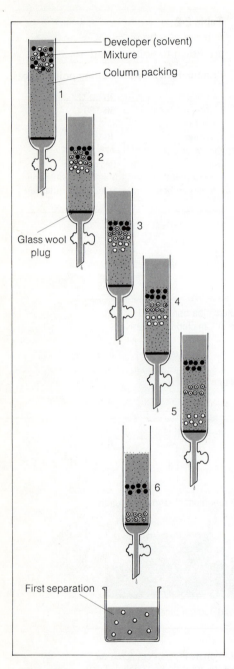

Developer (solvent)
Mixture
Column packing

1

2

Glass wool
plug

3

4

5

6

First separation

Figure 2-10
Separation of a three-component mixture by
column chromatography.

crystallization techniques in preparing chemically pure pharmaceuticals such as the widely used acetylsalicylic acid (aspirin), ascorbic acid (vitamin C), and diazepam (valium).

Chromatography: Separation and analysis of mixtures of chemical substances by chromatography work on the principle of *adsorption*, the tendency of a substance to "stick" to the surface of a finely divided solid. A solid support (solid phase) is packed into a cylindrical column, and a flowing solvent (mobile phase) is passed on through. Components of the mixture to be separated are placed on top of the column. As fresh solvent is passed continuously through from the top, the "stuck," or adsorbed components of the test mixture pass slowly down. The process involves a series of adsorptions and desorptions, a series of stickings and unstickings. Individual components of a complex chemical mixture will begin to separate into bands, moving down the column at speeds dictated by how tenaciously each substance sticks to the solid packing; the most firmly attached particles move the least. Should the components of the mixture be different-colored substances, then bands of different color appear; hence, the origin of the word *chromatography,* meaning "description of colors." (See Fig. 2-10.)

Perhaps an example will better illustrate what chromatography is about. But please don't try to retain each detail of the description. Just try to come away with some feel for the technique. Note that some of the other procedures we've introduced (filtration, extraction) show up here as well. Consider the leaves of Summer; they already contain Fall's colors, but the reds and yellows are overwhelmed by green coloring matter, the pigment called chlorophyll. These pigments can be extracted by grinding up green leaves with a mortar and pestle in a small amount of a 9:1 solution of two nonaqueous solvents, petroleum ether and benzene. The solvent extract is then freed of traces of water with a very effective drying agent, anhydrous (water-free) magnesium sulfate, which is then removed by filtration. Our cylindrical chromatography column is filled with confectioner's sugar (crushed and powdered limestone, the kind used on lawns, will also work well), and filled with petroleum-ether-benzene eluting solvent to the level of the solid phase. The sugar is not at all soluble in the mobile phase.

Now the solvent extract containing the dissolved pigments is poured onto the top of the column. As gravity causes the liquid to move down through the column, more fresh solvent is added at the top and movement continues down the column. Little attraction exists between the column packing (sugar) and the components of the solvent themselves (petroleum ether and benzene) where they come in contact. The pigments, however, are strongly attracted to the sugar support and their movement down the column is retarded. Most important, there are different degrees of "stickiness" among the pigments themselves. Therefore, the pigments spread into bands, a red band, a yellow band, and a green band. We have *developed* a *chromatogram.* If the red band were slowest in its migration down the column, that pigment was adsorbed most strongly.

Although our discussion has been limited to column chromatography, the technique of adsorption-desorption takes many other forms. Chromatographic separations can be made on sheets or strips of cellulosic, or glass-fibered papers, or on thin layers of powdered adsorbents spread on glass plates. A tremendously versatile and very important modification is gas-liquid chromatography, a form of column chromatography in which the test mixture is separated in the vapor phase. Because the technique serves to isolate and purify chemical substances, the highest stamp of purity is often the statement that a substance is "chromatographically pure." It is invaluable in chemical, biological, and medical research. Chromatography is employed in studying metabolic changes brought about by normal and abnormal cell function in the human body. The techniques is widely used in the pharmaceutical industry.

Melting Point: The melting point of a pure crystalline solid is the temperature at which the solid begins to change into a liquid (under normal pressure of the atmosphere). For pure crystalline substances, the solid-to-liquid transition is quite sharp, taking place within 0.5°C, and since the presence of impurities often cause a marked lowering of the melting point, the melting temperature has become invaluable to the chemist for purposes of identification and determination of purity (Table 2-3). A simple technique for obtaining melting points involves placing a very small sample of the solid in a thin-walled glass capillary tube. After gently packing the powder down by tapping, the capillary is gradually heated in a temperature-controlled bath of some kind, such as mineral oil (up to perhaps 200°C) (Fig. 2-11). Silicone oil (to about 350°C) or metal blocks can be used to obtain still higher temperatures for visually observing the temperature at which melting occurs. If the melt is allowed to cool, solidification generally takes place at the same temperature as melting. For a pure substance, the melting and freezing points are essentially the same.

☐ Elements, Compounds, and Chemical Properties

A pure substance is either an **element** or a **compound.** If it is an element, it is one of the hundred or so kinds of atomic building blocks that are known. About 88 occur in nature, and the others have been prepared synthetically. Atoms univerally consist of negative particles called *electrons* that surround a central core, or *nucleus,* in a prescribed fashion. The nucleus contains positively charged *protons* and electrically neutral *neutrons,* both of which have masses about equal to the mass of hydrogen, the lightest element. All atoms of each element contain *nuclei* with a given number of protons. For example, all atoms containing nuclei with 11 protons (11 positive changes in the nucleus) are atoms of sodium, while all those with 17 protons (17 positive charges in the nucleus) are atoms of

Table 2-3
Some characteristic melting points

Substance	Melting point, °C
Mercury	−39
p-Dichlorobenzene (moth balls)	53
Urea	133
d-Glucose (dextrose)	146
Norethynodrel (Enovid)	169
Nicotinic acid (niacin)	236
Morphine	254
Lead bromide	373
Sodium chloride	801

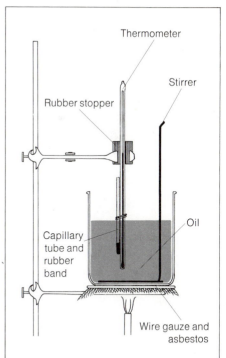

Figure 2-11
Gradual heating and efficient stirring are necessary if an accurate capillary melting point point is to be obtained.

chlorine. The number of protons in the nucleus is commonly referred to as the atomic number Z for that element. Therefore, atoms of the same element all have the same atomic number, or Z value. But atoms of the same element *can* have different weights or mass numbers N, equal to the sum of the protons and neutrons in the nucleus. Such atoms with the same Z values, but different N values (same numbers of protons but fewer or greater numbers of neutrons) are widely found in nature and are called **isotopes.** There are over 700 such representatives for just over 100 elements .

A **compound substance** is made up of atoms of more than one kind of element in some definite chemical combination. For example, the compound sodium chloride (table salt) is made up of equal numbers of sodium atoms and chlorine atoms chemically combined. The elements in a compound can be separated, but not by the physical methods we have described so far. Chemical methods are required, and these necessitate some explanation of the chemical characteristics or chemical properties of pure substances.

Chemical properties have to do with the way in which substances, both element and compound substances, enter into chemical transformations called chemical reactions. An atomic and molecular shuffling goes on when substances are changed into new ones. For example, if the white, cubic salt crystals of sodium chloride are heated to just above their characteristic melting point, say $810°C$, and an electric current is passed between two graphite electrodes, placed in the melt, two new substances are produced. One is an extremely reactive silvery liquid that solidifies to a soft metallic solid (melting point $97.8°C$) when removed from the electrolytic cell. The other is an extremely toxic greenish-yellow gas, and very reactive. Both are elemental substances; the soft metal is the element sodium; the toxic gas, the element chlorine. We've described a *chemical property* of sodium chloride, namely its decomposition by an electric current. One chemical property of sodium metal is its ability to decompose water and produce two substances, sodium hydroxide and hydrogen gas. A few more examples of chemical properties will serve to further illustrate the point. Hydrogen can be burned in chlorine producing the same acidic substance found in stomach acid in humans; iron rusts in moist air, while an iron alloy known as stainless steel does not; marble statues are attacked by the sulfurous smogs of our industrial cities; bronze statues develop a characteristic greenish "patina." (See Fig. 2-12.)

Taste and odor are chemical senses, or suggest chemical properties of substances in that "tastiness" and "odoriforousness" have to do with chemical interactions that trip a nervous response and send the brain a signal. At present we lack complete knowledge about this problem, but the weight of evidence suggests a chemical basis is best for understanding taste and odor.

The Chemical Elements Have a Periodic Way About Them

Scientific method requires two fundamental features: (1) systems of classification and (2) proper tools. Information gained from measurement and observation only becomes scientifically meaningful when systematic classification can be effectively introduced. When one can assign a unique identity to iron, cobalt, and nickel as atomic substances because of the chemical and physical properties peculiar to each, and then go on to show how each relates to the other because of properties they hold in common, a scientist has truly practiced his craft.

Essential tools for doing science have always provided tremendous stimulation at the time of their introduction: for example, physical tools such as the thermometer, the pneumatic pump, the discharge tube, and the chromatograph, as well as conceptual tools such as kinetic-molecular theory and mathematics. The periodic system for arranging nature's elements has proven to be a most effective conceptual tool leading to the prediction and discovery of new elements and new relationships between elements.

At present we believe there are 105 identified elements (see Table 2-4). We've hedged a bit here and said "believe" because numbers 104 to 106 are not yet officially documented and physical and chemical information about them is still sketchy. Of these 106 elements, 88 are found in nature, mostly in combined rather than free form, either within the earth's crust, or dissolved in the oceans of air and water. Most of the elements can be reasonably classified as *metallic*; a smaller number are described as *nonmetallic*; a bare handful fall into a difficult-to-designate in-between category variously referred to as *semimetals* or *metalloids*. We'll classify 16 elements as nonmetals. Of these, 6 are referred to as noble, rare, or inert gases, entering into chemical combination with great difficulty, and not very often at that. All but these 16 are classified as metals. There are 8 borderline semimetals. Of the metallic elements, the heaviest are radioactive or unstable, spontaneously decomposing into lighter ones, some very rapidly, some very slowly.

Direct examination will generally suffice to establish an element as a metal or a nonmetal. Does it have a lustrous appearance? Is it gaseous? Malleable and ductile? Conductor or electricity? Heat conductor? Under ordinary conditions of temperature and pressure, all gaseous elements are nonmetallic; all metallic elements except mercury are solids at these same temperatures. Metallic elements are generally dense, malleable, ductile, and exhibit a characteristic luster. The nonmetals, when they are not gaseous, are usually lumpy substances, forming dull-colored powders when crushed. Metals usually conduct heat and electricity well. Consider the group of elements in the far left IA family (see Fig. 2-13): lithium (Li), sodium (Na), potassium (K), rubidium (Rb), and cesium (Cs). All are metals, the so-called *alkali* metal family of elements; those lying lowest in the family are more "metallic." Moving one column right to the IIA family of

Figure 2-12
Stone decay in the industrial atmosphere of the Rhein-Ruhr. Comparison of a recent photo with one taken early in this century.

Table 2-4

The chemical elements

Elements	Chemical symbol	Atomic number	Approximate atomic mass	Year of discovery	Elements	Chemical symbol	Atomic number	Approximate atomic mass	Year of discovery
Actinium	Ac	89	227	1899	Mercury	Hg	80	200.6	ancient
Aluminum	Al	13	27	1827	Molybdenum	Mo	42	96	1778
Americium	Am	95	241	1944	Neodymium	Nd	60	144	1841
Antimony	Sb	51	122	ancient	Neon	Ne	10	20	1898
Argon	Ar	18	40	1894	Neptunium	Np	93	237	1940
Arsenic	As	33	75	1250	Nickel	Ni	28	58.7	1751
Astatine	At	85	210	1940	Niobium	Nb	41	93	1801
Barium	Ba	56	137	1808	Nitrogen	N	7	14	1772
Berkelium	Bk	97	249	1949	Nobelium	No	102	254	1958
Beryllium	Be	4	9	1798	Osmium	Os	76	190	1803
Bismuth	Bi	83	209	1793	Oxygen	O	8	16	1780s
Boron	B	5	11	1808	Palladium	Pd	46	106.4	1803
Bromine	Br	35	80	1826	Phosphorus	P	15	31	1669
Cadmium	Cd	48	112.4	1817	Platinum	Pt	78	195	1735
Calcium	Ca	20	40	1808	Plutonium	Pu	94	239	1940
Californium	Cf	98	252	1950	Polonium	Po	84	210	1898
Carbon	C	6	12	ancient	Potassium	K	19	39	1807
Cerium	Ce	58	140	1860	Praseodymium	Pr	50	141	1879
Cesium	Cs	55	133	—	Promethium	Pm	61	147	1902
Chlorine	Cl	17	35.5	1774	Protactinum	Pa	91	231	1917
Chromium	Cr	24	52	1797	Radium	Ra	88	226	1898
Cobalt	Co	27	59	1735	Radon	Rn	86	222	1900
Copper	Cu	29	63.5	ancient	Rhenium	Re	75	186	1925
Curium	Cm	96	242	1944	Rhodium	Rh	45	103	1803
Dysprosium	Dy	66	162.5	1886	Rubidium	Rb	37	85.5	1861
Einsteinium	Es	99	253	1952	Ruthenium	Ru	44	101	1827
Erbium	Er	68	167	1843	Samarium	Sm	62	150	1879
Europium	Eu	63	152	1896	Scandium	Sc	21	45	1879
Fermium	Fm	100	255	1953	Selenium	Se	34	79	1817
Florine	F	9	19	1886	Silicon	Si	14	28	1824
Francium	Fr	87	223	1939	Silver	Ag	47	107	ancient
Gadolinium	Gd	64	157	1880s	Sodium	Na	11	23	1807
Gallium	Ga	31	70	1875	Strontium	Sr	38	87.6	1808
Germanium	Ge	32	72.6	—	Sulfur	S	16	32	ancient
Gold	Au	79	197	ancient	Tantalum	Ta	73	181	1802
Hafnium	Hf	72	179	1923	Technetium	Tc	43	98	1937
Helium	He	2	4	1868	Tellurium	Te	52	127.6	1782
Holmium	Ho	67	165	1878	Terbium	Tb	65	159	1843
Hydrogen	H	1	1	1766	Thallium	Tl	81	204	1861
Indium	In	49	115	1910s	Thorium	Th	90	232	1828
Iodine	I	53	127	1811	Thulium	Tm	69	169	1879
Iridium	Ir	77	192	1803	Tin	Sn	50	118.7	ancient
Iron	Fe	26	56	ancient	Titanium	Ti	22	48	1791
Krypton	Kr	36	84	1898	Tungsten	W	74	184	1781
Lanthanum	La	57	139	1839	Uranium	U	92	238	1789
Lawrencium	Lw	103	257	ancient	Vanadium	V	23	51	1801
Lead	Pb	82	207	ancient	Xenon	Xe	54	131.3	1898
Lithium	Li	3	7	1817	Ytterbium	Yb	70	173	1878
Lutetium	Lu	71	175	1907	Yttrium	Y	39	89	1794
Magnesium	Mg	12	24	1755	Zinc	Zn	30	65.4	ancient
Manganese	Mn	25	55	1774	Zirconium	Zr	40	91	1789
Mendelevium	Md	101	256	1955					

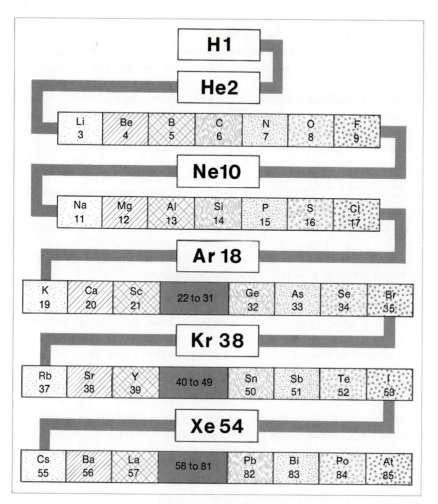

Figure 2-13
One version of the Periodic Table of the elements showing the principal family (descending) and periodic (transverse) relationships.

elements, we come to beryllium (Be), magnesium (Mg), calcium (Ca), strontium (Sr), and barium (Ba), the so-called *alkali earth metals*. Each resembles its neighboring alkali metal element in a systematic fashion, and there are family resemblances within the group of elements, too. In other words, both horizontal and vertical relationships exist; and there is even the hint of diagonal order as well. (See the Periodic Table in the front of the book.)

Horizontal, Vertical, and Diagonal Relationships

Let's illustrate: metallic sodium reacts vigorously with water, even with moisture in the air, forming sodium hydroxide and liberating hydrogen gas; hence, sodium must be stored under an inert, protective liquid, usually a petroleum distillation fraction such as light mineral oil. Potassium and rubidium are so reactive that the hydrogen gas liberated spontaneously ignites. By the time you get down the list to cesium, the metal bursts into flames simply on contact with moist air. The members of the neighboring alkaline earth metals are much harder, denser, and higher melting than the corresponding members of the alkali metal group.

Magnesium is used as a structural metal in aircraft because of its lightness and strength; its horizontal neighbor, sodium, can be about as easily deformed as a piece of clay. Reactivity toward water follows the same top-to-bottom trend among the alkaline earth metals, but always to a lesser degree than the respective alkali metals. Perhaps magnesium is closer to lithium, its diagonal neighbor, than to sodium in that regard; sodium vigorously reacts with cold water, but magnesium reacts rapidly only with hot water or steam. We will have more to say about the reasons behind such behavior after some background in atomic structure and the electronic arrangements within the atoms has been discussed.

The periodic nature of the classification can be seen by noting that exactly 8 horizontal elements after lithium, we arrive back at the next family member, sodium; 8 elements after that, potassium. In going from potassium to rubidium, we pass 18 elements. Something got stretched in there somehow. Another 18 gets us from there to cesium. Periodic regularity holds. And perhaps instead of laying the classification chart out flat, it ought to be put end-to-end in a descending spiral drum. That suggestion has some merit. Now move right, across to the VIIA family, referred to as *halogens.* These are nonmetallic, and more so the *higher* in the family the element lies.

Vertical trends, horizontal trends, and diagonal trends—in short, a system of classification for the chemical elements. By studying the chemical elements, how they occur, their separation and isolation, methods for purification, and characteristic physical and chemical properties, we have at hand the means to a very sensitive understanding of the continuity that exists in nature. Furthermore, no less than 24 elements have been shown to play a role in animal life.

Collecting and Classifying Elements

Chemistry's first collected group of elements was Greek and it was composed of but four elements: earth, air, fire, and water with nothing periodic or systematic about them. They were almost metaphysical elements, hardly the basis for establishing a science of substances. However, by the seventeenth and eighteenth centuries (2,000 years later), the search for the elements of natural substances, the indivisible atoms of the Greeks, was well along. As we've already noted, the British scientist, Robert Boyle, had an important hand in the early business; so did the Frenchman, Antoine Lavoisier. This same period saw elements first grouped into "families" having common properties. The early years of the nineteenth century produced numerical relationships between the apparent mass for the atoms of an element relative to the mass of equal numbers of hydrogen atoms (atomic mass). In 1860 an historic congress at the German city of Karlsruhe led to construction of a system of classification for all of nature's elements, the periodic system for the chemical elements. History has heaped its accolades on the Russian, Dmitri Mendeleyeff, with only passing mention of Lother Meyer of Germany who was almost codiscoverer (Fig. 2-14). (As Vince Lombardi said, "Winning may not be everything, it's the only thing," or the sequel, "Winning may not be everything, but being second is nothing.")

The periodic system was essentially complete by 1871 at a time when little was really known about "atomic research." Chemistry was only just emerging from the kitchen into the laboratory of the professional chemist. At the time, the very simplest of laboratory methods, techniques, measurements, and tools were still employed. Consequently, Mendeleyeff's discovery of periodic behavior must be regarded as an intellectual achievement, a conceptual triumph in science (Fig. 2-13). Here was a discovery of the first rank that took into account the simple relationships (horizontal and vertical) that existed among the known elements. And that could not be denied. The power of this tool for predicting the existence of still-to-be-discovered elements had far-reaching consequences. Mendeleyeff's system left room for the undiscovered elements; it also predicted relative atomic masses and physical and chemically properties with amazing accuracy.

Our modern understanding of the atom tells us that elements can be uniquely designated according to atomic number which spells out the number of positive charges, or protons, in the nucleus. That was also a discovery of the first rank by made by a young British scientist, Henry Moseley in 1914. Atomic numbers locate elements in their present slots in the periodic table, according to the number of protons in the nucleus; isotopic forms of an element all sit in the same periodic slot. The atomic numbers form an uninterrupted progression from 1 to 106.

The universal classification system for the elements has become the basis for modern chemistry. However, unlike the tablets Moses brought down from the mountain which became the faith of a people, a new generation of scientists refused to accept the gift of these universal 88 elements on faith. Nature with only 88 building blocks? With only 88 ultimate particles? There must be a subtlety and a simplicity yet to be discovered here. The twentieth century brought with it the discoveries of the subatomic structure of the atom.

Figure 2-14
Lother Meyer and Dmitri Mendeleyeff provided the critical insight that led to the collection of the elements into a Periodic Table or system (in about 1869-1870).

☐ Making Use of Numbers

Measurement is the source of all of the information upon which our knowledge and understanding of the universe is based. Preciseness is involved. It is all right for you to describe a traffic light as red or green, but how do you make that into a scientific description? After all, light is a form of energy. Something more exact is needed. To say just "red" is unsatisfactory. How red is red? When you

Metric System

Meter (m) = 39.37 inches

Centimeter (cm) = 0.01 m

Millimeter (mm) = 0.001 m

Kilometer (km) = 1000 m

Liter = volume occupied by 1 kg water

Milliliter (ml) = 0.001 liter

Gram (g) = weight of 1 ml of water at
    $4°C$

Kilogram (kg) = 100 g

Ton (metric = 100 kg = 2204.62 lb

English System

Yard = 0.9144 m

Inch = 2.54 cm

Mile (U.S.) = 1.609 km

Liquid quart (U.S.) = 0.9463 liter

Cubic foot (U.S.) = 28.316 liters

Ounce (oz) = 28.35 g

Pound (lb) = 0.4536 kg

Ton (short) = 2000 lb = 907.185 kg

Ton (long) = 2240 lb = 1.016 metric tons

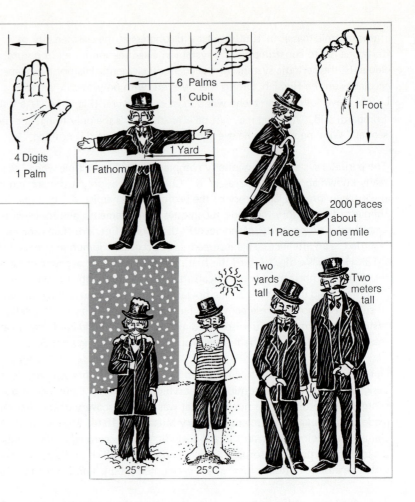

Figure 2-15
Man as a measuring rod (top). Thinking
metric (bottom).

say green do you mean a greenish blue or a yellowish green? Well, what **do** you
mean? You had better try to place a more exact description on your observation
by putting a numeric designation on some characteristic of light such as
wavelength: 6,500 Å. Fine! Now I know exactly "how red." How about hot?
"It's hot today" is all right if you wish to complain about the heat, but that's
unsatisfactory for a physician who would prefer to know whether your body
temperature is 98.6°F or 103°C. Where possible, scientists, especially physical
scientists, develop and build their concepts upon facts quantitatively, not
qualitatively, described.

Numbers and Systems of Measurement

Whether you've thought about it or not, you generally use two kinds of numbers, one a strictly arithmetic quantity, the other a physical quantity. Arithmetic numbers are defined exactly, for example, 2 + 2 = 4, and likewise, the $\sqrt{2}$ = 1.4142136... and π = 3.1415927.... *Physical* number quantities, on the other hand, are experimentally arrived at and are more or less inaccurate, depending on the experimenter and his measuring device. Most physical quantities have a tag or label, a *unit* of measurement. It is 400 *miles* to San Francisco from Los Angeles; we can cover that distance by car in 8 *hours*; our average speed is 50 *miles per hour.*

In the sciences, three standard sets of units have commonly been in use at one time or another: (1) the SI or International System, which you may see listed as the mks system, is a *metric* system, based on the meter length, the kilogram mass, the second, and the degree Kelvin; (2) the cgs metric system, which is the original metric system that arose after the French Revolution, is based on the centimeter length, the gram mass, the second, and the degree Kelvin; (3) the English or British system, sometimes called the native system, is based on the foot length, the pound mass, the second, and the degree Fahrenheit. (See Fig. 2-15.) Because of their considerable convenience, metric units have long since replaced native units in all scientific studies throughout the world with the exception of some engineering applications. Metric measure has also been accepted for practical use in nearly every country as well, except for a few of the still-to-emerge nations such as Barbados, Burma, Gambia, Ghana, Jamaica, Liberia, Muscat and Oman, Nauru, Sierra Leone, South Yemen, Tonga, Trinidad . . . and the United States.[1] The metric system now coming into widest use in the sciences is the SI, or International System, which was adopted in Paris in 1960 by the Eleventh Conference on Weights and Measures and has been in regular use by the United States Bureau of Standards since 1964.

Something about Units and Dimensions

Before going on to the International System itself and its standard units, it is worth saying something about the concept of units and the dimensions they add to otherwise simple arithmetic quantities. A dimensionless quantity has no unit, or more correctly, is a quantity whose number value is independent of any choice of units. But note that a dimensionless number can also arise from a ratio of two quantities that happen to be expressed by the same unit. For example, if you take the ratio of two numbers both expressing grams per milliliter, that is, divide

---

[1] As of this writing, these are the only countries among the family of nations that do not now use or have not made a firm commitment to use metric measure. At present in the United States, it is only under study.

density by density, the units cancel each other and all you are left with is a dimensionless number

$$\frac{(X \text{ g/ml})}{(Y \text{ g/ml})} = \frac{X}{Y}$$

Length is a one-dimensional concept: it is a geometric idea that cannot be understood or expressed in terms of any other simpler idea. Length must have the units of length, and that's all there is to that. Area is a two-dimensional concept having the dimensions of length squared. Volume? It must have the dimensions of length cubed. What we have just done is transpose an entirely geometric concept of the dimensions of space to the dimensions of a physically measurable quantity, volume.

Something about Equalities and Equations

Let's carry our growing numbers game a bit further. Consider the simplest arithmetic equality, or equation you can think of, perhaps $X = Y$. You know that $3 + 2 = 4 + 1$ where $3 + 2 = X$, and $4 + 1 = Y$. If $X = Y$ is a scientific equality expressing physical quantities, not just an equality of numbers, then the equality says that a physical quantity X equals another physical quantity Y so that the number values of both X and Y will be the same if the units are the same. Try our 400-mile trip from Los Angeles to San Francisco. Distance, a unit of length, equals the product of speed and time.

$$\text{distance} = (\text{speed})(\text{time})$$

$$\text{length} = \frac{\text{length}}{\text{time}} (\text{time}) = \text{length}$$

$$400 \text{ miles} = \frac{50 \text{ miles}}{1 \text{ hour}} (8 \text{ hours}) = 400 \text{ miles}$$

Another example of such an $X = Y$ physical equality relates mass, volume, and density. The volume of an object is the ratio of its mass to its density.

$$\text{volume} = \frac{\text{mass}}{\text{density}} = \frac{\text{mass}}{\text{mass/volume}} = \text{volume}$$

The density of water is 1 gram per cubic centimeter. If we have 500 cubic centimeters, about half a liter or about a pint of water, that quantity of water must have a mass of 500 grams because volume = mass/density.

$$500 \text{ cm}^3 = \frac{\text{g}}{\text{g/cm}^3}$$

and

$$\text{cm}^3 \left(\frac{\text{g}}{\text{cm}^3} \right) = \text{g}$$

$$(500 \text{ cm}^3) \frac{1 \text{ g}}{1 \text{ cm}^3} = 500 \text{ g}$$

Equations in the physical sciences express equalities among physical measurements and must be dimensionally consistent in terms of units: miles = miles; cubic centimeters = cubic centimeters; grams = grams.

Measuring Length

The fundamental unit of length in the SI system is the meter (m) which is approximately equal to 39.37 inches. It was originally defined as one ten-millionth of the distance from either pole to the equator, and later as the distance between a pair of engraved markings on a standard platinum-iridium metal bar kept in a temperature-controlled vault near Paris. The meter was redefined in 1960 as 1,650,763.73 times a particular wavelength in the visible spectrum of the element krypton, namely the orange-red line which is equal to 605.78210×10^{-9} meter. Because of the very small distances between atoms in molecules and the very long distances in space travel, some important multiples and submultiples of the meter should be noted (Fig. 2-16). Their particular designation is established by addition of the appropriate prefix.

$$
\begin{aligned}
\textit{mega}\text{meter} &= 10^6 \text{m} = 1 \text{ M} \\
\textit{kilo}\text{meter} &= 10^3 \text{m} = 1 \text{ km} \\
\textit{centi}\text{meter} &= 10^{-2} \text{m} = 1 \text{ cm} \\
\textit{milli}\text{meter} &= 10^{-3} \text{m} = 1 \text{ mm} \\
\textit{micro}\text{meter} &= 10^{-6} \text{m} = 1 \text{ } \mu\text{m} \\
\textit{nano}\text{meter} &= 10^{-9} \text{m} = 1 \text{ nm}
\end{aligned}
$$

Another unit of length commonly used is the **angstrom** (Å), which is equivalent to 10^{-10} meter or 10^{-8} centimeter. That turns out to be the order of magnitude of interatomic dimensions.

Expressing Big and Small Exponentially

How big is big and how small is small? How do we express such sizes and dimensions? There is a commonly used standard notation involving superscripts, or exponents, of the base number 10 as a multiplication factor. The exponent indicates how many times some number is multiplied or reduced by the factor 10. Take some very large number such as the speed with which light travels through a vacuum, 186,000 miles per second. That number can be written in successive multiples of the number 10 in exponential notation:

$$
\begin{aligned}
186,000 &= 186,000 \times 10^0 = 186,000 \times 1 = 186,000 \\
&= 18,600 \times 10^1 = 18,600 \times 10 = 186,000 \\
&= 1,860 \times 10^2 = 1,860 \times 100 = 186,000
\end{aligned}
$$

Figure 2-16
The picture at the top shows the atoms in a metal as seen through a scanning electron microscope. The picture at the bottom shows a view of New York from a plane. Clearly, it would be difficult to use the same system of measurement for both if it were not for exponential notation.

$$= 186 \times 10^3 = 186 \times 1000 = 186{,}000$$
$$= 18.6 \times 10^4 = 18.6 \times 10{,}000 = 186{,}000$$
$$= 1.86 \times 10^5 = 1.86 \times 100{,}000 = 186{,}000$$

We can properly describe the speed of light as 1.86×10^5 miles per second. That number can also be expressed as 3.00×10^8 meters per second, which is $3.00 \times 100{,}000{,}000$ or $300{,}000{,}000$ meters per second.

For a very small number such as the distance between two adjacent atoms in a water molecule, the situation is reversed, and we divide by 10 instead of multiplying:

$$1.54 \text{ Å} = 1.54 \times 10^{-10} \text{ m} = 1.54 \times \frac{1}{10^{10}} \text{ m} = \frac{1.54}{10{,}000{,}000{,}000} = 0.000000000154 \text{ m}$$

$$1.54 \text{ Å} = 1.54 \times 10^{-8} \text{ cm} = 1.54 \times \frac{1}{10^8} \text{ cm} = \frac{1.54}{100{,}000{,}000} = 0.0000000154 \text{ cm}$$

$$1.54 \text{ Å} = 1.54 \times 10^{-4} \mu = 1.54 \times \frac{1}{10^4} \mu\text{m} = \frac{1.54}{10{,}000} = 0.000154 \mu$$

$$1.54 \text{ Å} = 1.54 \times 10^0 \text{ Å} = 1.54 \times \frac{1}{10^0} \text{Å} = \frac{1.54}{1} = 1.54 \text{ Å}$$

The elementary particles of which atoms are composed are very small. For example, atomic events depicted in bubble chamber photographs take place over distances on an order of magnitude of 10^{-15} meters across time intervals on the order of 10^{-23} second At the other end of the spectrum of universal dimensions is the radius of the universe itself which is presently known to stretch out some 10^{26} meters distant.

Should you have to multiply two numbers containing such exponential notation, the exponents add.

$$(3.00 \times 10^8)(2.00 \times 10^6) = (3.00 \times 2.00)(10^8 \times 10^6) = 6.00 \times 10^{14}$$

If you have occasion to divide two such numbers, the exponents substract

$$\frac{(3.00 \times 10^8)}{(2.00 \times 10^6)} = (1.50)(10^8)(10^{-6}) = 1.50 \times 10^2$$

Accurate and Precise Measurements

You should always keep in mind that no measurement can ever be ***absolutely*** correct. The accuracy and precision of any measurement are restricted by the limits of both instrument and observer. We learn to minimize random errors by taking care and by repeating experiments; we also learn to understand systematic errors and assign reasonable uncertainty to our experiment's results. To a greater or lesser degree, observations are always approximations whether we're talking about big or small aspects of the universe. Science has always dabbled with both ends of the measuring stick, so to speak. Even at the early stages of scientific and philosophical observations of the world, there was concern about the microcosm of ultimate particles, or atoms, as well as the macroscopic frontier offered by distant stars.

Measurements must be made, information accumulated, and criteria established for the accuracy and precision of the information, all in order to arrive at reasonable evaluations of what's been done. One must have some sense of the limitations of the experimental measurement or procedure and the uncertainties of the measuring device, be that you and your ruler, or you and your laser. **Precision** expresses the degree to which you are able to rely on your result . . . its reproducibility. **Accuracy** is the degree to which you have approached the true value; in other words, how correct are you? Consider the markings on a balance during a particular weighing operation. The scale is calibrated in tenths of a gram; the pointer reads 31.6 grams. What that means is simply that the mass on the balance is more nearly 31.6 than 31.7 or 31.5. You might be tempted to guess as to where the arrow lies in-between, say, on the 31.7 side of 31.6, perhaps 31.63, but that is a value judgment on your part. Someone else may feel that it is 31.64 or 31.62. Who can really say? The precision of the instrument only allows for 31.6 with complete certainty; use of an additional decimal place, as in 31.63, has an uncertainty built into that last digit. Perhaps we would be best advised to state it as 31.63 ± 0.01 since it could be 31.64 or 31.62 depending upon who the estimator happens to be, or when you make the estimate (Fig. 2-17). In any case, the precision built into any measuring device and the

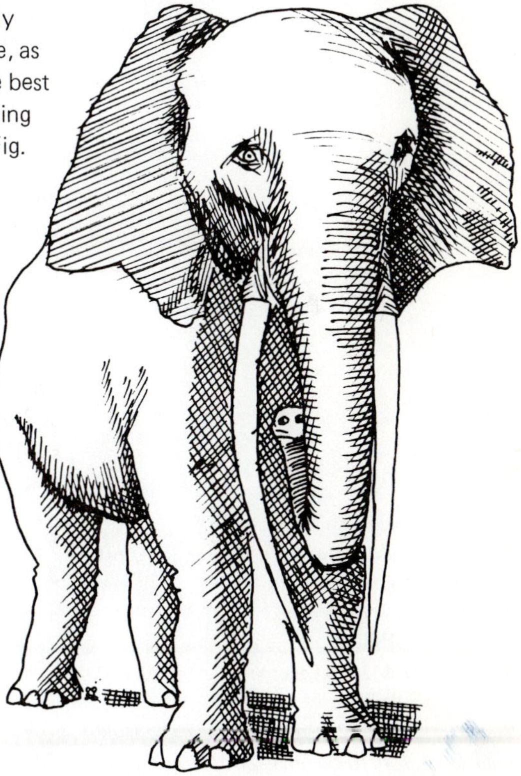

Figure 2-17
Precise measurement accurately made.

accuracy with which one uses it not only must be implicitly understood but must be explicitly stated whenever possible.

Significant Figures

Those digits in any numeric measurement that are known with certainty, together with the first estimated digit, are referred to as significant figures in common practice. The number of significant figures says a lot about accuracy in measurement. In the example cited, there are four significant figures, namely 3163, the first three (316) known with certainty; the last number (3) is the first estimated digit. A few simple rules will provide needed guidelines to cover significant figure problems in accuracy during calculations. For example, speed is measured as distance traveled per unit of time gone by, say, 125 miles covered in 1.5 hours.

$$\text{speed} = \frac{125 \text{ mi}}{1.5 \text{ hr}} = 83 \text{ mi/hr}$$

The division process will lead to a situation that can be carried out well beyond two significant figures. Why not 83.3 or 83.33, and so on? However, there is no justification for any derived number having more significant figures than the number known with the *least* degree of certainty. In this case, the number with the least number of significant figures is 1.5, having but two significant figures.

Let's look at the same problem in another way. Suppose you wish to drive 125 miles at a speed of 55 miles per hour. The trip will take you 1.5062 hours, or in ordinary terms, 1 hour 30 minutes and 3.612 seconds. Nonsense? Yes, of course. Even the most experienced driver knows that the time required to complete a journey of that length cannot be predicted with anything approaching that kind of accuracy. It is more realistic to say that the trip will take about 1.5 hours.

The rule, then, is to carry out the operation (division, multiplication, or addition as the case may be) and then **round off** the answer to the proper number of significant figures. Here are the rules for "rounding off":

1 If the last digit is less than 5, simply drop it.

2 If the last digit is greater than 5, drop it and add 2 to the preceding digit.

3 If the last digit is 5, drop it and add 1 if that addition makes the preceding digit even; if the digit preceding the last 5 is already even, then simply drop the 5 and do nothing else.

4 If the last digit is 0, simply drop it.

Of course, you needn't have gone through all that stepwise business since looking at the first four digits would have told you the answer. One final guideline has to do with zeros when they appear:

Take the number 27.4475160 and round it off stepwise to three significant figures.

Step 1: 27.4475160 becomes 27.447516 by Rule 4.

Step 2: 27.447516 becomes 27.44752 by Rule 2.

Step 3: 27.44752 becomes 27.4475 by Rule 1.

Step 4: 27.4475 becomes 27.448 by Rule 3.

Step 5: 27.448 becomes 27.45 by Rule 2.

Step 6: 27.45 becomes 27.4 by Rule 3.

5 Zeros left of the first non-zero digit are not significant, serving only to locate the decimal point.

6 Zeros after or in-between are significant.

As far as significant figures and exponential notation are concerned, note the following examples:

Thus, for the following numbers:

100	3 significant figures
101	3 significant figures
0.01	1 significant figure
0.11	2 significant figures
0.10	2 significant figures
1.01	3 significant figures
1.10	3 significant figures

1 The speed of light, 3.00×10^8 meters per second, has 3 significant figures.

2 The interatomic distance of 1.54×10^{-10} meters has 3 significant figures.

3 The mass of a proton, $1,673 \times 10^{-24}$ gram has 4 significant figures.

More SI Units of Measure

We've digressed a bit in order to show you how to handle notational problems with large and small numbers when they arise, and to suggest the need to be concerned with accuracy and precision in measurement. Let's go back to the other major units of measure in the SI system. The standard unit of mass is the kilogram (kg), defined by an object made of platinum-iridium stored in France that has a mass of 1 kilogram or about 2.2 pounds. A single gram (g) is 10^{-3} kilogram and a milligram (mg) is 10^{-3} gram or 10^{-6} kilogram. The mass of the universe is believed to be about 10^{30} kilogram; the earth's mass, about 10^{24} kilogram; and the mass of an electron, the lightest permanent particle, about 9.1×10^{-31} kilogram or 9.1×10^{-28} gram.

The standard time unit in SI is the second. Defined originally as 1/86,400 of a mean solar year, and later as a fraction of the earth's rotation about the sun during the tropical year 1900, the second is now defined as the interval occupied by 9,192,631,770 cycles of the microwave line of a certain cesium isotope (Cs-133) with wavelength very near 3.26 centimeters. The accuracy of the cesium clock can be maintained to better than 1 part in 10^{12}, or about 1 second in 30,000 years. We have to define time by such operational definitions; we know it passes: events happen, the sun rises, seasons come and go, young become old. Once you go beyond such conceptualizations of time as a backdrop upon which events are viewed, it becomes very difficult indeed to conceive of or describe what time is. Think about time for a bit; ask a friend what time is and see what kind of response you get.

Temperature is defined in the SI system by the Kelvin, or absolute, scale and the designation is K. (See Fig. 2-18.) The older cgs metric scale used the centigrade degree; it is well entrenched, so you should know about both. To interconvert:

$$K = C + 273.15$$

We should also briefly mention energy in the SI system, the unit of which is the joule. The thermochemical calorie is defined as 4.184 joules or the quantity of energy required to raise the temperature of 1 gram of water by $1°C$ in the

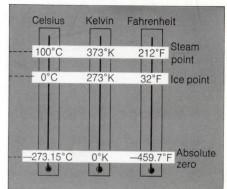

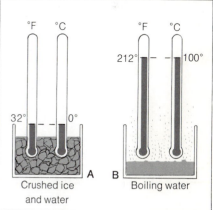

Figure 2-18

The old cgs metric scale of temperature was based on a comparison of the ice point and the steam point of water.

temperature range around 15°C. As was the case for the centigrade degree, the calorie is well-entrenched, and you'll have to know it right along with its SI equivalent, the joule.

Other common units derive from the standard units, for example, *density*, the mass of any substance per unit volume at any definite temperature. Densities are most commonly tabulated as grams per milliliter (g/ml). Mass is a fundamental unit; volume is length, cubed. The basic unit of volume is the liter (l) which is approximately 1.06 quarts; the milliliter (ml) is one thousandth of a liter and is equal to one cubic centimeter (cm^3) or the space defined by a uniform cube, 1 cm X 1 cm X 1 cm. In other words, 1 ml = 1 cm^3. A 1-liter volume therefore contains 1,000 milliliters, or 1,000 cubic centimeters.

□ The Unit Factor Method in Chemical Calculation

Here's a commentary on numbers and units that will prove very useful. It is frequently necessary to convert units of a particular physical measurement to some other set of units. Your measurement of volume may have been in liters, but in order to determine density, you require the volume in milliliters. The correct transposition can be carried out by introducing a conversion factor or ratio. We need to relate liter and milliliter; there is 1 liter for every 1,000 millliliter, or a ratio of

$$\frac{1 \text{ liter}}{1000 \text{ ml}} \quad \text{or} \quad \frac{1 \text{ liter}}{10^3 \text{ ml}}$$

If we were operating in reverse, transposing milliliters to liters, our ratio would be

$$\frac{1000 \text{ ml}}{1 \text{ liter}} \quad \text{or} \quad \frac{10^3 \text{ ml}}{1 \text{ liter}}$$

Take, for example, the conversion of 125 ml to liters. .

$$(125 \text{ ml}) \frac{1 \text{ liter}}{1000 \text{ ml}} = \frac{125 \text{ liters}}{1000} = 0.125 \text{ liter}$$

The check on the method is the equality of units, in this case, liters = liters. Moreover, in much the same way as we convert 79 cents into 0.79 dollars by a direct decimal "shift," *intra*metric conversions such as this can be made by simply moving the decimal point: 125 ml = 0.125 liter.

Complicating the matter somewhat, consider the volume in liters of 100 grams of a substance such as ink whose density is 0.25 grams per milliliter. Remember, density is stated in units of grams per milliliter for most solids and liquids. The required answer is volume in liters, given 100 grams of a solid. Our conversion factor here is the density of the solid, in ratio form.

Table 2-5
Densities for several pure substances

Substance	Density	
Liquids		
ether	0.714	g/ml
alcohol	0.789	
water	1.00	
chloroform	1.40	
bromine	2.93	
mercury	13.59	
Solids		
cork	0.20	mg/ml
aluminum	2.70	
iron	7.86	
lead	11.3	
platinum	21.4	
Gases		
ammonia	0.771	
carbon monoxide	1.250	
oxygen	1.429	
sulfur dioxide	2.927	
chlorine	3.214	

$$\frac{0.25 \text{ g}}{1 \text{ ml}} \quad \text{or} \quad \frac{1 \text{ ml}}{0.25 \text{ g}}$$

To obtain an answer in units of volume, multiply the mass of the substance in grams by the proper choice of the two ratios, namely

$$(100 \text{ g}) \; \frac{1 \text{ ml}}{0.25 \text{ g}} = 400 \text{ ml}$$

But we're not yet finished because we need an answer in liters, not milliliters so we continue.

$$(400 \text{ ml}) \; \frac{1 \text{ liter}}{1000 \text{ ml}} = 0.400 \text{ liter}$$

Or better, yet, the entire operation can be done in one step.

$$(100 \text{ g}) \; \frac{1 \text{ ml}}{0.25 \text{ g}} \frac{1 \text{ liter}}{1000 \text{ ml}} = 0.400 \text{ liter}$$

Try it again. Take a liquid substance such as carbon tetrachloride whose density is 1.595 grams per milliliter and determine the mass in milligrams of 0.010 liter of it. Needed conversion factors or ratios are the following: grams into milligrams, liters into milliliters, and density.

$$(0.010 \text{ liter}) \; \frac{1000 \text{ ml}}{1 \text{ liter}} \frac{1.595 \text{ g}}{1 \text{ ml}} \frac{1000 \text{ mg}}{1 \text{ g}} = (0.010)(10^6)(1.595) = 1.595 \times 10^4 \text{ mg}$$

$$= 15{,}950 \text{ mg}$$

Now try it on your own using the unit factor technique. Watch your significant figures and use exponential notation where it seems reasonable to do so:

1 Convert 10 cm^3 to liters.

2 Convert 1.55 kilograms to micrograms.

3 Show how you transform 186,000 mi/sec into 3.00×10^{10} cm/sec.

4 Determine the density of 20 ml of an alcohol sample that weighs 25.0 g.

5 What is the volume occupied by 0.35 kg of the alcohol sample in problem 4?

☐ **Questions to Answer . . . Problems to Solve**

1. Briefly define and illustrate each of the following terms:
    (a) matter   (e) mixture   (h) object
    (b) substance   (f) solution   (i) phase
    (c) atom   (g) material   (j) system
    (d) molecule

2. For each of the following, determine whether the best description is atom, molecule, or mixture. Draw on your practical experience where possible.

(a) vinegar	(h) oil	(p) Jello
(b) tap water	(j) gasoline	(q) sea water
(c) well water	(k) salt	(r) sunlight
(d) a penny	(l) cotton candy	(s) polyethylene
(e) iron	(m) air	(t) distilled water
(f) steel	(n) coffee	(u) stained glass
(g) coal	(o) Bufferin	

3. Distinguish between the following pairs of terms:
   (a) element and compound
   (b) homogeneous and heterogeneous
   (c) chemical change and physical change

4. Drawing upon your experiences, describe a change that is purely physical in nature; one that is chemical.

5. Determine whether each of the five human senses best describes a physical or chemical property of matter.

(a) chloroform	(g) aspirin
(b) nylon	(h) sulfuric acid
(c) freon	(i) octane
(d) jeweler's rouge	(j) Clorox
(e) borax	(k) asbestos
(f) tetraethyllead	(l) muriatic acid

6. Listed at the left are names of several common industrial and household chemicals. Using the index at the back of the book, look each up and find its chemical formula, and identify all of the elements present.

7. You have in your presence a white, crystalline substance which you strongly suspect to be common table salt. To the extent that your present experience in chemistry permits, how would you determine the truth of your suspicion.

8. Briefly distinguish between the following pairs of terms:
   (a) accuracy and precision
   (b) density and specific gravity
   (c) microscopic and macroscopic
   (d) millimeter and micrometer
   (e) 10^{-10} m and 1 Å
   (f) $0°C$ and $0°K$
   (g) log 3.00×10^{10} and 10×4771
   (h) a liter and a cubic decimeter

9. Offer a short analysis of the type of error that crops up in an experiment in which length measurements are often required and the meter stick used has inadvertently been graduated wrong.

10. Describe the type of error arising from the use of a carefully calibrated meter stick used by a diligent and conscientious experimentor who happened to be out partying last night and made a mistake in reading a measurement today.

11. From the following list of concepts, state which ones can reasonably be quantitatively, rather than qualitatively, assessed:
    (a) mass   (d) energy   (g) light
    (b) density   (e) error   (h) color
    (c) heat   (f) probability   (i) beauty

12. Calculate your height in meters, centimeters and millimeters, expressing each in common scientific notation (i.e., exponential notation); do the same for your weight in kilograms, grams and milligrams.

13. How would you go about determining your volume? Your average density?

14. Consider the 100-yard dash which you can do in 9.6 sec flat. Determine what your velocity was in cm/sec; determine the number of meters you could cover in 1.5 min if you could maintain your velocity constant.

15. There are exactly 6.023×10^{23} hydrogen atoms in exactly 1.008 grams of hydrogen. Determine the mass of a single hydrogen atom. If a single electron weighs 9.10×10^{-28} gram, what percentage of the atom is the mass of the nucleus remaining?

16. Determine the number of significant figures for each of the following:
    (a) 1975   (d) 186,000   (g) 0.1
    (b) 1.975   (e) 1080600   (h) 0.0000000001
    (c) 3.00×10^{10} (f) 0.00186   (i) 1 billion

17. Round off the following numbers to three significant figures:
    (a) 365,000   (c) 246,099   (e) 3.00×10^{10}
    (b) 1.745   (d) 0.00074559   (f) 1.151×10^{-2}

18. In each of the following, express your answer to the proper number of significant figures:
    (a) It takes 8 min for light to travel the distance from the Sun to the Earth at an average speed of 3.00×10^{10} cm/sec. Calculate the distance between the sun and the earth.
    (b) $(0.6625 \times 10^{-33})(2.466 \times 10^{15}) =$

    (c) $\dfrac{(3.00 \times 10^{8})}{(1.209 \times 10^{19})} =$

    (d) $\dfrac{(1.646 \times 10^{14})}{(3.00 \times 10^{8})^{2}} =$

19. Write out the proper conversion factors required for each of the following transformations:
    (a) liter to milliliter   (d) microgram to milligram
    (b) kilogram to milligram   (e) nm to Å
    (c) cm^{3} to dm^{3} (f) liter to cubic meter

John Dalton was a major scientific figure of the nineteenth century and it is upon his work that much of what is modern in science today is based. His atomic theory was one of the great achievements of the period.

Chapter 3

John Dalton and the Chemist's Atomic Theory

☐ Perceptions and Deceptions

1 "The science of the chemist is immediately concerned with the combination of atoms."

2 The notion of atoms was a lonely idea in history for a long time. But then John Dalton caught on, and after that so did a lot of others.

3 Multiple proportions is H_2O for washing and H_2O_2 for bleaching; CO from engine combustion and CO_2 from human respiration.

4 In ordinary chemical transformations, there is hardly any of the conversion of mass to energy predicted by Einstein.

5 "Were it not for number and its nature, nothing that exists would be clear to anybody either in itself or in its relation to other things . . . " and this Pythagorean doctrine has reappeared most significantly in Dalton's work.

☐ Old Ideas Under New Paint

The house that Newton built stood for 200 years, but by the beginning of the twentieth century it was clearly in need of remodeling. Einstein pointed that out in 1905. During that same dramatic period of scientific retrenchment, it also became evident that Dalton's atomic theory was in need of some remodeling. However, neither Newton or Dalton have been dishonored or dismissed as have Stahl and his phlogiston theory. Newton and Dalton's efforts were simply superceded, becoming part of a broader, more comprehensive understanding. Unshakable institutions were upset; new institutions emerged. The old conceptions were replaced by later choices. Perhaps when we take the time to look at the old as well as the new, we have a way of seeing, and then seeing again. There are the original achievements as shadows under the new coat of paint. Let's stop a moment, and take a look at John Dalton's powerful contribution to our modern understanding of atomic theory. Pure substances are composed of units called *atoms* that are directly involved in all chemical transformations. Our modern system of representation for atoms, molecules, and their transformations emerged from pictorial representations of elementary substances, each associated with specified relative masses. Furthermore, the basic idea behind all of our chemical computations depends directly on how given quantities of these atoms can be combined. John Dalton's atomic theory, which has played a significant role in the development of modern chemical science, is still basic to our understanding today.

☐ Atoms and Molecules

Explosive reaction: take hydrogen, mix it with oxygen, add a spark and BANG: a chemical transformation occurs. Water vapor is the product of that transformation. But is it all that simple? Hardly so. We need to know more about what takes place during such transformations, or chemical reactions. If that explosive transformation had occurred in the presence of a large amount of oxygen and much less hydrogen, the gaseous product would be a mixture of two substances. To be sure, you would find water vapor, but also some leftover, surplus oxygen molecules. Of course, we could reverse the situation, starting with a large amount of hydrogen molecules, ending with surplus hydrogen molecules in company with our newly made water vapor.

The reaction can also be put together in such a way that neither reactant is in excess. In that case, only water is present at the end of the reaction. To accomplish this feat, it is only necessary that hydrogen and oxygen be present in certain definite proportions according to mass. Look at the **pressure** of the resulting water vapor for a moment (at the boiling point, 100°C). The interesting point here is that the pressure of the gaseous product is quite different from that of the original gas mixture (at the same temperature). In fact, chemical reaction has effectively reduced the pressure by a third. What conclusions can we derive from that? The **number** of water molecules formed must be less than the total number of hydrogen and oxygen molecules initially present. That's reasonable. After all, pressure is determined by force and by the number of impacts on walls of the container. But so far we have no real clue as to why the pressure drop is one third. We can conclude, however, that the number of molecules must also be less by a third.

Burning hydrogen in oxygen chemically combines the two elements. Where there were **two** molecules before, only **one**, a new molecule, appears after: water vapor has formed. There should therefore be half as many water molecules as there were hydrogen and oxygen molecules to begin with. But the pressure didn't fall by half; it fell by a third. The pressure should have fallen by half **only** if two molecules (hydrogen and oxygen) form one molecule (water). (See Fig. 3-1.) Here, deeper insights must prevail. Not only does the water molecule consist of simpler parts called atoms, but so do hydrogen and oxygen in their natural gaseous state. You may well have anticipated that disclosure; a clue was left for you when we referred to hydrogen and oxygen **molecules** rather than atoms. There are several gaseous elements in nature composed of two atoms, pairs of atoms already in chemical combination.

We denote atoms of hydrogen and oxygen by their chemical symbols, H and O; if we have multiples of atoms in a molecule, the symbolism takes on the additional notation of subscript lowercase numbers. Hydrogen and oxygen form diatomic molecules, that is, two atoms per molecule: H_2 and O_2. The water molecule is composed of two hydrogen atoms in chemical combination with a single oxygen atom. That fact has been convincingly established by analytical procedures yielding percent composition data of namely an 8:1 mass ratio, oxygen to

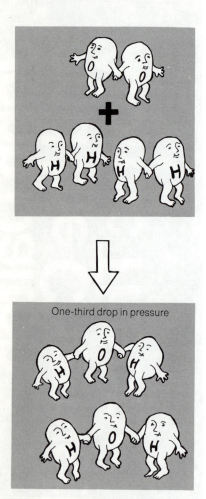

One-third drop in pressure

Figure 3-1
Three molecules become two. Two pairs of hydrogens combine with one pair of oxygens (that's three molecules) forming two sets of three-atom water molecules in the atomic shuffle. The pressure drops by a third.

hydrogen: 8 parts of oxygen for each part of hydrogen, resulting in 9 parts water. Each oxygen atom is 16 times as heavy as every hydrogen atom, and that means the real mass ratio is 16:2; the *simple* mass ratio is 8:1, so there must be two hydrogens, each having a relative mass of 1 mass unit each, combined with a single atom of oxygen, mass 16. Water is symbolically expressed as H_2O; our explosion process can be given as a chemical formalism called an **equation**.

$$H_2 + O_2 = H_2O$$

The equation is written as an equality, but if you look carefully you'll see that it doesn't add up. As it stands, there are 2 H's and 2 O's on the left, and 2 H's and 1 O on the right. If the equality expressed by the equation is to be maintained, we must have a pair of hydrogen molecules reacting with a single oxygen molecule yielding a pair of water molecules.

$$2 H_2 + O_2 = 2 H_2O$$

Now it adds up. The total numbers of atoms on both sides of the equality are equal; you'll find 4 H atoms + 2 O atoms = 4 H atoms + 2 O atoms. Finally, in order to write this as a proper equation for a chemical reaction, all that's required is to change the equality sign to an arrow

$$2 H_2 + O_2 \rightarrow 2 H_2O$$

Why there was a pressure drop of one third during this is now clear. We have one third fewer molecules present at the reaction's end, namely two molecules (both water) versus three molecules (two of hydrogen and one of oxygen).

Another Example

Some scientists believe all living organisms had their origins in a primordial broth full of all the necessary raw materials for producing life. If our primordial broth had nurtured an ammonia-based biology, perhaps a better example for our discussion here would have been the synthesis of the ammonia molecule (NH_3).

$$3 H_2 + N_2 \rightarrow 2 NH_3$$

Nitrogen, as it exists in nature, is also a diatomic molecule. Analysis tells us that ammonia has a 4.67:1 ratio of nitrogen to hydrogen. Nitrogen, however, is 14 times the relative mass of hydrogen, so the real mass ratio is not 4.67:1 but three times that, or 14:3. Therefore, ammonia has the symbolic formula NH_3. After all, you're not likely to find the fractions of atoms that a ratio such as 4.67:1 might suggest. Here, we really would expect a 50 percent pressure drop when hydrogen and nitrogen molecules chemically combine, but not because two molecules (hydrogen and nitrogen) produce one molecule (ammonia); rather because four molecules (three of hydrogen and one of nitrogen) produce two ammonia molecules (Fig. 3-2). Again, things have turned out to be other than they really seemed on first inspection.

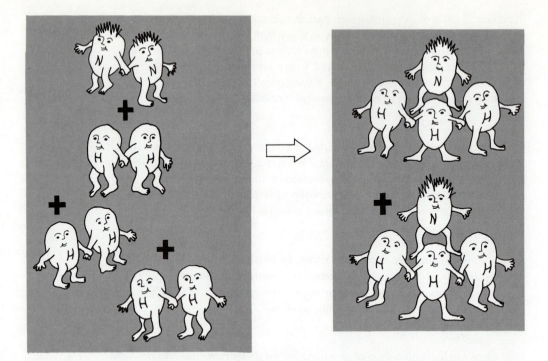

Figure 3-2
In the ammonia synthesis, four pairs of atoms get shuffled into two quartets and the pressure drops by a half.

Atoms exist. They have fixed relationships with each other; they have definite masses relative to each other. At the root of this discussion of water and ammonia molecules, chemical equations, and diatomic elements lies a physical idea of how gases behave (a subject we will deal with in Chap. 6). Gas behavior is fundamental to chemistry. All this because pressure signals *numbers* of molecules to us.

Conservation of Mass

Assume that all matter is made of atoms. Having done that, we can now begin to understand the nature of the four laws governing chemical change. The first of these basic laws is a conservation law suggesting, in the strongest possible way, that mass is conserved in *ordinary* chemical reactions. This means that in ordinary chemical transformations there is hardly any of the conversion of mass to energy predicted by Einstein's theory. *E* certainly does equal *mc²*; that's one of several shattering conclusions we must live with because relativity is a successful theory. But such processes where the conversion of mass *m* to energy *E* is significant are *not* ordinary; they are extraordinary (Fig. 1-15). They are nuclear and deserve the very special treatment they are given in Chap. 9. We are left with *ordinary* chemical reactions where that *E*-to-*m* conversion is insignificant, indeed not measurable at all. Take the best balance ever and try to measure the loss in mass that occurs when some ordinary chemical reaction gives up a million calories of heat; the amount of mass associated with that quantity of heat energy is 4.6 X

10^{-8} gram, or spelling it out more impressively 0.000000046 gram. You're hardly likely to recognize that amount of mass when it presents itself to you. A 75-watt light bulb may lose as much (or as little) as 10^{-12} gram of its mass during each minute of operation (Fig. 3-3). Little more than a specialized accommodation covering the behavior of mass in ordinary (not nuclear) chemical transformations can be offered here. Losses on the order of a few billionths of a pound will not be detectable in any convenient sense. If you're a doubter, as you might well be, the experimental proof is easily assembled in the simple electronic flashbulb. Flashbulbs are complete, isolated systems composed of oxygen gas and fine magnesium wire, all encapsulated in a transparent bulb. A tiny electric current causes the bulb to flash, at which point a great deal of heat and light are emitted; the magnesium and oxygen vanish; and a white powdery substance appears. Here is what happens

$$2\,Mg\,(solid)\;+\;O_2\,(gas)\;\rightarrow\;2\,MgO\,(solid)\;+\,heat + light$$

Compare the mass of the bulb after flashing with its mass prior to reaction. It's all the same. Mass has been neither created nor destroyed: it has only been transformed.

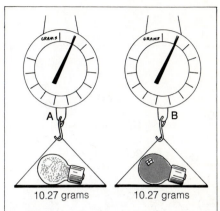

Figure 3-3
Flashbulbs provide the means for a simple demonstration of mass conservation during chemical reactions. There is no evidence of any gain or loss in mass, yet clearly a reaction has taken place.

Constant Proportions

A second important law governing reactions between atoms or molecules has to do with the proportion of each substance needed to form a new compound. When one goes to the trouble of forming a compound such as H_2O or MgO by synthesis, or when nature takes it upon herself to do that job, the quantity of hydrogen or magnesium needed to combine with a specific quantity of oxygen always turns out to be the same. For example, if you're talking about 16 grams of oxygen (the relative mass of the oxygen atom), then 2 grams of hydrogen (2 relative masses) will react, even if 20 or 200 grams of hydrogen are present. Only 2 grams react and the rest is just extra baggage. For 16 grams of oxygen, 24 grams of magnesium (1 relative mass) react, but never more. If you do have more present, it is just surplus magnesium.

Another way of looking at the **Law of Constant Composition** is in terms of different samples of the same substance. Take water (H_2O) again. In any 18 grams of water, there will always be 2 grams of hydrogen and 16 grams of oxygen present. Whether you prepare water in the laboratory, catch a bucket full of rain, melt an iceberg, or draw water from a well, the percent-mass composition will always be definite, namely:

$$\frac{2}{16+2} \times 100 = \frac{2}{18} \times 100 = 11.1\%\ H$$

$$\frac{16}{16+2} \times 100 = \frac{16}{18} \times 100 = 88.9\%\ O$$

Figure 3-4
Different sources of carbon dioxide in the picture? Yes, several. Whatever the source, CO_2 will always have a constant composition: 1 gram of C atoms for every 2.67 grams of O atoms.

And magnesium oxide? Synthetic or natural, it will always be

$$\frac{24}{24 + 16} \times 100 = \frac{24}{40} \times 100 = 60\% \text{ Mg}$$

$$\frac{16}{24 + 16} \times 100 = \frac{16}{40} \times 100 = 40\% \text{ O}$$

Ammonia? Yes, of course; 82 percent nitrogen and 18 percent hydrogen in NH_3.

When combining a definite amount of one element with another element, the first kind always finds exactly the proper amount of the second type—always. That, in turn, forces us to conclude that compound substances must be characterized by definite compositions. Because we've found no exceptions to this behavior, the law of constant proportions has become a foundation for chemical computations. Consider a few examples. When elemental carbon is consumed in an oxygen atmosphere, carbon dioxide forms; every gram of carbon will combine with exactly 2.67 grams of oxygen; 12 grams of carbon must combine with 32 grams of oxygen in these same circumstances. That relationship holds whether the source of the carbon dioxide is the natural environment, human respiration, oxidation of carbon or graphite, or when an antacid such as Alka-Seltzer dissolves in water (Fig. 3-4).

If carbon is consumed in a hydrogen atmosphere, methane forms. Three grams of carbon are required for combination with each and every gram of hydrogen. Twelve grams of carbon combine with 4 grams of hydrogen. That will be true in natural gas from a deep well, marsh gas bubbling from a dying Lake Erie, methane contained in sewage sludge or formed in the laboratory from carbon dioxide, as well as the synthetic product prepared industrially.

Multiple Proportions

When hydrogen combines with oxygen, an oxide we call water (H_2O) is formed. But there is another oxide of hydrogen known as hydrogen peroxide (H_2O_2), which is quite different from water. Casual comparison of the properties of H_2O and H_2O_2 tells us as much as we need to know about their differences. Pure H_2O_2 is a pale blue syrupy liquid that boils at 152°C, hardly the thin, colorless liquid that we expect to boil at 100°C. But more than that, pure H_2O_2 decomposes explosively with little more provocation than a few particles of the dust of some organic or inorganic impurities. Considerable use can be made of this energy release in processes ranging from fueling rocket engines (100 percent hydrogen peroxide) to bleaching wool (30 percent hydrogen peroxide) and hair (6 percent hydrogen peroxide) to simple disinfecting (3 percent hydrogen peroxide). Hardly water-like behavior. How is it possible that two elements combine to form such different compounds? Inspecting H_2O_2 will show that it conforms precisely to our law of constant proportions: 16 grams of oxygen combine with every gram of hydrogen—always—just as H_2O always has 8 grams of oxygen for every gram of hydrogen.

This brings us to one of nature's little subtleties, the **Law of Multiple Proportions.** Since both H_2O and H_2O_2 are combinations of hydrogen and oxygen atoms, shouldn't their two different combinations somehow be related? The law of multiple proportions tells us that in a series of compounds such as H_2O and H_2O_2, the quantity of oxygen combined with a given amount of hydrogen in H_2O is a simple multiple of the quantity of oxygen combined with that same given amount of hydrogen in H_2O_2. True? Yes, test it for yourself and see:

    For H_2O: 8 grams of O for 1 gram of H
    For H_2O_2:   16 grams of O for 1 gram of H

There is a simple, small, whole-number relationship, or multiplication factor, connecting H_2O and H_2O_2 in their respective element combinations: the factor, (ratio, multiple) is 8:16, or 1:2.

Nature is replete with illustrations of the law of multiple proportions. In fact, there are few of nature's element substances that don't partake of this polygamous practice. Nitrogen, for example, does it in fully half a dozen different ways from N_2O to N_2O_5, including NO, NO_2, N_2O_3, and N_2O_4. These oxides of nitrogen range from colorless, odorless nitrous oxide (N_2O) acting as a general anesthetic or propellent for the whipped cream on top of your deserts, to the brownish, noxious smelly air pollutant that is mainly nitrogen dioxide (NO_2) in air masses over urbanized areas. All obey the law of multiple proportions (see Table 3-1). The quantity of oxygen combined with a single gram of nitrogen in nitrous oxide (0.572 gram) is a simple multiple of the mass of oxygen combined with a single gram of nitrogen in nitrogen dioxide (2.28 gram), 0.572:2.28 or 1:4. It is a small whole-number ratio, a multiple of the number 0.572. Moreover it doesn't matter whether a comparison of N_2O_5 is made with N_2O or NO_2. NO against N_2O_4? Yes, that works in quite the same way; you can establish that for yourself. Carbon monoxide (CO) and carbon dioxide (CO_2)? Sulfur dioxide (SO_2) and sulfur trioxide (SO_3)? Yes, it holds for all these gaseous compounds (Table 3-2).

Table 3-2

Oxides of carbon and sulfur

Carbon oxides		Sulfur oxides	
CO	CO_2	SO_2	SO_3
12:16	12:32	32:32	32:48
1:1.33	1:2.67	1:1	1:1.5
$\frac{1.33}{1.33} = 1$	$\frac{2.67}{1.33} = 2$	$\frac{1}{1} = 1$	$\frac{1.5}{1} = 1.5$
1:2 ratio		2:3 ratio	

Table 3-1

Oxides of nitrogen

	N_2O	NO	N_2O_3	NO_2	N_2O_4	N_2O_5
Mass ratio	28:16	14:16	28:48	14:32	28:64	28:80
Grams of O per single gram of N	1:0.572	1:1.14	1:1.72	1:2.28	1:2.28	1:2.86
Ratio of grams O to smallest number of grams O in any of the oxides	$\frac{0.572}{0.572} = 1$	$\frac{1.14}{0.572} = 2$	$\frac{1.72}{0.572} = 3$	$\frac{2.28}{0.572} = 4$	$\frac{2.28}{0.572} = 4$	$\frac{2.86}{0.572} = 5$
Ratios	1	2 :	3 :	4 :	4 :	5

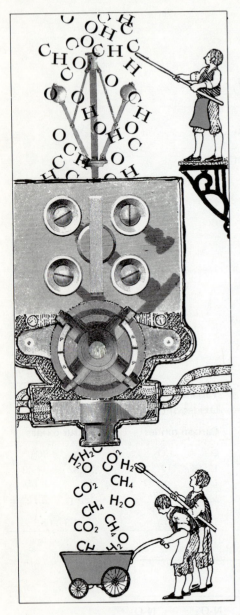

Figure 3-5
The law of equivalent proportions suggests that the possible pairing which occurs when three different elements combine with each other is *not* arbitrary.

Equivalent Proportions

The fourth law central to this theme of atoms and molecules is the **Law of Equivalent Proportions.** The idea is that there will be an **equivalent** relationship between the relative quantities of two elements when combined with each other and the quantities required when each then combines with a third element. If that seems like a mouthful of words, an example should bring it into focus for you. Consider a number of molecules with elements in common:

1 gram of H combines with 8 grams of O in H_2O
1 gram of H combines with 3 grams of C in CH_4

This demonstrates that 8 grams of O and 3 grams of C are equivalent, both combining separately with 1 gram of hydrogen (Fig. 3-5). When O and C combine, they will do so in an **equivalent** ratio of 3:8. The molecule formed is carbon dioxide (CO_2) and the mass ratio is 12:32, which is 3:8 when reduced to the simplest ratio. the equivalent ratio.

Try it again? Consider HCl and CCl_4. That's 1 gram of H for every 35.5 grams of Cl in HCl; as we have already noted, 1 gram of H combines with 3 grams of C in CH_4. Therefore, when CCl_4 forms, the equivalent ratio for C and Cl should be 3:35.5 or 12:142. $SiCl_4$? Also consider SiH_4 with 1 gram of H for 7 grams of Si; $SiCl_4$ must be 7:35.5 or 28:142. So it goes; simple number ratios demonstrating nature's connections. In this case, the Law of Equivalent Proportions.

☐ In Praise of John Dalton

The atomic theory that John Dalton proposed made possible many great advances in our perception of the restless universe. Those advances occurred during the entire nineteenth century, setting the stage for a twentieth-century revolution that took place just as the community of scientists began to focus their view inside the atom itself. Our perception of restlessness had changed anew. If all that seems like so much ancient history (after all, this Dalton business is getting on toward 175 years old) don't be fooled. Lucretius and the Greek notion of the atom is what's ancient history; Dalton's view is very contemporary by comparison (Fig. 3-6). The Greek point of view did contain the essential notion of indivisibility, however, even though the other ideas necessary for real progress were missing. Over the centuries, the poem of Lucretius has been reduced to an idea of atoms as being nothing more than something small.

Newton and Boyle wrote of their belief in particulate matter. But John Dalton first put the idea of atoms in a way that projected the connections between the theories and the accumulated experimental data of the day (Fig. 3-7). The laws governing chemical change sharply silhouette the essential facts having to do with the exact nature of chemical transactions. Dalton's atomic theory offered a successful explanation of these very laws. Dalton's atomic theory contained the following important principles:

1 Matter consists of ultimate particles called atoms (the principal theme of Dalton's theory).

2 These atoms are small, indivisible, and indestructible; they cannot be created nor destroyed (conservation of mass).

3 Atoms of any given element have identical characteristic properties and exhibit constant mass.

4 Molecules are formed from fixed numbers of atoms of the elements that were combined in their formation (constant proportions); these are the ultimate particles of compound substances.

5 Molecules have masses that are sums of the constituent element masses.

6 An atom of an element has the same mass in all its combinations; therefore, the composition of a molecule formed of two elements, A and C, may be determined from the composition of molecules formed when each combines with a third element, B (equivalent proportions).

7 When a single compound of two kinds of atoms, A + B, is known, it will generally be A + B. If more than one compound is known, then there will be A + B and 2A + B, or perhaps A + 2B, and so on (multiple proportions).

These principles led Dalton to a system for classifying pure substances as elements and compounds in terms of atoms and molecules. Assumptions 1 and 2 allowed Dalton to conclude the truth of Lavoisier's Law of Conservation of Mass; assumptions 3, 4, and 5 brought Dalton to the conclusion that compounds must have constant composition, settling one of the controversial scientific questions of his day. Dalton was the first to attempt to discover the relative masses of atoms through study of chemical compositions. From that study emerged a major revelation, the Law of Multiple Proportions, perhaps Dalton's single most important contribution to atomic theory. His work formed the substance of a new focal point for chemical analysis and the meaning of analytical data. Finally, the success of Dalton's theory brought about the second major modification in the original atomic theory that had come down from Greek antiquity. Lavoisier had already defined the chemical element. When Dalton translated that idea into atomic terms, belief in a continuity of matter was effectively abandoned. John Dalton consolidated all of his thinking on the subject into a book. The definitive published account appeared in 1808 under the title *A New System of Chemical Philosophy*:

Figure 3-6
Dalton is modern.

> Chemical analysis and synthesis go no farther than to the separation of particles from one another, and to their reunion. No new creation or destruction of matter is within the reach of chemical agency. We might as well attempt to introduce a new planet into

Figure 3-7
Reproduction of John Dalton's lecture diagrams and atom models. Note the symbols and relative weights, all compared to *one* for hydrogen.

the solar system, or to annihilate one already in existence, as to create or destroy a particle of hydrogen: All the changes we can produce, consist in separating particles that are in a state of cohesion of combination, and joining those that were previously at a distance.

Now it is one great object of this work, to show the importance and advantage of ascertaining the relative weights of the ultimate particles, both of simple and compound bodies, the number of simple and elementary particles which constitute one compound particle, and the number of less compound particles which enter into the formation of one more compound particle.

Dalton's theory received mixed reviews in London and Paris. It would be kind to suggest that the legendary British experimentalist, Sir Humphrey Davy, was simply "skeptical"; likewise, it would be a gross understatement to say that Berthellot, the famous French scientist and advisor to Napolean Bonaporte, only "would have none of it." But they loved him in Glasgow and Edinburgh, and it was all hearts and flowers in Turin and Stockholm where Dalton had his two strongest enthusiasts in Avogadro and Berzelius. Acceptance of the atomic theory after 1808 was not easy. Such things never are, and as we've noted before, it was 1908 before everyone "believed" in atoms.

"It's H_2O, John: not simply HO"

One of Dalton's principal objectives was to determine the mass of these atomic individuals directly. Atoms are small, however, and very restless. Consequently absolute measurement of mass seemed an all but impossible task. The road around the dilemma was to get at the relative masses of different atoms by measuring the mass of one element in combination with a second; all that was needed in addition was the relative number of atoms in the resulting compound. Water will serve again as our illustrative example. Analysis of a pure sample yields the results 11.1 percent hydrogen and 88.9 percent oxygen and the ratio 88.9:11.1 tells us that oxygen is responsible for eight times as much of what water is made of as hydrogen. If there is one hydrogen atom for every oxygen atom in water molecules, oxygen must be eight times more massive than hydrogen. But what if there are two hydrogen atoms attached to each oxygen atom? Then oxygen would be 16 times the relative mass of hydrogen. Hyrogen would be 1, oxygen would be 16.

Dalton missed the mark here. He assumed the simplest possible arrangement to be the most likely, namely that the water molecule is the combination of an atom of hydrogen and an atom of oxygen, forming HO. Unfortunately, Dalton had no way of clearly checking the basic assumption of his rule of "greatest simplicity." That a number of Dalton's formulas and all of his relative masses were incorrect is of no particular account today; what is important is the concept of relative masses and how to get at them. For example, in 1804 Dalton analyzed methane gas and obtained the mundane result 74.85 percent carbon and 25.5 percent hydrogen. If you now employ Dalton's genius and compare these same numbers on the basis of the amount of hydrogen combined with the same amount of carbon, they suddenly become very interesting numbers. Assuming C = 12, but using elemental analysis data from 1804:

> If C = 12 and H = 1, then 74.85 percent C must be 74.85 : 12 or 6.25, relative to 25.5 : 1 or 25.5 H. The 1 : 4 ratio that shows up for C : H fits methane, exactly as we know it today.

Mass-percent composition by analysis: C = 74.85%   H = 25.5%

Equivalent mass ratio: $C = \dfrac{74.85}{12} = 6.25$ $H = \dfrac{25.5}{1} = 25.5$

Atom ratio: $C = \dfrac{6.25}{6.25} = 1$ $H = \dfrac{25.5}{6.25} = 4$

CH_4 simple formula

For all nature's elements, a relative scale of atomic masses has been established by choosing a simple element as a reference standard and referring all the other elements to it. The chosen reference standard is the most common form of the element carbon, assigned a mass of 12; it has 12 atomic mass units (amu) per atom. A single amu has a mass of exactly 1/12 the mass of a single carbon atom of the reference kind (called C-12). Now an *average* carbon sample made up of the usual kind of carbon atoms that weigh 12 amu, along with the unusual carbon atoms that exist in nature, has an average atomic mass of 12.01115. That's just about 12 anyway so there really can't be a very big percentage of those unusual carbon atoms (mostly the C-13 variety). As it happens, a fairly large percentage of nature's different atoms have approximately integral average atomic masses (in atomic mass units) as well. Hydrogen has an average mass of 1.008, close enough to 1 for most purposes; lithium is 6.939, or about 7; nitrogen's mass is 14.0067, or 14, sodium is 22.990 or 23. (See Table 2-4.)

☐ Molecules and Moles

It is not very likely that any of us will have much luck at weighing a huge molecule such as a protein with a mass of perhaps a million amu or more, much less a single small molecule such as a nitric oxide molecule, mass 30 amu (see Fig. 3-8). Weighing out single atoms? Forget that. Well, what shall you do then if you want to do that experiment in the laboratory? How can you put together needed numbers of atoms or molecules? Remember that weighable quantities, perhaps as little as 0.1 gram will contain many hundreds of billions of particles.

It is possible to get your hands on at least the correct numbers of atoms and molecules by taking advantage of our system of relative atomic masses. For nitric oxide, we'll need to know the atomic mass for nitrogen and oxygen in amu. That's about 14 and 16 respectively. Now, if we could collect two piles, each containing equal numbers of nitrogen and oxygen atoms, it is reasonable to express the mass of the nitrogen pile as being 14/16 as great as that of the oxygen pile. Any pile of nitrogen atoms that contains the same number of atoms of oxygen will be 14/16 as massive. Simply stated, a pile of nitrogen atoms amounting to 14 grams

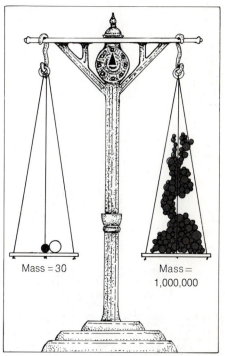

Mass = 30   Mass = 1,000,000

Figure 3-8
The most sensitive laboratory balance doesn't come close to detecting the presence of even the largest single molecules.

Table 3-3

Element	Atomic mass (amu)	Mass in grams of pile of atoms	Moles of atoms in that atom pile
Hydrogen (H)	1	0.01	0.01
Oxygen (O)	16	1.6	0.1
Sulfur (S)	32	32	1.0
Potassium (K)	39	78	2.0
Bromine (Br)	80	400	5.0
Uranium (U)	238	2380	10.0

will have as many atomic particles in it as a 16-gram oxygen pile (Table 3-3). Indeed, relative masses of different atoms or molecules will always consist of equal numbers of particles. Furthermore, it really does not matter whether we're talking gram units or kilogram units; 14 kilograms of nitrogen will contain as many atom particles as 16 kilograms of oxygen; kilogram piles merely have greater **total** numbers than gram piles.

The World of *N*

Create a number *N* (Fig. 3-9). Set *N* equal to the number of nitrogen atoms weighing 14 grams, or the number of oxygen atoms weighing 16 grams. *N* is the number of atoms in a 1-mole pile of atoms. That's true for molecules as well as atoms. Twenty-eight grams of nitric oxide contains *N* molecules, a mole of molecules. What we've said is that the mass of *N* atoms of an element is equal to its atomic mass in grams. Then 4 grams of a monatomic substance whose atomic mass is 4 must contain the same number of particles as 100 grams of a molecular substance of mass 100; 4 grams of the first substance on the laboratory balance contain as many atoms as a pile of the second substance 25 times as heavy. *N* helps us keep the numbers here on a large enough scale so that atoms and molecules can be reasonably handled by people. Single atoms and molecules are just too small, but one can reasonably manage to move *N* atoms or molecules.

Try a specific example. Copper burns in a sulfur atmosphere forming copper sulfide molecules; those same copper sulfide molecules can then be recycled back to copper atoms by reaction with molecules of hydrogen. One way the chemical equations describing that circuitous process can be written looks like this:

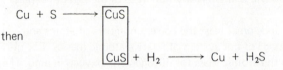

then

Start with *N* atoms of copper having a mass of 63.5 grams. You'll need exactly that number of sulfur atoms, or 32 grams. The maximum number of copper sulfide molecules of molecular mass 95.5 (by adding 63.5 to 32) produced *N* molecules, weighing 95.5 grams. Copper sulfide can react with the necessary

Figure 3-9

Creating *N*, the number of particles in a mole of particles.

quantity of hydrogen molecules—that's right, they're molecules (H_2's), not atoms (H's)—which must be N molecules. We get back exactly N copper atoms, that's what we started with, plus 34 grams or 1 mole of hydrogen sulfide molecules.

$$Cu + S \longrightarrow CuS \qquad CuS + H_2 \longrightarrow Cu + H_2S$$

$$\underbrace{63.5\text{g} \quad 32\text{ g}}_{95.5\text{ g}} \qquad 95.5\text{ g} \qquad \underbrace{95.5\text{ g} \quad 2\text{ g}}_{97.5\text{ g}} \qquad \underbrace{63.5\text{ g} \quad 34\text{ g}}_{97.5\text{ g}}$$

N is nothing more than a unit number of particles, like a dozen. Only instead of counting 12 particles, N contains some specific, very large number of very small particles, N particles, and they can be atomic, molecular, or whatever. In the same way that a dozen grapes, a dozen apples, a dozen grapefruits, or a dozen watermelons all weigh different amounts, mole quantities of atoms and molecules range from very light to very massive (Fig. 3-10). Whether it's 2 grams of hydrogen molecules (H_2), 18 grams of water molecules (H_2O), or 238 grams of uranium atoms (U) the number of particles is the same, the number of particles is N.

The mole is chemically convenient for us and from here on we shall refer to any quantity of a substance equivalent to its atomic or molecular mass in grams as a single **mole of atoms or molecules** of that substance. It follows that 1 mole of any substance must contain exactly the same number of particles as 1 mole of any other substance. Of course, by weighing out grams we are really counting particles for use in chemical transformations. Switching our terminology from grams to moles frees us of some confusing possibilities. A mole is a certain

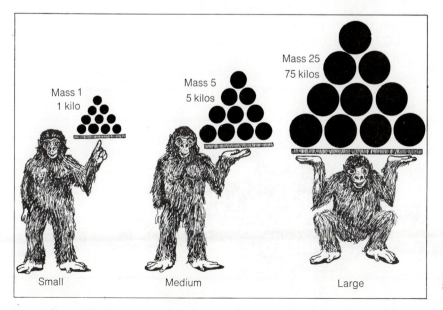

Mass 1
1 kilo

Mass 5
5 kilos

Mass 25
75 kilos

Small

Medium

Large

Figure 3-10
Same numbers, different masses.

number of units; in fact, it is *N* units. The crux of the matter lies in the fact that for a substance such as sulfur dioxide (SO_2) the oxygen content (2 X 16 amu) and the sulfur content (1 X 32 amu) are a match according to mass (32 versus 32). However, if you are *counting* instead of massing, oxygen easily outnumbers sulfur, 2 atoms for every 1.

Question: What exactly is the number of molecules in a mole? How many atoms are there in a mole of atoms? How big a number is *N*? To the best of our current knowledge, *N* is 602,277,000,000,000,000,000,000, alternately known as *Avogadro's number.* It is commonly expressed, using exponential notation, as 6 X 10^{23} particles. To give you some small idea of just how large that number of particles is, it has been estimated that Avogadro's number of grains of sand would fill a trench 3 feet deep and 11 miles wide, stretching from New York to San Francisco (Fig. 3-11). Consider a regular cube containing this number. Along each edge there must be on the order of 84,500,000 particles (because that number cubed gives a number very close to 6 X 10^{23}). How much does a single atom of the lightest element hydrogen weigh? Well, 6 X 10^{23} of these atoms weigh 1 gram. Therefore, using the more accurate values, we calculate the mass of a single H atom to be 1.673 X 10^{-24} gram

$$\left(\frac{1.008 \text{ g H}}{1 \text{ mole H atoms}}\right)\left(\frac{1 \text{ mole H atoms}}{6.023 \text{ X } 10^{23} \text{ H atoms}}\right) = \frac{1.008 \text{ g H}}{6.023 \text{ X } 10^{23} \text{ H atoms}} = \frac{1.673 \text{ X } 10^{-24} \text{ g H}}{1 \text{ H atom}}$$

In summary, an illustrative example or two will be very helpful:

1. First, consider 32 grams of O atoms, remembering that as it occurs in nature, it is a diatomic molecule.

   32 grams of O: is the molecular mass of O in grams

   is the mass of 1 mole of O molecules

   is the mass of 2 moles of O atoms

2. Then, consider 1 mole of H_2O molecules, remembering that each individual H_2O molecule contains three joined atoms, and that the molecular mass is 18 (H_2O = 2 + 16).

   18 grams of H_2O: is the molecular mass of H_2O in grams

   is the mass of 1 mole of H_2O molecules

Figure 3-11

San Francisco

Salt Lake City

BATHS

contains 2 moles of H atoms
contains 1 mole of O atoms
contains 6.023×10^{23} H_2O molecules
contains $2(6.023 \times 10^{23})$ H atoms
contains 6.023×10^{23} O atoms

3. Finally, consider 5 moles of N_2O molecules:

5 moles of N_2O: contains 10 moles of N atoms
contains 5 moles of O atoms
are $5(6.023 \times 10^{23})$ N_2 molecules
weighs $5(2.14 + 1.16) = 220$ grams

☐ **Questions to Answer . . . Problems to Solve**

1. Are you convinced of the atomic nature of matter? If so, why? If not, why not?

2. If you adopt Dalton's rule of greatest simplicity for nitrous oxide, what would be the simple chemical formula for the molecule? What would the relative weight of the nitrogen atom be? What would the formula for nitric oxide be?

3. In your day-to-day experience, can you describe an example or two of the law of conservation of mass that can be verified by a simple weighing procedure as for the electronic flash bulb.

4. Consider the following sets of experimental data. Then determine which of Dalton's principles cover that behavior; and indicate which of the laws of chemical change are illustrated by a particular statement or statements:
   (a) When 32 grams of sulfur (S) completely react with 32 grams of (O_2), 64 grams of sulfur dioxide are produced.
   (b) If 32 grams of sulfur were completely reacted with 48 grams of oxygen oxygen a different oxide, sulfur trioxide (SO_3) is produced.

Chicago   New York City

(c) And if 32 grams of sulfur were completely reacted with 64 grams of oxygen, sulfur trioxide forms but 16 grams of oxygen remain.

(d) When the two oxides, SO_2 and SO_3 were examined, the weight ratio of oxygen to sulfur in the two compounds was found to be $[S/2 O = 32/2(16) = 32/32 = 1/1]$ and $[S/3 O = 32/3(16) = 32/48 = 1/1.5 = 2/3]$, or $1/1$ in SO_2 and $2/3$ in SO_3.

(e) When carbon (C) is combined with oxygen, twelve grams of carbon react with 32 grams of oxygen; when carbon and sulfur react with each other, they form carbon disulfide, CS_2.

5. One technique that can be used in the purification of uranium involves the preparation of a fluoride, uranium hexafluoride, UF_6. For that fluoride, state the following:

(a) molecular weight in grams

(b) moles of fluorine atoms per mole of UF_6

(c) molecular weight

(d) weight percent composition of the component elements

(e) grams of uranium that combine with each gram of fluorine

(f) molecular formula for uranium hydride, knowing that when fluorine combines with hydrogen, HF forms

(g) molecular formula for uranium oxide, knowing that when hydrogen combines with oxygen, H_2O forms

6. Which of the following statements do you believe?

(a) A flask full of hydrogen gas at a particular temperature and pressure will weigh 1/9th as much as a flask filled with water vapor under exactly the same conditions of temperature and pressure.

(b) Twenty-eight grams of nitrogen gas as it occurs in nature contains the same number of molecules as 28 grams of carbon monoxide.

(c) A mole of oxygen atoms weighs the same as a mole of methane molecules.

(d) Carbon tetrachloride contains is better than 92 percent chlorine by weight.

(e) Ammonia is composed of hydrogen and nitrogen in a 1:4.67 weight ratio.

(f) Ten grams of water contain more molecules than ten grams of hydrogen peroxide.

7. If you were to distribute a mole of water among 3.5 billion inhabitants of the Earth, how many molecules would each receive? Would you think that would satisfy your thirst?

8. Are you sure all atoms of the same element weigh the same? What makes you so sure? How do you know?

9. Listed below are the symbols and percentages for the earth's ten most abundant elements. Identify each by name. ***Assuming*** you had exactly a 1-kg mass of this composition, how many moles of each of these ten elements would you have.

O	49.5%	Na	2.6%
Si	25.7%	K	2.4%
Al	7.5%	Mg	1.9%
Fe	4.7%	H	0.9%
Ca	3.4%	Ti	0.6%

10. Here is a set of definite proportions for four separate chlorine oxides. What can you do to show that these data illustrate multiple proportions:

	grams of oxygen	grams of chlorine
oxide 1	8	35.5
oxide 2	24	35.5
oxide 3	40	35.5
oxide 4	56	35.5

11. What do you think? Is Dalton's atomic theory still only a theory, or is it now pretty much experimental?

12. If Dalton had lived in Galileo's time (about two centuries earlier) and presented his atomic theory to the scientific community, do you feel he would have been subject to the same views by the inquisition and the church. In other words, do you think Dalton's theory was really radical in the proper context of his times? Was Dalton really a red-eyed scientific bomb-thrower as was Rutherford a century later and Galileo before him?

13. And how about some busy work to sharpen your understanding of the mechanics of atoms and molecules:

(a) Determine the number of moles for each case:

1.72 g of Ba
24.5 g of sodium
132 g of S
1 g of hydrogen gas
1.008 g of H
100 g of CuO
1000 g of H_2O

(b) Calculate the mass in grams for each of the following:

1 mole of chlorine gas, Cl_2
5.56 moles of water
20.0 g of potassium
3.097×10^1 g of P
0.0019 g of F_2
100 g of palladium
502 g of Co

(c) See if you can evaluate the number of grams per mole for each case

$PdCl_2$ $C_6H_{12}O_6$ NiCN
NaCl C_2H_6
I_2 $CaCO_3$

14. Here is a statement to think about for a moment . . . and when you've had time to do that, try and relate it to Dalton's atomic theory and the material in this chapter:

"Facts and experiments, however, relating to any subject, are never duly appreciated until in the hand of some skilled observer they are made to force the consequences of certain other operations which were never before undertaken."

Chemistry provides no real knowledge of what energy is. There is simply no picture available, however, the concept is useful and powerful, providing us with a means for perceiving action. We can feel the energy in the sweep of a wild river, yet the monolithic face of the mountain is hardly at rest. At the top, scientists from the Clavius moonbase view the monolith Moon-watcher had viewed from the Pleistocene. . . "sharp-edged and symmetrical . . . so black it seemed to have swallowed up the light falling upon it . . ." —2001: A Space Odyssey

☐ **Perceptions and Deceptions**

1 Rest isn't what you think it is. In fact, on a microscopic scale, rest simply isn't.

2 Force and acceleration go together, but we only witness the latter (acceleration) and we have to guess the former (force).

3 Energy: Transformed, degraded, interchanged, exchanged . . . Yes, certainly, but consumed? Never!

4 "Civilizations are characterized by the power of their energy converters. The shorter the time required to transport a cargo across a continent, or to flatten a city, the more advanced the civilization is said to be."

☐ **Rest: Stranger in the Physical World**

Our experience of the universe often results in incomplete judgments based on taking things at face value and trusting first impressions. For example, we have a notion of *rest* on a macroscopic scale which is easy to understand when comparing outward appearances: the raging Colorado River rapids, the monolithic structure of Halfdome at Yosemite. Halfdome is hardly raging. On a microscopic scale, however, there is nothing dead about the stone face of a mountain. We have simply been deceived by our impressions.

The universe is composed of tiny particles of matter that are always in motion. The air we breathe is nothing more than a collection of speeding particles moving randomly about. In liquids and solids the average motion isn't as fast, but the particles are still clearly on the move. They're just not able to travel very far before bumping a neighbor (more about such molecular overpopulations later). The deceptive nature of outward appearances teaches us to examine impressions derived from our sense experience more carefully. It may be appropriate to describe the sea of air around us as "foul" within the city limits or to talk of "clear" mountain air when hiking across the countryside, but both are inaccurate descriptions. "Foulness" has to do with pollutants mixed into the air: soot, sulfurous fumes, pollen, dust, oxides of nitrogen. "Clearness" has to do with cleaner air, some or all of those fouling agents being absent. Well, what's this *air* anyway?

The Pressure of the Atmosphere

Take a deep breath and hold it. Feel the pressure of the air in your lungs? Now breath out. Inhale. Exhale. You have just given a demonstration of air pressure while, at the same time, performing the most vital human operation possible with air: *respiration,* the supplying of oxygen to the lungs in order to keep yourself alive.

A bicycle pump is a simple air compressor, or air "squeezer" (see Fig. 4-1). If you've ever pumped up the air in a tire you may have noticed the pump

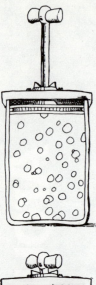

Figure 4-1
Pumps are air squeezers. Squeezing results in heating because the same number of molecules have been forced to occupy a smaller space.

getting warm, especially if you pushed the handle up and down rapidly. Pushing down on the pump handle or piston compresses the air, forcing open a valve, thus allowing air to flow into the confined space within the tire. First impression: the heating effect is due to friction between the inside walls of the pump and the moving piston in much the same way as heat is generated by rubbing your hands together. To a small degree that is probably true; a little heat may be produced by friction. However, most of it isn't. Proof? Disconnect the pump from the tire and push the air back out into the wide open atmosphere. Do it vigorously as before. Now the pump scarcely heats up at all. Second impression: most of the heating effect noted in pumping the tire up must have been produced by forcing more and more air into the fixed space inside the tire, in short, by compression. As a matter of fact, all gases are heated when compressed in this fashion. Squeezing more gas into the same volume has produced heat (Fig. 4-1).

By vigorously compressing a gas, one can attain very high temperatures. For example, heating air by means of violent compression is critical to the operation of the diesel engine (see Fig. 4-1). Air in the cylinder is compressed, gets very hot, and immediately ignites the fuel injected into it. No spark is needed as in the internal combustion, gasoline-burning engine.

What, then, is this stuff called air? We can squeeze it together although it resists being squeezed and immediately fills any new space given it. If the human ear were more sensitive than it actually is, we would all be audio witnesses to the ceaseless rush and racket of the air's particles as they beat on our eardrums. The beat or force on the outside of the eardrum is counterbalanced by a beat on the inside of the eardrum so that the net beat is zero. When you rise suddenly in an airplane or elevator or drive up a mountain, some discomfort in your ear is obvious because the net effect is not zero. It takes a while for the pressure on both sides of the eardrum to equalize.

The tiny particles of the air are mostly molecules of oxygen and nitrogen. They live a fast and furious existence, flying about, colliding with each other (almost), and bumping into the walls of whatever it is that contains them: eardrums, bicycle pumps, and the like. If the wall happens to be flexible, as an eardrum, or movable, as the piston in a bicycle pump, the rush of the molecules will push at the wall, causing it to move unless some opposition by nature prevents that from happening.

There is a theory known as the ***kinetic molecular theory***, which is based on the behavior of molecules in motion. (The Greek word for motion, and our theory's most salient feature, is ***Kinema***.) It applies not only to the mixture of molecules we call air but to collections of the individual components of the air, namely oxygen and nitrogen. We presently believe, and have for a long time, that it is applicable to all substances in the gaseous state.

☐ Kinetic Molecular Theory and Newton's Laws of Motion

From the moment Issac Newton proposed his theory of universal gravitation, its acceptance was assured. His book, ***Principia***, went through a number of revisions and his ideas became the talk of the drawing rooms and salons of Europe for a century after (hardly the way in which science filters down to people today). Wide public acceptance of Newton's ideas was due, in great measure, to his ability to simplify and connect nature's happenings in ways that could be experienced and understood. Can the same be said of kinetic molecular theory? The essence of that theory rests on a simple proposition: gas pressure is nothing more than the constant bombardment caused by the particles of the gas. Properties of gases depend on their possessing mass, on their expanding in all directions, unless otherwise constrained, and on their becoming more highly compressed in response to a compressing force.

The extent to which we are able to perceive the validity of the kinetic molecular theory has a great deal to do with Newton's laws. His law of inertia recognizes that all freely moving bodies keep the motion they possess:

A body at rest stays that way, and a body moving uniformly in a straight line also continues in that way unless something happens to *change* things (see Fig. 4-4).

Newton's second law can be stated in terms of the two key words, *change* and *motion*:

There is a constant relationship between changing motion and the force required to effect the change.

All particles in motion are governed by Newton's basic laws of science. Inertia and changing motion have to do with energy, momentum (more key words), and the motions of molecules. Therefore, Newton's two laws help provide a foundation for the kinetic molecular theory. That means these ideas are fundamental to any discussion of chemistry and deserve some attention here.

Experience suggests that in order to move horizontally here on earth, a body must somehow be pushed or pulled, mechanically or otherwise. Experience also suggests that when the push-pull mechanism is removed or turned off, the body will quickly come to rest. The obvious conclusion is that horizontal motion needs continuous propulsion. That conclusion, however, reached by many great thinkers since the time of Aristotle and first corrected by Galileo in the early part of the seventeenth century, is misleading. Galileo understood correctly that if frictional forces could be eliminated, a body would slide across a smooth surface without ever slowing to a stop, or slowing down at all.

Imagine what all of the neighbors thought on that day Galileo decided to drop some objects from the top of Pisa's leaning tower. Galileo was onto something

Figure 4-2
Galileo's experiment as it might have been conducted on the moon.

Figure 4-3
Max and Hedwig Born with the Physicist, Lise Meitner (center). The year was 1954.

all those doubters didn't know and wouldn't have believed anyway. Chuckle, if you like, at Galileo's surprised neighbors, but their incredulity was well-founded. At that time there was simply no basis whatsoever for faith in his imaginative predictions. Four hundred years later Galileo's experiment was successfully carried off on the moon's surface, where a hammer and a feather were shown to fall in an identical manner, according to his exact prediction and Newton's subsequent generalization (see Fig. 4-2).

Billiard Games and Kinetic Behavior

A fellow Italian by the name of Daniel Bernoulli had suggested a kinetic theory a century before the kinetic-molecular theory was first proposed. Bernoulli's ideas were based on Newton's laws set down some 50 years earlier, and were presented in the form of a billiard ball model. A billiard ball analogy for kinetic behavior is a very good one, one that has been effectively developed by Max Born, a colleague of Albert Einstein (see Fig. 4-3). Born began with a billiard game viewed as a series of applications of the law of inertia. The stroke of the cue speeds the ball on its way. Inertia keeps the ball going in much the same way your car persists in moving after the engine is shut down. Fortunately, since our billiard table is perfectly horizontal, gravity has no effect, since gravity only acts as a force in a vertical direction. Wind resistance and the little bit of friction between ball and cloth are also negligible for our purposes.

Now, suppose we replace the billiard ball with one of similar size made of styrofoam. Note the effect of the cue stroke. A stroke of the cue that might cause the billiard ball to slowly cover a long distance may give the styrofoam ball a smart blow, sending it suddenly and violently on its way, but the styrofoam ball comes as rapidly to rest again. Because of its greater mass, the much heavier billiard ball keeps right on rolling along. Its inertia is greater than that of the lighter styrofoam ball, and although it is less accelerated, it more persistently maintains its velocity. Stated another way, it is harder to bring about either an increase or decrease in the velocity of the more massive billiard ball.

If two billiard balls collide, as two particles in a gas might, part of the *momentum* of the first ball transfers to the second. The momentum of any body is the product of its mass and velocity. A massive ball moving slowly and a not-so-massive ball moving rapidly both generate considerable momentum. When our two billiard balls collide, their momentum will distribute between them in some definite way, but their *total* momentum will be unchanged. In other words, the mass-velocity product for the first added to the mass-velocity product for the second has the same numerical value before and after collision. The mass-velocity product for the first may well be less than it was originally and that of the second may be greater than it was, but their total momentum—the sum—is conserved (Fig. 4-4). While there are many situations where you may well gain something for nothing (a distant relative may leave you a fortune, or you may crawl through an income tax loophole to a clever profit) momentum is not one of them. The most—and the least—you can hope for is an even break. Momentum is conserved.

Motion Is Interesting When It Is Changing

This brings us to the hardest part of this discussion. Two concepts, namely force and motion, and their relationship, need explaining. Motion is of little interest unless it is changing. When we refer to motion "changing," we are talking about changes in speed, direction, and the like. For example, gas molecules suddenly and violently reverse their motion when they career off the walls of a container. In a similar fashion the billiard ball in our model does the same when it hits the cushion at an edge of the table. According to Newton's second law, the rate a at which motion is changing as time goes by is *proportional* to the applied force F, the particular push or pull as the case may be. "Proportional" simply means than there is a constant relationship. Concisely stated, F is proportional to a:

$$F \propto a$$

but $\propto$ can be replaced by $= m$ so that

$$F = ma$$

The proportionality constant m is the mass of the body in question and a is commonly referred to as the *acceleration,* the time-rate of change of velocity (see Fig. 4-5). Now we have all the components of a rigorous statement of Newton's second law, which may be rewritten as

$$a = \frac{F}{m}$$

Making use of our new of proportionality, if mass m is constant, then acceleration a is directly proportional to force F:

$$a \propto F$$

In simpler English, as the push or pull increases, the acceleration changes accordingly (see Fig. 4-6). On the other hand, if force F, the push or pull, is constant,

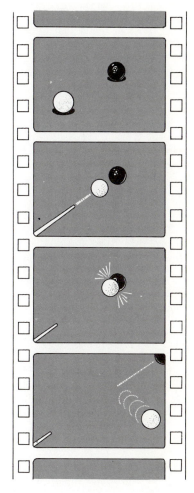

Figure 4-4
When billiard balls collide, momentum may well be redistributed between the colliding balls, but *total* momentum remains unchanged.

Figure 4-5
The young soccer star (far left) has just provided the needed foot-power to cause the ball's rapid acceleration (time-rate of change of velocity).

Figure 4-6
Clark Gable in action; his opponent in re-action. Newton's laws at work.

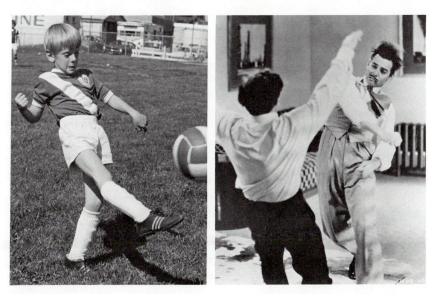

acceleration will be inversely proportional to the mass of the body being accelerated, namely,

$$a \propto \frac{1}{m}$$

We now have some basis for understanding the behavior of the billiard balls in our model. If we use the same push of the pool cue, a constant force, then the more massive billiard ball is more slowly accelerated than is the much less massive styrofoam ball. By the same token, a collision between a speeding foam ball will be as effective in accelerating another foam ball as will be the slowly moving billiard ball. Isn't this all related to Galileo's principle of inertia and our ideas of momentum? Bodies want to keep on doing what they are doing, moving or standing still. The greater the body's momentum, the stronger will have to be the influence of the changing force. The more massive ball is harder to get moving; once moving, it is harder to stop. Correct? You might well conclude that inertia is a property of mass. Again, you'd be right.

Newton's second law has now been dressed in the form of an equation, immediately lending it much stature, but we haven't said anything about our proportionality constant *m*, the mass. It must be defined more clearly. Matter, the stuff of the universe, has two characteristic properties. First, it has weight, or the property of being pulled toward the earth. Simply stated, matter is influenced by the force or pull of gravity. Second, it has inertia, or the capacity to resist an accelerating force. In other words, matter doesn't want to change the way it's moving. Both properties can be used to measure the mass of any pile of matter in the universe.

Our concept of matter as mass was an outgrowth of the age of Newton; the century that followed saw its fruitful development. Chemistry's development was thrust strongly forward by the concept of constant mass. Chemical changes were increasingly viewed as taking place through a shuffling about at the submicroscopic atomic level: lots of inner hustle and bustle while suffering no overall change in mass. The test for our continued complacency with the truth of that notion lay in the increasing skill at measuring mass.

☐ Energy? What's Energy?

Newton's two laws governing matter in motion can be applied to our description of the behavior of molecules in motion. To do this requires a preliminary discussion of the concept of *energy*. Energy applies to the behavior of just about every phenomenon in nature. The Law of Conservation of Energy comes about as close to being dogma in science as one is likely to find: to date, no exception has ever been documented. This law is a purely mathematical statement that says "some number" does not change when nature is changing. Just an abstract notion; there is no picture available from the world of our experience to enlighten us. One way to describe such a strange idea as this Law of Conservation of Energy is to repeat a short story that Richard Feynman (Fig. 4-7), famous scientist and teacher, tells his students:

Imagine a child, perhaps "Dennis the Menace," who has blocks which are absolutely indestructible, and cannot be divided into pieces. Each is the same as the other. Let us suppose that he has 28 blocks. His mother puts him with his 28 blocks into a room at the beginning of the day. At the end of the day, being curious, she counts the blocks very carefully, and discovers a phenomenal law— no matter what he does with the blocks, there are always 28 remaining! One day, however, the number appears to change—there are only 26 blocks. Careful investigation indicates that the window was open, and upon looking outside, the other two blocks are found. Another day, careful count indicates that there are 30 blocks! This causes considerable consternation, until it is realized that Bruce came to visit, bringing his blocks with him, and he left a few at Dennis' house. After she has disposed of the extra blocks, she closes the window, does not let Bruce in, and then everything is going along all right, until one time she counts and finds only 25 blocks. However, there is a box in the room, a toy box, and the mother goes to open the toy box, but the boy says "No, do not open my toy box," and screams. Mother is not allowed to open the toy box. Being extremely curious and somewhat ingenious, she invents a scheme. She knows that a block weighs three ounces, so she weighs the box at a time when she sees 28 blocks, and it weighs 16 ounces. The next time she wishes to check, she weighs the box again, subtracts sixteen ounces and divides by three. She discovers the following:

$$\text{(number of blocks seen)} + \frac{\text{(weight of box)} - 16 \text{ ounces}}{3 \text{ ounces}} = \text{constant}$$

Figure 4-7
Richard Feynman with his son on the morning in 1965 when he learned of his Nobel Prize award.

There then appear to be some new deviations, but careful study indicates that the dirty water in the bathtub is changing its level. The child is throwing blocks into the water, and she cannot see them because it is so dirty, but she can find out how many blocks are in the water by adding another term to her formula. Since the original height of the water was 6 inches and each block raises the water a quarter of an inch, this new formula would be:

$$\text{(number of blocks seen)} + \frac{\text{(weight of box)} - 16 \text{ ounces}}{3 \text{ ounces}} + \frac{\text{(height of water)} - 6 \text{ inches}}{\frac{1}{4} \text{ inch}} = \text{constant}$$

In the gradual increase in the complexity of her world, she finds a whole series of terms representing ways of calculating how many blocks are in places where she is not allowed to look. As a result she finds a complex formula, a quantity which has to be computed, which always stays the same in her situation.

Well, what has this little story to do with the Law of Conservation of Energy? The behavior of energy is exactly analogous to the behavior of blocks in the story; consequently, we can learn some important things from the analogy:

1. We talk of adding or removing energy, but only in a figurative sense. Energy cannot be looked at in any real material way. There aren't really any blocks. Professor Feynman introduced blocks only because they were useful in creating a mental picture of energy. We say, "A system has a certain energy constant," or "A system *possesses* energy."

2. Energy seems to come and go in the world of "Dennis the Menace." But in the real world one must be able to guarantee that all the energy being put in or taken out is accounted for because the law of energy is a *conservation* law.

3. There are many different kinds of energy, and mathematical statement for each, whether it be kinetic, thermal, chemical, or nuclear energy.

☐ Fuels Are Sources of Energy

Fuel is the commodity that keeps civilization "turned on," so to speak. If you want steam, you will need to buy coal or oil and use either of them to fire up a boiler; if you'd like to propel an automobile, you'll need gasoline; if you prefer a horse and carriage, hay will do the trick. Walking or jogging? How about steak and potatoes. Clearly, different types and amounts of fuels are required for doing various jobs. "Nonsense! says the skeptic, all that's required is to put a plug into the wall and on go the lights, vacuum cleaner, power drills, and I haven't had to buy fuel to feed a one of them." True, but don't be fooled. The electric bill from the power company comes without fail at the end of the month; power companies buy fuels to feed motors that drive turbines which produce the electricity. "Okay, but what about Niagara Falls? I'll go back to simpler times and erect a waterwheel below the falls; that will turn a generator for me and produce fuel-free electricity. Or let me heat my house by cleverly designing a reflector to catch the sun's rays. This time I haven't paid." True. You've gotten away free for the time being, but there is still a definite accountability, a balance sheet in nature that must be maintained like those blocks that "Dennis the Menace" tried to frustrate his mother with. In most cases the active feature of fuels originates in the sun's energies. As rich as that bank may seem, however, one is still making debits against the balance in the account, and the ledger will show we're all poorer for those debits.

Well, what kind of fuel should be used to fulfill the energy needs of a particular job? Before discussing which fuel is best for a certain job, it is simpler to discuss *jobs* that fuels do. To accomplish a job will demand fuel. To do two such jobs will require twice the fuel. Half a job? Why, half the fuel required for the original job is all that is needed. In short, fuel is meted out in proportion to the size of the job done.

Fuels are depositories for energy and become direct participants in doing jobs. There must be a balance between energy transfer from our source and the job

Figure 4-8
Energy transformations. How many can you identify in this Red Baron-like scenario?

it is doing: deposits must equal withdrawals. But now which jobs require energy? A vise, for example, can maintain a very large force for an indefinite period: virtually no fuel is needed after the initial few turns of the screw. The paperweight, once placed on a desk, has a job which is just about energy-free. In the locked position your car brakes do their job indefinitely with no apparent expenditure of energy. In short, steady motion does not need fuels: Newton's first law. The vise, paperweight, and brakes require no withdrawals from the energy bank. They represent inertia at work.

Let's now list some jobs that proportionately withdraw energy. Our experience tells us that one cannot lift a load without an input of energy, nor will a load rise by itself. If building pyramids were your thing, you would have been well-advised to feed your slaves; boring cannon suggested feeding one's horses; hydroelectricity needs falling water. To keep a vehicle on wheels moving, you would need to feed the man pulling, if the vehicle is a rickshaw; the horse, if it is a carriage; the engine, if its is an auto; and so on. A distorted watch spring stores energy for use in time changes as it unwinds; a distorted rubber band saves energy to drive an arrow with considerable force. Energy has been expended in these cases, generally for speeding the movement of an object. Heating a teapot full of water? Energy is again expended. In the same light there are several substances, some which you may not even be aware of, that provide a great deal of energy. (See Table 4-1.)

Once a job is completed you must be able to measure the energy transferred in order to properly account for the fuel proportionately consumed. You might think of it as a bank statement indicating a transfer of energy. The cost in energy for doing a job is known in familiar parlance as **work**. When we say something or other **possesses** energy, we mean it has the capacity to **do** work. But when we speak of work in the scientific sense, we have a more specialized meaning in mind, namely the product of distance and force. In a strict sense, the work **w** means the product of the force **F** and the distance **d** through which the point at which the force is applied moves, in the direction of the force.

$$w = Fd$$

So stated, work becomes a measure of the quantity of energy transferred from one account to another, from one place to another, all to the satisfaction of Mother Nature's energy accountant. For example, if you lift 5 pounds through a distance of 5 feet, an amount of work equal to 25 foot-pounds is done. Whether you do the lifting or a steam-operated crane does it, the same amount of energy will have to be expended.

Energy appears in many forms. We buy one, sell another. Heat energy can be converted at an appropriate electrical power station into electric current. A tightly wound spring and an extended rubber band convert strain energy (see Fig. 4-9).

Table 4-1

Thermal energy content available on burning

Substance	Approximate number of heat energy units when 1 kg is consumed
In an appropriate combustion furnace	
Coal (a form of carbon)	7,500
100 Octane gasoline (isoctane)	12,000
Wood (cellulose + lignin)	4,000
Alcohol (ethyl alcohol)	6,500
Rocket fuel (dimethyl hydrazine)	7,300
Rocket fuel (hydrogen)	30,000
Gun powder (potassium nitrate)	700
Natural gas (methane)	12,000
In an appropriate human furnace	
Corn flakes	4,000
Bread (rye)	2,500
Sugar (cane or beet)	4,000
Butter (natural)	8,000
Candy (chocolate)	6,000
Steak (sirloin)	2,500
Egg (grade A, medium)	1,500
Cheese (American)	4,500

Five pounds of bricks gain gravitational energy when raised five feet off the ground. It is chemical energy however, that we are really after here. Coal and oil can change their chemical energy to gravitational energy when they take a vehicle to a high elevation. An explosive can release chemical energy suddenly, producing heat and light; both are different energy forms. Our bodies easily convert the chemical energy of food into a variety of forms depending on whether we are winding springs, thinking, raising loads, or kicking soccer balls. Table 4-2 presents several comparisons of energy conversion, useful work, and the force-by-distance product.

Kinetic Energy, the Energy of Motion

The chemical energy released during the explosion in a cartridge of a gun chamber ends up largely as energy of motion in the speeding bullet. Energy of motion is commonly referred to as *kinetic energy* (K.E.). What do you do as you approach an onrushing hill in your auto? You accelerate, expending more gasoline, causing the engine to produce a greater power output. The auto presses forward faster, its greater momentum carrying it more easily up the hill. Forces brought into play by increased motion and greater momentum have done work in raising a weight, in this case a massive auto, to new heights.

Besides kinetic energy, the energy of motion, there is potential energy (P.E.), the energy of *latent* motion. Since conservation of energy *must* be maintained, it follows that the sum of the kinetic and potential energy within a given system will have a fixed value:

$$K.E. + P.E. = constant$$

Figure 4-9
Recovery of all that gravitational potential energy as kinetic energy of motion is about to make a twisted wreck out of the car.

Table 4-2

Jobs and the energy needed to do them[*]

Jobs	Student unit equivalents
1. Lifting one 2,500-lb volkswagen a distance of 10 ft: *Careful*! It's not quite the same as climbing 20 flights of stairs.	1
2. A 40-watt bulb in a reading lamp for 1 hr.	4
3. Heat 1 qt of water just to a boil.	10
4. Operation of an electric iron for 15 min.	10
5. Once boiling, allow 1 qt of water to boil away completely.	67
6. A student in a complete rest state, doing no more than maintaining body temperature and vital function for a 1-hr period.	0.0025

[*] Unit of measure is the stair-climbing "student unit." During an average day, a 125-lb female student (110 lb of student + 15 lb of books) climbs 20 flights of stairs, each flight being 10 ft, for a total 200-ft climb. Work done is (200 ft) (125 lb) = 25,000 ft-lb, or 1 student unit. *Remember: w = Fd.*

By the definition put forth in Chap. 1, we can call this a law since there are no known exceptions. Some examples will serve to illustrate this. The explosion in a revolver cartridge is a release of chemical potential energy. A mechanical shock exploded it, causing the formation of rapidly expanding gases that hurl the projectile: chemical potential energy has become energy of motion. An automobile driven to the top of a hill converts chemical potential energy into kinetic energy by burning gasoline inside the cylinders of an internal combustion engine. Arriving at the top, the mass now has gravitational potential energy, recoverable as kinetic energy. This energy is capable of doing useful (or useless) work when the mass falls to the rocks below (see Fig. 4-9).

Kinetic energy depends on both the velocity and the mass of a body. The fundamental relationship defined by Newton, $F = ma$, can be used to derive the rule that K.E. = ½ (mass) (velocity)^2: kinetic energy is half the product of the *mass* and the *square of the velocity*. For example, if you shoot at a target into which the bullets become embedded or trapped, kinetic energy is converted to heat. Now double the bullet's velocity. That's as effective as a fourfold increase in its mass because the velocity term in the K.E. equation is squared. Heat energy produced is proportional to the mass and the square of the velocity. Kinetic energy is defined as *half* of this product.

K.E. = ½ mv^2

If the meaning of that example eludes you, consider a second in which kinetic energy of motion is turned into heat. Take a ball of "Silly Putty" and imagine heaving it forcefully at a brick wall (see Fig. 4-10). That stops it, flattening it out at the same time. If you could have placed a thermometer into the wad of putty you would have observed the increased temperature indicating additional energy. In fact, if you could peek inside the putty at the molecular level, you would now see increased molecular motion. The energy of motion of the glob was partly used up in its distortion when it hit the wall, but there was also molecular motion within, and *that* increased. Another illustration? Strike a piece of iron rapidly 20 times using a hammer and anvil. Notice how warm the iron feels. This again indicates kinetic energy of motion turned into heat.

Figure 4-10
A "thought" experiment to be sure. But if you could look inside, things would be warmer after hitting the wall.

☐ Thermal Energy: Heat and Energy's Other Forms

Everything we have discussed so far emphasizes the importance that heat and thermal energy play in testing our idea of conservation of energy and energy conversions. Furthermore, thermal energy is often the go-between for energy stored in a chemical fuel being translated into useful mechanical work, something of particular concern to the chemist. Chemical fuels, whether coal, gasoline, kerosene, or hamburgers and french fries, supply varying quantities of heat energy (Fig. 4-11). The doing of mechanical work, in fact, often results in a heating effect. In the case of the molecules in our gaseous model for studying the behavior of matter (kinetic-molecular theory) any increase in the energy of the

THERE GO THREE KNIGHTS IN ARMOUR, FOUR DAMSELS AND A UNICORN

Figure 4-11
They're all just so many "hamburgers-and-french-fries" to our dragon friend.

gas simply serves to make it "hotter." As a loose generalization, its fine to think of heat as a form of kinetic energy at the molecular level.

Energy Exists in Many Other Forms

About a century ago kinetic energy was energy in its most elementary form and scientists worked at reducing all of energy's other forms to kinetic energy. When the going got rough, that is to say, when the connections became less than obvious, one could chalk off the difficulty as "attributable to kinetic energies of hidden motions." This works well with elastic energy, the energy in a stretched rubber band or a compressed spring, and for thermal energy as well. Rubber bands and bedsprings are made of atoms and molecules carefully arranged: if there is an attempt to make a change as in stretching a slingshot or taking a good bounce on an inner spring mattress, there will be a good deal of movement among the atoms and molecules. Some thermal energy will be produced along with some mechanical potential energy.

The picture is not as clear and simple when electrical energy is involved, as we will describe a bit later on. There's a pushing and shoving involved in electrical energy due to very tiny (even by atomic standards) electric charges. There is also the energy of light, radiant energy, perhaps more accurately described as a form of electric and magnetic (electromagnetic) energy than anything else. Nuclear energy has to do with the way subatomic particles are arranged within the *nucleus,* or central core of the atom itself. Since we don't know precisely what nuclear energy is, all we say about it is what it isn't: nuclear energy isn't electrical; it isn't kinetic; it isn't chemical. We do have some understanding, however, of its significance to modern man from two very different vantage points: nuclear weaponry since August 1945, and the energy crisis in the 1970s. What about chemical energy? Chemical energy falls into two categories: first is kinetic energy of those very tiny electrical units we've called electrons found inside the atom; second is electrical energy due to the interactions of these electrons with each other and with protons. A discussion of this kind of energy occupies most of the remaining chapters in this book.

Another kind of energy has come to be known as *mass energy*. Curiously, the ultimate in energy is found in simply "existing." All objects have energy merely from existing. A quantity of energy, completely independent, of the mass of an object, completely unconcerned with it, and completely ignorant of what it is can be obtained if the mass is known. Einstein found that out and stated the fact as a simple equation,

$$E = mc^2$$

where E = energy, m = mass, and c = velocity of light, a constant in nature. What Einstein *never* said was that *mass equals energy.* If c is unchanging, then there is clearly some proportional relationship between E and m (Fig. 4-12). A less confusing and misleading representation of the relationship is simply that *energy has mass.* When a mass of matter gets more energetic, in whatever way, its mass appears to increase. That mass increase has to do with the energy gained. On the other hand, if some object gives off radiation of a kind, mass appears to actually be emitted. The appearance is that the lost mass was spirited off as the radiation's glow. What kind of peculiar business is this anyway?

Some small mass is interchangeable with radiation; therefore, matter and energy are at least somewhat convertible. The opposite is also true, to a degree, namely that radiation can turn into mass. Energy has mass: mass and energy are inter-convertible; we are creating and destroying matter. Right? Correct! But what about that Law of Conservation of Energy that we've made such a big thing out of? How is it that suddenly we create and destroy matter with abandon? $E = mc^2$ is not part of our everyday understanding of chemistry and chemical energy. It is of a potentially more violent world, the atom's nucleus. But even in the midst of such extraordinary happenings energy is still conserved, because our idea of conservation since Einstein has simply been expanded a bit:

mass of matter   +   mass of energy   =   constant

Why was modification required? How come we didn't really get it right until

Figure 4-12
Einstein found a simple relationship between mass and energy. The year was 1905.

the twentieth century? The reason is simply that the energy change in any "usual" chemical happening has so little change in mass associated with it that you can't even measure it, let alone experience it. A speeding bullet weighs 1 ounce, perhaps, as it rests in a gun's chamber. Moving at 4,000 feet per second it may have a total mass of only 1.000000000001 ounces. It is only when an atomic bullet gets sprung madly from the atom's core at speeds approaching that of light itself, 186,000 *miles* per second as compared to 4000 feet per second, does the mass associated with energy become noticeable.

Chemical Energy in Particular

Chemical energy is "trapped" in those substances we consider primary fuel sources. Coal and oil are full of this molecular energy, packed into the atoms. When a shuffling of matter takes place at the atomic and molecular level, either more energy is added or some is lost. Matter can be transformed and energy changes are associated with these alterations. Events happen, or can be made to happen on an atomic and molecular level, and chemists study them. Most substances release some of their energy when they are burned; when we talk of burning, most often we mean burning with oxygen. Our concept of fuels and their energies, then, really has to do with a fuel package, molecules to be burned, oxygen molecules to do the burning. A certain number of thermal energy units are associated with each kilogram of the fuel package burned.

If food is your source of chemical energy, we can talk about a food-oxygen package along with an array of muscles and cells that effect transformations by turning food into useful work such as lifting and thinking (Fig. 4-13). Most foods, as you'll soon find out, are comprised of carbon, hydrogen, and oxygen atoms in a variety of arrangements. One particular sugar called glucose has a lot to do with muscle contraction and motion. A glucose molecule contains half a dozen carbon (C) atoms, a dozen hydrogen (H) atoms, and half a dozen oxygen (O) atoms; thus, it can be symbolically represented as $C_6H_{12}O_6$. When muscles go through the process of contracting and returning to their rest state, an atomic shuffle takes place: the carbon, hydrogen, and oxygen atoms that were glucose often end up as carbon dioxide (CO_2) molecules and water (H_2O) molecules. The oxygen needed for burning can be picked up by inspiration of air into the lungs.

Figure 4-13
The human machine at work, transforming fuels, doing jobs, in this case, jogging.

fuel package				*fuel products*			
$C_6H_{12}O_6$	+	$6\,O_2$	=	$6\,CO_2$	+	$6\,H_2O$	+ heat
one glucose molecule	+	*six* oxygen molecules	=	*six* carbon dioxide molecules	+	*six* water molecules	+ heat

total energy in = total energy out

Now consider this. If we're all so brim full of chemical energy, why do we get tired while holding a modest load overhead? In fact, you really can't even hold your arm extended above your head for too long a time. Why? Once a load has been lifted, isn't the situation akin to a load on a high shelf, or a hydraulic lift with the lift up, or a vise with a load locked into it? No, it's not the same thing. Try a simple experiment. First clench your teeth tightly; then cover your ears. You may actually sense or feel a low-keyed vibration from your muscles. When you hold a weight, you can never really hold it perfectly still. The load always manages to shift a bit up or down; in response to that movement your muscles are incessantly in action, using some chemical energy. Essentially, there is no net gain in gravitational potential energy, the load stays at about the same, and all that changes is chemical energy in the muscles into thermal energy which is dissipated or lost to your immediate surroundings.

Chemical energy, of course, can do much more than just give off heat and light. In batteries, such as the flashlight variety and the 12-volt lead storage automobile type, chemical energy is transformed on demand into an electric current. This, in turn, can be routed through wires and eventually delivered to a filament in a bulb, giving off light and heat, or to a mechanical starting device for getting a generator going. Part of the energy of the electric current generated by the battery can also be stored by making use of a second battery.

All of our ideas about chemical energy have to do with shuffling atoms and molecules. Nuclear energy also has to do with transformations within atoms. However, nuclear energies do not originate simply with the electrons in the atom, but with the nucleus itself. Certain elements in nature such as uranium, can eject atomic bullets with tremendous energies for their size or in some instances split into nearly equal-sized pieces. The energies potentially available here make the usual chemical reactions associated with electrons seem mundane indeed. Breaking apart atomic nuclei, a process known as **nuclear fission**, is not the only way to utilize this energy. The sun's monumental energy has to do with fusing small nuclei together in a process called **nuclear fusion**. That process, which you will no doubt recognize in its grimmer manifestation, the H-bomb, has the potential for virtually limitless cheap energy supplies for the future.

☐ Molecules in Action

Everything in the world is composed of atoms and molecules and their numerous combinations, all behaving in certain predictable ways. We can summarize this in sophisticated principles or laws. With energy in mind, let's take another look at the kinetic-molecular theory of behavior.

The billiard table establishes an almost ideal setting to examine the kinetic molecular theory: our billiard cloth is virtually friction free; the cushions are of such elastic character that balls rebound perfectly on impact with no loss of energy; there is no negligible wind resistance to contend with; and there are no hidden forces. A struck ball plies its zig-zag path for all time to come, since no

Figure 4-14
The familiar bicycle pump gets hotter as you work at pumping, not from friction, but mainly because of the compression taking place.

outside influence or force acts to change its motion. If a second ball is struck, its behavior will be about as uneventful, except if it happens to collide with the first ball. The two billiard balls are also as perfectly elastic as the table's cushions so that when they do occasionally glance off each other, heading off in new directions, their *total* energy remains unchanged. Now imagine a number of such balls rebounding and colliding, some moving off faster, some rebounding slower, all moving endlessly, always with no energy being lost. The total energy in the world of the billiard table is constant. This is our portrait, outlined by our idea of kinetic-molecular behavior, colored by our concept of energy. To complete the picture, simply add a third dimension. Remembering inertia, all that's required to keep the atoms and molecules in motion forever is to simply set them in motion.

Our perpetually moving molecules are no more than carriers of energy, or energy transfer agents. Nothing fills a space with quite the completeness and efficiency of a collection of energetic gas molecules. Squeeze them together a bit and the pressure that you note is simply an outside indication of inside behavior, of energetic particles now *more* intensively storming the walls of a suddenly smaller container. The hand in Fig. 4-14 does some work by rapidly compressing the space in which these energy carriers live. Remember, $w = F \times d$: work is the product of a force moved through a distance. Our pay for the work done takes the form of an increase in the speed of the molecules. We get hotter molecules, molecules with higher thermal energy. The job done on them resulted in a transfer of energy from the downward pushing hand to the gas molecules which then stored the added energy as heat. Sound familiar? That's something we already know about. A bicycle pump, operating on a compression principle, gets hotter as it works.

The kinetic-molecular theory explains what we already suspect form our experience. The pressure of a gas originates from the continuous movement of molecules along with exchange of momentum. If the pressure is increased suddenly, the molecular exchange of momentum increases and the temperature rises, registering the heat effect taking place. By the same token, if the temperature of the gas in the original container is allowed to rise, that will cause the pressure to increase because the added heat will increase molecular collisions against the walls of the container. If the volume of the container is fixed, an increase in heat content increases pressure. The corollary is also true: rapidly compress the gas and watch the temperature rise (see also Fig. 4-1).

Here is a small experiment. Take a rubber band and stretch it. You will note a definite heat effect. It gets warm. But don't try to feel the heat with your fingers because they're not sensitive enough. Instead, hold the rubber band between your lips, and now stretch it (see Fig. 4-15). Feels warm, doesn't it? When you allow the stretched band to contract back to its normal position, a pronounced cooling effect is observed. STRETCH, and the rubber band heats; RELAX, and the rubber band cools. If you want to pursue this further, try

Figure 4-15
The experiment works quite well, especially if you have a slightly wider than usual rubber band handy.

hanging a weight from a rubber band. It will stretch the band. What would you expect if you took a match and carefully warmed the stretched band so as not to chemically alter the rubber. Heat was given off when the band was stretched. If you add it back, the band should contract and the hung weight should rise. Try it. It really does work. When you remove the flame, the band stretches back down.

Figure 4-16
Can you tell whether this filmstrip is running forward or in reverse? Looks the same either way.

We can use the kinetic-molecular model to explain the behavior in the very large and complex molecules of which the rubber band is composed. To be sure, there are many complicating factors but we find that theory generally holds for complex solids such as a rubber band as well as for simpler gases. The rubber band is made up of very long chains of molecules, normally all twisted and knotted, much like cooked spaghetti. Stretching the band straightens the molecules into parallel strands, disrupting lots of the connectors bonding the strands together. That will result in the release of the energy normally used for such binding, now given off as heat. Warming the band while stretched causes the parallel chains to bump and make contact. Energy is being added. In this process, the chains tend to pull back together, giving them an opportunity to re-establish some of the broken bonds so that they are now better able to cope with the deforming weight.

☐ Disorganized Molecular Madness . . . and Something Called Entropy

Heating a gas, solid, or liquid means that large-scale macroscopic motions are being translated into small-scale microscopic motions within and between molecules. One interesting problem that arises with molecular motion due to heating is that the motion tends to be random, difficult to control, hard to orient, in short, inefficient. For example, much of the gasoline fuel consumed by an internal combustion automobile engine becomes wasted heat, radiating away, doing no useful work.

Heat is the energy associated with the random, disorganized, seemingly senseless motion of nature's molecules. However, there is also well-organized energy in the universe, energy with purpose, energy with direction, energy capable of being fully put to use. For example, the kinetic energy of motion of a fired bullet suggests total organization. If you don't believe it, fire the weapon straight up and watch most of the kinetic energy turn into gravitational potential energy. Chemical energy is virtually all of the available variety, energy just waiting to be put to use. For the most part, however, there is little we do to make direct use of chemical energy. Batteries produce electrical energy and electricity directly from chemical sources, a topic to be looked at more closely in Chap. 7. In most other familiar situations, chemical energy is first converted into heat. To show you more of what that means and perhaps why it is so, turn your attention to movies for a moment.

Because of the passage of time, or more exactly because of the forward direction of time, a film of some event run backwards looks pretty silly. You can certainly tell whether or not the film is running backwards. Now if the film happens to be of a molecular collision between a pair of billiard balls on our kinetic-molecular billiard table, the film looks like it is depicting an event that is forward-moving in time, when viewed in *either* direction. Figure 4-16 can be regarded as a 1-2-3 or 3-2-1 sequence and the two are indistinguishable. But a film showing a collection of **hot** molecules mixing with a collection of **cold** molecules would hardly be acceptable in reverse. At the end of the first reel, we have **cool** molecules. The likelihood of running in reverse, namely making half hot and half cold from a collection of cool is out of the question. Now imagine a bucket filled with a layer of black coal dust particles and a layer of white flour particles. You can easily mix the particles into a consistent gray mass by stirring, let's say in a clockwise direction (Fig. 4-17). But how shall we separate the particles once mixed? Why that's easy. Simply stir in a counterclockwise direction, thereby undoing what you've done. Ridiculous, of course. There are just too many particles to deal with; consequently, the process is not reversible. There is a beginning and an end that are clearly different; the film sequence of events can only be 1-2-3, and there is no way to reverse it.

Disorganization, randomization, disorder: that's the direction time takes us in. This disorganization or disorder has a great deal to do with **entropy**. In the world of our experience, entropy tends to increase to a maximum. Order naturally tends toward disorder in much the same way as the neatly shelved books of the library are in disarray by day's end. Our intuition would have allowed us to guess that and to predict the fate of the black and white particles in the bucket as well. Put a drop or two of cream in a cup of black coffee; place some food dye in water; burn a piece of wood; or simply live 70 years from birth to death. The chance of any of these processes taking place reversibly is incredibly unlikely. We are involved not with simply two billiard balls colliding but with the interactions of many, many particles. Our consciousness of irreversibility is what given us a sense of past and future: mixed comes after unmixed; unburned before burned; young, then old.

Heat Engines and Action Molecules

Without regard to specific design or function, all heat engines have certain general characteristics in common: fuel is transformed into heat and stored at an elevated temperature; work is done; and the unused quantity of heat exits to a low temperature storage area. This process can be illustrated with the help of Fig. 4-18. The useful work done by the engine is the difference between heat in and heat out. Usually there will be some kind of a working fluid, such as steam or air, present. The fluid will be restricted to a cylinder where it will be heated, causing it to expand against a piston which is then forced to move through a distance. Thus, work is done. The unused heat is finally exhausted as the cylinder piston contracts back to its original state. Then the entire circular process repeats . . . and repeats . . . and repeats . . . and repeats. In view of our growing preoccupation with energy supplies and demands, a particularly important illustration of one such engine is the four-stroke cycle built into internal combustion engines (Fig. 4-19) in most American and European automobiles.

Figure 4-17
Although you can run this sequence in reverse, what you'll see describes no *real* situation.

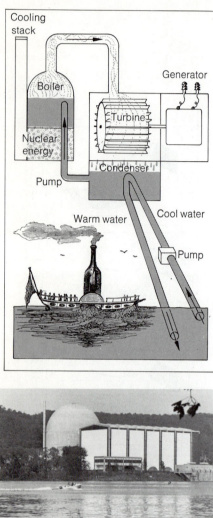

Figure 4-18

A heat engine at work (top). Fuel converted to heat, stored in a high temperature reservoir; heat withdrawn to do a job; unused heat collected in low temperature reservoir.

Nuclear reactors apply modern technology to classical methods of generating electricity (bottom). The steam powered turbine generator is a heat engine with nuclear fuel elements to supply heat for the high temperature reservoir.

It is not possible to achieve complete conversion of the energy stored in a fuel into the mechanical energy needed for power. That makes for an unfortunate loss. But what is even more distressing, and what most automobile drivers hardly realize, is that the maximum possible operating efficiency for the gasoline engine is very poor indeed. Most drivers have some idea of miles traveled per gallon of gasoline burned in the car's engine. Few perceive that less than a fourth of the available chemical energy of the fuel is ultimately converted to the energy of motion. That's a depressing and frustrating fact when you think of the hundreds of millions of cars on the roads and our present world economic dependence on fossil fuels.

You might expect that friction is the cause of the engine's low efficiency. After all, oil must be used to minimize friction between moving parts such as pistons and valves. Perhaps by clever design with fewer moving parts or development of better lubricating fluids we could build a much more efficient engine, one with an efficiency approaching 100 percent. Well, friction is certainly a consideration, but what we're up against here is a much more fundamental problem, a problem seated in the processes of converting energy from one form to another. A perfect engine would be able to convert all the chemical energy of the fuel into thermal energy, which would then make it possible to do mechanical work and move the vehicle. However, a perfect engine cannot be built. Why? Heat is a randomized form of energy, and in the conversion of heat energy into useful work much less than 100 percent is ever converted. There is a good deal of **waste** heat, as is plainly evident to anyone who has been around operating engines. Engines radiate lots of waste heat. In fact, automobile engines clearly must have cooling systems to help dissipate that waste heat.

This thermodynamic principle, that you can't build a 100 percent efficient thermal energy-to-mechanical work converter, is a product of vast experience. No exceptions to the principle have yet been found, and scientists and engineers today are pretty confident that none will be found either. The basis for the principle is our understanding of the disordered state of thermal energy. As we said before, in the world of our experience, entropy tends to increase to a maximum. Events proceed from order to disorder, spontaneously, not the other way around. What prospects are there for heat engines in the world of the future? Not terribly encouraging ones. New technologies are needed to convert chemical or nuclear energy *directly* in to work.

☐ Chance, Probabilities, Statistics . . . and Atoms and Molecules

What do we mean when we speak of chance, probability, and statistics in science? We've been hinting at reasons why chance and probability should play a role in science. If it appears odd to you that nature would leave it all to the whim of a chance happening, you're in good company. Many of the leading physical scientists of the last 100 years have felt funny about that, too. The fact of the matter seems to be that strict laws such as Newton's that apply to natural phenomena are not the absolute strictures scientists once thought they were. All the laws that govern matter and energy, that describe and predict the occurrences of phenomena in the natural world, are really laws of chance and probability.

Chance is a word we use every day, which signifies the likelihood or possibility of something occurring. There is a 50-50 *chance* of rain today: it is likely to rain today, or there is a possibility of rain. Because we lack the required information to be absolutely certain, a great deal of what we theorize about nature and generalize into laws is part of a sophisticated guessing game. The better our guesses, the sounder our theories and generalizations. Here, probability steps in to help us out. Probability theory offers a means for sharpening guesses; it lets us speak more rigorously when describing "chancy" situations; it permits stricter definition of what we can't strictly know; and it specifically states the average behavior for situations, such as tossing coins. In fact, this theory of probability actually did begin in a gambling way. In the seventeenth century, a superb mathematician, Blaise Pascal, was approached by a professional gambler about the question of how best to bet on throws of a pair of dice (Fig. 4-20).

In any honest coin-tossing game of chance, you cannot have the slightest inkling as to the expected outcome except that it will either be heads or tails. Intuitively, you would agree, without going to the trouble to test it, that if I toss a very large number of coins there is a strong likelihood of tossing an equal number of heads or tails. The probability of tossing a head is one half. That means the probability of a coin coming up heads or tails when it is tossed is a guess of the most likely fraction of a number of repeated tests yielding that specific result. Toss the coin a number of times; make a best guess of the number of those tosses

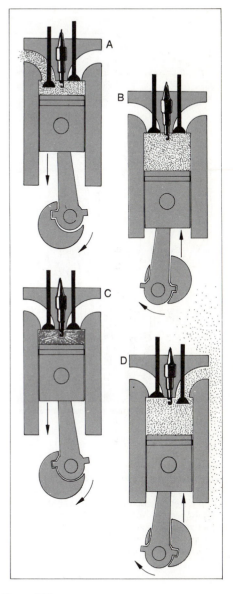

Figure 4-19
The four-stroke "auto" cycle is the heart of the internal combustion engine in most automobiles: intake-compression-ignition-exhaust.

Figure 4-20
Scenes at a Las Vegas crap game from a Hollywood film.

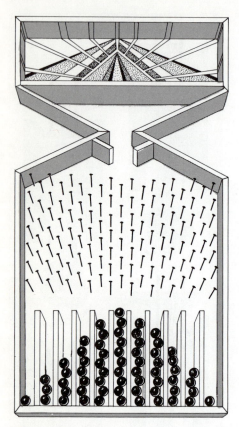

Figure 4-21
One way of demonstrating "normal distribution"
of events in a situation involving many events is
with a Galton's board. A collection of marbles
simultaneously released from the top bump
their way through the pegs, most ending up in a
a heap near the center. Some marbles will bump
their way toward the edges.

that will turn up heads. The *probability* of tossing heads, of having a head show up on any single toss, is given by a very simple relationship, namely

$$\text{Probability of tossing heads} = \frac{\text{Best guess of number of tosses that will turn up heads in a large number of tosses}}{\text{Large number of tosses}}$$

In 1,000 tosses of the coin, we might expect (remember, best guess) about 500 to turn up heads, so the probability *P* is

$$P \text{ head tosses} = \frac{500 \text{ head tosses}}{1,000 \text{ total tosses}} = 1/2$$

Some qualifications of our probability theory are necessary. We must stick to (1) *possible results* that are (2) *repeatable*. Tossing a head is a possible result, and we can certainly repeat the coin-toss operation in reasonable fashion again. In addition, in our 1,000 tosses of the coin we would not expect the number of head tosses to be exactly 500; it is more likely to be 490, 494, 506, or 510. Well, what shall the number be, then? If a choice is required, it would be most reasonable to say 500 heads. But any number of tosses between 490 and 510 gives a probability number very close to 1/2 anyway (Fig. 4-21).

$$\frac{490}{1,000} = 0.490, \text{ or just about } 1/2$$

$$\frac{510}{1,000} = 0.510, \text{ or just about } 1/2$$

Another way to test probability would be with a roll of pennies. The next time you have occasion to go to the bank, bring home a roll of pennies. Spread them out on the table and see how many happen to turn up heads and how many are tails. The probable distribution should be pretty close to the one in the coin toss, or about one half. See if you can explain why.

Where probability theory really pays off is in dealing with phenomena in nature; complicated cases involving not two possibilities as heads and tails, or only two interactions as pairs of billiards balls colliding, but many interactions involving many particles. In natural situations where one is dealing with large numbers of identical particles in different energy states, it is just not possible to predict how individual particles will behave. All we can really do is forecast *group behavior* for collections of interacting particles, whether they be atoms, molecules, or anything else. Place 100 gas molecules in a box that has been partitioned into a left side and a right side. The dominant distribution of molecules is uniform, 50-50. If there are 1,000 molecules, the various possible arrangements will place 500 on one side and 500 on the other. A million molecules, or 100 billion: our best bet increasingly is a unfiorm distribution. Furthermore, it should be clear why once the molecules are distributed, one cannot undistribute them. We can't separate the bucket of sand and charcoal particles into two neat piles of black and white. In situations where we cannot "know" nor even begin to guess, the theory of probability gives us **guessing power**. In areas where we are most ignorant, this "science of ignorance" gets us by. At nature's most fundamental levels, probability turns out to be one of the scientists most powerful tools.

□ Heat and Temperature

It is heat that makes things hotter or colder, depending on whether you are adding it or removing it. Temperature serves only as a heat indicator: temperature exists only as a property of some piece of matter or other. It has no existence by itself in the way that heat does. We can figuratively talk about temperature "effects," but we are really talking about the change that occurs in a body upon heating or cooling, *resulting* in a temperature change. That you are capable of *feeling* that one body is hotter than a second does not tell us anything much about heat content. A thimbleful of scalding water may be hot, indeed, but a bathtub filled with lukewarm water has a much greater heat content (Fig. 4-22).

Going back to billiard balls, bicycle pumps, and kinetic-molecular theory for a moment, our experience has shown that equal volumes of gases at identical temperatures exhibit the same gas pressure. That's because pressure was attributable to a storm of particles on the walls of the chamber. Therefore, pressure has to do with the total numbers of particles as well, and if you remember, to the square of their average velocity. Half of the product of mass and square of a particle's velocity measures the kinetic energy of motion (K.E. = ½ mv^2). This means that the pressure of a gas is proportional to the average kinetic energy of the particle of the gas. As a result, we can think of the "pressure of heat" when we talk of how full of heat or really hot something is.

When two equal volumes of gas mix, the volumes will exchange kinetic energy through myriad interactions between their respective molecules until they are now equal in kinetic energy. On the average, if one volume is a "hotter" and one is a "colder," the hotter will get cooler, and the colder, warmer. The temperature of one gas warms up while the other cools down: kinetic molecular theory in action. It would never be expected otherwise. You would not logically expect the volume of hot gas to get hotter yet, at the expense of the kinetic energy of the colder gas which would then be colder still. That would constitute an increased ordering and organization rather than greater disorder and randomness in nature, or a decrease rather than an increase in entropy.

We need not limit the argument to the molecules in a gas. That kinetic motion taking place in liquids and solids responds in essentially the same way. For example, consider the radiator depicted in Fig. 4-23. A thermometer has been placed on each of the radiator bars. The radiator is suddenly exposed to

Figure 4-22
Heat content has to do with quantity, not intensity. A cold bath for our hippo, if he had to depend on the heat content of the thimble to warm his tub.

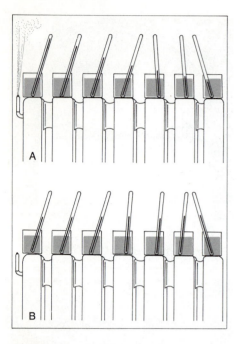

Figure 4-23
You can't go from a "cooler to a hotter,"
spontaneously. Only the other way.

rapid heating on one end, and then immediately isolated in such a way that none of the heat radiates away or is otherwise lost: a thought experiment, again. Initially, one end is distinctly "hotter" as the thermometers indicate. After a time, the heat has been unfirmly distributed, the hotter end cooling, and the colder end warming. The process is not reversible in the movie-film manner; you can't run it backwards. If you saw such a film, you'd recognize the error because that would constitute an **obviously** unreal process; it is the sequence indicated in the figure that you would **reasonably** expect.

□ **The Temperature Scale and Thermometry**

As thermometers, we humans are capable of only limited guesses as to hot and cold and are subject to often being "psyched" out in any case. Try this humbling experiment: place three bowls of water on a table, one hot, one lukewarm, one cold (Fig. 4-24). Place one hand in each of the two extremes, the hot water and the cold, for a few minutes. Now place both in the lukewarm water. Then ask each hand to tell you something about the relative temperature of the water. Obviously, something better is needed to measure the difference because one hand tells you the lukewarm is warm, the other hand tells you cool.

First, let's present an operational definition of scientific temperature so we can better talk about heat. Take two standard "hots," the melting point of ice and the boiling point of water, assign to the colder the identifying number "0" and to the hotter the identifying number "100." Divide the scale on the thermometer between these points into one hundred equal units. We'll call the units and numbers degrees Celsius, or "°C," for example, 0°C, the ice point, 100°C the boiling point, and 25°C about room temperature.

Most things in nature respond to temperature changes in a simple and direct fashion. We often experience expansion on heating, and contraction on cooling. This is the principle upon which the thermometer is based. Consider a liquid such as alcohol or mercury confined in a relatively large bulb, rising into a capillary column. Expansion will cause the liquid to rise still higher in the narrow column; contraction results in a fall in the liquid level in the capillary.

We noted earlier that numbers denoting temperature are a measure of the average kinetic energy that molecules carry about with them. Therefore, we should properly begin our scale at the beginning, the absolute zero of temperature, the point where kinetic energy has fallen to zero, the point where all molecules are "resting," in other words, where the gas pressure has dropped to zero. If we carefully watch how the pressure decreases as the gas is cooled across a range of reasonable temperatures, we can determine the unreasonable temperature called **absolute zero.** It lies about 273 degrees below the ice point or water, or below 0° on the Celsius scale.

Although the Celsius scale, formerly known as the Centigrade scale, is not an absolute scale, we will not discard it, since it is so firmly entrenched in scientific usage. We will, however, define a newer, absolute scale known as the Kelvin (K) scale. On the absolute scale, the ice point must be 273°K since it lies 273 degrees above absolute zero. The steam point thus becomes 373°K and room temperature, 25°C, is about $273^{\circ} + 25^{\circ}$, or 298°K. In fact, any degree reading on the Celsius scale becomes a Kelvin scale measurement by simple addition of the number 273.

The scale most widely used in the United States (but very few other countries) is the Fahrenheit scale. This scale is of little use to us in our present scientific discussion. It should be noted, however, that for every point on the Kelvin and Celsius scale there is a corresponding Fahrenheit temperature (see Fig. 4-25).

One further point about absolute zero is worth noting. It is clearly the ultimate in "coldness," a bottom limit on the energy scale. There have been many attempts at attaining this zero of temperature by all types of cooling schemes; but the closer we come to it, the more unreachable it gets. At levels of 0.001°K, within a thousandth of one degree of the absolute of zero, there has still been no indication that 0°K could be attained. In fact, if you pursue studies in the sciences a bit further, you'll find that absolute zero may be an unattainable *limit,* approachable yes, but not reachable. On the other hand, there is no known limit on the hot end of the temperature scale. Experiments have been carried out at temperatures registering in the millions of degrees. Interestingly, the effect of touching a very cold object is not unlike touching a very hot object. One experiences pain and tissue damage, and the medical treatments for both bear a similarity to each other. But don't take that too literally; a red hot metal coil on a stove at 600°C (873°K) is much the more dangerous than one cooled to -270°C (3°K). And how hot is hot? The center of the sun is believed to be about $20,000,000^{\circ}$K; a hydrogen bomb, about $100,000,000^{\circ}$K. Cold, on the other hand? Just plain old 0°K (see Fig. 4-25).

Conducting Heat

How fast is a fast molecule? What is the average speed of one of these energetic gas molecules at some given temperature, say room temperature? The mathematical answer to that question is startling: about 600 meters per second or about the speed of a rifle bullet. If you think about that for a moment, it should take only a split instant to detect various smells across a room: perfume, essence of skunk, or what have you. How do we then explain the relative "creepiness" or sluggishness of gas molecules for we do not detect smells instantly. In spite of a molecule's high speed, it just can't really seem to get started in its trip across a crowded room; it doesn't go far before it bumps into another molecule. Billiards again. A collision sends the molecule on some track other than its intended course. It's been sidetracked, or prevented from rapidly zipping

Figure 4-24
Sensations of hot or cold are subjective. Both feet are right when the hot foot says the pan of warm water is cold and the cold foot says the pan of warm water is hot. That's the way it seems.

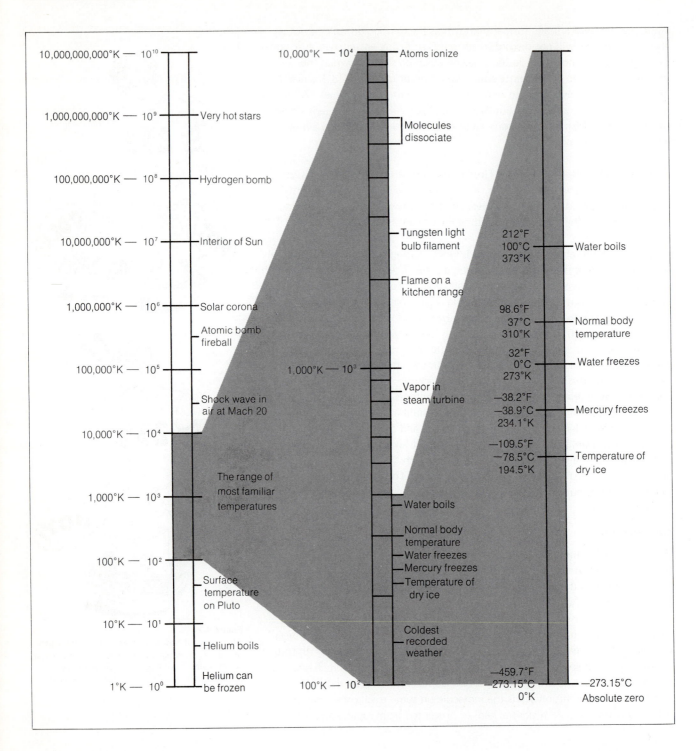

across the room. Molecules must bump their way across, through a series of successive collisions. They can't just zoom on through (Fig. 4-26).

Thermal or heat conduction in gases is slow, mainly because relatively few molecules are available for energy transfer, or heat transfer. Cotton, wool, and furs also conduct heat poorly for the same reason, namely they contain a large amount of air space. In effect, such clothing materials keep one warm, not because they themselves are poor heat conductors, but because they efficiently trap a blanket of air that keeps body warmth from dissipating away. The air is caught in the wide open space or weave in such materials as cotton, wool, and fur.

In gases and liquids the conduction of heat also, involves movement of particles, but they just don't travel very far before bumping into neighbors. Too many particles in too small a space: molecular over population. In solids the conduction depends on oscillating molecules being coupled to their nearest neighbors much like a shiver sent down your spine. Try holding an iron rod between your fingers while heating the opposite end in an open flame. Heat radiates and flows. You can feel it in the air about the other end and your fingers can sense it in the rod itself. Heat the rod long enough on the other end and soon you'll have to drop it. If you choose a copper rod instead, you will drop it a lot sooner because copper is a better conductor of heat. But a glass rod? Why you can heat one end until it is red hot and drippy while comfortably holding the other end. Glass is a poor conductor. Again, heat flows from warmer to cooler.

Heat and Mechanical Energy

One of our earliest experiences of heat in action is *friction*. We rub, and in rubbing, generate heat. That rubbing can warm your hands on a chilly day, give you a skin burn in a slide or fall, or start a camp fire for you (if you are patient). If you've ever felt the drill bit of a simple hand drill after drilling through a block of wood, you've come right to the edge of experimentally establishing the relationship between heat and mechanical energy. Those experiments began just at the turn of the nineteenth century. They were firmly established both in principle and practice by the mid-1800s and today constitute part of the

Figure 4-25
Temperature Ranges: (left) from hottest to coldest by orders of magnitude; (center) in the range of usual chemical experience; (right) in the range of usual human environment (opposite page).

Table 4-3
Heat conductivity numbers relative to air taken as 1*

Substances	Relative number
Air	1
Rubber	3
Asbestos	3
Wood	5
Water	22
Glass	42
Mercury	260
Lead	1,300
Iron	1,800
Aluminum	8,000
Copper	15,000
Silver	16,000

* That means silver is about 16,000 times better at heat transfer than air.

Figure 4-26
Bumping across, traveling by successive collision.

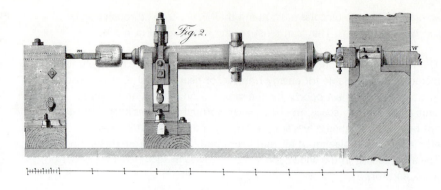

Figure 4-27
Warming Rumford's cannon (right). Determining the mechanical equivalent of heat while boring a cannon. Warming Rumford's 'can' (left). A cartoon showing the comforts of a Rumford stove.

Rotating shaft driven by descending weight

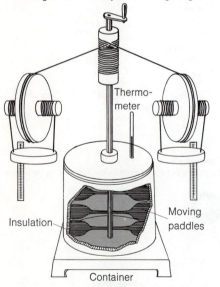

Figure 4-28
Joule's experiment for determining the mechanical equivalent of heat. The spinning paddle wheels heat the water in the tank by friction as the weights fall through a distance.

very footings of the house of science. The question was: What is the relationship between the quantity of heat produced by friction and the mechanical energy lost? Rumford and Joule supplied the basis for the answer.

Benjamin Thompson, Count Rumford of Bavaria, was a New Englander by birth (who chose the wrong side in the American Revolution and left for London in a hurry). He found himself at work in 1798 directing the boring of brass cannon for the Bavarian arsenal. Cannon manufacture involved casting a solid brass ingot in the desired shape and then making a proper bore with a drill bit and a team of horses (see Fig. 4-27). A very sharp drill bit produced a bore in short order and a modest supply of heat was generated. A dull drill bit, on the other hand, produced a very large amount of heat. The quantity of heat produced by a working drill bit in any fixed time period depended on how fast the horses moved about and on how many horses were at work. Rumford reasoned correctly: the generation of heat depended on the horses' ability to keep working. Heat was a form of energy, and although Rumford never said that, he was clearly onto it. He made measurements by placing kettles of water on top of the brass castings as the horses worked at turning the dull drill bit. Enough heat was generated in 2½ hours of boring to take 12 kilograms of water from the ice point to the steam point. The supply of heat was "endless" and 1 calorie of heat was found to be the equivalent of about 5 units of mechanical work, called joules.

The modern value for the mechanical equivalent of heat is about 4.184 of these joules, so-named because of the experiments of James Joule of England, brew-master turned scientist. His apparatus consisted of a cylindrical tank filled with water; down the center ran a rotating axle to which was appended a paddle system (Fig. 4-28). The axle assembly was caused to rotate by a weight hung on a pulley by a cord. Mechanical work done by the weight as it fell through a distance was converted into heat by friction, raising the temperature of the water. Through several experiments over 40 years, Joule was able to establish a value of 4.172, very close to the presently accepted value. Joule had succeeded in spelling out the proportional relationship between mechanical energy and heat.

☐ **Energy Reprise**

Energy is used in a variety of ways. We need food and warmth in order to survive, and a variety of thermal and mechanical energies for every kind of work imaginable. Our supplies of fuels, the energies built into "chemicals," is the other side of the coin. We are interested in matter and energy: by matter we mean nature's 88 elementary substances and their myriad combinations; by energy we mean that commodity mostly locked into the atom's outer electrons that allows us the means to action, or work, in addition to that very subtle and immense source locked into the nucleus. Our basic rule says that all energy debits and credits cancel: in other words, the total of all of the various forms of energy is constant because energy can neither be created nor destroyed but only transformed.

Without narrow limits, Newton's laws of motion and our understanding of how forces in nature behave, have provided us with strong experimental support for the credibility of conservation of energy. In its broader, post-Einstein context, conservation of energy goes well beyond a mere generalization from the experiments that supply us with our experience of the world; constancy of energy has become scientific dogma. Henri Poincaré, the French mathematician-physicist commented on just this aspect of energy:

As we cannot give a general definition of energy, the principle of the conservation of energy simply signifies that there is something which remains constant. Well, whatever new notions of the world future experiments may give us, we know beforehand that there will be something which remains constant and which we shall be able to call energy.

☐ **Questions to Answer . . . Problems to Solve**

1. If you place a thermometer in a woolen cloth and vigorously breathe into it several times, the mercury will clearly indicate a fevered condition. How is it possible that the exhaled air is more than normal body temperature?

2. A harmful pinging phenomena known as engine "knock" may occur during the compression stroke in a 4-cycle internal combustion engine. Can you suggest the possible cause of this "knock" phenomenon?

3. When a fire extinguisher of the carbon dioxide variety (compressed carbon dioxide gas) is activated and discharged, the nozzle becomes very cold and a snow-like mist is evident. Explain.

4. Cyrano de Bergerac's "villainous blasts of saltpeter from the rear" offered us early perception of space travel yet-to-come. Why do rockets indeed work in space in the absence of an atmosphere against which to push?

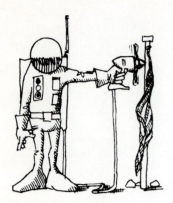

5. In one of the most famous of public suggestions, a TV commentator covering the first moonwalk in July 1969 suggested a fan to cause that first flag to wave when planted on the moon's surface. Why not?

6. What weighing technique might you use to demonstrate the constant nature of a hammer's mass when free of gravitation in space? What non-weighing technique might you use?

7. A VW and a Mack truck both roll, dead engine, down hill. You know which will get to the bottom first. The Mack truck . . . right? (Assume the only force acting is gravity.)

8. A person tends to tire rapidly while supporting a heavy load even though, strictly speaking, no work required. Why?

9. In the game of Russian Roulette played with a revolver containing six chambers and one cartridge, what is the probability that you'll win the first game? Winning means spinning the revolver, then firing the weapon, and finding that chamber to not contain the cartridge. If you play the game again without spinning the revolver, what are the odds of winning the second game? The third game? How do the odds change in the second and third game if you spin the revolver each time?

10. A series of happenings are described during the course of which a transformation of energy has taken place. For each, state the principal, before and after energy forms: for example, kinetic energy, chemical energy, thermal energy, electrical energy, gravitational potential energy, etc.
    (a) Your new 10-speed bicycle crashes into a immovable object and is demolished.
    (b) Exploded artillary shell is propelled to target by explosion gases.
    (c) Sunlight warms greenhouse.
    (d) Sunlight aids plant growth in greenhouse.
    (e) Sunlight gives greenhouse worker sunburn.
    (f) Heated steel bar glows red-hot.
    (g) Heated steel bar is allowed to sit on block of ice.
    (h) An accidently dropped book falls.
    (i) The falling book from the previous example lands on your toe.
    (j) Operate your car radio with the engine off.
    (k) Operate your car radio with the engine on.
    (l) While skating across the apparently frozen lake, you fall through.
    (m) An electric coil is used to bring a pot of water to boil.
    (n) Salt is spread upon an ice-covered road.
    (o) An inflated balloon is deflated.
    (p) A rubber band is stretched.

11. Try to track backward thoroughly the various energy stages passed in taking the sun's energy and converting it into coal.

12. A man, standing very erect, is half-way up on an escalator that is going down. He is climbing steadily but stays exactly in place relative to the ground. The man on the escalator claims he is working very hard. An observer on the ground says he isn't working at all. Who is right? Explain.

13. That extra pound of fat that placidly sags about your gut will provide 4300 calories of heat when burned. If your body weight remains constant on a food intake equivalent to 2800 calories, and you increase your diet by a 6-pack of beer a week (about 120 calories per can) and a single helping of potato chips with each beer (about 120 calories per helping), how much additional weight will you gain in a year?

14. Offer a qualitative explanation of why our 125 pound student friend can easily climb 200 feet of stairs (well, fairly easily) and in the process do 25,000 foot-pounds of work. But raise a 2500 pound VW a distance of 10 feet? No Way!

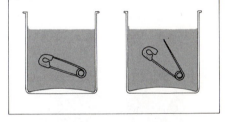

15. A pair of identical safety pins are individually placed in a pair of identical acid-filled beakers: one is open; one is closed. What was the fate of the added potential energy present in the closed safety pin when the pair of pins dissolved in the acid?

16. While standing perfectly still inside a fast flying jet aircraft, do you possess kinetic energy? Explain.

17. What is the fate of the original kinetic energy when
    (a) a bullet slams into a thick wooden block?
    (b) a hammer slams into a nail?
    (c) the end ball in a 5-ball "executive toy" slams into the other four?

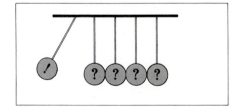

18. What is the fate of the original chemical energy when
    (a) A firecracker explodes?
    (b) gasoline is burned?
    (c) a chocolate bar is eaten?
    (d) a 12-volt auto battery starts an engine?

19. "I shoot the Hippopotamus
    with bullets made of platinum,
    Because if I use leaden ones
    his hide is sure to flatten 'em."

    What kind of energy transfer occurs when the lead bullet is flattened.

20. On one throw of a pair of dice, what is the probability of coming up with seven; with eleven; box cars (a pair of fours); not more than eight?

21. You have in your possession a well-shuffled deck of 52 playing cards. Determine the probability of drawing the ace of spades first; then any of the three remaining aces on the second draw.

22. Make up a table for all of the possible combinations for five flips of a coin. Determine the probability of winning the game by tossing a head only once in five tosses.

23. A small block of copper weighing 75 grams is heated to 100°C and immediately placed in 150 grams of water at 25°C. Determine the final temperature of the block of copper in the water when both register the same temperature, assuming no other loss or exchange of heat.

24. In the preceding question, if a simple heat engine were designed about that block of copper as our source of heat input and the room temperature water, acting as our exhaust reservoir, what maximum efficiency could be obtained?

25. Give a brief explanation of your understanding of each of the following terms, and include a simple example to illustrate your answer:
    (a) a reversible process
    (b) an irreversible process
    (c) a spontaneous process
    (d) randomization of energy
    (e) entropy
    (f) chance and probability in nature

26. Briefly discuss the concept of entropy in terms of Dennis, the Menace alone at play in his room with a box of red marbles, a box of white marbles and one of black marbles.

27. Two identical rubber bands, one stretched and one relaxed, are dissolved in a suitable solvent. Explain the relative temperature effects noted as a result of the solution process.

28. Remembering that temperature is a measure of kinetic energy, explain why a gas trapped in a cylinder becomes "hotter" when compressed by a piston.

29. The molecules of the air are an 80-20 mixture of nitrogen and oxygen. Do both kinds of molecules exhibit the same average kinetic energy, and if so, why?

30. Had ammonia been the stuff of life on our planet instead of water, and we'd set about the business of establishing a scale of temperature based on its freezing point (-78°C) and boiling point (-33°C) being the 0 and 100 degree units, how many degrees below 0 would the absolute zero of temperature be?

31. Explain why a metal bar feels colder than a piece of wood, both at the same temperature. Would you rather step barefoot on a cold metal surface, a wooden floor, or a shag rug, all at the same temperature? Why?

32. We have two identical blocks of metal. One registers a temperature of 27°C; the second is twice as hot. What temperature do you read for it?

33. Why would you expect to find the temperature of water at the bottom of Niagara Falls to be (higher than, the same as, lower than) the temperature at the top?

34. If you sit on a block of ice, you soon sense a certain "coldness" indicating a flow of cold from the ice to your bottomside in apparent contradiction of nature's usual behavior. Explain the paradox.

35. Explain the mode of operation of storm windows in helping to keep a house warm in winter.

36. What are the main heat sources in Rumford's horse-operated, cannon-boring boring experiments?

37. In what way was the universe less ordered after Humpty's fall? How did this manifest itself in terms of energy change and entropy?

38. With all of the available energy in the local environment distributed through the air, rivers, lakes and the like . . . especially the oceans . . . why is none of it really available in any practical sense?

39. Why isn't it possible to have a 100% efficient heat engine?

40. Is a man-engine, operating on food fuel more or less efficient than a Carnot type steam engine operating between 98.6°F and room temperature? Can you explain why?

41. Two containers of water sit on the same hot metal plate and exhibit identical temperatures. Therefore they must have the same heat content. True or false? Explain your answer.

Escher's study entitled *Cubic Space Divisions* shows girders intersecting each other at right angles, dividing each other into equal lengths, each forming the edge of a cube. In this way, space is filled to infinity with cubes of the same size. So it is with crystals, the lattice work uniformly filling all of the space within the crystal until the outer surface is reached.

☐ **Perceptions and Deceptions**

" I have amethysts of two kinds; one that is black like wine, and one that is red like wine that one has colored with water. I have topazes yellow as are the eyes of tigers, and topazes that are as pink as the eyes of a woodpigeon and green topazes that are as the eyes of cats. I have opals that burn always, with a flame that is cold as ice, opals that make sad men's minds, and are afraid of the shadows. I have onyxes like the eyeballs of a dead woman. I have moon-stones that change when the moon changes, and wan when they see the Sun. I have sapphires big like eggs and as blue as blue flowers. The sea wanders within them, and the moon comes never to trouble the blue of their eyes. I have chrysolites and beryls, and crysophases and rubies; I have sardonyx and hyacinth stones, and stones of chalcedony, and I will give them all unto thee, all . . ."

—*Oscar Wilde,* **Salome**

☐ **Evidence for Atoms and Molecules**

There is evidence for atoms and molecules. The Greeks first put us onto that idea in a qualitative way by suggesting that all matter was composed of discrete compositions of particles. Later, quantification became possible. Lavoisier's Law of Conservation of Matter was one quantitative generalization; Dalton's Law of Multiple Proportions, another (see Chap. 3). However, Dalton's suggestion that a molecule of water is formed when one atom of hydrogen and one atom of oxygen combine produced contradictory experimental results. The idea of a simple structure such as HO was nice, but quantitative analyses indicated the likely presence of two hydrogens, not one, for every oxygen atom. *174070*

Avogadro's Insight Produces a Law

If you study the gas phase synthesis of water by measuring the volumes of gaseous reactants and products (at standard temperature and pressure), you'll find that two volumes of hydrogen are needed to react with each volume of oxygen, producing two volumes of water. It was Avogardo who took us forward by a giant step when he hypothesized that a given volume of any gas (under the same conditions of temperature and pressure) contains the same number of molecules: a correct interpretation of the water synthesis reaction—two mole-cules of hydrogen and one molecule of oxygen, producing two molecules of water. Avogadro's analysis made still more sense after Cannizzaro suggested that the oxygen molecule was itself divisible into two identical atoms, each becoming part of two molecules of water. Hydrogen is similar. The smallest unit mass of hydrogen capable of independent existence in the free state is the hydrogen molecule (H_2); but half that mass, one hydrogen atom, is the mass of hydrogen capable of entering into chemical combination. In the formation of water, then, two hydrogen molecules combine chemically with one oxygen molecule:

Solid State Collections of Atoms and Molecules

Figure 5-1
Avogadro's Law guarantees that five 1-liter elephants will each contain identical numbers of gas molecules when measured at constant temperature and pressure.

$$2 H_2 + O_2 \longrightarrow 2 H_2O$$

Avogadro's hypothesis has been elevated to full, scientific law status:

At any particular fixed temperature and pressure, equal gas volumes contain identical numbers of molecules no matter what the nature of the gas (Fig. 5-1).

Defining the mass of the hydrogen atom as 1 amu established the mass of the hydrogen molecule as 2 amu; the quantities in grams are the masses of a mole of hydrogen atoms (H) and a mole of hydrogen molecules (H_2), respectively.

If the temperature should happen to be 0°C and the pressure 760 torr, a mole of hydrogen molecules will occupy 22,400 cubic centimeters, or 22.4 liters. That statement holds for a mole of any gaseous substance at that temperature and pressure. The number of molecules in 1 mole of molecules is defined as Avogadro's number *N,* or 6.023×10^{23}. From this we can determine that 1 mole of hydrogen molecules weighs 2 grams; 1 mole of oxygen molecules (O_2), 32 grams; 1 mole of chlorine molecules (Cl_2), 71 grams; 1 mole of bromine molecules (Br_2), 160 grams; and 1 mole of iodine molecules (I_2), 254 grams.

Enter Mendeleyeff

Last scene for this scenario: enter Mendeleyeff. The periodic table of the elements, created about a century ago, has become Dmitri Mendeleyeff's principal contribution to chemistry. Arranging the chemical elements from lightest to heaviest according to atomic weights placed those exhibiting similar physical and chemical properties into regular or periodic intervals. However, in the light of hindsight such patterns of regularity would be surprising if the *atoms* themselves were nature's smallest particles. Why wouldn't each one be unique? The true understanding of *periodicity* was first realized only after scientists perceived the atom's subatomic structure, those electrons, protons, and neutrons. The latter half of the nineteenth century saw the accumulation of evidence for such particles, but you won't get a peek at that subject until after the next chapter. We've another feature to present first.

☐ Molecular Shapes

Over 3 million pure substances have been isolated from natural sources or prepared in the chemical laboratory. Very precise structures have been determined for perhaps 30,000 of these substances. The pattern of atoms in a molecule or crystal is referred to as its **molecular** or **crystal structure.** For example, we can say we *know* the structure of the water molecule because we have data to back up that statement: both hydrogen atoms do *not* lie directly opposite each other, along a line passing through the oxygen atom, except occasionally, as the atoms vibrate; the water molecule is bent instead, with an average internal bond angle of 104.5°; generally, the two hydrogen atoms are equidistant from the oxygen atom, each being about 0.96 Å away; distances between adjacent atoms are known to within 1 percent, on the average, and in many cases to within 0.1 percent (Fig. 5-2). Again, these are data that we feel we *know* since all measurements have been firmly established by experimental observations.

From this example, we can see that a fair bit is known about molecular structure and the structure of crystals in general. Still, our perception of structure has only recently been clarified through the application of some powerful physical methods for studying atoms in molecules and crystals. Let's examine these techniques.

Seeing Atoms and Molecules Through New Eyes

Why discuss crystals anyway? Well, for one thing, the behavior of many of today's essential chemical compounds depends upon the presence of either very large crystals or collections of smaller ones. For example, transistorized radios and televisions uniquely depend on the properties of crystals. That is also true of electronic automobile ignitions, all types and kinds of electronic transmission lines, structural steel, cement and concrete, as well as table salt and sugar. By studying crystals, a beginning can be made toward understanding the forces that exist between atoms and molecules. Examine the neatly ordered and regular arrangements of atoms and molecules in crystals and an elegant model becomes available as an aid to the understanding of solid substances in general, be they crystalline or noncrystalline, microscopic or macroscopic, element or compound, living or nonliving.

What do we mean by "crystal" and crystalline? Let's start with a solid within which atoms are present as part of a regular, repeating arrangement in space. Everyone knows what *solid* means when we discuss solids, gases, and liquids. But watch out for the nuances in this science of crystals and crystallography because a solid substance such as glass is better defined as a very viscous liquid, in other words, not strictly a solid, and certainly not crystalline. A **crystal** is a systematically repeating, three-dimensional collection of atoms, periodically repeating itself throughout the entire volume.

An important consequence follows such a definition of a crystal. The immediate environment surrounding any collection of atoms will be in every way identical with any other surrounding environment. Check the squares surrounding one square on a checker board. A system of squares constitutes one kind of regular arrangement. The hexagonal arrangement of the honeycomb is another (Fig.5-3). In fact, there turns out to be a total of 11 ways in which one or two kinds of regular polygons can be so arranged that every vertex or edge of each polygon is surrounded by polygons in an identical manner to that surrounding every other vertex. The geometries are all kind of neat. You may notice the absence of

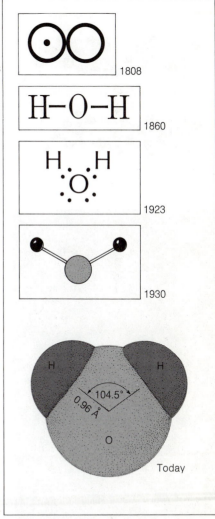

Figure 5-2
We've come to know the water molecule better over the years.

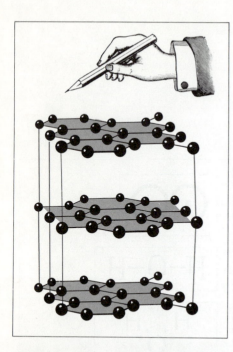

Figure 5-3
Graphite is also a crystalline variety of carbon.
It is the principal component of "lead" in lead
pencils. Strongly bonded in only two dimensions, graphite isn't diamond-like.

pentagons and heptagons, and the limitation of an eleven-sided structure (see Fig.
5-4). If you have a day or two with nothing to do but doodle, you can convince
yourself that these limitations are *requirements* of our definition of crystal,
namely: (1) same surrounding environment for all vertices, and (2) regular polygons.

Which Leads Us to Crystals and Symmetry

This is a good place to introduce **symmetry**. The concept appears in nature's
art as well as in man's art. (Symmetry is an important part of our discussion of
the molecules of life and biological activity in Chap. 14.) Symmetry is a consequence of the spacial arrangement of a regular collection of atoms in a crystal. Consider yourself as an outside observer stationed at some arbitrary point
within a crystal where one of those regularly repeating collections of atoms
is located. Look around you at any other location and you should see exactly
the same thing, as if you were in a hall of mirrors (Fig. 5-5). The practical feature of that perception is that there are directions within the crystal. Certain
crystals slice in certain directions; others conduct electricity in a certain
direction. Some transmit light in a certain direction. If you know anything
about gem stones and minerals, think how our understanding of this direction or symmetry immeasurably simplifies the work of the crystallographer
and allows the gemnologist to cut and polish stones without shattering them
(Fig. 5-6).

Now back to the regular arrangement of atoms in crystals. If you think that
this arrangement should result in a regular external appearance as well, you
are right. One thing you can say about crystals as you look at them without
aid of a microscope is that they have generally flat faces that are both extended and directed in space. Sometimes you have to look hard because of
the subtle ways in which crystals grow; nevertheless, the regularity is there.
It is there in the cubic structure of rock salt and copper metal, in the trig-
onal symmetry of cinnabar (HgS), tourmaline (a complex silicate), and in
the delicate and seemingly complex patterns found in snow crystals (Fig.
5-7). How do crystals become so complex? The answer is that crystals do
indeed grow, starting from tiny *seed* crystals. New atoms add at the crystal
faces in programmed fashion for as long as conditions of temperature and
pressure remain suitable and supplies of atoms remain available. Try it.
Grow some crystals yourself. You'll be surprised at what you can do with
a plain old mason jar and a piece of string right at home (Fig. 5-8).

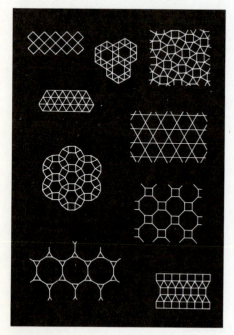

Figure 5-4
Regular polygons found in nature.

Figure 5-5
Tunneling through a model of a diamond crystal.

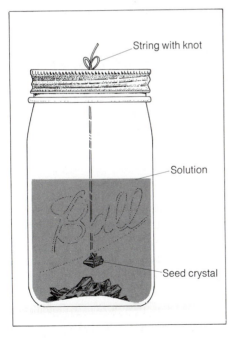

Figure 5-8
Growing crystals in a mason jar at home.

String with knot

Solution

Seed crystal

Figure 5-6
Popular diamond cuts: Emerald, Brilliant.

Figure 5-7
Snow crystals under the photographic microscope.

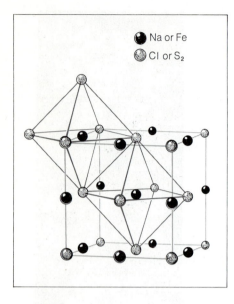

● Na or Fe
◉ Cl or S₂

Figure 5-9
Table salt and "fools" gold have similar crystal structures.

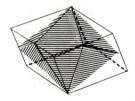

Figure 5-10
Inscribing hexagonal symmetry inside a rhombohedron.

Let's now take a quick look at a specific example to illustrate what we've been talking about. Pyrite, or iron sulfide (FeS_2), is a common mineral, valuable as a source of the metal, iron. Its characteristic yellow, almost golden, metallic appearance, has given it the name "fool's gold." Now consider this. Many compounds exhibit these same structural arrangements and inter-relationship, namely cubic and octahedral. It really doesn't matter very much what kind of atom; what does matter is where the atom is located. Common table salt (NaCl) and pyrite (FeS_2) have very similar crystal structures. We can consider interchanging sodium for iron, and chlorine for sulfur. In fact, let's just use dots and circles to show the spatial arrangement since that's really the key to the crystal structure (Fig. 5-9). Where are the atoms, not what kinds of atoms. The resulting structure is a regular cube in which dots (sodium or iron), sunk in the center of the cube's volume, find themselves surrounded at equal distances by circles (chlorine or sulfur). Each circle sits in the center of one of the six faces of the cube. Of course, the crystal doesn't stop there; the arrangement is a three-dimensional checkerboard, extending out into space. The dots and circles alternate continuously, and the regularly repeating collection of atoms looks like a block of 13 dots and 14 circles, or 14 dots and 13 circles, depending on where you start counting.

Getting back to our cubic-octahedral structure, whether you see one form or the other only depends on how you look at it. The cubic structure in fact has the octahedron built into it. Depending on the conditions available for growth, the corners of the cube can be sheared off, producing the octahedral appearance.

Each circle has 6 dots for nearest neighbors; each dot has 6 circles for nearest neighbors. All crystalline substances are put together like that. The tens of thousands of such substances are arranged into 236 spatial arrangements that fall into one of 7 crystal systems. One of these seven systems is the face-centered regular cube, characteristic of table salt and fool's gold (see Fig. 5-9).

☐ The Art and Science of Crystallography

The science of crystallography has been an honorable scientific pursuit for a long time. Its beginnings can be traced to the crystal studies of a French cleric, Abbé Rene Hauy, at the time of the French Revolution. Fortunately for the Abbé, he managed to keep his head after the overthrow of Louis XVI and Marie Antoniette in 1792, at a time when many others, including the great Lavoisier were losing theirs. A story has developed about the circumstances surrounding Hauy's discovery of the structure of calcite crystals. In some ways it parallels the events surrounding Newton, the falling apple, and the theory of gravitational attraction. While looking at a particular collection of minerals, Hauy supposedly dropped a group of calcite crystals. This particular group of calcite crystals had crystallized as hexagonal prisms (see Fig. 5-10). As the Abbé bent down to examine the shattered fragments, he found they were all perfect rhombonhedra, in every detail the identical shape of Iceland spar, a different crystalline form of calcite. Calcite is calcium carbonate, or limestone in one form. The idea came to Hauy that the rhombohedral fragments must be nuclei of *all* calcite crystals. To conclude the story, the old boy zipped home to his mineral collection and purposely busted a few more calcite crystals, some hexagonal, some acute rhombohedra, some irregularly torn from the quarry. He discovered that all produced rhombohedral fragments. Whether the calcite breakage story ever really happened isn't perfectly clear, but that is unimportant. The story of Newton and the apple was probably no more than a thought experiment either.

X-Ray Diffraction Allows Us To See Crystal Structure

About 60 years ago, a twentieth-century, German scientist, Max von Laue, aided by two assistants, devised a method for studying the internal structure of crystals which gave further evidence for Hauy's discovery. The technique, known as *X-ray diffraction*, proved for the first time that there was a regular arrangement of atoms in crystals. X-ray crystallography was recognized almost at once as a scientific discovery of the first rank. Analysis of crystals by this method brought the determination of crystal structures and the spatial arrangements of atoms in molecules from the realm of speculation to that of measurement. Within a year of the discovery, the structure of sodium chloride had been determined and the new science was off and running. By 1953 great discoveries were possible. That year, James Watson, a 23-year-old American biologist working in England with Francis Crick and Morris Wilkins, interpreted the double-helix structure of the DNA molecule from the X-ray diffraction photographs taken by Rosalind Franklin (see Fig. 5-11). That discovery opened the way to our understanding of genetic coding, making possible a great stride forward in molecular biology.

☐ Nature's Regular Polyhedra

The cube is probably the regular polyhedron most familiar to us. It has 6 square faces, 8 corners, and 12 edges. Many of nature's crystalline substances have atoms spaced in such a cubic arrangement. We've described two, salt and pyrites. Something must also be said about two other regular polyhedra, the tetrahedron and the octahedron. The octahedron has 8 triangular faces, 6 corners, and 12 edges (Fig. 5-12). There are many examples of molecular arrangements in nature where a central atom is bonded to six other atoms in an octahedral pattern. A tetrahedron has 4 triangular faces, 4 corners, and 6 edges. That arrangement also describes many of nature's molecular structures. First let's talk about octahedra and cubes, then tetrahedra and cubes.

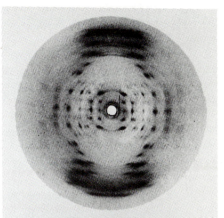

An X-ray photograph of crystalline DNA in the A form.

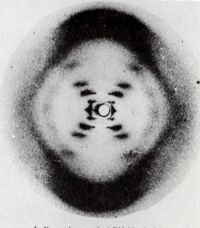

An X-ray photograph of DNA in the B form, taken by Rosalind Franklin late in 1952.

Figure 5-11
Rosalind Franklin's historic x-ray photographs of the A and B forms of DNA led directly to the correct double helix structure (see Chap. 14).

If you take the opaque, violet crystals of the iron salt known as ferric nitrate, $Fe(NO_3)_3 \cdot 6H_2O$, and the pale yellow crystals of a complex iron salt, potassium ferrocyanide, $K_4Fe(CN)_6 \cdot 4H_2O$, dissolve both separately in water, and then mix, a magnificent blue precipitate is formed. The blue substance is a pigment known as Prussian blue, $KFe_2(CN)_6 \cdot H_2O$. Now take a look at the crystal structure by means of X-ray diffraction analysis. X-ray studies show a simple cubic structure. In each corner of the cube is an atom of iron; along each edge is an iron-to-carbon-to-nitrogen-to-iron arrangement (Fe-C-N-Fe). Every iron atom forms six bonds that are directed in space toward the six corners of a regular octahedron (Fig. 5-13). The structure about the iron atoms has an octahedral arrangement within a cubic framework. We tried to show that earlier with our drawings of the iron pyrite structure (Fig. 5-9).

The structural relationship between the tetrahedron and the cube is readily seen in the diamond crystal (Fig. 5-14). Because the tetrahedral structure is characteristic of the carbon atom and many of the organic molecules that comprise living systems, it's of particular importance. Diamond is one of the hardest substances known; this particular crystalline form of carbon happens to be cubic, a discovery made very early in the history of X-ray crystal methods. There are carbon atoms in each corner of a unit cube, each bonded in a tetrahedral arrangement to four other carbon atoms. Because all of the carbon atoms in a diamond crystal constitute essentially a single molecule, the diamond crystal is very strong. To shear or shatter a diamond crystal requires the rupture of not a few, but lots of bonds. On the other hand, graphite, another crystalline form of carbon, ruptures certain of its bonds in one particular direction very, very easily (Fig. 5-3). That is the result of a *layered* structure in which molecular platelets readily slide over each other. Because of it's peculiar structure, graphite makes a good lubricant, particularly in space, where it won't freeze the way greases and oils do. Run your fingers over a pencil tip, notice how slippery it is, the lead in a lead pencil is graphite all right, but the manufacturer has put a little wax in there to help Mother Nature along. Graphite and diamond are simply two different crystalline modifications of the element carbon.

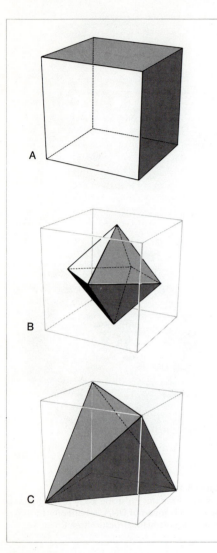

Figure 5-12
The cube, octahedron, and tetrahedron.

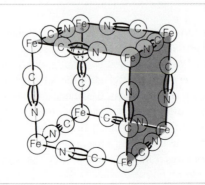

Figure 5-13
A pigment known as *Prussian Blue.*

As with sodium chloride and pyrites, copper is also found in nature as cubic and octahedral crystals. Each copper atom has 12 nearest, identical neighbors in the most efficient geometric arrangement possible for packing together regular balls, or atoms (see Fig. 5-15). It is this geometric arrangement of large numbers of identical nearest neighbors (12), often found in metallic substances, that accounts for the strengths of metals, and for other of their properties such as malleability, ductility, and compressibility.

☐ Molecular Architecture, Order, and a Portrait of the Solid State

For diamond crystals, the only spatial arrangement about carbon is tetrahedral. Consequently, diamond crystals can be looked upon as giant molecules of multiple carbon atoms, tetrahedrally directed into a continuous, three-dimensional cubic arrangement. Iron pyrites, on the other hand, is an alternating network or iron atoms and *pairs* of sulfur atoms. Each pair of sulfur atoms behaves as though it were a discrete component of the crystal's geometry, located at a single point in space. Many substances contain discrete molecular arrangements of molecules that occupy a single location in a crystal much as does an iron atom in pyrites or prussian blue, carbon atoms in diamond, or sodium ions in salt.

In short, there is a kind of orderliness in solids because atoms or groups of atoms (molecules or ions) exist in regular patterns that go on and on, until of course they stop, as you finally climb out of the inside of a crystal, having arrived at a surface layer of atoms. In two dimensions, it is much like an Escher print or

Figure 5-14
Alum crystals showing successive changes in form— cube to octahedron.

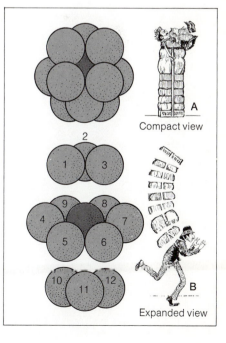

Figure 5-15
An exploded model of cubic close packing in crystals. They are like stacked cannonballs.

Compact view

Expanded view

A

B

2

1 3

9 8

4 7

5 6

10 12

11

Figure 5-16
Montreal landmark in winter mist. Moshe Safdie's apartment complex *Habitat* has a cube-on-cube crystalline regularity.

checker-board (see Chapter opening); in three dimensions, a good analogy might be identical high-rise housing units (Fig. 5-16). In fact, you can build yourself an elegant cubic crystal structure out of sugar cubes. If you start out with a 6 X 6 unit square cube and top it with a 5 X 5, 4 X 4, and so on, you'll come up with a three-dimensional arrangement in which each of the layers is stepped back one cube (Fig. 5-17). You've got the top half of an octahedron, and if you build the structure on a mirror, the other half of the octahedron would be reflected below.

Crystal Structure and Density

When crystals of ice are connected in frozen symmetry, we find the intricate details characteristic of snowflakes and the frosty window designs of winter (Fig. 5-3). Looking inside nature's frozen structure provides some real insight concerning a key property of ice, namely its unusual density. The density of ice is less than that of the water that forms when it melts. Molecules within the framework pattern are arranged hexagonally, with lots of empty space throughout; the whole structure isn't very tightly packed. Each water molecule is surrounded by four other water molecules in a three-dimensional tetrahedral arrangement. The hexagonal structure collapse when ice melts and the water molecules pack closer together. That accounts for the observation that water near its freezing point is denser than ice and explains why water expands, occupying more space on freezing, causing all sorts of problems from exploded containers to cracked roadbeds.

□ **The Limits of Orderliness and the States of Matter**

We've hardly been able to see actual single atoms, and why they should form into orderly arrangements is something we don't yet fully understand. Nevertheless, "orderliness" best describes the character of the solid state. Melt a few chips of a crystalline solid; the permanently ordered arrangements of atoms disappear, to be replaced by the momentary, localized kind of "orderliness" characteristic of liquids. Finally, apply heat to those now melted crystalline particles, allowing them to vaporize away into the gaseous state; the last remnants of order evaporate, right along with the last traces of liquid.

At temperatures ranging from just a shade above absolute zero, the atoms in crystalline solids lie close together, in neatly arranged patterns. They vibrate back and forth within some average, prescribed equilibrium position, the *interatomic distance*: for example, the 0.96 Å distance between hydrogen and oxygen atoms in water molecules. The atoms vibrate, but they cannot exchange places or slide past one another. Only at the surface of the crystal can atoms or molecules occasionally break away, directly into the gas phase.

As temperature progressively increases from the vicinity of absolute zero, the internal, kinetic energy of motion among particles in a solid begins to cause

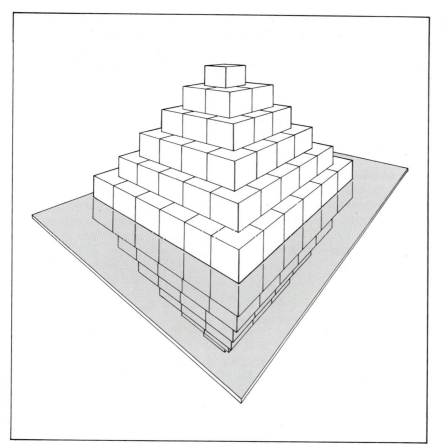

Figure 5-17
Reflections in a mirror. The octahedron.

some extreme agitation. Particles may strike each other; some can break free sliding past or dislocating other particles. Such thermal agitation causes the crystal to expand somewhat. Atoms or molecules in the liquid state are very neatly arranged and packed as closely as in crystalline solids, but they can move freely past one another. Consequently, the liquid state is somewhat less dense than the solid state: water is an exception, as we noted last chapter. Particles can also pass more easily into the gaseous state at the liquid surface than they generally can from the surface of a solid.

Continue raising the temperature, increasing the heat content within the liquid. When the internal energy becomes great enough to allow particles to escape freely into the gaseous phase at the liquid's surface, or anywhere else in the liquid for that matter, you have reached the boiling point. Eventually, the entire body of the liquid will become a collection of gaseous particles, widely separated separated, freely moving, totally independent, showing little or no interest in any neighbors. In our earlier discussions, we developed an all-purpose model for physical behavior known as the kinetic-molecular theory (billiard balls in collision; molecules in near-collision). Along with our notion of energy, we also began developing a more general perception of the restless world about us. We have added a continuous view of the three states of matter to our understanding.

☐ Questions to Answer . . . Problems to Solve

1. There is evidence for the existence of atoms and molecules! Put together a short summary in your own words in support of that contention.

2. The guy who wrote this book feels that Avogadro's hypothesis should be Avogadro's Law. What do you think about that? Justified?

3. There is a subtlety in Mendeleyeff's demonstration of periodic behavior that escaped him; there was a strong suggestion of **divisibility**, rather than indivisibility of atoms, all some twenty-five years before the discovery of the electron. Explain your understanding of that subtlety.

4. Indicate whether each of the following statements is reasonable, or unreasonable:
   (a) External form is not the only, nor even the most important characteristic of the crystalline state. It is only the most conspicuous.
   (b) The general properties of a crystal, such as density, melting point, and chemical composition, suggest the aggregate nature of the substance and do not involve any particular direction through the crystal.
   (c) A complex mineral, cordierite, $H_2(MgFe)_4Al_8Si_{10}O_{37}$, appears blue, or yellow-green, or blue-green depending on which way one views light passing through, and that must be a directional property of the crystals internal arrangement.
   (d) Crystals don't cleave at special places in a crystal, but in special directions through the crystal.

5. Based on your newly acquired understanding of the solid state, contrast the external appearance of a sheet of ice and a sheet of glass with your deeper perception of their respective internal structures.

6. Place the contribution of Hauy and von Laue in a contemporary perspective with regard to our understanding of crystal structure.

7 Lend us your understanding *why* the following phenomena:
   (a) A full, sealed soda bottle explodes on freezing.
   (b) A metal can be drawn into a wire or pressed into a sheet.
   (c) Diamond is a very hard, dense, substance.

(d) Lakes freeze from the top, down.

8. Referring back to the structural arrangement for salt and pyrite crystals,
    (a) Convince yourself that the smallest, regular repeating unit that makes
         up the entire crystal is 27 atoms, either 14 dots and 13 circles, or
         vice-versa.
    (b) And now that you can visualize it, see if you can explain it.

9. Break out the marshmellows from the pantry or the cherries and olives
    from the bar. With a box of toothpicks, build yourself
    (a) a regular cubic arrangement of atoms
    (b) an octahedral arrangement of atoms
    (c) a tetrahedral arrangement of atoms

10. Think of a number of things that
     (a) suggest both external and internal symmetry to you.
     (b) are externally symmetric but appear asymmetric when you look inside.
     (c) appear asymmetric to the eye but are symmetric inside.

11. Graphite and diamond are allotropes. Do you know of any others? If you
     don't, there are several other examples scattered through the succeeding
     chapters. See if you can't locate a few through the index.

12. Glass is best viewed as a super-viscous, perhaps *frozen* liquid. Can you
     think of any other examples of that state of affairs from the world of
     your experience?

13. Let's return to Chap. 4 and kinetic-molecular theory, and the concept of
     energy for a moment. How might you view the motion of atoms and
     molecules in the solid state? Now tuck that perspective away for a moment
     until you've had a chance to digest the next chapter on the liquid and
     gaseous state and we'll then try to tie the whole business together—solids,
     liquids, and gases—in one point of view.

14. Have you ever thought about the effects of pressure on solids?
     (a) For example, ice melts when you step on it with a skate blade and
          refreezes after you've skated away.
     (b) And dry ice never seems to melt at all.

15. How might you best describe the physical state of a rubber band?
     Crystalline? Amorphous? Half-frozen liquid? Or what?

16. What about the physical state of a pearl? Or a brass door knob? Or the
     lens of a giant telescope?

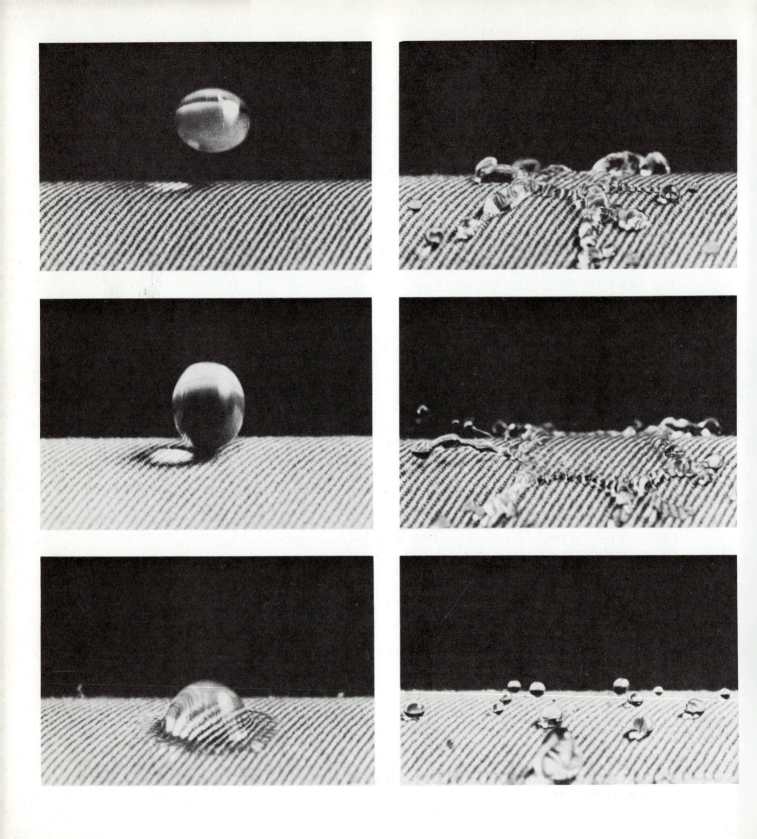

Chapter 6

The Fluid States: Gases and Liquids

□ **Perceptions and Deceptions**

1 Ordinarily, all gases behave in just about the same way. Want a one-word description of that behavior? Try **perfect**, or perhaps *ideal*.

2 The density of a gas is related to its molecular weight in a fundamental way

3 Liquids evaporate. That's cool! Solids evaporate. That's sublime!

4 The liquid surface is a very special place.

5 Gases are fluids; and liquids flow, too. Even solids have been known to creep.

6 We live submerged at the bottom of a sea of air.

□ **The Gaseous State and the Gas Laws**

The two most revealing characteristics of a gas: (1) its particles are independent, freely moving within what must be considered a very large volume compared to the volume of individual particles; (2) gases flow, completely filling space, whenever they are given the opportunity. We can describe gases according to their kinetic molecular behavior by two basic laws. The first law suggests that at a given temperature, the volume of any gas varies inversely as the pressure to which it is subjected. The second law suggests that at a given pressure, the volume of any gas varies directly as its absolute temperature. Those two ideas should be somewhat familiar to you from Chap. 4. But now let's place them into the kinds of formulas that are so much a part of the language of science.

The Boyle's Law Relationship

In much the same way as we did earlier for Newton's laws of motion, we can state the first of our two gas laws, *Boyle's Law*:

At some constant temperature T, the volume V is inversely proportional to the pressure P, or

$$V \propto \frac{1}{P}$$

But remember that $\propto$ is the same as $=k$, so

$$V = k\frac{1}{P}$$

A drop of water in free fall attempts to minimize its surface area by allowing for uniform distribution of molecular forces. As the drop (3X magnification) falls onto a cotton gabardine fabric that has been treated for water repellancy, it first breaks apart, but then quickly returns to its spherical shape. Treatment of the fabric prevented the water from penetrating and from forming any kind of adhesive forces between water molecules and the fabric surface.

which can be rearranged to

$PV = k$

In other words, for any gas that obeys our kinetic-molecular model perfectly, the product of pressure and volume, at any fixed temperature, will be constant. $PV = k$. Figure 6-1 provides a graphic representation of Boyle's Law.

Boyle's Law also states that pressure is proportional to density. How do we arrive at such a translation? Think about that for a moment. Density is the ratio of mass to volume (m/V). But in any given volume of gas, mass must be a constant. Therefore, density can be represented by $1/V$, multiplied by the **constant** mass; or in other words

$$d = \frac{m}{V}$$

But since m is a constant

$$d = m\frac{1}{V}$$

Remember that $\propto$ is the same as $= k$, or $= m$ in this case since mass is constant.

$$d \propto \frac{1}{V}$$

and since

$$\frac{1}{V} \propto P$$

then $d \propto P$

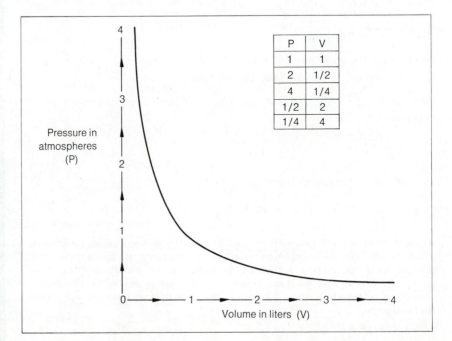

P	V
1	1
2	1/2
4	1/4
1/2	2
1/4	4

Pressure in atmospheres (P)

Volume in liters (V)

Figure 6-1
Boyle's Law graphically represented, showing the inverse relationship between pressure and volume at constant temperature.

Table 6-1

How pressure and volume change at constant temperature

Pressure, atmospheres		Volume, liters	Pressure-volume product, liter-atmospheres	
1		1	1	
2		½	1	
4	$V \propto \dfrac{1}{P}$	¼	1	$PV = k$
½		2	1	
¼		4	1	

That makes sense: put twice as many molecules into a given container and the pressure must double (Fig. 6-2).

The Charles' Law Relationship

Doing the same with our second gas law, *Charles' Law,* and representing the relationship graphically as we did for Boyle's Law, gives us Fig. 6-3.

Figure 6-3
Charles' Law graphically represented showing the direct relationship between temperature and volume.

Figure 6-2
If you increase the number of gas particles present in a flask at a given tamperature, the pressure will increase. Double the density, double the pressure.

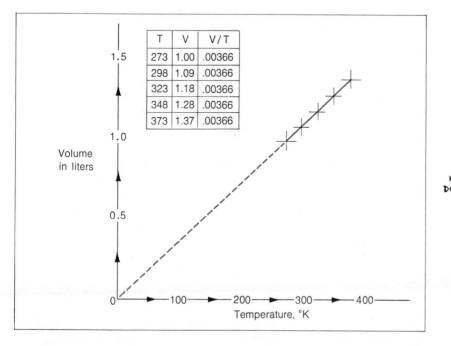

T	V	V / T
273	1.00	.00366
298	1.09	.00366
323	1.18	.00366
348	1.28	.00366
373	1.37	.00366

Volume in liters

Temperature, °K

THE PRESSURE MUST'VE DOUBLED IN HERE

YEAH! AND HAVE I GOT A HEADACHE TO PROVE IT

At some constant pressure *P*, *V* is proportional to *T*, or stated mathematically

$$V \propto T$$

Since $\propto$ means $= k$

$$V = kT$$

which can be rearranged to

$$\frac{V}{T} = k$$

The Ideal Gas Law Relationship

One important loose end can be tied together here. Remember that Avogadro's Law stated equal volumes of gas contain equal numbers of molecules, if both pressure and temperature are kept the same. Consider two gases occupying the same volume; if the temperature is also the same and one gas is at a greater pressure than the other, then that one volume must contain more molecules. The higher the pressure, the larger the number of molecules, if the volume and temperature are constant. The larger the volume, the larger the number of molecules, if pressure and temperature are constant. Putting Boyle's Law, Charles' Law and now Avogadro's Law all together into one equation

$$\frac{P \times V}{T} \propto \text{number of gas molecules designated as } n$$

Once again, since $\propto$ is the same as $= k$

$$\frac{P \times V}{T} = nk$$

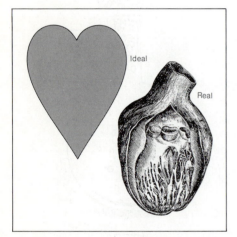

Ideal

Real

The constant k in this case has **universal** significance. In fact, it is referred to as the **universal gas constant,** R. The value of R may be calculated using the fact that 1 mole of any ideal gas under standard conditions of temperature and pressure (STP), $0°C$ and 1 atmosphere, occupies a volume of 22.4 liters

$$R = \frac{P \times V}{T \times n} = \frac{(1 \text{ atm}) (22.4 \text{ l})}{(273°K) (1 \text{ mole})} = 0.0821 \text{ l-atm/deg-mole}$$

The equation is quite general, describing the behavior of any "perfect" or "ideal" gas. We'll call it the perfect gas law equation, or simply the *Ideal Gas Law*:

$$\frac{P \times V}{T} = nR$$

Rearranging the equation gives the usual form for the Ideal Gas Law

$$PV = nRT$$

No *real* gas in nature exactly follows the behavior described by these *"idealized"* equations for *perfect* gases. A perfect gas is one which follows the ideal gas laws . . . exactly. That no such gases exist won't cramp our style at all, for what we are really after is a good model, one for comparing the behavior of real gases to ideal gas behavior. Some reasonable ideas have been suggested as to why real gases in nature do not behave "ideally." First, if according to the ideal gas laws, we continuously increase pressure and decrease volume (at constant temperature), the volume must approach zero as the pressure becomes very large. That is out of the question, because molecules of a gas will always occupy some finite space.

A second inconsistency lies in our assumption that molecules of a gas behave independently in whatever volume they happen to occupy: that is to say, they exhibit no attraction for one another. But molecules of a real gas are always attracting and repelling each other. For instance, at higher pressures interactions often become obviously significant. After all, gases liquify and attraction between molecules is therefore clearly implied. Nevertheless, it is safe to assume that the real gases with which we will be dealing can be adequately described by the ideal gas law equation (to the number of significant figures needed in our calculations and measurements). See Chap. 2. In other words, $PV = nRT$ is good enough for our immediate purposes.

STOP! Brief digression. When we speak of a law, for example, Boyle's Law, Charles' Law, Avogadro's Law, Ideal Gas Law, Newton's Law, an essential idea is provided by the word "constant." Many scientific laws can be reworded in terms of a **constant,** implying that a *fixed relationship* exists. Scientific laws express consistent, predictable, patterns of behavior . . . constant relationships. End of digression.

Density and Molecular Weight Calculations

Important ideas derive from the combined gas law relationships. For example, density is related in a straightforward manner to molecular weight. Direct calculation of the approximate molecular weight of an unknown substance by measuring its density is a modest laboratory procedure providing you can vaporize the substance without causing its decomposition (Fig. 6-4). Turn it into a gas; measure its density; then calculate its molecular weight. Let's begin.

$$PV = nRT$$

But the number of moles n is the ratio of the number of grams g of the substance to its molecular weight M,

$$\text{moles} = \frac{\text{grams}}{\text{molecular weight}} = \frac{\text{grams}}{\text{grams/mole}} = \text{moles}$$

$$n = \frac{g}{M} = \frac{g}{g/n} = n$$

so n is the same as g/M, and making that substitution

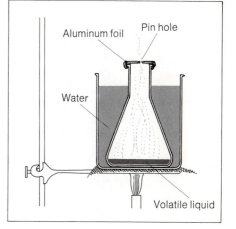

Figure 6-4
Vapor density measurements provide a convenient method for determining molecular weights.

$$PV = \frac{g}{M} RT$$

Rearranging terms,

$$M = \frac{g}{PV}RT \quad \text{or} \quad M = \frac{g}{V} \times \frac{RT}{P}$$

but g/V is density d so that

$$M = d \times \frac{RT}{P}$$

Molecular weight M is *calculated* by *measuring* density d since R is a constant, T is the known temperature of the experiment and P is the pressure of the gas at which the density is measured (usually atmospheric pressure).

Want to find the molecular weight of an unknown gas? Why, measure its density, under atmospheric pressure, at some fixed temperature

(1) $PV = n\mathrm{R}T$

(2) $PV = \frac{g}{M}\mathrm{R}T$

(3) $M = \frac{g}{V} \times \frac{\mathrm{R}T}{P}$

(4) $M = d \times \frac{\mathrm{R}T}{P}$

For example, in an experimental determination of the molecular weight of carbon tetrachloride vapor (Fig. 6-4), a 125-milliliter flask contained 0.629 gram of vapor. The temperature was 100°C and the vapor's pressure was 758 torr.

$$M = \frac{0.629 \text{ g}}{0.125 \text{ liter}} \times \frac{0.0821 \text{ liter-atm/deg-mole} \times 373 \text{ deg}}{1 \text{ atm}}$$

$$= 154 \text{ grams/liter}$$

How about establishing the molar volume for a perfect gas under standard conditions? We want to know the final volume occupied by 1 mole of a perfect gas at a final temperature of 373°K and pressure of 750 torr.

$$P = \frac{750}{760} = 0.986 \text{ atm} \qquad \mathrm{R} = 0.0821 \text{ liter-atm/deg-mole}$$
$$T = 373°\mathrm{K}$$

n = 1 mole

$PV = n\mathrm{R}T$

$$V = \frac{n\mathrm{R}T}{P} = \frac{(1 \text{ mole}) (0.0821 \text{ liter-atm/deg-mole})(373 \text{ deg})}{0.986 \text{ atm}}$$

V = 31.1 liters

☐ As If Boyle, Charles, and Avogadro Weren't Enough

Mixtures of Gases and Gas Pressures

John Dalton gets his two cents in here as well. Dalton insisted that for mixtures of gases, the total pressure reflects the individual contributions from the members of the mix. Here's an example. Fill two identical containers with separate samples of the pure components of a two-component (binary) gas mixture, both at the same pressure, say 1 atmosphere (see Fig. 6-5). Now allow the gases in each of the containers to mix. After the particles have had a chance to completely scramble, half of one gas and half of the other will be present in *both* containers: a reasonable assumption. The pressure of each gas will be half an atmosphere just as if the other weren't present; after all, each of the original gases is now distributed through a container (actually two *connected* containers) that is twice the volume of the original container. You know the pressure will decrease to one-half when the volume doubles. Therefore, in each container the pressure is still the same, 1 atmosphere. However the 1 atmosphere of pressure is due to the contributions of two gases in a mixture, each present in half the quantity of the pure gas component originally contained. But the total number of particles hasn't changed; neither has the total pressure. This observation has been labeled *Dalton's Law of Partial Pressures* which states that

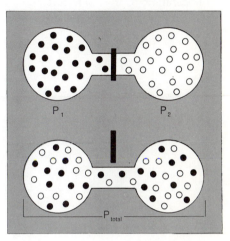

Figure 6-5
Neither gas knows the other is there. Each acts as if it were alone, exerting its own pressure. The total pressure is the sum of the individual or total pressures.

> Total pressure is the sum of the partial pressures.

The individual pressures are due to the different gases in the mix acting (like perfect gases) as if they were the only particles present. Want an equation? That's easy. Assuming the components of the mixture don't react with each other, so that our only concern is with the total number of particles present, we have

$$P_{Total} = P_1 + P_2$$

Next time you talk about the pressure of the atmosphere, remember what a mixture of gases you've really got. Mostly nitrogen (78.08 percent) and oxygen (20.95 percent), but also argon (Ar), carbon dioxide (CO_2), neon (Ne), helium (He), krypton (Kr), xenon (Xe), hydrogen (H_2), methane (CH_4), nitrous oxide (N_2O), carbon monoxide (CO), water vapor (H_2O), and others. Should your sea level barometer on a cold winter day ($0°C$) read 1 atmosphere, that total pressure is equal to the sum of the partial pressures due to the combined contributions of all the particles present.

Humidity, Absolutely, and Relatively

Dalton's Law of Partial Pressures is directly concerned with our personal comfort in humidity, the concentration of water vapor in the air. The mass of the small amount of water vapor present in any unit volume of the air (the concentration of water vapor) is called the *absolute humidity*. Ordinarily, the partial pressure

Table 6-2

Vapor pressure of water at temperatures between the ice and boiling points

Temperature, $^\circ$C	Pressure, torr
0	4.58
5	6.54
10	9.21
15	12.79
20	17.54
25	23.76
30	31.82
35	42.18
40	55.32
50	92.51
60	149.38
75	289.1
100	760.0

of water vapor isn't very much, perhaps no more than a few torr at most. Since the partial pressure due to water vapor at any air temperature cannot ever be greater than the vapor pressure for water at that temperature, on a relatively cold day, say 5°C, the partial pressure cannot exceed 6.54 torr; at 20°C, a comfortable room temperature, it cannot exceed 17.54 torr: and at 35°C, a really hot day, it cannot exceed 42.18 torr (see Table 6-2).

If it happens that the absolute humidity is such that the partial pressure is the same as the vapor pressure, the air is said to be saturated with water vapor. Whatever the ratio of the partial pressure to the vapor pressure turns out to be, that's referred to as the ***relative humidity***, and is commonly stated as a percentage.

$$\text{Relative humidity} = \frac{\text{partial pressure of water vapor}}{\text{vapor pressure at that temperature}} \times 100$$

If the relative humidity is 100 percent, the air is saturated with water vapor; zero relative humidity means "real dry" air, essentially no water vapor at all. A comfortable summer's day might be a warm 86°F (that's 30°C) with a dry 35 percent relative humidity,

$$\text{Relative humidity} = \frac{11.14 \text{ mm}}{31.82 \text{ mm}} \times 100 = 35\%$$

whereas a relative humidity of 70 percent at that same temperature would be very uncomfortable.

A saturated atmosphere, or 100 percent relative humidity, happens to be an important and useful limit. Such a condition can be established easily enough: introduce more water vapor into the air, increasing the partial pressure of water vapor; or cool the air to the point where the existing partial pressure now saturates the air. Consider a situation where the partial pressure is found to be 20.0 millimeters and the air temperature is 20°C, a situation leading to a calculated relative humidity of 114 percent.

$$\text{Relative humidity} = \frac{20.0 \text{ mm}}{17.5 \text{ mm}} \times 100 = 114\%$$

The partial pressure is greater than the vapor pressure, and the relative humidity greater than 100 percent; condensation takes place until an adjustment of the partial pressure at least down to 17.5 millimeter takes place. Because of this phenomenon clouds and fog form. The condensation we call ***dew*** forms in the same way when the earth's surface cools at night. If the partial pressure is very low, night temperatures may have to fall below 0°C before saturation levels of water vapor are attained; here condensed vapor takes the form of tiny crystals of ice or frost.

Torricelli's Emptiness and the Pressure of the Atmosphere

Gases react to volume, temperature, and pressure changes. But let's take a closer look at gas pressures in terms of our newly defined laws for gas behavior. We all know about the considerable pressure exerted by the air around us. This great mass of gases is on the order of 6×10^{15} tons, more than a kilogram for each square centimeter of the earth's surface. The Italian physicist, Torricelli, was first to determine the pressure due to that tremendous mass. Torricelli, a disciple of Galileo, gave the local inhabitants just cause to wonder about the student, as well as the teacher. Taking a vertical tube of some considerable length, Torricelli sealed it at the top, filled it completely with water, and then placed it, open end down, into a tub full of water. The level of the water in the tube immediately fell to a height of about 1,000 centimeters above the water level in the tub. "Torricelli's emptiness" remained above the water level in the tube. Containing little more than some water vapor and totally separated from the atmosphere, there could be no downward pressure acting on the top of the column of water standing in the tube. This raised the question of why the column of water in the tube remained standing. What was holding it up?

Figure 6-6
A vacuum "tugging" at Torricelli's "emptiness."

Torricelli's emptiness may now seem quite reasonable, but consider the logic of Franciscus Linus, a contemporary of Torricelli. He believed the so-called empty space at the top of the column contained an imperceivable cord. If you stretch this cord, it responds by pulling at any surrounding matter. This explained, for example, why matter climbed up a column at the insistence of a vacuum pump. It was being *pulled* up. Try placing your finger over one end of a straw while sucking on the other. Same idea. If all this seems like a frivolous digression, remember this, common sense would tell us that the idea of a vacuum "tugging" is more rational than the perception that suction is simply a response to pressure difference, even if the latter is actually correct (Fig. 6-6). If the straw collapses the outside pressure of the atmosphere did the collapsing, not the invisible cord. Similarly, water is pushed, not pulled, up a column by a suction pump.

The seventeenth century French scientist, Blaise Pascal, supplied the background for understanding pressure. He showed that when you increase the pressure on fluids in closed containers, the pressure increase is transmitted equally through the fluid (see Fig. 6-7). Hydraulic presses and car brakes work on that principle; Pascal's idea also helps us to understand Torricelli's problem. The pressure of the atmosphere is transmitted throughout the fluid in an open tub of water, forcing water up the tube. Since there is only "Torricelli's emptiness" or a near vacuum on the top of the column, there is little resistance, except that due to the mass of a column of water that particular height. Therefore,

$$h \times d = \text{pressure of the atmosphere}$$

where h is the height of the fluid in the column and d is the density of the fluid. The density is the proportionality constant in this case. In Torricelli's experi-

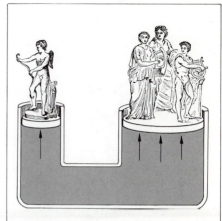

Figure 6-7
Pressure is transmitted uniformly through solutions.

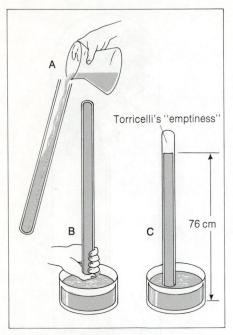

Figure 6-8
Building a simple mercury barometer.

Figure 6-9
Math supplies giant shoulders on which science stands.

ment, the water column stood at 1,000 centimeters. Since the density of water is 1 gram per cubic centimeter, the pressure of the atmosphere becomes 1,000 grams per square centimeter

$$(1000 \text{ cm}) \times \frac{1 \text{ gram}}{1 \text{ cm}^3} = 1000 \text{ g/cm}^2$$

This is a cumbersome experiment if you do it the way Torricelli did. You'll probably have to use the drainpipe on your house, checking the water level somewhere near the third floor. But the experiment can be repeated easily in the laboratory if you use mercury instead of water. Since mercury is 13.6 times as dense as water, the liquid in the column will now rise only 1/13.6 as high as the column of water in Torricelli's drainpipe. Fill a glass tube full of mercury; cover the open end, invert, and submerge it, open end first in a dish of mercury. If you are at sea level on a normal day, the column of mercury will fall until its top stands about 76 centimeters above the surface of the mercury in the dish. By the way, you have just built a barometer, and you also just measured the pressure of the atmosphere (Fig. 6-8). For the sake of uniformity, 76 cm is accepted as the standard pressure of the atmosphere at sea level, or 760 torr.

☐ Presenting Scientific Data: Tables and Graphs

Let's briefly pause to discuss the importance of tables for illustrating scientific data and graphical methods of data handling. We will illustrate our discussion with materials from the liquid state which follows.

Mathematics and science can be depicted as a pair of strangely related creatures, sustaining and enriching one another. But there's a catch. For while mathematics could do quite nicely without science, it is hardly likely that modern science could manage without mathematics (Fig. 6-9). In the absence of the logic and clarity which numbers and mathematical methods impart to science, there would be little chance of finding relationships in nature. A number of techniques are commonly employed in collecting and presenting scientific information. To begin with, data are tabulated. Data in Table 6-3 define the rate at which a sugar solution reacts when dissolved in aqueous acid (as in your stomach) as time passes.

This same data may be presented in graphical form. Coordinates in two dimensions referred to as x and y are commonly used. They serve to fix a point in a plane, for example, on a sheet of graph paper. As Fig. 6-10 shows, there is a *point of origin* and specified directions referred to as axes.

The very simplest relationship is direct proportionality. We saw an example of

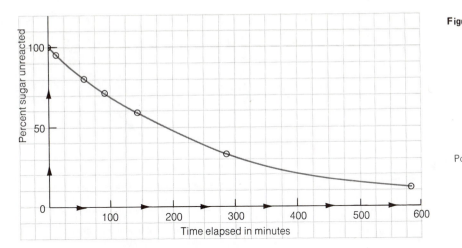

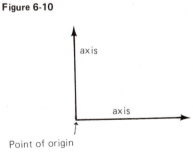

Figure 6-10

such a relationship in Charles' Law. As the absolute temperature of a gas changes, so does its volume (at a constant temperature). Thus, volume and temperature are directly proportional to each other. In the same manner, movement along the x axis causes proportional changes along the y axis. These are not equal changes, but proportional ones. (See Fig. 6-3.) Graphing the data in Table 6-3 along the vertical or y axis, we'll plot the sugar still remaining (percent sugar unreacted) versus time elapsed in minutes along the horizontal or x axis. Remember that our interest is in the entire curve, and in this case, it is not a straight line. It is a line that is constantly changing direction. It would be inappropriate and misleading to draw straight lines between adjacent points. A smooth curve is what is wanted. There is a clear relationship indicated by the smooth nature of the changing curve.

Let's now try to represent a second set of data, and at the same time, introduce another manipulative technique, namely **extrapolation**. Consider the manner in which the volume of a given mass of gas is affected by changing pressure; the temperature is kept constant and has no net effect on the pressure-volume relationshp, consequently we can forget temperature for the moment. A Boyle's Law plot of pressure versus volume (Table 6-4) produces the hyperbolic curve characteristic of inverse relationships; as the pressure increases, the volume decreases. In other words, double the pressure (1 atm to 2 atm) and halve the volume (22.4 liters to 11.2 liters) (Fig. 6-11). Extrapolation is the technique of extending a curve beyond the points allowed by the limits of the experiment. By extrapolation, the volume of gas in question could be determined under a pressure of 8 atmospheres as shown by the dashed line extending $P = 8$ atm. The actual experiment need not be done. However, a strong possibility for introducing error exists here because you are extending a curve whose direction is changing. A plot of pressure versus the *reciprocal*

Table 6-3
The reaction of sugar in aqueous acid solution

Time elapsed, min	Percent sugar unreacted
0	100
9.82	96.5
59.60	80.3
93.18	71.0
142.9	59.1
294.8	32.8
589.4	11.1

Table 6-4

Pressure, atmospheres	Volume, liters	$1/V$
1	22.4	0.0446
2	11.2	0.0892
4	5.6	0.179
8	2.8	0.357

Figure 6-11

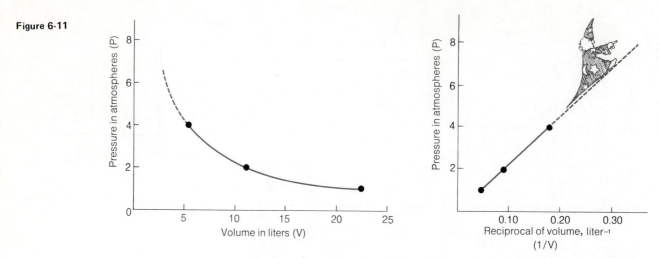

of volume is a straight line. Extrapolation of this line involves no guessing as to the direction of the line, therefore, a more accurate answer is possible.

☐ A Snapshot of the Liquid State

Based on our preceding discussion, we could appropriately describe the gaseous state as one of confusion; there are virtually no direct interactions between atoms and molecules. By contrast, things are all very neat and tidy in the solid state; atoms and molecules know their proper place, vibrating about a fixed position. Strong interactions are the rule with solids. The behavior of atoms and molecules in the liquid state is least understood of the three states of matter. We do know that molecular interactions in liquids are strong but that unlike gases, liquids will occupy some definite volume. A liter of water is still a liter of water whether it is in a liter-sized bottle or poured into a plain old 1-gallon bucket (see Fig. 6-12). A 1-liter container of water vapor, on the other hand, will become 4 liters of water vapor in a 4-liter container. On the other hand, molecular interactions aren't as strong as in solids; after all, liquids do flow readily, and they do conform to the shape of the container. So where are we with liquids? Somewhere in the middle ground, between states perhaps, but closer to the solid state. Let's take a candid view of some of the liquid state's more obvious features.

The Liquid Surface Is a Special Place

We could appropriately say that liquid molecules are "sticky," that is, each molecule is stuck to all of its neighbor molecules. In addition, all are pulling and tugging in every direction. The net result is that a molecule somewhere in the body of a liquid will be completely and uniformly surrounded so that the total force of the pull is zero (Fig. 6-13).

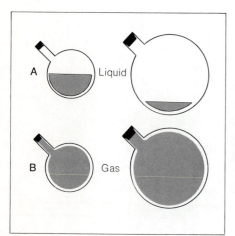

Figure 6-12
A liter of water is a liter of water, but a liter of air....well, that depends.

The layer of molecules at the surface of the liquid presents another story (Fig. 6-14). These surface molecules are surrounded by air above and liquid below. Consequently, there is an **unbalanced** pull of other liquid molecules below and around them. What happens, then, to these surface molecules?

Try this experiment. Let free-falling drops of water fill up a glass. Because of the force of gravity and the "squashiness" of molecules in the liquid state, the liquid takes on the familiar shape of its container. But we've a unique situation at the surface. If we magnify the surface, we see an obvious curvature at the boundary between the liquid and its solid container (see Fig. 6-15). In the case of water this curvature is concave due to the water piling up along the sides of the container. The water is said to **wet** the surface of the container. In some liquids, however, the intermolecular forces are greater between liquid and the solid surface. The familiar convex surface of mercury in a glass tube is an example. We say that such a liquid does not **wet** the walls of its container.

How about some more examples of wetability? Ever try to separate the stuck-together sheets of wet newspaper? Water molecules mix well with newspaper molecules; we say they "stick" or adhere to each other: the **adhesive** forces are great. But water and oil molecules don't mix well at all. The **cohesive** forces among water molecules or among oil molecules is much greater than any adhesive forces between the two so that water and oil separate, forming two distinct phases. Cohesive forces of attraction between **like** water molecules account for water molecules pulling in closest to each other. Therefore, water falls in spherical droplets of minimum surface area. You can easily observe the surface tension of liquids such as water. Take a needle and gently lay it on the surface; it will make no more than a depression, much as if a thin skin were covering the surface of the water. Drop the needle point first, however, and the skin gives away. The water was very penetrable when the surface was pierced. Ever thought about why it is you can carefully fill a glass of water to a level slightly higher than the edge of the glass? The surface tends to contract so that spilling is prevented. Or how about the bristles of a wet paint brush. What's holding them together? Yes, surface tension again.

Oil will lower the surface tension of water and a very small amount of oil will be drawn out into a very thin film coating the surface. True, but what about all of those little beads of oil floating about the surface of a bowl of chicken soup? Why aren't they spreading out over the surface in a thin film? They will if you allow the soup to cool off. As a matter of fact, if you let the pot of soup sit in the refrigerator overnight, you can remove an entire layer, not just a few globules, of solidified fat off the top. The faster moving molecules at the higher temperatures lowered the surface tension, the forces of attraction

Figure 6-13
Equal distribution of forces acting on molecules in the body of a liquid.

Figure 6-14
At the surface, equal distribution of forces is not the case, making the liquid surface a "special" place.

between neighboring molecules at the surface were broken up and globules of melted fat had an opportunity to form on the surface of the hot soup.

It is also interesting to note that the surface of smallest area will contain a given volume is a sphere. If a liquid has the freedom to assume its own shape rather than the shape of its container, as in a free falling drop of water, it will pull itself into the shape of a sphere. (See chapter opening.) An illustration of this phenomenon is the manufacture of lead shot. Molten lead is allowed to fall free from the top of a tower. The liquid lead droplets form nearly perfect spheres before they fall into the water at the bottom, which in turn serves to solidify and preserve the spherical form.

Liquids Flow

As we've seen, the surface of a liquid is rather special place. Below the surface, liquids can be looked at as being built of many sheets, or layers of molecules, like the seemingly endless number of sheets of mica that can be peeled from the surface of the mineral. Perhaps even more special is another characteristic property of liquids, their ability to flow. Liquids flow at the insistance of some force, often gravity. As you might expect, top layers flow more easily over layers further down. *Thin* liquids such as water flow easily through tiny cracks; thick liquids such as maple syrup and molasses flow very slowly; the flow properties of lubricating oils and greases hardly seem to "flow" at all, yet, they do. Tar flows; glaciers flow; even glass flows (Fig. 6-16).

Liquids also have a kind of elasticity to them. The swimming pool wasn't exactly a trampoline when you belly-flopped onto the water, but the lake always did seem elastic enough when you skip-bounded a flat stone or two off its surface. That curious synthetic material known as Silly Putty—shall we call it solid or liquid? If you roll it into a ball, it becomes rubbery and bouncy like rubber balls are supposed to be. You can throw it against a wall, and it will bounce back, just like any rubbery solid. But let the ball sit for a while and soon all you'll have is a puddle of putty; left to the more subtle force of gravity, it slowly relaxes and flows as any liquid will.

Liquids flow. That's typical of them. Place a stress on a liquid and you see movement in response to that force. Sometimes the movement is slow as in the case of Silly Putty; there are times when you can hardly notice flow at all. Here is another opportunity to point out the connection between solids and liquids. If something flows very slowly, perhaps it is better to talk about it in terms of solid flow rather than liquid flow. This really slow flow, this creepiness of solids suggests that the difference between solids and liquids is, in part, one of degree. The slow flow of solids, particularly in the case of metals, accounts for their ability to be rolled, pressed, and drawn.

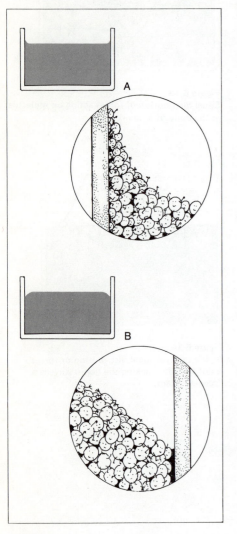

Figure 6-15
Wetting the surface (A). The familiar concave curvature of water molecules piling up along the walls of a glass container. The convex surface of mercury on glass is different (B).

Particles in Action

We now know something about what keeps liquid molecules together. But what are the conditions that make them break away from one another, particularly at the liquid surface? Collisions between molecules in the liquid, especially at the surface will result in an energy boost which allows some of them to break free of their entanglements with neighbors, moving into the space above the surface. This is **evaporation**. Water evaporates from an open bowl. The fate of the evaporated water molecules is an independent existence in the gaseous state. It is conceivable that a streaking water molecule may smack right back into the liquid surface, renewing its liquid connections. Nevertheless, on an average, more molecules escape the surface than return, and the process continues until all of the water has evaporated.

There's more to evaporation then this, however. If our bowl were very large and the room small enough, a stage would be reached where lots of water molecules would have found their way into the gas phase. Thus, the possibility that many water molecules will successfully strike back into the liquid's surface greatly increases. If the number of water molecules entering and leaving the liquid surface is equal, as may well happen, the room is said to have become *saturated* with water vapor. At that point, the measured pressure of water vapor, whatever the temperature happens to be, is referred to as the **vapor pressure** of the liquid at that temperature. Evaporation has not stopped. It is true that the level of water in the bowl isn't receding any further. However, if you could put identifying tags on those liquid phase water molecules in the bowl, and on the gas phase water molecules above the liquid surface, you'd find considerable activity and a constant interchange between the two phases (see Fig. 6-17). A state of **equilibrium** has thus been established. The rate at which molecules leave the liquid surface (through evaporation) is exactly equal to the rate of return from the gas phase (a process familiar to you as condensation). The measureable quantity here is known as the *equilibrium vapor pressure;* this is a characteristic physical property of a pure liquid substance at a given temperature.

Taking a still closer look at evaporation, water molecules tearing free of the liquid surface possess more than the average quantity of energy. Consequently, those left behind must possess lower-than-average energy. Higher-than-average escape; lower-than-average accumulate. Evaporation continues, and the average temperature of the liquid in the bowl falls. The rate of evaporation should slow with lower temperatures (lower heat content) since that means there is lower average energy. In fact, what actually does happen is that heat flows back into the bowl from the surroundings, replacing heat lost in creating energy-rich molecules suitable for evaporation. The process continues, often until completion, but certainly at least until an equilibrium between evaporation and condensation has been established (Fig. 6-17).

Figure 6-16
Viscous liquids flow.

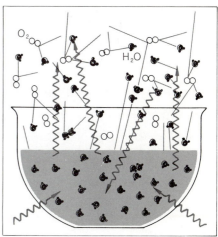

Figure 6-17
The equilibrium process in action. Evaporation and equilibrium vapor pressure. A constant collision of molecules.

Cooling accompanies evaporation. That should be familiar to you. When you march out of the water at the seashore you feel noticeably cooler. In fact, the warmer the air in comparison to the water, the cooler you'll feel. That's right, *cooler,* not warmer, because the rate of evaporation will be increased and the water molecules newly evaporated from the skin's surface will be hustled along out of the way by the breeze so that new water molecules can take their place in the vapor state. Interested in a desert refrigerator for cooling water? Why just fill a canvas bag with water and strap it to the outside of your car as you cross the Mojave Desert from Needles to Barstow along Route 66. The hot breeze will evaporate some of the water slowly seeping through the damp canvas, cooling the remaining water inside the bag. Want to cool or even freeze something in a hurry? Why just spray on a liquid such as ether or freon that evaporates faster than water. The team physician at the basketball or football game will often do that, using local freezing to numb pain due to minor injuries.

Perhaps the most important feature of evaporation and cooling has to do with maintaining body temperature. As we noted earlier, fuel consumption in cars ends up mostly as waste heat. That's true for an active human machine, too. Food is burned and most of the energy is released in the form of excess heat which must be dissipated if you are to stay at a cool and constant 98.6°F, or an average of 37.0°C. Unfortunately, the air around us is a poor heat-transfer agent. But evaporation of moisture from the skin's surface is a remarkably efficient absorber of heat. You clearly suffer on a hot, humid day because of the high moisture content already present in the air; sweat dripping off your brow just won't cool you off very much at all. But sweat evaporating off your skin into relatively dry air? That's cool! And if you fan yourself, that's cooler still, for you've assisted the removal of the moister air and replaced it with drier air, thus helping sweat evaporate.

Equilibrium Vapor Pressure

Through all this vapor pressure discussion, you may have noticed the careful emphasis on temperature. Increased temperature indicates increased kinetic motion among molecules in the liquid, and therefore increased numbers of surface molecules will have what it takes to break free and evaporate. Equilibrium vapor pressure deals with temperature. Water at room temperature, say 25°C, gradually evaporates; its equilibrium vapor pressure is about 24 torr. At 50°C, water evaporates much faster, its equilibrium vapor pressure having risen to 93 torr. At 100°C, the equilibrium vapor pressure is 760 torr, exactly the same as the pressure of the atmosphere, which means the water molecules can escape freely into the vapor phase. Evaporation is no longer a phenomenon limited to the surface. It happens throughout the liquid now. Individual molecules don't have to work their way through the molecular crowd: they form bubbles anywhere at all. We call this *boiling* (Fig. 6-18).

The boiling point of a liquid is the temperature at which the equilibrium vapor pressure of the liquid equals that of the atmosphere. If you're boiling water on Pike's Peak where the atmosphere is less dense, don't expect it to boil at 100°C; you won't need all that energy to overcome the pressure of the atmosphere; 97°C will do since the pressure is only 697 torr. In Death Valley, California, you'll have to do better than 100°C to bring water to the boil because the pressure of the atmosphere is greater. If all of this boiling hardly has the look of evaporation as we've been describing it, don't be misled; the same essential mechanism is at work for both evaporation and boiling (Fig. 6-19).

Does this vapor pressure phenomenon have something to do with the solid state as well? Absolutely! Dry ice—that's solid carbon dioxide—sends its molecules directly off the surface into the gaseous phase, a phenomenon known as *sublimation*. Carbon dioxide simply cannot exist in the liquid state under atmospheric pressure. Try and liquify carbon dioxide gas by cooling it. Instead of condensing, as steam does, it solidifies. Release a carbon dioxide fire extinguisher where you have trapped *liquid* carbon dioxide because of unusually high pressures; most of the carbon dioxide evaporates, using a lot of its heat content in the process, thereby lowering the internal energy, and the temperature, freezing the remaining liquid into a cloud of snow-like solid. Place a few crystals of iodine in an empty flask and stopper it; the presence of iodine molecules in the gas phase is almost immediately announced by the violet vapor. The violet color increases in intensity as more molecules break free of the crystal surface. After a while, an equilibrium vapor pressure is established in the closed flask and the

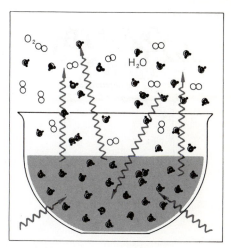

Figure 6-18
Boiling is a phenomenon not unlike evaporation.

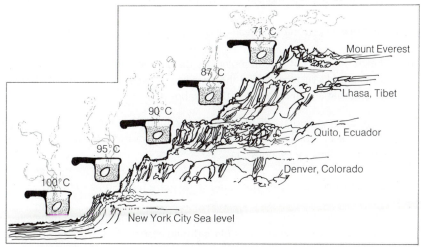

71°C   Mount Everest

87°C   Lhasa, Tibet

90°C   Quito, Ecuador

95°C   Denver, Colorado

100°C   New York City Sea level

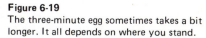

Figure 6-19
The three-minute egg sometimes takes a bit longer. It all depends on where you stand.

intensity of the violet-colored iodine vapor no longer increases. Large numbers of iodine molecules strike the crystal surface, condensing directly back into the solid state, equaling the number of iodine crystals which sublime into the gaseous state. Active molecules again, all busy going about the business of energy transfer.

☐ **Questions to Answer . . . Problems to Solve**

1. Spend a few moments connecting your thoughts about the relative "squashiness" of three states of matter: crystalline solids, gases, and liquids.

2. What evidence can you bring out to support the contention that
   (a) a liquid is a dense gas?
   (b) a liquid is a disordered solid?

3. What is Avogadro's law (guess? hypothesis? rule? law)? What does it mean?

4. Mix equal volumes of gaseous hydrogen and gaseous chlorine . . . a spark, a flash, an explosion . . . and chemical combination produces a new substance, hydrogen chloride. Avogadro's law in action:
   (a) If one liter of hydrogen combines with one liter of chlorine, one liter of hydrogen chloride formed. True?
   (b) If the original volumes were unequal, an excess of one of the gases would remain after reaction. True?
   (c) How many molecules of hydrogen would you expect to find in that liter of the gas? You say you need more information in order to answer that question? O.K., at 760 torr and 0°C.
   (d) And how many molecules of hydrogen chloride formed?

5. What makes you think molecules in liquids attract each other?

6. Sketch the paths of several molecules that are near the surface of a liquid, at the liquid's surface, and in the open space just above the liquid's surface . . . and that are all involved with neighbor molecules.

   Then, using your diagram and your understanding of kinetic energy changes taking place, explain (a) evaporation, (b) condensation, (c) vapor pressure, and (d) cooling by evaporation.

7. Why do some molecules in a liquid move extra fast? Some extra slow?

8. If heat content is a reasonable measure of kinetic energy of the molecules of a liquid, explain what takes place during evaporation. Why doesn't evaporation usually continue to completion without slowing down?

9. Would you expect temperature to affect the rate of evaporation? Explain why . . . both ways (increasing and decreasing).

10. What's boiling? And how is it different from evaporation?

11. Growing bubbles of liquid vapor are characteristic of boiling. Why do they usually form at the bottom, and then rise?

12. Around a growing bubble of liquid vapor, the liquid squeezes the bubble tending to collapse it; inside the bubble, liquid vapor tends to expand it:
    (a) Compare the internal and external pressure, assuming the bubble grows, expands, and rises.
    (b) How can you get an approximate value for the liquid pressure?
    (c) For a liquid to actually boil, you've got to get it hot. How hot?
    (d) Why doesn't a liquid normally get any hotter than its boiling point, even though you don't remove it from the burner? What happened to all of that extra heat energy?

13. What would you imagine the effect of increased temperature to be on surface tension and viscosity of liquids? Why?

14. Sweat. What is it; why is it; and how does it work?

15. Describe the behavior of liquid air, boiling point $-190°C$, in a teapot on a table.

16. The PV product is a constant for a gas whose temperature is held constant. That's Boyle's law. Boyle's law can be stated in perhaps a simpler form by considering changes in density instead of volume. Try it. Establish Boyle's law as a pressure-density relationship.

17. Heating a gas increases pressure, volume, or both. Whose law is that, and how can you explain such behavior?

18. Room temperature is $30°C$ today . . . warm. A smoothly polished metal can is cooled by adding cold water, and at a water temperature of $5°C$, the metal surface becomes fogged over. What is the relative humidity in the room today?

19. Explain why the sandbar stands firm under foot compared to the sand on the beach under foot.

20. What do you think about water leaking through a hairline crack in your car radiator? Will it be more or less obvious when the engine is hot?

21. Offer a reasonable explanation for each of the following:
    (a) Water is cooled in desert regions by keeping it in a tightly woven canvas bag which is wet on the outside.
    (b) The heat required to vaporize a gram of water is much greater than the heat required to melt a gram of ice.
    (c) Wet clothes may freeze when hung out to dry on a very cold day, but it still dries, and without ever thawing.
    (d) Gases vary widely in their masses and chemical properties, but are very similar in their physical properties.

22. Briefly explain your understanding of each of the following:
    (a) gas
    (b) liquid
    (c) solid
    (d) surface tension
    (e) viscosity
    (f) fluidity
    (g) partial pressure
    (h) relative humidity
    (i) perfect gas
    (j) STP
    (k) vapor pressure
    (l) boiling point
    (m) evaporation
    (n) frost
    (o) steam

23. When hydrogen chloride (HCl) gas is formed by reaction of hydrogen molecules (H_2) and chlorine molecules (Cl_2), there is no change in gaseous pressures between original gaseous reactants and the gaseous product at the reaction's end. Explain why?

24. Satisfy yourself that you fully understand, and can explain the following laws to someone else in the class:
    (a) Boyle's law
    (b) Charles' law
    (c) Avogadro's law
    (d) Dalton's law

25. Graph the adjacent data in the manner indicated:
    (a) Pressure versus volume
    (b) Pressure versus the reciprocal of volume
    (c) Then determine the volume occupied by the gas when the pressure reads 70 atmospheres; 10 atmsopheres.
    (d) Finally, decide which graph is the better for testing Boyle's law. Explain your choice.

pressure, atms	volume, liters
6.25	44.8
12.5	22.4
25.0	11.2
50.0	5.6
100.0	2.8

26. Determine the volume occupied by 1 liter of a gas initially at $0°C$ and 760 torr under each of the following sets of new conditions:
    (a) $0°C$ and 520 torr
    (b) $25°C$ and 760 torr
    (c) $100°C$ and 700 torr
    (d) $273°C$ and 1520 torr

27. There is a marked pressure drop when carbon dioxide (CO_2) gas is formed by reaction of carbon monoxide (CO) and oxygen (O_2):

(a) Explain what has happened and why.

(b) Do the same for the reaction in which ammonia (NH_3) is decomposed into its elements, nitrogen (N_2) and hydrogen (H_2).

28. Determine the volume of each of the following gases when measured at STP:

    (a) $0°C$ 1 atm   22.4 l

    (b) $27°C$ 700 mm   22.4 ml

    (c) $30°C$ 759 mm   250 ml

    (d) $273°K$ 760 mm   459 ml

29. Fill in the missing information in the following chart:

gas	V (ml)	T (°C)	P (torr)	n (moles)	grams
oxygen (O_2)	—	27	760	—	3
ammonia (NH_3)	50	25	754	—	—
methane (CH_4)	125	28	759	—	—
carbon monoxide (CO)	200	20	—	0.10	—
*——	224	0	760	—	0.44

*contains only carbon and oxygen

30. Graph the following data, drawing the best possible curve through the plotted points. Place time along the horizontal axis; concentration along the vertical. Then calculate the log of the concentration, and replot time against these logarithmic values. From these data, determine the existing reactant concentration after 1000 minutes had passed. By exprapolating the log concentration curve back to zero time, determine the initial concentration.

Time elapsed (min)	existing concentration
185	2.10
320	1.90
525	1.65
870	1.35
1200	1.10
1875	0.70
2315	0.55
3145	0.35

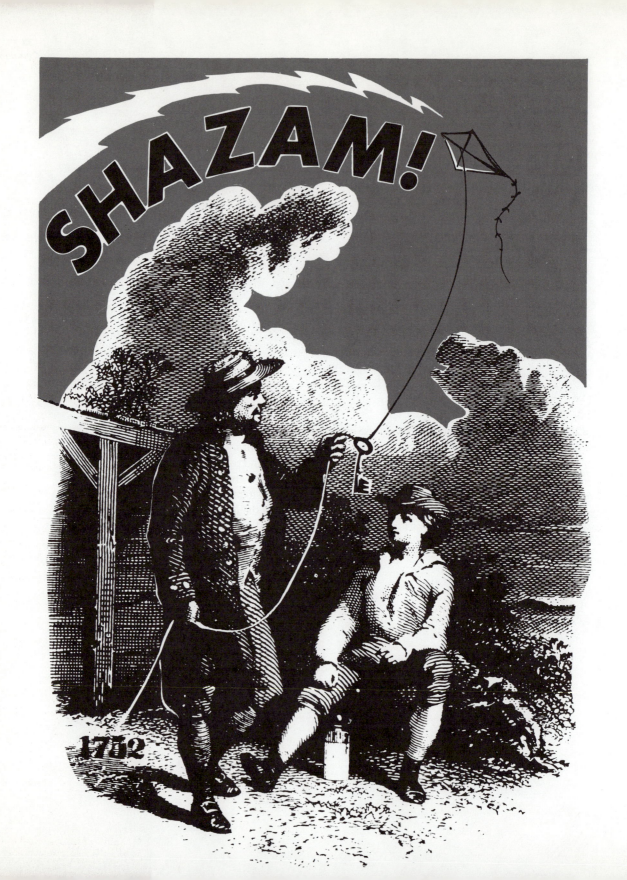

Chapter 7

The Microscopic World of Matter

☐ **Perceptions and Deceptions**

1 The electron is the littlest ion.

2 Cathode rays make great toys: you can bend them; play shadow games with them; spin paddle wheels with them; and find them just about everywhere if you know how to look.

3 Electrochemical cells aren't very complicated devices. They generally consist of two rods immersed in a solution. That's all? That's all!

4 If someone suggests you go fly a kite in an electrical storm, don't. Ben Franklin was lucky. Some other early electricians weren't.

5 "It was almost as incredible as if you fired a 15-inch shell at a piece of tissue paper and it came back and hit you."

☐ **The More Things Change . . .**

Scientists are tempted to talk of revolutions in science; of heretics and heresies leading to tremendous upsets, disorders, and eventually establishment of new hierarchies. Newton's revolution established a new understanding of nature, but the heretic of the piece was Galileo. He upset the old established order, the universe as it was supposed to be. Galileo destroyed the earth as the center of heaven. Einstein's revolution established a newer understanding of nature, but with limits that encompassed, not destroyed, the existing Newtonian view of nature. The heretic of the new revolutionary period was Rutherford. Einstein rearranged our ideas about space and time; that was difficult enough to understand in the beginning. Rutherford, however, dissolved all that we regarded as solid into so many specks floating in empty space. Things were no longer what they seemed to be. A tree was only a tree if you didn't look too closely.

John Dalton gave us a reasonable, consistent, explanation of the behavior of matter at the atomic level, an explanation that we all came to know and use. Dalton's atomic theory helped put the scientific seal of approval to the world of ordinary experience. To be sure, it was a revelation in its day, but never really a revolution. The origins of Dalton's theory were long-standing, traceable back to early Greek thought, and quite in keeping with all our preconceived notions that things in the universe were *substantial.* But just when the atomic dream of 2,500 years took on a new reality a century after Dalton, the real revolution fell upon us, destroying the old order forever as the twentieth century began. The atom turned out to be as empty as the solar system itself. Nobody had predicted how empty everything really is. After 1911 Rutherfordian solar system atoms took over from Daltonian billiard ball atoms.

To confirm the electrical nature of lightning experimentally, Benjamin Franklin made his famous kite experiment in June of 1752. As he described it, when thunderheads passed overhead . . . "the pointed wire will draw the electric finger from them, and the kite with all the twine will be electrified . . ." and, well, just don't you try it!

☐ Electrons Are Elementary Particles

The early history of the atomic theory was remarkable for its perception of indivisibility and atoms but was worlds apart from the views developed by the nineteenth-century atomists (Dalton and company). Nebulous speculation and the Greek legacy served as a starting point for the quantification that began with John Dalton. Moreover, these atomic notions received a tremendous boost with the further development of kinetic-molecular theory, thermodynamics, statistics, and probability. You could even crank out a pretty good estimate of Avogadro's number. Now all our quantitative understanding of atoms and their combinations had to be newly perceived, for under high magnification and sharp resolution atoms were not indivisible at all. Protons, neutrons, and electrons abound, and the number of subatomic particles doesn't end there. There is an entire family of "elementary" particles. Such particles perhaps come closest to being what the Greeks originally had in mind when they suggested "atoms," parts that have no parts. Here perhaps the splitting ends. A proton is elementary; so is the neutron and the electron. When we look closely through scientific eyes, atoms are not the indivisibles we had once anticipated. The **electron,** the particle of negative electricity, may well be the most important elementary particle from the chemist's point of view. No one has yet seen an electron; nevertheless we have strong support for its existence.

Guidelines for Describing Electric Charge

You're probably familiar with the concept of electric charge from very early experience and some of the simple guidelines for describing it. At one time or another you must have gotten a shock after walking on a nylon rug and then touching a metal doorknob. Then there is the old trick of picking up a piece of paper with a pocket comb. Or perhaps you've rubbed two glass rods with a silk cloth or a piece of fur; the rods repel each other. However, rub one rod with silk and one with fur, and now the glass rods attract. Essentially, whenever you rub certain objects together they become "electrically" charged, that is, they have acquired some property which allows objects to attract other objects. There are two kinds of electric charge, negative and positive, and any object that has electric character exhibits either one or the other. The simple guidelines are:

1 Like charges repel each other.

2 Opposite charges attract each other.

3 Electric charge is neither created nor destroyed; no electrical "creation" takes place.

4 Net charge on an object is due to charge distribution and arrangement.

Hence, there is **positive** electricity (+) and *negative* electricity (−), and that's that, as far as the essentials needed for understanding electrically charged matter. You have all you need to know about *neutral*, or apparently uncharged matter in nature, too. What neutral really means for bulk matter is *equal* *numbers of positive and negative charge,* and therefore apparently no charge at all. If bulk matter is charged, the distribution of positive and negative charges must be unequal. The old rules of algebra work here too; five positives neutralize five negatives and we're left with algebraic and electrical neutrality.

Coulombs Law

A force exists, then, between electric charges, and where there is a force, there is a law governing that force. And as you might have guessed, that means another constant. In this case the constant helps define the way in which the force depends on: (1) how much charge there is, and (2) the distance separating the charged objects. Let's start out with a hair comb and a fragment of paper. You can charge the comb by running it through your hair a few times. As comb and paper get closer to each other, the attraction between them gets stronger. That's *inverse* behavior: smaller distance, larger force (Fig. 7-1). A French scientist and military engineer, Charles Augustine Coulomb, was able to experimentally establish that the force F of attraction for unlike electric charges, or repulsion for like electric charges, is inversely proportional to the square of the distance d separating them. Here is the formula stating the experimental relationship

$$F \propto \frac{1}{d^2}$$

What that rather neat looking equation says is that the force F gets large as d^2 gets small (inverse relationship) because $1/d^2$ must be getting larger. Coulomb was also able to show that the force F between the two charged objects was proportional to the product of the amount of the electric charges q_1 for one object, and q_2 for the other

$$F \propto q_1 q_2$$

It is also interesting to note here that if F has a positive numerical value in any calculation, the force is one of repulsion because it would indicate $q_1(+)q_2(+)$ or $q_1(-)q_2(-)$ for the product $q_1 q_2$; both give a positive algebraic result. On the other hand, a negative value for F means attraction since that must arise from $q_1(+)q_2(-)$ or $q_1(-)q_2(+)$ for the product (opposite signs attract). Putting these ideas together with the proportionality involving force and distance, we get

$$F \propto \frac{1}{d^2} \qquad \text{(first proportional relationship)}$$

$$F \propto q_1 q_2 \qquad \text{(second proportional relationship)}$$

$$F \propto \frac{q_1 q_2}{d^2} \qquad \text{(combined proportional relationship)}$$

Here is our old friend, the proportionality sign again. Remember that $\propto$ means =k; therefore,

$$F = k \frac{q_1 q_2}{d^2}$$

Note that the inverse square dependence shows up in gravitation and several other important phenomenological situations. Coulomb's Law takes the same form as Newton's well-known Law of Universal Gravitation.

Figure 7-1
Coulomb's Law is an inverse-square relationship. The force between two electric charges (attraction or repulsion) varies *inversely* as the square of the distance between them.

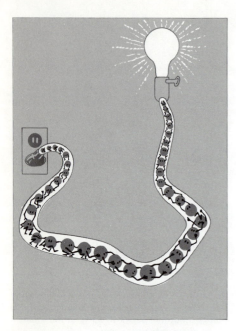

Figure 7-2
The "flow" of electricity when the current is switched on, isn't much of a flow at all. Vibrations might be a better word, or perhaps transmission.

Figure 7-3
High-power transmission lines carrying electricity "marching like soldiers, single file across the landscape."

$$F = k \frac{m_1 m_2}{r^2}$$

Newton had also perceived that the force of attraction between a planet and it's sun, just as between any two bodies of matter, has to be proportional to the product of their masses. Further, that force must be inversely proportional to the square of their distance apart. In fact, it was just this knowledge of Newton's gravitational mechanics and familiarity with Newton's *Principia* that brought the first suggestion of the inverse square law to the attention of Joseph Priestley. Priestley was a British chemist, displaced to America by political and religious unrest in his homeland. Coulomb experimentally confirmed Priestley's contention and then went on to complete the design of that law.

This is Coulomb's Law. It can be used to define the basic unit of electric charge. That unit is called the coulomb, the quantity of electrical charge moving through a wire in 1 second when the current in the wire is measured at 1 ampere. In household terms, the ampere or *amp* is about that amount of electrical current required by a 100-watt light bulb. (See Fig. 7-2.) One coulomb is the quantity of electrical charge buzzing quietly through a 100-watt bulb in a single second. Small amount of charge, right? Wrong! As one coulomb of negative charge moves through the light bulb filament in each second, it is moving through a structured arrangement of positive charges; at any single instant, the net result is electrical neutrality. Negative charges are hardly flowing through the filament like water through a faucet. Rather, they have to bump along through the filament, each jostling or pushing the one ahead, the whole line advancing in crowd-like fashion. Throw the wall switch on and the room lights up. Current has flowed from the light switch to the filament but the electrons at the switch didn't do all the work. They told neighbors who told neighbors, and so the message got sent.

Transmission may be a better word than flow for describing electricity's movement from any one point to another (Fig. 7-3). But collect all of the negative charge in a single coulomb in one place and ZAP! For example, if you take two objects, separated by a distance of 1 meter, and on each object place a unit charge of 1 coulomb, forces on the order of a million tons would be exerted by each object on the other. We never realize such forces because of the fact that you cannot get that kind of **net** electrical charge together in one place. Even if we could, how would we keep two such charges from pushing themselves apart? It's pretty difficult to maintain a charge of even 1/1,000 of a coulomb on an ordinary object. The spark you get when you touch a doorknob after walking across a nylon carpet on a dry day is something less than 1/1,000,000 of a coulomb.

Lightning discharge in a severe electrical storm may produce an accumulated net charge of perhaps 100 to 200 coulombs, and that accumulation is only possible because of the very large volume of the type of clouds typical of thunder storms (Fig. 7-4).

☐ Batteries, Electrolytic Cells, and Faraday

From the light switch on the wall, let's move on to the ubiquitous batteries. Dry cells like flashlight batteries and wet cells like your 6- and 12-volt auto type lead storage batteries are the most familiar, instant sources of electrical current, and therefore electrical potential energy. The reactions taking place inside succeed in converting chemical potential energy into electrical potential energy. Each battery has two terminals, one positive (+) and one negative (−). If you connect two batteries with copper wires, (+) to (+) or (−) to (−), nothing very exciting happens. But connect them in series, (+) to (−) to (+) to (−), and we get a lot of heat along with considerable sparking; in addition, the copper wire is likely to melt. Some transformation or other has certainly taken place: chemical energy into electrical, then into heat, sound, and light. Current flows when the electrical circuit is completed, the single requirement being an *electric* potential difference between the two terminals. A 12-volt auto battery suggests a 12-volt electric potential difference; a 1½ volt dry cell used in emergency lighting lamps suggests a 1½ volt potential difference between terminals.

Figure 7-4
Nikola Tesla, the electrical-engineer inventor, contributed many discoveries in the field of high voltage. Here he sits in apparent unconcern as one of his giant induction coils discharges away in Hollywood style (left).

In trying to repeat Franklin's experiment (see Chap. opening), Georg Richmann, professor at St. Petersburg, was killed by lightning that struck his ungrounded apparatus. He thus became the rist martyr to the new electrical science (right).

Figure 7-5
A miniature mercury battery.

Voltage is nothing more than the measured amount of work done for each bit of electric charge transferred: the electric potential difference between the two terminals of the battery. Recalling Chap. 4 for a moment, remember that work performed per unit of time is power. Therefore voltage tells us how powerful the battery is (Fig. 7-5).

You can generate a feeble flow of electricity by simply taking a lemon from the refrigerator, a paper clip, and a length of copper wire about the size of a paper clip. Try it. Build yourself a "lemon" cell. Straighten a paper clip and a piece of copper wire; rough up the surfaces with a piece of steel wool. Then push the wires straight through into the heart of the lemon. The ends of the two *electrodes* (that's what they are called, electrodes) should be close, but not in contact. To test your lemon cell touch the electrode ends to the tip of your tongue. Taste sour? Slight tingling sensation? You'll find no taste or sensation if you touch your tongue to only one of the wires. If you don't have paper clips and copper wire handy, try two forks, one stainless steel, the other silver plate.

Want to generate a stronger current? Well, you can do that right at home, too, by building a pile of properly connected cells, cells in series. You could make up a series of connected lemons, but that becomes a bit awkward. Try a pile of pennies and nickels instead. Put pairs composed of a nickel and a penny in piles connected by a small piece of newsprint paper (absorbent cotton will do as well) soaked with salt water and squeezed damp dry. A dozen or so of these separated pairs will do (see Fig. 7-7). Wet a finger on one hand and touch the bottom coin; wet a finger on your other hand and touch it to the top coin. Truly shocking, isn't it. Certainly a somewhat stronger total current has been generated by twelve

Figure 7-6
Investigating the effects of the "lemon" cell.

Figure 7-7
Alessandro Volta arranged a "pile" of zinc and silver discs separated by brine-soaked paper. This battery generated a continuous flow of electricity, ushering in the electrical age as the nineteenth-century began.

cells versus our single lemon cell. Oh, by the way, remember to take the pile apart, or else you'll discover why it is that batteries get used up fast.

Electrolysis

Chemical reactions can be used to generate electricity, but what is perhaps more interesting and more important to our immediate purpose is that electricity can do some chemical things to help us get to know our elementary particle, the electron. Decomposing a pure substance by means of an electric current is called *electrolysis.* Make use of a battery's electric current to decompose water into hydrogen and oxygen: first place two thin platinum electrodes (bars) into a beaker of water; then connect the electrodes by means of copper wires to the terminals of the battery and close the circuit, allowing current to flow; bubbles of oxygen gas appear immediately at one plantinum bar while bubbles of hydrogen gas appear at the other electrode; now add a small amount of vinegar, bicarbonate of soda, or "Drano" to the water and the electrolysis speeds up considerably (see Fig. 7-8). That electrical experiment turns out to be very important for up to the time of Dalton, water was believed to be an elemental substance because it just couldn't be decomposed. Its electrolytic decomposition, disproved that dramatically, producing two elements, oxygen at one electrode and hydrogen at the other, and in the exact proportions in which the elements were combined to form water (see Chap. 3).

Now consider a somewhat more complicated electrolysis. Instead of decomposing plain water with two inert, unreactive platinum electrodes, decompose a solution of copper sulfate dissolved in water, using copper metal electrodes and our battery as a source of electric potential energy (see Fig. 7-9). Let current flow. Pretty soon it will be obvious that a mirror-like coating of bright new copper is being deposited on one of the electrodes. At the same time, the other electrode is becoming pitted and corroded. If you carefully weigh the two electrodes, you'll find that the amount the newly coated electrode got heavier will just equal the mass lost by the corroding electrode. Copper has been transferred from one electrode to the other through the good offices of the copper sulfate solution. The electroplating industry is built upon such electrochemistry.

Michael Faraday Found Evidence for Electrons

The first quantitative experiments bearing on electrolysis were conducted by Michael Faraday who studied the electrolysis of aqueous copper sulfate solutions (Fig. 7-10). Faraday found the first direct evidence for the electron's existence. Electrons flowing out of the battery's negative terminal into one copper electrode place a net negative charge on that electrode. Faraday called that electrode the *cathode.* Copper from the copper sulfate solution accumulated on the cathode. By carefully weighing the cathode before and after electrolysis, noting the quantity of current that passed through the electrolysis cell, and observing the time that elapsed during passage of current, Faraday came up with two remarkable perceptions. He found that the number of grams of copper deposited on the

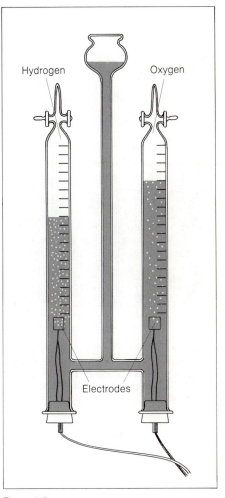

Figure 7-8
A demonstration of the electrical decomposition (electrolysis) of water into its elements; hydrogen, and oxygen evolve in a 2:1 ratio by volume (remember Avogadro's Law).

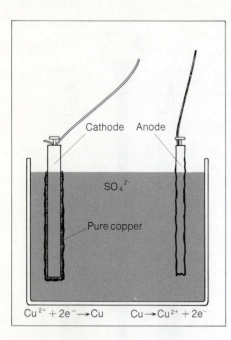

Figure 7-9
Electroplating copper metal onto a copper electrode during the electroysis of a copper sulfate solution. The other copper electrode corrodes in the process.

cathode was directly proportional to: (1) the amperes (speed of the current) passed through the cell; and (2) the time period for any given current to flow. Double the amperes, double the grams deposited; halve the time and halve the number of grams deposited; double the amperes and halve the seconds and yes, that's right, no change. Therefore,

grams of copper $\propto$ current

grams of copper $\propto$ time

In short, the chemical change Faraday observed was proportional to the product of current and time:

grams of copper $\propto$ (current) (time)

There is a gem buried in here. Current is the amount of charge transferred during any given interval of time. If we're talking about current in amps and time in seconds, current can then be expressed as ***amount of charge per second.*** Therefore,

grams of copper $\propto$ (current) (time)

grams of copper $\propto \dfrac{\text{(amount of charge)}}{\text{(second)}}$ (second)

grams of copper $\propto$ (amount of charge)

The amount of charge is measured in coulombs, and we end up with Faraday's result: the number of grams of copper deposited is a direct measure of the chemical change taking place during electrolysis, and that's proportional to the quantity of electric energy transferred. There is a relationship between the particles of electricity and chemical change. Electrons must somehow play a key role in chemical transformations. Let's continue.

The amount of copper deposited is simply proportional to the amount of electricity passing through the cell. In other words, 1 gram of copper, one bucket of charge; 2 grams of copper, two buckets of charge; after all, 2 grams of copper do contain twice as many copper atoms as 1 gram. Each atom of copper has a definite number of unit electric charges associated with it. These are electrons, or atoms of electricity. As each atom of copper plates out on the cathode, it carries along a definite quantity of these atoms of electricity.

How about equations for all this electrochemistry? Yes, a few are in order, especially since chemical equations are so much a part of the formalism of the science. First, the electrolysis of water. The overall reaction is

$$2\,H_2O \longrightarrow 2\,H_2 + O_2$$

At the individual electrodes, electrons are gained and lost

$$4\,H^+ + 4\,\text{electrons} \longrightarrow 2\,H_2 \qquad \text{(gain)}$$

$$2\,H_2O \longrightarrow 4\,H^+ + 4\,\text{electrons} + O_2 \qquad \text{(loss)}$$

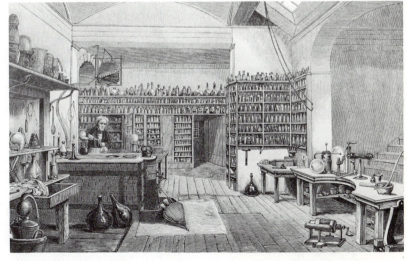

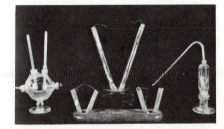

Figure 7-10
Michael Faraday, an experimental genius,
an unparalleled lecturer, a nineteenth-century
prophet of modern science, in caricature
(upper left). Faraday's laboratory at the
Royal Institute in London (upper right).
Michael Faraday, the chemist (lower right).
Prospectus for Christmas lectures for children
(bottom left). Faraday's apparatus (bottom
center).

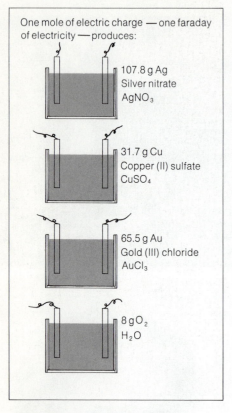

One mole of electric charge — one faraday of electricity — produces:

107.8 g Ag
Silver nitrate
$AgNO_3$

31.7 g Cu
Copper (II) sulfate
$CuSO_4$

65.5 g Au
Gold (III) chloride
$AuCl_3$

8 g O_2
H_2O

The electrochemical jobs 1 Faraday of electricity (96,500 coulombs) can do. Deposit 1 mole of silver atoms from a silver nitrate solution.

The net result is expressed by the overall reaction. Note that four electrons and four protons (H^+) come and go, canceling each other.

Second: electrolysis in copper sulfate solution. At the individual electrodes, electrons are gained and lost

$$Cu^{++} + 2 \text{ electrons} \longrightarrow Cu \qquad \text{(gain)}$$
$$Cu \longrightarrow Cu^{++} + 2 \text{ electrons} \qquad \text{(loss)}$$

Note the overall effect: copper ions deposit as copper metal; copper metal dissolves as copper ions.

Faraday Didn't Quit Here

He went on and measured the number of grams of a whole variety of elementary substances liberated from their chemical combination during electrolysis by identical quantities of electric charge. This is what Faraday found. The quantity of any substance (copper from copper sulfate in solution; hydrogen or oxygen from water) depended on two things: atomic mass and combining capacity, or *valence,* as he now began to call it. Faraday had again run smack into the electron, the definite quantity of electricity. The amount of electric charge associated with a single gram of hydrogen (a single atomic mass of hydrogen) is referred to as the *Faraday* of electricity. A Faraday (F) is the electric charge of 1 mole of electrons.

Hydrogen atoms have a combining capacity of 1; according to the new terminology, hydrogen atoms are *monovalent*. The amount of charge associated with a single atomic weight or mole of oxygen weighing 16 grams, is 2 Faradays of electricity; the oxygen atom has a combining capacity or valence of 2; it is divalent; 2 moles of electrons. That result is exactly in keeping with what we know for both formation of water from its elements, and electrolytic decomposition of water *into* its elements; 1 gram of hydrogen is equivalent to 8 grams of oxygen, both being associated with equivalent quantities of electricity, 1 mole of electrons, 1 Faraday each. Similarly 2 grams of hydrogen (2 moles of hydrogen atoms) are required to combine with 16 grams of oxygen (1 mole of oxygen atoms) in the water molecule, producing 18 grams or 1 mole of water molecules. Remember, you just can't have HO (Dalton's style). It has to be H_2O.

In Summary of Faraday's Laws

Faraday of electricity is the electric charge of a mole of electrons (Fig. 7-11). It is equal to 96,500 coulombs. That means you can generate a Faraday of electricity by pushing 96,500 amperes through a cell for 1 second (a coulomb is an amp-second), 1 ampere for 96,500 seconds, or any combination in between.

96,500 coulombs = 1 Faraday = 96,500 amp-seconds
1 F = (96,500 amp) (1 sec) = 96,500 coulombs
1 F = (5 amp) (19,300 sec) = 96,500 coulombs

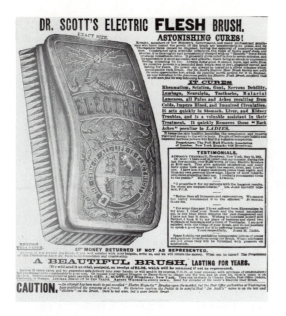

Figure 7-11
Some of the quackery associated with the early days of electrical science is illustrated by these magazine advertisements from a century ago.

For hydrogen and oxygen atoms, we have the following.

$$2 \text{ F} = (10 \text{ amp}) (19{,}300 \text{ sec}) = 2 \times 96{,}500 \text{ coulombs}$$
$$5 \text{ F} = (2.5 \text{ amp}) (193{,}000) = 5 \times 96{,}500 \text{ coulombs}$$

1 gram of hydrogen needing 1 Faraday is 1 mole of hydrogen atoms.
8 grams of oxygen needing 1 Faraday is ½ mole of oxygen atoms.

To form molecules of water, the arrangement must be

2 grams of hydrogen needing 2 Faradays is 2 moles of hydrogen atoms.
16 grams of oxygen needing 2 Faradays is 1 mole of oxygen atoms.

But because hydrogen and oxygen are diatomic molecules as they naturally occur, everything has to be doubled.

4 grams of hydrogen needing 4 Faradays is 4 moles of hydrogen atoms,
    or 2 moles of hydrogen molecules.
32 grams of oxygen needing 4 Faraday is 2 moles of oxygen atoms,
    or 1 mole of oxygen molecules.

Finally,

$$2 \text{ H}_2 + \text{O}_2 \longrightarrow 2 \text{ H}_2\text{O}$$

Through the last few chapters at least, you've been aware that hydrogen and oxygen atoms combine in the ratio 2:1. Your perception should now include the understanding of the electrical equality as well. The complete decomposition of water, according to the balanced equation, requires passage of 4 Faradays of electricity through an electrolysis cell.

$$2\,H_2O \xrightarrow[\text{4 F}]{\text{electricity}} 2\,H_2 + O_2$$

The combining capacity for chlorine, however, is 1. It is a univalent atom and the amount of charge associated with a single mole of chlorine atoms weighing 35.5 grams is 1 Faraday. So HCl for hydrochloric acid is quite legitimate, then, whereas HO for water wasn't. In the electrolytic decomposition of hydrochloric acid we expect 1 gram of hydrogen gas bubbling off of one electrode for every 35.5 grams of chlorine bubbling off the other. That's just the way it works:

$$2\,HCl \xrightarrow[\text{2 F}]{\text{electricity}} H_2 + Cl_2$$

Copper generally has a combining capacity of 2. It is a divalent atom with an atomic mass of 63.57. That means that 2 Faradays of electricity will deposit 63.57 grams of copper; each Faraday will deposit 63.57/2 or 31.78 gram of copper. In other words, the ratio of the atomic mass of an element to its combining capacity, or valence, is the number of grams of that element freed from chemical bondage in an electrolytic reaction using 1 Faraday of electricity. Aluminum has a valence of 3; therefore, 1 Faraday of electricity through an electrolytic cell liberates approximately 27/3 or 9 grams; 3 Faradays liberate 1 mole of atoms of aluminum metal weighing 27 grams (see Table 7-1).

☐ **Making an Important Electrical Connection**

There is an important thread that runs between the Faraday of electricity and Avogadro's number:

Table 7-1
Electrical equivalents

Element	Approximate atomic mass	Valence or combining capacity	Grams electrochemically liberated from chemical bondage by 1 Faraday
Hydrogen	1	1	1
Chlorine	35.5	1	35.5
Silver	107	1	107
Oxygen	16	2	8
Magnesium	24	2	12
Copper	63.5	2	31.8
Aluminum	27	3	9
Gallium	69.7	3	23.2
Germanium	72.6	4	18.2

1 mole of hydrogen atoms (combining capacity 1; univalent) associated with 1 Faraday of electricity; 1 mole of hydrogen atoms per 1 mole of electrons.

1 mole of oxygen atoms (combining capacity 2; divalent) associated with 2 Faraday of electricity; 1 mole of oxygen atoms per 2 moles of electrons.

1 mole of aluminum atoms (combining capacity 3; trivalent) associated with 3 Faraday of electricity; 1 mole of aluminum atoms per 3 moles of electrons.

For every atom involved, there is an *equivalent* number of electrons on the move:

1 hydrogen atom   1 electron
1 oxygen atom   2 electrons
1 aluminium atom   3 electrons

For every mole of atoms, an equivalent number of moles of electrons, or Faradays of charge, are on the move. Let's look at this more closely.

Transfer of 1 Faraday of electricity moves Avogadro's number of atoms of electricity N or 6.023×10^{23} electrons. If twice Avogadro's number of atoms of electricity move ($2N$) then 2 Faradays of electricity have been transferred. The Faraday of electricity is Avogadro's number of electrons.

The point is we can now estimate the numerical value for the unit charge on the electron. Passage of 96,500 coulombs of charge results in electrolysis of 6.023×10^{23} atoms of hydrogen, silver, or any other element with a combining capacity or valence of 1:

96,500 coulombs/mole = F
6.023×10^{23} atoms/mole = N

$$\frac{F}{N} = \frac{96,500 \text{ coulombs/mole}}{6.023 \times 10^{23} \text{ atoms/mole}} = 1.60 \times 10^{-19} \text{ coulombs/atom}$$

Since a monovalent atom (an atom whose combining capacity is 1) transfers 1 electron per atom during electrolysis:

$$\frac{1.60 \times 10^{-19} \text{ coulomb/atom}}{1 \text{ electron/atom}} = 1.60 \times 10^{-19} \text{ coulomb/electron}$$

This number value for the unit electric charge, the electron, is not especially important for our purposes. The real significance still to come is; independent confirmation from data on *free* electrons themselves, out of solution, and therefore in the absence of any atomic associations. We get the same number value (as we will see in our discussion of Millikan's oil drop experiment later in this chapter). From that independent confirmation has emerged a tremendous sense of confidence in the plausibility of the picture that is developing here: universality of electrons.

☐ Anions and Cations

There is another important topic to be worked through here. The facts as we recognize them today and as Michael Faraday recognized them more than a

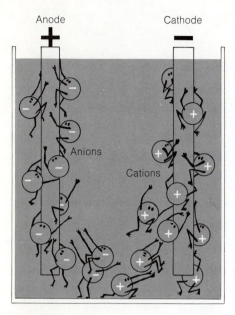

Anode

Cathode

Anions

Cations

Figure 7-12
Anions and cations.

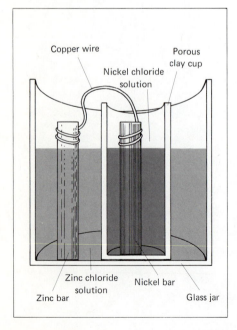

Copper wire

Porous
clay cup

Nickel chloride
solution

Zinc chloride
solution

Nickel bar

Zinc bar

Glass jar

Figure 7-13A
A battery recipe.

century ago, suggest that atoms in solution carry the moving electric charges, or atoms of electricity. Charged atoms are called *ions*. They are positive or negative, depending on the net distribution of plus and minus charges within the atom. A copper atom is electrically neutral. The copper ion is a positive ion or *cation*, so named because it migrates toward the opposite electrode in solution, the negative cathode. A chlorine atom is electrically neutral. The chloride ion is negative, and referred to as an *anion*, so named because it migrates to the cell's positive electrode, the anode (see Fig. 7-12).

We'll label the ions: copper, Cu^{++}; chloride, Cl^-. The double positive charge hung onto the copper ion is consistent with our idea that it will require 2 Faraday of electricity transferred at the cathode to neutralize its charge. A mole of metal atoms weighing 63.6 grams is produced. One Faraday of electrons produces only half as much copper metal. A single negative charge on chloride is also consistent with our ideas. Transfer of 1 Faraday of electrons at the anode is required to produce a mole of neutral chlorine atoms weighing 35.5 grams. Putting these two ideas together, half as many copper ions carry sufficient charge to neutralize twice as many chloride ions in solution during electrolysis. If we succeed in dissolving solid copper chloride by stirring some into water as well as we can, the same *ionic* situation will exist.

$$CuCl_2 \longrightarrow Cu^{++} + 2\,Cl^-$$

Some ions are complex combinations of atoms carrying a net electric charge. They are often referred to simply as complex ions. For example, when water dissociates, positive hydrogen ions (H^+) and negative hydroxyl ions (OH^-) are produced. Sodium nitrate produces positive sodium ions (Na^+) and negative nitrate ions (NO_3^-); potassium sulfate dissolved in water is a mixed association of potassium ions and sulfate ions ($SO_4^=$).

$$H_2O \longrightarrow H^+ + OH^- \text{ (hydroxide ion: 2 atoms)}$$
$$NaNO_3 \longrightarrow Na^+ + NO_3^- \text{ (nitrate ion: 4 atoms)}$$
$$K_2SO_4 \longrightarrow 2\,K^+ + SO_4^= \text{ (sulfate ion: 5 atoms)}$$

Remember what was said earlier. You can expect only very limited success at electrolysis of water unless you add water soluble salts or other substances such as sulfuric acid that dissociate into ions in solution. Ions form easily when salts are dissolved in water; large collections of ions make transfer of charge possible. In fact, if you carefully use colored ions such as blue copper sulfate ($CuSO_4 \cdot 5\,H_2O$ dissolved in water) or yellow potassium chromate (K_2CrO_4 dissolved in water) you can actually witness the happening. A small amount of blue Cu^{++} ions, or yellow $CrO_4^=$ ions, is placed in an electrolysis cell containing dilute sulfuric acid (colorless ions)[1]. Throw the switch, thus

---

[1] Enough gelatin should be dissolved into the cell solution to minimize the normal rate of diffusion.

closing the circuit. Current flows. The blue or yellow crawls across towards the cathode or anode. There you are, witness to the event, ions moving along at a rate of about 2 inches per hour. Unimpressed? Think that's slow? See how fast you can move through a crowd like that. Times Square on New Year's eve at midnight? Why that's not nearly as crowded.

Perhaps to summarize our discussion of electrical behavior in solution we can work our way through the operation of a simple battery. Remember that a battery is a chemical source of electricity. Metallic zinc has a combining capacity of 2, forming divalent zinc chloride.

$$Zn\ (s)\ +\ Cl_2(g)\ \longrightarrow\ ZnCl_2(s)$$

Nickel metal behaves in similar fashion

$$Ni\ (s)\ +\ Cl_2(g)\ \longrightarrow\ NiCl_2(s)$$

In aqueous solution both metal chlorides dissolve, forming positive metal ions and negative chloride ions

$$ZnCl_2(s)\ \longrightarrow\ Zn^{++}\ +\ 2\ Cl^-$$
$$NiCl_2(s)\ \longrightarrow\ Ni^{++}\ +\ 2\ Cl^-$$

Build a battery (Fig. 7-13) by putting a nickel bar into a nickel chloride solution, all in a porous clay cup. Placing that entire cup arrangement into a large glass jar containing a zinc chloride solution and a zinc bar completes the other half of the cell. Half the *circuit* for flow of current is established by connecting a conducting wire (copper will do nicely) between the two metal bars; the other half of the current is established by flow of ions between the porous cup and the glass jar.

Immediately on connection of the wire, an electric current is produced. Positive nickel ions pick up electrons, nickel metal plates out on the nickel electrode, and the green nickel chloride solution becomes depleted and more faint in color. Meanwhile, the zinc electrode becomes etched as zinc dissolves, forming a greater concentration of zinc ions in solution within the glass jar. If there are enough materials present, when 29 grams of nickel has deposited 1 Faraday of current will have flowed; when 65 grams of zinc has dissolved, 2 Faraday will have flowed. What has happened is this:

1   Nickel cations (positive) migrate to the cathode (negative), are neutralized by electrons, and plate out as nickel metal.

2   More electrons flow into the cathode from the anode where they have been picked up from the zinc metal, leaving zinc cations behind to dissolve into the existing zinc chloride solution.

3   There is an excess of negative chloride ions in the nickel chloride cell where nickel plated out. They migrate through the porous cup to

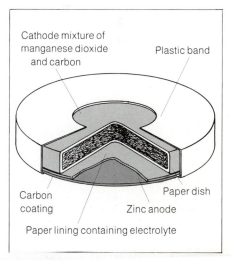

Figure 7-13B
Two different versions of the ubiquitous Le clanché cells. One is the standard D-type flashlight battery.

neutralize and balance the excess of positive zinc ions, newly formed and dissolved.

4. It happens all the time, until the cell depletes some required cell component, either electrode materials or ions in solution.

Why doesn't it work the other way, zinc plating out and nickel dissolving? For the time being, just accept this as the chemical characteristic of this particular cell: nickel plates out; zinc dissolves. The physical laws that are the basis of this chemical characteristic will come a bit later (ionization potential and electron affinity versus atomic size and nuclear charge). Perhaps you also want to know why it is Ni^{++} and $2\ Cl^-$. Why not $2\ Ni^-$ and Cl^{++}, or $Ni^=$ and $2\ Cl^+$. Patience for a bit longer, and we'll develop some rationale for the experimental facts, namely Ni^{++} and $2\ Cl^-$.

☐ **Pride of Place**

No real attempt has been made to give "pride of place" to any of the nineteenth-century electrical scientists who got us to the brink of the discovery and identification of the electron by J. J. Thomson in England in 1897. It was one of the most colorful, fascinating, and important periods in all of modern science, beginning in 1785 with Coulomb's experiments. It also marked the beginning of the age of electricity in motion, electrodynamics, as well as the end of a great era of investigation of static electricity that included the homespun nostalgia of Ben Franklin's kite experiments (see Chapter opening and Fig. 7-4). Galvani's discovery in 1786 that a frog's legs twitched convulsively when touched to a source of electricity led to the study of "animal electricity" (see Fig. 7-14). There was intense interest in Volta's first batteries, and a flurry of research, in a fashion not seen for nearly another century until the burst of activity surrounding the discovery of X-rays in 1895 and radioactivity in 1896. Here in the battery was a ready, reliable, and continuous source of electricity. No longer was it necessary to depend on cranking up those monstrous electrical machines. Davy and Faraday, Groves, Oersted and Ampere, Maxwell, Helmholtz, Hertz, Tyndall, Crookes, Thomas Edison and Marconi, Charles Steinmetz, Langmuir and Coolidge, the General Electric Company, Siemans, and the Eveready battery. It was a colorful, enlightened period that spanned the end of the nineteenth century and the first years of the twentieth. Experiment was king. It was a time in which science changed from the hobby of the privileged class to a professional pursuit. Science emerged from the kitchens and salons of Europe into the newly developing university and institutional research laboratories. It is a period worthy of deeper attention and interest. The practice of science went modern.

☐ **Turning the "Atom of Electricity" into the "Electron"**

The atom of electricity was a principal clue to one of the central mysteries of modern science, how matter works. A second clue was discovered by the per-

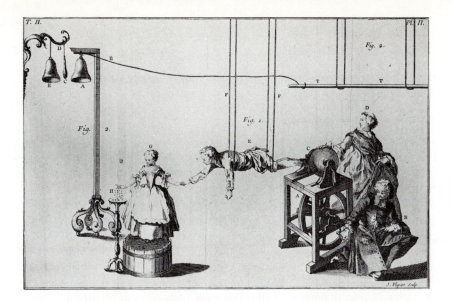

Figure 7-14
A   Galvani's experiments with frogs and the whole subject of "animal electricity" touched off a generation of popular lecturers who played upon the sensational aspects of the science.

An electric "Rube Goldberg" generator: C turned by wheel and crank—the charge, caused by a dry hand, is drawn by the feet of the boy suspended by silk ropes and transmitted to the girl standing in a tup of dried pitch, whose hand attracts and repels.

In the upper part of the illustration, a charge drawn from an electrified gun barrel causes alternate attraction and repulsion of the clapper and a jingling of the bells.

ceptive Mendeleyeff in his periodic arrangement for the chemical elements, published in 1871. Armed with hindsight, periodic behavior can only truly be understood in terms of subatomic particles, common to all elements.

To actually get at the electron itself, free of its entangling alliances with other atomic components and nearest neighbors, that was a real problem. The behavior of electrolyte solutions and the whole business of batteries and electrolysis, did indicate the presence of atoms of electricity and told us something about their complex involvement. But now instead of looking at electrical behavior in liquids, examine conduction of·electricity in gases. The early perception of the atom of electricity had depended upon a technological development, the battery. The new perception also depended upon technology in advance of science: (1) the discharge tubes that were at first only curiosities, scientific toys; and (2) improved vacuum pumps.

The air around us is a collection of fast-moving molecules in random motion. Their chief behavioral characteristic is collision with each other and with the walls of whatever it is that contains them. A metal plate in air is continually bombarded by particles of the gas. If it were possible to jar an electron loose from the metal's surface through a smashing collision with a flying air particle, there is little likelihood of its escape. There are simply too many particles in the vicinity; too many random collisions would occur so that it just couldn't get very far away. However, if you first pump most of the surrounding gas particles out and then cause electrons to break free, they will literally come *streaming* off. As was true for liquids, high-voltage currents pass through gases because charged ions are in motion. There are positive and negative ions. The positive ions are similar to those found during electrolysis in solution (charged atoms). Ions such as these give us bright red neon lights and pale green neon lights (and other colors, too). The positive ions are called *canal rays.* The negative ions are

Figure 7-15
William Crookes with one of his highly evacuated discharge tubes; a caricature from *Vanity Fair.*

far less massive than any atom we know, and they are singly charged. We have identified them as electrons.

The Discharge Tube Phenomenon

In the second half of the nineteenth century, a number of scientists noticed the pale green glow that filled a sealed glass tube when passing a current of electricity through air at low pressure (Fig. 7-15). Now the only way current can flow through the circuit is if electrons stream across the tube, from one metal plate to the other, bridging the intervening space. Walk across a dry nylon rug while scuffing your feet and touch your finger to a metal doorknob; you can feel and perhaps see the tiny bluish spark jump the gap between finger and knob. The lightning discharge between a charged cloud and the earth is a more visible example of electrical phenomena in air. Such discharges, great and small, are characteristically staccato, crackling, sparking phenomena. But pump the gas in the tube out so that there is little more than a few thousandths of the original air pressure inside the tube, and the static discharge jumping from one metal plate to the other gradually smooths out. At very low pressures it becomes a greenish, fluorescent glow.

Study the greenish glow inside the discharge tube and you'll find some unusual and intriguing phenomena. First, the source of the glow seems to be the cathode, or negative electrode. Because of that, we'll call whatever it is that's streaming off the cathode, *cathode rays*. Second, these streaming cathode rays seem to be totally independent of the particular cathode metal. Identical cathode rays are produced from a zinc cathode as from an iron or copper cathode. Third, an object placed in the path of the cathode rays casts a shadow much as it would with a light source. Apparently, cathode rays also travel in straight lines. Fourth, a carefully balanced paddlewheel arrangement in the path of the stream of cathode rays spins about, suggesting a particle nature for the beam. And fifth, if the discharge tube is placed in an electric field, the path of the cathode rays will bend toward the field's positive pole, a clear indication of the negative electric nature of these curious rays. Magnetic deflection also takes place.

The definitive studies that clinched this electron business were carried out by one of the truly great experimental and theoretical scientists of modern times. His name was Joseph John Thomson. In 1897, Thomson designed a modified version of the discharge tube. The anode was a metal disk (Fig. 7-16) with a thin slit running across and through it. Just beyond was a second slit disk, carefully aligned with the first along the axis of cathode tube. When Thomson turned the juice on, electrons came streaming off the cathode toward the anode. Almost all of the electrons smashed into the anode, except for the thin, regular high-speed band passing through the two slits, zipping down to the other end of the glass tube. There, a patch of light was produced on the fluorescent coating of the inside surface. Thomson stuck a piece of ruled paper to the glass at

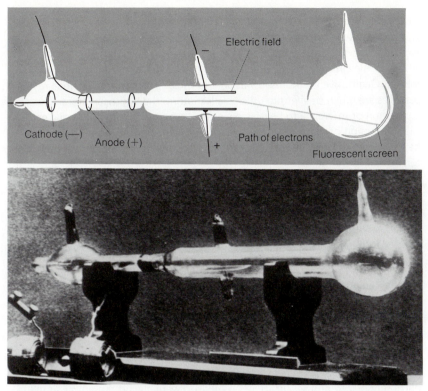

Cathode (—) Anode (+) Electric field Path of electrons Fluorescent screen

Figure 7-16
Schematic representation of Thomson's discharge tube with the stream of electrons coming off the cathode and being bent as they pass through an electric field.

Figure 7-17
Thomson's original discharge tube with which he discovered the electron in 1897.

the wide end in such a manner that the position of the band of fluorescent light could be exactly located. If this description sounds somewhat familiar, that's because such a discharge tube is close to the basic design of the modern television tube, the image being produced by the fluorescence resulting from a beam of electrons.

J.J.'s Results

The first thing Thomson did was to show that the band of cathode rays could be bent by applying an electric field across the two horizontal plates located in the center of the discharge tube; if the upper plate was electrically positive, that was the direction of the bending; if the electric charge on the plates was reversed, the bending was toward the lower. He then placed the discharge tube directly into a strong magnetic field; when the electric field was off, the magnetic field could bend the beam of cathode rays. Thus, charged particles are subject to the bending forces of both electric and magnetic fields (see Fig. 7-17). You can balance the magnetic field bending by switching on the electric field and adjusting it to the right strength. That information (the required field strength to balance the two fields, electric and magnetic, acting on a beam of negatively charged particles) allowed calculation of the ratio of the charge on the electron to its mass. A reliable determination of a very important number was now known, the ratio of the unit electric charge *e* for the atom of electricity to its mass *m*. Of course, the ratio of *e:m* turned out to be exactly the same, whatever the cathode metal, which meant that cathode rays are common to all matter. Qualitatively, Thomson was able to establish that these cathode ray particles are much smaller than the smallest atom, the hydrogen atom. The conclusion or inference to be drawn was that the atom could not be the end to the subdivision of matter in the universe. The electron was therefore assumed to be a component of all atoms, and perhaps an *elementary* particle. All that turned out to be the case.

You may ask whether we cannot at some future date expect the electron to be subdivided, too. How can we be so certain it is at last, an elementary particle? Well, if you must have the proof, hold on for another chapter and you'll be a true believer, too.

□ The Famous Oil Drop Experiment

With the ratio of *e:m* already established, an American, Robert Millikan of the University of Chicago, set about the business of evaluating *e*. Once *e* is known, *m* is automatically known by straightforward calculation. In what must be described as a really neat experiment (in Millikan's day it was probably described as a really "swell" experiment), Millikan was able to show that electric charges purposely placed on the surface of an oil drop were always present as simple whole number multiples of a single minimum value. This minimum value must be the quantity associated with the charge on one electron (see Fig. 7-18). The oil drop experiment began with a fine mist of oil (produced with an atomizer), electrically charged during formation by friction. A very few of these fine, charged drops were allowed to drift through a tiny opening into the space between two electrified plates. Illuminated by an electric arc outside the apparatus and viewed through a microscopic eyepiece, a charged oil drop appeared as a bright star against a black sky. The oil drop fell through the distance between the two plates because of the force of gravity. But if a potential difference in the vertical direction were put across the plates, the uniform electric field produced would act as a force opposite to the force of gravity. The time it takes for an oil drop to fall the distance between two horizontal hairlines on the microscope eyepiece with no opposing electric potential force acting was determined in this manner. This was set against some new velocity due to the strength of an applied field. Comparison of these values allowed Millikan to directly calculate the charge on the drop. The value would vary from experiment to experiment, from oil drop to oil drop. But the value was always a simple, whole-number multiple of 4.8×10^{-10} electrostatic units (esu). Millikan concluded that this must be the smallest charge, the unit electric charge, the charge on the electron.

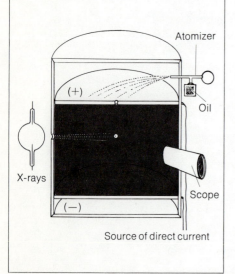

Figure 7-18
Schematic representation of Millikan's experimental determination of the unit charge on the electron—the famous "oil-drop" experiment.

Again, you have the opportunity to ask an embarrassing question: "What is there in Millikan's experiment that excludes the possibility of charges smaller than the unit charge *e*?" The answer is nothing; however, not a single experiment has been able to undermine our great confidence in *e* as smallest. Perhaps the most satisfying thing to do here is to remind ourselves that *e* can be defined in terms of two other universal constants of nature, F and *N*. Calculating the ratio of the Faraday of electricity to Avogadro's number (*N*) a few pages back gave us an independently derived number value for *e*, the unit charge on the electron. It turned out to be 1.60×10^{-19} coulomb. That can be expressed in Millikan's electrostatic units by making use of a simple conversion factor (an esu is small, 3 billion times smaller than a coulomb):

$$1 \text{ coulomb} = 3.0 \times 10^{19} \text{ esu}$$

Therefore,

$$\frac{1.60 \times 10^{-19} \text{ coulomb}}{1 \text{ electron}} \quad \frac{3.0 \times 10^{9} \text{ esu}}{1 \text{ coulomb}} = 4.8 \times 10^{-10} \text{ esu/electron}$$

The agreement with Millikan's result is beautiful.

Famous oil drop experiment value for $e = 4.8 \times 10^{-10}$ esu/electron
F/*N* value for $e = 4.8 \times 10^{-10}$ esu/electron

Combining Millikan's value for *e* with Thomson's ratio for *e/m* we can calculate the electron's mass, *m*.

Thomson's value for $e/m = 5.3 \times 10^{17}$ esu/g
Millikan's value for $e = 4.8 \times 10^{-10}$ esu

$$\frac{e}{m} = 5.3 \times 10^{17} \text{ esu/g}$$

$$\frac{4.8 \times 10^{-10} \text{ esu}}{5.3 \times 10^{17} \text{ esu/g}} = m \ 9.1 \times 10^{-28} \text{ g}$$

and

$$9.1 \times 10^{-28} \text{ g} \cong 1/1,837 \text{ mass of a single hydrogen atom}$$

The picture we have today looks something like this. If we take the simplest and smallest atom and rip off an electron, we are left with a positively charged hydrogen ion. That process, removal of electrons, is one kind of ionization. Since atoms are electrically neutral to begin with, the hydrogen ion left behind after ionization must be electrically positive, a positively charged ion. The mass of the hydrogen ion turns out to be close to 2,000 times that of the electron that spun off. Taking the relative mass for the lightest atom as 1, the mass of the hydrogen ion must be approximately 1 as well, since ripping out an electron reduces the total mass by only a very small amount. We can write a chemical equation for the ionization process:

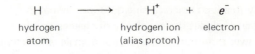

H ⟶ H⁺ + e⁻

hydrogen   hydrogen ion   electron
atom   (alias proton)

☐ Ernest Rutherford's New Atomic Model

Having gotten this far, we must next ask about how and where one places these fundamental, electrically opposite charges (positive ions and negative ions) for they are clearly principal atomic ingredients. Well, some of Thomson's work had suggested that the number of electrons might be roughly equal to the atomic mass of the element in question. Therefore, one would expect to find an equal number of positive charges if electrical neutrality is to be maintained. In such a situation, in order for stability to be maintained within the atom, the electrons were pictured as being embedded in a large mass of positive charge. This effectively snared them as so many seeds stuck in a watermelon. The atom was a massive, positive pink pulp with enough very light, negative, black seeds dispersed throughout to make the whole business neutral. (Of course, Thomson never imagined a watermelon model; his analogy was a plum pudding.)

Sound alright for an atomic model? Simple and reasonable? Yes, but with a fatal drawback. How shall we keep all of these negative and positive charges lying randomly about? Won't they all be drawn in and crash upon each other? Perhaps one can arrange a delicately balanced pattern of pluses and minuses; a kind of equilibrium balance of coulombic, inverse square forces. Yes, but that would indeed be an unstable arrangement. Any small disturbance, let alone something the likes of a collision, would upset the balance of electrical attraction and repulsion and lead to collapse. No, atoms just aren't like watermelons. But if they are not properly modeled after watermelons, and if they're no longer solid, uniform, and billiard-ball like things, what kind of atomic conceptualization can we have? Ernest Rutherford provided the new view; the year was 1910; things haven't been the same since.

Rutherford got his kicks from shooting atoms. He would use as his bullets, very high energy, relatively massive alpha (α) particles, particles spontaneously emitted from the then newly discovered *radioactive* elements such as radium and thorium. It has already been shown that these α-particles were in fact helium ions that had erupted from deep inside the radioactive elements with extremely high velocities. They were also electrically positive, having a double positive charge upon them, presumably leaving two electrons somewhere behind in the radioactive atom. So we have Rutherford's shooting gallery and his magic bullet, the α-particle, doubly charged, positive, some 7,500 times as massive as the electron.

The experiment was simple enough in its design (Fig. 7-19). Find out how these

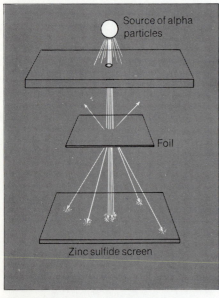

Figure 7-19
Rutherford's experiment. Nearly all the alpha particles pass through the foil or experience only small deflections. A very few are deflected through large angles and that was, as Rutherford said . . .''incredible.''

bullets are deflected by whatever it is they encounter on their trip through a few layers of atoms. Such information should supply a qualitative picture of what kind of arrangement exists inside. Rutherford's student, Geiger and "young Marsden," were given the assignment. As Rutherford himself recalled the incident years later:

> . . . I had observed the scattering of α-particles, and Dr. Geiger in my laboratory had examined it in detail. He found, in pieces of heavy metal, that the scattering was usually small, of the order of one degree. One day Geiger came to me and said, "Don't you think that young Marsden, whom I am training in radioactive methods, ought to begin a small research?" Now I had thought that, too, so I said, "Why not let him see if any α-particles can be scattered through a large angle?" I may tell you in confidence that I did not believe that they would be, since we know that the α- particle was a very fast, massive particle, with a great deal of energy, and you could show that if the scattering was due to the accumulated effect of a number of small scatterings, the chance of an α-particle's being scattered backward was very small. Then I remember two or three days later Geiger coming to me in great excitement and saying, "We have been able to get some of the α-particles coming backward . . ." It was quite the most incredible event that has ever happened to me in my life. It was almost as incredible as if you fired a 15-inch shell at a piece of tissue paper and it came back and hit you. On consideration, I realized that this scattering backward must be the result of a single collision. . . it was impossible to get anything of that order of magnitude unless you took a system in which the greater part of the mass of the atom was concentrated in a minute nucleus. It was then that I had the idea of an atom with minute massive centre, carrying a charge. . . . .

Table 7-2

Scattering of Alpha-Particles Sent Through a Gold Foil by Geiger and Marsden

Angle of deflection	Experimental count
150°	33
135°	43
120°	52
105°	70
75°	211
60°	477
45°	1,435
30°	7,800
15°	120,570
10°	502,570
5°	8,289,000

☐ **Questions to Answer . . . Problems to Solve**

1. Briefly comment upon each of the following statements:
   (a) A "normal" atom exhibits no electric charge even though many of its component parts are "charged."
   (b) Rubbing a glass rod with a piece of fur produces a charged glass rod.
   (c) Ben Franklin was probably more lucky than smart.
   (d) *e/m* has the same value for all cathode materials in all kinds of discharge tubes.
   (e) In the famous oil drop experiment, the value of *e* is always an integral multiple of some single small value.

2. A hydrogen ion is placed next to an electron. What would you expect to happen? What law governs such physical behavior, and what mathematical form does that law take? How about placing a hydrogen ion in the vicinity of an α-particle—what then?

3. Michael Faraday discovered the basic experimental relationships that determined how much of any particular element deposits or is generated in an electrolysis. What are they? And doesn't that directly implicate electricity in chemical change?

4. The equivalent weight of an element is the ratio of atomic weight to valence, or combining capacity. For example, copper has an equivalent weight of 63.5/2 = 31.75. What's that all about, electrochemically?

5. Fill in the blanks in the following table:

element	atomic weight	combining capacity	grams freed from combination by one of charge
hydrogen	1	1	1
lithium	7	1	—
magnesium	24	—	12
barium	—	2	68.5
—	40	2	—
sulfur	32	—	16
chromium	—	3	17.33
manganese	55	—	27.5
—	51	5	—

6. If oxygen has a combining capacity of 2, what is the apparent valence of
   (a) N in NO; N in N_2O
   (b) C in CO_2; C in CO
   (c) Mn in Mn_2O_3; Mn in Mn_2O_7

7. Identify each of the following:
   (a) the electrode in a cell with a positive charge; the one with a negative charge.
   (b) an anion; a cation
   (c) hydroxide ion; hydrogen ion
   (d) proton; α-particle
   (e) electron; "atom" of electricity
   (f) battery; electrolytic cell

8. What do you mean when you say something is "electrically neutral?"; When you say something is "negative?"; positive?

9. What is your understanding of each of the following terms?
   (a) electron
   (b) ion
   (c) $F = k \dfrac{e_1 e_2}{d^2}$
   (d) voltage
   (e) $\dfrac{F}{N} = e$
   (f) combining capacity
   (g) electrical equivalents
   (h) nitrate ion
   (i) corrosion
   (j) electroplating

10. What do you think about copper rivets for the iron plates of an ocean-going tanker? Would you be better advised to use iron rivets in copper hull plates, electrochemically speaking?

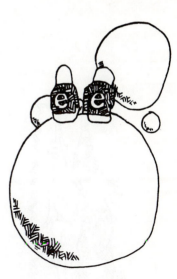

11. Chemical evidence of long standing suggests that single atoms, ar atoms acting in small groups, are the carriers of electricity in solution. The charge on these ions are all multiples of one basic unit, the "atom" of electricity, or electron. Reconstruct the case for this contention based upon your understanding of the chapter.

12. Physical evidence of more recent vintage has offered a picture of the basic unit charge on unencumbered, gas phase electrons. Reconstruct the case for for that contention based on your understanding of the chapter.

13. And having answered the preceding question, what is the evidence that suggests to you that the basic unit of charge for "associated" electrons in solution, is the same as that for "free" electrons on the gas phase?

14. What is the exact size of the unit of positive charge left on an atom of hydrogen after it ionizes, losing an electron, and becomes a hydrogen ion?

15. How will you go about accomplishing each of the following:
    (a) making a positive ion; a negative ion; an electron.
    (b) generating a stream of electrons; a potential difference; an electric current.
    (c) copper plate an iron ring; refinish a chromium surface.
    (d) electrochemically produce hydrogen; chlorine.

16. Your window air-conditioner draws 10-amps of current:
    (a) Determine the quantity of charge, in coulombs, passing in _____ minutes.
    (b) Would that be a "shocking" experience? How shocking?
    (c) Can you calculate the number of electrons that actually flow past a fixed point in the circuit in one second?

17. If the symbol for a chloride ion is Cl^-, what is the formula for a hydroxide ion? And how do you generate one? How about generating a nitrate ion? Sulfate ion?

18. A 3-amp current flows for one hour and twenty minutes through an electrochemical cell. Determine each of the following:
    (a) The number of coulombs that flowed.
    (b) The Faradays of electricity that passed through.
    (c) The maximum number of grams of copper metal that could be deposited from a copper sulfate solution.
    (d) The maximum number of moles of aluminum that could be deposited from solution.
    (e) The maximum number of liters of hydrogen gas evolved, as measured at STP, of course, in the electrolysis of water.

19. If hydrogen has a combining capacity of 1, what is the apparent valence of
    (a) N in NH_3; N in N_2H_4
    (b) C in CH_4; C in C_3H_8
    (c) B in B_2H_6; B in B_5H_{11}

20. A total of 0.108 g of silver metal deposited from a silver nitrate solution in an electrochemical cell. The cell was in operation for 7.2 hr. Determine each of the following:
    (a) The electrode to which the silver ions, Ag^+, migrated.
    (b) The total number of coulombs that passed through.
    (c) The amperage for the current being generated.
    (d) The number of grams of iron metal that could be deposited from Fe^{3+} ions.
    (e) The number of moles of oxygen gas that could be generated.

21. Making use of a carefully drawn and labeled diagram, design a complete, battery-powered cell, that could succeed at electroplating a coating of copper onto an iron ring.

22. Go back into the chapter and bone up on the following . . . and then give a brief description *in your own words* of
    (a) Thomson's discharge tube experiments establishing *e/m*.
    (b) Millikan's famous oil drop experiment.
    (c) The α-particle scattering experiments.

23. How do you know that electrons . . .
    (a) have mass?
    (b) are negatively charged?
    (c) are subatomic particles?
    (d) are "elementary" particles?

24. A hydrogen atom and a hydrogen ion have approximately the same mass. How come?

25. Briefly explain or identify each of the following:
    (a) discharge tube   (d) *e/m*   (g) helium nucleus
    (b) cathode ray   (e) esu   (h) hydrogen ion
    (c) lightning   (f) α-particle   (i) periodic law

26. A cylindrical arrangement for the periodic table might make the beauty of the scheme more obvious. What do you think about that?

27. Using Geiger and Marsden's data for the scattering of α-particles, by gold atoms in a foil (Table 7-2), calculate the percentage that were scattered an angle greater than 75°. Are you impressed? And what was the significance of that experiment again?

28. Try to briefly explain . . .
    (a) why J. J's plum pudding model for the structure of the atom was significant.
    (b) why J. J's model was an unreasonable representation.
    (c) why Geiger and Marsden's scattering experiments were significant.

29. Make a comparison of J. J's model and Rutherford's plantary system model for the atom.

30. Try the following:
    (a) Differentiate between atomic number and atomic weight; which is of more fundamental significance, and on what evidence do you base that answer?
    (b) Pick several elements at random; look up their atomic number; compare compare that to their atomic weights.
    (c) Determine the maximum number of unit positive charges possible for the hydrogen atom; the helium atom.

31. In the year 1815, an English physician by the name of William Prout' suggested that all known elements were varying combinations of hydrogen atoms . . . multiples of a unit mass of the lightest element:
    (a) Can you speculate a bit about why he might have thought that?
    (b) In what way does this wrong hypothesis have a very modern ring to it?

New Ways of Thinking

☐ **Perceptions and Deceptions**

1 "Light brings us the news of the universe."

2 Light added to light can mean brighter light or no light at all.

3 Rutherford's planetary model was nice. But planets aren't charged particles; electrons are.

4 The old theory became the limit to which the new theory exceeded. That's just as it should be.

5 Electrons in atoms leave their own special kind of fingerprint.

6 The twentieth century has witnessed a shift in scientific allegience: proof has been replaced by plausibility.

☐ **What is Light?**

In trying to build some understanding of the universe, we find ourselves faced with a house of cards. The most basic theories, the most pervasive facts, the most fundamental ideas, are bottom cards. It is a simple enough matter to take off a top card without disturbing the entire framework of the house of science: exchange Thomson's plum pudding model for Rutherford's planetary system and what we've done is to put on a new roof. But try and replace a bottom card and the whole house must be rebuilt anew. This chapter is about bottom cards. Light is one of them.

"Light Brings Us the News of the Universe."

Light is the way we know of distant places and next door; the black-and-white vault of the heavens on a starry night and the myriad colors in the rainbow arching across a wet summer sky; the Mona Lisa and the flowers of Spring; chlorophyll and photosynthesis, life itself. Light is a form of radiation. The general term is *electromagnetic* radiation. Classification of electromagnetic radiations is according to wavelength, ranging from the very long radiowaves and beyond, to the very short X-rays, gamma rays, and cosmic rays. The human eye responds only to one relatively small segment of the total range of radiations, the *visible region* of the electromagnetic spectrum.

The successes of chemistry in the nineteenth century provided most scientists with a satisfactory belief in matter as being composed of atoms. As the twentieth century began, the quantum theory, one of two great new physical theories was being composed by the German physicist Max Planck. In 1918, Planck was awarded the Nobel Prize for this work. Orchestration of Planck's quantum theory was undertaken by Albert Einstein and Neils Bohr. Einstein won the Nobel Prize for his work on the photoelectric effect in 1921. In 1922, Bohr was given a Nobel Prize for his work on the quantum model of atomic structure.

Our perception of "visible" light comes through the central nervous system. But most light, most radiations, are invisible and must be detected by secondary means, electrically, thermally, chemically. Radiowaves are styled no differently by nature than visible light and cosmic rays. Perhaps we suspect visible light to be somehow different, but that's just not so. It only happens to be more familiar, and therefore more comfortable.

Nothing in the Universe Moves Faster than Light

Let's see about light—radiation—and the claim that it must be assigned a key position in our house of cards. Perhaps most remarkable is its unique speed. Nothing in the universe moves faster than light. Light smoothly flows along at a very definite, very fast, 3×10^{10} cm a second in a vacuum, and nearly that in air. That means it makes the 93 million mile trip from sun to earth in about 8 minutes. Of course, our sun is relatively close. It takes about 4 years for light from the nearest star to hit you in the eye and tell you it's there (Fig. 8-1). But the actual speed isn't very important at all. What is important is that nothing can go faster. That's right. Nothing. We have understood that must be so ever since Einstein's famous theory of relativity. Relativity theory says nothing can move faster than light (when measured in a vacuum), for mass increases rapidly as a moving body approaches that speed. At the speed of light, a moving body would have infinite mass . . . which means it would have infinite energy . . . which is meaningless. The speed of light is a universal limit, and every substantive bit of matter in the universe moves less quickly than that. Most bodies move a *lot* less quickly; for all practical purposes, we can't even begin to measure mass increases due to increased speed as predicted by Einstein's theory. For example, a one-ton truck moving 70 miles per hour still weighs one ton, and even if it could be moved at supersonic speeds of say 1000 miles per hour . . . still one ton. When we talk of approaching the speed of light, we're approaching ***186,000 miles per second*** and nothing familiar, like cars and trucks or even jet airplanes, comes close to that.

Figure 8-1

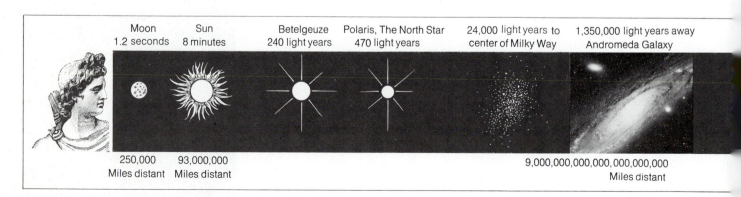

| Moon
1.2 seconds | Sun
8 minutes | Betelgeuze
240 light years | Polaris, The North Star
470 light years | 24,000 light years to
center of Milky Way | 1,350,000 light years away
Andromeda Galaxy |

250,000 Miles distant 93,000,000 Miles distant

9,000,000,000,000,000,000,000 Miles distant

The Mysterious, Non-existent "Ether."

Light moves without dragging the medium through which it travels. It's kind of movement is referred to as a travelling wave. We say that "waves can propagate through a *material* medium." Note how water waves move rapidly along causing the water to move up and down; but the water itself moves little more than that. The wave front moves forward, but place a cork on the water or watch a boat bobbing on the waves and see how little their forward motion is (Fig. 8-2). However, whereas sound moves in waves through the medium of the air and wave fronts propagate through a water medium, light spreads out in waves and moves through *empty* space. What medium is supporting its vibration? Presumably none. That caused a lot of trouble among scientists for a long time. After all, how were they to explain something moving through nothing? It was a hard pill for scientists to swallow. Therefore scientists at first created the "ether," a medium for light to travel through. They just couldn't accept that something was moving through nothing. But that theory wore thin in the last years of the nineteenth century and mostly collapsed on evidence from a famous experiment.

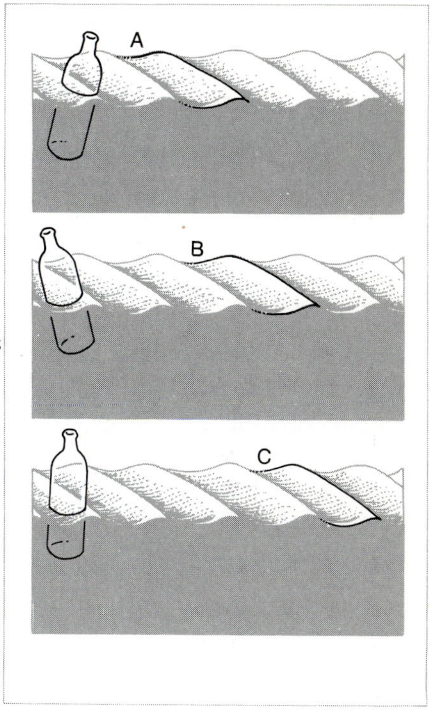

The Michelson-Morley ether drift experiment demonstrated that we really can't tell whether we are in motion or at rest with respect to this "ether" medium. Think about rowing a boat or paddling a canoe upstream; you have to overcome the resistence due to the drift of the river (the medium). The same is true when moving through air (Fig. 8-3). But this mysterious ether medium didn't drift. Light wasn't slowed by passage through this medium; perhaps the best conclusion to draw was simply that no "ether" medium existed. Einstein's famous theory supported that conclusion.

Light's Complementary Aspects

Now there is a paradox here, and it is a very important one. Light behaves sometimes as if it has a wave nature, but these waves sometimes have particle properties, too. Einstein was famous for his theory of relativity, but it was for his explanation of the *photoelectric effect* that he was awarded the Nobel Prize. The photoelectric effect has to do with the particle nature of light. Shine the right kind of light on a metal surface and electrons come spilling off. Something substantive, particulate, seems to be knocking electrons free. These particles of light were dubbed *photons.* What to do about the theory of light. Is light to be regarded as waves or particles? A compromise is required between the granulated view of light and its continuous wave nature—between light's two *complementary* aspects. This new understanding of light leads us to a new understanding of matter in general, especially the behavior of electrons. The new understanding is called **quantum mechanics.**

Figure 8-2
It's not the wave that moves, but the wave *front*. The bobbing motion of the bottle indicates just how little transverse movement there is.

Figure 8-3
Midshipman First Class Albert Michelson at the U.S. Naval Academy, photographed while making a self-portrait. His experiments earned him the reputation "master of light."

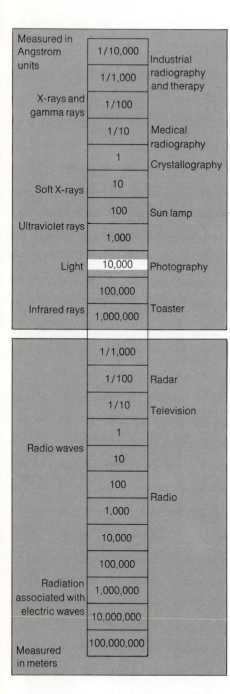

Figure 8-4
Diagramatic spectrum of electromagnetic radiations.

So light really isn't what we thought it was. When we changed our view of light, we replaced a bottom card. Light—radiation—is not a separate concept from matter. Our connection is energy, an old friend from an early chapter. Since Einstein, we know matter can disappear in a burst of radiation, and radiation can be condensed into particles of matter. That has had a profound influence on our lives. Perhaps we can go so far as to suggest that all one needed for creation of the universe was a very forceful command "Let There Be Light." And after that, it's all a matter of progressive condensation. How will it all end? Yes, in a flash of light. So much for speculations on beginnings and endings. We've a lot to talk about. Fiat lux!

☐ Spectral Properties and Harmonic Motion

Take a polished glass prism and carefully allow light from the Sun to fall upon it. The light will be resolved into a characteristic rainbow spectrum of its component colors. Newton did that in the seventeenth century. Now take a second prism, and you can cause the entire spectrum to recombine into a beam of ordinary white sunlight again. Newton did that, too. You can duplicate the experiment on a cloudy day, or if you are a night person, by inspecting white light from a glowing solid. Use a carbon arc, or a white hot metal rod, or a molten liquid metal. The white light splits into a rainbow spectrum again (Table

Table 8-1
Identifying regions in the electromagnetic spectrum

Type of radiation	Source	Relative wavelengths, and energy	
Cosmic rays	Interstellar space	10^{-14} m	Shorter wavelengths correspond to higher energy
Gamma rays	Atomic nucleus	40^{-13} to 10^{-10} m	The *blue* end of the spectrum
X-rays	X-ray tubes, bouncing electrons off metal targets	$\sim 10^{-11}$ to 10^{-8} m	
Ultraviolet rays	The sun, incandescent solids, gaseous discharge	$\sim 10^{-7}$ m	
Visible rays	The sun, other hot stellar bodies, hot gases, incandescent solids	$\sim 10^{-6}$ m	Direction of corresponding energy decrease
Infrared rays	Warm bodies, glowing solids	$\sim 10^{-4}$ m	
Microwave & radio waves	Radar, TV, microwave, standard broadcast	$\sim 10^{-2}$ m	Longer wavelengths correspond to lower energy
Electric waves	Electric power, current, transmission lines	$\sim 10^{2}$ m	The *red* end of the spectrum

8-1, Fig. 8-4). Such spectra are called **emission** spectra. They are continuous; all the colors simply blend, one into the next. Curious about any effect due to the nature of the radiation emitter? Forget it. The cinders in the fireplace, glowing red hot, and at the same temperature as a red hot metal poker sitting in their midst. Same glow; same heat. *Red* radiation is all the same, glowing cinders or metal poker.

The wave motion of light can be represented by a graphical pattern called a sine curve (Fig. 8-5). You can see that the wave moves forward all right, by looking at a series of wave patterns at different times. But any point on the wave does nothing but move up and down, like the bobbing cork. It is perhaps familiar to think of it in terms of uniformly jangling a rope anchored at one end. A transverse wave travels along a taut rope, tracing out **simple harmonic motion.** The maximum height of the wave above the position of the rope prior to jangling is known as the *amplitude* of the curve. You may have noticed that the amplitude is also the depth of the wave's hollow. Hump and hollow both measure **amplitude.** The distance between successive humps, or between successive hollows, is the **wavelength** (λ). The **frequency** (ν) of the waves is the number of humps (or hollows) passing a fixed point per unit of time.

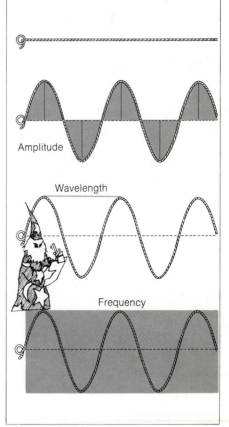

The relationship between frequency and wavelength is the following: frequency is inversely proportional to wavelength: the smaller the wavelength, the higher the frequency:

$$\nu \propto \frac{1}{\lambda}$$

Now introduce our old friend, "=k" for $\propto$

$$\nu = k\frac{1}{\lambda}$$

The proportionality constant k, in this relationship, is none other than that universal constant, the speed of light, leaving us with a neat and powerful little equation:

$$\nu = c\frac{1}{\lambda}$$

$$\nu = \frac{c}{\lambda}$$

$$\nu\lambda = c$$

So a simple harmonic wave has three principal features:

1 The wavelength λ, the distance between consecutive humps (or hollows).

2 The frequency ν, the number of such waves passing by per second.

Figure 8-5
The motion of jiggled rope, anchored at the end, will trace out a typical sine curve.

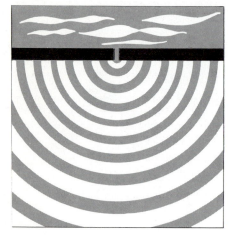

Figure 8-6
Water rippling through a wide break (top).

Water rippling through a narrow break. Little or no interference is evident (bottom).

3 The speed with which the wave travels. In the case of light in a vacuum (or air), that's "c."

Therefore, c = $\nu\lambda$, and since c is a constant in a given material (vacuum or air) the frequency is inversely proportional to the wavelength.

More About Light Waves: Bending and Interference

Waves in general have two more characteristics that play an important role in what's coming. First, they appear to bend around corners, and second, they interfere with each other just as water does. Water will ripple through a wide break in a barrier (Fig. 8-6). But a narrow break causes bending of the waves as they ripple through the barrier; and if the break through which the ripples pass is less than a wavelength in width, then waves tend to ripple out in all directions. Light does these very same things: after all, light is wave-like. Yet, on first examination of light waves, where is the bending? Sunlight passing through only a pinhole is a tremendously large number of wavelengths across, and should behave as water rippling through a very large opening. By light standards, there is little to bend around because the opening is so wide. But now try a much smaller hole; try looking at a flashlight some distance away from you through a very fine screen, or perhaps streetlights through an umbrella on a rainy night. What you see is a pattern, a **diffraction pattern.** Compare that to just look-ing at the flashlight in a darkened room through a pinhole in a cardboard. There all you see is light without bending; no diffraction.

The second important characteristic is interference. When waves arrive together, overlapping the net effect is addition. The result is either amplification of the wave . . . if it's a light wave, that means brighter . . . or cancellation of the waves . . . if it's a light wave, that means darker. If two very small side-by-side pinholes are illuminated, light spreads out or is diffracted in all directions from both, and waves march out in military fashion . . . hump, hollow, hump, hollow. Now place photographic plate at some distance from the light source and let's see what happens. We get an alternating pattern of bright-dark-bright-dark. These fringes are caused by interference of the ripples moving forward from the two holes, overrunning each other. Let's look at two identical waves that travel exactly the same distance before running together at the film plate. They arrive . . . hump, hollow, hump, hollow . . . and overlap just that way, resulting in HUMP, HOLLOW, HUMP, HOLLOW . . . Interference (superposition in this case) has resulted in doubling of the amplitude, or intensity of the wave. Now consider two waves that arrive at the photographic plate on top of each other, but out of phase . . . hump, hollow, hump . . . and hollow, hump, hollow . . . . Cancellation is the result. The humps cancel the hollows, being equal and opposite; the result is no light at all due to interference (Fig. 8-7). Gray areas between occur when the humps and hollows amplify and cancel less than completely. Our rule of thumb is light + light produces more light if two ripples are in phase; light + light produces less light if the two ripples are out-of-phase.

☐ The Black Box

From your own experience, it should be evident that a certain level of energy, or intensity of heat must be present for a warm body to radiate enough light for you to be able see it. That red-glowing poker was a hot body, but you don't glow on a cold winter day, even though you are radiating heat like mad. The surface of the sun that we see glows white-hot, registering very high temperatures. What then is in all this radiation, heat, and visible "glow"? Qualitatively, as temperature and heat content increase, the intensity of the radiation given off increases. Furthermore, the most intense radiation shifts from longer to shorter wavelengths; that is from the red (longer) end of the spectrum to the blue (shorter) end; or to put it still another way, from lower to higher energy. (Refer to Table 8-1 again). Infrared radiation, at wavelengths longer than visible light, is often referred to as *heat radiation* because it radiates from all bodies not hot enough to be *obviously* hot, or luminous. That's the red end of the electromagnetic spectrum. Ultraviolet radiation, at wavelengths shorter than visible light, generally accounts for summer suntans and sunburns: the blue end.

Take a look at the graphic representation of this discussion (Fig. 8-8). It shows the wavelength of radiations for warm bodies plotted against the intensity of those radiations, the radiant energy per unit wavelength. At very low temperatures, below 4000°K, almost all the radiant energy falls into the infrared region. Very little is visible light, or light in the 4000-7500 Å region. The surface temperature of the sun is about 6000°K; note the maximum in the curve peaks at about 5560 Å, well into the visible range. A large percentage of the sun's radiated energy is in the visible region, a fact easily confirmed on any clear day. The family of curves in these figures can be drawn out of experimental data for each radiation temperature you'd care to measure. For *any* radiating substance, no matter what its composition, the same curve is obtained at the same temperature. Remember our earlier example of the red hot poker in the red hot coals: same heat, same glow, same radiation—yet different substances.

There seems to be a certain kind of universality about the emission of light. Again, we're using the word light in the general sense of radiation. Scientists can study a perfect model, or perfect radiation emitter called a **black body.** In all likelihood you've got at least one black body in your own home—your furnace. The best radiator is the best absorber, a perfectly black body. A tiny hole in a black box is such a perfect absorber, for whatever light enters the box is fated to bounce around inside until it is completely absorbed. Open the door to the furnace, with its soot blackened walls, and see just how black, black is. Inside the

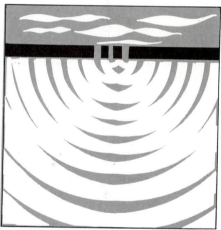

Figure 8-7
The wave fronts impinge on each other causing interference that produces reinforcement and cancellation where the wave fronts cross.

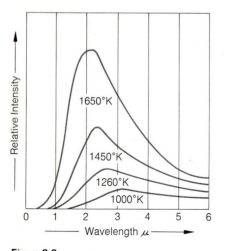

Figure 8-8
Graphic representation of radiations from warm bodies: wavelength versus intensity.

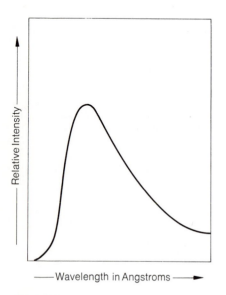

Figure 8-9
Radiations from inside the furnace.

entire collection of radiations is achieved as any entering light gets bounced around and absorbed. Eventually, a complete sampling finds its way back out the opening, through the furnace door, which has now become a perfect radiator. The typical radiation spectrum looks like the family of curves we've just been describing (Fig. 8-9).

☐ **"h"**

The radiation exiting from the open furnace door turned out to be very important, theoretically. It was a signal for an entirely new way of looking at the universe. Those radiating waves announced a marked departure from a traditional or classical level of understanding, the view of the physical world for 200 years since Newton. Let's see how that came about.

Two very useful radiation laws emerge from our discussions of the black box. First, the total energy radiating from a hot body was found to be directly proportional to the fourth power of the absolute temperature. The detail of that observation needn't concern us, but there are some very practical consequences. For example, it is therefore possible to get an accurate estimate of the surface temperature of the sun and other bright stars. To determine the temperature inside a blast furnace, why simply stand back and take a *measured* look inside. Second, we also know that the peak in the family of curves shifts toward shorter wavelengths with increasing temperature. This allows us to calculate the temperature of stars and furnaces, and other radiating bodies. Some nice correlations show up: one is that surface of the sun is 6000°K by either calculation. That certainly makes scientists happy—corroboration by two different techniques.

But just here, we run into trouble. For no matter what kind of mathematical handstands, backflips or contortions you are capable of, classical theory—light as waves—fails to represent the experimental picture faithfully. One isn't likely to feel overly confident if one's theory is only *approximately* like the experimental results. But that turns out to be the case here. Some of the theory is O.K., fitting the experimental data nicely. However, a significant inconsistency shows up in the short wavelength, ultraviolet end of the radiation spectrum. The spectrum for solar radiation, perfect black body radiation, or radiation from a glowing hot poker are not adequately described by any classical law. After you get to the peak in the curve, classical theory says energy must continually increase to shorter and shorter wavelengths. In other words, classical theory suggests "no peak at all," only a continual, steep climb right on off the graph at some distant infinity (Fig. 8-10). Of course, that's not what we actually see.

A Discovery of the First Rank

This apparent radiation catastrophe in the ultraviolet region only exists because the theory at the time was incomplete. A better understanding was needed. In the year 1900, Max Planck, a German physicist, discovered an empirical expression (a mathematical equation) that did completely represent the experimental radiation curves for an ideal radiator: at long wavelengths; at short wavelengths; at high temperatures, at low temperatures—peak and all. Nevertheless an equation is not an explanation. True, Planck's empirical equation was a real step forward, accurately describing the data as it did, yet what was the meaning of it? Planck now set out to accomplish the more difficult task.

The problem was fundamental, and Planck's thinking was exactly right. What makes it both fascinating and really "bottom card" fundamental is the fact that continuous spectra of radiation from suns and stars, glowing rods and black boxes, depend only on temperature. Such spectra are completely free of any dependence on the nature of the chemical properties of the radiating substance. Iron rods and hot gases, graphite or ceramic; its all the same, at the same temperature. That smacks of relationships like universal gravitation, which has nothing to do with chemical composition. Planck's empirical radiation formula was a great success; that was in mid-October. By mid-December, he had the theoretical understanding to fit the mathematical equation that described the experimental results (Fig. 8-11). Up went the curtain on the future . . . even though no one quite realized it at the time. But Planck suspected. He remarked to his son on a walk through a wood in the suburbs of Berlin:

> "On this walk he explained that he felt he had possibly made a discovery of the first rank, comparable perhaps only to the discoveries of Newton."

Planck's new view of the sun's ray did not represent the usual train of light waves. Light waves, to be sure, were still ripples propagating along, but no longer, or ever again, was that ripple of waves to be viewed as *continuous*. Planck suggested a stream of particles called *photons*. A new word; a new idea: **Photon.**

Not a particle in the old sense but a quantity, package, particle of energy, of electromagnetic radiation characterized as waves with prescribed wavelength and frequency. There is a definite quantum of energy corresponding to each and every frequency of light. And the only place you'll be likely to find half a quantum of red light is wherever it is you think you can get your hands on half an atom of potassium. The quantum of light, the photon, corresponds to the atom of energy, available in different sizes, as are the atoms themselves; but no fractions, please. No half an atom; no half a quantum.

Planck proceeded. He said that photons of different frequencies (ν) are carriers of different quantities of energy. The photon's energy (E) will be proportional to its particular frequency of vibration:

$$E \propto \nu$$

Doing our proportionality constant thing again,

$$E = k\nu$$

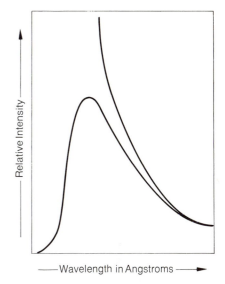

Figure 8-10
Irreconcilable behavior for a radiating black body.

Figure 8-11
A charcoal sketch of Max Planck done in 1932.

In honor of Planck, we'll call the proportionality constant k, *Planck's constant* . . . well, why not . . . and designate it as "**h**." That now gives us another famous equation, one relating radiant energy to its frequency:

$$E = h\nu$$

Now, having assumed that energy exists as quanta, how does that explain the shape of the radiation curve? We know Planck's equation works, but what about his explanation? Let's begin with his relationship, $E = h\nu$. Radiant energy moves about, packaged or quantized, and each pack is proportional in energy content to its frequency. Light waves in the longer wavelength, infrared region, exhibit lower frequencies, therefore their energy packs are smaller. Remember wavelength and frequency are inversely proportional. Visible lightwaves have shorter wavelengths, higher frequencies, and their energy packs are larger than those infrared radiations. Ultraviolet light waves are shorter still, higher frequency, and still higher in energy per pack. Rule: no half packs. Energy is absorbed or emitted in exactly whole quanta. No other way (Fig. 8-12).

Placing Radiation in the Perspective of Probability

To really make sense of all of this you must understand one thing about Planck. His lifelong scientific interest was thermodynamics, especially the second law of thermodynamics. Remember our discussions about entropies and probabilities back in Chapter 4. Humpty dumpty broke up irreversibly and the coal dust and white sand, stirred grey, couldn't be unstirred without absolutely prohibitive expenditures of time and energy, all because of the tremendous number of particles and events involved in those happenings. Second law of thermodynamics! Planck solved this radiation dilemma by placing radiation in the prospective of probability, too.

Qualitatively, his argument would begin by considering not one or ten or a thousand, but all the unthinkable number of vibrating electrons that make up the subatomic surface of a glowing body. Each electron vibrates at its own unique frequency, describing a particular pattern of simple harmonic motion. Those vibrations that make extravagant energy demands have little chance of success; those vibrations that make modest demands have a better chance of achieving theirs. Both ends of the experimental curve, and Planck's empirical duplicate, fall off toward zero. Remember we are now considering our black body radiation curve (Fig. 8-10) to be a curve representing the probable distributions of all the many vibrations (energies) possible (Fig. 8-13). In the short wavelength end of the energy spectrum there is little chance of receiving a great burst of energy even though each burst would be very large: very energetic quanta, but low probability of emission due to low populations of such energetic electrons. On the other hand, at long wavelengths there is a much better chance of receiving what amounts to just about nothing: the probability of emission here is higher because

Figure 8-12
Buying and selling packaged energy.

of the higher population of electrons, but the energy quanta emitted are so very small they hardly count for very much. The maximum in the curve lies inbetween the low and the high energy region; in going from low to high energies, the distribution curve passes through a maximum; here is where all the action is because here is where the population density is at a maximum.

"h" Is Very Small and Has Strange Units

Planck's constant h shows up continually in all sorts of scientific experiments and observations. We measure it in a variety of ways and find (most recently) that it is 6.626×10^{-27} erg-seconds or

.00000000000000000000000000006626 erg-seconds

"h" is small. Very small. That in itself is interesting and suggests certain things as we'll note in a moment. But perhaps of greater significance are the units associated with h, namely erg-seconds. Ergs are energy units. What we have is a universal constant whose nature is the product of energy and time. Now when was it that you last felt the inclination to multiply energy by time? Divide energy by time to be sure. In your travels, that is commonplace. Simply divide the energy produced by your automobile by time and obtain the vehicle's horsepower. **Horsepower** is no more than energy output per unit time. Multiplication of energy by time, however, seems a bit strange on first inspection. Let's look closer.

Since Einstein and his famous theory of relativity, time has taken on new meaning. We live in a three-dimensional, space-occupying universe, but clearly events happen across intervals in time. As three-dimensional beings, we operate in a world of events that happen in an absolute four-dimensional universe. This fourth dimension is referred to as *space-time.* Now a quantity such as energy that we commonly view as having an instantaneous existence in three-dimensional space, really needs help to make it in a four-dimensional universe. By time-multiplication energy acquires a kind of universal thickness. Take a three-dimensional chunk of space, the state of Connecticut. Therein live more than two million persons. Now consider a chunk of four-dimensional space-time: the state of Connecticut between 1965 and 1975. Our description changes and we are now talking about twenty million person-years (two million persons across ten years). If we are to honestly picture the human composition of the universe in four dimensions, we need units that are limiting in space, and in time, too. That applies to the other contents of space as well. Energy is ergs in three-dimensional space, but it's got to be erg-seconds in space-time, or the four-dimensional universe (Fig. 8-14). That quantity is called action, and the units of h, erg-seconds, are the units of action.

Energy and time: the two components of action. Now the question is where in

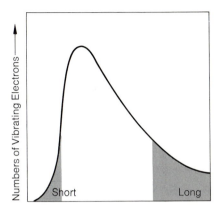

Figure 8-13
Black body curve representing the distribution of energies among large populations of particles: electrons on the surface of a glowing body.

3-dimensional space

Breadth

Width

Length

Time
4-dimensional
space

Figure 8-14
Multiplying by time.

all the realm of nature will we find energy sporting both components? What we're after is energy, uniquely identified with some definite time period. Perhaps propagating light waves with their period vibration. Atoms emit light in wave packages. We're not usually privileged to witness the discontinuity because we are dealing with a host of atoms all doing their thing. Many are emitting waves all the time and it all looks very continuous indeed. But each wave is made up of definite packages of energy with some characteristic period of vibration; a certain number of *ergs* with a particular period of vibration in *seconds.* The units of action. Sodium, mercury, helium, hydrogen, iron, oxygen; the ergs are all different; so is the period of vibration. But in every case, the erg-second product multiplies out to 6.626×10^{-27} erg-seconds or an integral multiple of it. Very short wavelengths such as cosmic rays from deep space; very long waves such as radio waves; 6.626×10^{-27} erg-seconds. Absorption of energy rather than emission? Yes, equally discontinuous.

□ 1905—Einstein Rediscovers "h"

What we have since Max Planck is the idea of an atom of energy, something common to all radiation processes, a quantum of action. There are eighty-eight elements freely distributed through nature, and there are unique atoms identified with each variety. Sodium atoms are not chlorine atoms. But there is only one quantum of action, h. We are confident of the truth in that statement whether talking visible light from a firefly, or thermal radiations that aren't visible at all. But we are left in an awkward state if you think about it for a moment: how in the universe can radiation be a smoothly flowing, continuous wave phenomenon, and at the same time, a discontinuous hail of particles? We know both perceptions are correct from a pile of accumulated facts. What shall we do about the paradox?

The year 1905 is notable because that was the year Einstein's famous theory was published. In that same year Einstein published a less famous work, but one of great significance to this new quantum concept in science, for which he was awarded a Nobel prize 16 years later. This paper had an auspicious title: "On a Heuristic Point of View Concerning the Generation and Transformation of Light." It was about the **photoelectric effect** (Fig. 8-15). When ultraviolet light is allowed to fall on a metal such as a freshly sanded zinc plate, electrons spill off its surface. That fact is experimental, but not especially surprising. Ultraviolet light is electromagnetic radiation, one form of energy. The truly remarkable feature is the kinetic energy of the bumped electrons. That depends only on the frequency (and wavelength) of the light, and is completely independent of the light's intensity. Increase the intensity and all you do is increase the *number* of bumped electrons, not their energy. From any classical understanding of the wave nature of radiation, we'd expect greater intensity, greater amplitude, and bumped electrons accelerated to greater speeds. After all it is the bigger waves at the ocean that more forcefully toss you off your feet. But those are not the facts for light. All the bumped electrons have the same speeds.

As far as the energy of the bumped electrons is concerned, *how much* light doesn't matter, only it's frequency. If the wavelength (frequency) of light falling on a metal isn't of a certain minimum energy, no electrons are bumped at all. Visible light won't do for zinc unless it's way down toward the blue, or ultraviolet region. We're best advised to use light of wavelengths shorter than 3500 Å, which is the effective photoelectric threshold wavelength for zinc. It is 2600 Å, for silver; and 2000 Å for platinum. Potassium is photosensitive in the visible region, its threshold wavelength being about 7000 Å.

Einstein Had a Way with Words

Heuristic was a nice word to use (Fig. 8-16). It refers to some devise or scheme, helpful in developing a concept—the quantum concept for example—that is not yet perfectly clear or in final form. A good description of the state of the art, circa 1905. The 26-year-old Einstein went on to explain the photoelectric effect. A beam of light is a bolt of energy, and in any such beam, light is packaged in units called *quanta*. The magnitude of each peak is simply stated in units of $h\nu$ where ν is the frequency of the light beam. Remembering that $\nu = c/\lambda$, the packs are hc/λ and $E = hc/\lambda$. The only thing the energy E depends on is the wavelength (λ) because h and c are constants.

Here we are then. A quantum of energy, $h\nu$, can be transferred to an electron at the metal's surface. To bump the electron, work must be done; the kinetic energy of the now suddenly free electron must be $h\nu - W$, the energy transferred to the electron by the incoming quantum from the light beam ($h\nu$), less the amount of energy expended as work W in getting free:

$$E_{\text{kinetic energy}} = E_{\substack{\text{quantum}\\\text{transferency}}} - W_{\substack{\text{energy-work factor characteristic}\\\text{of metal in question}}}$$

$$\text{K.E.} = h\nu - W$$

Here is one surprising illustration of the heart of the photoelectric effect: higher frequency light means higher energy free electrons; greater intensity light means greater numbers of free electrons. Sirius, is the head of the constellation Canis Major, the Great Dog, and is one of the stars nearest earth. Even so, its distance is great enough that light waves resulting from radiating atoms take 8¾ years to get here. As the light waves spread out, the energy carried along spreads out In a widening circle, but the frequency of the light remains unchanged. After the almost nine year trip, this now feeble light wave, more powerfully bumps electrons

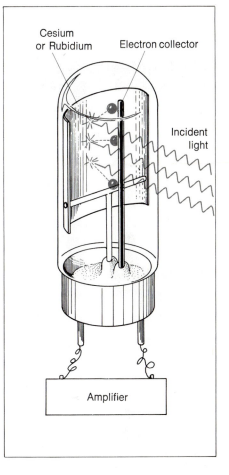

Figure 8-15
A schematic representation of a photocell and the photoelectric effect.

Figure 8-16
Our view of the universe was strange and new after 1905. Einstein's pronouncements were ''heady'' stuff indeed.

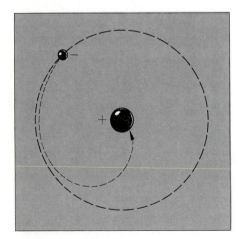

Figure 8-17
Rutherford's hydrogen atom would collapse whereas real hydrogen atoms do not.

free than does a full dose of sunlight. Sirius is a bluer star—shorter wavelengths—than the sun. The greater distance of Sirius from us does not weaken the electron-bumping capacity of the light that does get here; it simply reduces the number of effective electron-bumps.

Einstein's photoelectric effect provided the means for experimenting with and applying certain pieces of Planck's conceptual framework that had grown out of black body radiation. It is interesting to note the fact that Einstein wasn't initially aware of Planck's work, done five years earlier. However, Einstein's incisive views had a lot to do with the gathering awareness of the quantum of action among scientists of the day, and its ultimate impact. Putting the photoelectric effect into Planck's style, we can state that electromagnetic radiation propagating through space is packaged energy called photons. On meeting an electron, either the entire package of energy is transferred to the electron, or none at all. If you have light waves supplying one quantum to a billion atoms, you might expect to find the atoms absorbing one billionth of a quantum each. What is observed is that one atom in a billion absorbs one entire quantum, and all the rest have none. Smacks of statistics and probability, doesn't it. The gift that light waves bear to atoms is not a billionth of a quantum, but a billionth of a chance to win one whole quantum.

The developing quantum theory made it possible to get a giant step closer to understanding atomic structure and through the photoelectric effect, quantum theory provided the basis for a large number of significant practical applications. Among them one can count a variety of alarm and signal systems, the proverbial ''seeing eyes''; temperature control devices; automatic furnace control in the event of flame failure; sound reproduction on motion picture film . . . and the like (Fig. 8-15).

☐ The Rutherford Atom Was a Great Success, But . . .

The one great redeeming virtue of Rutherford's atom model lay in its value as an heuristic device . . . that word again. It promoted considerable thought and experiment almost at once. Here was a nice, picturesque theme, but not one we could live with for very long. Rutherford's model was predicated on the success of the α-particles scattering experiments. Those beautiful experiments of Geiger and ''young Marsden'' nurtured formulation of the theory and at the same time built in the requirements for obsolescence within a few short years. The scattering experiments showed a definite dependence on an inverse square law in the vicinity of that small, dense, positively charged nucleus. But what shall we do about those little negative electrons moving about the nucleus in a manner approximating the way planets move about the sun? A solar system arrangement is O.K. for *neutral* planets moving around an equally neutral sun, but electrons are moving charges and there are special laws governing the behavior of that kind of particle. A negative electron moving about a positively charged nucleus is constantly accelerated by the electrostatic force of attraction of the oppostie electric charges. Its much like swinging a stone overhead on a string; it all goes round in a circle until the string breaks because the centripetal force has become too great. But according to very well established and understood classical theory, such a circular acceleration must be at the expense of energy, by radiation. As the electrons lose energy, Rutherford's atom should *gradually* collapse (Fig. 8-17).

It was also known that atoms do in fact sometimes radiate, and when they do, they emit light. But there was something strange, for the light emitted by atoms in glowing gases was not continuous; instead, it was split into very clearly defined "spectral lines." Here was a bright line spectrum, not a continuous spectrum (Fig. 8-19). That was unexpected for if a hydrogen atom is falling apart, with its electron collapsing into the nucleus, a collection of hydrogen atoms should be in various stages of collapse, and we should see all of the various corresponding colors. Collapse of the electron into the nucleus should take place in a blaze of continuous color. Further, if you calculate the time for complete collapse from theory, it should all happen in a flash, not a blaze, perhaps only a hundred-millionth of a second being required. Contrary to fact? Sure! Hydrogen atoms exist, and they do so *permanently.* Classical theory must be incomplete.

Classical mechanics was fine for describing movement in a macroscopic world. However, it could not adequately describe the hustle and bustle at the atomic level. In the year 1913, a young Danish physicist (he was 28), Niels Bohr, showed us how to modify the traditional physical theory in such a way as to accept nature's facts (Fig. 8-20). He combined the quantum theory, newly learned from Planck and Einstein, with Rutherford's classical rendering of the atom's composition. The shockingly irreverent way in which Bohr was able to rationalize this

Figure 8-18
Schematic of continuous and line spectra.

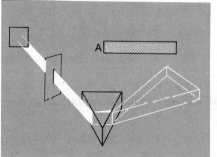
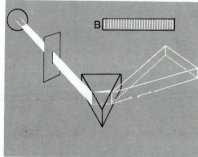

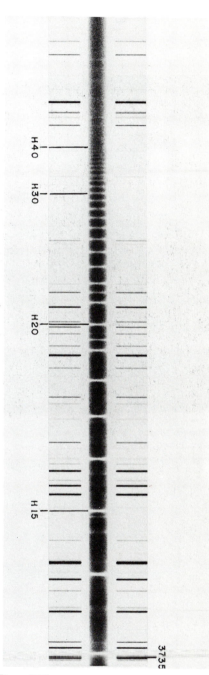

Figure 8-19
Part of the spectrum of the star HO193182 showing lines in the hydrogen spectrum at the edge of the visible region 3600-3900Å.

paradox of stable atoms that should instantly suffer a firey collapse was itself eventually shown to be naive. But Bohr's theory was the first application of the quantum hypothesis to questions of atomic structure, and the effect was electric.

Figure 8-20
Niels Bohr lecturing, during his first visit to the U.S.

☐ "On the Constitution of Atoms . . . ;" by Niels Bohr

Bohr had to make three principle assumptions:

1. Let's accept Rutherford's basic construction of a nuclear atom. But only a few of all the possible circular orbits are allowed, and electrons moving in any one of that select group of stable orbits must do so without any radiation being given off. No conventional electromagnetic radiation—no light of any kind—is given off in spite of what *classical* theory says.

2. Now turn to the allowed orbits, the select few. We'll have to establish very special selection rules for these few stable electron race tracks and to do that, let's turn to quantum behavior as our guiding principle. Electrons revolving about nuclei in stable orbits must never tamper with the preeminence of h, the quantum of action, or some simple whole number multiple of h such as 2h, 3h, 4h, . . . nh. The integer n will later be called the principle quantum number and it must be a whole number multiple of h. So the smallest possible orbit for orbiting electrons is $n = 1$; the next smallest allowed electron track is $n = 2$, and so on; and the only permitted orbits are those with action values of nh where n is always a whole number.

3. Electrons racing at Hialeah may be permitted to race at Tropical Park under certain conditions. That is to say electrons are permitted jumps between orbits, but in all cases these will be accompanied by a change in energy in the form of quanta. When an electron moves to an empty orbit, one quantum level further from the nucleus, say from $n = 2$ to $n = 3$, a quantum of energy must be absorbed by the electron. If the electron in the $n = 3$ level is too excited to stay there, it can jump back to an unoccupied $n = 2$ level, giving up one quantum of energy in the form of emitted radiation.

And if it all seems incredible, even Bohr noted at the time that it . . . "is in obvious contrast to the ordinary ideas . . . but appears to be necessary in order to account for experimental facts."

It was well-known that hot, excited, gaseous atoms radiated only certain frequencies of light. The characteristic bright-line spectrum of gaseous hydrogen and sodium vapor were not continuous but made up of colored bands on a black background. Each line is a representation of radiation of one particular wavelength, or frequency of light (Fig. 8-19). Hydrogen has its own fingerprint pattern of bright lines, and all the other elements do too. That is in marked contrast to the complex radiations we noted for white hot solids, or radiations emanating from a black box. In those cases we got the continuous range of "black body" radiation.

Hydrogen is the simplest atom. Its lone electron orbits a nucleus with a single positive charge. In the frequency range of the electromagnetic spectrum visible to the human eye, hydrogen gas shows a characteristic set of four lines. These lines arise from stimulated hydrogen atoms, vibrating and radiating light at a number of unique frequencies: hence, a set of distinct visible lines. There are sets of lines in the infrared and ultraviolet regions, too. These frequencies are the natural frequencies of vibration for the atom. They fall into a regular number series that can be represented by a simple formula. The formula says that the frequencies for the series of lines that we see (the visible series) are directly proportional to the difference between the inverse square of the number 2, and the inverse square of the succeeding integers, 3, 4, 5, and 6.

$$\text{frequency} \propto \left(\frac{1}{2^2} - \frac{1}{n^2}\right) \qquad \text{where } n = 3, 4, 5, \text{ or } 6$$

Doing our proportionality thing,

$$\text{frequency} = k\left(\frac{1}{2^2} - \frac{1}{n^2}\right)$$

The proportionality constant, is known as the **Rydberg constant** and is commonly designated R . . . not in any way to be confused with the universal gas constant which is also usually R.

$$\text{frequency} = R\left(\frac{1}{2^2} - \frac{1}{n^2}\right)$$

Fortunately, we know the value for the Rydberg constant (R) very precisely. Its equal to 3.289×10^{15}. Therefore, we can calculate the line frequencies for hydrogen and compare them to the experimentally observed values. Here's the way it looks for the four lines in the visible series:

$$n = 3 \quad \text{frequency} = R\left(\frac{1}{2^2} - \frac{1}{n^2}\right) = 3.289 \times 10^{15}\left(\frac{1}{2^2} - \frac{1}{3^2}\right)$$

$$= 3.289 \times 10^{15}\left(\frac{1}{4} - \frac{1}{9}\right) = 4.569 \times 10^{14}$$

$$n = 4 \qquad\qquad\quad = 3.289 \times 10^{15}\left(\frac{1}{2^2} - \frac{1}{4^2}\right)$$

$$= 3.289 \times 10^{15}\left(\frac{1}{4} - \frac{1}{16}\right) = 6.168 \times 10^{14}$$

$$n = 5 \qquad\qquad\quad = 3.289 \times 10^{15}\left(\frac{1}{2^2} - \frac{1}{5^2}\right)$$

$$= 3.289 \times 10^{15}\left(\frac{1}{4} - \frac{1}{25}\right) = 6.908 \times 10^{14}$$

$$n = 6 \qquad = 3.289 \times 10^{15}\left(\frac{1}{2^2} - \frac{1}{6^2}\right)$$

$$= 3.289 \times 10^{15}\left(\frac{1}{4} - \frac{1}{36}\right) = 7.310 \times 10^{14}$$

You need not be overly concerned with the calculations themselves. What is important are the results obtained. A comparison of calculated and measured frequencies reveals perfect agreement as shown in Table 8-2.

Fantastic agreement, but so what? Well, here is the 'so what.' Bohr was able to predict from theory, based on his three assumptions, the value for the proportionality constant R, the Rydberg constant. He got a value of 3.290×10^{15}. Near perfect agreement. Buried deep inside Bohr's prediction for the Rydberg constant was the quantum factor. In final, Bohr-polished form, the equation reads

$$\text{frequency } (\nu) = R\left(\frac{1}{n^2_{\text{final}}} - \frac{1}{n^2_{\text{initial}}}\right)$$

The two quantum numbers are n_f, the final resting place for the orbiting elect electron, its home track, and n_i, the initial location of the orbiting electron, its excited state. For the visible series, n_f was equal to 2 and n_i was equal to 3, 4, 5, 6.

Any Theory Worth Its Salt, Ought To Be Able To Predict As Well As Confirm

Let's see how good a predictor Bohr's theory turned out to be. Permitted orbits are stable orbits, and an electron can zoom about ad infinitum without ever radiating a single quantum of light energy. Radiation only takes place during a move from a higher energy track to a lower energy orbit. Consequently, for light to be emitted, an electron first has to get bumped up an orbit so there is potential available for falling back down. Emission spectra are due to excited atoms, and each bright spectral line marks a definite shift of an electron between orbits, occurring at one natural wavelength.

A second series of lines was also known to exist for excited hydrogen atoms at lower energies, in the longer wavelength, infrared region. Bohr's theory successfully explained both these two series, and strongly suggested the existence of other spectral series at still shorter and still longer wavelengths. Experiments eventually confirmed these predictions, too.

Putting it all together, Bohr's theory (1) succeeded at accounting for stability of the hydrogen atom, and all other atoms by analogy, (2) established a basis for understanding the existence of the families of lines in the hydrogen spectrum, and (3) predicted the spectroscopic Rydberg constant R whose number value was already precisely known by experiment. Of all the Bohr theory's permitted orbits, the lowest in energy lies closest to the nucleus. Normally this is where the electron in the hydrogen atom hangs out and we say that such an atom is in the "ground state," its most stable condition. That being the case, there is no way a ground state atom can radiate energy since the electron has no place to fall into. Therefore, for a hydrogen atom (or any other atom) to emit quanta of energy the electron must sit in a higher energy orbit. You may ask, "But how does an electron get into a higher Bohr orbit so it can fall back down?" Absorption of energy is the answer, and that takes place through collisions with the hotter atoms in any mass of gas atoms, in a spark, in an electric discharge, or perhaps during absorption of energy from light of the right frequency.

However excitation happens, an electron in higher orbit can now radiate surplus quanta when it falls lower. Should an electron fall from a third orbit to a second, that's one quantum jump. Should it fall from the third to the first, the quantity of energy emitted will be the sum of the two possible step-wise jumps, third to second, second to first. In fact each spectral series corresponds to collapse of the electron into a different *final* energy level. Here is a schematic representation in the form of an energy level diagram (Fig. 8-21).

Table 8-2

Calculated versus measured frequencies for the four lines in the visible series for hydrogen

Calculated	Measured
4.569×10^{14}	4.569×10^{14}
6.169×10^{14}	6.169×10^{14}
6.909×10^{14}	6.909×10^{14}
7.311×10^{14}	7.311×10^{14}

Reading from left to right: Wolfgang Pauli, Werner Heisenberg, Erwin Schrodinger.

The visible series marks a collapse to the n = 2 level from n = 3, 4, 5, 6; you might have anticipated that series to be higher energy (ultraviolet) since it would require more to lift the electron out of its most stable, ground state condition in the first place. Don't forget, emission or absorption of energy is all the same as far as the electron is concerned, except with direction reversed: n_f to n_i; n_i to n_f.

Perhaps it's less imaginative, but it is also equally less misleading as we'll see shortly, to make this same representation in the form of an energy level diagram. Same idea but now stretched out, and included is the energy needed to jump the electron from n_f to n_i in electron-volts (Fig. 8-23). Note what energy is

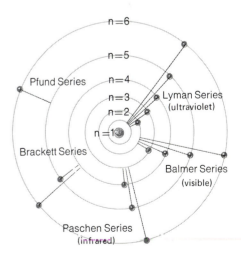

Figure 8-21
Schematic representation of energy levels for electrons in atoms.

required to jump the electron from n = 1 (ground state energy) to n = ∞ (infinity), the point where the electron is free of any influence of the nucleus, and that means it completely ionized; remember

$$H \longrightarrow H^+ + e^-$$

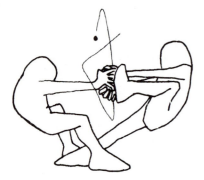

That's what we mean by n = ∞: 13.60 eV of energy are required. Bohr calculated that, too, from his theory, and by some pain-staking experiments arrived at a confirming value of 13.54 eV. Again, pretty good. All in all, a great success. A few words of caution before the neat representation of circular orbits and arrangements of electrons rising and falling becomes indelibly inscribed in your mind. All we've actually said so far is that atoms have well-defined, *permitted* energy levels, and quanta radiate away or are absorbed when some change in those energy levels takes place. All the rest is nothing more than pedagogic fiction —useful in getting a feel for the subject when communicating understanding, in postulating, in predicting—but not to be confused with reality.

☐ **"Monday (classical) and Tuesday (quantum) rules."**

If it appears to you that classical ideas about matter and energy in the universe are at loggerheads with the quantum hypothesis, be careful. Newton and Newton's laws have hardly been overthrown. The behavior of electrons in their permitted energy levels can be described classically, by the same laws that govern cars and trucks (well, not quite). It is only when electrons change from one energy level to another that they do so in a totally new way, as far as our understanding is concerned. Perhaps that seems rather arbitrary; nonetheless such a *dual* view has provided the basis for a coherent and more comprehensive theory. However, one cannot help but retain a sense of empathy for the pragmatic capitalist who practices one religion during the week and another on weekends. How shall we rationalize the sermon on the mount with the word from the lab?

The truth of the matter is both views must be right. It may well be that the fine-grained, quantum phenomena make for a more intimate view of nature's style than the coarse-grained view provided by our traditional perceptions. However, difficulties crop up especially when the two domains come together. Bohr grappled with this very problem and suggested a guideline known as the **Correspondence Principle.** The new and the old ways of viewing nature mesh: quantum hypotheses turn into classical laws when quantum numbers become very large. Under such a restriction, there is effectively no difference between the basic assumptions of both points of view. The old order has been incorporated into the new view of things. The electron hardly does different things one day than the next. It's all a matter of how you describe what it is the electron is doing. As one famous chronicler of this scene described it:

"I run down the stairs on Tuesday and slide down the bannister on Wednesday; but if the staircase consists of innumerable infinitesimal steps, there is no essential difference in my mode of progress on the two days. And so it makes no difference whether the electron steps from one orbit to the next lower or comes down in a spiral when the number of steps is innumerably great. The succession of lumps of energy cast overboard merges into a continous overflow. If you had the formulae before you, you would find that the period of the light and the strength of radiation are the same whether calculated by the Monday or the Tuesday method—but only when the quantum number is infinitely great. The disagreement is not very serious when the number is moderately large; but for small quantum numbers the atom cannot sit on the fence. It has to decide between Monday (classical) and Tuesday (quantum) rules. It chooses Tuesday rules."

What then shall be the criterion for Monday rules and Tuesday rules? Let's look to our two universal constants, the speed of light c and Planck's constant h. In Einstein's famous theory, he suggested c = 3.00 X 10^{10} cm/sec as the upper limit on the speed of any material particle, or the movement of energy through space. Classical treatment is quite adequate when speeds are small compared to the speed of light. Otherwise, the non-classical, relativity treatment must be used. Planck's constant, the quantum of action, is 6.626 X 10^{-27} erg-seconds. It is a small number. Whenever anything shows up having the dimensions of action, classical laws apply if it is very large compared to h. Otherwise the non-classical, quantum treatment must be used.

☐ Bohr's Energy Levels Are Real. Here's Proof

The experimental confirmation of Bohr's permitted energy levels for electrons about the nucleus was elegantly demonstrated in what is known as the Franck-Hertz Experiment, so named for the two German physicists who performed it in 1914 (Fig. 8-22). The work showed that energy in atoms is discontinuous, stepwise, or quantized . . . just as Bohr said. Here is what they did. Merucry atoms, in the form of mercury vapor, were bombarded with electrons in a tube at a low pressure. Franck and Hertz measured the kinetic energy of the electrons before they ran through the mercury vapor, and again afterwards. If the electrons lost energy, it should be because they collided with mercury atoms along the way. When slow electrons were used to begin with, then slow electrons came through the purple haze with virtually no loss in energy. *Explanation:* hitting a mercury atom whose mass is close to a million times the mass of an electron is like hitting a wrecking ball with a bee-bee. The collision is perfectly elastic; no energy is transferred from electron to mercury atom; after passing through the mercury vapor, the kinetic energy of the electron is essentially unchanged.

If, however, you turn around and zap the mercury vapor with higher speed electrons, a marked transfer of energy is observed. Let's assume that the slow electrons had an average kinetic energy of 3 electron-volts, hardly enough to move a mercury atom as the experiment showed. Therefore, afterwards we are left with 3 eV electrons. But if we up the energy of those incoming electrons to 6 eV, the departing electrons have only 1.1 eV. Something has happened. Energy is of course quantized and mercury accepts 4.9 eV; 6 eV went in; 1.1 eV came

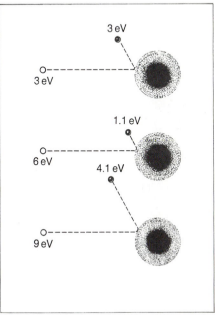

Figure 8-22
In the Franck-Hertz experiment, mercury vapor was bombarded with electrons. The results confirmed Bohr's ideas about "permitted" energy levels for electrons.

out; 4.9 eV were transferred. Mercury atoms are very particular and will have nothing to do with a paltry sum like 3 eV . . . or even 4 eV. They shunned those energy packs completely. Only 4.9 eV is minimally acceptable. O.K. Let's try 9 eV. How many eV come through? Yes, 4.1 eV. Again, 4.9 eV were absorbed. So it goes. Mercury in our Franck-Hertz experiment does in fact have a stable, permitted energy level with an energy 4.9 eV above the ground state energy level.

There is a nifty little addendum to this experiment. Bohr suggested that . . . radiation or absorption of energy, it's all the same. Therefore, when the atom decides to fall back to the ground state energy level from its excited, higher energy state, exactly 4.9 eV should radiate away. That is what was found. A characteristic green line whose wavelength is 2536 Å is emitted for which $E = hc/\lambda$ supplies the confirming calculation, 4.9 eV. Nice. Bohr must have been pleased for here was direct evidence of quantization of energy in atoms that would be very hard to deny.

☐ Then the Bohr Theory Changed!

The Bohr theory is one of the pivotal achievements of modern science. It is virtually indispensable to one's first understanding of the physical sciences in general, chemistry in particular. The Bohr theory successfully demonstrated the need for Planck's quantum of action and how it was related to the atom's insides. Perhaps the Bohr theory's greatest success was the tremendous burst of scientific activity that it initiated.

In the decade following their first proposal, Bohr's ideas underwent considerable development, modification and change. The Bohr theory led to deeper understanding, produced further experimentation, and suggested subsequent need for modification. Newton's theories underwent no significant change for 200 years. But now suddenly, these were modern times, and science began to witness an unprecedented acceleration of events. One decade was sufficient to bring about tremendous change. Here are the developments most important to the evolution of the Bohr theory. The essence of the matter is that we ended up with not one, but four of those quantum numbers. It takes four quantum numbers to give a complete description of the electron. It all worked out like this, at the time:

First: The first quantum number was Bohr's principal quantum number, *n*. Today *n* refers to the principal *energy level* for the electron. As we'll see a bit later, it is a moot point to argue whether it is the energy level that's quantized or the roving electron. In any case, it was the radial distance between electron and nucleus that had to be quantized (Fig. 8-23).

Second: Look very closely at the spectroscopic lines in hydrogen (Fig. 8-24). Each of the four single lines in the visible series turns out to be not single at all. All four are split, separate and distinct, but each only ever so slightly different from the principal spectral line. What that immediately implies is ever so slightly

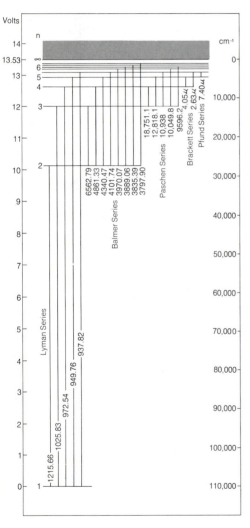

Figure 8-23
The quantum number model for describing the hydrogen atom. Wavelengths and transitions are shown for the principal spectral lines.

different energies. A Bohr energy level is really a group of energy sub-levels, each just slightly different. This could be explained by postulating elliptical rather than simply circular Bohr orbits for electrons. So now a second quantum number was needed to fingerprint the new component of the electron's energy that was causing the observed *splitting* of the principal spectral lines. At the time, it was ascribed to the electron's angular momentum.

Third: It was also known that if you caught a group of gaseous atoms while radiating quanta in a magnetic field, single spectral lines split into a variety of multiple line patterns. That had to do with the fact that the extranuclear electron produced its own magnetic field, which had to be quantized, too. A third quantum number was required to fingerprint that magnetic property.

Fourth: One more. It was thought that as the electron revolves about the nucleus, it spins on its axis. That's exactly analogous to the earth spinning about the sun while revolving around its own axis. If you study the behavior of a top or a gyroscope you'll see what's involved. A fourth, *spin* quantum number was necessary to characterize the atom completely. Further, it turns out to be important, if you are a spinning electron, to know whether you're spinning clockwise or counterclockwise.

Every electron is the same as every other electron. After all, haven't we designated electrons as elementary particles? Well, true enough. But inside any atom, no two electrons can be strictly identical in the following sense: they can't have all four of these identifying quantum numbers the same. Two the same? Yes, that's O.K. Three? O.K., too. But quantum theory puts this restriction on electrons in the *same* atom. No two can have all four quantum numbers equal. Strictly forbidden. That's called the *Pauli Exclusion Principle*. The four quantum numbers effectively constitute a non-classical fingerprint for all the electrons in an atom; the Pauli Principle keeps 'em honest.

☐ Some Necessary Bookkeeping

Right along with the development of the Bohr theory has come a bookkeeping system for keeping track of electrons in atoms, and their quantum number descriptions. The imaginary shells within which electrons are contained as they move about the atomic nucleus possess discrete energy level labels in the atom. The picture we've painted so far is that of a layered, onion arrangement. At the core is the nucleus; the first layer circumscribing it is referred as being at the $n = 1$ quantum level, or K shell. The other principal quantum levels also have capital letter designations; $n = 2$ is the L shell; $n = 3$, the M shell; $n = 4$, the N shell; $n = 5$, the O shell. Only two electrons are permitted in the K shell; eight are permitted in the L shell; eighteen in the M shell; thirty-two in the N shell; fifty in the O shell. Electron occupancy is governed by a simple $2n^2$ rule where n is the principal quantum number.

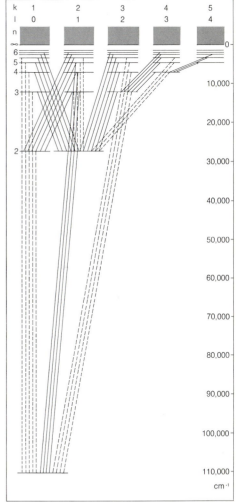

Figure 8-24
Closer inspection of principal spectral lines reveals a more complicated picture. The splitting of the principal lines (the fine line structure) is due to a whole host of other transitions.

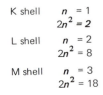

K shell $n = 1$
           $2n^2 = 2$

L shell $n = 2$
           $2n^2 = 8$

M shell $n = 3$
           $2n^2 = 18$

All the shells except the first divide into sublevels: the L shell consists of two sublevels; M has three; N has four: O has five. The K shell, then has up to two electrons occupying one principal energy level. For the second principal energy level, the L shell level, the lower energy of the two permitted sublevels has a two electron-capacity; the second sublevel contains up to six for a total of eight electrons in all—remember $2n^2 = 2(2)^2 = 8$.

Consider the M shell; a maximum of eighteen electrons according to $2n^2$, filling three discrete energy sublevels; the lowest energy sublevel can contain two electrons; next lowest sublevel can contain as many as six; and the highest energy sublevel, up to ten. You can see the kind of progression involved here. The N shell contains $2n^2 = 32$ electrons; and perhaps before we get any more details, let's stop to summarize the bookkeeping for the current theory in tabular form (Table 8-3).

□ Visiting with Mendeleyeff . . . Again

Now let's pause to try and put together some understanding of an earlier notion: chemical properties have to do with arrangements of electrons in atoms. We'll end up with a qualitative picture, but that will do quite nicely for our purposes here. What we are after is a modest connection between chemical properties and electronic structure. Remember that the total number of electrons in shells is equal to the number of positive charges on the nucleus, which equals the atomic number Z for the element.

Figure 8-25

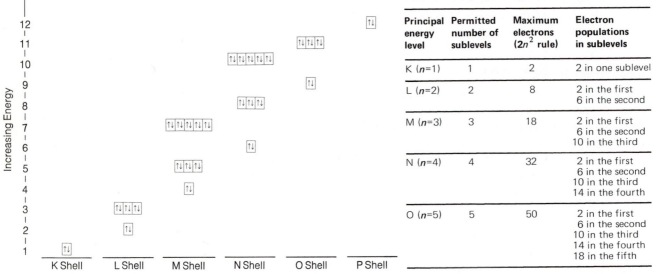

Table 8-3
Permitted "house plan" for electrons in atoms, including energy level labels

Principal energy level	Permitted number of sublevels	Maximum electrons ($2n^2$ rule)	Electron populations in sublevels
K (n=1)	1	2	2 in one sublevel
L (n=2)	2	8	2 in the first 6 in the second
M (n=3)	3	18	2 in the first 6 in the second 10 in the third
N (n=4)	4	32	2 in the first 6 in the second 10 in the third 14 in the fourth
O (n=5)	5	50	2 in the first 6 in the second 10 in the third 14 in the fourth 18 in the fifth

Building Up the Periodic Table of the Elements

Begin with hydrogen (Z = 1): one electron, one proton. There is no difficulty in assigning the electron to the K shell when the atom is in the **ground state.** Hydrogen atoms are extremely reactive, so much so in fact that you'll not find any uncombined H atoms anywhere except under extreme conditions.

With two electrons and two protons, the situation is quite different. Helium is extremely stable, so much so that you'll not find helium atoms chemically combined with anything else anywhere, except under extreme conditions. No more than two electrons are permitted in the K shell and that seems to be a reasonable decree based on the unusual stability achieved. Perhaps the qualitative implication of hydrogen's reactivity has something to do with a craving for the placid state of helium. By acquiring an electron any way it can, hydrogen achieves the helium arrangement and is suddenly stabilized . . . perhaps. The helium arrangement has two electrons in the same principal quantum level, with the same zero angular momentum quantum number, and identical magnetic properties, too. Three of the four quantum designations for the pair of electrons are the same. What distinguishes the two electrons, and makes the two energy levels ever so slightly different are their spin quantum numbers, one clockwise spin orientation, the other one counterclockwise. Again, please remember, this is a qualitative view. Don't try to ascribe too much reality to quantum number descriptions.

A third electron finds it impossible to gain entry into the K shell; it is full—remember only two electrons allowed. Lithium (Z=3) will have two electrons in an inside K shell and one electron, the third, at a new principal energy level, the n = 2 quantum level in the L shell. There are two things you might take note of here. First, this third electron, being alone at a greater average distance from the nucleus, will be less strongly held under the nucleus' dominating influence. It can therefore more easily be lost than those electrons in the K shell, allowing the atom to ionize, and to end up with the stable helium configuration (filled K shell—two electrons).

$$Li \longrightarrow Li^+ + e^-$$

This is one rationalization for lithium's strong chemical affinity for fluorine (Z = 9) which is only one electron short of the ten needed to fill the inner K shell (two electrons) and the outer L shell (eight electrons), achieving the neon structure (Z = 10). Neon is totally unreactive, inert, and helium-like. So helium and neon are close relatives, both featuring filled outer electron shells, the K shell in helium, the L shell in neon.

The second thing you should perceive here is this. If indeed helium and neon are alike because of their outer electron shell structures, shouldn't lithium be just like hydrogen in some ways? After all, both have a single outer shell electron,

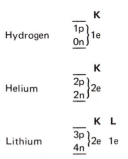

where p = proton, n = neutron, e = electron

H with its single K shell electron, Li with its single outer L shell electron. The answer is yes, *in some ways.* Hydrogen also ionizes to form a positive ion (+1); hydrogen is chemically reactive toward fluorine, and HF and LiF have certain similarities in common.

We jumped from Z = 3 (lithium) to Z = 10 (neon). What went on in-between? Well, placing a fourth electron with the third, fills the lower energy of the two L shell sublevels, and describes beryllium (Z = 4). The next six electrons all fall into the higher energy L shell sublevel taking us successively through boron (Z = 5), carbon (Z = 6), nitrogen (Z = 7), oxygen (Z = 8), fluorine (Z = 9), ending finally at *all-filled-up*, Z = 10 neon. It is worth noting one additional fact here: these last six electrons in neon are thought to be all *spin paired* or separated into three pairs of two each. To put it another way, that six-electron sublevel is made to consist of three pairs of electrons, all of equal energy with each pair spin-paired. What does spin-paired mean? Two electrons differ only in their spin orientation, the sign of their spin quantum number, positive or negative; clockwise or counterclockwise. We've thus subdivided the sublevels into pairs of electrons.

Beyond the L Shell

All the elements up to and including argon (Z = 18) are constructed in a straight-forward fashion as we have described for the first ten. After neon (Z = 10) with its filled complement of eight L shell electrons, no more electrons are permitted into the L shell for ground state atoms. The K shell, of course, was filled long ago at helium (Z = 2). An eleventh electron must go into the third principal quantum energy level, lying still further from the nucleus in the M shell. Are the chemical properties for sodium (Z = 11) similar to lithium? You bet. Six electrons further on brings us to chlorine (Z = 17), which is in many chemical ways similar to fluorine: seven outer shell electrons, two in the lowest energy M shell sublevel and five in the next lowest. Argon (Z = 18) is chemically similar to neon; both have the two electron-six electron sublevel arrangement in their outer shell (L shell for neon; M shell for argon); both elements are essentially inert.

Note that argon has achieved the stability associated with having the filled shell two electron-six electron sublevel arrangement, but that the entire M shell is not filled. There is a third energy sublevel capable of accommodating ten more electrons for a total of eighteen M shell electrons in all. Potassium (Z = 19) has one more electron than argon (Z = 18). However, in the ground state potassium atom, that electron is not part of the vacant M shell sublevel. The first energy sublevel within the next shell, the N shell, has a lower energy label. Following a *lowest first* pattern for the energy levels and sublevels in ground state atoms, potassium has this arrangement: K shell filled with two electrons; L shell filled with eight electrons, occupying two sublevels in a two electron-six electron grouping; M shell has eight of eighteen possible electron-occupants filling two of three sub-

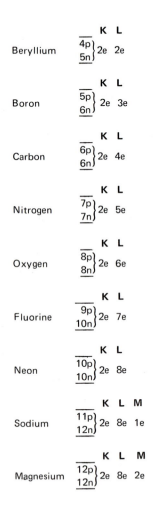

		K	L	M
Beryllium	4p / 5n	2e	2e	
Boron	5p / 6n	2e	3e	
Carbon	6p / 6n	2e	4e	
Nitrogen	7p / 7n	2e	5e	
Oxygen	8p / 8n	2e	6e	
Fluorine	9p / 10n	2e	7e	
Neon	10p / 10n	2e	8e	
Sodium	11p / 12n	2e	8e	1e
Magnesium	12p / 12n	2e	8e	2e

levels in the two electron-six electron arrangement; N shell, one lone electron in the lowest of four possible sublevels. Is potassium, with one outer shell electron, chemically similar to sodium and lithium? Yes, it is.

Relative energy level labels for isolated, gaseous ground state atoms can be illustrated with the aid of a diagram (Fig. 8-25). Each block containing up-down arrows indicates the spin-pairing of the electrons within a sublevel. If you carefully examine the table, you'll see that the nineteenth and twentieth electrons (potassium and calcium) are placed in the lower sixth (first N sublevel shell), ahead of the higher energy seventh (third M sublevel shell).

☐ Periodic Properties and Electronic Structure

We have placed the electrons in ground state atoms into fictitious shells, according to their principal quantum energy levels and sublevels. The electrons themselves are thought to be spread at various distances from the nucleus. In a qualitative way, the chemical characteristics of atoms have to do with the nature of such distributions and arrangements of the electrons (Table 8-4).

The Group A Elements

Only hydrogen deserves special periodic attention among all the elements. For reasons that will become clear shortly, hydrogen ought to be placed separately in the periodic table of the elements. Lithium, sodium, potassium, and rubidium belong to a family of elements known as the Group IA or alkali metal family elements. As the name "family" implies, they are all related by their chemical and physical properties, principally because of their unique electronic arrangement. All react with hydrogen to yield very active **hydrides:**

$$2\,Li + H_2 \longrightarrow 2\,LiH$$
$$2\,Na + H_2 \longrightarrow 2\,NaH$$

All form **oxides** of the general formula M_2O.

$$4\,Na + O_2 \longrightarrow 2\,Na_2O$$
$$4\,K + O_2 \longrightarrow 2\,K_2O$$

All react with water to form strongly alkaline, caustic, hydroxide solutions along with the evolution of hydrogen gas.

$$2\,K + 2\,H_2O \longrightarrow 2\,KOH + H_2$$
$$2\,Rb + 2\,H_2O \longrightarrow 2\,RbOH + H_2$$

In aqueous solution salts of all four metals yield the corresponding, solvated positive ions.

$$RbCl \longrightarrow Rb^+ (aq) + Cl^- (aq)$$
$$LiCl \longrightarrow Li^+ (aq) + Cl^- (aq)$$

		K	L	M	N
Aluminum	13p, 14n	2e	8e	3e	
Silicon	14p, 14n	2e	8e	4e	
Phosphorus	15p, 16n	2e	8e	5e	
Sulfur	16p, 16n	2e	8e	6e	
Chlorine	17p, 18n	2e	8e	7e	
Argon	18p, 20n	2e	8e	8e	
Potassium	19p, 20n	2e	8e	8e	1e
Calcium	20p, 20n	2e	8e	8e	2e
Scandium	21p, 24n	2e	8e	9e	2e

$$\begin{matrix} \text{LiCl} & \text{KCl} \\ \text{NaCl} & \text{RbCl} \end{matrix} \quad \xrightarrow{\text{in water}} \quad \begin{matrix} \text{Li}^+ \text{(aq)} & \text{K}^+ \text{(aq)} \\ \text{Na}^+ \text{(aq)} & \text{Rb}^+ \text{(aq)} \end{matrix} + \quad \text{Cl}^- \text{(aq)}$$

The IA family of elements in their free states are all extremely reactive because of their ability to "give up" one outer electron. That property also has to do with alkalinity; hence the name *alkali* family. The order of reactivity turns out to be Cs > Rb > K > Na > Li. One reason is that the outer shell electron in cesium is farthest from the electrostatic attraction of the positively charged nucleus; lithium's electron on the other hand is most tightly bound (Fig. 8-25). Cesium promptly catches fire in open air, reacting violently with both oxygen and moisture; lithium is reactive, but hardly the violent sort characteristic of cesium. Rubidium, potassium, and sodium lie in-between and have graduated properties. Conductors of an electric current? Remember our discussions of the movement of electricity in the last chapter? Good conductors have free electrons, electrons easily donated on simple chemical demand. The group IA elements fill that bill.

The left-side-of-the-table elements in general are "metallic". So are those comprising the big middle-block elements in the center of the table. What 'metallic' means in terms of characteristic physical properties is malleability and ductility; a lump of the element can be hammered into sheets and drawn into wires. 'Metallic' also means highly conducting, both electricity and heat. Metallic generally means lustrous. Right-side-of-the-table elements are considered non-metallic elements. There is also a diagonal group of intermediate-in-property semi-metallic elements ranging from boron and silicon through tellurium and polonium. By and large, metallic properties are most obvious for the elements lying lower left; elements occupying the upper right are most markedly non-metallic.

Each alkali group element is preceded in the periodic table by an element best described by the profile of an eight-electron shell; therefore unusual stability, and a general lethargy toward chemical reaction. Couldn't care less about entering into chemical combination. Cs (Z = 55), Rb (Z = 37), K (Z = 19), Na (Z = 11), Li (Z = 3) are preceded respectively by Xe (Z = 54), Kr (Z = 36), Ar (Z = 18), Ne (Z = 10), He (Z = 2). As a family these elements from He through Xe are referred to as the noble gas elements.

The VIIA family of elements are referred to as the halogens. F, Cl, Br, I are all characterized by a seven electron subshell content, just one electron away from noble gas, 8-electron shell stability. All four VIIA elements are efficient electron grabbers; contrast that with the electron-donating alkali metal family members. As the group IA elements are metallic, the properties of the group VIIA are characteristically non-metallic—but decreasingly so with atomic number.

Elements in IIA and VIA exhibit family-related properties as you follow them up and down the periodic table, too. Each in IIA is characterized by two outer

Table 8-4 The Periodic Table

	I A	II A	III B	IV B	V B	VI B	VII B		VIII		I B	II B	III A	IV A	V A	VI A	VII A	0
1	1 H																	2 He
2	3 Li	4 Be											5 B	6 C	7 N	8 O	9 F	10 Ne
3	11 Na	12 Mg											13 Al	14 Si	15 P	16 S	17 Cl	18 Ar
4	19 K	20 Ca	21 Sc	22 Ti	23 V	24 Cr	25 Mn	26 Fe	27 Co	28 Ni	29 Cu	30 Zn	31 Ga	32 Ge	33 As	34 Se	35 Br	36 Kr
5	37 Rb	38 Sr	39 Y	40 Zr	41 Nb	42 Mo	43 Tc	44 Ru	45 Rh	46 Pd	47 Ag	48 Cd	49 In	50 Sn	51 Sb	52 Te	53 I	54 Xe
6	55 Cs	56 Ba	57–71 *	72 Hf	73 Ta	74 W	75 Re	76 Os	77 Ir	78 Pt	79 Au	80 Hg	81 Tl	82 Pb	83 Bi	84 Po	85 At	86 Rn
7	87 Fr	88 Ra	89–103 **															

57 La	58 Ce	59 Pr	60 Nd	61 Pm	62 Sm	63 Eu	64 Gd	65 Tb	66 Dy	67 Ho	68 Er	69 Tm	70 Yb	71 Lu

Lanthanide series

89 Ac	90 Th	91 Pa	92 U	93 Np	94 Pu	95 Am	96 Cm	97 Bk	98 Cf	99 Es	100 Fm	101 Mv	102 No	103 Lw

Actinide series

shell electrons; each in VIA is characterized by six. The two left families, IA and IIA, and the last five, up to the noble gases, IIIA-VIIA, are related to each other in a special way: no unfilled *inside* shells. And as you might anticipate, there is a pronounced systematic transformation in properties going *across* the periodic table, from left to right, through the *periods* of elements.

The Group B Elements

The very large block of B family elements, IIIB through VIIB, IB, and the group VIII elements, taking up the entire middle of the periodic table, all *do* have space available for electrons inside the outermost shell. Each has some special, inside electron arrangement. That's a complication of sorts; still, it all makes sense in terms of figuring out how and why certain elements are related. For example, the first horizontal row from $Z = 21$ to $Z = 30$, scandium to zinc, is referred to as the first transition metal series. We placed electrons 19 and 20 in the first N shell sublevel, leaving still empty an inside M shell sublevel, capable of accommodating ten electrons. Potassium ($Z = 19$) and calcium ($Z = 20$) were just like sodium ($Z = 11$) and magnesium ($Z = 12$). But electron 21 gets placed back down into that third sublevel of the inside M shell. There are outer shell electrons, two of them, in the N shell; however, as we go from scandium to to zinc, we're filling that inner M subshell. Markedly different properties result. As a group these elements are referred to as *transition elements.* Note also a very special group of *inner transition elements* within the transition elements, known as the *lanthanide* and *actinide* elements, where we're filling a shell two layers deep (Fig. 8-25).

Our understanding of the periodic table is stronger now. Chemical properties depend on the distribution of electrons in atoms. Certain arrangements lead to inert gas stability; one electron more than that produces the highly reactive, alkali metals; an electron less results in highly reactive, nonmetallic halogens. And the Pauli Principle? Its limiting statement on an accommodation of electrons in energy levels was of critical importance to the advance of chemistry and to our understanding of atomic structure.

☐ Henry Moseley Performed a Key Experiment

Something should be said about the perception that *atomic number,* not atomic mass is the fundamental *raison d'etre* for the order of the elements in the periodic table (Table 8-4). It was Henry Moseley, while working in Rutherford's laboratory in 1913, who performed the key experiments showing that atomic number measures nuclear charge and electron content for the atoms. He found that when atoms of an element were blasted with a high speed stream of electrons, radiations of very short wavelength, in the X-ray region of the electromagnetic spectrum, were emitted. The radiation spectra consisted of sharp lines characteristic of the particular element being bombarded. The stream

Table 8-5

Wavelengths for the principal K-lines in the X-ray spectrum of some typical elements[*]

Element	Atomic number	Atomic weight	Wavelength of K-line
Manganese	25	54.93	2.10
Iron	26	55.85	1.93
Cobalt	27	58.94	1.79
Nickel	28	58.69	1.66
Copper	29	63.54	1.54

[*]Note that the atomic *weight* does not progress systematically with respect to the K-lines. Atomic number is the systematic ordering for the elements.

First at McGill University, then at Manchester, and later at Cambridge University, Ernest Rutherford turned out of his laboratories more than a dozen Nobel Prize winners trained in nuclear science. He himself won the Nobel Prize for chemistry in 1908 for his work on radioactivity. . . . "the greatest transformation of all," he liked to quip, referring to himself (a physicist by training and disposition) winning the Nobel Prize in chemistry.

Rutherford was a great teacher and his world famous laboratories set the tone and style for training a generation of scientists in the early years of the twentieth century.

Moseley was a Rutherford student whose researches were sadly interrupted by the opening of hostilities as World War I began in 1914. He managed to complete and publish his key paper on X-ray spectra and atomic weights with Rutherford before joining the British Expeditionary forces in 1915. He died in action in August of that year.

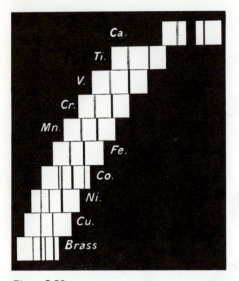

Figure 8-26
X-ray lines for a number of successive elements
as obtained by Moseley.

of electrons succeeded in knocking out an inner, K shell electron, leaving a
lower energy space available. An electron falling into the space radiates its extra
energy as an X-ray sized quantum. There was a clear relationship between the
wavelength of radiation emitted and atomic number (Fig. 8-26). For example,
Moseley made a graph of his data, plotting frequency against atomic number
squared. Moseley got a straight line when he connected the points.
The experiment was decisive. Moseley was himself an unfortunate victim of the
abortive British Gallipoli campaign in World War I during the summer of 1915
. . . at age 27.

☐ "Wavicles"

We conclude this chapter, with all of its truth-is-stranger-than-fiction ideas, with
the biggest fairy tale of all. It's called the theory of **quantum mechanics.** Newton's
theory was incorporated into the more pervasive, relativistic ideas of Einstein
after 1905. The Bohr theory developed, and during the period between 1923 and
1927, it too became part of a more pervasive theory, the new mechanics based
on the quantum of action. Quantum Mechanics is the most fundamental view we
have today for understanding the constitution of matter and energy in the
universe. Of course that is not to say it is the last word. In its day Newton's
theory held that same pre-eminent position. And in a much more limited way, the
Bohr theory was best in its day, too. Today the conventional view is a very unconventional set of ideas broadly termed "quantum mechanics."

Once upon a time . . . that's the way any forthright fairy tale should begin . . . I
think it was 1923, we understood electrons to be particles and we knew
photons exhibited wave properties. Electrons could do tricks like spin paddle
wheels, and clever people could measure their mass. Photons were light radiations,
and we could measure their intensity, wavelength, and frequency as with any
upstanding wave. Two things happened in 1923. One involved an American,
Arthur Compton, working in Rutherford's laboratory . . . did everybody work
in Rutherford's laboratory in those days? Seems so! The other involved a young
French physicist, Louis de Broglie.

We know from Einstein's explanation of the photoelectric effect that quanta
are packs of energy, hν in size. The question that arises is whether the quantum
of energy also has momentum associated with it. After all Newton's laws
certainly suggest considerable association of energy and momentum. We can
explore that possible association in a qualitative way. If you follow this simplified
calculation, I think you'll see a connection. Momentum is defined as the product
of mass and velocity. We know that from Chap. 4.

momentum = (mass) (velocity)
momentum = $m \times v$

Now ever since Einstein's famous theory, we know that energy is the product

of mass and velocity of light, squared:

$$E = mc^2$$

or,

$$m = \frac{E}{c^2}$$

Plug *m* into our equation for momentum and we now have

$$\text{momentum} = \frac{E}{c^2} \, v$$

Let's assume photons have momentum. Since photons only move with the speed of light, substitute their velocity *v* with c, the speed of light. That's reasonable, and the equation now becomes

$$\text{momentum} = \frac{E}{c^2} \, c$$

And making the appropriate cancellations:

$$\text{momentum} = \frac{E}{c}$$

But for a quantum of light, since Planck, $E = h\nu$ or in terms of wavelength rather than frequency, $E = hc/\lambda$

$$\text{momentum} = \frac{hc}{\lambda c}$$

Again, make the appropriate cancellations:

$$\text{momentum} = \frac{h}{\lambda}$$

Momentum has traditionally been an aspect of **particle** behavior; but our equation now suggests momentum has a wave nature, too.

In 1923, Arthur Compton found that a beam of high energy quanta, photons in the X-ray region, can be bounced off an electron in much the same way as when you try to hit the eight ball into the side pocket (Fig. 8-27). The change in wavelength of the scattered photons due to collision with electrons was what one would have predicted if photons were particles having a momentum described by the equation

$$\text{momentum} = \frac{h}{\lambda}$$

The photons in Compton's pool table style scattering experiments behaved very particle-like to say the least. There is momentum associated with a quantum of light.

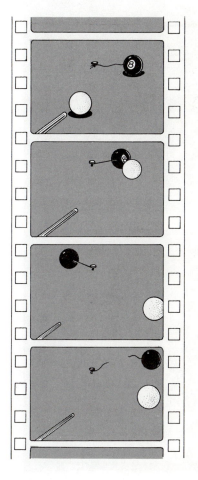

Figure 8-27
The Compton experiment confirmed the suggestion that photons have particle properties.

In that same year, Louis de Broglie proposed that as photons behave as particles or waves, so electrons must also exhibit this ambivalent behavior. Electrons should have wave properties. The reasoning is the same. For a particle like an electron of mass m, Einstein says $E = mc^2$; for a light quantum, Planck says $E = h\nu$. Setting the two equations for E equal to each other:

$$E = mc^2; \quad E = h\nu$$

$$mc^2 = h\nu$$

$$mc^2 = \frac{hc}{\lambda}$$

Making the appropriate cancellations:

$$mc = \frac{h}{\lambda}$$

Substituting the more general term v instead of c for velocity

$$mv = \frac{h}{\lambda}$$

The wavelength λ for an electron of mass m is given by the simple expression

$$\lambda = \frac{h}{mv}$$

The hypothesis that there are matter waves exhibiting measurable wave properties, such as wavelengths for substantive matter like electrons was confirmed in a classic 1926 experiment. Electrons were struck against a metal surface and scattered about. The scattered electrons showed a diffraction pattern as they passed through the arrangement of metal atoms in its crystal structure. The experimenters were two Americans working at the RCA Laboratories, Clinton Davisson and Lester Germer. A few years later, the experiment was repeated by a German, Otto Stern, using a molecular beam of sodium atoms in place of the electron beam. Again diffraction phenomena were observed. It was clear! Particles of matter no larger than electrons and atoms were more than what we had thought. Particles in motion have waves associated with them (Fig. 8-28).

What does it all mean? Waves? Particles? As one famous scientist has quipped . . . "perhaps as a compromise we had better call it a **wavicle.**" Our photon has properties of diffraction and interference expected for wave forms of light; but it also has momentum enough to play at a form of electron pool. The electron has mass and yet has a wavelength associated with it. "Wavicles," then, is about right. What's needed is a wave theory for matter that encompasses this wave-particle duality . . . quantum mechanical behavior.

De Broglie's thesis provided one guess why it was that the energy levels in the Bohr theory were quantized, or only specifically allowed. It was a naive guess by present standards of sophistication that has since been discarded. But it

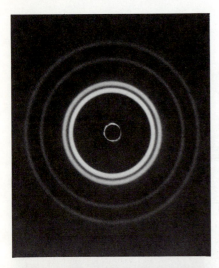

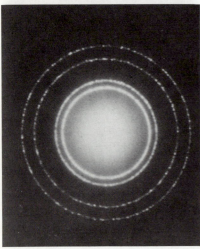

Figure 8-28
If particles are wave-like they ought to give well-defined diffraction patterns. Davisson and Germer demonstrated that for electrons. X-ray diffraction pattern (top) and electron diffraction pattern (bottom).

succeeded in directing our thinking onto the right track. Assume that the electron's orbit about the nucleus is of just the proper size to be an integral number of wavelengths. Going uniformly about the circle, only certain wavelengths will produce a continuous wave, exactly in phase (Fig. 8-29). That led Erwin Schrodinger, an Austrian physicist, to the complete generalization of the Bohr theory.

Schrodinger understood that although it was perfectly human to want to know which opposing behavior is the correct behavior—wave or particle—neither was *exclusively* correct. He perceived that we cannot describe the microscopic world of atoms and actions in the same terms and with the same models used in describing the macroscopic world of cars and trucks. The very fact that there is a wave-particle dilemma attests to that. Schrodinger's answer was mathematical, his equations corresponding fairly well with reality. But there is no physical model, only the mathematical one. There is no picture you can paint, conjured up from your experience. We can measure the energy of state 1 and state 2, and determine ΔE, the energy difference between the two states, and the $h\nu$ quantum of energy associated with that difference. But we are not permitted to know what happened when the photon was being emitted. What does the electron look like while it falls from the higher energy level to the lower? We know the higher; we know the lower; but we can't experience the event. All we get is a signal that the event took place; we know a quantum of light is emitted (or absorbed). What we have to do is learn not to ask: "Which model is correct?" or even try to imagine any model at all. We can't have it *both* ways . . . because it isn't both ways. Schrodinger's ideas and equations are of fundamental importance to the new quantum theory that developed after 1925, which we call quantum mechanics.

There is a very practical application of the wave-particle *duality* known as electron microscopy. It's worth mentioning briefly before moving on because electron microscopy has proven to be such a very powerful aid to the physical scientist. The electron microscope was established in principle the moment the wave character of the electron was perceived. An optical microscope makes use of light waves to produce the image of an object; an electron microscope uses a beam of electrons. Since electron waves are very much smaller than light waves in the visible region, microscopes of far higher resolving power are possible. The optical microscope cannot render details smaller than half the wavelength of light, but the wavelength of a beam of electrons is about one ten thousandth that of a light wave. So we have electron microscopes and they make magnificent images of nature (Fig. 8-30). The electron beam draws sillhouettes of the object for us on a fluorescent screen as much as 40,000 times enlarged, or if we choose to use photographic techniques, magnifications as high as 1,200,000 times can be obtained.

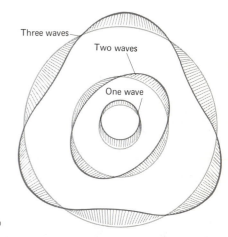

Figure 8-29
Circular wave motion.

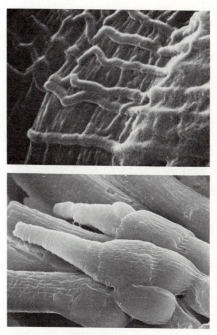

Figure 8-30
Electron micrographs from nature. Dendrites on the outer segment of a cone from a mudpuppy (top). Visual cone from the retina of the mudpuppy (bottom).

□ Reality and Uncertainty

The first break with the comfortable reality of our common experience came with Planck and Einstein. It promptly led to Niels Bohr with his circumspect perception of electrons racing round the atomic nucleus in quantized orbits. Broglie and Schrödinger, however, showed these electron-raceways to be waves, acting as guidelines for the electrons in their movement in the vicinity of the nucleus. (Fig. 8-29) The new descriptions produced results. We've never had such close accommodation to the properties of nature's atoms. Still, one is left with a quizzical "It somehow just doesn't seem right" feeling deep down . . . just a bit uncomfortable. But what you must remember is that modern theory in physical science has now progressed well beyond our daily experience and conventional ways of thinking. Model-building based on what we "know" just won't do. The quantum theory has indeed produced an unconventional concept, the existence of a smallest unit of energy that is a totally meaningless concept in the macroscopic world of our daily experience. At the microscopic level, the quantum theory has brought about radical changes in our fundamental thinking about the universe.

In 1927, the German physicist, Werner Heisenberg, showed us why we had to adjust to this diabolical scheme. He proposed an **Indeterminacy Principle,** the sense of which is this: We can exactly identify the position of a particle, or we can correctly measure the velocity of a particle, but we cannot determine precisely both the position and velocity of a particle *simultaneously.* For example, we can locate an electron precisely but not state its exact energy level. On the other hand, we can label an electron exactly as to energy level, but not locate it precisely. The frustration of quantum mechanics restated.

Consider determining the temperature of the water in your aquarium. You've probably got a big fat glass bulb thermometer, and that's entirely satisfactory for measuring the temperature in a five-gallon aquarium, or an eighty-gallon bathtub for that matter. But can you use the same thermometer to measure the temperature of the water in a thimble? Well, yes . . . if you are content with a certain margin of error and aren't going to make fancy claims like "The exact temperature is . . . " However, if exact temperature is what you're after, the aquarium thermometer is no good. It takes up so much heat out of the thimble itself that the measured level is considerably less that what it was we'd started out to measure. The measuring device is fouling up the measurement.
It's just the nature of measurement to involve the observer in the observation . . . and that involvement must always be reduced to some acceptable minimum impact. Well, then let's use a smaller thermometer, one that will make a smaller distrubance on our measurement, perhaps a thermocouple. That's the right idea in our daily, macroscopic environment. We can minimize the impact of a measurement by miniaturizing the measuring device to the point where the disturbance is less than the limits of experimental error in general.

Figure 8-31
The measuring device is fouling up the measurement.

But we're really stuck for it on the submicroscopic scale of atoms and molecules. Remember? Planck told us, and Einstein concurred, that we can't lower the amount of energy required to make a measurement to anything less than one single quantum. No way! And as far as our ability to exactly measure the motion of the electron in an atom? Well that's like trying to use our aquarium thermometer to determine the body temperature of an amoeba. But the real trauma lies in the fact that while we actually can get a thermometer small enough to accurately measure the amoeba's temperature, there is no way of getting less than a quantum of energy.

A diabolical scheme, no? We are prevented from observing what doesn't exist. We can't locate the electron in the atom . . . exactly. But that's O.K. All we have to do to be able to live with this is change what it is we regard as "complete description" of the universe. We must not limit our description of the universe to data drawn from direct or indirect sense observations. As one famous philosopher-scientist put it: "The description should include nothing that is unobservable but a great deal that is actually unobserved." The moon exists whether we are looking at it or not; and though we're not permitted to observe the electron's fall between two energy levels in an atom, we can recognize that the event happens.

So the Bohr atom was swallowed up by de Broglies waves, and then the electron, with its definite location and exactly measured velocity and momentum, dissolved into indeterminacy. All we have left is a measure of probability. Our model for the atom has become a probability pattern representing the shape and density for the time average distribution of the electron about the nucleus. That works out just fine.

☐ **Questions to Answer . . . Problems to Solve**

1. Offer a brief explanation of the following phenomena:
   (a) A glowing puddle of molten sodium gives off a continuous spectrum.
   (b) Sodium vapor produces a bright line spectrum.

2. We observe a surprising regularity in the visible spectrum emitted by excited hydrogen atoms. That regularity can be described by a single empirical relationship, namely

$$v = R\left(\frac{1}{2} - \frac{1}{n^2}\right)$$

   (a) Explain what the formula means.
   (b) Out of the Bohr theory came predictions of a "series" of spectral series based on the empirical relationship, one in the ultraviolet region, and

others at wavelengths beyond the visible region. Explain the existence of these series.

(c) Out of the Bohr theory came a theoretical prediction of the spectroscopic constant R. What was the significance of that fact?

3. The quantum theory suggested that light is composed of packs of energy called photons.
   (a) Describe Compton's experiment and his results.
   (b) What is the meaning of it all?
   (c) In what way is the momentum of a photon a function of the wavelength of the light?

4. If a photon is a particle, it is hardly the ordinary variety. You can't weigh a photon on a bathroom scale since they only exist at the speed of light. Examine your understanding of the wave properties of these speedy particles, covering the following points:
   (a) The principal features describing a wave, namely frequency, wavelength, and velocity.
   (b) Interference and diffraction.
   (c) Continuous and bright line spectra.

5. Periodic behavior should allow you to predict the properties for elemental bromine, knowing the same properties for the other members of the halogen family. Try predicting, and check your results against data in the Handbook of Chemistry and Physics (available in library or lab):

element	physical description	m. p.	b. p.	density at STP	ionization energy
fluorine	pale yellowish gas	−223	−187	1.695 g/l (gas)	17.42
chlorine	greenish yellow gas	−102	−35	1.3 g/ml (solid)	13.01
bromine	——	——	——	1.557 g/ml (liq)	——
iodine	violet black	+114	+184	4.93 g/ml (solid)	10.44

6. A practical manifestation of the photoelectric effect is the electric eye, or photocell. Cesium metal or cesium oxide is coated on one side of the cell and a potential is applied. Light striking the coated side bursts an electron free, completing the electric circuit, and for cesium atoms, 3.9 eV are required:
   (a) Using the fundamental Planck equation, determine what wavelength of light will do that job. (An electron-volt is equivalent to 1.6×10^{-12} erg).
   (b) Should you use visible light, an infrared lamp, or an ultraviolet source?

7. See what you can do with the following questions:
   (a) Although one observes doubly ionized helium atoms, one never observes doubly ionized hydrogen. Why not?
   (b) Would you *expect* to see doubly ionized lithium atoms? Is it possible under any circumstances?
   (c) Would you think that the emission spectrum of hydrogen ions (H^+) and helium ions (He^{++}) might exhibit certain similarities? Why? How about hydrogen atoms and He^+ ions?

8. How many electrons *per atom* can be at a principal quantum level, or in a specific shell? How many can fill a subshell? Orbitals have been likened to a housing arrangement for electrons. How many electrons can be so housed in orbitals?

9. A hydrogen atom is very complex, even though it is the simplest atom. Its very complex emission spectrum attests to that. And by the way, why do you think the spectrum is so complex, being composed of those several spectral series?

10. A hydrogen atom is struck by some sort of high energy particle causing its electron to reach the $n = 5$ energy level. After a while, the electron's energy decreases to the $n = 2$ energy level, emitting visible light. What was the energy of the photon emitted? If the electron's energy had fallen to that of the ground state, what would the emitted energy have been?

11. Consider the Bohr theory:
    (a) Why was it necessary?
    (b) What were its principal assumptions?
    (c) How was it modified in the years immediately after 1914?
    (d) Why has it been more or less abandoned in favor of the quantum mechanical view?

12. Lithium salts find extensive applications in fireworks demonstrations because lithium atoms have a strong red emission line in the visible spectrum at 6710 Å. Calculate the energy associated with an excited lithium atom dropping back to the ground state in (a) ergs; (b) electron-volts; (c) kcal/mole.

13. In order to produce the proton in the following dissociation,

$$H \longrightarrow H^+ + e^-$$

a total of 13.527 eV is required per mole of atoms. Calculate
    (a) the energy per atom;
    (b) the energy in kcal/mole;
    (c) the photons of minimum wavelength to do the job.

14. Describe the evidence for the existence of energy levels in atoms.

15. Describe the Franck-Hertz experiment. What was its significance? Predict the kinetic energy of 4.5 eV electrons exiting from a fog of mercury atoms after collision. How about 5.5 eV electrons? 10 eV electrons?

16. Based on the positions of the elements in the periodic table, identify the atoms of:
    (a) metallic character
    (b) non-metallic character
    (c) ease of loss of electrons
    (d) empty inside subshells
    (e) inert gases

17. You are a member of a chemical debate society and you've been given the task of defending the position that hydrogen belongs as first member of the IA alkali metal family of elements. Defend that contention! Then defend the opposite contention, that it ought to be first of the halogen family, the VIIA elements.

18. Helium has only two outer shell electrons. All of the other inert gases have eight. Yet helium is a full-fledged member of the inert gas family. Explain.

19. Here are some data. See if you can explain the obvious trends based on your newly developed understanding of atomic structure:

Ionization Energy in Electron-volts Required for Removal of a Single Electron.
$(M \longrightarrow M^+ + e^-)$

Li	C	F	Ne
5.39	11.26	17.42	21.60
Na	Si	Cl	Ar
5.14	8.15	13.01	15.76
K	Ge	Br	Kr
4.34	8.13	11.84	14.00
Rb	Sn	I	Xe
4.18	7.33	10.44	12.13

(a) Moving down through the four families, ionization energies steadily decrease.
(b) Moving across the four periods, ionization energies steadily increase.
(c) The ionization energy for hydrogen is 13.527 eV. Why is it so much higher than that for the other IA family members?
(d) The ionization energy required for removal of the second electron from lithium is 75.60 eV. Why should it be some fifteen times greater than for removal of the first electron?

20. Making use of the periodic table of the elements identify
    the following elements as metallic, non-metallic, or semi-metallic:
    (a) aluminum (Al)   (f) iodine (I)
    (b) barium (Ba)   (g) molybdenum (Mo)
    (c) boron (B)   (h) selenium (Se)
    (d) cesium (Cs)   (i) uranium (U)
    (e) germanium (Ge)   (j) zinc (Zn)

21. Give a brief explanation of why the kinetic energy of the "bumped"
    electron in the photoelectric experiment has less energy than the light that
    bumped it.

22. Since Moseley, we've known that the properties of the elements are a
    periodic function of their atomic number. Explain Moseley's work, and the
    meaning of that statement.

23. Explain the principal reason for observed similarities between the elements
    lithium, sodium, and potassium. Would you expect beryllium, magnesium,
    and calcium to be similar? How about comparing oxygen, sulfur and
    selenium to fluorine, chlorine, and bromine?

24. Briefly explain your understanding of each of the following:
    (a) $2n^2$ rule   (f) $Z = 19$
    (b) shells, subshells, and orbitals   (g) Al^{3+}
    (c) K, L, and M shells   (h) noble gas configuration
    (d) transition elements   (i) group IA elements
    (e) alkali and halogen families (j) group B elements

25. You must have realized by now that one of the things scientists do is
    propose theories, even before all the facts are in. But that's O.K. because
    those discarded theories prove to be useful stopping points for developing
    keener perception. Where does the redeeming virtue in the following
    theories lie?
    (a) Thomson's atom model
    (b) Rutherford's atom model
    (c) Bohr's atom model

26. One of the frustrations of science is the perception of beauty. On the one
    hand, the Bohr theory produces a beautiful physical model for atomic
    behavior. But the beauty in quantum mechanics lies in its success at
    explanation, no physical model being possible at all. Explain briefly.

□ **Perceptions and Deceptions**

1 Alchemy is a modern profession . . . and Ernest Rutherford and Frederick Soddy were the first of the new breed of alchemists.

2 A horizon is a limit beyond which we cannot see . . . but about which we can speculate. That's the way it was in those early years of radioactivity and nuclear structure . . . lots of speculation about unseen events.

3 Speeding α-particles spend a lot of their time and energy making neutral atoms into ions.

4 Atomic nuclei are full of lots of strange subatomic particles, not simply protons and neutrons.

5 Interfering with the atomic nucleus has strongly interfered with the course of natural history.

6 A gram of radioactive material produces about as much heat as a couple of tons of coal.

7 The very largest machines are needed to push around the very smallest particles.

□ **Radioactivity Is a Property of the Nucleus**

The history of radioactivity is intimately connected to Wilhelm Röntgen's accidental discovery of X-rays, along with the great discoveries that opened up this century: Planck's quantum hypothesis, Einstein's photoelectric effect, Rutherford's nuclear atom, Bohr's theory, and Moseley's determination of atomic number as the natural order of the elements. Before 1940 the prospects for finding elements beyond atomic number 92 did not appear promising. But then numbers 93 and 94 were prepared synthetically. Today the count runs to about 106. Those at the tail end of the series, from 84 to 92 and beyond, and any new ones you may read about next month or next year, will likely be unstable, or **radioactive.** Consequently, the synthetic elements beyond 92 are absent from today's roll call of the elements in nature. The radioactive elements spontaneously emit certain radiations resulting from changes taking place in their nuclei.

Reprise! Atomic number is the essential label for nature's elements. It is the number of unit positive charges (protons) in the nucleus and is equal to the number of unit negative charges (electrons) moving about the nucleus of a

Of all the amazing stories that make up modern science, none has been more so in the public view than the discoveries concerning the structure of matter and the atomic nucleus. It all began with those mysterious X-radiations emanating from within. Suddenly, there seemed to be a lot of truth in the predictions of the science fiction writer: Jules Verne, H. G. Wells, Arthur Clarke—**Amazing Stories** is the cover from a science fiction magazine published in June 1928.

Getting at the Heart of Matter

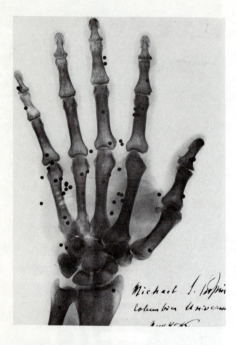

Figure 9-1
Professor Michael Pupin of Columbia University was asked to "X-ray" the hand of a New York attorney accidentally shot. Done in February of 1896, it's one of the earliest medical X-rays.

neutral atom in what we now understand (but cannot depict) as quantum mechanical style. Chemical reactions are generally believed to be a function of changes taking place among the outer electrons, so it follows that chemical properties are a function of atomic number. Inner electrons are different from outer electrons because they are held more tenaciously by the opposite charge on the nucleus. The innermost electrons, placed in the *K* shell, are almost completely insulated against chemical change, except in the case of the very lightest elements such as hydrogen and helium which have only *K* shell electrons. Moseley showed that removing these otherwise secure *K* shell electrons resulted in characteristic X-rays being emitted when another electron falls into the hole left behind. (See Fig. 8-26.) So to get an atomic number, just compare the characteristic X-rays produced by bombardment of metallic targets with high speed electrons. The lines in the X-ray spectrum progressively shift to shorter wavelengths as the atomic number of the element being bombarded increases. However, the end-of-the-table elements not only give off X-ray photons of energy *without* being bombarded at all, but also give off α-particles and β-particles from time to time, becoming *transmuted* into other elements, eventually stable ones. Here was transmutation of the elements, the alchemist's dream in modern garb.

The New Rays of Professor Röntgen

The last days of 1895 and the first weeks of the year that followed were a dramatic period in science. Professor Röntgen's rays were pure science fiction, though clearly there was no fiction here. Röntgen had been experimenting with cathode rays generated in Crookes type discharge tubes. His astonishing discovery has been recorded in his own words in a newspaper interview some six months after the event. It is an interesting period piece, documenting one of the most important discoveries in modern science (Fig. 9-1).

"Now, Professor," said I, "will you tell me the history of the discovery?"

"There is no history," he said. "I have been for a long time interested in the problems of the cathode rays from a vacuum tube as studied by Hertz and Lenard. I had followed theirs and other researches with great interest, and determined as soon as I had the time, to make some researches of my own. This time I found at the close of last October. I had been at work for some days when I discovered something new. I was working with a Crookes tube covered by a shield of black cardboard. A piece of barium platinocyanide paper lay on the bench there. I had been passing a current through the tube, and I noticed a peculiar black line across the paper. The effect was one which could only be produced, in ordinary parlance, by the passage of light. No light could come from the tube because the shield which covered it was impervious to any light known, even that of the electric arc."

"And what did you think?"

"I did not think: I investigated. I assumed that the effect must have come from the tube, since its character indicated that it could come from nowhere else. I tested it. In a few minutes there was no doubt about it. Rays were coming from the tube which had a luminescent effect upon the paper. I tried it successfully at greater and greater distances, even at

2 meters. It seemed at first a new kind of invisible light. It was clearly something new, something unrecorded."

Röntgen's Rays Are X-rays

Certain substances exhibit **fluorescence,** the property by which energy is absorbed from an ultraviolet source and then emitted as visible light. If you are a rock hound, you know that certain rocks do that. Barium platinocyanide is known to be fluorescent. But in Rontgen's experiment there was no such light source present. Perhaps cathode rays could produce the same optical phenomenon, but it was well-known at the time that they were not capable of traveling more than a few centimeters in air. Röntgen made the correct judgment. Fluorescence here was not the usual fluorescence but was due to **X-rays,** a new ray of unknown nature. Rontgen continued his study. In seven short weeks he was able to describe just about everything we know to this day about X-rays.

X-rays can easily pass through a variety of substances from sheets of paper to lead foil. Flesh is transparent to these penetrating rays, more so than bone; so we have the basis for a new medical technique: bones can be photographed without removing them from surrounding flesh. Place a hand upon a protected photographic plate, one covered with heavy black paper to exclude all light. X-rays passing through hand and paper expose the plate, showing differences in density according to whether they passed through bone, cartilage, muscle, or just plain flesh. Within weeks, laboratories of the physicists were jammed with physicians bringing in their patients for medical X-rays. And there the patients sat, having broken bones X-rayed to the accompaniment of a maze of buzzing sounds, strange glows, and weird illuminations, all the while exposing themselves for half an hour at a time to strange radiations with little knowledge of their hazards (see Fig. 9-2).

Figure 9-2
First application of X-rays in America on February 3, 1896. At Dartmouth College a young patient's fractured arm was photographed (bottom). Early medical X-ray equipment constructed in 1896-1897 (top).

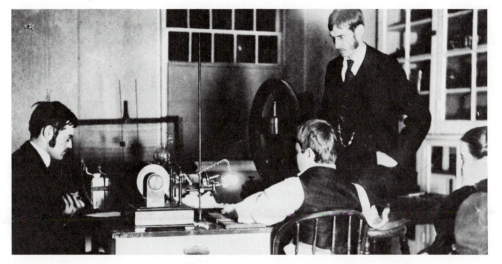

THE MARCH OF SCIENCE.

INTERESTING RESULT ATTAINED, WITH AID OF RÖNTGEN RAYS, BY A FIRST-FLOOR LODGER WHEN PHOTOGRAPHING HIS SITTING-ROOM DOOR.

THE NEW ROENTGEN PHOTOGRAPHY.

"LOOK PLEASANT, PLEASE."

Figure 9-3
"Oh, Röntgen, then the News is true,
   And not a trick of idle rumour,
That bids us each beware of you.
   And of your grim and graveyard humour."
"The March of Science." From *Punch*, March 7, 1896 (top).
"Look Pleasant, Please." From *Life*, February 27, 1896 (bottom).

Professor Röntgen's discovery was the first modern scientific event to be given banner, front page headlines in the newspapers of the day. The publicity and coverage parallels the news stories surrounding the atom bomb and the moon landing. Story followed story for weeks and weeks. There was a strange fascination for these mysterious rays. Victorian spinsters went fully clothed into their baths in the belief that the mad scientists had penetrating rays that could see through stone walls and peep around corners. Here, too, was an entry into the world of Jules Verne and modern science fiction (Fig. 9-3).

☐ Radioactivity: The Spontaneous Transmutation of the Elements

France has always been a country with a deep sense of national pride. After vintage French wines, the three-star restaurants in the Michelin Guide, and fashions by Dior, perhaps nothing has been more rewarding than French science. Lavoisier and Pasteur were giants; radioactivity was a giant discovery, and all-French in its origins. The principals were Henri Becquerel, and a husband and wife team, Pierre and Marie Curie.

Becquerel's Flight Into History . . . .

As with Röntgen's discovery of X-rays a few months earlier, this discovery took the form of an experimental accident to a prepared mind. Becquerel was an expert on the subject of fluorescence. Röntgen had showed the source of the X-rays in the discharge tube to be the fluorescent spot at the other end of the tube where the beam of cathode rays struck the glass wall. Turning the power off caused the spot to fade while the X-rays ceased. Becquerel was curious. Did the fluorescent glow at the spot where the cathode rays hit the glass have anything to do with X-rays and their ability to photograph all those "inside" bones? Sure enough! Becquerel turned up a salt of the element uranium that was indeed fluorescent, and gave off penetrating rays that exposed photographic plates. But that turned out to have nothing to do with the observed fluorescence; rather, it was due to the spontaneous disintegration of the atomic nucleus. His own words describe the great discovery; the first communication is dated 24 February 1896:

With the double sulfate of uranium and potassium, of which I possess some crystals in the form of a thin transparent crust, I was able to perform the following experiment:

One of Lumiere's gelatine-bromide photographic plates is wrapped in two sheets of very heavy black paper, so that the plate does not fog on a day's exposure to sunlight.

A plate of the phosphorescent substance is laid above the paper on the outside and the whole exposed to the sun for several hours. When later the photographic plate is developed, the silhouette of the phosphorescent substance is discovered, appearing in black on the negative. If between the phosphorescent substance and the paper there is placed a coin or a sheet of metal pierced with an openwork design, the image of these objects can be seen appearing on the negative (Fig. 9-4).

A second note appeared 2 March 1896:

Among the preceding experiments, some were prepared on Wednesday the 26 and Thursday the 27 of February, and, as on these days the sun appeared only intermittently, I held back the experiments that had been prepared, and returned the plate-holders to darkness in a drawer, leaving the lamellas of the uranium salt in place. As the sun still did not appear during the following days, I developed the photographic plates on the first of March, expecting to find very weak images. To the contrary, the silhouettes appeared with great intensity. I thought at once that the action must have been going on in darkness.

Photographic plates wrapped in paper and kept in drawers were exposed. Plates wrapped in aluminum foil produced images that were somewhat weaker but quite distinct as well. (If you use a disk of metallic uranium instead of the uranium salt, the effect is stronger still.) It was clear that the uranium salt had exhibited the same fantastic property as Professor Röntgen's rays, but these rays had been generated spontaneously. This was the first discovery of natural radioactivity.

What Immediately Followed Was to Become the More Famous Work

Marie Curie and her husband found a second element, thorium, gave off the same X-type radiations. That was really significant. This strange phenomenon was not unique to uranium. Furthermore, thorium and uranium were very heavy elements (at the end of the atomic number line) perhaps implying special properties for these most massive of the elements. In addition, the intensity of the X-radiations was directly proportional to the quantity of the radioactive element present in the salt sample or particular ore being investigated. Possibly most important of all was the discovery that the quantity of radiation was completely independent of whether you made measurements hot, cold, under water, in the dark, chemically combined or pure metal, other things present or not. Whatever, emission of X-rays depended only on the number of uranium atoms present.

Next came the discovery of two new elements, both radioactive, from the uranium oxide ore known as **pitchblende**. The Curies found the ore to be several times more radioactive than predicted, based upon the uranium atom content. Two other elements present in the pitchblende (bismuth and barium) were not radioactive. What conclusion can be drawn? Well for one, the presence of new elements *more* radioactive than uranium itself! In July 1898, **polonium** was discovered, and six months later, **radium**. Polonium was several hundred times more radioactive than uranium; radium was still more radioactive, showing twice the radioactivity of polonium. From several tons of pitchblende the Curies chemically concentrated and prepared a gram of pure radium bromide. The great unanswered question was what it all meant. How were these X-rays being violently and spontaneously ejected from the atom's nucleus? What was going on inside these radioactive atoms that were in other ways so typical, chemically (Fig. 9-5)?

Röntgen, Becquerel, the Curies: X-rays, radioactivity, radium and polonium: all

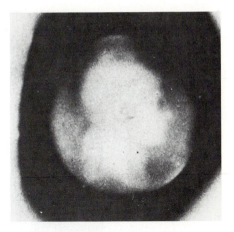

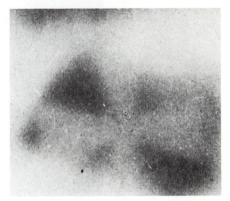

Figure 9-4
Bequerel's original researches into radioactivity with a coin and a cross, faintly seen on the photographic plates.

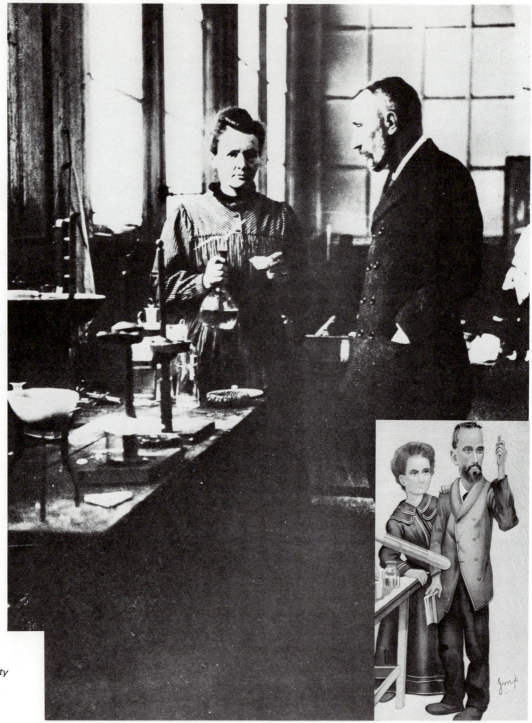

Figure 9-5
The Curies in their laboratory; caricature from *Vanity Fair* (inset).

across the short span of a few years. And if you think that's mind-bending, remember what else happened in the midst of all that, and because of it: J. J. Thomson discovered the electron (see Chap. 7). One of the really exciting things about the discovery of X-rays and radioactivity was that these rays, generated by a cathode discharge or emitted spontaneously from radioactive substances, produced *ions*. They produced ions in the air or just about anywhere else they traveled. These rays were powerful, *ionizing* radiations. In fact, Thomson discovered that you could measure radioactivity by the amount of ionization.

□ The New Alchemy

Radioactivity turned out to be much more complex than these early discoverers believed. For example, these radiations were made up of not one, but three kinds of rays, *alpha* (α), *beta* (β), and *gamma* (γ) rays. Of the three, the most penetrating were least ionizing, or least effective at knocking electrons off of atoms in their path:

Gamma-rays are most penetrating, being able to pass through thick lead plates at distances several feet from the source. They are electromagnetic radiations very much on the order of Röntgen's X-rays, ranging in wavelength from 10^{-10} m

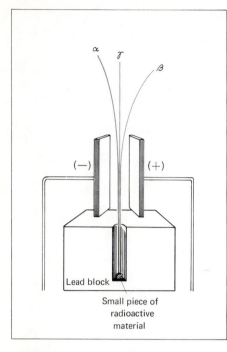

Figure 9-6
Separating alpha, beta, and gamma rays on passing through a magnetic field.

down to 10^{-13} m. They do not cause ionization of surrounding atoms.

Beta-rays will penetrate sheets of paper and metal foils such as aluminum, travelling short distances of a foot or two in air. They are effective at ionizing gases, making them conducting, and have been shown to be high-speed electrons with velocities ranging from 30 percent to 99 percent of the speed of light.

Alpha-rays are the least penetrating of the three. They don't stray much beyond a few inches from the source and are stopped cold by a thin metal foil or a few thicknesses of tissue paper (see Table 9-1). It was demonstrated that these particles are doubly charged helium ions moving about 5 percent of the speed of light (when unaccelerated). The α-particle was Rutherford's nuclear bullet for penetrating the atom and establishing the planetary model (see Fig. 9-6). So here we are with a strange, violent, explosive world to explore. Charged atoms of a light element, helium, exploded from nuclei of much heavier atoms, leaving new transmuted elements in their place.

Examining This Strange World Within

An atom of radium, element 88, splits loose an α-particle from its nucleus, and in doing so, transmutes itself into radon, element 86. The radioactive decomposition succeeds in producing a new element whose chemistry is entirely unique and unrelated to the old one. Compare the behavior of radium with that of radon. Radium is a dense, typically reactive metallic substance that falls at the bottom of IIA, the alkaline earth family, in the periodic table. As with its predecessors, radium forms compounds in which the metal is characteristically divalent: $(BeCl_2)$, $(MgCl_2)$, $(CaCl_2)$, $(BaCl_2)$, and $(RaCl_2)$. Any collection of radium atoms, chemically combined or otherwise, will lose particles, leaving behind a growing collection of radon atoms. Radon is very dense, chemically inert, belonging to the noble gas elements in the far right column of the periodic table: helium, neon, argon, krypton, xenon, and radon. A chemical equation—a *nuclear* chemical equation—can be written to describe the event.

$$^{226}_{88}\text{Ra} \longrightarrow {}^{222}_{86}\text{Rn} + {}^{4}_{2}\text{He}$$

Check the notation carefully. It will be used extensively in describing chemical reactions in this chapter. The convention places the atomic mass of the atom

Table 9-1
The three particles in radium emanations and other radioactive decompositions

Name	Identity	Relative charge	Relative mass	Penetrating power
α-ray	He^{++}	+2	4	1
β-ray	nuclear e^-	−1	1/1837	100
γ-ray	electromagnetic radiation	0	intrinsic	1000

as the superscript and the atomic number as the subscript. Together these numbers identify the proton-neutron composition of the nucleus. More will be said about neutrons shortly. For the moment, all you need to realize is that if atomic number designates the number of protons on the nucleus, and atomic mass is the total number of protons and neutrons, their difference identifies the neutron content. Examples: Radium (atomic mass 226, atomic number 88) has a nuclear composition of 88 protons and $226 - 88 = 138$ neutrons; radon (atomic mass 222, atomic number 86) has 86 protons and $222 - 86 = 136$ neutrons; helium (atomic mass 4, atomic number 2) has two protons and $4 - 2 = 2$ neutrons. Eliminating an atom of helium from a radium atom subtracts 4 from radium's atomic mass and 2 from its atomic number. That leaves you with an element of atomic mass 222 and atomic number 86, describing the element radon $^{222}_{86}$Rn. The parent atom, radium, has given birth to a daughter (see Table 9-2).

Here's another parent-daughter relationship, uranium atoms giving off helium atoms from their nuclei

$$^{238}_{92}U \longrightarrow {}^{234}_{90}Th + {}^{4}_{2}He$$

Note that the α-particle, $^{4}_{2}$He, makes up the nuclear difference between an atom of uranium and an atom of thorium.

The naturally abundant form of radioactive $^{232}_{90}$Th slowly decomposes by elimination of α-particles. You ought to be able to determine the new element left behind as the helium ion departs. If you figured it to be radium because the atomic number of the new element is 88, you're correct. Here's the nuclear equation

$$^{232}_{90}Th \longrightarrow {}^{228}_{88}Ra + {}^{4}_{2}He$$

But wait a minute. Radium was 226 – 88, not 228 – 88, and didn't we write thorium as 234 – 90, not 232 – 90? What's going on? Well, the atomic numbers are the same. That puts 88 in the radium slot in the periodic table and 90 in the thorium slot, but in both cases the neutron count is different. Look at radium: $226 - 88 = 138$ neutrons in the first case, and $228 - 88 = 140$ neutrons in the

Table 9-2
Nuclear assembly for three different atoms

Element	Atomic mass	Atomic mass	Protons	Neutrons
Uranium "parent"	238	92	92	146
Thorium "daughter"	234	90	90	144
Helium	4	2	2	2

second case. What shall we do about that? We must of course accept two different kinds of radium atoms because their existence is experimental. Their usual chemistry is the same because the number of extranuclear electrons is the same. Remember? Atomic number equals protons in nucleus which equals number of outer electrons in the neutral atom. So the difference lies only in the total mass because there are different numbers of neutrons. Atoms of the same element having different atomic masses, as in these two kinds of radium and thorium atoms, are called *isotopes.* Most of nature's elements have two or more isotopic forms. Just glance ahead for a moment to Table 9-4.

Nuclear transmutation also takes place by β - particle elimination, or loss of an electron from the nucleus of an atom. Beta-particles are indistinguishable from *ordinary* extranuclear electrons. Think of the neutron with its one unit of mass and neutral electric character as being made up of a proton of unit mass and an electron of negligible mass. That amounts to a neutral particle of one mass unit. When β-emission frees an electron from the nucleus of a parent atom, a proton from the breakup of the neutron is left behind. As a result, the atomic number goes up by one, and that's all. The atomic mass stays just about the same since loss of an electron amounts to essentially no loss at all. For example, a radioactive isotope of lead produces an isotope of bismuth when β-emission takes place.

$$^{210}_{82}\text{Pb} \longrightarrow {}^{210}_{83}\text{Bi} + e^-$$

It's worth noting that the new atom will be an *ion*, unless the expelled electron

Table 9-3

The uranium-radium family tree

Element	Symbol	Particle emitted	Half-life
Uranium	$^{238}_{92}\text{U}$	α, γ	4,510,000,000 years
Thorium	$^{234}_{90}\text{Th}$	β, γ	24.5 days
Protactinium	$^{234}_{91}\text{Pa}$	β, γ	1.14 minutes
Uranium	$^{234}_{92}\text{U}$	α, γ	267,000 years
Thorium	$^{230}_{90}\text{Th}$	α, γ	83,000 years
Radium	$^{226}_{88}\text{Ra}$	α, γ	1,620 years
Radon	$^{222}_{86}\text{Rn}$	α	3.823 days
Polonium	$^{218}_{84}\text{Po}$	α	3.05 minutes
Lead	$^{214}_{82}\text{Pb}$	β, γ	26.8 minutes
Bismuth	$^{214}_{83}\text{Bi}$	β, γ	19.7 minutes
Polonium	$^{214}_{84}\text{Po}$	α	0.000164 seconds
Lead	$^{210}_{82}\text{Pb}$	β, γ	21 years
Bismuth	$^{210}_{83}\text{Bi}$	β	4.85 days
Polonium	$^{210}_{84}\text{Po}$	α, γ	138.4 days
Lead	$^{206}_{82}\text{Pb}$	——	stable

emitted from the nucleus can be slowed down and captured into a "bound" state. Mass and nuclear charge must always be conserved.

Emission of γ - rays during radioactive transformations affects neither the atomic mass nor the atomic number but frequently accompanies α- or β- decay. That process is simply photoemission of some particular short wavelength quantum at the high-energy end of the spectrum.

☐ Half-lives and the Radioactive Decay Series

Perhaps all the elements that exist were here on that day when the universe was born but in all likelihood there were actually more elements than there are today. However, the really unstable ones have long since decayed and disappeared. Those radioactive elements that remain are forever moving in a downhill direction, energy-wise, constantly being transmuted toward ultimately stable elements. At some distant moment the last uranium atom will decay and we'll be left with synthesis as our only means of obtaining atoms of Z = 92 just as is true today for all those elements heavier than uranium. That's true for radium and thorium, as well as the elements beyond bismuth.

The different radioactive elements vary in their stabilities. We talk about their relative stabilities in terms of their respective half-lives, or the time it takes for half the radioactive atoms present to change. Radium—226 is modestly unstable. If you have a stockpile of 1,000 atoms, you'll have 500 left 1,620 years from today. And 1,620 years after that, 250 will remain; 125 will still be left after a third 1,620 year period passes, and so on. Why 1,620 years? Because that's the half-life for the $^{226}_{88}$Ra isotope of radium. That means in any pile of $^{226}_{88}$Ra atoms it's even money that any one atom will decay in the next 1,620 years; and of those that don't, the odds are fifty-fifty that they'll split in the next 1,620 years. The probability of decay is 0.5 (Fig. 9-7).

Radon, the daughter element, $^{222}_{86}$Rn, is far less stable, decomposing with a half-life of approximately 4 days into an isotope of polonium. Every four days, half the radon present decays. Here today; half here 4 days later; only a quarter left 4 days after that. Measure the pressure *P* due to gaseous radon atoms in a container (at constant *V* and *T*, of course) and after 4 days it falls to *P*/2, then to *P*/4 in a total of 8 days; and so on. The new daughter atom, polonium, is even more unstable. It has a half-life of only 27 minutes, and so the decompositions go until it all finally ends with transformation into a stable isotope of lead, in this case, $^{206}_{82}$Pb. We can describe the behavior of this half-life characteristic of radioactive decay by drawing a generalized curve on a graph that fits all these decaying elements perfectly. Graph the number of parent atoms present versus time elapsed in half-lives, or the time required for half the parents to decay into daughters. It could be seconds; it could be centuries. Let's call it $t_{1/2}$ whatever it is. Our plot for a million molecules with half-life of $t_{1/2}$ is shown in Fig. 9-8.

IF HALF OF YOU AIN'T OUTA HERE IN 1620 YEARS I'LL THROW YOU OUT!

Figure 9-7

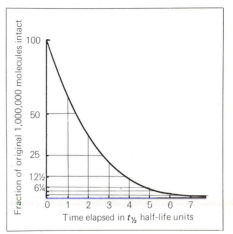

Figure 9-8
Radioactive decay.

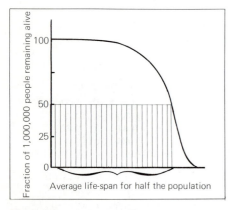

Figure 9-9
When it comes to half-lives, people just aren't the same as radioactive elements.

Here's a small subtlety in this "decay law" describing radioactive behavior. We are dealing with the probability of any single atom decaying. It may or it may not. But in a statistically representative group of such atoms we can say that if the half-life is 50 years, essentially half are gone after 50 years have passed. The half remaining are strong and healthy, and no different than they were 50 years earlier. Not so for any statistically representative group of people. Half the students in your class may be dead 50 years from now, but the other half won't be in such good shape either and it's doubtful if *any* will be left alive 50 years after that. People-decay follows a different decomposition law than that governing decay of radioactive atoms (see Fig. 9-9).

If you trace the descent of radium-226 and its daughters, ten generations can be identified before the lineage ends at a stable isotope of lead. Some of the transmutations involve α-particles, some β-particles, and sometimes both. Often during α- and β-decay, gamma rays are emitted as well. But the decay series actually began five generations before radium-226 with uranium-238. Remember it was from pitchblende, the uranium-bearing ore, that radium and polonium were isolated and identified by the Curies. The entire 15-generation uranium-radium decay series takes us from $^{238}_{92}U$ through $^{226}_{88}Ra$ to $^{206}_{82}Pb$ (see Table 9-3).

In addition to the radioactive elements belonging to the uranium-radium family, and three other such decay series involving the heavier elements in the periodic table, there are a few other naturally-abundant isotopes of radioactive elements. Samarium-148 has a half-life of hundred millions of years; a potassium isotope with a half-life of hundreds of millions of years produces a daughter, argon, found in the atmosphere; Rubidium and lutetium also have abundant long-lived radioactive isotopes. And there are others.

☐ Isotopes of the Elements

In studying radioactive decay and natural transmutations of the heavier elements, how shall we explain things like *three* kinds of lead in the uranium-radium family tree; what shall we do with three kinds of polonium? Bismuth and uranium show up twice each, a heavier and a lighter. We've already indicated that as far as common chemical properties are concerned, these isotopic forms all qualify as lead and polonium, or bismuth and uranium. No new slots in the periodic table are necessary. If the isotopes have the right atomic number (the right number of protons in the nucleus and electrons about it) they qualify; 82 for lead, 83 for bismuth, 84 for polonium, 92 for uranium. Most of the "stable" elements exist in groups of isotopes as well.

A question that you might ask is: "How shall we examine these mixtures of atoms?" How do we analyze a bag of lead isotopes, copper isotopes, or neon isotopes? The obvious answer is to take advantage of the only difference between isotopes, their relative masses. Some are heavier than others because some have more neutrons. Remember that the study of cathode rays, those beams of negative ions in the discharge tube, led to discovery of the electron and measurement of the charge-to-mass ratio, e/m. If we use a discharge tube similar in design to J. J. Thomson's tube for determining e/m (see Chap. 7), electrons can be knocked out of gaseous atoms to create positive ions. Electrons coming off the cathode effectively bump other electrons out of neutral, gaseous atoms that happen to get in their way. As a result, a beam of positive ions, or **canal rays** moving in the opposite direction to the flow of the cathode rays is created (see Fig. 9-10).

The mass and charge of those beams of positive ions can be determined by causing them to be deflected in electric and magnetic fields. To be able to do this proved tremendously important to the separation and identification of isotopes of the elements, and to chemical analysis in general. The technique is called **mass spectrometry.** The instrument used in this technique today, a mass spectrograph, is a far cry from those early models that established the principles and practice of mass spectrometry. For one thing, atomic masses and individual atoms could be determined for the first time by using just a tiny speck of material, with an accuracy approaching a few parts per million. Until this discovery was made practical in the early 1920s, atomic weights were all determined chemically: find out how much of an element combines with a given amount of another of known atomic weight; call H = 1 and O = 16 and take it from there. Because of the importance of atomic weights to the study of chemistry, the value of the mass spectrograph with its capacity for sorting atoms and molecules according to mass cannot be overestimated.

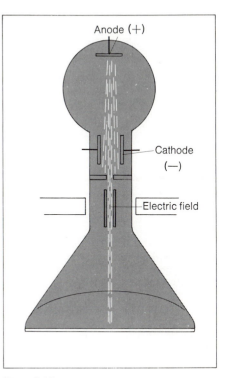

Figure 9-10
Canal rays move in the opposite direction to the flow of cathode rays. They are streams of positively charged ions.

How a Mass Spectrograph Works . . . In Principle

Start with an evacuated chamber containing a small quantity of gaseous atoms or molecules (Fig. 9-11). Neon was studied first so let's use it to illustrate our discussion. Neon atoms are allowed to leak through a pinhole and between a pair of electrodes which changes them into ions by removing an electron. These ions are then caused to accelerate uniformly through slits by a potential difference which selects only ions of about the same average energy for passage. From there the selected beam of positive ions moves through the field of a powerful electromagnet that bends the beam from its intended path. The force to which any ion responds as it moves through this system is proportional to its own electric charge. If we assume, for simplicity's sake, that only one electron was bumped off, then the bending force is proportional to $+e$. As is true for all moving bodies, the ion's inertia is proportional to its mass $m.$ The deflection of the beam of positive ions passing through the fields is determined by e/m, the ratio of the charge on the ions to its mass. However, for ions of identical charge, the mass difference will determine the deflection, light ions being deflected farther. Measure the deflection, e is a constant, and therefore the deflection is

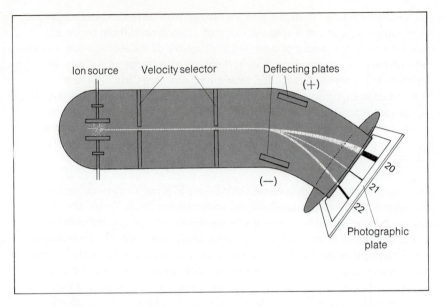

Figure 9-11
Schematic representation of the mass spectrograph. The photographic plate shows separation of the isotopes of neon, mass 20, 21, and 22 respectively.

proportional to *e/m*, or *e* (1/*m*). Taking this one step further, deflection is inversely related to relative mass.

Here, then, was the way to experimental determination of absolute masses for atoms and absolute atomic weights. Natural neon separates into three beams which can be made to fall on a photographic plate. The main beam contains 90.92 percent of the neon ions having a relative mass of 20. There is a less intense band on the plate at the location indicating mass 22, containing 8.82 percent of the neon ions. A faint band appears in-between at mass 21, accounting for 0.26 percent of the neon ions. These same results can be obtained electronically as a chart recording or a computer print-out.

Average Isotopic Masses

So we have three kinds of neon atoms, neatly resolved and quantitatively measured, all chemically and spectroscopically the same but having different atomic masses and whole number masses at that. That's really interesting because for the longest time the chemical determination of atomic weights always gave *almost* whole number values. For example, neon's was carefully determined to be 20.179; sort of 20, but not quite. But now we know. Plain old everyday neon is a mix of three neon isotopes, and when we determine the mass, what we're determining is the average mass of neon 20, 21, and 22 according to their distribution in nature. The average is 20.179. Take a look:

$^{20}_{10}$Ne . . . 90.92% = 0.9092 (20) = 18.184

$^{21}_{10}$Ne . . . 0.26% = 0.0026 (21) = 0.0546

$^{22}_{10}$Ne . . . 8.82% = 0.0882 (22) = 1.9404
                                          20.179

Neon wasn't bad. We could live with 20.179 as being close to 20. But what do we do with chlorine, atomic mass 35.453? The mass spectrograph and the isotope concept solve our problem. The natural abundance of chlorine in nature is a mix of $^{35}_{17}$Cl and $^{37}_{17}$Cl, and the mix is distributed as follows:

Chlorine-35 . . . 75.53% = 26.4358

Chlorine-37 . . . 24.47% = 9.0539
                          35.4894

The average mass is 35.4894. In the mass spectrograph, two bands show up, one about three times the intensity of the other. Table 9-4 lists a number of other elements and their isotopic distribution in nature. A very few elements such as gold and iodine are 100% of a single isotopic mass.

Table 9-4
Stable isotopes in nature

Element	Atomic number	Isotopic mass	Nuclear symbol	Percent natural abundance	Experimental average atomic mass
Hydrogen	1	1	$^{1}_{1}$H	99.9844	1.008
		2	$^{2}_{1}$H	0.0156	
Lithium	3	6	$^{6}_{3}$Li	7.42	6.941
		7	$^{7}_{3}$Li	92.58	
Oxygen	8	16	$^{16}_{8}$O	99.76	15.9994
		17	$^{17}_{8}$O	0.037	
		18	$^{18}_{8}$O	0.20	
Potassium	19	39	$^{39}_{19}$K	93.10	39.102
		40	$^{40}_{19}$K	0.0119	
		41	$^{41}_{19}$K	6.89	
Molybdenum	42	92	$^{92}_{42}$Mo	15.05	95.94
		94	$^{94}_{42}$Mo	9.34	
		95	$^{95}_{42}$Mo	15.79	
		96	$^{96}_{42}$Mo	16.56	
		97	$^{97}_{42}$Mo	9.60	
		98	$^{98}_{42}$Mo	24.00	
		100	$^{100}_{42}$Mo	9.66	
Iodine	53	127	$^{127}_{53}$I	100	126.9045
Gold	79	197	$^{197}_{79}$Au	100	196.9665

The Isotopic Principle Resolved an Old and Unsettling Supposition

Prout, a contemporary of Dalton, suggested at the beginning of the nineteenth century that atomic masses for the elements were multiples of the mass of hydrogen, the lightest element: Prout's Hypothesis. That's a fair assumption if you pick your elements carefully. Check the list of atomic masses (Chap. 2) and you'll find lithium, carbon, nitrogen, oxygen, sodium, sulfur, uranium, and many others to be very close to whole numbers. Perhaps there is merit in the suggestion that atoms are built of hydrogen building blocks. But what could Prout or anyone else do with chlorine, whose atomic mass was chemically determined as 35.5. The mass spectrograph showed there was no such mass 35.5, but rather a mix of mass 35 and mass 37, distributed so as to average out to 35.5. To the disappointment of just about every chemist from Prout to Mendeleyeff, and on into the early years of this century, this very appealing idea couldn't quite hold water. It just wasn't possible to construct a theory for the elements in which one, or at best a very few basic particles in combination accounted for all. Still, Prout's hypothesis was a rare idea in principle and became established in practice (in modified form) when it was realized that all atomic nuclei are made of common constituents: not hydrogen atoms as had been suggested, but protons and neutrons.

One last note about the masses of the atoms before we go on. Except for carbon, atomic masses for the isotopes of the elements are still not quite whole numbers. We'll see why a bit later in this chapter. Since 1964 the accepted convention for relative atomic weights is to consider the relative mass of the $^{12}_{6}C$ isotope of carbon as the standard of reference, mass 12.0000. A single atomic mass unit (amu) is defined as 1/12 that of the carbon-12 isotope.

☐ Dating—with Radioactive Carbon

High-energy cosmic ray neutrons in the upper atmosphere collide with nitrogen nuclei, causing stable nitrogen-14 isotopes to become transformed into a radioactive isotope of carbon, carbon-14, with half-life of 5668 years:

$$^{14}_{7}N \ + \ ^{1}_{0}n \ \longrightarrow \ ^{14}_{6}C \ + \ ^{1}_{1}H$$

In a period of time estimated to be about 500 years, carbon-14 becomes part of the terrestrial carbon cycle. Thus, during the lifetime of the radioactive isotope, it enters all living things, a fact which has led to one of the most fascinating applications of the modern study of radioactivity, *radiocarbon dating*. It is primarily the work of an American chemist, Willard Libby, developed after World War II. Here is how it works.

Carbon dioxide is the photosynthetic food of life for plants. Carbon-14 reacts with oxygen in the atmosphere right along with the stable, carbon-12 isotope, producing a wind-mixed distribution of radioactive carbon-14 carbon dioxide and *regular* carbon-12 carbon dioxide:

$$^{14}_{6}C + O_2 \longrightarrow ^{14}_{6}CO_2 \qquad \text{(unstable carbon isotope)}$$

$$^{12}_{6}C + O_2 \longrightarrow ^{12}_{6}CO_2 \qquad \text{(stable carbon isotope)}$$

Photosynthesis fixes both isotopic forms of carbon in plants, and in that way carbon-14 is introduced into animals as well. A balance is eventually established between carbon-14 intake and its radioactive decay in living materials. Death of the organism, whether plant or animal, completely removes it from the life cycle and the radiocarbon clock begins to tick. The *ticking* is based on the 5,668-year half-life. After 5,668 years, there will only be half the radiocarbon atoms left; another 5668 years pass and there are only half again as many. Carbon-14 inexorably decomposes. The extent to which decay has proceeded measures the time elapsed since removal of the organism from the life cycle—in short, since death. Cells are being constantly replaced in the living organism. Therefore, the carbon-14 composition at the moment of death should be the same as the average carbon-14 composition of the atmosphere. As long as the organism lives, constant replenishment for decomposing atoms takes place. It is death that seals the system from further replenishment and starts the clock winding down.

Charcoal is a perfect substance for carbon-14 dating. Since humans are the only animals that can make fire, and since a fire's charcoal remains are chemically inert to just about everything, carbon-14 dating is also perfect for studying human history. In Fig. 9-12 the 14,000-year-old gravesite has been dated by carbon-14 analysis of scraps of charcoal and wood found in it. Flesh, skin, hair, horn, nails and other carbonaceous animal remains serve to date objects and places. California's giant sequoias have been dated at 2,900 years, and Egyptian tombs at 4,900 years; the oldest living things today, the Bristlecone pines of the

Figure 9-12
The age of this 14,000 year old burial site was determined by radiocarbon dating (left). Linen wrapping from the Dead Sea Scrolls containing the Book of Isaiah has been dated as about 1900 years old (right).

American southwest may be as old as 7,000 years. By taking wood specimens from a buried forest in Wisconsin, the date of the last great ice age in North America has been determined to be 11,500 years ago. Archeologists found the trees all facing in the same direction, knocked down by the movement of a glacier.

Crater Lake in Oregon was likely formed as a result of the eruption of Mount Mazama some 6,500 years ago, as determined by dating pieces of charcoal from trees killed in that eruption. Other findings in Oregon date Man as being present some 9,000 years ago. The amazing wall paintings in the Lescaux Cave in France have been dated from nearby remains of campfires to be perhaps 15,000 years old. The Dead Sea scrolls have been dated by their linen wrappings as 2,000 years old, going back to the second century B.C. Recently, American archeologists in Greece have dated findings in the Franchthi Cave at 20,000 B.C.

☐ Artificial Disintegration and Man-made Transformations

About a quarter-century after Becquerel's discovery of natural radioactivity, and nearly a decade after his own proposal of a nuclear atom, Ernest Rutherford succeeded in artificially disintegrating atomic nuclei. The year was 1919. Nitrogen nuclei were smashed with speeding α-particles emitted from a small plug of a radioactive element such as radium, placed in nitrogen gas. Protons are produced and the helium ions are seen no more. Rutherford correctly concluded that the nitrogen nucleus captured the α-particle, followed by elimination of a proton. Expressed as a nuclear equation, Rutherford's experiment looks like this:

$$^{14}_{7}N + ^{4}_{2}He \longrightarrow ^{17}_{8}O + ^{1}_{1}H$$

The α-particle hits the nitrogen nucleus and a proton is ejected. If you add up the protons and neutrons, it should be clear that the atomic number of nitrogen increases by 1 from 7 to 8, and the atomic mass increases by 3. The new nucleus is an isotope of oxygen. Transmutation has occurred:

Atomic number: $7 + 2 - 1 = 8$
Atomic mass: $14 + 4 - 1 = 17$

$$^{14}_{7}N \longrightarrow ^{17}_{8}O$$

However the transmutation did not take place naturally. It was artificially produced by smashing a nuclear projectile into a nucleus. To get at the nucleus and fracture it into parts one faces the necessity of first pushing through a crowd of electrons, then overcoming the concentrated positive charge of the nucleus. But because of the electron's relatively small size and high speeds, that's not really a problem. Now having gotten by the electrons, how will you break in the door and then succeed at breaking up what's inside? Remember, the nucleus is positively charged. The measured energy of naturally emitted particles like α-particles is on the order of millions of electron-volts. Why not try just such an energetic particle? Use an α-particle emitted from one nucleus to bash into a second. That's just what was done.

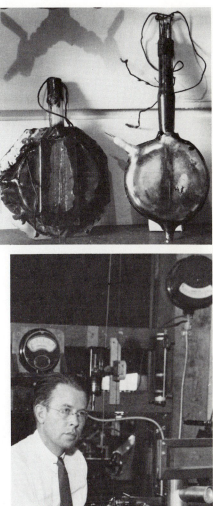

So the first nuclear bullet was an α-particle ejected from a radioactive element. For good reasons, one would like to propel particles into the nucleus that have a smaller positive charge than the doubly charged helium ion. That would decrease the electrostatic repulsion between like-charged nuclei. Large machines called accelerators were developed to zing highly energetic, less massive, *singly* charged protons into a nucleus. For example, both lithium and boron isotopes can be disintegrated by proton bullets, producing lots of helium atoms.

$$_{3}^{7}\text{Li} + {}_{1}^{1}\text{H} \longrightarrow {}_{2}^{4}\text{He} + {}_{2}^{4}\text{He}$$

$$_{5}^{11}\text{B} + {}_{1}^{1}\text{H} \longrightarrow {}_{2}^{4}\text{He} + {}_{2}^{4}\text{He} + {}_{2}^{4}\text{He}$$

Chadwick's Neutrons

In 1932 an Englishman, James Chadwick, working in Rutherford's laboratory, discovered an electrically neutral nuclear particle with a mass just about equal to the proton. The neutron's symbol is $_{0}^{1}n$. Each neutron particle present in an atomic nucleus makes a contribution of one unit of mass to the total mass of the isotope. Neutrons were first produced by bombarding beryllium with α-particles as indicated in the nuclear equation which follows. An isotope of carbon is the daughter element, and, as is always the case, the total budget of atomic masses and atomic number on both sides must balance.

$$_{4}^{9}\text{Be} + {}_{2}^{4}\text{He} \longrightarrow {}_{6}^{12}\text{C} + {}_{0}^{1}n$$

Chadwick's neutron source is still widely used today. Simply mix beryllium with a good α-emitter such as radium or polonium and out spin neutrons.

The main characteristic of the neutron is *neutrality*. This lack of electric charge of either kind gives it the ability to move through large masses of matter with ease. As we saw in Rutherford's scattering experiments α-particles collide with and are deflected from nuclei. Neutrons are not subject to any such electrical forces and therefore are not slowed or deflected, except when they effectively bash into a nucleus. The result is penetrating power, 10^{12} or more times that of the α-particles with which Rutherford had first succeeded at artificial disintegration. Neutrons penetrate the electron cloud about the nucleus without much difficulty. They enter the nucleus with as much ease as if they had fallen into a hole. And although neutrons are not ions themselves and

Figure 9-13

The first cyclotrons, built in 1932 are hardly more than toys when looked at today. Yet they successfully demonstrated the principle and the practice (top).

Ernest Lawrence, the founding father of the cyclotron atom smashers, works at a second generation cyclotron in 1934. The switchboard in the background has to do with magnet control (bottom).

Huge steel ingot to be forged into a 400,000 lb cyclotron magnet yoke (right).

produce virtually no ions directly, they are a form of ionizing radiation because of the other particles produced on their high-energy trips through matter. For example, in living tissue neutrons make protons from hydrogen atoms, a process that can be very damaging to an organism. In fact, neutrons are one of the kinds of radiation that are most effective at causing biological damage. That has interesting and important implications in atomic reactions, peaceful and otherwise, as we shall soon see.

As you may have noticed from the neutron's nuclear symbol, $_0^1n$, it makes no contribution to the atomic number; therefore, absorption of neutrons is useful in making many elements radioactive without changing their chemistry. Radioactive cobalt, a β - and γ - emitter with a half-life of 5.25 years, is made by reacting the natural, stable isotope, cobalt-59, with neutrons:

$$_{27}^{59}\text{Co} + _0^1n \longrightarrow _{27}^{60}\text{Co} + \gamma$$

But entirely new elements can be produced by neutron capture. For example, radioactive phosphorus can be produced by bombing the otherwise stable sulfur-32 with high-energy neutrons:

$$_{16}^{32}\text{S} + _0^1n \longrightarrow _{15}^{32}\text{P} + _1^1\text{H}$$

Finally, if you want to try your hand at the alchemist's trick and prepare gold from base metals such as mercury or lead, a neutron-induced reaction will do it it—but beware the cost. It's hardly an economic process:

$$_{80}^{198}\text{Hg} + _0^1n \longrightarrow _{79}^{197}\text{Au} + _1^2\text{H}$$

In this case the gold isotope is stable, but note the strange isotope of hydrogen produced. It has mass 2, not mass 1, and is referred to as *heavy hydrogen* or **deuterium.**

Nuclear Hardware

Large machines are needed to accelerate these nuclear bullets to sufficient speeds to gain the energy needed for breaking and entering atomic nuclei. Rutherford's early experiments were potluck sorts of things. Most of the α-particle bullets scattered, only a few hitting their intended target; focusing was a problem. One would like to be able to control the track of the bullet into the target. Beginning in 1932, a generation of giant machines grew up, each producing greater energies and higher controls. Perhaps the best-known type of particle accelerator is the *cyclotron.* It was the first machine to develop energies of more than a million electron-volts (Mev) (Fig. 9-13). The largest operates today at the National Accelerator Laboratory at Batavia, Illinois, producing energies in the range of 200×10^9 electron-volts, or 200 BeV (Fig. 9-14).

If you can propel atomic particles and subatomic particles to tremendous velocities, accurately directing them into a target with energies in the billion

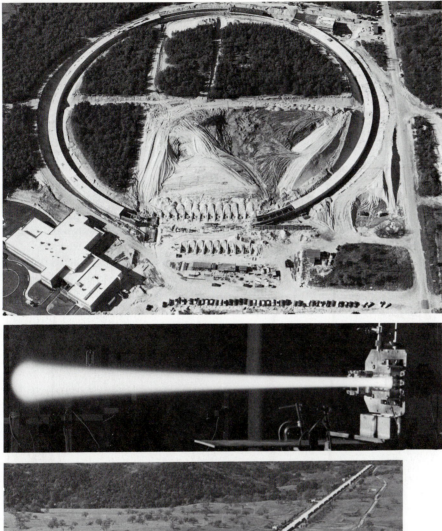

Figure 9-14
Cyclotron under construction at the Brookhaven
National Laboratories on Long Island (top).

A beam of high energy particles (deutrons) is
allowed to spill from the cyclotron across the
room at Brookhaven (middle).

All particle accelerators are not cyclotrons.
Here is the two mile long *linear* accelerator at
Palo Alto, California (bottom).

electron-volt range, how will you watch the event? How can you recognize even the simpler events such as counting particles emitted from a uranium atom, or radon gas glowing in a tube? What methods of detection and quantification can be used for such violent happenings? Remember Heisenberg's Principle of Indeterminacy from the last chapter? Imagine two types of detection. First is the type that gives a signal precisely noting the time of the event but little information about exactly where it occurred; the particle's track is pinpointed in time, not space. The second type pinpoints the particle's path through space but tells little about its trip through time. The Geiger counter is a device of the first kind; the cloud chamber, a device of the second kind.

A Geiger counter consists essentially of a metal tube filled with a gas (see Fig. 9-15). Sealed into the end of the tube is a metal wire that acts as an anode; the wall of the cylinder serves as cathode. A voltage is maintained across the two terminals so that a discharge doesn't quite take place. When charged particles such as α-particles enter through a mica window, electrons are produced which rush toward the wire anode, along with cations that rush toward the cathode, producing more ions as they go. There is a very rapid increase in the number of ions, resulting in a discharge. The avalanche of ions produces a sudden surge of current which can be audibly amplified as a click on a loud speaker or registered as a number on an electric counter. Either way, the nuclear events can be counted in this fashion. A scintillation counter makes use of fluorescence produced by the event so that one can count events visually. Using special cells called photomultiplier cells (the principle here is Einstein's photoelectric effect), exceedingly rapid detection is possible; therefore very fast processes occurring on the order of a millionth of a second are recorded.

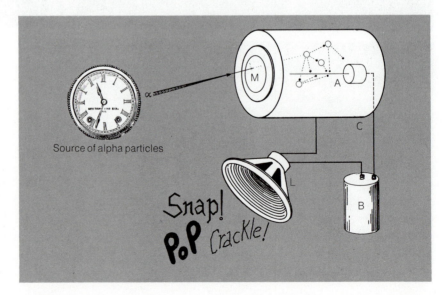

Source of alpha particles

Figure 9-15
Schematic representation of a Geiger counter. Nuclear events can be detected audibly or counted electronically.

The cloud chamber is another device for witnessing nuclear events. If you go back and review our earlier discussion of humidity (Chap. 6), you'll realize why it is that rapid cooling of the air, for example as night falls, often leads to very unstable, supersaturated air, the water content not having time to properly condense. The situation is so unstable that even a slight impurity such as a dust particle can trigger condensation. If the particles are small and light, the droplets of condensation are finely suspended as fog. In the cloud chamber, a piston is rapidly moved downward, cooling the gas rapidly and supersaturating it with water vapor. Tracks that are visible and photographable are made by ions as they traipse through the unstable vapor, triggering condensation and leaving a thread of a cloud behind (Fig. 9-16).

☐ Energy Is Conserved in Nuclear Reactions

It is true that some chemical reactions absorb energy; it is also true that many others liberate energy. Take the formation and decomposition of water as an example. If you take 2 moles of hydrogen gas and 1 mole of oxygen gas, allow them to thoroughly mix, and then allow one small electric spark to pass through, a violent explosion takes place, and 2 moles of water as well as a great deal of heat are formed. *Conclusion*: 2 moles of water are in a lower energy state than 2 moles of hydrogen and 1 mole of oxygen, the energy difference being roughly equal to the heat liberated to the immediate environment in the chemical process.

$$2\,H_2\,(g)\ +\ O_2\,(g)\ \xrightarrow[\text{spark}]{\text{electric}}\ 2\,H_2O\,(g)\ +\ 2\,(-58\ \text{kcal/mole})$$

Remember that heat liberated is minus, by convention, so $\Delta H = -58$ kcal/mole. To do the thing in reverse, you'll need a like amount of energy input:

$$2\,(58\ \text{kcal/mole})\ +\ 2\,H_2O\,(g)\ \longrightarrow\ 2\,H_2\,(g)\ +\ O_2\,(g)$$

This is typical of the order of magnitude for energy in the "usual" chemical reactions involving the extranuclear electrons. Compare these energies with those liberated or consumed in nuclear reactions. There is a factor of 10^6 or more; that's right, energies often in excess of a million times greater for nuclear versus chemical reaction.

The Mass Defect, An Interesting Aberration

Our discussion of nuclear energy begins with Einstein's famous conservation law, $E = mc^2$. Since 1905 we have been conscious of the proportional relationship that exists between mass and its energy equivalent. Any large scale release in energy must be accompanied by some significant change in mass for those nuclei participating in the event. Our discussion is limited to nuclei: protons and neutrons, or *nucleons*. When we precisely measure atomic masses keeping in mind our new understanding of isotopes, almost whole-number values are obtained. But if we look carefully, an interesting and very important aberration referred to as the *mass defect* turns up here. Measure the exact mass of a neutron;

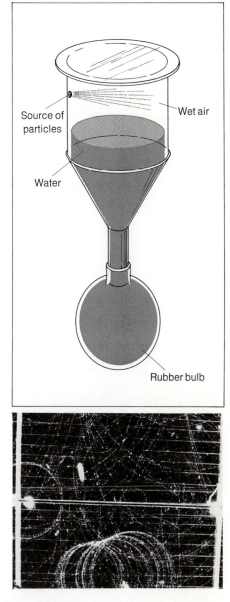

Figure 9-16

Schematic representation of a simple cloud chamber. A glass cylinder contains wet air over a piston of water that can be driven up by squeezing the rubber bulb. To operate, squeeze bulb, wait, release bulb. Tracks appear as lines of water drops (top).

Cloud chamber photograph of the spiral tracks left by a subatomic particle (bottom).

do the same for a proton. Now figure out how much any one nucleus, made up of a given number of neutrons and protons, should weigh. You know what? The whole is *not* equal to the sum of its parts. It is somewhat smaller. What shall we do about that? Well, we must explain it because it is an experimental fact. Here is the helium nucleus, $^4_2$He; two protons, two neutrons.

carefully measured mass of single proton = 1.0072766 amu

carefully measured mass of single neutron = 1.0086654 amu

2 protons   = 2 (1.0072766) = 2.0145532 amu

2 neutrons = 2 (1.0086654) = 2.0173308 amu

mass sum for separate nucleons in a single $^4_2$He = 4.0318840 amu

But if you weigh a single helium nucleus, it is 4.0014026. The difference, then, is

mass of combined singles   = 4.0318840 amu

mass of helium nucleus   = <u>4.0015026 amu</u>

difference   = 0.0303814 amu

Well, but do we really have to worry about little things like that? After all, what's a couple of hundredths of a single atomic mass unit? Think of Avogadro's number and all that. It must be a very small consideration, right? No! Not so at all. That kind of a mass difference makes for a tremendous energy difference because of the huge size of the proportionality constant c^2 in the Einstein equation $E = mc^2$. A single amu has an energy equivalent of 931 million electron-volts, which means 28.3 million electron-volts for that 3/100 or so of an amu.

$$0.0303814 \text{ amu} \frac{931 \text{ MeV}}{1 \text{ amu}} = 28.3 \text{ MeV}$$

That's enough fuel to heat your home for a couple of years. And compare 28.3 million electron-volts with the energy required to ionize or dissociate the outer electron in a hydrogen atom. Right! Only 13.6 electron-volts (not *million* electron-volts, but electron-volts); a difference by a factor of 10^6.

Nuclear Binding Energies, a Glue of Sorts

Well, where is the missing energy in the bound nucleus? It's the glue holding it all together; it is the nuclear binding energy. A total of 28.3 million electron-volts per nucleus is about an average of 7 million electron-volts per nucleon; remember, there are four nucleons in the helium atom. If it were possible to bring together two protons and two neutrons and form a helium nucleus, a loss of energy amounting to 28.3 million electron-volts would be emitted. All four nucleons would stay glued together because each is short the 7 million electron-volts required to be free, and that's the state of affairs until such time as that amount of energy becomes available. So if you prefer, it's all right to think of binding energy as the energy required to break the nucleus into pieces.

Try your hand at the calculation of binding energies. The oxygen-16 isotope
has a nuclear binding energy of 127.6 million electron-volts. See if you can
verify that. Go through the stable nuclides of all the elements and obtain
the average binding energy per nucleon (about 8 million electron-volts for
oxygen nucleons) and you'll find something very interesting. The average
binding energy per nucleon lies between 7 and 9 million electron-volts for most
all the nuclei of the stable nuclides of known elements. Check that out on the
graph showing average binding energy per nucleus versus mass number (Fig.
9-17). The curve rises to a maximum of about 9 million electron-volts with
iron and nickel, mass 55 and 57. These are most stable, and not surprisingly,
are common components of meteors and are major constituents of the earth's
core.

You may have caught a glimpse of the lighter elements on the graph, up to
about Z = 20. The nuclei have just about equal numbers of protons and neutrons;
but beyond 20, things seem to push toward greater and greater numbers of
neutrons. Perhaps that's best illustrated graphically by plotting numbers of
protons versus numbers of neutrons. For a simplified explanation, look at
the more massive nuclei with their apparently disproportionate numbers of
neutrons as having to do with electrostatic repulsion. Protons are positively
charged and repel each other, inhibiting their further accumulation in the
nucleus (Fig. 9-18).

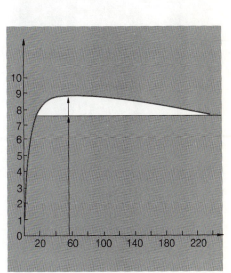

Figure 9-17
The curve of binding energy.

☐ Fission Is A Word Biologists Use

The year 1932 saw the identification of the neutron in theory and its confirmation in experiment. Those events set the proper tone for our understanding of
the nucleus and how to attack it for further information. The years immediately
following the discovery of the neutron were also notable and clearly marked for
history by an impeccable German chemist, Otto Hahn, and his colleague,
Fritz Strassmann. In 1938, uranium nuclei were split when bombarded by
neutrons. The event takes place with considerable release of energy, and the
emission of more neutrons. Emission of more neutrons is the real hooker
because it allows for an immediate chain reaction, in theory. On January 6th,
1939, in the midst of the uneasy peace in Europe between Munich and the
beginning of the Anschluss, Hahn and Strassman reported that barium (Z = 56)
and krypton (Z = 36) were present in uranium samples irradiated with neutrons.

$$^{238}_{92}\text{U} + ^{1}_{0}n \longrightarrow ^{239}_{92}\text{U} \longrightarrow ^{145}_{56}\text{Ba} + ^{94}_{36}\text{Kr}$$

On January 16, ten days later, two Jewish emigrés from Hitler's Germany
explained the fission hypothesis. Lise Meitner, then in Stockholm, and her
nephew, Otto Frisch, at Bohr's institute in Copenhagen, suggested:

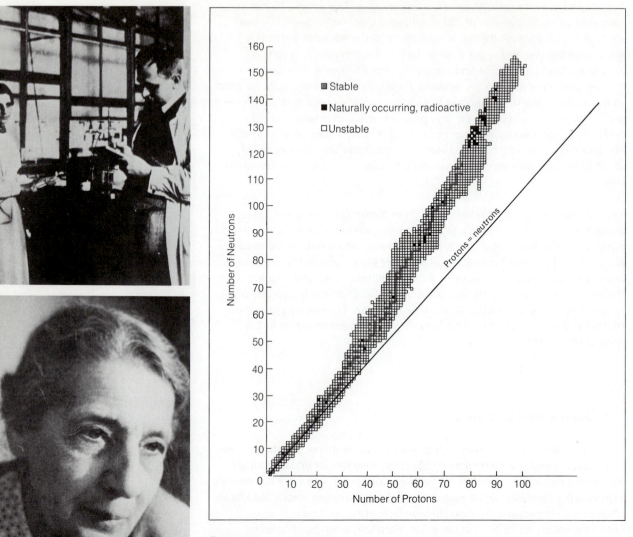

Figure 9-19

Lise Meitner in Otto Hahn's Laboratory in Germany (top).

Ms. Meitner, years later in the United States, after having to leave Germany in 1938 because of the Nazis (bottom).

Figure 9-18
Plotting numbers of protons versus numbers of neutrons.

It seems possible that the uranium nucleus has only small stability of form, and may, after neutron capture, divide itself into two nuclei of roughly equal size. [Fig. 9-20].

Here was *fission,* for the first time applied to atomic nuclei splitting into large pieces of roughly equal size. Frisch himself asked one of the biologists working at the Bohr Institute for the word they use to describe the process whereby one-celled organisms split.

This was a whole new ball game. No more nibbling away of the nucleus to smaller pieces as with α-particle elimination in the uranium-radium decay series. Here was a major disruption of the heart of the atom in one megalithic swoop. Fission takes place. Two drops of "nuclear fluid" now exist where only one was present before. Two hundred million electron-volts are liberated per atom as compared to perhaps 2 million electron-volts in early artificial transformations such as Rutherford's experiments, and at least a million times more energy than is commonly released in ordinary chemical reactions.

The Liquid Drop Fission Model

Before that January of 1939 faded, Niels Bohr, who was then in the United States, and John Wheeler of Princeton University, worked out the theoretical principles of this nuclear fission process based on their "liquid drop" model for the nucleus. Formally published in September 1939 (Hitler's armies had crossed the Polish border on September 1) it became the last major document in nuclear chemistry and physics to be published until 1946 because of World War II. Bohr and Wheeler believed fission to be due to a standoff between opposing forces. Think of the nucleus as a drop of liquid. Let us suppose that the nucleus behaves as molecules in a real liquid. There is a surface tension due to the strong forces between nucleons just as there is a surface tension due to intermolecular interactions. These nucleon forces tend to make the nucleus spherical much as intermolecular forces account for the spherical shape of water drops. Imagine the atomic nucleus to be an electrically charged drop of "nuclear fluid." It is conceivable that the positive protons may repel each other, elongating the ends of the atom, overcoming the surface tension, and finally splitting in half (Fig. 9-20).

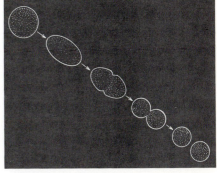

Figure 9-20
The liquid drop model for the fission process suggested that *capture* of a neutron results in instability...and fission.

It is just because of surface tension that a drop of nuclear fluid tends to maintain its spherical shape. To stimulate its rearrangement through electrostatic repulsion, we'll smash a neutron into it. Breakup results in two smaller droplets. Uranium-238 behaves like a Bohr-Wheeler nuclear droplet containing 238 particles, some neutral, some positively charged, all moving about, and all in contact with each other. Hit the droplet with a 1-million electron-volt neutron and fission takes place. For uranium-235 or plutonium-239 nuclei, fission takes place with such facility that even very slow, very tired neutrons of energy 1 electron-volt or less will be quite sufficient (not a million electron-volts). For lighter nuclei, surface tension forces have the edge; however, for heavier nuclei, electrostatic forces are more in control.

Figure 9-21
Uranium fission. Whereas deformation of a liquid drop would most likely result in breakage into two equal pieces, uranium fission produces two fragments of unequal size.

Here is the picture of the Bohr-Wheeler model as Bohr himself depicted it. The liquid drop oscillates because of the added energy from the neutron collision, then passes through the deformation sequence: spherical, eliptical, dumbbell, finally deformed droplets. At the end of the process, two spherical fission fragments move apart due to plain old electrostatic repulsion (Fig. 9-21). Now being perceptive, you've noticed the two drops are unequal in size; the two uranium fragments are krypton and barium. As with most models in science, the liquid drop model for the nucleus is not a perfect analogy. It is a good one if we consider the collective behavior of large numbers of protons and neutrons as in heavy, fissionable nuclei. For light elements with few nucleons, it doesn't fit the experimental data well at all.

When the Nucleus "Fissions," Neutrons Are Released

The 200 million electron-volts released when the nuclear liquid splits in two originated in part from electrostatic repulsion between a pair of half-sized, positively charged nuclei lying at close quarters to each other. The two fission fragments will have slightly less mass; remember, $E = mc^2$ for the original uranium nucleus + neutron. The small mass lost (less than 0.1 of one percent) must be multiplied by c^2, therefore, you get a big energy release. What is at least as important as the big blast of a nucleus flying apart is the release of two to three neutrons per nucleus. They make a chain reaction possible which immediately makes fission of any more uranium atoms possible, and perhaps an explosion. Fission of uranium-235 releases an average of 2.5 neutrons for every split nucleus. If you think about that multiplication factor for a moment, a lot of uranium atoms will be split, suddenly releasing a lot of energy (Fig. 9-22).

The 0.7 percent of the uranium-235 isotope present in natural admixture with 99.3 percent of the 238 isotope is a more fissionable material. However, *slow* neutrons must be provided. What that means is if you are going to separate uranium-235 from uranium-238, and use this highly fissionable isotope to start a chain reaction, you'll have to figure out how to slow down the neutrons jumping out of the nucleus so they'll be able to get together with unsplit nuclei. What's needed is a moderator, something for the neutrons to bounce off, causing

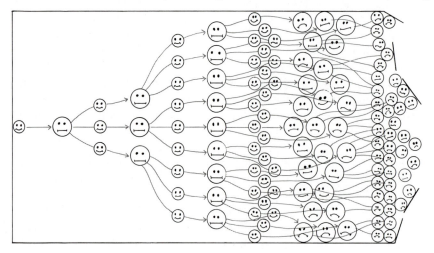

Figure 9-22
The "chain" reaction depends on the multiplication factor provided by production of 2 or 3 neutrons per uranium nucleus fission.

them to lose some of their energy. Now from what you know of Newton's laws, billiard balls, and collisions, you'd best choose a collision partner for the neutron that's about its own size. Collision with something too big will result in a perfectly elastic collision and no energy loss. Collision with something too small will slow the neutron down very little. Ideally, a proton with mass virtually identical to the neutron is what we want. But unfortunately protons and neutrons react, producing an isotope of hydrogen called deuterium.

$$^1_1H \; + \; ^1_0n \; \longrightarrow \; ^2_1H$$

About one in 7,000 hydrogen isotopes are the heavier deuterium or D atoms. That's right, deuterium has become such a well-known isotope we have a private symbol for it. That being the case, there must be a similar ratio of D_2O present in in H_2O. In fact, deuterium oxide, or *heavy water* can be separated (with some difficulty) from plain old water. Perhaps deuterium atoms in D_2O could be used as our moderator. That works very well at slowing down neutrons. However, the first self-sustaining chain reaction used the element carbon in the form of graphite to control the neutron buildup.

"The Day Tomorrow Began"

The first successful nuclear chain reaction was conducted under the old west stands of the University of Chicago's football stadium. A graphite-moderated uranium pile was constructed under strict wartime secrecy. The director was an Italian emigré named Enrico Fermi, forced to leave Italy by the rising tide of fascism in the late 1930s. The pile was constructed of graphite bricks in which were embedded plugs of natural uranium. A clandestine photograph taken in November 1942 (Fig. 9-23) shows alternating layers of all graphite blocks (even-

Figure 9-23
Clandestine photo taken during construction of the first nuclear reactor at the University of Chicago, November 1942. Wartime secrecy prevailed at the time....almost (top).

The Day Tomorrow Began (left).

Caricature of Enrico Fermi, the "Italian Navigator" (below).

numbered) and graphite blocks embedded with uranium slugs (odd-numbered). At 57 layers the pile became critical, or capable of sustaining a chain reaction. Gary Sheehan, the staff artist for the Chicago *Tribune,* recreated the December 2, 1942 scene, "The Day Tomorrow Began," depicting the dramatic, first test. The three standing on top of the pile in the upper right were referred to as the suicide squad. It was their job to flood the pile with a solution of cadmium salt in case things got out of hand among the fissioning uranium nuclei inside the pile. Cadmium is an excellent neutron absorber. At the base of the pile is a lone man controlling a long cadmium rod whose removal from the pile allowed a gradual approach to the self-sustaining state. Without that cadmium rod absorbing neutrons, the pile would go out of control. In fact, rumor has it that in typical army fashion, there was a cover story ready to be released about some large arsenal blowing up accidentally, if the pile didn't quite work properly and a chunk of Chicago went up in what would have been the first nuclear explosion. But all went well. The key figure in the painting is Fermi himself, the "Italian navigator," standing on the balcony ordering the calculated withdrawals of the control rod. An oscilloscope record of the neutron intensity showed the exponential rise in the curve that was achieved between 3:00 and 3:30 P. M. indicating the reaction to be self-sustaining. Here was one of the great discoveries of modern science and it could not be announced to the world because of the wartime crisis. Publication consisted of a single telephone message, in cryptogram, that read, "The Italian navigator has landed in the new world. The natives are friendly." The test of CP-1 (Chicago Pile-1) was a success.

☐ There Are Large-scale Consequences to Large-scale Energy Release

Enrico Fermi's reactor established the experimental verification needed to substantiate what had been predictable in theory from the moment Hahn and Strassmann's studies on fission products for uranium isotopes were reported. Fermi's reactor also produced two new fissionable materials. Many of the released neutrons had been slowed, sustaining the chain reaction in the pile; many others were captured by uranium-238 nuclei while they still had high speeds, producing heavier uranium isotopes:

$$\ce{^{238}_{92}U} + \ce{^{1}_{0}n} \longrightarrow \ce{^{239}_{92}U} + \gamma$$

Uranium-239, being loaded with excess neutrons, then successively eliminated two β - particles, producing two new synthetic elements, neptunium-239 and plutonium-239.

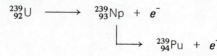

Plutonium-239 turned out to be a more fissionable material than uranium-235, yielding an average of 2.7 neutrons per fission. It was a uranium-235 type bomb that destroyed the city of Hiroshima on August 6, 1945; plutonium-239 was the fissionable material in the bomb dropped on Nagasaki three days later.

There is a critical mass or size for a nuclear pile. To bring about a self-sustaining chain reaction you must be able to control two key factors: (1) production of fission neutrons; and (2) their loss by (a) captured neutrons not resulting in fission, (b) capture of neutrons by other materials present, and (c) escape of neutrons from the sample before capture. Should too many neutrons be absorbed (without fission) or escape, too few would be left to sustain the fission reaction. If too few neutrons escape or are captured, the reaction builds too rapidly to control. For example, if the control rod in Fermi's reactor is removed to the point where the reproduction factor is only slightly larger than one-for-one, neutron intensity increases continuously. Nothing more need be done. It all happens by itself. For uranium-235, the critical mass is about the size of a grapefruit. Bring together a ball of uranium-235 of that size, under controlled conditions, and you have self-sustaining release of energy. Under conditions of no control, you have an atomic bomb on your hands.

Engineering a Fission Bomb As An Offensive Weapon

That was a national goal of the United States government between 1940 and 1945. The primary motivation for putting these discoveries to use in developing instruments of destruction came directly from the scientists themselves. After Hahn and Strassmann's experiments, a flurry of research interest and activity in the first months of 1939 established the fission principle. One could argue that the principle had been established as early as 1905 with Einstein's famous theory and equation $E = mc^2$, but that's a naive oversimplification. The real thrust for developing fission as a weapon was the realization by the community of nuclear scientists that Nazi Germany might equally be capable of developing weapons of such potential destructive power. Einstein made all of this known to Franklin Roosevelt in a famous letter in August 1939. Out of Roosevelt's response to the scientific initiative grew the Manhattan project, Fermi's pile at the University of Chicago, a test blast at Alamagordo, New Mexico in July 1945, and President Truman's decision to drop two bombs on Japan. The social and cultural shock waves of that decision still reverberate through our collective consciousness.

To build the bomb was a technical achievement. It had to be two different sizes at two different times. In storage and delivery it had to be "too small" so that the neutrons released would mostly escape and not support a successful chain reaction. If it were "too big" at this stage, it would be all over at this stage, for a bomb that is too big must explode. The problem to be solved was how to make it suddenly too big at just the right moment. To accomplish this, two subcritical masses of fissionable material, say uranium-235, are suddenly driven together. By suddenly, we mean so fast that the bomb doesn't explode until the two masses, each perhaps 7/8 critical size (each the size of a *small* grapefruit) are completely pushed into each other making a 1¾ critical mass (a *large* grapefruit). The gun-type design (Fig. 9-24) makes use of a TNT charge to drive a uranium-235 disk along a drive shaft, the end of which is a uranium-235 plug.

Explosion of a few pounds of fissionable material suddenly releases what can only be described as an enormous amount of energy. A searing river of radiation is generated, followed by a violent shock wave due to the sudden expansion of super-hot gases. Fission products, high-energy γ- and X-rays, and high-energy neutrons spill out in all directions, producing ionization that is damaging to all life in its path. Many of the fission products are radioactive and long-lived. Scattered by prevailing winds from one part of the world to another, they constitute a random and uncompromising hazard as precipitation washes down the skies into the local biosphere, into the air we breathe, into the food chain. Some of these radioisotopes cause harmful genetic and somatic aberrations. Strontium-90 is just such a radioactive isotope. It is produced in abundance from fissioning either uranium-235 or plutonium-239. Being chemically related to calcium, strontium-90 eventually shows up in the body, incorporated in bone, and is especially hazardous to young children. Slowly decaying by β-emission, it can cause bone cancer, leukemia, and other acute problems.

The Controlled Use of Fission in Nuclear Reactors

The necessary technology has been well-developed since the end of World War II for nuclear production of electric power (Fig. 9-25). Note that the source of electricity is still the traditional turbine. All the nuclear reactor does is supply energy for heating water to steam. The actual electric generators are still the same old steam turbines found in traditional coal-burning plants. Remember what

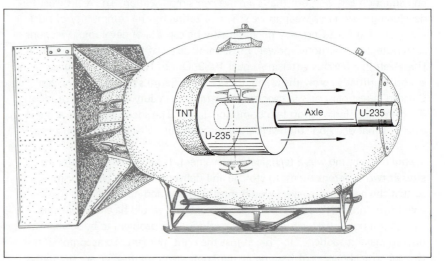

Figure 9-24
A bomb-type atomic device.

we said back in Chap. 4 about thermal energy, randomization, and efficiency. Thermal efficiencies are low. Ideally, one would like to achieve direct conversion of nuclear energy into electrical energy but that is yet to come. Nuclear fuels offer the potential for easing the crisis in fossil fuels that has been steadily developing since the early 1960s. In fact, more than half the money committed to new electric power facilities in the United States and Europe is nuclear. Perhaps it is here, in the human use of nuclear power, that atomic energy will finally overcome the tainted, inhuman necessity of its birth. But there are social costs here as well. What will we do with nuclear wastes, and what of the spector of accidents as nuclear power plants proliferate? Questions without easy answers at the moment.

☐ Fusion and the Carbon Cycle

Fusion of the lightest elements also produces large-scale release of nuclear energy. But that's nothing new; fusion has been going on in the universe for years. In fact, to the best of our educated guesses, it's been going on for as long as there has been a universe. The sun's energy comes from fusion of four hydrogen atoms into a helium nucleus with release of 26 million electron-volts of energy and formation of two positive electrons, or *positrons.*

$$4\,{}^{1}_{1}\text{H} \longrightarrow {}^{4}_{2}\text{He} + 2\,e^{+} + 26\,\text{MeV}$$

We haven't talked about *antimatter* such as positrons, and will defer that discussion to another course. Suffice it for our purposes here to say that there is a fascinating world of opposites, such as e^{+}'s opposed to e^{-}'s, clearly and reasonably (but sometimes fleetingly) fitting into the scheme of things as we understand it today. Table 9-5 lists a few of these strange *opposite* particles, and a few other subatomics.

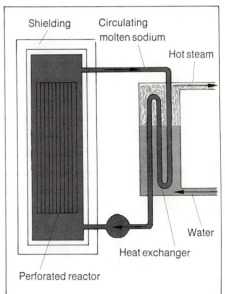

Figure 9-25
A closed-cycle nuclear reactor. Molten sodium is often used as the circulating heat transfer fluid.

Table 9-5
Some of nature's elementary particles

Name	Charge and symbol	Mass relative to the electron's mass	Life expectancy outside the nucleus
Omega	Ω + or −	3282	fleeting
Xi	Ξ +, o, −	2583	fleeting
Lambda	λ o	2181	fleeting
Neutron	${}^{1}_{0}n$	1837	unstable
Proton	${}^{1}_{1}\text{H}$	1835	stable
Meson	K +, o, −	966	fleeting
Muon	μ + or −	207	fleeting
Electron	e + or −	1	stable
Neutrino	ν	0	stable
Photon	ν	0	stable

The Fusion Principle

The problem here is *not* to find neutrons with the right speed for bringing nuclear oscillation and splitting into droplets. It's quite the opposite. What is wanted is energy to overcome electrostatic repulsion, pushing two light nuclei close to the point where nuclear binding forces can take over and pull them together. Accomplishing that releases energy. Take another look at the graph in Fig. 9-18. How shall two nuclei be fused together? Well, the sun does it in part with tremendously high heat causing collisions of such large magnitude that nuclei do get close enough to each other; gravitational forces are also involved.

There is good evidence that at the center of our sun temperatures exceed $20,000,000°$ and nuclear particles are forced together under exceedingly high pressures. Once begun, the fusion process itself provides the continuing heat that helps to fuel the process. The only limiting factor is the supply of fusible atoms. Hydrogen bombs are simple enough in principle and in practice have been the only large-scale energy release by nuclear fusion to date. Controlled fusion reactors are still experimental. For fusion, you need only surround a fission bomb with low molecular weight atoms such as metallic lithium. Explosion of the fission bomb creates the right environment for the fusion process to begin.

Controlled Fusion Power

As a means to clean electric power production fusion requires overcoming some severe engineering restrictions. But there are essentially no radioactive wastes to get rid of, and fusion fuels are limitless compared to fission fuels. The high temperature required is a major restriction for it would first melt, then vaporize, any container or reactor. And then what will you do with the additional heat due to the successful fusion process? Fusion reactors are all quite experimental for the moment and depend on new principles, mainly magnetic fields, and what is referred to as *plasma* physics. A whole mess of high-speed nuclei and electrons are *pinched* in a magnetic field, and under such circumstances, fusion may take place. Here is the nuclear chemistry of one fusion process under study (Fig. 9-26).

$$^2_1H + {}^3_1H \longrightarrow \left\{ \begin{array}{c} 3 \text{ neutrons} \\ + \\ 2 \text{ protons} \end{array} \right\} \longrightarrow {}^4_2He + {}^1_0n + 17.6 \text{ MeV}$$

Humans have long been curious about the sources of the Sun's energy, perhaps for as long as they have been able to think. In 1939 it was satisfactorily established for the first time that thermonuclear processes were at the core of the matter, and in that year, two physicists, Hans Bethe in the United States and C. von Weizacher in Germany proposed a theory for those processes known as the *carbon cycle.* Carbon begins the cycle, and ends it; the net result is liberation of about 25 million electron-volts, the disappearance of 4 protons, and formation of a helium atom.

Step 1: $^{12}_6C + {}^1_1H \longrightarrow {}^{13}_7N + \gamma$

Step 2: $^{13}_7N \longrightarrow {}^{13}_6C + e^+$

Step 3: $^{13}_6C + {}^1_1H \longrightarrow {}^{14}_7N + \gamma$

Step 4: $^{14}_7N + {}^1_1H \longrightarrow {}^{15}_8O + \gamma$

Step 5: $^{15}_8O \longrightarrow {}^{15}_7N + e^+$

Step 6: $^{15}_7N + {}^1_1H \longrightarrow {}^4_2He + {}^{12}_6C$

Figure 9-26
Princeton University fusion-type reactor, The Symmetric Tokamak.

The sun manages to convert in excess of 600 million tons of hydrogen into approximately 600 million tons of helium every second. And in every passing second, more than 4 million more tons of matter is converted to energy. But don't despair. It has been comfortably estimated that the sun has enough of a hydrogen surplus to fire its energy-producing fusion processes for at least 30,000,000 more years.

□ Radiation, Radioisotopes, and Medicine

In the opening section of this chapter Professor Röntgen's amazing rays were discussed at some length. We noted the almost immediate translation into medical practice that took place with this scientific development. An equally rapid and significant reduction to practice took place with the first synthetic preparation of **radioisotopes**. Artificial radioisotopes became available between 1929 and 1935, the years when the cyclotron was undergoing rapid development. Unstable radioisotopes, decaying by α-, β-, and γ-ray emission, are medically useful either as tracers or radiation sources in treatment. Their utility is based on two features, both of which we've had occasion to view earlier in this chapter. First, the chemistry of the radioisotope is the same as the chemistry of

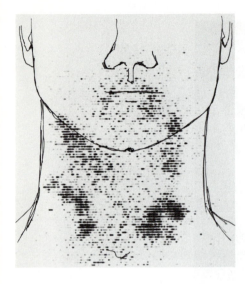

Figure 9-27
Photoscan 72 hours after administration of gallium-67 citrate shows location of bilateral malignant lymph tissues in throat (darkest areas) (above).

Specially designed respiration mask used with carbon-14 breath analyzer to measure rate of metabolism in cows (below).

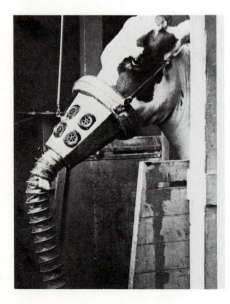

the stable isotope; second, its mode of decay serves as a telltale, identifying both position and quantity. Radioisotopes are important as diagnostic, clinical treatment, medical, and scientific research tools for today's scientists. Being absorbed just as any stable isotopes would be, the radioisotopes proceed to concentrate in particular cells or organs of the body. Table 9-6 summarizes some of the principal isotopes in use today and their medical application (Fig. 9-27). Exposure to large doses of radiation in a very short period of time is clinically referred to as *acute radiation syndrome.* The symptoms have been studied both in animal experiments and with humans. The survivors of Hiroshima and Nagasaki, along with the case histories of many who didn't survive have been closely examined. Some time after the entire body, or large portions of it, have been bathed in penetrating gamma radiations, the syndrome can be observed in varying degrees depending on radiation dosage as summarized in Table 9-7.

Table 9-6

Radioisotopes in medicine

Type of study	Isotope(s) in use
Metabolic studies: by means of breath analyzers for $^{14}CO_2$; types of anemia; specific glucose activity; fat metabolism; enzyme systems; cardiac output.	Carbon-14
Hematology: spleen, bone marrow and liver; iron metabolism; construction and destruction of red blood cells; polycythemia; B_{12} deficiency	Iron-52; Iron-59; chromium-51; phosphorous-32; cobalt-60
DNA and RNA precursors in the transfer of genetic information	Tritium
Radioautographing of bone marrow cells	Tritium
Kidney, liver, thyroid function; lung scan.	Iodine-131
Bone and brain scanning	Strontium-84; strontium-90; gallium-68; arsenic-74
Whole body scans	Iodine-131; fluorine-18; iron-52; potassium-40
Cancer therapy by direct X-ray and isotope implantation	Yttrium-90; strontium-90; cobalt-60; cesium-137

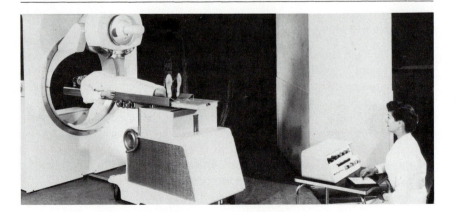

Table 9-7

Acute radiation syndrome

Dose*, rads	Effect	Comments
0-25	Not detectable	
25-100	Blood changes, but little obvious effect on person.	Lymph nodes and spleen damage; blood count drops; bone marrow damage.
100-300	Blood changes, vomiting, fatigue, loss of appetite.	Antibiotic treatment may be necessary due to danger of infection; some minor radiation sickness; but recovery can be expected.
300-600	In addition to effects already noted, diarrhea and hemorrhaging; severe gastrointestinal damage; epilation; sterility.	Antibiotics and blood transfusions required; bone marrow transplant; recovery in 50% of cases at 500 rad level.
greater than 600	In addition to effects already noted, severe damage to the central nervous system; possible circulatory and respiratory failure.	Beyond 600 rad, death is almost certain, possible bone marrow transplant at 600; up to several thousand rad, death occurs in a few days to a few weeks.

* After Hurst and Turner; *Elementary Radiation Physics* (New York: Wiley, 1970), Table 8-1; the basic unit for radiation dosage is the rad.

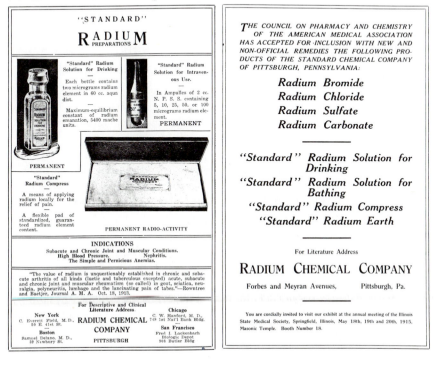

Figure 9-28
A tragedy of innocence.

☐ **Questions to Answer . . . Problems to Solve**

1. Complete the following chart by filling in the appropriate columns:

Element	Atomic mass	Atomic number	Protons	Neutrons	Electrons
hydrogen					
deuterium					
tritium					
carbon-14					
cobalt-60					
cesium-137					
lead-208					
radium-226					
uranium-238					

2. Try your hand at completing the following nuclear reactions:

$$^{9}_{4}Be + ^{4}_{2}He \longrightarrow \underline{\hspace{1cm}} + ^{1}_{0}n \qquad ^{9}_{4}Be + ^{1}_{1}H \longrightarrow \underline{\hspace{1cm}} + ^{2}_{1}H$$

$$^{9}_{4}Be + ^{2}_{1}H \longrightarrow \underline{\hspace{1cm}} + ^{1}_{0}n \qquad ^{9}_{4}Be + ^{1}_{1}H \longrightarrow \underline{\hspace{1cm}} + ^{4}_{2}He$$

3. Here are a few more nuclear reactions for you to complete:

$$^{7}_{3}Li + ^{1}_{1}H \longrightarrow ^{7}_{4}Be + \underline{\hspace{1cm}}$$

$$^{7}_{3}Li + ^{1}_{1}H \longrightarrow ^{4}_{2}He + \underline{\hspace{1cm}}$$

$$^{6}_{3}Li + ^{1}_{1}H \longrightarrow ^{4}_{2}He + \underline{\hspace{1cm}}$$

4. Do a couple more?

$$^{27}_{13}Al + ^{1}_{0}n \longrightarrow ^{28}_{13}Al + \underline{\hspace{1cm}} \qquad ^{27}_{13}Al + ^{2}_{1}H \longrightarrow ^{28}_{14}Si + \underline{\hspace{1cm}}$$

$$^{27}_{13}Al + ^{1}_{1}H \longrightarrow ^{4}_{2}He + \underline{\hspace{1cm}} \qquad ^{27}_{13}Al + ^{4}_{2}He \longrightarrow ^{30}_{15}P + \underline{\hspace{1cm}}$$

nucleus	disintegration
thorium-232	alpha
radium-228	beta
actinium-228	beta
thorium-228	alpha
radium-224	alpha
radon-220	alpha
polonium-216	alpha
lead-212	beta
bismuth-212	beta
polonium-212	alpha
thallium-208	beta
lead-208	stable

5. Besides the uranium-radium decay series, there are three others in nature. One begins with thorium-232, goes through eleven generations, ending at the stable lead-208 isotope. Write equations for each step.

6. The actinium series begins with uranium-235 and goes through ten steps to a stable isotope of lead-207. The first six steps involve the following decay sequence: alpha, beta, alpha, alpha and beta, alpha, and alpha. What isotope is produced?

7. The atomic mass for the nitrogen-14 atom is 14.00307 amu which is 99.63 percent of the natural abundance of the element. The other 0.37 percent is the nitrogen-15 isotope, 15.00011 amu. Determine the average binding energy per nucleon for both isotopes, the mass defect for both, and the apparent atomic mass for nitrogen as it is found in nature.

8. How much energy is liberated in Rutherford's famous first artificial nuclear

transformation?

$$^{14}_{7}N + ^{4}_{2}He \longrightarrow ^{17}_{8}O + ^{1}_{1}H$$

N-14 = 14.00307   O-17 = 16.99914

He-4 = 4.00260   H-1 = 1.00797; proton = 1.00728

9. Consider the fusion reaction between lithium atoms and protons according to the equation:

$$^{7}_{3}Li + ^{1}_{1}H \longrightarrow ^{4}_{2}He + ^{4}_{2}He$$

  (a) Using the amu values given below, and the proper conversion factor taken the chapter, determine the energy in MeV's for both reactants and products:

     Li-7 = 7.01601

      H-1 = 1.00797; proton = 1.00728

     He-4 = 4.00260

  (b) Is the reaction exothermic or endothermic? How much energy is absorbed or released?

  (c) If a mole of lithium atoms and a mole of protons were involved, how much energy in calories would be absorbed or released?

10. Speaking of fission:

  (a) Explain why there is a "critical" mass.

  (b) Do you think the shape of a critical mass is important? Why?

  (c) Are you better-advised to use uranium-235 than uranium-238 for bombs? Why?

  (d) Uranium-238 is converted to plutonium-239 in a nuclear pile. What is the significance of that?

  (e) Explain the heavy metal end of the graph in Fig. 9-30 showing average binding per nucleon.

  (f) Do you understand why it would be fruitless to study the energy release in splitting atoms of iron.

11. Speaking of fusion:

  (a) Fission is necessary initially. Why?

  (b) Explain the very light element end of the graph in Fig. 9-30 showing average binding energy per nucleon.

  (c) Do you understand why it would be fruitless to study the energy release in fusing atoms of iron?

12. Fusion reactions taking place in the Sun are believed to be the sources of its enormous energy:

  (a) Without referring back to the text, see if you can fill in Bethe's classic six-step explanation for the Sun's energy.

$$^{12}_{6}C + ^{1}_{1}H \longrightarrow (\underline{\quad}) + \gamma$$

$$(\underline{\quad}) \longrightarrow ^{13}_{6}C + e^{+}$$

$$^{13}_{6}C + ^{1}_{1}H \longrightarrow (\underline{\quad}) + \gamma$$

$$(\underline{\quad}) + ^{1}_{1}H \longrightarrow ^{15}_{8}O + \gamma$$

$$^{15}_{8}O \longrightarrow (\underline{\quad}) + e^{+}$$

$$(\underline{\quad}) + ^{1}_{1}H \longrightarrow ^{12}_{6}C + ^{4}_{2}He$$

(b) Having completed the historic cycle, write the overall reaction showing what was consumed and the products.

13. Consider the fusion reaction involving lithium and deuterium, producing two alpha-particles and a neutron:

$$^7_3\text{Li} + ^2_1\text{H} \longrightarrow 2\,^4_2\text{He} + ^1_0n$$

(a) Using the graph in Fig. 9-30, see if you can predict whether or not the process is energy releasing or not.
(b) Then, making use of the data (left), actually determine the energy released, or absorbed. (*Remember*: Its the energy of the products less the energy of the reactants.)
     He-4 = 4.00260

He-4 = 4.00260   Li-7 = 7.01585
n-1 = 1.00867   H-2 = 2.01410

14. Describe the Bohr-Wheeler liquid drop nuclear model. According to this theory, what kinds of forces hold the nucleus together; what kinds of forces are responsible for nuclear fission? Illustrate your discussion by using the obvious analogy to a drop of water. Explain why the liquid drop nuclear model is not a completely accurate description.

15. What is it about radioisotopes that makes them particularly valuable in diagnostic medicine? In therapeutic medicine? In medical and scientific research?

16. One of the newer techniques used by the research chemist involves "tagging" molecules with radioactive atoms. For example, the energy transfer agent in human cells is a complex molecule called ATP. It has three very reactive phosphate groups, phosphorus atoms surrounded by four oxygens.

Can you imagine or speculate in what way a radiophosphorus atom at any one of the three phosphorus atom positions in the molecule might be useful in studying energy transfer and cell metabolism?

17. What makes a proton a better bullet for bringing about nuclear change than an alpha-particle? Why is a neutron better than a proton? Could we use an electron? Why?

18. Consider the proton-neutron theory for the structure of the nucleus:
(a) describe the inside of the helium-4 nucleus; the argon-40 nucleus; the uranium-238 nucleus.
(b) Speculate on possible reasons why the heavier elements might have many more neutrons than protons does as uranium-238.
(c) And while you're speculating, how do you explain beta-decay or loss of electrons from the nucleus? Didn't the proton-neutron model exclude such particles from the nucleus?

19. Briefly explain how the cloud chamber works in detecting nuclear particles.

20. How does the Geiger counter work in detecting nuclear particles?

21. Explain how we've learned to live with fractional atomic weights.

22. If you allow chlorine atoms to slowly bleed into the vacuum chamber of a mass spectrograph, you'll find atoms with a mass of 35 and some with a mass of 37, yet chemically, both kinds remain chlorine. How so?

23. Give a brief explanation of how a mass spectrograph works; see if you can illustrate your discussion with a simple schematic diagram, properly labeled.

24. Picture this! You've just completed a mass spectral determination of atomic bromine. The mass spectrum shows two large peaks of just about equal intensities at mass values of 79 and 81. How would you interpret these data in terms of isotope distribution and average atomic mass?

25. Determine the mass change on emission of
    (a) an alpha-particle   (d) an alpha and a beta particle
    (b) a beta-particle   (e) a beta-particle and a gamma ray
    (c) a gamma ray

26. Of the three principal particles eliminated from the parent during radioactive decay, alpha-particles, beta-particles, and gamma rays, which
    (a) is electrically neutral
    (b) is most massive
    (c) is most penetrating
    (d) is deflected toward the positive pole in an electric field
    (e) is deflected the most in a magnetic field
    (f) is most ionizing
    (g) was used by Rutherford to effect artificial disintegration
    (h) was originally discovered by J. J. Thomson
    (i) is most similar to Röntgen's rays
    (j) has a relative mass of approximately 1

27. The half-life of a radioactive isotope is understood to be the time required for half the material present to decay. What's wrong with the idea of measuring radioactivity in terms of the time it takes for radioactive atoms to decay completely, instead?

28. You have at your discretion a radioisotope whose half-life is 900 seconds:
    (a) Draw a graphical representation of the decay profile for the isotope, plotting time against fraction of the atoms left.

(b) What percentage of the original pile of atoms is present after an hour?

(c) If you'd started with one million atoms, how many would you have left after three hours?

29. Explain the carbon-14 method for determining the age of carbonaceous materials to a classmate.

30. A similar method has been worked out for dating the Earth's crust by means of the uranium-radium decay series that begins with uranium-238 and ends with lead-208. Can you imagine how that might work? (*Hint*: where you find uranium ore deposits, you'll find lead, too.)

31. An archeological dig uncovers the charcoal remains of a prehistoric campfire. The ratio of carbon-14 to carbon-12 was found to be 25 percent of that in a living tree. Determine the approximate age of the campfire.

32. A radioactive pollutant produced in atmospheric testing of fissionable materials is strontium-90. Its half-life is 28 years. How many years will it take for the strontium-90 level to fall to approximately 1.5 percent of its original level?

33. Do you think it might be difficult to prepare pure uranium-238? How about radium-226? What about radon-222? Why? (*Hint*: consider their respective $t_{1/2}$ values given in the uranium-radium decay series.)

34. Cesium shows only one single peak at amu 133 in the mass spectrometer. What conclusion do you draw? Are you absolutely positive about that?

35. The natural abundance of uranium in nature is approximately distributed among three isotopes, 99.28 percent of 238, 0.71 percent of 235, and 0.01 percent of 234. Determine the average isotopic mass for uranium in nature.

36. The natural abundance of antimony in nature is a mix of two isotopes, mass 121 and mass 123. The average atomic mass is 121.75. Calculate the percent composition of the two isotopes.

37. Even though you now understand the not-so-anomolous, fractional nature of atomic masses for the average abundance of the elements, how come even the **pure** isotopic masses still deviate slightly from exact whole numbers?

Chapter 10

□ Perceptions and Deceptions

1 No classical laws of physics or chemistry can explain why two atoms share a pair of electrons.

2 "An octet of electrons around an atomic nucleus is peculiarly stable."

3 Beware the apparent simplicity of the chemical formula. Much more is implied.

4 If it weren't for chemical bonds, not the least of our troubles would be the gaseous state everything would be in.

5 The concept of resonance is much like understanding mules: not horses—not donkeys. They are a unique crossbreed that can perhaps be better understood if you know a little about both.

□ From the Chemist's Point of View

There is a binding force between atoms; consequently, there are polyatomic molecules in nature. Similarly, there is a binding force between molecules; consequently, there are aggregated states of matter. The properties of matter are determined by the characteristics of these binding forces, these chemical bonds. We can illustrate what we mean by considering the molecular structure of water and the ambivalent architecture about elemental carbon.

Plants and animals are watery things. In fact, our particular life form can be defined in terms of two kinds of hydrogen-to-oxygen bonds acting within the piles of molecules we call water. There is the internal O—H bond within the molecule itself; its properties are interesting, but not unexpected. The surprise is the external O---H—O bond in which a hydrogen atom finds itself connecting two other atoms; that's called the *hydrogen bond.* Were it not for such hydrogen bonding, water would be a gas at room temperature. However, because of hydrogen bonding, water molecules collect in extensive three-dimensional aggregates.

Let's compare water with methane, the principal constituent of natural gas: (1) the molecular weights are nearly the same (18 versus 16); (2) both contain hydrogen and one other kind of atom, oxygen or carbon; (3) a measure of the volume of a water molecule reveals it to be about the same as a methane molecule; yet water freezes at $0°C$, methane at $-184°C$; water boils at $100°C$, methane at $-162°C$. The great difference has to do with hydrogen bonding. Hydrogen bonding explains why lakes freeze from the top down in winter, a profound fact for life in the aquatic environment. When water freezes, an open hexagonal structure of

If all you want to do is represent the arrangement of atoms in space, then a chemical bond can simply be a straight line. But if you wish to show how bonds break and new bonds form, more is needed. The electron pair model for the chemical bond, first proposed by Gilbert Lewis (right) and subsequently popularized by Irving Langmuir (left), became accepted and known as the Lewis-Langmuir theory in 1923.

The Nature of Chemical Bonding

Figure 10-1
Our present understanding of the nature of the chemical bond is the work of Linus Pauling.

lower density than the liquid phase is formed (see Fig. 5-5). As a result, ice forms first on the surface of a body of water. That in turn shields life within from the severe conditions of winter, while at the same time altering climatic conditions. Hardly the behavior of most liquids which generally become more dense when they solidify; the solid then sinking in the liquid.

In Chap. 5 we pointed up the difference between two forms of elemental carbon, graphite and diamond (see Fig. 5-3). The graphite structure was made up of parallel layers of uniformly packed hexagonal plates. Consequently, graphite has lubricant properties: the weakest chemical bonds are those between carbon atoms in different layers; mild stress on the system results in slippage of layers over each other; but within any one of the neatly fitted layers, all the carbon atoms are strongly bonded. Not so for the diamond structure where we saw a three-dimensional tetrahedral structure with every carbon atom uniformly and identically bonded to each of four other atoms as though it were at the center of a three-sided pyramid (see Fig. 5-3). That makes for a mighty structure. Diamonds are used as abrasives and on cutting edges; they are hardly graphite-like at all.

The point is this. If we are to understand the physical and chemical properties of matter, the best place to begin is with an understanding of chemical bonding and the nature of the chemical bond. That perception will reveal why solid water is the ice we know and why graphite is different from the crystalline modification of carbon called diamond. Curious about why a very simple collection of atoms such as helium is a gas to a temperature within 4° of absolute zero? Again, chemical bonding (or the lack of it). Proteins, the building blocks of living systems, are complicated collections of atoms. We know their structures depend on internal chemical bonds between atoms within these large molecules and external chemical bonds between molecules close by each other. In some situations, all that really counts is just the shapes of things. That's also because of the nature of chemical bonding.

The last chapters in this book will describe lots of the details of chemistry in practice for you. Perhaps they are best understood in terms of one of the science's most powerful and pervasive theories, the theory of the chemical bond. The chemist's point of view about chemical bonding is in great measure the work of a young man from Oregon, working at the California Institute of Technology in the early 1930s. Linus Pauling (Fig. 10-1) suggested:

> That there is a chemical bond between two atoms or groups of atoms (when) the forces acting between them lead to the formation of an aggregate with sufficient stability . . . for the chemist to consider it as an independent molecular species.

☐ Little Cubes, Littler Cubes, Littlest Cubes

Chemical bonding and the structure of molecules are easy enough to understand providing you've picked up a reasonable sense of atoms and atomic structure along the way. As a prologue to our continuing discussion let's pause and recall some of those earlier perceptions and at the same time introduce a couple of new twists that we'll now need. To begin with, it should be confirmed that we are believers in atoms. They exist. But beware the structural formula. Remember that's just a clever device for conveniently communicating information about atoms and molecules. The reality of the whole atomic-molecular conceptualization of matter lies in experimental facts, convincingly pointing out the existence of atoms and molecules. As we've seen earlier, it has almost gotten to the point where we can begin to collect photos for a family album of single atoms.

Equal volumes of gases contain equal numbers of gas molecules if you count them under the same conditions of temperature and pressure. For example, when 4 grams of hydrogen react with 32 grams of oxygen, yielding 36 grams of water, the actual number of hydrogen molecules reacted equals the number of water molecules formed:

$$2\,H_2 \quad + \quad O_2 \quad \longrightarrow \quad 2\,H_2O$$

In this case, it is twice Avogadro's number of molecules (twice N). Knowing N, the mass of a single atom or molecule can be easily determined. A single water molecule weighs very little indeed. Water molecules have a molecular weight of 18; the mass of 6.023×10^{23} (N) water molecules is 18 grams.

$$\left(\frac{18 \text{ grams of } H_2O}{N \; H_2O \text{ molecules}}\right)\left(\frac{N \; H_2O \text{ molecules}}{6 \times 10^{23} \; H_2O \text{ molecules}}\right) = 3 \times 10^{-23} \text{ grams/}H_2O \text{ molecules}$$

Model Building With Sugar Cubes

Table sugar (or sucrose) has the chemical formula $C_{12}H_{22}O_{11}$ with molecular weight 342. Therefore the mass of a single table sugar molecule is about 5.7×10^{-22} gram, a calculation that you can check out on your own. With that information, a reasonable estimate of the size of a single sucrose molecule can be made. Here's how.

First: sucrose has a density of 1.59 g/ml. A little cube of table sugar molecules 1 cubic centimeter in volume weighs 1.59 grams. If we take a very small cube out of our cubic centimeter, say a chunk that is 1 cubic *millimeter*, it ought to weigh 1/1,000 of the original cube (Fig. 10-2). After all, 1 cubic centimeter = (1cm)(1cm)(1cm), whereas 1 cubic millimeter = (0.1 cm)(0.1 cm)(0.1 cm) = 0.001 cm³. So our smaller cube weighs 0.00159 or 1.59×10^{-3} gram.

Second: if our smaller sucrose cube (it will hardly do for sweetening a cup of coffee) weighs 1.59×10^{-3} grams, it contains 2.8×10^{18} molecules per cubic millimeter.

$$\left(\frac{1.59 \times 10^{-3} \text{ g sucrose}}{1 \text{ mm}^3}\right) \left(\frac{1 \text{ molecule sucrose}}{5.7 \times 10^{-22} \text{ g sucrose}}\right) = 2.8 \times 10^{18} \text{ molecule/mm}^3$$

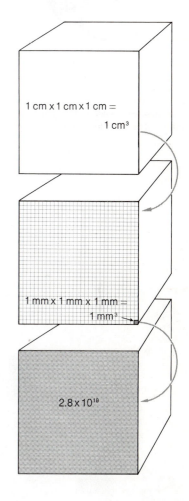

1 cm x 1 cm x 1 cm = 1 cm³

1 mm x 1 mm x 1 mm = 1 mm³

2.8×10^{18}

Figure 10-2

A model for sucrose molecules based on neatly stacked "little cubes." Begin with a 1 cm³ cube. Assume that cube divided into 1000 smaller cubes. And each of these is made of still smaller cubes, about 2.8×10^{18} of them filling each of the 1000.

Figure 10-3
In a manner of speaking, the "glue" of chemical combinations is supplied by the outer electrons.

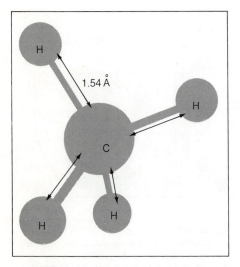

Figure 10-4
Average bond lengths between two connected C-H atoms within a molecule of methane.

Third: what do sucrose molecules look like? Little cubes all neatly piled into a big cube? Hardly, but it won't change our qualitative estimate here if we go ahead and assume a single table sugar molecule to be a cube. Pile up 2.8×10^{18} of these smallest cubes and you'll have a sugar cube 1 millimeter by 1 millimeter by 1 millimeter, the dimensions of our smaller, or intermediate cube. That being the case, the smallest cube must be made up of 1.41×10^6 molecules on an edge because $(1.41 \times 10^6)^3$, or $(1.41 \times 10^6)(1.41 \times 10^6)(1.41 \times 10^6) = 2.8 \times 10^{18}$. And a single sucrose molecule would spread itself along an edge of our smallest cube for a distance of 7.1×10^{-7} millimeters/molecule:

$$\left(\frac{1 \text{ mm}}{1 \text{ smallest cube edge}}\right)\left(\frac{1 \text{ smallest cube edge}}{1.4 \times 10^6 \text{ molecule}}\right) = 7.1 \times 10^{-7} \text{ mm/molecule}$$

Finally: when we measure atomic and molecular dimensions, our unit is the angstrom, and the qualitative length of a sugar molecule along an edge is about 7.1 angstroms. That's small as distances go, but fairly large as far as molecules are concerned:

$$\left(\frac{7.1 \times 10^{-7} \text{ mm}}{1 \text{ molecule}}\right)\left(\frac{10^{-3} \text{ m}}{1 \text{ mm}}\right)\left(\frac{1 \text{ Å}}{10^{-10} \text{ m}}\right) = 7.1 \text{ Å/molecule}$$

Of course, there aren't any cubic sucrose molecules! We've been model-building again. The qualitative picture is about right, though, giving us a very useful perception of molecular size.

Binding Atoms

Molecules are composed of combinations of atoms stuck together in certain allowed, geometric patterns in space. The concept of combining capacity helps us to understand why Dalton's HO formula for water had to be wrong and why methane is composed of hydrogen and carbon in a CH_4 combination: never CH_2; never CH_6. The outer electrons surrounding the nucleus are the source of the glue for chemical combination, supplying atoms with sticking power (Fig. 10-3). Chemical combination is electrical in nature, resulting in preferred average distances or bond lengths between consecutive atoms within a molecule (Fig. 10-4). Specific spatial arrangements which can be studied in terms of the ***bond angle*** lying between three consecutive atoms (Fig. 10-5), along with the elements of symmetry within any molecule (Fig. 10-6) also result from the electrical nature of atoms. Chemical binding (or perhaps we ought to stick to the word "bonding" while understanding "binding") is an electrical phenomenon mostly of the outer electrons.

☐ **Atoms Look Like . . .**

At first, atom models depicted electrons as being much the same as planets orbiting the sun in the heavens. The Bohr Theory was better, providing a closer fit between theory and experiment by introducing the quantum description for

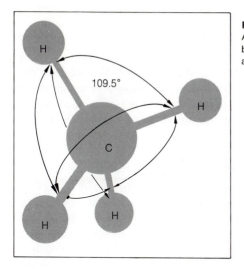

Figure 10-5
Average bond angle lying between three consecutive atoms in a methane molecule.

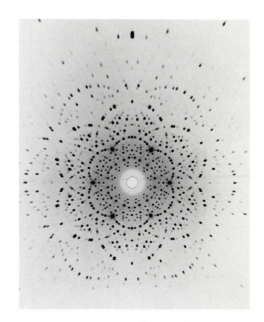

Figure 10-6
Note the almost flower-like symmetry present in a crystal of the mineral beryl, uncovered in its X-ray diffraction pattern.

electrons, now placed in shells or energy levels. Quantum mechanics gave atoms an exact, mathematical description, providing a still better, more accurate model. Perhaps right here a good portrait will be of some additional help. It is true that the fuzzy balls we referred to as probability patterns are a lot less elegant than mathematical descriptions of matter waves. However, it's worth keeping in mind that ever since Heisenberg told us about the Principle of Indeterminacy, an electron-cloud or electron-density pattern is apparently about the best we can hope for in our mind's eye view of such high-speed, submicroscopic atomic events.

Imagine for a moment that you can photograph an electron in motion. If you took a few thousand pictures and superimposed the single dot indicating the location of the electron in each photo onto one single photo you'd see what we mean by an electron-cloud or probability pattern. The lowest energy level electrons placed in any shell look like a sphere, symmetrically distributed around the nucleus; they're called *s*-type electrons (Fig. 10-7). Note how the electron distribution trails off toward the outside edge. Electron waves never die, they just fade away; atoms do not have sharp boundaries but the location of maximum electron density is fairly clear. If you are looking for an electron in the lowest principal quantum energy level (*K* shell), look at a distance of about 0.53 Å from the nucleus in hydrogen. That's where the *s* sublevel has its maximum electron density. At about 1 Å out from the nucleus you are much less likely to locate the electron.

For an *s*-type electron placed in the second shell (*L* shell), the radial distance from the nucleus is still greater, and for *s* orbitals placed in the next shell (*M*

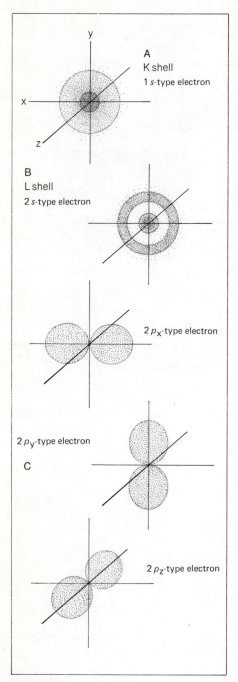

Figure 10-7
s- and *p*-type electron cloud patterns. The boundary lines have been drawn in to mark 90% of the electron-density.

shell) it is greater still. All *s*-type electrons are described by fuzzy, symmetric spheres that thin out and vanish as one recedes away from the nucleus, after passing through the region of maximum density. That can be shown to best advantage graphically (Fig. 10-8). Electrons in the slightly higher *p*-type energy sublevels come in sets of three, projected in space, mutually perpendicular to each other. To round out the qualitative picture, we should also include electrons in *d*-type energy sublevels; they come in sets of five. However, if we go on like this, the picture gets more complicated than necessary for us; *s* and *p* energy sublevels will do for our purposes here.

We now have an electronic picture of the atom along with a pictorial view of electrons in an atom. Let's try to put these ideas to use in describing chemical bonding. Atoms occupy space, each kind having its own characteristic volume (Fig. 10-9). When atoms combine to form molecules, some molecules such as the carbon dioxide molecule turn out to be linear; others like the water molecule are bent; the bending (or lack of it) is responsible for the molecule's unique properties. Still other molecules, as ammonia, are pyramid-shaped and continually flip-flop inside-out and back again like an umbrella in a high wind. Silica in sea sand is structured like little three-sided tetrahedra (pyramids), all neatly packed together. Some big molecules are uniformly twisted like spiral staircases; others are about as ordered as a bowl of spaghetti. Some molecules cause diseases because of their size and shape; others cure diseases for the very same reasons. Some molecules dictate blond hair and blue eyes because of their structure and geometry; others cause hemophilia and sickle cell anemia for the very same reasons. Let's examine some of the bonds in our chemical portfolio.

☐ Electrovalence and Electron Transfer

Geography probably has little to do with the origins of modern chemistry, but in the case of chemical bonding an awful lot of it rode out of the West, particularly from California. As has been true of all the great scientific discoverers, Linus Pauling also had giant shoulders upon which to stand (Fig. 10-10) and if he saw farther than others it was partly because of the work of another California chemist, Gilbert Lewis, two decades earlier (1916). Lewis explained chemical combination: a theory of **valence.** The essence of the theory was the suggestion that in order to achieve stability in chemical combination, eight electrons, an octet of "outer" electrons, should be available to an atom through transfer (electrovalence) or sharing (covalence). Achieving the electron configuration of the noble gases results in unusual stability, favorable energy distribution, and chemical bonds whose properties can easily be studied. There are, to be sure, very unstable bonds, suffering only a fleeting, transitory existence, but we won't worry about those for the moment. We'll stick with the general qualifications Pauling's definition places on chemical bonding, namely,

sufficient stability . . . for chemists to consider it as an independent molecular species.

Figure 10-9
Relative volumes occupied by atoms; approximately drawn to scale.

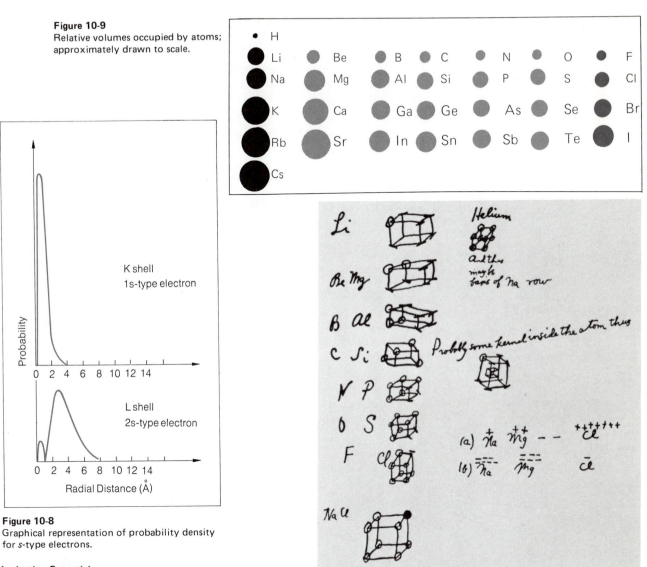

Figure 10-8
Graphical representation of probability density for *s*-type electrons.

Figure 10-10
Notes made by Gilbert Lewis on the arrangement of electrons around the atomic nucleus.

Ionization Potential

Chemical combination arises by achieving an octet of "outer" electrons, thus providing noble gas design through direct electron transfer from one atom to another. The energy required to remove an electron from an atom, its **ionization potential**, is one of two important aspects of electron transfer. The second aspect is **electron affinity**, the energy associated with one atom *acquiring* an electron from another. You've met ionization potentials before. For example it takes 13.6 electron-volts to remove an electron from hydrogen, leaving a hydrogen ion:

$$H \longrightarrow H^+ + e^-$$

What does that mean? If you don't pump a minimum of 13.6 electron-volts into the gaseous hydrogen atom, the electron will simply jump up and then fall down again in a blaze of color (Fig. 10-11, see also Chap. 8). Consider atoms of the element lithium, a metallic element in the second period of the table of the elements. Of its three electrons, only one is readily available, placed in the outer *L* shell. Remember, two electrons are all the *K* shell can handle; that's the helium core. A total of 5.392 electron-volts is required to remove the third, outer-shell electron. It is possible to take out a second electron, breaking into the inner *K* shell and disrupting the stability of the helium core; but look at the additional energy that's needed: 5.392 electron-volts remove the first electron; 75.62 electron-volts remove the second; 14 times as much!

Step 1:   Removal of the first electron from the *L* shell

$$\text{Li} \longrightarrow \text{Li}^+ + e^- \qquad 5.392 \text{ eV needed}$$

Step 2:   Removal of the second electron necessitates breaking into the *K* shell.

$$\text{Li}^+ \longrightarrow \text{Li}^{++} + e^- \qquad 75.62 \text{ eV needed}$$

The important perception lies in the fact that removal of the second electron takes place from what is now a positively charged lithium ion (Li^+). You must overcome forces of electrostatic attraction between positive ions and negative electrons before removal can be effected. That is not the case with the first electron which was removed from a neutral atom.

It is often the practice to draw in the outer-shell electrons as a memory aid in first courses on chemical bonding; we'll do that for a while. The reaction for the ionization of the lithium atom looks like this.

$$\text{Li} \cdot \longrightarrow \text{Li}^+ + e^-$$

The lithium ion formed is positively charged, having one less electron than usual. Sodium and the other alkali metal family elements are similar because they all have: (1) a complete inner core of appropriate noble gas configuration; and (2) one transferable outer electron.

$$\text{Li} \cdot \longrightarrow \text{Li}^+ + e^- \qquad 5.392$$
$$\text{Na} \cdot \longrightarrow \text{Na}^+ + e^- \qquad 5.138$$
$$\text{K} \cdot \longrightarrow \text{K}^+ + e^- \qquad 4.339$$
$$\text{Rb} \cdot \longrightarrow \text{Rb}^+ + e^- \qquad 4.176$$
$$\text{Cs} \cdot \longrightarrow \text{Cs}^+ + e^- \qquad 3.893$$

Note the periodic trend in ionization potentials. It is obviously easier to remove outer electrons from the influence of the positive nucleus when they are at greater distances, separated by additional inner principal quantum shells. That's the case for rubidium or cesium in contrast to lithium or sodium.

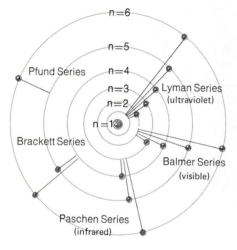

Figure 10-11

Electron Affinities

Electron affinities are not as clear-cut (experimentally) or as well-defined (conceptually) as ionization potentials. Still, electron affinity is a useful model. It can be generally defined as the energy associated with the process of acquiring an electron that has been released elsewhere. Thus the complete electron-transfer requires both an electron donor and an electron receiver (Fig. 10-12). Consider the structure of fluorine atoms and fluoride ions. A fluorine atom has seven electrons placed in its outer shell: two are *s*-type and five are *p*-type. With our new notation, the process looks like this:

$$:\ddot{F}\cdot \ + \ e^- \ \longrightarrow \ :\ddot{F}:^-$$

neutral fluorine   negative fluoride
   atom   ion

Note that the fluoride ion is negatively charged, having assumed one more electron than its neutral complement. If fluorine, as the first member of the halogen family of nonmetallic elements, behaves in a certain fashion, chlorine, bromine, and iodine can be expected to behave similarly.

$$:\ddot{Cl}\cdot \ + \ e^- \ \longrightarrow \ :\ddot{Cl}:^-$$
$$:\ddot{Br}\cdot \ + \ e^- \ \longrightarrow \ :\ddot{Br}:^-$$
$$:\ddot{I}\cdot \ + \ e^- \ \longrightarrow \ :\ddot{I}:^-$$

Oxidation-Reduction and Electrovalence

The chemist has a special name for the overall process coupling ionization potential and electron affinity. Loss of electrons is referred to as *oxidation,* gain of electrons as *reduction: oxidation-reduction* (Fig. 10-13). The two processes go hand-in-hand; lithium atoms are oxidized to lithium ions; fluorine atoms are reduced to fluoride ions. Oxidation took place and oxygen wasn't necessary at all; fluorine or chlorine, or any one of a number of other atoms do quite nicely.

Now, having coupled electron donors and electron acceptors together let's see just what electrovalence means. Consider sodium chloride, plain old table salt. Sodium atoms are strong electron donors, giving up electrons in the presence of strong electron acceptors. The converse is also true, for chlorine atoms that are properly isolated from each other don't do very much. But bring chlorine atoms together in the presence of a strong electron donor and oxidation-reduction immediately takes place, producing equal numbers of *cations* and *anions.* Remember, those are terms for positive and negative ions described in Chap. 7.

$$Na\cdot \ + \ :\ddot{Cl}\cdot \ \longrightarrow \ Na^+ \ + \ :\ddot{Cl}:^-$$

Sodium atoms have been oxidized; chlorine atoms have been reduced; electrons have been transferred. Sodium ions have an oxidation number of +1; chloride ions have an oxidation number of −1. The familiar chemical equation, however, is written somewhat differently:

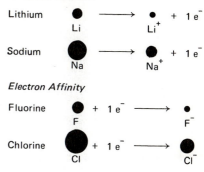

Ionization Potential

Lithium   Li   ⟶   Li$^+$ + 1 e$^-$

Sodium   Na   ⟶   Na$^+$ + 1 e$^-$

Electron Affinity

Fluorine   F + 1 e$^-$ ⟶   F$^-$

Chlorine   Cl + 1 e$^-$ ⟶   Cl$^-$

Figure 10-12
The electron-transfer process.

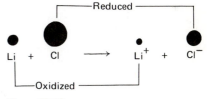

Li + Cl   ⟶   Li$^+$ + Cl$^-$

Figure 10-13
Oxidation-reduction.

$$2\,Na \;+\; Cl_2 \;\longrightarrow\; 2\,NaCl$$

Chlorine is a diatomic molecule, the atoms being held together by covalent forces that we'll explain shortly. On the other hand sodium chloride is an ionic compound, a three-dimensional cubic structure of alternating sodium and chloride ions held together by electrostatic interactions due to their electric charges. That pattern extends uniformly through space to the limits of the crystal's surfaces. Take a moment to refer back to the discussions on the solid state described in Chap. 5. Note that we've never referred to sodium chloride as a molecule, although the NaCl formula for sodium chloride certainly seems to warrant that. After all, it is a combination of atoms of sodium with atoms of chlorine producing sodium chloride. Nevertheless as we've tried to indicate, sodium chloride is only a formula on paper. The true situation is a three-dimensional crystalline salt structure. There is no discrete entity we can call NaCl, not even when the crystal structure is disrupted by dissolution in water. There are "free" ions in solution, slightly encumbered by some occluded water molecules stealing a ride.

This phenomenon is electrovalence, or chemical combination through electron transfer. Sodium atoms lose electrons, becoming 10-electron sodium ions with filled outer *L* shells. In losing an electron, each sodium atom has gained the 10-electron neon configuration. Chlorine atoms gain electrons, becoming 18-electron chloride ions with the argon configuration of electrons. Note the apparent stability achieved by acquiring the noble gas core configuration of filled outer-electron shells.

When lithium and fluorine react, a significant part of the driving force can be described in terms of electrovalence. The lithium ion has achieved the stable helium configuration; fluoride ions have gained the neon configuration.

$$Li\cdot \;+\; :\!\overset{\cdot\cdot}{\underset{\cdot\cdot}{F}}\!\cdot \;\longrightarrow\; Li^+ \;+\; :\!\overset{\cdot\cdot}{\underset{\cdot\cdot}{F}}\!\overset{\cdot}{:}$$

$$2\,Li \;+\; F_2 \;\longrightarrow\; 2\,LiF$$

Take a look at fluorine and sodium for a moment, separated as they both are from neon by one electron; it helps in understanding why fluorine is an electron acceptor and why sodium is an electron donor. Electrically speaking, each ends up where neon is at, by gaining or losing an electron. You could argue that perhaps sodium atoms ought to try and gain seven more and get to argon, or that fluorine lose seven and get back to helium. But if you think about it you'll sense the improbability of those processes.

There are many other examples of electrovalence. Most involve electron donors from the left, or metallic side of the periodic chart, and electron acceptors from the right, or nonmetallic side. Magnesium oxide (MgO) is one.

$$Mg\colon \quad \overset{\cdot\cdot}{\underset{\cdot\cdot}{O}}\colon \;\longrightarrow\; Mg^{++} \;+\; :\!\overset{\cdot\cdot}{\underset{\cdot\cdot}{O}}\!\overset{=}{:}$$

$$2\,Mg + O_2 \longrightarrow 2MgO$$

Electrovalence Is Only Part of the Binding Picture

Ions generally have single or double charges. When you get beyond the point of giving up or taking on one or two extra electrons, a minor dilemma arises. Should atoms be viewed as giving or receiving electrons? Here are the electron dot structures for atoms of the second period elements.

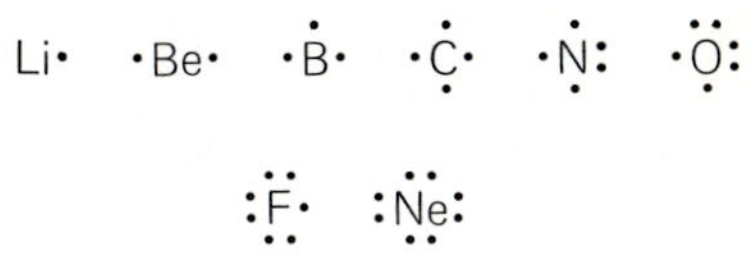

$$\text{Li·} \quad \text{·Be·} \quad \text{·}\overset{\cdot}{\text{B}}\text{·} \quad \text{·}\overset{\cdot}{\text{C}}\text{·} \quad \text{·}\overset{\cdot\cdot}{\text{N}}\text{·} \quad \text{·}\overset{\cdot\cdot}{\underset{\cdot\cdot}{\text{O}}}\text{:}$$

$$\text{:}\overset{\cdot\cdot}{\underset{\cdot\cdot}{\text{F}}}\text{·} \quad \text{:}\overset{\cdot\cdot}{\underset{\cdot\cdot}{\text{Ne}}}\text{:}$$

Carbon has four outer electrons. What to do. Give up four? Gain four? Which way to go? Carbon does neither, choosing instead to *share* electrons, combining through **covalence** instead (Fig. 10-14). In so doing, the resulting chemical combinations are now hardly salt-like. They are obviously molecular, as you will see. This is the other half of the valence theory. Electrovalence successfully explains why magnesium oxide is an ionic solid with the familiar sodium chloride crystal structure; covalence successfully explains why carbon dioxide is a gaseous collection of molecules under the same conditions of temperature and pressure. To write an electrovalent representation for carbon dioxide is about as wrong as talking about magnesium oxide molecules.

□ Covalence and Electron Sharing

Covalence theory is a justification for stable chemical combinations based on sharing of electrons. Through sharing electrons, stable octets and electron-shell configurations can be drawn that help explain the stability of many molecules. The simplest molecule is the hydrogen molecule. It is the stable arrangement for hydrogen in nature. Hydrogen molecules are commonly found in the chemistry laboratory, stored in appropriate gas cylinders. Under those conditions hydrogen molecules can be stored indefinitely. This is not so for hydrogen atoms. Covalence theory offers an explanation for the energetically favored combined state (hydrogen molecules) based on sharing electrons. Each hydrogen atom has its single electron; two electrons are required to achieve the stable helium configuration. All that is needed, then is for two hydrogen atoms to share their electrons.

$$\text{H· + ·H} \longrightarrow \text{H:H}$$

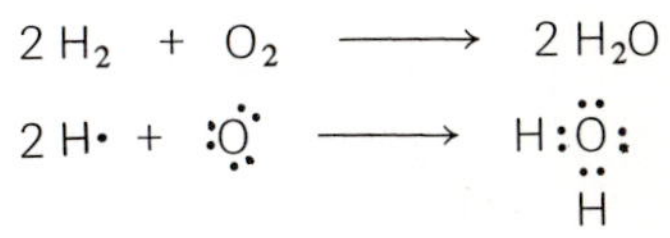

Each hydrogen atom has the filled shell configuration of helium. The molecular combination is much lower in energy and therefore more stable than are two uncombined atoms. Since hydrogen has only a single *s*-type electron in the *K* shell, only one covalent bond is possible. Thus, the hydrogen ion is a univalent species.

Oxygen is generally divalent; nitrogen tends to be trivalent; carbon, quadrivalent: all possible because electrons in the (*L* shell) $n = 2$ shell have four bonding sublevels. The oxygen atom in the water molecule finds its complement of eight electrons by sharing between two of its outer shell electrons and two electrons from a couple of hydrogen atoms.

$$2\,H_2 \;+\; O_2 \;\longrightarrow\; 2\,H_2O$$

$$2\,H\text{·} \;+\; \text{:}\overset{\cdot\cdot}{\underset{\cdot}{O}}\text{·} \;\longrightarrow\; H\text{:}\overset{\cdot\cdot}{\underset{\cdot\cdot}{O}}\text{:}$$
$$\phantom{2\,H\text{·} \;+\; \text{:}\overset{\cdot\cdot}{\underset{\cdot}{O}}\text{·} \;\longrightarrow\;} H$$

Figure 10-14
Covalence, the *sharing* of electrons.

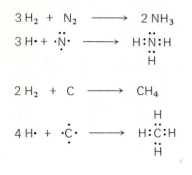

$$3\,H_2 + N_2 \longrightarrow 2\,NH_3$$

$$3\,H\!\cdot + \cdot \overset{\cdot\cdot}{\underset{\cdot}{N}}\!\cdot \longrightarrow H\!:\!\overset{\cdot\cdot}{N}\!:\!H$$
$$\qquad\qquad\qquad\qquad H$$

$$2\,H_2 + C \longrightarrow CH_4$$

$$\qquad\qquad\qquad\qquad H$$
$$4\,H\!\cdot + \cdot \overset{\cdot\cdot}{\underset{\cdot\cdot}{C}}\!\cdot \longrightarrow H\!:\!\overset{}{C}\!:\!H$$
$$\qquad\qquad\qquad\qquad H$$

Each hydrogen then has its complement of two. The nitrogen atom in the ammonia molecule finds eight electrons by sharing electrons with three hydrogen atoms. Each hydrogen is then satisfied, having two electrons. For the carbon atom in methane, a similar mutually satisfactory arrangement through electron-sharing is possible.

In all three cases, the bonding electrons are completely accounted for: two for hydrogen; eight for oxygen, nitrogen and carbon. Further, in every case these product molecules (H_2O, NH_3, CH_4) are more stable than the reactant species (H_2, O_2, N_2, C).

Here is an ever-so-slightly more sophisticated notation for molecular structures. Whenever an electron-pair bond exists between two atoms we'll draw a line. Note that electrons not directly involved in bonding are left as pairs of dots.

Once in a great while you may see a free electron, unpaired and not apparently involved in bonding, but those are very special cases, and will be an important part of a later discussion.

When a pair of atoms share a pair of available electrons, the atoms can bond. That's why H_2 exists. But now consider a pair of chlorine atoms. Each has seven electrons available; each has a single slot in one of its four energy sublevels in which an electron can be placed in order to get to a filled argon-like configuration. Electrons are shared.

$$:\!\overset{\cdot\cdot}{\underset{\cdot\cdot}{Cl}}\!\cdot + \cdot\overset{\cdot\cdot}{\underset{\cdot\cdot}{Cl}}\!: \longrightarrow :\!\overset{\cdot\cdot}{\underset{\cdot\cdot}{Cl}}\!:\!\overset{\cdot\cdot}{\underset{\cdot\cdot}{Cl}}\!:$$

Each now has eight and so both have happily arrived at argon. Chlorine molecules have lower energy and are more stable than chlorine atoms; using our new notation, write it as $:\!\overset{\cdot\cdot}{\underset{\cdot\cdot}{Cl}}\!-\!\overset{\cdot\cdot}{\underset{\cdot\cdot}{Cl}}\!:$. A bit later on when you are thoroughly comfortable with electron complements for the more familiar atoms and molecules, we'll drop the dots altogether, writing Cl–Cl, or simply let it go as Cl_2. Again, beware the beguiling simplicity of the chemical formula. Clearly much more is implied. Please remember that!

Understanding What's In a Formula and a Reaction

Right along with understanding chemical formulas and chemical reactions comes a developing awareness of electronic structure for simple covalent molecules and ionic substances. Hydrogen reacts with chlorine producing the covalent hydrogen chloride molecule.

$$H_2 + Cl_2 \longrightarrow 2\,HCl$$

$$H\!:\!H + :\!\overset{\cdot\cdot}{\underset{\cdot\cdot}{Cl}}\!:\!\overset{\cdot\cdot}{\underset{\cdot\cdot}{Cl}}\!: \longrightarrow 2\,H\!:\!\overset{\cdot\cdot}{\underset{\cdot\cdot}{Cl}}\!:$$

When hydrogen chloride reacts with ammonia, the two covalent reactants combine, producing an ionic structure, ammonium chloride (NH_4Cl). The product is a salt-like structure, existing as a pair of "free" ions, either in solution or when put together in a crystalline arrangement in the solid state.

The ammonium ion (NH_4^+) is formed by a proton transfer reaction in which the hydrogen ion bonds to the unshared electron pair on nitrogen, leaving the negative chloride ion behind. That constitutes a new kind of electron-shared chemical bond in which one species, the nitrogen atom of the ammonia molecule, supplies both of the shared electrons. The proton brought nothing with it but the positive charge. Interestingly, once the proton makes the fateful trip to nitrogen, all four hydrogen atoms are then indistinguishable and the positive charge becomes a *net* charge on the entire complex ammonium ion. Rather than write the ionic products as two separated species, we'll write such structures as *ion-pairs.* That more nearly approximates the existing physical relationship. The ammonium ion is made up of four equivalent, covalent N-to-H bonds, paired to the chloride ion in an ionic type of bond: an ion-pair.

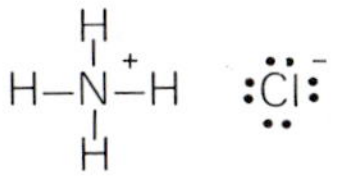

Fluorine forms single bonds in much the same way we described for chlorine:

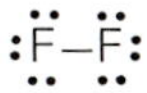

Molecular oxygen requires special comment. There are six electrons available for bonding in each oxygen atom: a total of twelve. On first impulse you might perhaps assume a double bond between the two oxygen atoms through sharing pairs of electrons:

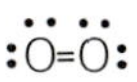

However, that turns out to be an incorrect model for describing the facts. Molecular oxygen's chemical reactivity is so great that gaining a stable octet of electrons by such an arrangement is probably *too* artificial. A more realistic representation gives each oxygen an odd, unpaired electron.

That's a radical departure from the octet rule we've been discussing. In fact, let's use the word **radical** here to imply the availability of an energy sublevel with a free, or unpaired bonding electron present. That makes molecular oxygen a "diradical." (More about that situation when our discussion turns to oxygenation of the blood during animal respiration.) However, oxygen follows the octet rule in the usual fashion when combining with atoms of the other elements. In its compound substances, oxygen is all but completely octet-prone. Check the arrangement of the outer electrons in water (H_2O), or take a look at the oxygen atom in ethyl alcohol (CH_3CH_2OH).

$$H-\overset{\overset{\displaystyle H}{|}}{\underset{\underset{\displaystyle H}{|}}{C}}-\overset{\overset{\displaystyle H}{|}}{\underset{\underset{\displaystyle H}{|}}{C}}-\overset{..}{\underset{..}{O}}-H$$

CH_3CH_2OH

In Summary

Valence refers to the combining capacity, or number of possible bonds that can be formed with other atoms. Electrovalence refers to bonding through electron transfer; covalence has to do with bonding through electron sharing. Stability in any chemical combination, and consequently stable bond formation, is depicted as revolving about one central theme, the octet rule, or the approach toward a filled outer-shell, noble gas configuration. Helium neon, argon, krypton, and xenon generally form no bonds. Still you may have heard rumors about xenon tetrafluoride (XeF_4), and krypton compounds, too. Hang on to that perception until Chapter 12 when we'll air one of the fascinating chemical developments of the 1960s. Fluorine generally single-bonds, having seven of eight core electrons; oxygen commonly forms two bonds, but watch out for molecular oxygen with its "radical" structure; nitrogen usually forms three bonds, but sometimes four as in NH_4^+ ions; carbon is tetravalent, forming four bonds.

☐ Multiple Bonds Between Atoms

Go back to carbon dioxide, the molecule we used to get us off into a discussion of covalence, for a moment. How shall we arrive at a satisfactory octet structure for both oxygen and carbon in carbon dioxide? We do have to introduce *multiple* bonds between atoms.

$$\cdot \overset{\displaystyle \cdot}{\underset{\displaystyle \cdot}{C}} \cdot \;\; + \;\; 2\cdot\overset{..}{\underset{..}{O}}: \;\;\longrightarrow\;\; :\overset{..}{\underset{..}{O}}::C::\overset{..}{\underset{..}{O}}:$$

That's a satisfactory arrangement. Each oxygen atom has eight electrons in a shared arrangement; so does the central carbon atom. Using our line representation for bonds, we can write the equation as follows:

$$C \;+\; O_2 \;\;\longrightarrow\;\; O=C=O$$

Note that we have written carbon dioxide as a linear molecule. The linear arrangement is partly a consequence of the double bonds which restrict bending or twisting about the carbon atom by the two oxygen atoms. The water molecule is similarly bonded; a central atom (O), surrounded by two others (H's). However, bonding to the central atom is single, not double, and the atoms fall naturally into a bent arrangement as $H-\overset{..}{\underset{..}{O}}_{H}$. Therein lies the world of difference in properties. But we don't want to make too much of the consequences of the double bond's presence, or of the octet rule for that matter. In fact, this entire picture is going to have to be modified. As we'll try to show, molecules such as nitric oxide (NO), known for over 200 years, are quite stable, yet can't be explained by the octet rule; and molecules such as the formaldehyde molecule have oxygen double-bonded to carbon, yet are bent. Nevertheless, the octet rule and the multiple bond picture drawn from it, give us a good model for a start.

An acetylene torch in use.

Here Are Some Examples

Armed with this new perception of multiple bonds, we are now in a position to begin to see and understand some other diatomic molecules such as nitrogen with its five bonding electrons, oxygen with its six, and fluorine with its seven. Nitrogen forms a very stable *triple* bond between two atoms, making use of three connecting pairs of electrons.

:N:::N: :N≡N: N≡N N_2

The acetylene molecule (C_2H_2) is a simple triple bonded carbon structure, perhaps best known for its use as a high-energy fuel for the oxyacetylene torch. The energy is locked up partly in that triple bond. Satisfied the bonding requirements for carbon and hydrogen in acetylene? Yes, check it and see.

H:C:::C:H   H—C≡C—H

Another interesting triple bond molecule with a simple structure is hydrogen cyanide (HCN). It is probably best known to you for its very nasty behavior in destroying the blood's oxygen-carrying capacity: cyanide poisoning. It is highly toxic when taken internally as the soluble salt (NaCN) or ingested via the lungs as the gas (HCN). But that isn't very important relative to hydrogen cyanide's industrial use as a raw material in the preparation of synthetic fibers (topic for Chap. 13). Check the covalences here, too.

H:C:::N: H—C:::N: H—C≡N   HCN

An example of a simple, double bonded, carbon structure is the ethylene molecule (C_2H_4) which has the unusual property of causing fruit such as bananas and tomatoes to ripen.

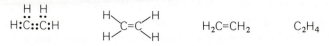

$H_2C=CH_2$ C_2H_4

Valence requirements satisfied? Yes. Everything seems in order: four bonds to each carbon; hydrogens all singly bonded.

□ Why Should a Couple of Atoms Share a Pair of Electrons?

Good question! Why should a couple of atoms share a pair of electrons between them? How shall we explain why these valence bond ideas fit this theory for the covalent bond? We really have no basis for expecting that any force of attraction should suddenly come into being whenever atoms share electrons. But the fact is experimental, and the nagging question is why? Quantum mechanics supplies a very successful answer which we can qualitatively sketch in a way that avoids the pitfalls of some very difficult mathematics. Fuzzy clouds, electron densities, and probability patterns will become our forte here. Be careful, however. As with valence bonds and octets of electrons, these will provide no more than models that will allow us a closer look at the nature of chemical bonding. We'll examine a few simple models, trying to gain some understanding of the forces of attraction in hydrogen and methane. More complicated molecules are just too difficult to handle, even qualitatively. **Molecular orbital models** are descriptive approximations, but they turn out to be pretty good ones. The trouble, of course, is that quantum effects really have no *ordinary* explanation. Remember, as we've tried to emphasize before, the trouble is not with the molecules . . . they're all right . . . it's our inability to accurately describe them that causes difficulty for us.

No Ordinary Explanation

We'll begin with a coulombic discussion. The very simplest molecule is a complex of interactions. Molecular hydrogen is made up of four charged particles, two electrons and two protons. In each isolated atom, before any combination or bond formation takes place, the single most important force is the electrostatic attraction between proton (+) and electron (−) (Fig. 10-15). As the two atoms are brought near each other, additional interactions are evident: the electron of one atom is attracted to the nucleus of the other; the two electrons repel each other; and the two nuclei repel each other. In the ensuing battle between attractive and repulsive forces, the most effective turn out to be the forces of attraction between positive nuclei and negative electron clouds. The two atoms are drawn together to the point where repulsive forces between the two positive nuclei become significant and call a halt. We've arrived at a preferred distance across which attractive and repulsive forces are held in balance. The two hydrogen atoms now find themselves in stable combination where the energy of the system is at its lowest level (Fig. 10-16). The internuclear distance, or the average bond length in the hydrogen molecule (the H-H bond) is 0.74 Å. Bond energies are also important in characterizing chemical combinations; in the case of molecular hydrogen, it takes 103.5 kcal per mole to separate the two atoms in the molecule. That much energy is needed to cleave the H-H bond symmetrically. Finally, what

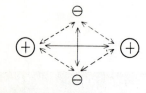

Figure 10-15
The hydrogen molecule: two positively charged nuclei and two negatively charged electrons interacting.

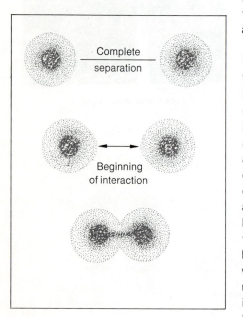

Figure 10-16
Two hydrogen atoms coming together to form a stable combination, the hydrogen molecule. A combination of s-type atomic orbitals.

does our sketch of the hydrogen molecule look like? Kind of like a slightly tapered football perhaps? That's the picture we get from our quantum mechanical description of two hydrogen atomic orbitals combined into a hydrogen molecular orbital. Two separated *s*-type energy sublevels have overlapped in a way favorable to bonding; two atomic orbitals have become a molecular orbital.

This molecular orbital approximation, when applied to other molecules, turns out to be a very elegant technique for generally understanding and predicting molecular structures. The very simplest *s*-orbitals that overlapped into the model of the hydrogen molecule required no particular thought about direction. We imagined both clouds simply approaching, overlapping, and finally settling into the most comfortable position, 0.74 Å apart. A bonding molecular orbital was formed in which electron density concentrated in the region between the two nuclei.

The Water Molecule Requires a More Complicated Model

The water molecule requires a more complicated model since it involves *p* atomic orbitals in oxygen. As we've seen, these *p*-type energy sublevels were depicted as running off into space at right angles to each other. The water molecule is made up of three atoms, two hydrogens and one oxygen. Bring each of the two spherical *s* atomic orbitals of the two hydrogen atoms up to the two available *p*-orbitals in oxygen along the proper linear direction. Overlap and combination of these models is allowed to take place. There are six of eight possible *L* shell electrons in the oxygen atom; two more, and oxygen achieves argon stability. These six electrons are thought to be arranged into four orbitals, a single *s*-orbital and three *p*-orbitals. The rule is this: when we add electrons into orbitals while going from simple to more complex atoms, the final picture must show the electrons placed lowest energy first. So oxygen's *s*-orbital fills with a pair. The next four electrons are added to the three equal but higher-energy *p*-orbitals. Here is another rule: put one electron into each of these three equivalent *p*-orbitals before you introduce a second to fill any completely. The final arrangement looks like this:

$$\text{2s} \quad \textcircled{$\uparrow\downarrow$} \qquad\qquad \text{2p} \quad \textcircled{$\uparrow\downarrow$} \; \textcircled{$\uparrow$} \; \textcircled{$\uparrow$}$$

2 s
lower energy

2 p
higher energy

The arrows indicate that the electrons have opposite spin number signs (+ or −). The other possibility for the *p*-orbitals would place two pairs in two orbitals, leaving the third completely empty. It doesn't happen that way.

We can project two *p* orbitals in oxygen, the two with available space for overlap and bonding, the two that are free to share electrons with hydrogen, along the *x* and *y* direction. Presume the one set of paired electrons (the filled orbital) lies in the *z* direction; it's not necessary to draw it in. Please keep in mind that the

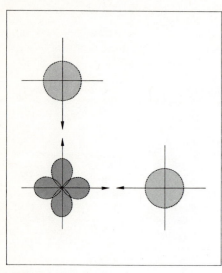

Figure 10-17
P-type atomic orbitals in oxygen available for combinations with *s*-types in hydrogen.

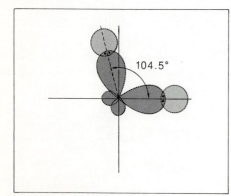

Figure 10-18
The atomic orbitals combine, forming the molecular orbitals in water.

pair of electrons is there, although not involved in bonding. That's true, too, for the pair of *s* electrons: uninvolved. Now look at the two *p*-orbitals that have the space available (Fig. 10-17). The *s*-orbital hydrogen electrons are made to approach, overlap, and bond, and the preferred configuration is a bent water molecule with an internal bond angle of 104.5°. The average H-O bond distance is 0.96 Å, and of course, it's the same for both H–O bonds (see Fig. 10-18).

Question: why isn't the internal bond angle 90°? According to the angular orientation of three mutually perpendicular *p*-orbitals it ought to be. Here is one likely answer. The two sets of bonding electrons that are formed can repel each other slightly, spreading the angle within the molecule to something greater than a right angle, namely from 90° to 104.5°. Take a look back at our simple valence bond formulas for the water molecule, and see how consistent they are. The two covalent H-O bonds are indicated; and so too are both the pairs of electrons on oxygen that are not involved in bonding. A second, and perhaps better answer to the original question can be drawn from viewing the water molecule in terms of those two lone electron pairs, the nonbonding electrons we mentioned. Water molecule models could have an electronic distribution that is tetrahedral, or 109.5°. However, due to repulsion between the lone electron-pairs, the angle closes down to the observed value of 104.5°. Which is the best explanation: closing down or spreading? The general consensus among scientists today is that closing down from 109.5°, based on lone-pair repulsion, is *most* likely. However, it's interesting to look at both views, two seemingly reasonable ways of explaining the same experimental result (Fig. 10-19).

What kind of bonding would you expect for the ammonia molecule? Well, let's begin with nitrogen's complement of five outer shell electrons: two paired *s* electrons; three unpaired *p* electrons:

Therefore, overlap and sharing with three hydrogen *s* electrons is reasonable. (See Fig. 10-20.) The bond angle closes down to 107.3° due to bonding versus nonbonding electron-pair repulsions, much as in the water molecule. Ammonia is also pyramid-shaped because of the influence of the electron-pair on nitrogen *not* involved in bonding. Hydrogen fluoride should be easy enough for you to sketch out. You'll have three pairs of electrons on fluorine not involved in bonding, and one available *p*-orbital for overlap with the single hydrogen *s*-orbital.

Reprise

In order to put together a model for a covalent bond between two atoms, you'll need two electrons and an available orbital in both atoms, usually in an outer shell. The two atoms of our model can now form a shared electron-pair bond, or simply produce an atom with one outer-shell orbital already containing an electron pair. All the other atom has to do now is produce an empty orbital, thus allowing possible formation of a covalent bond between the two atoms.

The model bonds we've built for ammonia, water, and hydrogen fluoride by linear combination of *s*- and *p*-orbitals are called *sigma* bonds. They are the single bonds. The linear combination of two *s* atomic orbitals in a hydrogen molecule also produces a sigma bond; combination of two *p* atomic orbitals in fluorine produces a sigma bond, too. When we introduce multiple bonds (the double and triple bonds in oxygen, nitrogen, ethylene, and acetylene) the additional bonds are referred to as *pi* bonds. These pi bonds are produced by combination of *p*-orbitals that we picture as taking place laterally rather than linearly (see Fig. 10-21).

□ **Bonding with Carbon Atoms Is Special**

The trouble with methane is that all of its four C-H bonds are identical; in fact, they are indistinguishable. Bond lengths are all 1.54 Å. The valence bond picture doesn't really give a very satisfactory picture. The molecule is not planar, or flat; the six H-C-H bond angles are all the same, namely 109.5°. Six H-C-H bond angles? Yes, that's right. Six! Because the structure is tetrahedral. There is a central carbon atom to which four hydrogens are attached in a uniform, tetrahedral structure. All well and good. But how shall we rationalize that

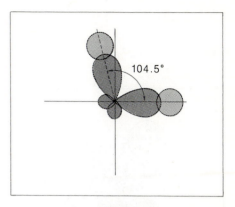

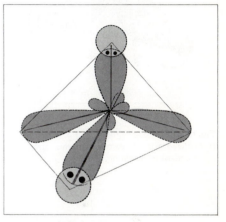

Figure 10-19
Two different models explaining the 104.5° bond angle in the water molecule (top). Electron-pair repulsion; and (bottom) repulsion of bonding electrons.

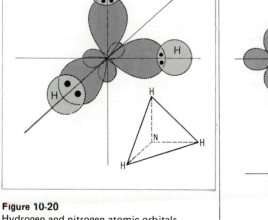

Figure 10-20
Hydrogen and nitrogen atomic orbitals combined in the ammonia molecule.

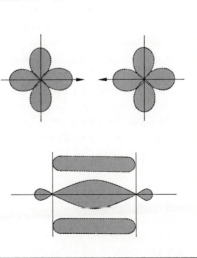

Figure 10-21
Linear combination gives rise to the central central sigma bond; lateral combination produces the pi-bond.

structure in the light of the carbon atom and its four valence electrons as they are apparently placed in *s*- and *p*-orbitals within the *L* shell? We'd expect a pair of *s*-orbital electrons and two more in two of three *p*-orbitals.

But on that basis, we should predict anything but four equivalent C-H bonds when hydrogen shares electrons with carbon. We could jump one of the two *s*-orbital electrons into the empty *p*-orbital. That yields four possible bonding sites where there were only two before, but not four equivalent positions. Remember, there is a difference in energy between *s*- and *p*-orbitals. That difficulty is overcome by recognizing the fact that all four bonds are equal in energy; that the electron distribution for the four shared pair bonds is entirely uniform. Therefore, all four orbitals must also be exactly equivalent to explain this; their energies must be exactly the same. The process of equalization has a fancy name and shows up in pictures of many bonding situations. It's referred to as *hybridization*. The four new bonds are *hybrids* with *s* and *p* character; all four are equal and tetrahedrally directed in space (Fig. 10-22). You may say, "Oh well, all that is nothing more than an explanation after the fact." True enough! But then that's part of what science is about, and hybridization is a very strong model indeed. Many, many structures can be understood as a result of this model; it is a successful conceptualization. In fact, in a very general way, bonding theory itself constitutes one of the really great strengths of modern theoretical chemistry. Bonding theory stands out perhaps more than any other single development in chemistry during the last 50 years.

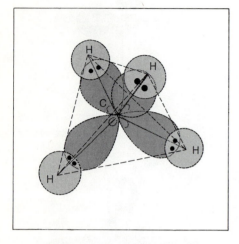

Figure 10-22
Hybridized orbitals account for the tetrahedral arrangement in methane.

☐ Covalent Bonds with an Ionic Profile

When hydrogen atoms bond with each other, or when chlorine molecules are formed, the region of high electron density where the bonding orbitals overlap lies equidistant between the nuclei. It is therefore reasonable to write H:H or H—H; :C̈l:C̈l: or Cl—Cl. The reason is that in both cases each atom exerts an equal and opposite influence on the shared electron-pair. When you consider the hydrogen chloride molecule, however, the center of highest electron-density is thought to be shifted toward the chlorine atom, imparting *partial* ionic character to the hydrogen chloride molecule. The chlorine atom becomes slightly more negative and the hydrogen atom slightly more positive. Such a molecule is said to be *polar*. Polarity is indicated in the following fashion, making use of the squiggly Greek letter, *delta*:

$$\overset{\delta+}{H}\overset{\delta-}{-Cl}$$

The extent to which different atoms are believed capable of exercising control over a shared electron-pair is related to their *electronegativities*. The greater the electronegativity, the greater the control or attraction for the pair; the most electronegative elements lie upper right in the periodic table; the least, lower left. When we imagine the most electronegative elements bonding with the least, the very great difference produces positive and negative ions, the more electro-negative atom taking with it the pair of electrons. Thus, cesium chloride exists as a pure example of an ionic structure:

$$[Cs^+] \; [:\!\ddot{C}\!\ddot{l}\!:]$$

The water molecule is considered covalent and polar. It has a negative end, presumably because of oxygen's electronegativity in addition to two positive poles since electrons have been drawn away from the hydrogens. Polarity is very important in understanding the ability of water molecules to hang together in a three-dimensional network. The water molecule has partial ionic character because of electronegativity differences as well as those external hydrogen bonds we mentioned very early in this chapter. The positive pole of one water molecule is attracted to the negative pole of another . . . and on and on and on (Fig. 10-24).

An orbital portrait for the nonpolar hydrogen and chlorine molecules might look like this:

bonding *s*-orbitals
electrons in region of highest
electron density where
they overlap

bonding *p*-orbitals
showing
electron pair

The polar hydrogen chloride molecule would be better represented by showing the shared electron-pair removed toward the center of the chlorine atom *p*-orbital:

Briefly re-examine an earlier comparison: the linear carbon dioxide molecule and the bent water molecule. Bond polarity and electronegativity are important. Oxygen atoms in carbon dioxide are electronegative. Why then is carbon dioxide not polar? The twin bonding orbitals from carbon to each of the two oxygens lock the molecule into a linear arrangement. Removal of electrons from carbon due to the electronegativity of one oxygen is exactly offset by the equal and opposite removal of electrons from carbon on the other side. It's very much as two teams of horses pulling against each other with equal force. If none of the harnessing equipment breaks, nothing is done. Equal and opposite forces cancel (Fig. 10-24).

Because of the bonding in the water molecule the equal forces do not act in exactly opposite direction and there is a resultant force. We owe much of our style as living things to that resultant force, since we are very water-oriented organisms.

Here's one for you to think about. Can you perceive of ions in solution? You know, like the dissolved ions that carried the charge and completed the circuit

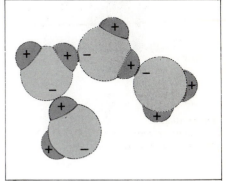

Figure 10-23
Water is a hydrogen-bonded collection of polar H_2O molecules.

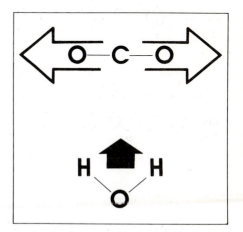

Figure 10-24
Comparing dipolar forces in CO_2 and H_2O.

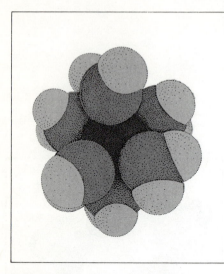

Figure 10-25
The hydrated sodium ion finds itself surrounded by half a dozen water molecules in solution.

for us back in our discussion of electrochemical cells a couple of chapters ago? What do you think about the possibilities of unattended protons in solution, and free-swimming sodium ions? In fact, can you now begin to imagine or sketch in your mind the manner in which salts dissolve into ions? The water molecule is polar: a fat, fuzzy ball that can attach its positive or negative end into an electrostatic interaction as the opportunity arises. The sodium ion in solution is surrounded by a number of water molecules; it might be better described as a *hydrated* sodium ion (Fig. 10-25).

$$Na\text{-}Cl \longrightarrow [Na^+]\,[:\!\overset{\cdot\cdot}{\underset{\cdot\cdot}{Cl}}\!:^-]$$

Crystals of sodium chloride dissolve in water because water molecules lower the energy within the crystal, by electrostatically interacting with positive sodiums and negative chlorines. The ions are continually attracted away until dissolution is complete, or until there just isn't any more room in solution because the limits of solubility have been passed.

☐ There Are Exceptions to the Octet Rule

Perhaps the most incredible thing about the octet rule is that across the row of elements making up the second period there are virtually no exceptions. Second period elements have stable, lower energy *s*- and *p*-orbitals that can accumulate eight electrons. When that happy situation is attained, everything is very stable indeed, in fact so stable, the situation can be likened to the stable noble gas configuration. But now step on down into the third period and the octet rule begins to lose some of its luster. Still a good rule, but now watch out for exceptions. Let's look at sulfur.

The octet rule is very much in evidence for simple sulfur-containing compounds such as hydrogen sulfide (H_2S). The orbital arrangement and bonding for the outer shell electrons in H_2S is much the same as for oxygen and water. Two bonding sites are available.

But how shall we explain a series of sulfur molecules such as SF_2, SF_4, and SF_6? SF_2 is no trouble; it's much the same as H_2S except the overlapping orbitals are fluorine *p*- and sulfur *p*-orbitals whereas in H_2S the molecular orbitals were due to *s*- and *p*-orbital overlap. But SF_4 and SF_6? It seems clear that sulfur does more than simply follow rules. Sulfur is a leader. Sulfur has the capacity to share electrons with more than the number of atoms allowed by the octet rule. The violation of the octet rule is, however, not an aberration, but an explainable perception based on atomic theory. At the end of the third period lies the noble gas, argon, with its *s*- and *p*-orbitals. But third period elements have a set of five *d*-orbitals that lie inside . . . and are empty.

If one of the paired *p* electrons "jumps" into a *d*-orbital, there are now four

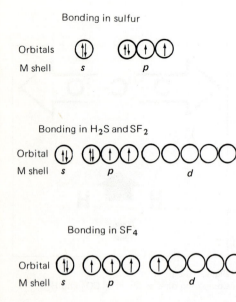

hybrid orbitals available for bonding.

Again, "jumping" one of the paired *s* electrons into a second *d*-orbital results in six hybrid orbitals available for bonding.

By using *d*-orbitals for sharing electrons . . . extra bonds, not possible otherwise form. That extra bond potential explains why the sulfuric acid structure H_2SO_4 is possible. The sulfur atom is hardly the divalent structure of our expectations based on a simple understanding of H_2S.

$$H-\overset{..}{\underset{..}{O}}-\overset{\overset{\textstyle :\overset{..}{O}:}{\|}}{\underset{\underset{\textstyle :\overset{..}{O}:}{\|}}{S}}-\overset{..}{\underset{..}{O}}-H$$

Bonding in SF_6 and H_2SO_4

As far as SF_6 and H_2SO_4 are concerned, the eight-electron octet rule has seemingly graduated to a twelve-electron rule. Or more simply put, here we have an exception.

☐ Resonance: A Neither-Here-nor-There Bonding Concept

We've been busily spinning yarns about valence bonds and molecular orbitals as though they really are the stuff of atoms and molecules. They are of course no better than approximations, useful models, tools in the chemist's arsenal. There are however certain molecules for which we can draw no satisfactory structure picture based on anything said so far. Take for example what happens when you apply the octet rule and valence bond ideas to the structure of the carbonate ion. The sodium carbonate crystal structure is ionic, and dissociates in water into hydrated sodium ions and carbonate ions:

$$Na_2CO_3 \longrightarrow [Na^+][CO_3^=][Na^+] \longrightarrow 2\,Na^+ + CO_3^=$$

A structure for carbonate can be drawn as a flat, ionic species with a single negative charge on two of three oxygen atoms due to the presence of extra electrons . . . seven instead of six. All four atoms are surrounded by an octet of electrons.

Such a structural approximation is hardly adequate because it implies one key point not born out by experiment. It suggests two different kinds of bonds between oxygen and carbon: one, a single bond; the other a double bond. When chemists look inside carbonate ion only one kind of bond is found. And most interestingly, the properties of that one kind of bond lie somewhere between single and double bond character . . . perhaps a hybrid or intermediate bond, a $1\frac{1}{3}$ bond. There are three equivalent carbon-to-hydrogen bonds. But what kind of formula or formalism shall we use to represent such a situation. Easily done! No new model needed. The slight-of-hand that makes the new case fit the old model is the combining of the more-than-one structural formula needed. For carbonate ion, there are three possible structures, the one real structure being a hybrid, or intermediate thereof.

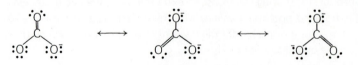

We've given the twelve o'clock oxygen the double bond 1/3 of the time, the four o'clock oxygen has it 1/3 of the time; and 1/3 of the time, the eight o'clock oxygen. Which means that on an average we can expect to see each bond at any time with 1⅓ bond properties. The three resonance hybrids, as they are called, easily change, one into the other, by simply shifting a pair of electrons from bonding status to non-bonding status. That forces other electron-pairs to shift as well in order to sustain the demands of the octet rule. For example, structure I shifts into structure II.

Resonance is nothing more than an accommodation of these electron-dot and valence bond formalisms to the facts of the matter. Two or more formulas are combined to better represent the real thing. The little double headed arrow serves to indicate to you that the formulas should be superimposed in your mind. Not strictly the one; not really the other—resonance hybrids. Perhaps it is helpful to remember that a mule is an animal, a unique member of nature's menagerie. But a mule is also understandable as a cross between two other unique species, horses and donkeys. Not strictly the one; not really the other. A mule is a mule.

The same arguments work out very well for sulfate ion. Six equivalent structures can be drawn, and we best understand the sulfate ion as a resonance hybrid thereof:

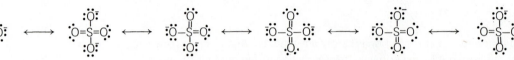

And what might you guess about the sulfur-to-oxygen bond? Single or double? Right. Experimentally, about 1½ bonds; a hybrid of two double bonds and two single bonds.

But perhaps the broadest interest with the deepest implications for this resonance phenomenon must be accorded to one further example, the benzene molecule. And the structure story of benzene stands as one of the great triumphs of bonding theory. Simple covalent structures will not serve to reasonably represent C_6H_6, the benzene molecule. A physical examination will reveal that all twelve atoms lie in a plane, hardly what you'd expect for a molecule with a skeleton of tetrahedral carbon atoms; further examination reveals that the bond angles are 120° which puts the main structure into the form of a hexagonal ring; and there is only one kind of carbon-to-carbon bond with a length of 1.40 Å, somewhere between the single bond value of 1.54 Å and the double bond value of 1.33 Å. Well to begin with, we can draw a basic ring structure. That will satisfy some of the physical requirements.

But we still have to cope with the octet rule and the fact that the molecule is flat. So we'll introduce a system of alternating single and double bonds. That leaves us with the classical structure for benzene. However, resonance theory suggests the possibility of a second structure equally satisfactory:

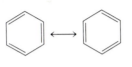

The actual structure is a resonance hybrid, a flat hexagonal molecule with only one kind of C-to-C linkage of about $1\frac{1}{3}$ bond character. And here again, we can get some help for our better understanding by drawing the structure in a new way in which the dashed line indicates the apparent equality that really exists between the bonds:

The benzene story is legend. It happened the year the Civil War ended, involving the learned professor at the Belgian University of Ghent, Auguste Kekulé. The principle involved was the stuff dreams are made of. As the story goes, Kekulé had a dream. He had been much concerned of late about structural chemistry as he was in the midst of preparing his lectures in chemistry for publication. He dozed before the fireplace. The benzene structure problem danced in his head. He dreamt of long snake-like chains of carbon atoms, and was suddenly struck by a remarkable revelation as the head of one molecule "gripped its own tail and the picture whirled scornfully before my eyes." (Fig. 10-26.) A cyclic structure rather than an open chain. It remained for Kekulé but to work out the details of the valences to produce the classical model of the hexagonal ring with its

Figure 10-26
A humorous representation of the benzene ring in the reports of the "thirsty chemical society" in 1886.

Figure 10-27
Auguste Kekulé was a marvelous subject for the caricaturists of his day.

CH₄	NH₃	OH₂	FH
– 161	– 33	+100	+19
		SH₂	
		– 61	
		SeH₂	
		– 42	
		TeH₂	
		– 2	

alternating double bonds. Kekule had studied architecture and so perhaps it was no coincidence that his thoughts drifted in such a graphic manner. And besides, with such a marvelously funny countenance (Fig. 10-27), you'd have expected something weird and Freudian, such as dreaming about snakes biting their tails and the like.

☐ **Questions to Answer . . . Problems to Solve**

1. In your own words, put together a brief statement of what it is you understand by each of the following terms:
    (a) resonance   (e) bond angle   (i) pi bond
    (b) hybridization   (f) bond length   (j) multiple bond
    (c) atomic orbital   (g) bond energy
    (d) molecular orbital (h) sigma bond

2. Draw an electron-dot structure for each of the following, being sure to honor the octet rule:
    (a) H_2, P_4, S_8 (d) H_2S (g) H_3PO_4
    (b) H_2O (e) H_2SO_4
    (c) H_2O_2 (f) H_3P

3. For each of the following, draw the appropriate electron-dot formulas:
    (a) NH_3 (c) CH_4 (e) CH_3NH_2
    (b) N_2H_4 (d) CH_3OH (f) HCN

4. Carbon monoxide (CO) has a melting point and boiling point of – 199°C and – 191.5°C respectively. Does that suggest anything to you about chemical bonding in CO? Compare that to magnesium oxide (MgO) with melting point and boiling point of 2800°C and 3600°C respectively.

5. Carbon dioxide is a non-polar molecule. What does that suggest to you about its molecular architecture?

6. What's a hydrogen bond? Explain the effect of hydrogen bonding on the boiling points of liquids that hydrogen bond.

7. Explain the vast difference in the physical properties of graphite and diamond in terms of chemical bonding and atomic architecture.

8. Water isn't anything like its periodic neighbors going across or down the table. Compare boiling points for example. What boiling point might you have expected? Would you care to comment about that?

9. Can you anticipate a situation in which the two electrons in two hydrogen atoms might not form a stable bond? (*Hint*: Remember Wolfgang Pauli!)

10. Briefly explain and illustrate each of the following:
    (a) electronegativities
    (d) ionization potential
    (b) polar molecules
    (e) electron affinity
    (c) ion pairs

11. Sulfur dioxide causes us much grief as an air pollutant in heavily industrialized areas and locations. Draw the electron-dot formula.

12. Sodium hypochlorite is the active ingredient in "clorox," a well-known laundry bleach. Draw the electron-dot formula. And see if you can explain the situation that it finds itself in when in a gallon container of aqueous solution.

13. And here's a tough one. Try your hand at the electron-dot formula for carbon monoxide. (*Hint*: One possible structure puts a positive charge on carbon and a negative charge on oxygen.) It should be comforting to know the structure next time you find yourself asphyxiated in a freeway traffic jam some warm afternoon.

14. Sodium and chlorine both find themselves in the same period in the periodic table of the elements. For each, define the number of outer shell electrons, and the number of electrons that actually enter into chemical combination in their most characteristic reactions.

15. Consider the element sodium:
    (a) Compare the electron structures of the atom and the ion.
    (b) Compare the relative volumes of the atom and the ion.
    (c) Why is it unlikely that you'll find a negative sodium ion?
    (d) Why is it unlikely that you'll find a dipositive sodium ion?

16. Qualitatively assess which of the following bond ionically and which bond covalently:
    (a) LiF (lithium fluoride)
    (e) KBr (potassium bromide)
    (b) MgO (magnesium oxide)
    (f) CBr_4 (carbon tetrabromide)
    (c) CO (carbon monoxide)
    (g) BN (boron nitride)
    (d) NF_3 (nitrogen trifluoride)

17. Try and pick the polar molecules from the following pairs and see what you can do with an explanation of why you chose the way you did:
    (a) CO and CO_2
    (b) H_2 and HCl
    (c) CH_4 and $CHCl_3$

18. Based on your understanding of electronic structure, why is H_2O O.K. but not H_3O? Why is NH_4^+ O.K. but not NH_4?

19. What does an **s**-orbital look like? How about a **p**-orbital? And in what way do the three separate **p**-orbitals differ?

20. How come there is H_2 but not He_2? Why CH_4, but not CH_2 or CH_6?

21. Describe how the pi bond in oxygen (O_2) is formed through proper combination of atomic orbitals. Do the same for the two pi bonds in nitrogen (N_2).

22. Draw a molecular orbital picture that shows the bonding in H_2, F_2, O_2, and N_2. Do the same for HF, H_2O and NH_3.

23. Why is the modern resonance structure for benzene a better picture than Kekule's "classical" pair of structures? Or to put it another way, what experimental evidence favors the one view over another?

24. Situations arise in which covalent bonds form through electron-sharing where one party to the bond contributes all. Such a case was the ammonia molecule reacting with a proton to form the ammonium ion:

$$NH_3 \; + \; H^+ \; \longrightarrow \; NH_4^+$$

Another such case, but with a different twist is the boron trifluoride molecule (BF_3) reacting with fluoride ion. See if you can work out the electron-dot formula for BF_3, and write the equation . . . including electron-dots . . . for its reaction with fluoride ion.

25. Try your hand at a brief explanation of this statement: "We distinguish between two limiting kinds of chemical bond, the purely ionic and the purely covalent, though recognizing that any actual bond may partake of some of the qualities of each."

26. Don't you kind of get the feeling that there is a certain kind of cleverness inherent in molecules? Why just look at the subtlety with which they behave:
    (a) How about an anthropomorphic view of atoms and molecules? Nonsense?
    (b) Is it better to view the bonding business simply in terms of the properties of the atoms involved?
    (c) Are we wrong in talking of chemical bonds in familiar terms as though referring to old friends?

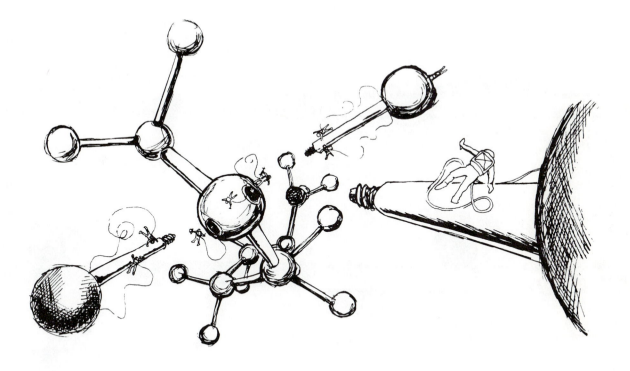

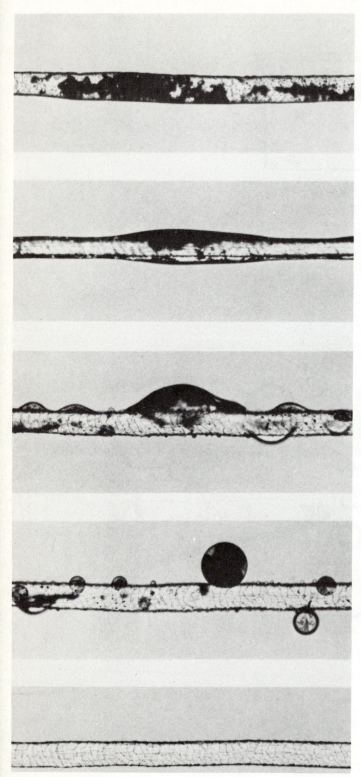
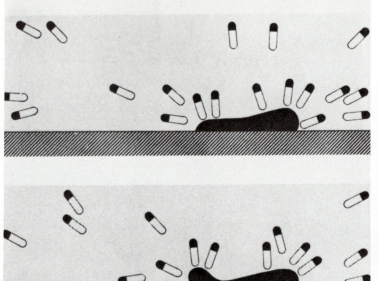
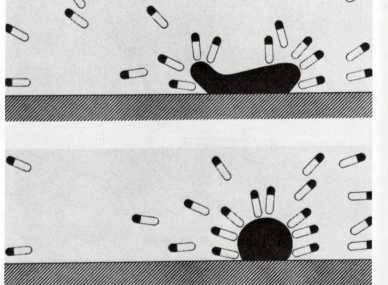
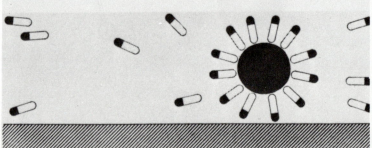

Chapter 11

There's Nothing Quite Like Water

☐ **Perceptions and Deceptions**

1 "The only naturally occurring *inorganic* liquid is essential for the maintenance of *organic* life."

2 *An American Indian Proverb:* The frog doesn't drink up the pond in which he lives.

3 Local joke: "The Cuyahoga is the only body of water in the world that should be declared a fire hazard." And on June 22, 1969, the Cuyahoga burst into flame.

4 If you're a fish, dissolved oxygen is good for you; if you're a steamboiler, dissolved oxygen is bad for you.

5 Ice floats . . . fortunately.

6 Your stomach rebels if its hydronium ion concentration gets out of line. That's called "acid indigestion."

☐ **A Congenial Environment**

Millions of years ago simple, single-celled organisms evolved within a tepid, watery broth, and life began . . . we think. The milieu was congenial for life, affording protection from the severe effects of air and sunlight. Day and night, summer and winter were nothing more than slow warmings and coolings in the waters. Oxygen dissolved into the waters and became accessible to the organisms; soluble foods were served up by the waters and cellular wastes transported away. The primordial seas controlled the chemical environment needed for life.

As life moved free from the seas to become air-breathing, terrestrial, and multicellular, the compatible salt sea environment went right along with it. That soup of nutrients, dissolved gases, salts, and chemicals excised from the seas performed vital functions such as control of acidity, food supply, temperature, and transport of wastes. Here, then, was no bland liquid occupying intracellular and extracellular space. Water was a most active liquid. No other liquid, in fact, no other substance, is so well suited to carrying on the tasks required in support of life. If you're less than certain of that, just remember two facts: water was here first, long before evolution succeeded at producing even the simplest living forms; consequently, life has been conditioned by water's ubiquitous presence. Second, the average adult human is 65 to 70 percent water; living organisms in

The washing process, schematically and under the microscope (150X) shows how soap molecules concentrate around oily dirt. Mechanical action (a little elbow grease or a washing machine) separates the soap-dirt complex from the fiber.

general range from 50 to about 95 percent water content. Why, just look at yourself.

Don't forget plasma, saliva, and gastric juices, too. Water promotes digestion, or biological hydrolysis, in which proteins and carbohydrates are broken down; it also promotes biosynthesis in which large biomolecules are constructed from smaller molecules carried within the body's cells. If all that isn't enough water for you, we take in a couple of liters a day in what we eat and drink. Most solid foods average about 50 percent water, and we produce another couple of liters or so of water just through the normal metabolic combustion of foods.

So life on planet earth is of necessity a watery business of metabolic pathways and processes. Water is bound to life as solvent, dispersant, irrigant, lubricant, and reactant. This extraordinary physiological liquid owes its properties to several peculiarities that altogether make it something quite unique. We've already briefly discussed the water molecule and the aggregate features of water in the last chapter, but there is so much more of importance to be said. Let's summarize the out-of-the-ordinary properties and central ideas as best we can and see where that takes us. For example, water has an unusually high boiling point. The heat required to vaporize a given quantity of water is also surprising. Its specific heat is very high as anyone who has watchfully waited for the proverbial pot to boil knows; so, too, is its surface tension, that property causing the pond's surface to dimple under the water strider's legs. Water climbs up walls and through them, phenomena we call capillary action and osmosis. Its solvent properties are second to none (Table 11-1).

☐ Peculiar Properties

Compare the heat of vaporization and the boiling point for water with those very same properties for two of water's companions from primordial times, ammonia (NH_3) and methane (CH_4). Water survives and is abundant in its natural liquid form. Ammonia hasn't survived, nor has methane because neither can survive at what have become *normal* atmospheric conditions. Life on earth is what it is because of what water is (see Fig. 11-1).

The **heat of vaporization** is directly related to the energy needed to disrupt the forces that pin single water molecules together by their positive and negative ends. Remember the last chapter? The telltale internal $H-O_{\diagdown H}$ bond angle of 104.5° and the marked difference in electronegativity between oxygen and hydrogen were examined. Electrostatic forces of attraction exist between the positive poles, or ends of some water molecules, and the negative poles of others. These intermolecular forces of attraction are the very important hydrogen bonds. Water is a network of molecules hanging together in three dimensions through hydrogen bonding. The network is regular, arranged almost tetrahedrally with each water

---

Water in the human body

Nervous tissue	~85% water
Liver	~75% water
Muscle	~75% water
Skin	~70% water
Connective tissue	~60% water
Adipose tissue	~30% water

Table 11-1

Comparing water with two of its prebiotic ancestors

	Water H_2O	Ammonia NH_3	Methane CH_4
Molecular weight	18	17	16
Boiling point, °C	100	−33.4	−161.5
Heat of vaporization, cal/g	539	327	122

Figure 11-1

molecule stuck to four others (Fig. 11-2). That's especially true in the solid state, as ice.

Peculiar Properties and Hydrogen Bonds

The last chapter began with a discussion of hydrogen bonds. This chapter does, too. What is it that's terribly important about these hydrogen bonds? They're not very strong: only about 5 percent the strength of the intramolecular or internal O—H bond in water. But that's just the point. They do break easily. In fact, individual hydrogen bonds are forever breaking and forming again so that the average lifetime of any one isn't much more than a split second. Bonds break, new bonds form. At −180°C, the hydrogen bond network in ice is complete, just about entirely intact. At any higher temperature, a certain percentage are broken: about 15 percent at 0°C, the melting point. Raise the temperature still higher; more hydrogen bonds break. But even at the boiling point their presence is still in evidence; for example, note the high heat of vaporization.

The properties of water depend on hydrogen bonding in several ways. First: water requires a larger input of heat energy than just about any other liquid in order to get it to evaporate. That's advantageous for higher animals, maintaining constant body temperature by dissipating excess heat through evaporation of sweat. Similarly, surface waters evaporate slowly in the summer, keeping rivers,

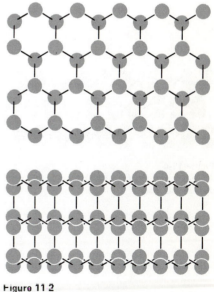

Figure 11-2
The regularity of neighboring water molecules. The top structure is a tetrahedral arrangement, and the bottom structure is the top and side views of ice.

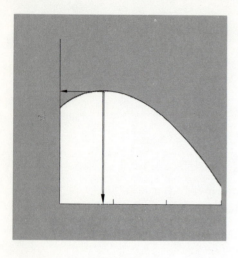

Figure 11-3
The densest water is *not quite* the coldest.

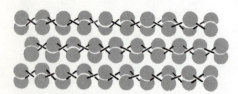

Figure 11-4
As the regularity of the ice structure collapses, density increases.

lakes, and ponds from drying up and killing the life forms present. Second: the high **specific heat** of water is important to an organism's temperature control mechanism, as well as for climate control and climate stabilization. Water has a high specific heat, requiring 1 calorie to raise the temperature of 1 gram 1 degree Celsius. That may not seem like much but 1/10 as much heat will do the same for 1 gram of iron (see Chap. 2). So lots of heat has to be added to water to raise its temperature, or subtracted to lower its temperature. Therefore, small amounts of water absorb large amounts of heat, and large bodies of water take a long time cooling. The warm waters of the Gulf Stream keep much of Western Europe warmer than the corresponding region of Eastern North America.

Third: ice floats! The solid form of water is less dense than the liquid; what's more, the maximum density is attained at 4°C and it decreases as the temperature falls to the freezing point. In cold weather surface water freezes first, leaving the liquid trapped below nicely blanketed, insulated from further cooling. The very coldest waters between 3°C and the freezing point (0°C) are less dense than water at 4°C (see Fig. 11-3). Therefore these waters rise to the surface, cool further because they are in direct contact with the colder atmosphere, finally freezing at the surface. If it were otherwise, lakes would freeze from the bottom up, thawing slowly in spring and summer with little possibility for protecting life. Surface pools would be commonplace in summer, yet bottom waters would remain frozen. This strange density inversion causes lakes to turn over twice a year allowing waters to aerate, another factor favorable to life. But the question is: why is there this anomolous effect? Most crystalline substances give up regularity when they melt; higher energy and more random arrangements tend to produce lower densities. But the ice structure has an open, hexagonal framework, thereby accounting for its low density (see Fig. 11-4). As kinetic energy increases—as the temperature rises—hydrogen bonds generally break, and the open structure collapses, resulting in compacting of the framework, and increasing the density. At 4°C, compacting is at its maximum. After that, as the temperature rises further, molecular commotion wins out over compacting and then density lowers in the normal fashion.

Water Is a Terrific Solvent

Another property peculiar to water is its ability to dissolve substances. Water is about as close as we can come to a universal, all-purpose dissolver, or solvent for other substances. It's really good at dragging other substances into solution, especially if the substances are ionic or "water-like" in character—lots of *OH* character. Particles of a salt such as sodium chloride are held together by the strong attractions between opposite electric charges extending through the crystal structure. Water molecules lower the effectiveness of those internal forces through strong electrostatic attraction between their own positive and negative ends and the sodium and chloride ions with which they come in contact. The tendency to form stable, hydrated Na^+ ions and Cl^- ions helps overcome those internal ionic forces, allowing salt crystals to dissolve in water (see Fig. 11-5).

But a substance need not be ionic in order for water to dissolve it; if it's "water-like," that may be sufficient. A large variety of covalently bonded molecules are soluble in water, providing they are polar and their molecular weights aren't too large. Solute-solvent hydrogen bonding is very important here. For example, ethyl alcohol (old *legal* alcohol) is polar, and water-like (*OH* character) to such an extent that it dissolves easily into water with formation of strong hydrogen bonds to water. Acetic acid has a polar carboxyl group, making it very soluble; it is commonly found in 3 to 4 percent aqueous solutions, better known as vinegar. However, as the hydrocarbon portion of the molecule (substantially characterized by hydrogen and carbon atoms alone) becomes larger, solubility falls off markedly. Consequently, *n*-butyric acid with four carbon atoms per molecule (and characteristic rancid butter odor) is only modestly soluble. Benzene isn't very soluble at all; but substitute a water-like OH group for one of the six benzene ring hydrogen atoms and you now have the modestly water-soluble phenol molecule. The more OH's the merrier. As the number of OH groups in a molecule increases the solubility usually does, too; in fact, the relatively high molecular weight sugar molecules are very water soluble. Solubility of sugar turns out to be very important biologically. The breakdown of sugars by the body's cells provides both energy and raw materials for synthesis of other molecules required in life processes. But as you may have anticipated, solubility has even more to do with the hydrogen bonding between the solvent (doing the dissolving) and polar OH groups on the solute molecules (being dissolved).

Perhaps we should note right here that hydrogen bonding isn't limited to water or the water-like OH group. Other electronegative atoms such as nitrogen stuck on hydrogen will do it. Nitrogen enters into hydrogen bond formation; therefore ethylamine and aniline exhibit water-solubility, too.

But there is nothing quite like water and its OH, or hydroxyl group, for demonstrating hydrogen bond character.

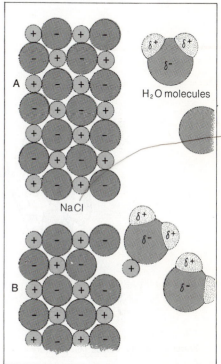

Figure 11-5
Dissolving.

Temperature Affects Solubility

It should be noted that solubility is markedly affected by temperature. Generally, solubility increases with increasing temperature—not always, but generally. That raises yet another of water's unusual properties. Since increased temperature favors solubility, a desirable solvent property is a relatively high boiling point. Otherwise, before much more solute has a chance to dissolve, the solvent will have evaporated or boiled away. For any given quantity of solvent a point is reached where the solvent has become loaded, or saturated with solute for that temperature. We measure **solubilities** in terms of grams of solute dissolved in 100 grams of solvent; a glance at the graph in Fig. 11-6 will give you some idea of the order of magnitude in question. As the temperature increases, solubilities generally will increase, too; but be careful, for evaporation of the solvent will act at cross-purposes here. Water is an unusual solvent; evaporation takes place slowly; because of hydrogen bonding, water stays liquid much longer. The increase in its vapor pressure with increasing temperature is less drastic than for most other common liquids. Thus, water stays *liquid* at higher temperatures; and its boiling point is substantially higher, too.

The Properties of a Solution

The properties of a solution differ from those of the pure solvent because there are dissolved solute particles present: molecules or ions. Such solution properties, referred to as *colligative properties,* produce some very pronounced effects. For example, the presence of solute particles in a given solvent *depresses* the freezing point and *elevates* the boiling point of the particular liquid solvent. The presence of salt on roadways causes ice to melt; ethylene glycol or alcohol in your car radiator prevents water freeze-ups in winter. Want water to boil at a higher temperature? Why, simply dissolve some salt in the water.

Hydrates and Water of Hydration

Another interesting thing often happens when certain solutes are dissolved, forming aqueous solutions. Many water-soluble salts separate as crystals in which water molecules are fixed in definite proportions, when their aqueous solutions are allowed to evaporate. The compounds are called *hydrates,* and the fixed water molecules, *water of hydration.* One common example is the striking blue crystals of copper sulfate pentahydrate ($CuSO_4 \cdot 5H_2O$). Heating the crystals drives the water molecules off, producing the powdery white, anhydrous salt.

$$CuSO_4 \cdot 5H_2O \longrightarrow CuSO_4 + 5H_2O$$

The reverse of that reaction works quite well, too. Anhydrous salts such as copper sulfate pick up water, yielding back the blue hydrate. In fact, anhydrous salts like sodium sulfate (Na_2SO_4) and calcium chloride ($CaCl_2$) are often used as **dessicants**, or drying agents. These hygroscopic salts can remove small amounts of water from a moist environment, or they can dry a "wet" liquid other than water.

Water-containing hydrates all have characteristic vapor pressures. Because of that, some hydrates spontaneously lose water of hydration. No heating is required. All that's needed is a high enough vapor pressure—higher than the pressure due to water vapor in the surrounding atmosphere. The process is called *efflorescence*; sodium sulfate decahydrate, for example, gradually loses water, becoming anhydrous sodium sulfate on a warm day.

Calcium chloride, as we've just noted, is *hygroscopic.* At the same time, calcium chloride is *deliquescent*, which means that it can remove water from the

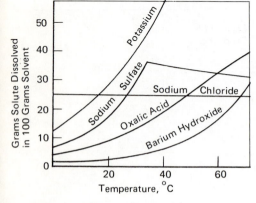

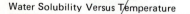
Water Solubility Versus Temperature

Figure 11-6
Solubilities.

surrounding atmosphere to dissolve itself, forming a solution. A dish of anhydrous calcium chloride will first form the dihydrate, then eventually turn itself into a puddle of calcium chloride solution.

How Do You Explain the Solubility of Gaseous Molecules

Carbon dioxide and oxygen are hardly anybody's idea of polar molecules. True, carbon dioxide does have a fair solubility in water, a characteristic to which carbonated beverages will attest. But that's mostly attributable to a chemical reaction with water. As for oxygen, its solubility is very low, though still greater than most other gases such as nitrogen or methane; we know from our experience just how important the availability of dissolved oxygen is to living creatures. Generally speaking, however, gases tend to be less soluble substances and temperature increases cause solubility to lower still further. If you want to keep a gas dissolved in a liquid, do as the soda bottlers: keep pressure high and temperature low (see Table 11-2). Note the sudden effervescence produced in uncapping a warm bottle of soda as compared to one from the refrigerator or cooler.

One important aspect of gas solubility has to do with our still incomplete understanding of how general anesthetics such as ether and nitrous oxide (laughing gas) work. Studying the physiology of a number of gases capable of producing anesthesia and narcosis appears to require no chemical action whatsoever. There is some good qualitative evidence indicating that *any* gas could produce anesthesia at high enough pressures. Animal tests with mice have shown that a large number of gases can knock out mice at sufficiently high gas pressures. Table 11-3 gives a comparative analysis of the mouse power of several gases in terms of their respective knock-out pressures.

Table 11-2
Water solubility of several gases

Gas	g/liter at STP
Helium	0.018
Nitrogen	0.029
Carbon monoxide	0.044
Oxygen	0.069
Nitric oxide	0.098
Carbon dioxide	3.35
Sulfur dioxide	228
Hydrogen chloride	625
Ammonia	890

Effect of temperature on the solubility of oxygen in water

Temperature, °C	g/liter at 1 atm
0	0.069
30	0.036
60	0.023
90	0.008

Table 11-3
Relative mouse knock-out power for several gases

Gas	Gas pressure required, atmospheres
Chloroform	0.008
Ether	0.032
Xenon	1.1
Nitrous oxide	1.5
Krypton	3.9
Argon	24
Hydrogen	85
Helium	190

Gases were awarded a mouse knock-out if the rodent, knocked off his feet in a test chamber, failed to get off the canvas after taking a 10 second count.

☐ Things to Think About While Doing the Wash

Besides being a great dissolver, water is a terrific disperser. Of course, "dispersing" is not quite the same thing as "dissolving," but dispersion does involve breakup of large particles, as in solution. And dispersion is the key to understanding the action of soaps and detergents, as well as the theory behind the effectiveness of washing agents in general. Here again, hydrogen bonding plays a significant role. Let's begin by taking a look at a family of organic molecules known as fatty acids.

Heads and Tails

Fatty acids are stretched out relatives of acetic acid and *n*-butyric acid, both of whom you've just met. Stearic acid, for one, has a hydrocarbon portion that stretches out to a length several times that of acetic or butyric acid.

$$CH_3-COOH \qquad\qquad CH_3CH_2CH_2-COOH$$

acetic acid $\qquad\qquad\qquad\qquad$ *n*-butyric acid

$$CH_3CH_2CH_2CH_2CH_2CH_2CH_2CH_2CH_2CH_2CH_2CH_2CH_2CH_2CH_2CH_2CH_2-COOH$$

stearic acid

The long hydrocarbon chain is nonpolar and water-insoluble. Down at the other end of the molecule sits a carboxylic acid, or carboxyl group, which is highly polar and water-soluble. As you can see, the progression from acetic to stearic produces a molecule that is mostly the nonpolar portion from one that was mostly the polar portion. Stearic acid is essentially a water-soluble, carboxylic acid head with a long, water-insoluble tail. Soaps can be loosely identified as sodium salts of fatty acids such as stearic acid; sodium stearate is a good example.

stearic acid $\qquad$ COOH

sodium stearate $\qquad$ COO$^+$Na$^-$
(a stearate soap)

Forming Structures Called Micelles

There is virtually no initiative on the part of the sodium stearate to get dissolved in water because of the large hydrocarbon portion of the molecule. You just can't take a teaspoon of ivory soap and dissolve it as you would sugar. On the other hand "soap solutions" can be prepared, but they are not true solutions. Soaps are easily dispersed in water, forming structures called *micelles* (Fig. 11-7). **Micelles** are spherical structures in which the polar carboxyl group with its negative electric charge is oriented toward the surrounding water medium while the nonpolar hydrocarbon group makes up the inside structure. As you can see in Fig. 11-7, the micelles themselves have an overall negative charge which keeps them all suspended in the water medium because they repel each other.

Water

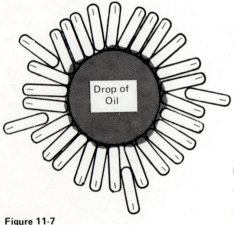

Drop of
Oil

Figure 11-7
Micelle structures.

Where does hydrogen bonding fit into this picture? Water exerts tremendous cohesive forces because of internal hydrogen bonding. Water molecules like each other. Just try and stuff a nonpolar molecule like the long hydrocarbon tail of a soap particle in-between the regular, hydrogen-bonded structure. Water doesn't care for nonpolar structures, forcing them into micelles. In the washing process, dispersed soap particles find a dirt particle built around a small part of last night's supper or other grease and congregate around it. The fat-soluble group (insoluble in water) is attracted, bonding to the hydrocarbon tails collected in the micelle structure. The impurity has been removed from the water, suspended, and then separated away. A little elbow grease or the mechanical agitation supplied by a washing machine helps. Essentially, we've succeeded in building a bridge across the interface between two incompatible, mutually insoluble states of matter, the nonpolar fat and the polar water (see Chapter opening).

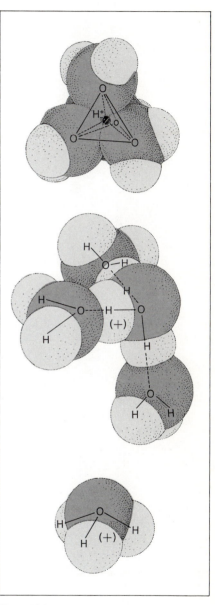

☐ Ionization and Proton Transfer in Water

Water is a definite aid to the dissociation of salts such as sodium chloride into hydrated "free" ions.

$$Na^+Cl^- \longrightarrow Na^+ + Cl^-$$

Sodium chloride and most other salts already exist as ions in the solid state, and as we've seen, water's function in dissolving the salt is to lower the energy within the crystal. Many molecules are also encouraged to ionize when dissolved in water. That's right, covalently bonded molecules, not only ionic structures. For example, hydrogen chloride is a colorless, covalent gas at room temperature, but when dissolved in water it ionizes through reaction with the solvent itself.

$$HCl + H_2O \longrightarrow H_3O^+(aq) + Cl^-(aq)$$

The essence of that process is addition of protons from hydrogen chloride ($HCl \rightarrow H^+ + Cl^-$) to water molecules producing hydrated ions.

$$H^+ + H_2O \longrightarrow H_3O^+(aq)$$

Ionization has taken place, but not in quite the same way as when sodium chloride dissolves in water. A proton has been transferred from hydrochloric acid to water and the water molecules now find themselves in new form as *hydrated* protons; in fact, the proton is thought to be hydrated by an average of not one but four water molecules into an $H_9O_4^+$ or $H(H_2O)_4^+$ structure (see Fig. 11-8). However there is no need to pack on all that baggage; one water molecule will do to illustrate our discussion. So in solution, then, we have hydronium ions, $H_3O^+(aq)$ or $H(H_2O)^+(aq)$.

There are many sources of hydronium ions. Hydrogen fluoride, dissolves in water, partially ionizing through proton transfer.

$$HF + H_2O \longrightarrow H_3O^+(aq) + F^-(aq)$$

Figure 11-8
Hydronium ions are *hydrated* protons: the hydrated proton model, $H^+(4H_2O)$ (top), the $H_9O_4^+$ model (middle), just plain H_3O^+ (bottom).

Hydrogen nitrate partially ionizes, too.

$$HNO_3 + H_2O \longrightarrow H_3O^+(aq) + NO_3^-(aq)$$

Hydrogen sulfate partially ionizes twice, stepwise.

$$H_2SO_4 + H_2O \longrightarrow H_3O^+(aq) + HSO_4^-(aq)$$
$$HSO_4^- + H_2O \longrightarrow H_3O^+(aq) + SO_4^=(aq)$$

Water Ionizes All By Itself . . . A Little Bit

To a very, very small extent, the water molecule is capable of undergoing the selfsame proton transfer reaction.

$$H_2O + H_2O \longrightarrow H_3O^+(aq) + OH^-(aq)$$

It comes about because the hydrogen atom is relatively small, its electron being very much dominated by the influence of the strongly electronegative oxygen atom. The positive hydrogen can jump to the negative oxygen of a neighbor water molecule.

But in 1 liter of water near 25°C, that entire process occurs to such a limited degree that at any instant, there is only 1.0×10^{-7} mole $H_3O^+(aq)$ and 1.0×10^{-7} mole $OH^-(aq)$, both very small amounts.

The ionization of water is an **equilibrium process**, as indicated by double arrows that show the reaction proceeding in both directions.

$$H_2O + H_2O \rightleftharpoons H_3O^+(aq) + OH^-(aq)$$

The smaller arrow means the forward reaction proceeds to only a slight extent. Reversibility is suggested. Why not hydronium ions transferring protons to hydroxide ions to produce unionized water molecules? There is no reason why not; and both processes do go on all the time. What we see when we look is an equilibrium state of affairs where the speed of the left-to-right reaction equals the speed of the right-to-left reaction. In this example there are mostly unionized water molecules. We say that the equilibrium lies way left as shown by the relative lengths of the two arrows. In fact, at room temperature the concentrations of $H_3O^+(aq)$ and $OH^-(aq)$ (the right side of the equilibrium) are negligible, only 0.0000001 mole in 1 liter of each solution. That concentration is expressed as 1.0×10^{-7} molar in $H_3O^+(aq)$, or 1.0×10^{-7} mole per liter; the solution is also 1.0×10^{-7} molar in $OH^-(aq)$, also 1.0×10^{-7} mole per liter.

Concentrations in solution are generally expressed as the molarity *M*, or moles of solute per liter of solution. Brackets are often used to indicate molarity. For example, writing [H_3O^+] means hydronium ion concentrations in moles per liter, molar solutions. A 0.1 *M* (pronounced 0.1 molar) hydronium ion solution simply means 0.1 mole of H_3O^+ is present in a liter of solution.

☐ Aqueous Acids, Aqueous Bases, and the pH Scale

Muriatic acid and lye; citric acid and milk of magnesia; vinegar and ammonia; sulfuric acid and sodium hydroxide. We are all more or less familiar with acids and bases (Fig. 11-9). But what is it we mean besides sour and soapy? Well, one reasonable model for explaining acid-base character is in terms of proton donors and proton acceptors. In any acid-base reaction, both proton processes must take place; no donors without acceptors. Recall the acid behavior of hydrogen chloride, donating protons to water which must of necessity act as a base, or proton acceptor.

$$HCl + H_2O \longrightarrow H_3O^+(aq) + Cl^-(aq)$$

That's moderately interesting. Now look at some more proton donors: nitric acid (HNO_3) and sulfuric acid (H_2SO_4). There's some real excitement here because in every one of those proton-transfer reactions, the *same* hydronium ion species (H_3O^+) is always found. You may ask, "But what else can form in a proton-transfer reaction taking place in water other than hydronium ions (along with solvated anions)?" Nothing else. In aqueous solution, the acid properties of any substance are really properties largely due to the presence of H_3O^+(aq). For hydrochloric acid, nitric acid, and sulfuric acid, the equilibrium lies so far right that H_3O^+(aq) and solvated anions are all there is: no unionized species present to speak of. For every single mole of hydrochloric acid molecules placed into solution, there is essentially a single mole of H_3O^+(aq) ions present. However as we've seen, that's not always the case. When water molecules donate a proton to other water molecules, very few hydronium ions form. The equilibrium is way left. Still other substances are intermediate, the equilibrium lying somewhere in-between, producing a more limited concentration of hydronium ions. Hydrogen chloride is essentially 100 percent ionized in aqueous solution; a 0.1 *M* acetic acid solution is about 1.3 percent ionized; plain old water, all alone, contains only about 1.0×10^{-7} mole of hydronium ions per liter of solution.

Figure 11-9
Advertising for Victorian *soaps*.

Acidic-Basic-Neutral

The acid-base reaction involving two water molecules is known as the *autoprotolysis* of water and has become the standard for judging all other acid-base reactions in aqueous solution. At 25°C, the OH^- and H_3O^+ concentration is 1.0×10^{-7} mole per liter of solution. When that condition exists, it is referred to as a *neutral* solution, neither acidic or basic. Neutral solutions contain equal numbers of proton donors [H_3O^+(aq)] and proton acceptors [OH^-(aq)]; their respective concentrations are 1.0×10^{-7} *M*. We therefore, say the *pH* is 7.

Acid-base character for aqueous solutions is stated in terms of special hydrogen ion concentration units called **pH.** As the hydronium ion concentration increases, the proton-donating capacity of the solution increases, and we say the solution has become **acidic.** Add hydrogen chloride to water, and the concentration of $H_3O^+(aq)$ particles becomes greater than 1.0×10^{-7} mole per liter.

$$HCl + H_2O \rightleftharpoons H_3O^+(aq) + Cl^-(aq)$$

On the other hand, should an excess of hydroxide ions appear such that their concentration exceeds the neutral level of 10^{-7} **M**, then the solution is said to be **basic.** For example, when sodium hydroxide dissociates in water,

$$Na^+OH^- \xrightarrow{\text{in } H_2O} Na^+(aq) + OH^-(aq)$$

As you can see, hydronium ions and hydroxide ions are intimately related. They will always be present in equal amounts in pure water according to the forward, or left-to-right reaction in our autoprotolysis equilibrium expression. They will react with each other wherever they find each other, forming undissociated water molecules in the reverse, or right-to-left neutralization reaction in that same equilibrium expression.

K_w, the Ion Product for Water

Another way of expressing the marriage between hydronium ions and hydroxide ions is through the **product** of their respective molar concentrations. In neutral water, each is 1.0×10^{-7} **M;** therefore, the ion product is 1.0×10^{-14} **M.** We call that K_w. Please remember that when you multiply in exponential notation, you add.

Table 11-4
The pH scale*

$[H_3O^+(aq)]$	pH			$[OH^-(aq)]$	$K_w = [H_3O^+(aq)] [OH^-(aq)] = 1.0 \times 10^{-14}$
1.0 **M**	0			1.0×10^{-14}	
1.0×10^{-1}	1			1.0×10^{-13}	
1.0×10^{-2}	2	increasing $H_3O^+(aq)$	increasing acidity	1.0×10^{-12}	$(1.0 \times 10^{-2})(1.0 \times 10^{-12}) = 1.0 \times 10^{-14}$
1.0×10^{-3}	3			1.0×10^{-11}	
1.0×10^{-4}	4			1.0×10^{-10}	
1.0×10^{-5}	5			1.0×10^{-9}	$(1.0 \times 10^{-5})(1.0 \times 10^{-9}) = 1.0 \times 10^{-14}$
1.0×10^{-6}	6			1.0×10^{-8}	
1.0×10^{-7}	7			1.0×10^{-7}	
1.0×10^{-8}	8			1.0×10^{-6}	
1.0×10^{-9}	9			1.0×10^{-5}	
1.0×10^{-10}	10	decreasing $H_3O^+(aq)$	decreasing acidity	1.0×10^{-4}	
1.0×10^{-11}	11			1.0×10^{-3}	
1.0×10^{-12}	12			1.0×10^{-2}	
1.0×10^{-13}	13			1.0×10^{-1}	
1.0×10^{-14}	14			1.0 **M**	

*Concentrations given in moles/liter.

$$K_w = [H_3O^+][OH^-] = (1.0 \times 10^{-7})(1.0 \times 10^{-7}) = 1.0 \times 10^{-14}$$

The ion product for water is 1.0×10^{-14} at $25°C$; it is a constant in nature. Carefully note that as either ion changes in concentration, the other ion must change in the opposite sense, since their product K_w must stay constant. Consequently, if $H_3O^+(aq)$ rises to $1.0 \times 10^{-4} M$, the $OH^-(aq)$ molar concentration must fall to $1.0 \times 10^{-10} M$ because

$$K_w = 1.0 \times 10^{-14} = [H_3O^+][OH^-] = (1.0 \times 10^{-4})(1.0 \times 10^{-10}) = 1.0 \times 10^{-14}$$

Such an aqueous solution will be acidic because the $H_3O^+(aq)$ concentration has risen above the neutral level of $1.0 \times 10^{-7} M$. The same argument holds for a basic solution. For example, when the $H_3O^+(aq)$ concentration falls to say $1.0 \times 10^{-9} M$, the OH^- concentration must rise above the neutral level to $1.0 \times 10^{-5} M$.

$$K_w = 1.0 \times 10^{-14} = [H_3O^+(aq)][OH^-(aq)]$$

$$[H_3O^+(aq)] = 1.0 \times 10^{-9}$$

Therefore,

$$[OH^-] = \frac{K_w}{[H_3O^+(aq)]} = \frac{1.0 \times 10^{-14}}{1.0 \times 10^{-9}} = 1.0 \times 10^{-5} \text{ molar}$$

Again, please remember that in exponential notation, division means subtraction of exponents.

Now let's see where that leaves us with our pH scale. We generally define both acidity and basicity in terms of **pH** which measures *only* the concentration of the hydronium ion, the proton donor. Our definition of K_w says that's okay because if you define $H_3O^+(aq)$, you've also set $OH^-(aq)$. Take a look at Table 11-4. High pH number values (beyond 7) mean lower hydronium ion concentrations, basic solutions; low pH number values (below 7) mean higher hydronium ion concentrations, acidic solutions. Substances that are better proton donors than water will be acidic since they will donate protons to water molecules, producing higher levels of hydronium ions than water is capable of producing by itself. Vinegar is mildly acidic, a 1 molar solution having a pH of about 4.7 at $25°C$.

$$CH_3COOH + H_2O \rightleftharpoons H_3O^+ + CH_3COO^-$$

Muriatic acid is strongly acidic, a $1 M$ solution having a pH of about 0 at $25°C$.

$$HCl + H_2O \rightleftharpoons H_3O^+(aq) + Cl^-(aq)$$

Note the difference. The weaker acid, acetic acid, must be incompletely dissociated. Each is present in $1 M$ concentration but acetic acid's equilibrium lies much farther left; it is less-than-completely ionized; 1 mole of acetic acid molecules produces fewer hydronium ions in a liter of solution than 1 mole of hydrogen chloride molecules.

Table 11-5
pH of some of nature's aqueous fluids

Fluid	pH
Gastric juice	1.2-3.0
Lemon juice	2.3
Grapefruit juice	3.2
Urine	5-8
Saliva	6.4-6.8
Cow's milk	6.6
Seawater	7.0-7.5
Blood plasma*	7.4
Pancreatic juice	7.8-8.0

*Must not vary beyond 7.35-7.45.

Sodium hydroxide is essentially fully dissociated into ions in a dilute solution, a 1 *M* solution having a pH of about 14. Ammonia is not completely ionized and a 1 *M* solution has a pH of only about 11.6.

$$Na^+OH^- \xrightarrow{\text{in water}} Na^+(aq) + OH^-(aq)$$

$$NH_3 + H_2O \rightleftharpoons NH_4^+(aq) + OH^-(aq)$$

Acidity and basicity are terribly important because there is little in nature that is neutral. Nature's watery fluids are generally acidic or basic and must stay that way within very narrow limits. Drastic variations in pH will often destroy the biological efficiency of a fluid. In the case of blood, even a small variation is extremely dangerous. Should arterial blood fluctuate outside the very narrow range of pH 7.35 to 7.45, severe physiological consequences, such as the death of the organism can be expected (see Table 11-5 and Fig. 11-10).

☐ When Acids and Bases React

The whole concept behind equilibrium and reversibility suggests "direction." When two molecules of water react, one is behaving as a base, or proton acceptor, the other as an acid, or proton donor. But then it all depends on how you look at it because the products of that autoprotolysis, hydronium ion and hydroxide ion, are respectively an acid and a base to each other in the reverse process.

$$H_2O + H_2O \rightleftharpoons H_3O^+(aq) + OH^-(aq)$$

An equilibrium is established, but it's an awfully lopsided affair. Just look at how many hydronium and hydroxide ions there are in pure water: 50 percent? 5 percent? Hardly. We said that about one part in 10,000,000 is all you can expect. So the direction is clearly spelled out and as weak as the water molecule is as an acid and a base, that's how strong an acid is the hydronium ion and how strong a base is the hydroxide ion. The direction is clearly right-to-left; in fact, bring strong acid and strong base together and WHAMMO! A virtually complete *neutralization* producing undissociated water molecules and a considerable quantity of heat.

$$H_3O^+(aq) + OH^-(aq) \longrightarrow 2H_2O + heat$$

The heat of neutralization is about 13,000 calories per mole of H_3O^+ and OH^- at 25°C. Water molecules, for their part, are very, very weakly acid or basic, and show little tendency to donate or accept protons. Nature's acid-base direction is stronger to weaker, as you might expect.

Once upon a time, neutralization reactions were considered to be acid-base reactions producing salts and water. For example, consider the reaction between sodium hydroxide, a strong base, and hydrochloric acid, a strong acid. Sodium chloride, a salt, and water are the products.

Figure 11-10
Talk about "severe physiological consequences"......

$$NaOH + HCl \longrightarrow NaCl + H_2O$$

The reaction can be carried out by first dissolving solid sodium hydroxide in water; an aqueous solution of sodium ions and hydroxide ions is produced.

$$NaOH\ (aq) \xrightarrow{\text{in water}} Na^+(aq) + OH^-(aq)$$

Then an aqueous solution of hydrochloric acid can be prepared by bubbling gaseous hydrochloric acid into water, producing hydronium ions and chloride ions.

$$HCl + H_2O \longrightarrow H_3O^+(aq) + Cl^-(aq)$$

Now consider the products of the reaction. Common table salt or sodium chloride is completely ionized in solution and exists as hydrated sodium ions and chloride ions.

$$NaCl \longrightarrow Na^+ + Cl^-$$

When our two reactants, aqueous sodium hydroxide and aqueous hydrochloric acid, are mixed, the only reaction that takes place is between hydronium ions and hydroxide ions.

$$H_3O^+(aq) + OH^-(aq) \longrightarrow 2\ H_2O$$

Sodium ions and chloride ions are nonparticipants. Here is the essence of the neutralization reaction of the strong base, OH^-, with the strong acid, H_3O^+. Any such proton-transfer process that proceeds past 50 percent completion must be thought of as neutralization. In aqueous solution, all at strong acid-strong base neutralizations are really nothing more than reactions between the hydronium ion and hydroxide ion, gone essentially to completion. Sulfuric acid? Hydrofluoric acid? Nitric acid? In aqueous solution, they're all $H_3O^+(aq)$. Lithium hydroxide? Calcium hydroxide? Potassium hydroxide? In aqueous solution, they've all gone to hydroxide ions. The heat of neutralization is about 13,000 calories per mole for any combination of acids and bases, corresponding to the heat of neutralization for $H_3O^+(aq)$ and $OH^-(aq)$.

Reaction of a weak acid such as acetic acid with hydroxide ion proceeds to completion.

$$CH_3COOH + OH^- \longrightarrow CH_3COO^- + H_2O$$

Yet at equilibrium there is a significant quantity of OH^- ions present, and such solutions are obviously alkaline or basic. That's typical of reactions of weak acids with strong bases. The salt that can be separated is quite different from an "ordinary" salt, say NaCl. Pure sodium chloride, when dissolved in water, is neutral; it is neither acidic nor basic. However, pure sodium acetate is quite different because the anion of the original weak acid **hydrolyzes** in a reaction with the solvent, producing hydroxide ions.

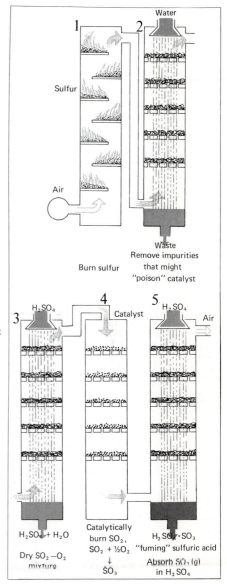

Figure 11-11
Schematic of industrial process for sulfuric acid synthesis.

$$CH_3COO^- + H_2O \rightleftharpoons CH_3COOH + OH^-$$

The same logic can be applied to the reaction of a weak base and a strong acid.

$$NH_3 + H_3O^+ \rightleftharpoons NH_4^+ + H_2O$$

Again, the reaction proceeds to completion, yet at equilibrium there are significant concentrations of hydronium ions present and such solutions are acidic. A hydrolysis reaction between the solvent and the cation of the original weak base produces hydronium ions, and an acidic solution.

$$NH_4^+ + H_2O \rightleftharpoons NH_3 + H_3O^+$$

☐ Body Fluids and Buffers

The suggestion has been made that pH must be maintained within closely prescribed limits to insure proper biological function. How is this accomplished? Certain salts of weakly acidic substances have the chemical capacity to **buffer** or protect fluid systems in the biosphere against substantial changes in pH or acidity. Two buffer systems maintain the pH limits of the two major fluid systems in living organisms. The intracellular fluids that push through muscle are controlled by the equilibrium that exists between a pair of inorganic phosphate salts of phosphoric acid (H_3PO_4). Sodium dihydrogen phosphate (NaH_2PO_4) and disodium hydrogen phosphate (Na_2HPO_4) make up the buffer system.

$$H_2PO_4^-(aq) + H_2O \rightleftharpoons H_3O^+(aq) + HPO_4^=(aq)$$

Organic phosphates such as certain glucose phosphates and the more complex ADP and ATP phosphate molecules also help out, but we'll hold discussion of these for a later chapter.

The second buffer system is based upon the abundance of carbon dioxide in animal respiration. Extracellular fluids such as the blood depend upon the hydrogen carbonate-carbonic acid buffer system produced when carbon dioxide dissolves in water. Shifting of that equilibrium keeps the level of acidity within the narrow 7.35 to 7.45 limit we mentioned earlier. Carbon dioxide exhibits considerable solubility in water, in great measure due to the formation of an unstable, weakly acidic species known as carbonic acid.

$$CO_2 + H_2O \rightleftharpoons H_2CO_3(aq)$$

The reaction is reversible, and an equilibrium is established between the forward and reverse processes. As with all acidic substances, carbonic acid is a proton donor to the solvent, water.

$$H_2CO_3(aq) + H_2O \rightleftharpoons H_3O^+(aq) + HCO_3^-(aq)$$

Of course, neither of these two equilibrium reactions can be detached from the other and to get an overview of what's going on, we'll have to combine them.

$$CO_2 + H_2O \rightleftharpoons H_2CO_3 \text{(aq)} + H_2O \rightleftharpoons H_3O^+\text{(aq)} + HCO_3^-\text{(aq)}$$

Equilibrium is established between carbon dioxide on the extreme left and carbonate on the extreme right, in the form of the hydrogen carbonate ion. If hydrogen carbonate ion doesn't ring a bell for you, remember that common baking soda is sodium hydrogen carbonate, or sodium bicarbonate, the salt of the weakly acidic, carbonic acid.

$$Na^+HCO_3^- \xrightarrow{\text{in water}} Na^+\text{(aq)} + HCO_3^-\text{(aq)}$$

If the blood becomes too acidic, the excessive quantities of hydronium ions react with hydrogen carbonate ions, neutralizing them and forcing the equilibrium to move left, forming more carbon dioxide and water. Look at the overall carbon dioxide/hydrogen carbonate equilibrium again; see if that isn't reasonable. The formation of an overabundance of hydronium ions puts a stress on the blood, the buffer system compensating accordingly by swinging left, adjusting the pH to within its normal limits.

Let's consider what happens when the opposite situation occurs. The hydronium ion concentration drops, causing the blood to turn excessively basic. In response, more carbon dioxide dissolves by reacting with the excess base, forming more hydrogen carbonate ions. This reduces the basicity, bringing the pH back into adjustment. Again, the buffer system has shifted in response to a stress placed upon it. It is the shifting of the position of an equilibrium left-to-right or right-to-left that permits maintenance of an essentially constant chemical environment. The buffer system depends on the ratio of carbon dioxide to hydrogen carbonate ions; carbon dioxide either dissolves or is released accordingly during respiration. If a high rate of metabolic activity is maintained for an excessive period of time, the buffer system can be overloaded; too much carbon dioxide will enter the bloodstream, resulting in excessive carbonic acid, excess hydronium ions, and a condition known as acidosis. On the other hand, if you breathe more rapidly than necessary (that's called hyperventilation) too much carbon dioxide is removed from the blood turning it basic, a condition known as alkalosis. Either condition may lead to death (Fig. 11-12).

☐ **The Salt Balance in Nature's Aqueous Fluids**

Aquatic organisms are keenly sensitive to salt concentrations in their environment. Those animals that crawled out of the primordial broth at an early evolutionary state and eventually walked away from the seas still carry that same sensitivity. There is a salt gradient that gradually builds from rivers and lakes to brackish waters, back toward the sea environment. Anywhere along that gradient, living organisms must stay within certain close limits. At each stop along the way, different salt concentrations and tolerances are found. In the aquatic environment, because of the narrow limits of salt concentration, salt water and seawater are a lethal environment for freshwater species. When the salt balance is out of whack,

Figure 11-12
The severe activity of long-distance running has caught up with Russia's Hubert Pyarnakivi, collapsing at the end of a 10,000 meter race in Philadelphia.

Table 11-4

Comparing Blood and Sea Water (g/l)

	Blood	Sea Water
Na^+	3.3	10.7
K^+	.15-.20	0.4
Ca^{++}	0.10	0.4
Cl^-	3.5-3.7	19.3
$SO_4^=$	.16-.34	2.7
$CO_3^=$	1.5-1.9	0.07

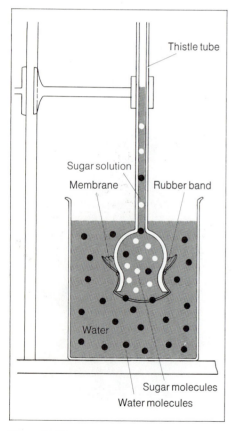

Figure 11-13

Osmosis. Pure solvent diffuses through the membrane, diluting the solution.

it places us in a potentially precarious position with possible severe physiological consequences. Let's take a closer look at living organisms and their dependence on the salt balance in their local environment.

Rainwater is relatively pure, except when it falls through smog and dust; through the ground, it dissolves a variety of minerals. Most freshwater bodies such as lakes and rivers contain perhaps a few hundredths of a percent dissolved substances, but by and large, they are simply water. The seas, however, run at about 3.5 percent dissolved salt. In freshwater, calcium ions and carbonate ions are species predominantly present; in seawater, sodium, magnesium, chloride, and sulfate are most prominent, but virtually all the mineral elements are represented at least in trace quantities. Their biological activity varies and may serve critical physiological functions for living organisms. As we noted earlier, blood plasma is in many ways similar in composition to dilute seawater, making for some interesting speculations regarding the origins of life (see Table 11-4).

Living organisms must be able to control the movement of dissolved minerals into tissues. Cell membranes tend to be selectively permeable: some particles move through with abandon; others are carefully regulated; still others are entirely excluded. The whole selection process is referred to as *osmosis* (Fig. 11-13). Cell membranes can do lots of other fancy tricks, too. Most are able to pump ions across concentration gradients existing in fluids separated by a membrane. In human beings the kidneys serve to remove metabolic wastes from the blood, maintaining pH and ionic balance through selective transfer and removal of sodium and hydrogen ions. Operating on the same principles, but using synthetic membranes, artificial kidneys are now commercially available. They are widely used in treating acute renal failure (Fig. 11-14).

□ Hard Times and Hard Water

If water is such a terrific solvent, it must create a number of solubility problems. After all, water dissolves just about everything in sight to a greater or lesser extent. At least some of those dissolutions ought to cause us hard times because they are unexpected and unwanted. For example, water contains dissolved oxygen, which is okay if you're a fish, but something to be gotten rid of before you can pump water into a boiler system.

Water dissolves about 38 parts per million of oxygen at 25°C and atmospheric pressure; not a very large amount by what we normally regard as water-soluble. Nevertheless, that's sufficient to keep the ecology of a river, stream, or lake in balance. It's quite another matter as far as industrial equipment is concerned. Unless dissolved oxygen is removed prior to feeding water into a boiler, severe corrosion problems such as rusting can be anticipated. Preheating water to a high enough temperature generally "deaerates" it. Remember what we said about

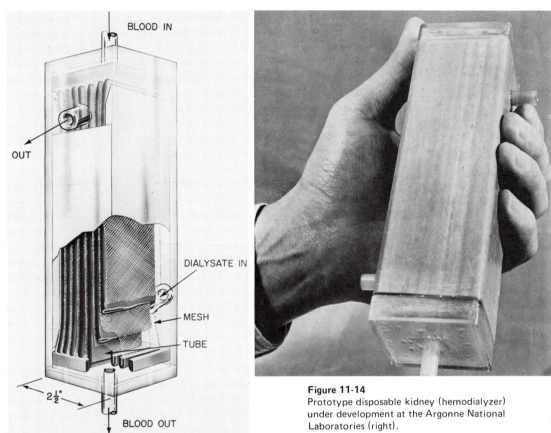

BLOOD IN

OUT

DIALYSATE IN

MESH

TUBE

$2\frac{1}{2}''$

BLOOD OUT

Figure 11-14
Prototype disposable kidney (hemodialyzer)
under development at the Argonne National
Laboratories (right).

Cut-away schematic view (left).

solubility of gases and the effect of temperature: gas solubility decreases with
increasing temperature.

If you are a "Coca Cola" bottler or a brewmaster, **hardness** in water will be a
serious concern because of the unwanted, insoluble solids that will form in your
product. Suspect trace amounts of iron in your water? You'll find out soon
enough with the appearance of that telltale rust-like ring in your toilet bowl and
other plumbing fixtures. If man-made pollution of natural waters has reached
crisis proportions, it is principally because of the ease with which water dissolves
and absorbs, thereby making it difficult and expensive to recover all those
materials back again.

That salt gradient we mentioned raises a problem with respect to municipalities
and drinking water. Some 4/5 of the world's population lives within 200 miles
of the oceans. As one moves inland the salt content decreases until finally
brackish waters turn to freshwaters. Salt water is about 3.5 percent or about

35,000 parts per million sodium chloride. Water begins to taste distinctly salty when the salt content reaches a level of only about 500 parts per million, or 0.05 percent. That makes for some hard problems in cities like New York: the ocean is right there but can't be used. Undoubtedly there is an economic advantage and convenience to be able to just take Hudson River water as it flows by, purifying it first. However, the Hudson is brackish for up to 20 miles from its mouth, so the river has to be diverted some distance upstream.

Calcium carbonate (along with a close relative, magnesium carbonate) has an unfortunate habit of dissolving in even weakly acid solutions to produce hard water. Limestone and marble are different forms of calcium carbonate. Lime (CaO) for a variety of industrial and agricultural uses is produced by simply heating limestone to a high temperature.

$$CaCO_3 \longrightarrow CaO + CO_2$$

Marble, of course, is the favorite of the sculptor and the builder.

Ca^{++} and Mg^{++} Make Water Hard

The chemistry of hard water is fairly straightforward once acids, bases, and water solubility have been discussed. Let's begin our lesson in hard water chemistry with limestone in dilute acid; that means react calcium carbonate with hydronium ions.

$$CaCO_3 (solid) + H_3O^+ \longrightarrow Ca^{++} + HCO_3^- + H_2O$$
$$\text{as ions in solution}$$

Calcium ions are produced in solution along with a recent friend, the hydrogen carbonate (bicarbonate) ion. Magnesium carbonate does essentially the same thing. Now, if acid ground waters are allowed to percolate through an underground bed of limestone, the waters will accumulate significant concentrations of calcium ions and magnesium ions as well. Such waters are said to be hard. It is extremely difficult to get any significant soaping or foaming

Table 11-6

Composition of dissolved minerals in certain natural fluids[*]

Dissolved ion	River water	Seawater	Blood plasma
Na^+	6.7	30.4	35.4
K^+	1.5	1.1	1.3
Ca^{++}	17.5	1.2	1.2
Mg^{++}	4.8	3.7	0.4
Cl^-	4.2	55.2	39.0
$SO_4^=$ and HSO_4^-	17.5	7.7	—
$CO_3^=$ and HCO_3^-	33.0	0.4	22.7

[*] Parts per million (ppm) by weight. 10,000 ppm = 1%.

action (suds) in such hard waters. Not only is cleansing action impaired, but soap is wasted because calcium ions tend to precipitate "solubilized" salts of fatty acids soaps. The first thing the soap does is react with the calcium ions; then, only after they are all reacted and removed from solution will any cleansing action begin.

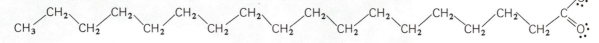

The stearate anion: solubilized as the Na$^+$ salt; gummy precipitate as the Ca^{++}/Mg^{++} salt

Calcium or magnesium ions react, forming insoluble, gummy precipitates. Their most visible form may be the proverbial "bathtub" ring.

One way of "softening" hard water is to run it through an ion exchanger, replacing the calcium and magnesium ions with sodium ions. Sodium ions don't interfere with the cleansing action of soaps. Hard water is allowed to slowly flow through a column packed with particles of some natural clays called zeolites or some synthetic ion-exchange resins. These are complex, insoluble structures in which certain pathways down through the packed column are filled with sodium ions. As they pass by, calcium and magnesium ions replace the sodium ions of the zeolite or the resin, and the sodium ions are carried on through with the water (see Fig. 11-15).

Using Detergents in Place of Soaps

A second approach directed at reconciling our preoccupation with washing machines and the hardness in most freshwaters has been the widespread use of detergents in place of soaps. Detergents clean in essentially the same fashion as soaps do; they dissolve organic dirts in a hydrocarbon portion, using an ionic portion to then solubilize or drag it into solution. The difference in these surface active agents or **surfactants** lies in the ionic end-group which is generally a sulfate rather than a carboxylic acid salt.

Detergents became very popular in the United States after World War II. They worked in hard water without precipitating; in fact, wide public acceptance of detergents was based on their favorable behavior in hard water. "DUZ Does Everything" became a household word. Unfortunately, many of these detergents were not easily biodegradeable; they weren't broken down rapidly enough by natural degradative processes. Consequently, streams and rivers "sudsed and foamed" as the waste waters, with their higher and higher concentrations of these washday miracles, spilled into the aquatic environment (Fig. 11-16). That problem has been more or less overcome by modifying the structure of the detergent molecules, producing a generation of biodegradeable detergents.

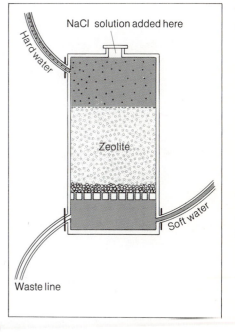

Figure 11-15
Ion-exchange.

Figure 11-16
Foam caused by the presence of detergents in
the stream.

A second problem emerged in the 1960s. Detergent manufacturers had found
that inclusion of inorganic phosphates markedly improved the overall performance
of detergents. Addition of the low-cost phosphates improved the overall cost-
effectiveness of the product as well. They work like this. The phosphates take
care of the hardness in the water by effectively sequestering (removing) calcium
and magnesium ions, leaving the detergent to do its stuff in what is now
"softened" water. In the late 1960s public awareness of the effect of phosphates
in promoting growth of algae was recognized. Premature eutrophication reared
its slimely head. "Algal blooms" are still a problem for us today. In part, the
problem is cultural as well as technological because of our preoccupation with
cleanliness in the United States today (see Fig. 11-17).

□ Water Pollution: An Old Problem with a New Imperative

Water is survival. Archeologists pick at the bones of peoples, nations, and
civilizations that died when the waters failed. Water is a limited resource, one
that must be managed with wisdom. Our predecessors were no better supplied
with water than we are today, and our successors will have no more of it to
tamper with tomorrow.

Water cannot be viewed in the same way as other natural resources. Once it's
spoiled, what replacement will you find for it? What substitute? We are living
organisms, consisting of better than 70 percent water, entrained into a steady
state of equilibrium, an essentially constant state of affairs. Should you fail to

maintain the minimum daily water requirement for that steady state, you will surely start down the road to eventual degeneration and death. The average American needs about 4 million gallons of water to see him through a 70-year life span. The word *need,* however, reflects more than simple biological need. The demands of industrialization and the consumer society swell the word *need* out of all proportion. Our modern water needs are all but insatiable (see Table 11-7). Therefore, we must not pollute or ruin our greatest and most necessary resource. Yet how are we to prevent it?

Of course we may have access to more water than we think. It is true that ¾ of the surface of the earth is covered with water. That's enough water to completely cover a flat uniform sphere the same size as our planet to a depth of close to a 1,000 feet. Still only a fraction of all that water is useable: about 3 percent if freshwater; 97 percent lies in the salty seas. Even the most careful and efficient salt removal requires huge amounts of energy to produce minor quantities of freshwater. Of the 3 percent freshwater, 75 percent of that is not really useable, lying as it is down in deep wells 2,500 feet beneath the earth's surface as well as in the polar ice caps and glaciers. So water is no longer a giveaway, especially in view of a still-expanding world population.

Table 11-7
Some water equivalents*

Product or process	Water needed, gal
Manufacture 1 phonograph record	2½
Process 1 gal of milk	5
Process 1 lb of sugar	48
Hen feed to produce 11 eggs	40
Manufacture Sunday *New York Times*	150
Manufacture 1 lb synthetic rubber	300
Grow 1 ton corn for cattle feed	350,000

* Of the 1,600 gal of water required per day per person, only 9 percent waters your garden, cooks your food, or fills your tub. The other 91 percent is used to satisfy the technical demands of our modern society.

Figure 11-17
Dead and dying algae along the banks of Lake Minnetonka. Excessive nutrients are responsible.

Pollution Means Chemical Alteration of Natural Water Resources

Water, by definition, is a pure substance of definite composition. But natural waters already contain much in the way of dissolved matter, largely because of water's marvelous solvent properties. The seas are salty. Rivers, lakes, and well waters contain a variety of substances that account for hardness and cause aesthetic problems. Our understanding of pure water in the natural environment is different from what we theoretically mean by "pure" water. Pollution is whatever makes natural waters unnatural, undesirable, unpleasant, and unhealthy for living organisms. Pollutants lower the quality of the water, and right along with that, its fitness for balanced support of life. Drinking water may taste bad; or the growth of water lilies and aquatic weeds may go unchecked; or the beaches may be covered with oil and dead fish and smell disgusting. Beer cans litter the deepest ocean floors, and the immortal bottle is submerged everywhere. The lakes are turning into swamps before their time.

The water pollution problem is one that has followed man through history. Here is no new trauma. On man's first boat ride it's likely that something was discarded over the side. From the very beginning man has been cleansing himself in the waters, and using the waters to dilute, dissolve, and decompose his refuse. The waters transport and they assimilate. As long as demand were small, localized, and unconnected, nature was able to "fix" it and restore the waters. But Western civilization spawned the industrial revolution, invented the water-borne sewage system, and nurtured societies that began to live in large, connected communities by the waterways. By the middle of the nineteenth century, the sewage problem had reached crisis proportions. The Thames was an open sewer as it flowed through London, and good luck to you if you lived in the next town downstream. Michael Faraday decried the stinking condition of the Thames (see Fig. 11-18). In 1868 the British Parliament passed the River Pollution Prevention Act, eventually accepted by all the industrialized nations. As a result, direct pollution by toxic substances and disease-bearing bacteria has been essentially eliminated.

Classifying Water Pollutants

A century later, the pollution problem is still very much with us because of two factors: (1) world population is growing geometrically in the face of a constant water supply; (2) tampering with the very delicate and complex balance in nature creates ecological problems of unforeseen magnitude and direction. According to the United States Public Health Service, there are eight classifications for water pollutants:

1. Oxygen-demanding wastes.   Aerobic decomposition of organic wastes of both plant and animal origin depletes available oxygen dissolved in natural waters. That happens at the expense of the oxygen requirements for the natural biologic processes. Dissolved oxygen is a necessary requirement for both plant and

Figure 11-18
Pollution of our lakes and rivers is not a new problem. This cartoon from the British humor magazine *Punch* appeared in 1842; Professor Faraday had just been appointed to a commission to clean up the River Thames.

animal life in the waters. Biodegradation goes on all the time, too, as large and complex molecules are broken down into the smaller and simpler ones, but degradation demands oxygen. Oxygen depletion below some minimum level leads to disappearance of plant and animal life and severe alteration of the biosphere. For example, when oxygen levels fall too low, anaerobic microorganisms (those that don't need oxygen) replace aerobic microorganisms (those that need oxygen) and a complete new biochemistry takes over. Let's look at this further. Under normal aerobic conditions, carbon, nitrogen, phosphorus, and sulfur end up as oxygen-containing carbon dioxide (CO_2), nitrate (NO_3^-), phosphate ($PO_4^\equiv$), and sulfate ($SO_4^=$). Under anaerobic conditions, methane (CH_4), ammonia (NH_3), phosphine (PH_3), and hydrogen sulfide (H_2S) are produced, making for an obnoxious-smelling, heavy, sludge-producing situation.

2. **Infectious agents.** A variety of bacterial and viral agents from raw sewage and other organic wastes can be transmitted by water. Typhoid fever, dysentery, cholera, and hepatitis are examples.

3. **Plant nutrients.** When waters become enriched through the availability of excessive quantities of nutrients such as phosphates in detergents and human

excreta, a natural process known as eutrophication gets out of hand. The natural aging of a lake into a bog (and eventually into a meadow) is speeded up. For example, it has been estimated that Lake Erie has aged 15,000 years in the last fifty.

4. Organic chemicals.   Insecticides and pesticides, soaps and detergents, paints and solvents, fuel oils and fuel additives, food additives, and pharmaceuticals all fall into this category. Large-scale industrial, agricultural, and domestic use creates new water pollutants and potential environmental hazards with each new organic chemical synthesized and introduced.

5. Other minerals and inorganic chemicals.   Strip mining in Missouri produces acid runoffs; millions of pounds of detergents filter through the sewers and septic tanks washing phosphates into the Potomac's growing algal slimes; the Cuyahoga and the Raritan could be mined for the inorganic sulfates and chlorides spilled into them by heavy industry along their shores. Industry uses mercurial compounds heavily, and their pollution of rivers, streams and oceans has only recently been recognized (Fig. 11-19).

6. Sediment.   Land erosion from improper farming methods, mining, forestry, industry, channel building, and dredging operations produce sediments that reduce the stream's ability to assimilate oxygen-demanding wastes. As the bottom silts over, fish and aquatic plants find their normal environment altered. You'll have to look deep and far to locate even a lowly sandworm living in most shipping ports and busy harbor bottoms.

Figure 11-19
The burning Cuyahoga River. June 30, 1970.

7. **Radioactive wastes.**   If that's not a major problem today, look for it to develop into one. As nuclear power plants proliferate and medical and industrial applications of radioactivity grow, the need for mining and processing radioactive ores increases.

8. **Heat.**   Changing the temperature of a body of water by only a few degrees can radically alter the ecological balance in a river or stream. Predators move into the warm waters and have no natural enemies to control them. New forms of algae and other flora multiply too rapidly. Thermal pollution follows industry's seach for water as coolant and remover of waste heat (Fig. 11-20).

Waters are used and reused, and more pollutants pour in. A gallon of Monongahelia water passes along the Ohio, into the Mississippi and eventually into the oceans. Perhaps even the oceans are no longer the great assimilators we once thought. *Nobody lives upstream any more.* The environmental changes that take place are often slow and reversible, given enough time. But we don't leave things alone long enough for that; consequently, the costs of water treatment prior to returning it to the environment must be considered a small price to pay. Sedimentation, filtration, aeration, flocculation—whatever can be done to resuscitate the constant supply of water—must be done. Water pollution cannot be allowed to continue as a free practice. We all live downstream from someone else.

There is a danger in trying to dramatically draw your attention to the issues of "water pollution" and the "environmental crisis" by raising up the usual tired cliches. That was not true a decade ago; or even five years ago. Saving the environment used to be a battle cry. (Whatever happened to Earth Day?) Too many magazine articles, newspaper stories, television specials, and political

Figure 11-20
"Fingers" of hot water can be seen diffusing into the Connecticut River from the cooling system of a nuclear power plant in these twin photos, the second a *thermogram.*

speeches have numbed the senses. Something is wrong, all right. That's clear enough. But the fever has paled. Nevertheless the water pollution problem is still a major part of the environmental crisis, and both continue unabated. Any successes we have had can be counted as little more than a holding action.

☐ **Questions to Answer, Problems to Solve**

1. Water has several peculiar characteristics such as its density, its high boiling point and heat of vaporization, and its solvent properties. Discuss each one . . . in your own words.

2. Can you offer a reasonable explanation of why the heat of vaporization for water is several times greater than the heat of fusion?

3. Lakes and ponds "turn over" twice a year in Spring and Fall. That's important because it allows bottom waters to aerate at the surface, a requirement for life. Based on your understanding of water's weird density characteristics, explain that behavior. While you're at it, you might as well explain why such bodies of water freeze from the top, down.

4. Offer an explanation of each of the following phenomena:
   (a) Your line of laundry, hung out to dry when the temperature is below freezing, freezes . . . but still it dries, without first thawing.
   (b) A desert water bag made of tightly woven cord, or canvas, serves up cool water in spite of the great heat.
   (c) Water boils at temperatures below 100°C on top of Pike's Peak, some three miles above sea level. Water boils above 100°C in Death Valley, well below sea level.
   (d) After you stop vigorously exercising, you feel chilled as the sweat evaporates off your skin.

ICE COLD TOO

5. If you fill a glass to the very brim with water at 0°C, will the level overflow, recede, or what as the glass of water warms to room temperature?

6. How about this one! Fill another glass with a mix of water and ice cubes, all at 0°C, to the very brim. As the ice begins to melt, do you think the level will overflow, recede, or what?

7. If Dalton had been right about the structure of water being HO, would you expect the properties of water to be vastly different? (*Hint:* perhaps a comparison with HF or HCl would be valid here.)

8. What's a saturated solution? How can you determine very simply whether a solution is saturated or not? What effect does temperature have on solubility? Is that always true? What about the effect of temperature on gas solubilities?

9. With your new understanding of solubility and hydration, see if you can develop a simple understanding of the sudden change in the solubility curve for sodium sulfate.

10. Three familiar hydrates are listed below:

<table>
<tr><td>epsom salts</td><td>$MgSO_4 \cdot 7H_2O$</td></tr>
<tr><td>alum (kalinite)</td><td>$KAl(SO_4)_2 \cdot 12H_2O$</td></tr>
<tr><td>Glauber's salt</td><td>$Na_2SO_4 \cdot 10H_2O$</td></tr>
</table>

(a) Determine the percent water in each.
(b) Write a chemical reaction for their thermal decomposition.
(c) How does thermal decomposition differ from efflorescence?
(d) How does efflorescence differ from deliquesence?

11. Carefully distinguish between the following pairs of terms:
(a) efflorescence and effervescence
(b) efflorescence and deliquescence
(c) hydration and hydrolysis
(d) solute and solvent
(e) hydrogen ion and hydronium ion

12. A white crystalline solid is placed in an open dish and allowed to sit overnight. In the morning there is only a puddle of clear liquid. Assuming no supernatural occurrence, explain what most likely took place.

13. A second white crystalline solid is placed in an open dish and allowed to sit overnight. In the morning, blue crystalline substance has replaced it. Again, what may well have taken place?

14. What is the pH of each of the following solutions?
(a) an 0.10 M HCl solution; an 0.001 M solution of HCl.
(b) an 0.10 M NaOH solution; an 0.001 M solution of NaOH.

15. Considering the pH of the gastric juices in your stomach to be about 2:
(a) What is the hydronium ion concentration of the solution?
(b) What must the hydroxide ion concentration be?

16. The acidity of a given solution is diminished simply because it has been diluted.
(a) Why is that so?
(b) Would the pH become larger or smaller?

(c) To what final volume would a liter of solution have to be diluted to change the pH by one pH unit?

17. Lemon juice lightens the color of tea. But so will grapefruit juice, vinegar, and hydrochloric acid, too. Explain what that would imply about the cause of that effect and why all these substances in aqueous solution accomplish the same thing. What is the active species?

18. What is it about strong and weak acids and bases in aqueous solution that makes them strong or weak?

19. Contrast the dissolution and dissociation of hydrogen chloride and sodium chloride in water.

20. The chemistry involved in neutralizing 1 mole of HNO_3 with 1 mole of NaOH produces about 13.8 kcal of heat. One mole of HCl or HF produces exactly the same number of calories in reaction with 1 mole of NaOH. Do you find that result strange? What's going on?

21. Sulfuric acid is special in one sense. When it ionizes, or dissolves in water, two moles of hydronium ions can be produced for every mole of H_2SO_4. It is a "polyprotic" substance. Write the two-step reaction. Phosphoric acid (H_3PO_4) is another polyprotic acid. Write out the three equations involved in its dissociation in water.

22. Here's a strange one for you. Assume our liquid of life is ammonia, and perhaps we look like the space traveler in Fig. 11-1.
And the cry of the ancient mariner has become "Ammonia, ammonia, everywhere . . . "
(a) Based on the physical properties of ammonia, is "Ammonia, ammonia, everywhere" too far fetched? What kind of planet would the Earth have to be? What do you think . . . would N_2 be the life support O_2 is?
(b) In your new ammonia world model, write the autoprotolysis reaction for your new universal solvent. Will sodamide ($NaNH_2$) be a basic substance as was sodium hydroxide? And isn't the ammonium ion (NH_4^+) the acid counterpart to the hydronium ion? How about dissolving ammonium chloride (NH_4Cl) in liquid ammonia . . . is the solution acidic?

23. What is the pH of a neutral solution? What is a buffered solution? How do buffers work, and why are they important in nature?

24. Using the CO_2/HCO_3^- buffer system, explain the buffering action that goes on in blood. Now see if you can explain how the $H_2PO_4^-/HPO_4^=$ buffer system might work in the presence first of an excess of acid (H_3O^+); then in

the presence of an excess of base (OH⁻). Try doing it by analogy to the blood example, and write some equations to help your explanation.

25. Comment briefly on the following statements:
    (a) There really isn't very much in the way of chemically pure water available in nature.
    (b) Blood plasma is similar in composition to dilute sea water.
    (c) Semipermeable cell membranes can do lots of tricks.
    (d) Carbonated beverages become flat on standing open.
    (e) Carbonated beverages inadvertently made with hard water will not be pleasing.

26. Speaking of "hardness" in natural waters:
    (a) What do we mean?
    (b) What ions are principally responsible?
    (c) Why is it objectionable?
    (d) What can be done about it?

27. The pH inside your stomach is normally in the acid range of about 1-2. Should the acid run-off from an open pit coal mine drop the pH of a lake or stream to perhaps only 4-5, all the living inhabitants of the water will likely die. Explain.

28. Go back over that list of eight categories for classifying water pollutants:
    (a) Can you come up with illustrative examples for each out of your own experience, or that you know about?
    (b) What categories should be of most immediate concern?
    (c) Do you think the water pollution problem and the environmental crisis are . . . . . .
        I. hackneyed, oversold phrases.
        II. still serious problems but ones we are coping with.
        III. sorely underestimated problems, threatening our very survival on Earth.
    Try and defend each contention separately.

29. Comment upon the statement that "the quality of life is intimately linked to the quality of the environemnt" and briefly discuss that with respect to water quality.

30. What is eutrophication? Explain its occurrance. Why does the addition of phosphates stimulate eutrophication problems in the aqueous environment? What is biochemical oxygen demand (BOD) all about?

31. To what extent do you feel the environmental crisis in this country is a problem in population or in affluence? Compare.

The Earth viewed from Apollo. There is a growing realization of the fragility of the life-sustaining environment of our spaceship, Earth. One need only view the pale cloud-shrouded planet through the eyes of the moon-bound astronauts to perceive astronomer Fred Hoyle's comment: "Once a photograph of the Earth taken from outside is available, once the sheer isolation of the Earth becomes plain, a new idea as powerful as any in history will be let loose."

Chapter 12

☐ **Perceptions and Deceptions**

1 "We can't Put It Together. It Is Together."

2 The periodic table is a highly successful effort at organization of the substantial number of elements known to us.

3 Getting a "fix" on nitrogen is something plants do quite well, and since 1908, we know how to do that, too.

4 The proverbial "lick of salt" recovered from a prehistoric sea.

5 The nobility of the inert gases has been somewhat tarnished.

6 A system at equilibrium will tend to shift under stress in such a way as to restore the original equilibrium, Le Chatelier's Principle—powerful stuff.

7 A rusty nail is one that has been oxidized.

☐ **Some Aspects of the Earth**

Our planet is an extraordinarily complex chemical entity. While it is easy enough to visualize the earth's surface or regions near the surface, evidence of its internal structure and composition are less easily obtained. We have to reconcile ourselves to indirect evidence based on studies by geologists and geophysicists. *Geochemistry* is a study of the chemistry of the earth and its 6-mile deep envelope of surrounding air. Samples for study are obtained by scratching at the part of the earth called the crust.

The Internal Structure of the Earth

In simplified terms, it might be compared to a golf ball with a fluid center. There is a thin outer crust, perhaps 5 to 65 kilometers in thickness. The average thickness is about 15 kilometers and all of our presently available supply of mineral resources is contained therein. Our animal and vegetable resources depend on the thin soil cover right at the surface. The deepest penetrations of the crust have been about 35 kilometers (2 miles) in a South African mine shaft, and an 80-kilometer (5-mile) Texas oil well. Neither comes close to penetrating the second layer. The *mantle,* underlying the crust, extends down to about 2,900 kilometers below the surface. There is a boundary region at the base of the crust called the *Moho* or *Mohorovicic discontinuity.* Our knowledge of this area is primarily from the observation that a sudden change takes place in the velocity of earthquake waves in that region.

The mantle extends to where the *core* begins, constituting 83 percent of the earth's total volume and 68 percent of its mass. Geologists speculate that during the early history of the earth there was only one surface layer, a primitive mantle from which the crust developed during succeeding geologic epochs through volcanic events. The mantle today is the source of most of the earth's internal energy; it is responsible for the forces that bring about spreading of the ocean floors, continental drift, and major earthquakes. Composed of dense silicates (complex silicon-oxygen structures) of magnesium and iron under very high pressures, it is also likely that the mantle contains aluminum, sodium, potassium, and calcium. We know this from seismic density measurements and chemical examination of meteorites, which are supposed to have closely related compositions (Fig. 12-1).

Here then is what we have: a relatively light layer of crust floating on an underlying layer of mantle. Of course, the crust isn't floating on any *usual* liquid. The mantle is solid rock; but don't be deceived. As with many materials subjected to long periods of stress, *plastic flow* occurs as a response to variations in pressure due to weight differences in the overlying region. (Remember our silly putty of Chap. 4.) Place a heavy object such as a hammer on the surface of the solid tar in a barrel of tar. After a period of time, the hammer not only sinks into the tar, but eventually falls to the bottom. Yet if you drop the hammer onto the tar, the surface shatters the same way as glass would (Fig. 12-2).

The earth's core extends downward for more than 3,000 kilometers from the mantle to the geometric center and appears to be divided into a liquid outer core and an extremely high-density, solid, inner core. It is assumed to be metallic, mostly iron, but with some nickel. Again, we know all of that from seismic data and analysis of meteorite materials; of course, you must remember such data are qualitative in nature and indirectly obtained. Therefore the exact composition of the earth's core continues to be a problem that geophysicists and geochemists are working on today.

As you already know, the earth's atmospheric envelope is composed primarily of oxygen and nitrogen, along with several other elements in much smaller concentrations. Table 12-1 lists the elements we are totally concerned with in the continental crust and Table 12-2 lists the principal elements in the atmosphere. It is interesting to note the apparent lack of any useful organizational scheme with respect to the elements and their abundance. There is quite a mix of the inert and the active, the rare and the commonplace, those that are useful and widely applicable, those that have no apparent utility or need.

Describing the Chemistry of the Elements

It is the custom among chemists to make a somewhat arbitrary distinction between inorganic and organic chemistry. As with all such scientific separations this one is done for convenience. The element carbon is unique in the way it forms bonds, leading to literally millions of chemical combinations. That is in marked contrast to the behavior of most other elements which have produced a

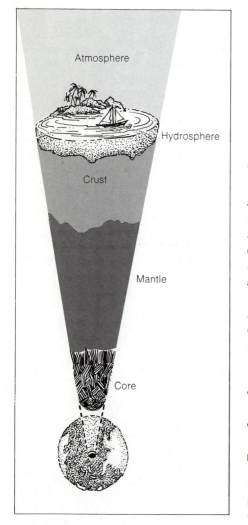

Figure 12-1
Our spheroid, third from the sun.

grand total of perhaps a tenth that many combinations. The chemistry of carbon will occupy us completely in the two chapters that follow this one. In this chapter we'll first concentrate on three gaseous elements, hydrogen and oxygen, and nitrogen. Virtually every element in nature combines in one way or another with hydrogen or oxygen. Nitrogen is the apparently passive *major* component of the atmosphere, yet it turns out to be quite important in its combined or "fixed" forms.

We'll then describe a couple of representative metallic elements taken from the alkali and alkaline earth families, followed by one or two of the halogens and the noble gases in order to see just what's with the nonmetals. Taken together, these descriptions will give us a pretty good view of both ends of the periodic table. Some attention must also be paid to the big block of elements in the extended mid-section of the periodic table, the transition elements, as well as the lanthanides and actinides. Boron, silicon, and sulfur deserve special attention because their chemistry has some considerable bearing on the study of carbon yet to come but we'll defer that until next chapter. A great deal of the vitality and fascination of chemistry is most evident when doing just what we're about to do . . . describing the chemistry of the elements.

Table 12-1

Average composition of the earth's continental crust

Element	Percent by weight
O	46.59
Si	27.72
Al	8.13
Fe	5.01
Cu	3.63
Na	2.85
K	2.60
Mg	2.09
Ti	0.63
H	0.13
P	0.13
Mn	0.10
S	0.052
Cl	0.048
Cr	0.037
Ni	0.020
Co	0.001
Other	0.200

Gutenberg in *McGraw Hill Encyclopedia,* 3rd ed., Vol. 4, (New York: McGraw-Hill), p. 364.

Table 12-2

Average composition of the earth's atmosphere near the surface

Components	Fraction by volume
Major components	
N_2	0.78084
O_2	0.20946
A	0.00934
CO_2	0.00033
H_2O	highly variable
O_3	variable
Lesser components	
Ne	1.1818×10^{-5}
He	5.24×10^{-6}
Kr	1.14×10^{-6}
CH_4	1.6×10^{-6}
H_2	5×10^{-7}

*Other gases such as NO, CO, H_2O, and NO_2 also exist in small amounts.

†*McGraw-Hill Encyclopedia of Science and Technology,* 3rd ed., Vol. 1, (New York: McGraw-Hill, 1971), p. 79.

Figure 12-2

☐ The Chemistry of Hydrogen and Oxygen

Physical-Chemical Properties. Hydrogen

Hydrogen is a colorless, odorless, tasteless gas composed of diatomic molecules. With a density only about 1/15 that of air, it is the lightest gas. Therefore, a balloon filled with hydrogen gas behaves according to Archimedes Principle: it rises. Remember it was Archimedes who very early in the history of science observed that the buoyant force acting on an object in a fluid (in this case the fluid is air) is equal to the mass of the fluid the object displaces. The only element with a lower melting and boiling point than hydrogen is helium (see Table 12-3). Liquid hydrogen is thin and colorless, the lightest of all known liquids. Yet as you might expect, there is no crystalline solid less dense either. Such low melting points and boiling points suggest weak forces of attraction between molecules (weak intermolecular forces).

The hydrogen atom has an atomic number of 1 and an average mass of just slightly more, 1.00797, because of the three isotopes. Protium, or regular hydrogen with mass 1 comprises 99.98 percent of the natural element; deuterium, mass 2, makes up the remaining 0.02 percent with only a trace of the third isotope, tritium, mass 3. There is one proton in the nucleus and a single orbital electron. The distinction between isotopes is according to whether there are zero, one, or two neutrons present as well. Remember we refer to hydrogen's electron as a $1s$-type electron (see Chap. 8). Because that energy sublevel—the $1s$ sublevel—can contain a second electron of opposite spin number hydrogen atoms are always found in pairs (in *spin* pairs) in the form of H_2 molecules in the free state. H_2; never H.

Hydrogen molecules are very reactive. Under the proper circumstances, many other elements enter into combination with hydrogen. However, hydrogen in the free state is a very minor component of the earth. In the combined state, however, it makes up 0.76 percent of the weight of the earth's crust; 13.5 percent of the atoms of the earth's crust are hydrogen, a percentage exceeded only by oxygen and silicon. Most of the combined hydrogen atoms on the earth are found in seawater. Furthermore, hydrogen is believed to constitute 90 percent of the atoms of the universe; in fact, thermonuclear energy produced by fusion reactions of hydrogen nuclei is believed to be the source of most of the energy radiated by sun and stars in the solar system.

Physical-Chemical Properties. Oxygen

Oxygen is eighth in the periodic lineup. It, too, is a colorless, odorless, tasteless gas composed of diatomic molecules, O_2 in this case (see Table 12-3). Interestingly, oxygen condenses to a pale blue liquid, and on freezing, it turns to a pale blue crystalline solid. There are three isotopes, mass 16, 17, and 18. Mass 16 is the common one, composed of eight protons, eight orbital electrons, and eight

Table 12-3

Characteristic physical properties of diatomic molecules

Molecule	Density, g/l	Melting point	Boiling point
H_2	0.08988	−259	−253
O_2	1.429	−218	−183
N_2	1.2506	−210	−196
Cl_2	3.214	−101	−34.6

neutrons. Again, sharing electrons leads to filled orbitals and diatomic molecules.

Just about every element except the inert gases enters into chemical combinations with oxygen, too. However, in marked contrast to hydrogen, oxygen is present in large amounts on the earth in its free, molecular form as the lesser of the two major components of the atmosphere. About 49.5 percent by weight of the earth's crust is oxygen, mostly combined as silicates, oxides, and water. There is also oxygen outside the earth's atmosphere, but since 98 percent of the matter of the visible universe (stars, nebulae, interstellar space) is hydrogen and helium, the oxygen concentrations are relatively small (Fig. 12-3).

Preparing Hydrogen Gas

A number of methods can be employed for the preparation of hydrogen gas. The simple **laboratory procedure** involves the reaction of zinc metal with dilute hydrochloric acid (Fig. 12-4).

$$Zn + 2HCl \longrightarrow ZnCl_2 + H_2(g)$$

Figure 12-3
One of the largest lighter-than-air crafts ever built, the German Zeppelin, the Hindenburg, containing 7,063,000 cubic feet of hydrogen, exploded and burned at Lakehurst, New Jersey, on May 6, 1937.

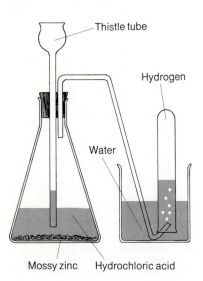

Figure 12-4
Laboratory preparation of hydrogen.

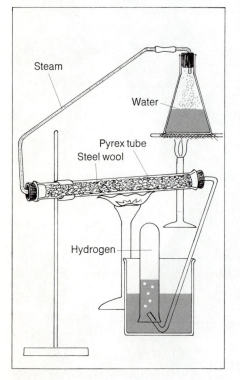

Figure 12-5
Preparing hydrogen by the action of steam on steel wool.

In a somewhat more sophisticated procedure, the action of steel wool on steam can be used, the iron reacting with oxygen, freeing hydrogen gas (Fig. 12-5).

$$3\,Fe \;+\; 4\,H_2O \longrightarrow Fe_3O_4 \;+\; 4\,H_2\,(gas)$$

A **commercial process** that can be easily demonstrated in the laboratory is the electrolysis of water, containing a little dissolved sodium sulfate (Na_2SO_4) or potassium hydroxide (KOH). (See Chap. 7 if you've forgotten about electrolytes.) Although the process is comparatively expensive, very pure hydrogen is produced.

$$2\,H_2O\,(l) \longrightarrow 2\,H_2\,(g) \;+\; O_2\,(g)$$

Hydrogen is produced by a very **large scale industrial process** using hydrocarbon raw materials such as natural gas, gasoline, or fuel oils. High temperatures are required along with a special nickel catalyst to make the reaction go easily.

$$C_3H_8\,(g) \;+\; 3\,H_2O\,(g) \longrightarrow 3\,CO\,(g) \;+\; H_2\,(g)$$

The carbon monoxide that forms can be used as a fuel to produce more hydrogen, by passing it over an iron oxide catalyst along with water vapor.

$$CO\,(g) \;+\; H_2O\,(g) \longrightarrow CO_2\,(g) \;+\; H_2\,(g)$$

The entire process is referred to as the *steam-hydrocarbon process.* With an annual production of 100,000,000,000 cubic feet of hydrogen gas in the United States alone, excluding the huge amounts consumed in the manufacture of ammonia, methyl alcohol, and petroleum refining, it's obviously got to be a pretty important process. The steam-hydrocarbon process, has replaced a widely used process that now may enjoy a rebirth in popularity due to the energy crisis and the general uncertainty about world petroleum supplies: the *steam-water gas process.* Here, coke or coal is treated with steam at elevated temperature, producing carbon monoxide and hydrogen.

$$C\,(s) \;+\; H_2O\,(g) \longrightarrow CO\,(g) \;+\; H_2\,(g)$$

water gas

The water gas may then be stripped of hydrogen, using the carbon monoxide to produce more hydrogen (according to the preceding equation) or the water gas mixture may be burned directly, serving as a very high-energy fuel.

Preparing Oxygen Gas

Oxygen may be simply prepared in the **laboratory** by heating potassium chlorate mixed with a little manganese dioxide catalyst to speed up the process (Fig. 12-6).

$$2\,KClO_3\,(g) \longrightarrow 2\,KCl\,(g) \;+\; 3\,O_2\,(g)$$

Mercuric oxide can also be used.

$$2\,HgO\,(g) \longrightarrow 2\,Hg\,(l) \;+\; O_2\,(g)$$

Oxygen is produced **commercially** by liquefaction (a process that goes back to Priestley and Lavoisier) and distillation of air. Electrolysis of water can also be used. (See Chap. 7.)

The Analysis of Hydrogen and Oxygen

Principles of gaseous behavior can be applied. Burn hydrogen in an oxygen atmosphere, thus converting it to water; then measure the reduction in volume that takes place. Remember,

$$2\,H_2\,(g)\ +\ O_2\,(g)\ \longrightarrow\ 2\,H_2O\,(g)$$

Three moles of gaseous reactants produce two moles of gaseous products. Therefore, the volume of hydrogen must equal two thirds of the total reduction in volume. Oxidation may be carried out by passing an electric spark across two platinum electrodes stuck down into the gas mixture.

Finally, determination of chemically bound hydrogen, particularly in organic substances such as hydrocarbons, is usually carried out by burning the compound in a stream of oxygen at elevated temperatures. The water formed on combination is absorbed by a dehydrating agent and the amount of hydrogen is calculated from the increase in weight of the adsorption tube.

Oxygen can be qualitatively identified by the glowing wooden splint test; it bursts into flame since oxygen supports combustion better than air. But you can be fooled here, for this test won't tell you whether you have a tube full of oxygen or nitrous oxide (laughing gas) which gives the same result (Fig. 12-8). Quantitative analysis is carried out by absorption techniques.

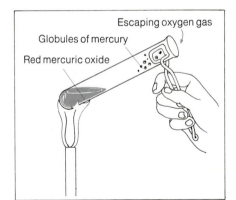

Escaping oxygen gas

Globules of mercury

Red mercuric oxide

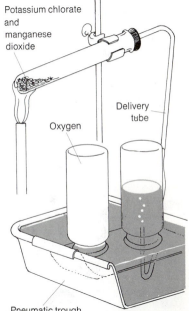

Potassium chlorate and manganese dioxide

Delivery tube

Oxygen

Pneumatic trough

Figure 12-8
Demonstration of the effects of nitrous oxide at the Royal Institution (left). Modern analytical techniques were developed in the French laboratories of St. Claire De Ville.

Figure 12-6
Preparing oxygen by decomposition of mercuric oxide (top).

Figure 12-7
Laboratory preparation of oxygen (bottom).

Reactions of Hydrogen and Oxygen

At ordinary temperatures, hydrogen gas is generally unreactive. However, under the proper conditions, hydrogen eagerly combines with most of the other elements. For example, a flask full of a 2:1 mixture of hydrogen and oxygen will still be just that next week or next year. No reaction takes place unless a platinum catalyst is present or an electric spark is introduced. When the reaction does take place, water forms violently, releasing a great deal of heat.

$$2 H_2(g) + O_2(g) \longrightarrow 2 H_2O + heat\ (115.6\ kcal\ evolved)$$

When the reaction takes place in an oxygen-hydrogen torch, welding temperatures close to 3000°C are produced; the heat of the reaction is in turn used to help sustain these high welding temperatures. If you burn hydrogen in an atmosphere of fluorine instead of oxygen, the reaction is extremely violent under virtually any conditions.

$$H_2(g) + F_2(g) \longrightarrow 2 HF(g) + heat\ (128.4\ kcal\ evolved)$$

Hydrogen undergoes a very useful kind of reaction in which it behaves as a powerful ***reducing*** agent. Chemical reducing agents add electrons to other species, thus lowering their apparent oxidation state. Note the liberation of copper metal from combination with oxygen: reduction of copper oxide. In fact, in many cases reduction with hydrogen turns out to be an important route to preparation of very pure metals. For example, many metallic elements occur naturally as oxides, and can be set free in that fashion (Fig. 12-9).

$$metal\ oxide + hydrogen\ gas \longrightarrow pure\ metal + steam$$

$$CuO + H_2(g) \longrightarrow Cu + H_2O(g)$$

$$Fe_2O_3 + 3H_2(g) \longrightarrow 2Fe + 3H_2O(g)$$

Some of the metals that can be produced from their respective oxides in this way include copper, silver, bismuth, mercury, tungsten, iron, nickel, and cobalt. Chemical reduction plays an important role in life processes, too, as we'll have occasion to discuss in Chap. 14.

In another important type of reaction, hydrogen can simply be added into another molecule. Such processes, called ***hydrogenations,*** occur in the presence of special hydrogenation catalysts. For example, methyl alcohol (wood alcohol) is the product formed when carbon monoxide reacts with hydrogen; ethyl alcohol (fermentation alcohol) can be produced from acetaldehyde. Methyl and ethyl alcohol are both prepared industrially on a large scale in this manner.

$$CO + 2 H_2 \longrightarrow CH_3OH$$

$$CH_3CHO + H_2 \longrightarrow CH_3CH_2OH$$

Hydrogenation is very much in the public's interest today as a method of altering certain chemical characteristics of animal fats, vegetable oils, and a whole range of petroleum, tar, and coal-related products (more about that in the next chapter).

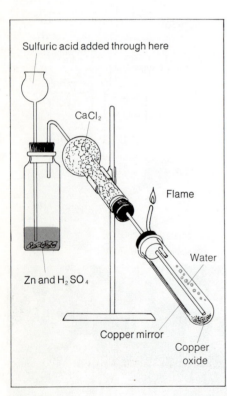

Sulfuric acid added through here

CaCl$_2$

Flame

Water

Zn and H$_2$SO$_4$

Copper mirror

Copper oxide

Figure 12-9
Copper mirror by reduction of copper oxide in a stream of hydrogen.

Now to oxygen. Practically everything reacts with oxygen; in fact, because it is so available, it is perhaps the most widely used *oxidizing* agent, effectively removing electrons, raising the apparent oxidation number of elements. Fluorine is the only element that does a better job than oxygen as an oxidizing agent. What better illustration than the oxidation of hydrogen (oxidation state for H = 0) to water (oxidation state for H = +1). Most metals form one or more oxides when heated in an atmosphere containing oxygen gas. This may explain why many of the elements in the earth's crust occur as oxides. All that sand (SiO_2), for example, all that iron ore (Fe_2O_3), and even water (H_2O) can be correctly viewed as simple oxides. Complex silicates such as the sodium aluminum silicate known as feldspar ($NaAlSi_3O_8$) are among the most abundant oxygen-containing substances making up most rocks and salts. Garnet is a magnesium-iron-aluminum silicate.

The oxygen-acetylene torch produces welding temperatures in excess of 3000°C.

$$2\ HC{\equiv}CH\ +\ 5\,O_2\ \longrightarrow\ 4\,CO_2\ +\ 2H_2O\ +\ \text{heat (621 kcal evolved)}$$

Imagine the application of such a vigorous oxidizer in aerospace situations; liquid oxygen is commonly used in burning rocket fuels. Animal respiration is a different kind of burning, but it is oxidation nonetheless, only now the catalysts are large organic molecules called enzymes.

Two peculiar *oxygen* substances are hydrogen peroxide and ozone. Hydrogen peroxide, (H_2O_2) is markedly different from that other compound of hydrogen and oxygen, namely water. Hydrogen peroxide is a powerful oxidizing agent in its own right, reacting vigorously with many substances, especially organic compounds. Widely used as a bleaching agent in industry and the home, hydrogen peroxide also has antiseptic properties for just the same reason, its oxidizing power (Fig. 12-10).

Figure 12-10
The availability of "bleaching" agents and technology in the nineteenth century made white fabrics a significant element of Victorian style. J.A. McNeill Whistler's "The Girl in White."

Ozone is a Special Form of Oxygen

There is a second elemental form of oxygen (an *allotropic* modification) called ozone. A high-energy triatomic species, the ozone molecule has the formula O_3. However, whereas oxygen gas is colorless, condensing to a pale blue liquid, ozone is decidedly blue to begin with. Both the liquid and solid are an opaque blue-black, not much different from ink. Ozone has a characteristic pungent odor, familiar to many persons because it forms during an electric discharge in air, as in an electric storm (Fig. 12-11). Ozone has been used in low concentrations to sterilize contaminated drinking water in Philadelphia and Paris, and to inhibit growth of molds in cold storage rooms for furs and foods. Possibly the most important feature of ozone's behavior is demonstrated continuously in the earth's upper atmosphere. At vertical distances greater than 13 miles above the surface, ozone is formed by the action of ultraviolet radiation from the sun acting on oxygen in the air.

$$\text{ultraviolet energy}\ +\ 3\,O_2\ \longrightarrow\ 2\,O_3$$

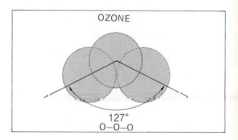

OZONE

127°
O–O–O

Because these radiations are absorbed and utilized in ozone formation, they are prevented from reaching the planet's surface, making life as we know it possible on earth. Appreciable concentrations of such ultraviolet radiations would be fatal to man.

□ Nitrogen Chemistry

Nitrogen, as the diatomic molecule, N_2, is the most abundant component of the atmosphere. It is a common atmospheric constituent of our sun, the stars, and the large planets. As it occurs in nature, there are two isotopes, N-14 and N-15, with the average mass of the natural abundance being 14.007. The mass 15 isotope is widely used as a tracer in chemical reactions involving *nitrogen*-containing substances. The element is found in the combined form as Chile saltpeter, or sodium nitrate ($NaNO_3$). Combined nitrogen also occurs significantly in plants and animals in the form of complex molecules called proteins.

Obtained by the fractional distillation of liquid air, nitrogen gas condenses to a colorless liquid that freezes into a white solid at very low temperatures (see Table 12-3). In its elemental form, N_2, it will not usually react under ordinary conditions with most common substances. However, at elevated temperatures, it does combine directly, forming nitrides with a number of elements such as lithium and aluminum.

$$6\,Li + N_2 \longrightarrow 2\,Li_3N \quad \text{(lithium nitride)}$$
$$2\,Al + N_2 \longrightarrow 2\,AlN \quad \text{(aluminum nitride)}$$

Oxide formation is carried out on purpose by passing air through an electric arc at 1000°C, producing small yields of nitric oxide, (NO); the nitric oxide can then be recovered and converted to nitrates. Nitrates are important for growing food. Paradoxically they are also needed for making war. In addition, oxides of nitrogen form accidentally, with little control, producing both industrial and automobile pollution.

$$N_2 + O_2 \longrightarrow 2\,NO$$

The large-scale industrial preparation of ammonia which combines hydrogen with nitrogen takes place by the widely used *Haber* or the modified *Haber-Bosch process*. The *Ostwald process* converts ammonia to nitrates. Both ammonia and nitrates are significant in agriculture. Altogether, nitride, oxide, and hydride formation constitute processes referred to as *fixing* or *fixation* of nitrogen. Atmospheric nitrogen is returned to the soil (we'll soon see how it leaves the soil) either by chemically fixing the element into compounds that will be used as fertilizers or through biological fixation by means of microorganisms.

Hydrazine (H_2NNH_2) can perhaps be viewed as the nitrogen analog of hydrogen peroxide (HOOH). It is also a liquid at room temperature but with a musty, ammonia-like odor. Hydrazine has a violently explosive nature giving it some

Figure 12-11
Electric discharge in air off an insulator material.

considerable space-age notoriety as a rocket fuel. For example, in the presence of strong oxidizing agents such as hydrogen peroxide, using copper salts as catalysts, a highly exothermic reaction takes place.

$$H_2NNH_2\,(l)\ +\ 2\ HOOH\,(l)\ \xrightarrow[\text{salts}]{\text{copper}}\ N_2\,(g)\ +\ 4\ H_2O\,(g)\ +\ heat\ (148.6\ kcal)$$

We could reasonably consider nitrogen's highly variable valence or combining capacity to be its uniquely defining property. For example, nitrogen and its compounds run the gauntlet from the -3 state to the $+5$ state, and few other elements can beat that record. Table 12-4 offers a brief summary of the many oxidation states of nitrogen.

☐ Ammonia Synthesis and Nitrogen Fixation

Ammonia forms during decay of most nitrogen-containing organic materials, announcing its presence by its pungent odor and irritating effect on the mucous membranes. Millions of tons are synthesized each year for a large number of applications: nitric acid, drugs, plastics, dyes, fertilizers, refrigerants, and, of course, household cleaners. The ammonia molecule is pyramid-shaped, polar, and forms hydrogen bonds, producing characteristic properties that are in many ways similar to water. Note the boiling point, freezing point, the heat of fusion, and the heat of vaporization, all of which are abnormally high. Since ammonia acts as a base to water, aqueous ammonia solutions tend to be characteristically alkaline. Ammonia is the proton acceptor.

$$NH_3\ +\ H_2O\ \longrightarrow\ NH_4^+\ +\ OH^-$$

If you want to actually be a witness to a proton-transfer reaction involving ammonia molecules just place reagent bottles of aqueous ammonia and hydrochloric acid side-by-side and remove the stoppers. Ammonia and hydrochloric acid in the vapor phase react immediately forming white fumes of ammonium chloride.

$$NH_3\,(g)\ +\ HCl\,(g)\ \longrightarrow\ NH_4^+Cl^-\,(s)$$

Fertilizers, Fixation, and Food

At the beginning of the nineteenth century, the English economist, Thomas Malthus, predicted that production of food supplies could not keep up with population growth. Malthus believed that war and disease would result, killing off the overpopulation unless people voluntarily limited reproduction. At the beginning of the twentieth century, the English physicist, William Crookes predicted that mankind now *really* did face imminent starvation. Chilean nitrate deposits, supplying two thirds of the world's nitrogen fertilizer resources in 1900, were fast running out. Nitrogen, which is essential to plant growth, just wasn't available in the soil in any sufficient quantities to sustain the intensive farming needed to support the massive demands of growing populations. Was Malthus'

Table 12-4

The many states of nitrogen

Representative compound	Formula	Apparent oxidation state	Comments
Ammonia	NH_3	-3	Prepare by direct combination from the elements; a source of nitric acid for fertilizers and explosives.
Hydrazine	H_2N-NH_2	-2	High energy fuel; drag racers like the tremendous energy kick they get out of it, too.
Diimine	$HN=NH$	-1	It's novel, highly energetic, unstable, and experiences only a transitory existence; but it's been of great use to the chemist of recent years for both practical (synthetic) and theoretical (understanding) reasons.
Nitrogen	$N\equiv N$	0	The nitrogen cycle begins with this gaseous component of the atmosphere. "There is no atom of nitrogen in the air that has not at some time or other in its existence throbbed through the tissue of a living plant or animal, not once, but many times."
Nitrous oxide	N_2O	$+1$	Laughing gas is a local anesthetic of limited use that has found some notoriety in the drug subculture. As early as the nineteenth century, one chemist described that aspect of the gas after breathing 16 quarts of it. "This gas raised my pulse upwards 20 strokes, made me dance about the laboratory as a madman, and has kept my spirits in a glow ever since."
Nitric oxide	NO	$+2$	A colorless gas that has the distinction of being the most stable of the oxides of nitrogen. Even at temperatures approaching $1000^\circ C$, it is little decomposed.
Dinitrogen trioxide	N_2O_3	$+3$	The least stable of the oxides, existing in pure form only in the solid state at very low temperatures; a pale blue solid or an intense blue liquid.
Nitrogen dioxide	NO_2	$+4$	Notable for the ease with which the reddish brown gas combines into the colorless dimer: ($2NO_2 \rightleftharpoons N_2O_4$).
Dinitrogen pentoxide	N_2O_5	$+5$	Forms colorless crystals that have been known to explode; it is an acid anhydride, picking up water.

Figure 12-12
Populations.

prediction finally to mature a century later? (See Fig. 12-12.)

Despite the seemingly insufficient supply of nitrogen in the earth, there's lots of nitrogen in the atmosphere. We know that 80 percent of air is nitrogen; that is to say, above every square meter of Earth's surface there sits more than 6,000 kilograms of it, or about 20,000,000 tons of nitrogen above each square mile of the earth's surface. We have a plentiful supply then, readily obtained by distillation; but we do not have the means for easily fixing it.

In the early years of this century, a German chemist, Fritz Haber turned his attention to this problem of making atmospheric nitrogen available in chemical combination (Fig. 12-14). Actually, there were some chemical schemes known for combining or fixing nitrogen with oxygen or hydrogen but none was very efficient or economic. Direct combination of the elements could possibly provide the production potential that obviously was going to be required in the twentieth century to suppress the predictions of Malthus and Crookes. Here is the essence of the synthesis:

$$N_2 + 3H_2 \rightleftharpoons 2NH_3 + \text{heat (21.8 kcal)}$$

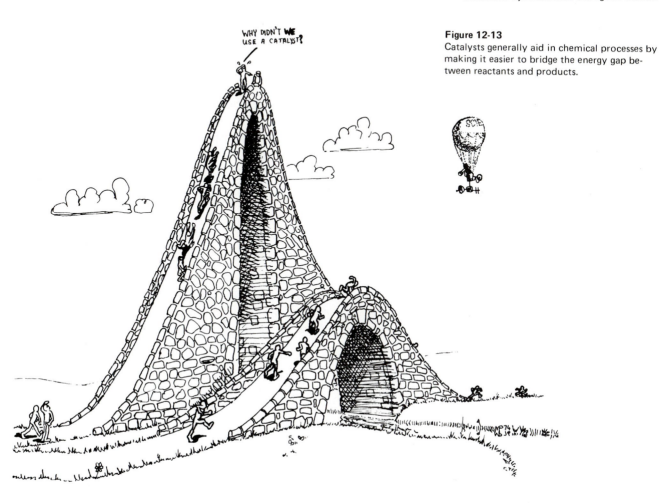

An analysis of the equation will let us see how Haber beat the problem, while at the same time allowing us to explore some of the features of another very important topic, chemical equilibrium.

The Ammonia Synthesis and Chemical Equilibrium

The equation for the ammonia synthesis states that two diatomic molecules combine to form a polyatomic molecule and that three volumes of hydrogen molecules combine with one volume of nitrogen molecules. Matter is conserved: two moles of ammonia molecules (34 grams) can be produced from one mole of nitrogen molecules and three moles of hydrogen molecules (28 grams + 6 grams = 34 grams). The synthesis of ammonia takes place with the evolution of heat. It's exothermic. But perhaps the most interesting feature of the equation is its reversibility which indicates that formation of ammonia proceeds right along with simultaneous decomposition back into its elements. When the forward reaction (always reading from left to right) takes place at the same rate as the reverse (always reading from right to left) we say that a state of chemical equilibrium has been achieved. When the rate of formation of ammonia from its elements exactly equals the rate of decomposition back into its elements, we have arrived at a state of equilibrium.

Many Factors Control the Position of a Chemical Equilibrium

For example, in Haber's early trials the best he could do was produce a situation in which less than 1 percent of his equilibrium reaction mixture was ammonia, more than 99 percent being the uncombined elements. If only something could be done to upset that equilibrium, to shift the equilibrium to 99 percent ammonia with only 1 percent uncombined reactants left. What can be done? Well, changes in the position of a chemical equilibrium can be brought about by (1) altering the speed of the forward and reverse reactions; (2) concentration changes will do that; (3) so will temperature changes; and (4) pressure changes in gaseous reactions.

To begin with, let's consider nitrogen, hydrogen, and ammonia, in equilibrium with each other. When the rate of ammonia formation is equal to the rate of ammonia decomposition, a state of chemical equilibrium has been established. However, change one or more of the reactants or products and the entire equilibrium picture is altered. *Add more nitrogen* to the system: the system will try to adjust to this alteration by absorbing the increase through additional reaction, forming more ammonia, while shifting to a new equilibrium position of say 10 or 20 percent ammonia instead of just one percent; the system has shifted in such a way as to accommodate the stress produced by the increased nitrogen concentration. *Add hydrogen*: more ammonia forms for just the same reason. *Add both nitrogen and hydrogen*: still better yields of ammonia form. Looking at the ammonia side of the equation, *removal of ammonia* will aid its own further formation because nitrogen and hydrogen will then combine to form the equilibrium concentration of ammonia being removed.

The equation has still more to say. Evolution of heat accompanies ammonia synthesis; the reaction is exothermic. Consequently, temperature can be used to effect a more favorable equilibrium (see Table 12-5). Take away the heat formed in the process, let's say by cooling the reaction flask, and the yield of ammonia increases. Think of it this way: heat brings about the decomposition of ammonia into its elements; that's what the equation says as you read the reverse reaction from right to left. Removing heat increases the speed with which ammonia is formed, bringing about an overall change that is equivalent to adding nitrogen and hydrogen: more ammonia; a more favorable equilibrium. Okay, then, for an exothermic reaction involving an equilibrium state, cooling it favors the forward process. But be careful: if you cool it too much, the reactants become sluggish; a certain minimum heat level is always needed to develop a reasonable rate of reaction. Too high a temperature is no good either because ammonia will break

Table 12-5

Data on percentage of ammonia present at equilibrium

Temperature, °C	Pressures, atm		
	1	100	1000
200	5	80	98
400	0.5	30	50
600	0.05	4.5	20

up into products. So we are forced into a compromise, an optimum situation as far as speed and yield are concerned. Choose a moderate temperature.

Pressure changes are also very important in determining where the equilibrium lies when dealing with gaseous materials (see Table 12-5). The equation states that four volumes of gaseous reactants (three of hydrogen; one of nitrogen) are somehow shuffled into two volumes of gaseous products (two of ammonia). Since larger pressures favor smaller volumes, a pressure increase favors an equilibrium state in which more product is formed.

Catalysts help here, too, speeding up formation of ammonia by getting us to the equilibrium position sooner. Generally speaking, catalysts alter the rate of both the forward and reverse reactions in equilibrium reactions without undergoing any observable changes themselves (Fig. 12-13). Fritz Haber and an industrial colleague, Carl Bosch, experimented widely with catalysts and found that if gaseous nitrogen and hydrogen were passed through a bed of mixed iron oxides (Fe_2O_3/Fe_3O_4), ammonia synthesis was heavily favored. Coupled to that, if the temperature was held between $400°$ to $550°C$ and the pressure maintained in the vicinity of 100 to 1000 atmospheres, the conversion could be on the order of 50 percent. The equilibrium is most favorable at low temperatures, but even with the best available catalysts (iron metal promoted with potassium and aluminum oxides) elevated temperatures are required in order to generate reasonable rates of reaction. In addition, as soon as you begin to raise the temperature, ammonia decomposition becomes more favorable. Therefore, a compromise on conditions is what's needed. Moreover, if you recycle the unconverted nitrogen and hydrogen, the overall ammonia synthesis becomes even more favorable, and very economic indeed.

Haber was, of course, familiar with the work of the Frenchman, Le Chatelier, who had succeeded in defining the laws governing chemical equilibrium systems directly in terms of "response to stress conditions." Changing temperature, pressure, and concentration place stress on the system causing the position of the equilibrium and the relative ratio of reactants to products to change. A kind of internal chemical compensation takes place.

☐ Nitric Acid and Its Salts

Haber's ammonia synthesis solved our needs for fixed nitrogen in agriculture. As a matter of fact, by 1974 there were close to 300 synthetic ammonia plants in operation around the world and more than a hundred under construction. But there is a twist of irony here because fixed nitrogen is also necessary for waging war. It is a component of every known explosive except atomic explosives. When war broke out in Europe in 1914, it was Haber who suggested that in times of peace, the scientist belongs to the world, but in times of war, to his country. It was Haber's fate to be most closely associated with the successful development

Figure 12-14
Fritz Haber, a controversial chemical giant because of the times in which he lived: the ammonia synthesis was an important factor in World War I; and World War I witnessed the introduction of gas warfare.

of gas warfare by Germany in 1915, followed a year later by similar developments by the Allies. In 1918, the year the "war to end all wars" ended, Haber was awarded the Nobel Prize in Chemistry for the ammonia synthesis, a great scientific discovery and invention in the benefit of mankind. Still, many people at that time criticized the choice of Haber because of his scientific involvement in World War I (Fig. 12-14).

The onset of World War I produced an allied blockade of Germany, cutting off needed supplies of synthetic nitrates for explosives. However, Germany had the internal capability to produce ammonia directly from the elements through Haber's process, and nitrates as well because of the invention another famous German Chemist, Wilhelm Ostwald, made in the year 1900 (Fig. 12-15). The *Ostwald process* for preparing nitric acid and nitrates began with ammonia being catalytically oxidized in the presence of air to nitrogen dioxide which was then dissolved in water, forming a 68 percent aqueous nitric acid solution:

Step 1. $4\,NH_3\,(g) + O_2\,(g) \xrightarrow{\text{(Pt cat)}} 4\,NO\,(g) + 6\,H_2O\,(g)$

Step 2. $2\,NO\,(g) + O_2\,(g) \longrightarrow 2\,NO_2\,(g)$

Step 3. $3\,NO_2\,(g) + 3\,H_2O \longrightarrow 2\,HNO_3 + NO\,(g)$

Note the important acid-base reactions that also take place: first, nitric acid (HNO_3) reacts with water;

$$HNO_3 + H_2O \rightleftharpoons H_3O^+ + NO_3^-$$

then nitric acid reacts with ammonia, forming the nitrate salt, ammonium nitrate;

$$HNO_3 + NH_3 \longrightarrow NH_4^+,NO_3$$

Figure 12-15
The gun and blasting powders manufactured by E. I. DuPont and his progeny on the banks of Delaware's Brandywine Creek (below). Early DuPont gunpowder was manufactured in separate buildings to prevent destruction of the entire facility in a single blast. Each building had a blow-out wall facing the open creek (bottom, opposite page). The "Powder Monkey" pictured on the opposite page was an early and a young user of gunpowder. This particular young man worked on the U.S.S. New Hampshire during the Civil War in 1861.

Nitric acid is a colorless liquid, boiling at 86°C, having a specific gravity of about 1.52. The acid freezes to a snowy solid that melts at −47°C. When concentrated solutions of nitric acid are distilled, nitric acid decomposition takes place. The acid strength becomes progressively weaker until it reaches 68 percent nitric acid. At this point, the liquid solution boils and distills at 120.5°C. Should you distill a nitric acid solution that is less concentrated than 68 percent, the residual liquid remaining behind in the pot gradually increases in acid strength, becoming progressively stronger until it again hits the 68 percent nitric acid level. This *constant boiling* 68 percent solution is the article of commerce.

Nitric acid is chemically unstable. Both heat and sunlight can bring about its decomposition to oxygen and nitrogen dioxide.

$$4\,HNO_3 \longrightarrow 4\,NO_2 + O_2 + 2\,H_2O$$

Nitric acid attacks protein materials such as your own skin, causing painful wounds, leaving behind a characteristic yellow discoloration. It is a powerful oxidizing agent, reacting energetically with metals and nonmetals alike. Organic materials such as turpentine are quickly oxidized, igniting violently, when combined with nitric acid. A 1:3 mixture of nitric acid and hydrochloric acid forms the powerful oxidizing agent and solvent known to the alchemists as *aqua regia* (royal water) because it readily dissolves gold and platinum and other noble metals that are impervious to most other chemical actions. Aqua regia is still used today.

If nitric acid is a powerful oxidizer, you might well expect the nitrate salts to be similarly inclined. Nitrates such as potassium nitrate (KNO_3) possess this explosive property, vigorously oxidizing many substances with which they are mixed. In fact, one of the most important chemical discoveries of all time (perhaps invention is the better word for it) was that useful work could be done by a mixture of potassium nitrate (KNO_3), charcoal (C), and sulfur (S) in certain proportions. The impact on human civilization of this discovery, *black powder,* has to be classed along with the prehistory inventions of pottery and the wheel, and the twentieth-century fixation of nitrogen. Black powder and similar incendiary explosive mixtures have been used in pyrotechnic devices for amusement and for war long before anyone thought to apply the way they release energy to the useful production of mechanical work. Perhaps black powder dates back to the thirteenth century; yet in the modern sense it's closely connected with Haber's synthesis of ammonia (Fig. 12-16).

But try to keep it in mind that explosives *do* have peaceful applications such as mining, dredging, and construction; in fact, it was to supply safe-to-use high

Figure 12-16
Gunpowder, the villainous theme of many old-time movies.

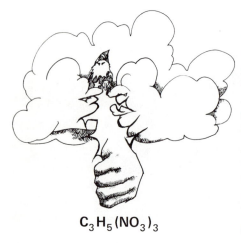

$$C_3H_5(NO_3)_3$$

explosives for just such purposes that Alfred Nobel invented dynamite in 1864. What he found was that the dangerously explosive nitroglycerin, made by treating glycerin with nitric acid, could be absorbed into a kind of natural clay called diatomaceous earth (*kieselguhr,* in German).

$$C_3H_5(OH)_3 \;+\; 3\,HNO_3 \longrightarrow C_3H_5(NO_3)_3 \;+\; 3\,H_2O$$

A relatively inert, solid explosive that now had to be purposely shocked was produced. Nitroglycerin by itself was an oily liquid that tended to detonate if you just looked at it cross-eyed. Today, dynamite is made by absorbing nitroglycerin onto wood pulp; various amounts of sodium and ammonium nitrate are added oxidants. Some 3 million pounds of nitroglycerin are used daily in the United States alone. Of course, Nobel's great discovery was immediately put to use by belligerents on all sides in all wars ever since. Nobel's frustration at the uses to which his ingenuity had been put caused him considerable anguish and led him to establish the Nobel prizes through the terms of his will after his death in 1895. His legacy created five prizes: Peace, Literature, Medicine and Physiology, Chemistry, and Physics. (More recently, a sixth prize in Economics was created.) The science prizes were clearly stated to be given only for inventions in the *benefit* of mankind.

☐ Nitrogen Fixation and Nature's Nitrogen Cycle

All animals and most plants are incapable of assimilating atmospheric nitrogen directly, owing to the extreme unreactivity of the nitrogen molecule; most organisms just can't seem to perform that little trick. But fortunately, there are a few genuine *nitrogen-fixers.* Their importance should not be underestimated, for without them, no organisms, including us, could exist. These nitrogen-fixers are: the blue-green algae; Azotobacter; Clostridium; and possibly the best-known, Rhizobium, a group of microorganisms that fix nitrogen *only* in the nodules of the roots of certain higher leguminous plants including peas, beans, alfalfa, soya, and clover. There is a growing body of chemical evidence supporting the idea that biological fixation is a progressive reduction, lowering the oxidation state from nitrogen to ammonia.

$$N{\equiv}N \longrightarrow HN{=}NH \longrightarrow H_2N{-}NH_2 \longrightarrow 2\,NH_3$$

nitrogen	diimine	hydrazine	ammonia
(N is 0)	(N is −1)	(N is −2)	(N is −3)

That's not to say diimine or hydrazine ever really occur in plants as such. Nothing more is intended here beyond a reasonable working model.

So far, all of the nitrogen-fixers that have been studied contain certain common elements: *ferredoxin,* a powerful reducing agent, always shows up; a complex enzyme called *nitrogenase,* containing both iron and molybdenum shows up too; and there is a highly reactive, energy-transfer agent we'll call *ATP* for the time being. The reduction of nitrogen to ammonia appears to occur while the nitrogen molecule is specifically bound to the enzyme, nitrogenase. It is worth mentioning the magnitude of biological nitrogen fixation: on the order of 100 million tons per year plus a trivial amount formed as a result of electrical discharge in the atmosphere. From the point of view of the government, the farmer, or anyone anywhere standing in line for bread, nature's techniques for fixing nitrogen into the soil through microbial action just won't do. Too slow. Rhizobium can fix atmospheric nitrogen all right, but population pressures won't allow us the luxury of simply leaving it to nature. Still, one cannot help but appreciate and admire nature's style and efficiency. Nature is really good at it, so good in fact that we've had difficulty in chemically copying the essence of what bacteria do so well.

Fixed nitrogen is essential to plant and animal growth primarily because nitrogen's eventual incorporation into amino acids, peptides, and proteins (a topic for the next chapter). However, there's more to the story. All plants and animals die at the end of their season, but the scheme of nitrogen combinations and interconversions continues. Things keep on chemically changing through an underlying cyclic theme (Fig. 12-17). This *nitrogen cycle* consists of four steps: (1) ammonification; (2) nitrification; (3) denitrification; and finally (4) the freeing of nitrogen as ammonia from organic molecules in plants, animals, and microbial substances. Nitrification is essentially bacterial oxidation of ammonia to nitrate,

Figure 12-17
Nature's nitrogen cycle.

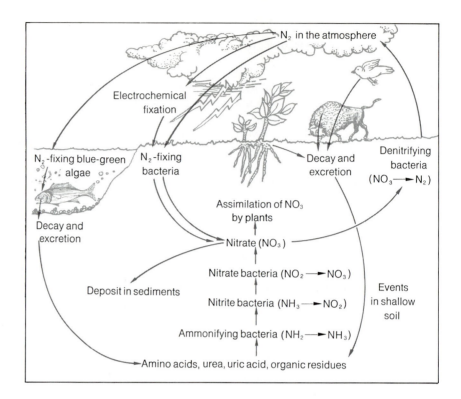

which is the principal source of nitrogen available to higher plants. Denitrification principally involves the nitrogen in nitrate being reduced first to nitrous oxide, then to ammonia; finally molecular nitrogen is formed. There are two kinds of nitrogen fixation: chemical fixation by man, and natural fixation by microorganisms.

The nitrogen cycle reasonably explains how the relatively inert nitrogen molecule effectively moves through the living world. In that regard, it is worth noting that in all of nature, the most biologically independent cells are the nitrogen-fixing blue-green algae found in the soils and the seas. They are believed to have been the first organisms out of the water and up onto the land during the long evolutionary process. That interesting hypothesis is based on a unique observation: after the great eruption of the volcano Krakatoa in 1883 had decimated all life on certain adjacent oceanic areas, the blue-gree algae were first to reestablish themselves.

☐ **Automobiles Fix Nitrogen, Too**

The air found within the earth's atmospheric envelope, the 12-mile high jacket geologists call the troposphere, is closely controlled by meteorological happenings and geographical conditions. When these combine in just the right way, air stagnation results, preventing dilution of the volatile effluents rising off the earth's surface. Wind velocity is a factor; so are thermal convection currents and the location of landforms such as mountains, valleys, and bodies of water. On a normal kind of day, for example, daylight warming (rising air currents) produces mixing at depths of 1,000 to 3,000 feet. However, if the barometric pressure is high and cooler air at the surface is being held down by warmer air above, pollutants can be trapped in the lower zone where human activity occurs: from 1,000 feet down to ground level. The classic Los Angeles *photochemical* type smog is a direct consequence of such temperature inversions (Fig. 12-18). A second type of smog is the sooty, sulfurous London variety. Los Angeles smog was not particularly noteworthy before the automobile really took over after 1945; London smog has been around since the industrial revolution first got cranked into high gear some 400 years ago.

Products and processes that pollute and contaminate air include: oxides of carbon, sulfur, and nitrogen; smoke and dust arising largely from industrial burning of fossil fuels (gasolines, oils, coal); smelting; the manufacture of tens of thousands of organic and inorganic products; petroleum refining; and last, but not least, the nearly 100 million cars in use in the United States today. The incomplete burning that takes place in all those automobile engines contributes the lion's share of these contaminants. In Los Angeles county alone, an average of 8 million gallons of gasoline are burned by four million automobiles each day,

Figure 12-18
The ubiquitous automobile (right).

Panoramic view of San Francisco in July, blanketed by an eye-watering layer of smog (below).

Figure 12-19
Industrial smokestacks in Rochester show the difference that electrostatic precipitators make to the environment.

exhausting 12 million grams of lead from the antiknock compounds present. It has been estimated that close to 3 trillion grams of lead have been exhausted into the airs of North America since knock-inhibiting additives were introduced in 1923. Then, too, there are forest fires, dust bowls, leaf-burning, cigarette-smoking, erosion, evaporation, and all those cans of aerosol everything: 200 million civilized people and their by-products in the "effluent society" doing what it does best!

Los Angeles and London Smog

Two principal categories of pollutants make for bad air: noxious gases and aerosols producing dense haze. Both the Los Angeles and London types of smog are stable suspensions of particulate matter and toxic gases. It is important to realize at the outset that in such a situation synergistic effects are likely to show up, producing key chemical and biological reactions. *Synergistic* means that the sum of the effects due to the gases alone plus the particles alone exceeds the expected effects of the combined mixture: one plus one is greater than two, in a manner of speaking. Even slight changes in just a single component in the atmosphere can cause astonishing changes in the whole system.

Automobile-born air pollution begins with oxides of nitrogen entering atmospheric air chiefly by direct fixation of the elements during engine combustion. Nitric oxide (NO) is the principal species initially formed. In the atmosphere's photochemical soup, nitric oxide is then converted to nitrogen dioxide (NO_2) whose unique role we'll use here to illustrate a bit of the complex chemistry mixed up in this obnoxious piece of science.

Nitrogen dioxide exists in the atmosphere over most urbanized areas. In order to briefly place urbanization in perspective, in 1800 more than 85 percent of the population in the United States was rural; by the year 2000, more than 85 percent of the population will be urban in spite of urban blight, in spite of the rush to the suburbs. High, persistent nitrogen dioxide concentrations are strongly suspect in terms of the deleterious effect of air pollution on human health and on the growth of all kinds of vegetation. Pure nitrogen dioxide gas is also highly colored, reducing atmospheric visibility; it is principally responsible for the creamy-yellow-to-brown cast characteristic of discolored, smoggy air masses in and around urban areas (Fig. 12-18).

Equally important is nitrogen dioxide's role in photochemical formation of other noxious air pollutants. We know nitrogen dioxide absorbs visible light because it is itself a reddish-brown color. But what we can't see is that it also efficiently absorbs ultraviolet light in the 3000 to 4000 Å region reaching the vicinity of the earth's surface. Wavelengths of light in that region of the electromagnetic spectrum have sufficient energy to cause dissociation of nitrogen dioxide to form nitric oxide and atomic oxygen. About 70 to 75 kcal per mole are required, easily available from ultraviolet light in this region. However, the really critical phenomenon occurs when this dissociation takes place in an urban atmosphere heavily laden with certain gasoline-range hydrocarbons; additional reactions take place between these hydrocarbons, nitrogen dioxide, nitrous oxide, molecular oxygen, and atomic oxygen. Some of the products of these reactions are powerful eye-irritants; others cause substantial crop losses; a number are known to be extremely hazardous to the health of older people and anyone with chronic respiratory or heart disfunction. It has been estimated that more than 100 million dollars in crop losses occur per year in California alone; more than 4,000 excess deaths occurred in the London killer smog of 1952.

If sulfur dioxide happens to be present in these dirty airs, either from industrial or human combustion of high sulfur-containing hydrocarbon fuels, the usually slow conversion of sulfur dioxide to sulfuric acid and sulfates becomes quite rapid. Stable, submicron-sized aerosol particles form, scattering light, thereby further reducing visibility, while making the air more obnoxious to breathe. What has become increasingly clear is that in the absence of nitrous oxide, and therefore nitrogen dioxide as well, none of these things happen. Despite high oxygen concentrations in the atmosphere, oxidation reactions are *normally* slow; however, such reactions as the sulfur dioxide to sulfuric acid oxidation zoom along with the greatest of ease in polluted atmospheres.

Ozone and PAN-Formation

It is interesting to note the role played here by ozone, that allotropic form of oxygen. Ozone is responsible for rapid conversion of nitrous oxide to nitrogen dioxide; in fact, the reaction between nitrous oxide and ozone is so rapid that they can coexist for only a few minutes at most.

$$NO + O_3 \rightleftharpoons NO_2 + O_2$$

Where does the ozone come from? Atomic oxygen from the photochemical dissociation of nitrogen dioxide freely reacts with molecular oxygen in the presence of an inert third body such as atmospheric nitrogen.

$$N_2 + O + O_2 \rightleftharpoons O_3 + N_2$$

All in all, smog formation is a complex phenomenon characterized by multiple interdepencies, both chemical and physical.

When sunlight acts on air containing incompletely combusted gasoline hydrocarbons and nitrogen oxides, a group of organic nitrogen compounds called *peroxyacylnitrates* or *PAN's* are formed. These photochemical reaction products play a key role in air pollution, especially because of their biological activity; they also constitute a secondary route to further nitrogen dioxide formation from nitrous oxide. Somehow, during atmospheric oxidation, highly energetic free radicals such as $CH_3\overset{O}{C}-COO\cdot$ form which then react with nitrogen dioxide, producing peroxyacetylnitrate (PAN).

$$\underset{\text{CH}_3\overset{\displaystyle O}{\overset{\|}{\text{C}}}-\text{OO}\cdot + \text{NO}_2 \longrightarrow \text{CH}_3\overset{\displaystyle O}{\overset{\|}{\text{C}}}-\text{OO}-\text{NO}_2}{}$$

The mechanism by which *PAN*-formation occurs is presently speculative, but the end result is not. Exposures to PAN concentrations measured in parts per hundred million can cause visible crop damage; PAN concentrations in parts per million can cause severe eye irritation; and PAN concentrations of a few hundred parts per million are lethal to certain small animals after exposure for only a few hours. So the ubiquitous automobile is guilty, spilling the needed reactants into the air where sunlight causes the photochemical process to take place, and away we go, all the way to PAN-formation. Moreover, it doesn't even end there because PAN reacts with nitrous oxide, forming still more nitrogen dioxide, a seemingly endless downhill run.

$$\text{NO} + \text{CH}_3\overset{\displaystyle O}{\overset{\|}{\text{C}}}-\text{OO}-\text{NO}_2 \longrightarrow 2\,\text{NO}_2 + \text{CH}_3\overset{\displaystyle O}{\overset{\|}{\text{C}}}-\text{O}\cdot$$

Plant damage from air pollutants, especially the photochemical smog type, now extends across the United States from California to New Jersey, and also occurs in many foreign countries. Up to 1970 in the United States alone, well over half a billion dollars damage to agriculture has been documented. PAN is toxic to lettuce, alfalfa, and spinach, and to ornamental plants such as petunias and snapdragons. Lettuce damage appears as a silvering under the leaf. By comparison, ozone kills cells on the top surface of the leaves, damage showing up as a kind of stippling; a few hours of exposure to air containing 0.5 parts per million ozone produces lesions on grape leaves. The action of nitrogen dioxide is a bit more subtle, there being no such outward signs; but low concentrations markedly stunt the growth of young plants.

☐ Most Elements Are Metallic

The ammonia synthesis and the nitric acid processes have given us a few insights into the nature of chemical reactions. Our view in earlier chapters was that a chemical reaction was a "chemical shuffle" of sorts; decidedly an over-simplification. We now perceive more complex features such as a sensitivity to control by outside forces and factors. The effect of temperature, pressure, and concentration of material on the conversion of reactants to products at equilibrium is quite pronounced. However, the equilibrium state isn't the whole story either and in the next chapter we'll offer yet another feature of chemical reactivity: some insight into what takes place on the way to equilibrium. However, this is a good place to show you a few additional chemical reactions, and at the same time, introduce you to the metallic elements.

Practically all of nature's elements react with hydrogen and oxygen (which are notably nonmetallic) in one way or another. True, things may have to get heated up and churned about, or brought into intimate contact: a soup of gaseous or liquid reactants in a pressure cooker, a flask, or flowing through a tube.

We'll even have to invoke the magic of a catalyst. But once begun, some of these apparently stodgy, seemingly difficult reactions really "go." Just note the reaction of hydrogen and oxygen. Once you get it going, it goes explosively. All of the elements we refer to as *metallic* form oxides when burned in oxygen. Magnesium burns violently in air (only 20 percent oxygen) with release of a considerable amount of energy in the form of light and heat. As a matter of fact, you're well-advised not to look directly at the glow produced by a burning ribbon of magnesium; it's a blinding light. On the other hand, iron rusts, oxidizing slowly in air, thus producing iron oxide (Fig. 12-20).

The way elements combine with oxygen varies according to periodic arrangements into families. For example, the elements of the first family, the alkali metals, can be characterized by formation of oxides with two metal atoms for every one oxygen atom.

$$4\,Li + O_2 \longrightarrow 2\,Li_2O$$
$$4\,Na + O_2 \longrightarrow 2\,Na_2O$$
$$4\,K + O_2 \longrightarrow 2\,K_2O$$

Although these are *not* all the actual products of oxidation, writing simple formulas for the metal oxides provides a good model for comparing the different families of metallic elements. The actual state of affairs is much more complex; but our simplified model provides us with the basis for making some reasonable comparisons.

In the second family of metallic elements, the alkaline earths, also form simple oxides but now we find only one metal atom for each oxygen atom.

$$2\,Be + O_2 \longrightarrow 2\,BeO$$
$$2\,Mg + O_2 \longrightarrow 2\,MgO$$
$$2\,Ca + O_2 \longrightarrow 2\,CaO$$

Iron belongs to that broad group of metallic elements filling in the extended mid-section of the periodic table, the transition metal elements. Here the oxides are mixed and many. Nickel and zinc form only one kind of oxide; copper forms two; vanadium and manganese form several.

Aluminum falls just beyond the transition metal elements in the periodic table. It forms an oxide, Al_2O_3, with interesting similarities to iron oxide (Fe_2O_3), yet as we shall see, in marked contrast. The element uranium is a transition metal but one of a special group known as the *actinides,* and generally considered separately when discussing properties.

The Alkali Metals

Let's take a closer look at the alkali metals, the most reactive of the metallic elements. Their reactivity can be described and understood in one way that's

Figure 12-20
A rust-caked cleat on the deck of a World War II liberty ship in the Hudson River mothball fleet.

already been suggested, namely ionization potential. If you measure the energy needed to remove the single outer shell electron from the control of the nucleus, you'll find that relatively little is required for the alkali metals. Further, it is easiest to remove the outer electron from the heaviest member of the family. Consequently, the alkali metals have combining capacities, or oxidation states of +1, forming salts such as sodium chloride and oxides such as sodium oxide that readily react with water to yield strongly basic or alkaline hydroxides.

$$Na_2O + H_2O \longrightarrow 2\,NaOH$$

The upshot of it all is that the elements do not exist in nature in uncombined form. Sodium and potassium are principal components of the earth's crust in the form of their salts, the chlorides, nitrates, silicates, and phosphates. By and large, the salts tend to be soluble in water. Seawater, we noted earlier, is about 3.5 percent sodium chloride; presumably the large land deposits of alkali metal salts were left behind as ancient seas evaporated.

In terms of world commerce and economics, sodium hydroxide and sodium chloride are the two most important alkali metal compounds. It has been said that one can judge the wealth of nations by their sodium hydroxide production. Sodium hydroxide is a white, water-absorbing, water-soluble solid that is strongly alkaline and corrosive to the skin. A crust of sodium carbonate (soda ash) forms on the surface by reaction with carbon dioxide in the atmosphere.

$$2\,NaOH + CO_2 \longrightarrow Na_2CO_3 + H_2O$$

The lime process for manufacture of sodium hydroxide makes use of the extremely water-insoluble calcium carbonate which forms and precipitates, causing the equilibrium to continually favor a shift to the right, with more sodium hydroxide formation.

$$Na_2CO_3 + Ca(OH)_2 \longrightarrow 2\,NaOH + CaCO_3$$

Calcium hydroxide, or slaked lime reacts with sodium carbonate, forming sodium hydroxide and the insoluble carbonate of calcium. It's an old reaction originally studied by the famous french scientist, Bertholet, who was perhaps the first science advisor to a chief of state while serving with Napolean in his Egyptian campaign. But perhaps the more important preparative process today is the electrolysis of salt solutions.

Sodium chloride has been around literally since day one. When the first animals emerged from the primordial broth onto dry land, salt came right along, and is part of man's earliest written and unwritten history.

Solid salt is generally mined, or recovered from seawater by solar evaporation. It is a transparent, crystalline, high-melting substance with a moderate solubility in water. World production is about 60 million tons per year, one third of which is United States production. Its uses are legion, but primarily as a raw material for manufacturing of other compounds of sodium and chlorine. The element sodium is itself an important article of commerce and is gotten by an electrolytic process (Fig. 12-21).

Whereas the oxides of the active metals tend to form soluble hydroxides in pedestrian fashion in reaction with water, the metallic elements themselves put on a spectacular show, one that is explainable in terms of the periodic arrangement. Metallic sodium is lustrous when freshly cut, but rapidly corrodes in air, forming an oxide coating. A bit of sodium dropped into a beaker of water produces a violent reaction in which hydrogen gas and sodium hydroxide are produced as the metal sputters about the surface.

$$2\,Na + 2\,H_2O \longrightarrow 2\,NaOH + H_2$$

In order to keep air and water from sodium, it is generally stored in bottles or cans under mineral oil. Potassium reacts more energetically, igniting the liberated hydrogen gas instantly; rubidium and cesium are much more violent still.

Moving to sodium's periodic neighbor, you'll find direct reaction with water slowed considerably. Magnesium does, however, react rapidly with steam and with hydrogen ions in aqueous acid solution.

$$Mg + 2\,H_2O \longrightarrow Mg(OH)_2 + H_2 \text{ (only slowly)}$$

$$Mg + 2\,HCl \longrightarrow MgCl_2 + H_2 \text{ (rapidly)}$$

That's the way it seems to go, in a qualitative sense. Metallic properties increase in going from top to bottom through periodic families of elements, and decrease from left to right across the table. Most metallic? Bottom left. Nonmetallic? Upper right.

The Core and Crust Metals: Iron and Aluminum

Iron makes up the bulk of the earth's core, while aluminum is the commonest element in the earth's crust in the form of bauxite (the hydrated oxide) and cryolite (Na_3AlF_6). Iron and aluminum both form oxides based on a combining capacity of 3. As a result, we have iron oxide (Fe_2O_3) and aluminum oxide (Al_2O_3). But there the similarity ends; only the formulas are similar. Iron oxide is a soft, reddish, flaky substance. In a moist air environment or an aqueous medium, especially seawater, there is often an unwanted formation of this oxide on iron or iron alloy surfaces. Such *corrosion* processes leading to *rust* formation cost billions of dollars per year in maintainance in the United States alone. If that seems to be a lot, consider this: most metals are iron or iron alloys, steels of one sort or another, and air and moisture are ever present. The trouble with rust is that it tends to flake off when formed, constantly exposing fresh metal surfaces to continuous rusting (corrosion) until eventually it has all crumbled away. Therefore, paint you must, in order to protect the metal surface, unless you use aluminum metal.

Process	Important Products
Ammonia-soda (Solvay)	
$2\,NaCl + CaCO_3 \longrightarrow$	$Na_2CO_3 + CaCl_2$
Chlorine-caustic (electrolytic)	
$2\,NaCl + 2\,H_2O \longrightarrow$	$2\,NaOH + H_2 + Cl_2$
Downs-sodium (electrolytic)	
$2\,NaCl \longrightarrow$	$2\,Na + Cl_2$
Mannheim-sulfate	
$2\,NaCl + H_2SO_4 \longrightarrow$	$Na_2SO_4 + 2\,HCl$
Nitrosyl chloride	
$3\,NaCl + 4\,HNO_3 \longrightarrow$	$3\,NaNO_3 + Cl_2 + NOCl + 2\,H_2O$
Cyanamid-electrolytic	
$2\,NaCl + CaCN_2 + C \longrightarrow$	$CaCl_2 + 2\,NaCN$
Chlorate-electrolytic	
$NaCl + 3\,H_2O \longrightarrow$	$NaClO_3 + 3\,H_2$

Figure 12-21

Plain old salt is one of our most important raw materials.

Aluminum reacts rapidly with oxygen, too; in fact, even faster than iron does, but the aluminum oxide coating that forms at the metal's surface is a tough clingy substance. And when several layers of aluminum oxide particles coat the metal's surface, oxygen is effectively excluded and no further reaction can take place. No flaking occurs for the metal is now completely protected. What's more, the thin coating of aluminum oxide does not visually detract from the metal since it has a grayish metallic appearance. So you don't have to paint for protective covering or aesthetic purposes. Aluminum has been a choice construction material, unusually suited for many purposes where the rigid structural requirements of iron and steel aren't needed. Its low density makes it light, and its self-protecting properties (oxide formation) make it a highly desirable, aesthetically appealing facing for skyscrapers or airplanes (Fig. 12-22).

Unfortunately there's an ironic twist to the aluminum success, and it's this. Just the very properties that are such an advantage have become an environmental hazard in the form of the immortal 12-ounce beer and soda cans either with aluminum tops or made entirely of aluminum. The old *tin* cans used to just rust away if left to weather along a country road or at the bottom of a lake. But aluminum survives.

☐ Coordination Chemistry and the Transition Elements

There is much more to be said about iron and a number of closely related elements. Iron is special in that it is one of the block of metallic elements in the extended mid-section of the periodic table of the elements. All 61 are metals just like potassium and calcium at the beginning of the first long period (the fourth period) because of the presence of one or two electrons in an outside shell. Still, that's not what's special. Their unique properties are due to electrons placed in unfilled *inner* shells. All 61 transition elements are characterized by a growing population of electrons within the energy level just inside the atom's outer shell. Sodium and magnesium are all electron-filled from the inside out. That's not true for the gang of transition elements in the middle. Only when the expansion into that inside shell is completed, does the electron population again resume building into the outer shell in pedestrian fashion. The periodic properties that began with the alkali IA and alkaline earth IIA metals, continue upon reaching group IIIA, (Al, Ga, In, Th) the first family just to the right of the block of transition elements.

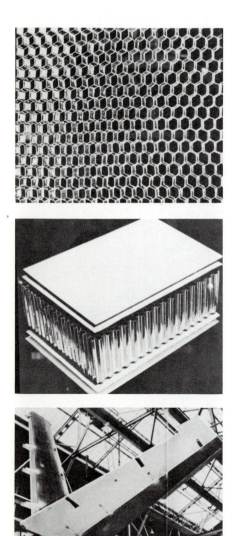

Figure 12-22
Aluminum foil, fastened together with a plastic adhesive into a honeycomb-like mesh (top). The mesh is then joined on both sides to a sheet metal skin (middle). The resulting aluminum "sandwich," being very light weight, stable and mechanically resistant, is used in the fuselage and wings of jet aircraft (bottom).

Coordinated Silver Ions

Of all the distinguishing features of the transition metal elements, the most important may well be the ability to enter into the special kind of bond formation that gives rise to **coordination compounds.** Such substances are generally stable compounds in which a central metal atom or ion finds itself complexed to a cluster of ions and molecules. The usual result is a charged complex, capable of reacting with an oppositely charged counterion to form an ionic crystal. For example, silver ions in solution, say from dissolved silver nitrate, will precipitate as insoluble silver chloride in the presence of even trace amounts of chloride ions.

$$Ag^+ + Cl^- \longrightarrow AgCl \ (s)$$

In the presence of ammonia, the silver ion becomes instead the central ion in a coordination complex involving a pair of ammonia molecules.

$$Ag^+ + 2\,NH_3 \rightleftharpoons Ag(NH_3)_2{}^+$$

In fact, the tendency toward complex formation with ammonia is so great that even if dissolved chloride (say as sodium chloride) is present, no insoluble silver chloride forms. All that's required is the presence of an excess of ammonia. Or, if you've already precipitated a mess of insoluble silver chloride, the precipitate immediately dissolves when an excess of aqueous ammonia is introduced.

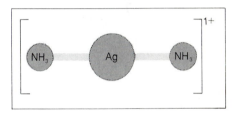

$$AgCl \ (s) + 2\,NH_3 \rightleftharpoons Ag(NH_3)_2{}^+ + Cl^-$$

Coordinated Copper Ions

Anhydrous copper sulfate is an opaque white solid that forms a beautiful blue, hydrated coordination complex with five water molecules.

$$\underset{\text{colorless}}{Cu^{++}SO_4^=} + 5\,H_2O \rightleftharpoons \underset{\text{blue}}{Cu(H_2O)_5{}^{++},SO_4^=}$$

You'll find the formula more commonly represented as $CuSO_4 \cdot 5H_2O$; but that formula doesn't tell the real story of this coordination complex. As the sulfate, the formula would more correctly be $CuSO_4 \cdot 4H_2O \cdot H_2O$. Four water molecules lie in the same plane as the four oxygen atoms of the sulfate group; the fifth water molecule is hydrogen-bonded in the lattice structure. If you heat the blue crystals in a watch glass, a white powder is first produced.

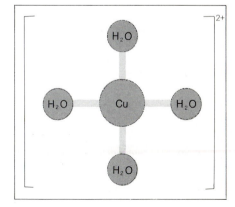

$$\underset{\text{blue}}{CuSO_4 \cdot 5H_2O} \rightleftharpoons \underset{\text{opaque}}{CuSO_4 \cdot H_2O} + 4\,H_2O$$

On further heating, copper sulfate may be completely dehydrated to the virtually white, anhydrous salt.

$$CuSO_4 \cdot H_2O \rightleftharpoons CuSO_4 + H_2O$$

Invisible Ink, Blood, and Chlorophyll . . . to Mention a Few Complexes

Colors are often prominent characteristics of transition metal ions and coordination compounds. One example that you can have some fun with is the use of cobalt chloride solutions as an invisible ink. Consider the equilibrium between the aqueous cobalt chloride complex and the anhydrous salt.

$$2\ [Co(H_2O)_6]\,Cl_2 \rightleftharpoons Co(CoCl_4)\ +\ 12\,H_2O$$

The pale pink, almost colorless complex in dilute aqueous solution is all but invisible when used to write on white paper. Gentle warming of the paper shifts the equilibrium to the right by driving out the complexed water molecules, forming the easily identified blue cobalt chloride complex. However, if you now allow the paper to sit about at room temperature for a while, all is soon invisible again as the anhydrous complex picks up moisture from the atmosphere, regenerating the colorless *aquo* or aqueous form. Looking across the rows of transition metal elements reveals a rainbow of other colored ions produced in solution; we'll meet more of them as we continue on.

Coordination compounds are widespread in nature and widely used in industry. The Syrians and Egyptians were using naturally occurring coordination compounds as dyes thousands of years ago. Phthalocyanines were among the earliest synthetic dye substances. It is clear that the mode of action of many enzymes catalysts that are essential for life processes depends on formation of metal ion coordination complexes; iron is by far the most important. Your blood is red (arterial) or blue (venous) because of an iron complex called hemoglobin. The chief *heme* proteins are the hemoglobins and myoglobins, cytochromes, and some enzymes such as catalase and peroxidase. Ferredoxins are relatively small proteins containing iron complexed to sulfur, especially important in green plants, algae, and all photosynthetic bacteria. Plant chlorophyll is a magnesium ion coordination complex structurally related to hemoglobin. Iron complexes along with molybdenum ions, catalyze the fixation of nitrogen in nature. One coordination complex of very recent interest has been the cobalt complex, vitamin B_{12}, the antipernicious anemia factor. (See Fig. 12-23.)

Alfred Werner and the Coordination Theory

The idea of a ***privileged*** central metal atom or ion surrounded by a group of tightly bound molecules or ions was first suggested by the Swiss chemist Alfred Werner in 1893. The success of Werner's coordination theory puts him in a class with Kekule and van't Hoff before him, and Pauling after him as far as our present day understanding of molecular architecture is concerned (We'll meet Kekule, van't Hoff, and Pauling in the next chapter.) Werner was a brilliant chemical practitioner and theorist. He was faced with a need to explain a perplexing experimental fact. Cobalt can have a combining capacity of 3 forming a simple ionic salt, cobalt chloride. In much the same way that any salt may be

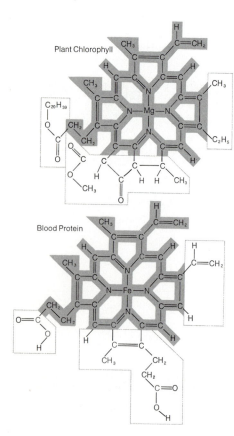

Plant Chlorophyll

Blood Protein

Figure 12-23
Chlorophyll structure (top).
Hemoglobin structure (bottom).

expected to pick up water to form a hydrate, cobalt chloride picks up ammonia, binding itself respectively to 6, 5, 4, or 3 ammonia molecules in a series of coordination complexes.

$CoCl_3 \cdot 6 NH_3$
$CoCl_3 \cdot 5 NH_3$
$CoCl_3 \cdot 4 NH_3$
$CoCl_3 \cdot 3 NH_3$

The really intriguing part was the question of why there was such arbitrariness about the number of ammonia molecules (3 NH_3's to 6 NH_3's). Furthermore, if you dissolve these cobalt complexes in water and add silver nitrate, you get strikingly different quantities of the insoluble silver salt, silver chloride, precipitating. Why not 3 moles of silver chloride in each case? After all, aren't there 3 moles of chloride available? Here's what you get experimentally:

$CoCl_3 \cdot 6 NH_3 \longrightarrow$ 3 moles AgCl precipitate

$CoCl_3 \cdot 5 NH_3 \longrightarrow$ 2 moles AgCl precipitate

$CoCl_3 \cdot 4 NH_3 \longrightarrow$ 1 mole AgCl precipitate

$CoCl_3 \cdot 3 NH_3 \longrightarrow$ no precipitate at all

Well, obviously (to Werner) the three chlorine atoms were not bound to metal in the same way. Werner suggested correctly that transition metal atoms could bind to some constant number of neighbors. In this case, cobalt ions form octahedral complexes with six surrounding groups. For $CoCl_3 \cdot 6NH_3$, all three chlorines were loosely held as in ionically bonded salts such as NaCl; for $CoCl_3 \cdot 3 NH_3$, all three chlorine atoms are tightly held, hardly like the ionic interactions in sodium chloride at all. Perhaps we could better understand the molecular structure for these species as follows:

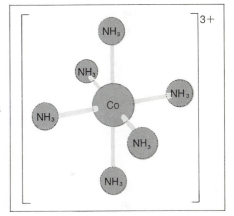

$[Co(NH_3)_6]^{+++}, 3Cl^-$

$[Co(NH_3)_5Cl]^{++}, 2Cl^-$

$[Co(NH_3)_4Cl_2]^+, Cl_2$

$[Co(NH_3)_3Cl_3]$

The first has six ammonias; all three chlorines are simple ionic chloride ions, precipitating in the usual fashion when excess silver ions (as silver nitrate) are introduced. The structure of the cobalt complex ion is shown at the right. For each successive chloride ion substitution, one ammonia group is replaced.

Werner said there are two kinds of chemical combination, a primary kind with which cobalt forms the trichloride, cobalt chloride, and a secondary kind that allows coordination with six other groups (6 ammonias). Extension of that view led to our considerable understanding of the structure and behavior of transition metals in their combinations.

Another important point that comes up here has to do with possible alternate spatial arrangements of six different groups coordinated about the metal atom or ion. For example, in the case of $[Co(NH_3)_4Cl_2]^+$, the two chlorines can be on the same or opposite sides of the octahedron. That makes for electronic

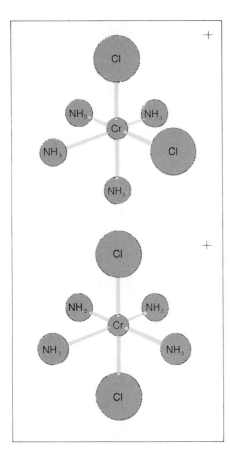

differences, and results in slightly different properties. The two *isomers,* as such compounds are called, differ only in the spatial geometry or arrangement of atoms. Most evident immediately are their different colored solutions: the *trans* form, in which the chlorines are opposite, is green while the *cis* form, in which the coordination complex has the chlorines on the same side, is violet. Moreover, it was the existence of these two differently colored forms of identical chemical composition that set Werner to wondering about what could be the basis of it all. As the next two chapters will show, such spatial isomers are common in nature and of great importance in living systems.

One last remark about transition elements. Looking at the entire block of transition metal elements reveals ten subgroups of which the first, the scandium subgroup, is perhaps most interesting. It contains not four, but 30 elements: scandium ($Z = 21$) and yttrium ($Z = 39$) are followed by lanthanum ($Z = 59$) and 13 more elements through lutetium ($Z = 71$); then follows actinium ($Z = 89$) and 13 more elements through lawrencium at $Z = 103$. The 14 elements from lanthanum to lutetium are referred to as the *lanthanides* or *rare earth* elements. It should be pointed out that geochemically they are neither rare, nor of the earth. Cerium, for example, is more abundant than lead; yttrium is more abundant than tin. Until recently, the only use for these elements was in glass manufacture. However, substantial interest has developed in the electronics industry, most notably for color television cathode ray tubes. Europium and yttrium are used as color phosphors (in the red region). All 14 are depicted in the periodic table as occupying the same slot. The 14 elements from actinium to lawrencium are referred to as the *actinides;* all 14 actinides fill one slot (Fig. 12-24). A one-slot arrangement seems reasonable because of the remarkable similarity among the elements in these two groups, especially the lanthanides. In fact the lanthanides are so alike, separating them from each other is difficult and tedious. The actinides are the heaviest elements in the periodic table, are mostly synthetic, and basically unstable.

☐ Carbon Monoxide Is a Little Neutral Molecule

Carbon monoxide is the little, neutral molecule with the tremendous biological impact. Looking at the molecule, you might never expect that: it is colorless, odorless, tasteless; a simple 1:1 combination of carbon and oxygen, formed upon incomplete combustion of organic material as the burning of wood or gasoline-range hydrocarbons in an internal combustion engine. Yet it is this molecule, especially in high concentrations, that dangerously reduces the ability of the bloodstream to carry vital oxygen to body tissue. Highest concentrations of carbon monoxide are found in urban areas having dense auto traffic; therefore, the greatest potential hazard exists where the greatest possible number of people could be affected. Unfortunately, carbon monoxide is only very slowly further oxidized in the atmosphere to the less harmful carbon dioxide.

GEOCHEMISTRY? . NEVER HEARD OF IT

Figure 12-24

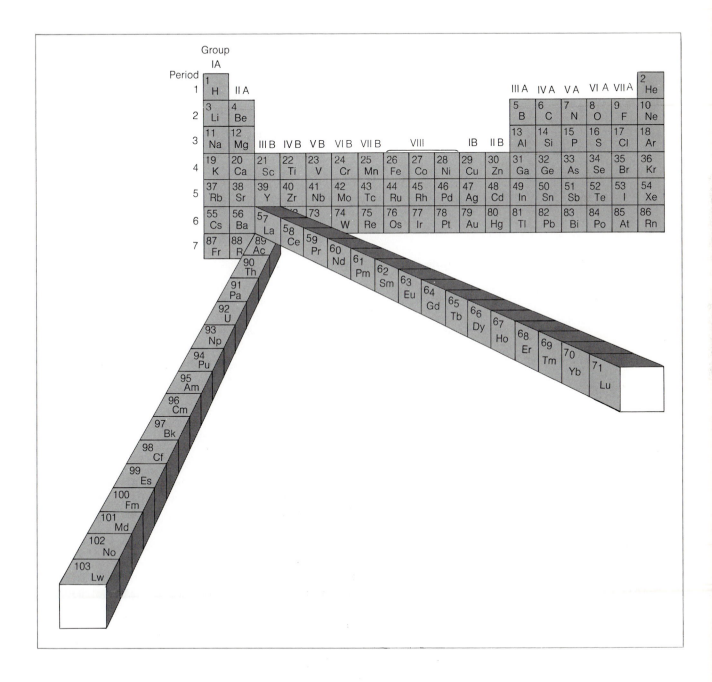

Carbon monoxide successfully competes for the available bonding sites on blood hemoglobin, displacing necessary oxygen. There is a complex equilibrium established that depends on the carbon monoxide concentration in the local air. Acute effects of high concentrations depend on the carbon monoxide levels, time of exposure, and physical activity, progressing from no apparent affects, to drowsiness, to altered behavior patterns, to impairment of vision, judgment, and motor acuity, finally ending in cardiac and pulmonary distortion, respiratory failure, and eventual death.

On the face of it, carbon monoxide is an unseemly molecule for such a sinister role. Carbon monoxide is generally an inert molecule; furthermore, when it does combine, the combination is often molecular, which is to say the carbon monoxide molecules remain as individuals. For example, when carbon monoxide combines with transition metal atoms, metal carbonyls are formed: nickel carbonyl is a colorless liquid, boiling at $43°C$; iron carbonyl is a yellow liquid, boiling point, $103°C$; vanadium carbonyl forms stable black crystals that turn into a yellow solution when dissolved. All are deadly poisons. The chemical bonding in all of these cases involves electrons drifting into and out of the metal and carbon-to-oxygen bonds (Fig. 12-25).

$Ni(CO)_4$ (colorless liquid)

$Fe(CO)_5$ (yellow liquid)

$V(CO)_6$ (black crystals)

Carbon Monoxide Bonds to Iron

Iron is the most important and widespread of the transition metals, playing a key role in living systems, especially as iron-containing proteins. It is to iron that carbon monoxide binds in the blood protein hemoglobin. When oxygen is displaced in that process, the vital oxygen transport function is disrupted. The effects, as we've noted, can be disastrous. Hemoglobin is the main chemical component of red blood cells, transporting oxygen via the arterial network from lungs to body tissue through formation and dissociation of an oxygen-hemoglobin complex. A simplified equation for the established equilibrium will do for our purposes.

$$\text{hemoglobin} + \text{oxygen} \rightleftharpoons \text{oxyhemoglobin}$$
$$\text{Hb} + \text{O}_2 \rightleftharpoons \text{HbO}_2$$

As you might anticipate from our discussions of Haber's ammonia synthesis and Le Chatelier's principle, increasing the concentration of dissolved oxygen in the blood shifts the equilibrium to the right. That's exactly what goes on in the lungs where there's lots of available oxygen. A shift to the left takes place if there is a decrease in oxygen concentration as in active body tissue where some of the oxyhemoglobin dissociates back into free oxygen and hemoglobin. The extent to which oxygen dissolves in an aqueous medium such as blood is limited and insufficient for support of normal body function. Typically, a liter of blood at $37°C$ ($98.6°F$) cannot dissolve more than 3 milliliters of oxygen gas; however, in the presence of the iron protein transport of about 70 times that amount of gas takes place because of oxyhemoglobin formation.

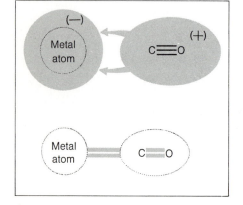

Figure 12-25
Electron-drift.

The erythrocytes, or red blood cells, are disk-shaped, and about 33 percent hemoglobin by weight. An average adult human being has on the order of 10^{12} of these red blood cells containing close to 1,000 grams (2.2 pounds) of hemoglobin. A simple red blood cell will contain about a quarter of a million hemoglobin molecules, each made up of some 10,000 carbon, hydrogen, nitrogen, oxygen, and sulfur atoms along with four important iron atoms. The four iron atoms are the biochemical key to oxygen-binding activity. They are located at the center of this large group of atoms forming the heme or pigment portion responsible for blood's red color. Each heme group is in turn wrapped into a protein chain, and all four chains are referred to as *globin.* Four oxygen molecules can bind to the four iron atoms in four heme groups tied into four protein chains. However, we'll just keep it simple and represent the equilibrium as we did by the previous equation, using Hb as the symbol of hemoglobin (Fig. 12-26).

Carbon monoxide also combines with hemoglobin's iron atoms, forming carbon monoxyhemoglobin which effectively short-circuits and poisons the oxygen-transport capabilities of the blood. In a qualitative sense, carbon monoxide adds to iron in just about the same way as it would in forming a simple inorganic complex such as iron carbonyl. Electrons flow back between metal and carbon monoxide and a stable complex results. The wrapping of the heme proteins turns out to be important, too, but we'll leave that for a later discussion. Although oxygen does all that carbon monoxide does, if hemoglobin is given the chance to select, it chooses carbon monoxide, much to our human disadvantage.

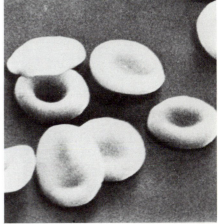

Figure 12-26
Characteristic donut-shapes of normal red blood cells.

$$Hb + O_2 \rightleftharpoons HbO_2$$
$$Hb + CO \rightleftharpoons HbCO$$

The relative proportions of hemoglobin combined with oxygen or carbon monoxide will be proportional to the relative concentrations of both gases present, but at 37°C, there is a proportionality factor of about 200 in favor of carbon monoxide. In other words, when the relative concentrations of carbon monoxide and oxygen are 1:1, about 200 times more carbon monoxyhemoglobin (HbCO) will form than oxyhemoglobin (HbO_2); that's potentially very deadly.

A good case in point occurred in the fall of 1969, when the United States government attempted to put a stop to the flow of drugs from Mexico, especially "grass," by tightening up the security at points of entry along the common border with California. The attempt was abortive. Fantastic traffic jams developed and resulted in hundreds of autos sitting, literally for hours, with engines at idle, waiting to clear through the road blocks. Border guards were actually asphyxiated by carbon monoxide, and the program had to be dropped. Think about that next time you're stuck in traffic on a hot summer's day with your windows rolled down . . . all those engines idling . . . and you begin to feel drowsy and headachy.

It is interesting to note in passing the hereditary condition found almost exclusively among Blacks, called *sickle-cell anemia.* That genetic disease involves certain mutational alterations that affect the hemoglobin molecule within the erythrocytes. The name derives from the characteristic shape of the red-blood cells (sickled) when in the deoxygenated condition. In the presence of large concentrations of carbon monoxide the equilibrium shifts away from the oxygenated form toward the carbon monoxide form. As a result, more of the sickled, deoxygenated species piles up, further accentuating the manifestations of the disease (Fig. 12-27).

☐ Characteristic Nonmetallic Chemistry of the Halogens

In marked contrast to the metallic elements, each of which has very few electrons in the outermost shell, the halogen family of elements is characteristically nonmetallic. That state of affairs arises by virtue of an almost complete (all but one) complement of outer-shell electrons that characterize their behavior. A high degree of stability is attained when six *p* electrons are placed in an outer electron shell. As a result, there is a really strong tendency to add one or two additional electrons when four or five are already present. As we noted in the Chap. 10 which dealt with chemical bonding, the nonmetallic halogen atoms easily pick up an electron, thus forming halide ions; there is a strong affinity for electrons. We also saw that same kind of stable filled shell configuration characteristic of halide ions achieved by halogen atoms through electron sharing. Thus, it is reasonable to assume that diatomic molecules should be the rule for the halogens.

The chemistry of the halogens and their compounds is totally nonmetallic, changing progressively with increasing size. Moreover, in this VIIA family of elements more than any other except the lithium-to-cesium elements in IA, such family traits are especially pronounced. Although there is a much greater change between fluorine and chlorine (the first and second row elements) than between any other pairs, that same first-row, periodic exception shows up with most of the other elements as well. The principle defining characteristics of VIIA elements are the ability to form halide ions and extreme electronegativity. Note the strikingly predictable flow of properties within the family (see Table 12-7).

Fluorine constitutes some 0.03 percent of the earth's crust, principally as the minerals cryolite (Na_3AlF_6) and fluorspar (CaF_2). Chlorine and bromine are primarily found as halide salts in concentrated salt deposits such as Great Salt Lake and the Dead Sea. Iodine deposits are usually in the form of iodate salts such as sodium iodate ($NaIO_3$). Astatine is a short-lived radioactive element which, when prepared, doesn't choose to stay around very long anyway. Fluorine (F_2) and chlorine (Cl_2) are yellowish-green, noxious gases; bromine (Br_2) is a corrosive red liquid with a very high vapor pressure; iodine (I_2) is a deep violet, almost metallic-looking solid. All are fantastically effective oxidizing agents; in fact, fluorine is just about the best there is. Uses for members of this family of elements in their variety of compound forms are legion: refrigerants; gasoline additives; insecticides; pesticides; pharmaceuticals; photosynthesis; household bleaches for

Figure 12-27
Elongated red blood cells in a sickle cell crisis magnified 8700X.

Table 12-6

Halogen properties*

Halogen	Physical state	Color	Melting point, °C	Boiling point, °C
F_2	gas	greenish-yellow	−223	−188
Cl_2	gas	yellowish-green	−102	−34.6
Br_2	liquid	reddish-brown	−73	58
I_2	solid	violet	113	183

*What do you think the properties of astatine would be like?

fabrics; industrial bleaches for paper, wood pulp and natural fibers; disinfectants; and in many vital body functions as for example, thyroxin, an iodine-containing compound of the thyroid gland which is critical to proper metabolic behavior in humans.

Because all the halogens are such good oxidizing agents, isolating them as free elements from their natural combined forms requires some very strong chemistry; in fact, for fluorine no oxidizing agent is strong enough to do the job and so it must be **won** by electrolysis of molten cryolite or liquid hydrogen fluoride to which an ionic fluoride, KF, has been added as electrolyte. Remember that in the electrolysis of water, an electrolyte was also added because pure water, and pure liquid hydrogen fluoride, are not good conductors of electricity; both are covalent, hydrogen-bonded liquids (hydrogen fluoride boils at 20°C) (Fig. 12-28).

$$2\,HF\,(l) \; \rightleftharpoons \; H_2\,(g) \; + \; F_2\,(g)$$

Chlorine is produced on a large scale, industrially, by electrolysis of brine solutions (see Fig. 12-29) or by electrolysis of molten salt (see Chap. 7).

$$2\,Na^+Cl^-\,(l) \; \longrightarrow \; Na\,(l) \; + \; Cl_2\,(g)$$

In the laboratory, chlorine is easily prepared and collected by reacting aqueous hydrochloric acid and manganese dioxide, the manganese dioxide, serving to oxidize the chloride ions released by hydrochloric acid molecules.

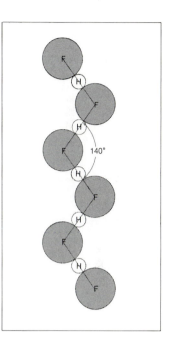

Figure 12-28
Hydrogen-bonded hydrogen fluoride chains.

Table 12-7

Some properties of the halogens

Element	Outer-shell electronic structure	Potential for halide ion formation		Electro-negativity
F_2	$2s^2 2p^5$	$F_2\,(g) \; + \; 2e \; \longrightarrow \; 2\,F^-$	2.85 volts	4.0
Cl_2	$3s^2 3p^5$	$Cl_2\,(g) \; + \; 2e \; \longrightarrow \; 2\,Cl^-$	1.36 volts	3.0
Br_2	$4s^2 4p^5$	$Br_2\,(g) \; + \; 2e \; \longrightarrow \; 2\,Br^-$	1.07 volts	2.8
I_2	$5s^2 5p^5$	$I_2\,(g) \; + \; 2e \; \longrightarrow \; 2\,I^-$	0.54 volts	2.5
At	$6s^2 6p^5$	——	——	——

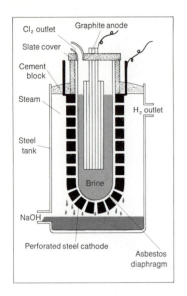

Figure 12-29
An electrolytic cell for the manufacturer of chlorine.

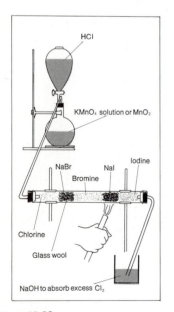

Figure 12-30
Oxidation-reduction of the halogens and the halide ions.

$$HCl\ (g)\ +\ H_2O\ \rightleftharpoons\ H_3O^+\ +\ Cl^-$$
hydrochloric acid
or "aqueous" HCl

$$4\ H_3O^+\ +\ MnO_2\ (s)\ +\ 4\ Cl^-\ \longrightarrow\ Cl_2\ (g)\ +\ MnCl_2\ +\ 6\ H_2O$$

The same principle serves for preparation of bromine in the laboratory. Chlorine can be used as the oxidizing agent for freeing bromine from its salts.

$$Cl_2\ +\ 2\ Na^+Br^-\ \longrightarrow\ 2\ NaCl\ +\ Br_2$$

Chlorine oxidation is also the basis for the commercial preparation of bromine from seawater. Of course, the bromine formed is also a good oxidizing agent and so you might want to know why the reverse reaction doesn't occur, namely, bromine freeing chlorine from sodium chloride. The answer is that the stronger oxidant sits higher in the family tree; hence, fluorine oxidizes chloride ions or chlorine bromide ions; but bromine won't touch chloride ions, nor chlorine, fluoride ions.

Yes $\begin{cases} F_2\ +\ 2\ Cl^-\ \longrightarrow\ Cl_2\ +\ 2\ F^- \\ Cl_2\ +\ 2\ Br^-\ \longrightarrow\ Br_2\ +\ 2\ Cl^- \end{cases}$

No $\begin{cases} Br_2\ +\ Cl^-\ \longrightarrow\ \text{no reaction} \\ Cl_2\ +\ F^-\ \longrightarrow\ \text{no reaction} \end{cases}$

Following this developing trend down through the halogens, one would expect bromine to be able, in its turn, to oxidize iodide ions to elemental iodine. That is the case and Fig. 12-30 is a classic demonstration pointing up the increasing strength of the elemental forms as oxidizing agents as you rise through the family and the decreasing resistance to oxidation of the halides as you move down the family.

Iodine is prepared commercially somewhat differently than the other halogens because as the iodate salt, IO_3^- ($NaIO_3$), it is in a higher oxidation state (+5) than the elemental form (always taken as zero oxidation state) and therefore must be *reduced.* Chilean nitrate deposits yield iodate that can be treated with sodium bisulfite ($NaHSO_3$) according to the following reaction:

$$2\ NaIO_3\ +\ 5\ NaHSO_3\ \longrightarrow\ I_2\ +\ 2\ Na_2SO_4\ +\ 3\ NaHSO_4\ +\ H_2O$$

Be sure to take note of the fact that while iodine atoms were being reduced, sulfur atoms were being oxidized from the +4 state in sulfite ($NaHSO_3$) to the +6 state in sulfate (Na_2SO_4 and $NaHSO_4$).

Halogen Processes and Products

The most familiar and important compounds of the halogens are the halogen acids such as hydrochloric acid (HCl), the oxyhalogen acids such as hypochlorous acid (HOCl), and the alkali and alkaline earth metal salts such as sodium chloride (NaCl). Perhaps the most striking uses for chemically combined halogen are in gasolines and photography. If you treat sodium chloride with concentrated sulfuric acid, hydrogen chloride gas is produced, which, when dissolved in water, becomes hydrochloric acid, the industrial *muriatic* acid.

$$NaCl \ (s) \ + \ H_2SO_4 \ \longrightarrow \ NaHSO_4 \ + \ HCl \ (g)$$

Hypochlorous acid (HOCl) is a very powerful oxidizing agent and as its sodium salt solution, aqueous sodium hypochlorite (Na^+, OCl^-), is commonly found in the household as laundry bleaches such as "Clorox."

Chlorine and bromine easily add to multiple carbon-to-carbon bonds found in ethylene-type molecules. For example, the synthesis of ethylene dibromide.

$$CH_2{=}CH_2 \ + \ Br_2 \ \longrightarrow \ BrCH_2CH_2Br$$

Ethylene dibromide (EDB) has a very special importance with regard to the energy crisis and the environment since it is used as a lead *scavenger* in gasolines containing lead antiknock compounds. Tetraethyl lead (TEL) is such an organometallic compound, functioning as a combustion modifier in gasoline, essentially upgrading and improving the quality (octane rating) of the fuel. But the engine combustion process converts the lead atoms to abrasive, nonvolatile lead oxides which will produce severe engine damage if not removed. With ethylene dibromide present, the lead is removed or "scavanged" along with other combustion products in the exhaust as the volatile lead bromide. That's okay for the engine, but there is considerable concern for the long-range effects of continually dumping large, concentrated doses of lead into the environment. On the other hand, in terms of short supply of gasoline for a mobile economy geared toward fuel consumption, removal of lead from gasoline means going to higher-grade fuels or spending more money and energy to upgrade poorer fuels in other ways than by addition of TEL and EDB.

Silver halides in light-sensitive emulsions can record an image; these compounds constitute the basis for conventional black-and-white photography. The black and white photographic process has to do with formation of visible images by action of light or other forms of radiation on light-sensitive silver halide coated systems. Most forms of black-and-white photography make use of light to bring about a change in the silver halide, followed by treatment with a chemical developer to convert the now exposed and activated silver halide to silver metal. Bright features of the subject produce more exposure than the dark parts, a negative is produced, and the photo-reproduction at this point is entirely in reverse. Materials used are usually an emulsion of finely divided silver bromide mixed with a small amount of silver iodide in gelatin placed as a thin layer on some kind of paper or transparent film. After exposing the emulsion in the camera, the sheet is developed, fixed by washing in a solution which dissolves the unexposed silver halide, washed again with water, and dried. A positive print is made from a negative by projecting the reversed image onto an emulsion-coated paper, and going through the entire sequence again as before. A modified form of this scheme is the one-step, combined polaroid process. Developer and fixer perform both operations at once, and positive prints are gotten directly from the camera. (See Fig. 12-31.)

☐ The Nearly Noble Gases

The family of noble gas elements includes helium, neon, argon, krypton, xenon, and radon. All are found in the atmosphere in measurable concentrations, although radon, the last one, is an unstable, short-lived radioactive element. Next to hydrogen, helium is the most abundant element in the sun's atmosphere. All of the main-sequence stars have similar chemical compositions. A high cosmic abundance of helium is understandable in terms of the energy-producing thermonuclear processes taking place in the interior of the stars; these processes bring about the transmutation of hydrogen to helium. Helium is probably the second most abundant element in the entire cosmos.

There are two really interesting features about the noble gases. First, none of the six family members were really known until the end of the nineteenth century. Just see if you can find that extreme right-hand column in Mendeleyeff's periodic table, or any other one for that matter, in the 25 years that followed 1871. Yet in just about every other way, the old periodic tables are otherwise entirely familiar to us. Helium had been identified as a new element by the astronomer, Sir Norman Lockyer in the 1860s, but it wasn't until 1894 that isolation and positive identification was made. Argon was actually the first, and within five years all had been reported. Question: where should these elements be placed in the periodic table? There was no space left, certainly not six similar spaces. Because of their utter intransigence at entry into chemical combination, they were dubbed **inert** or **noble** and given a family slot of their own, off by themselves (Fig. 12-32).

The second interesting feature about this family of elements has to do with why we thought we couldn't get them to react. Filled electron shells was the stated explanation; those outer **p** electrons. We could also happily explain away ionic and covalent bonding in a simplistic, yet workable, scheme as either electron transfer or electron sharing that led to an octet of electrons and filled outer shells. Well, we still make use of that modeling scheme, but we now have to accept a new experimental fact, the existence of noble gas compounds. The noble gas

Before Development

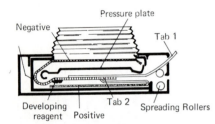

Film pack positioned in camera has pressure plate separating negative (which faces lens) from positive. Pod containing developing reagent is attached to No. 2. After exposing negative, tab No. 1 is pulled, moving exposed negative to face positive.

Development

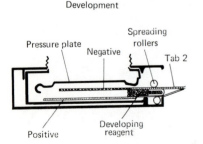

When tab No. 2 is pulled, negative and positive are pulled through rollers, bursting pod, spreading developing reagent between positive and negative; that starts processing. Film assembly is then pulled out of camera where processing takes place.

Figure 12-31
The polaroid film "pack" process represented schematically.

elements are not so noble; not nearly as inert as we'd all led ourselves to believe. In 1962 a Canadian chemist, Neale Bartlett, working at the University of British Columbia observed that oxygen gas could be oxidized by platinum hexafluoride, producing a heretofore unknown ionic substance of oxygen and platinum hexafluoride.

$$O_2 + PtF_6 \longrightarrow (O_2)^+(PtF_6)^-$$

Interestingly, xenon has an ionization potential that suggests it can give up electrons with about as much facility as oxygen; sure enough, when xenon vapor was allowed to mix with platinum hexafluoride, the analogous reaction took place immediately, producing an ionic solid, $Xe^+(PtF_6)^-$. Here was the first chemical combination of a noble gas element ever to be observed. As is usually the case with moments of high excitement in science, that was just a beginning. The direct chemical combination of xenon and fluorine followed, producing three stable xenon fluorides, (XeF_2), (XeF_4), and (XeF_6). These experiments were carried out at the Argonne National Laboratories near Chicago. At 400°C, with a fluorine pressure of 8 atmospheres and a xenon pressure of 1.2 atmospheres, almost pure xenon tetrafluoride was produced. Today, there are literally dozens of well-documented compounds of xenon, krypton, and radon. However, preparation of compounds of the three lighter noble gas elements has yet to be accomplished.

Two more things about noble gases. First is a well-known physical feature of noble gas chemistry namely the use of these gases, neon in particular, in lighting. As you know from our discussions of the discharge tube, when an electric current is made to pass through a glass tube containing a small amount of a gas at low pressure, light can be emitted. The excited atoms of the gas are giving off the unique color(s) of its spectral lines. The discharge tube has become a vapor lamp. Neon gives off a bright red glow; if the vapor lamp is shaped into long tubes and bent into letters and other decorative forms, we have the all-too-familiar hallmark of Western civilization's city culture, neon lighting.

Second, and perhaps more exciting, is a much newer device called a laser. An intensely energetic beam of light that has a narrow frequency range and so contains only a single color is produced by pumping energy into a neon-filled tube at low pressure between two special optical mirrors. Being able to generate this unique one-directional beam of identical photons or energy packages results in the potential for all sorts of applications, especially for telecommunications where the laser beam serves as a carrier wave. Lasers have found uses in a variety of civil and aeronautical engineering applications where it is necessary to line things up exactly; the coherent beam of the laser with its almost exactly parallel sides makes a very straight reference line. Also, as the wave front emerges from the laser, it can be focused to a pinpoint of light, and this property, along with the high energy of the laser beam, makes it useful for producing small holes called microwells used in the performance of certain types of eye operations. For example, a detached retina may be fixed by creating a small burn on the

Figure 12-32
William Ramsay, from the *Vanity Fair* series of caricatures. He was one of the principals in the discovery and exploration of the properties of the noble gases.

back wall of the eye, the scar tissue that forms acts as a weld for the previously detached retina.

□ **Questions to Answer, Problems to Solve**

1. In what form would you expect to find each of the following elements in nature: hydrogen, sodium, magnesium, aluminum, carbon, nitrogen, oxygen, fluorine, neon?

2. Briefly describe how you might go about preparing the pure elements mentioned in question #1. Where possible, write chemical equations illustrating these processes.

3. Describe the industrial preparation for ammonia and nitric acid, using equations to illustrate your answer where possible.

4. What's dynamite? What's nitroglycerin? How is dynamite different from nitroglycerin . . . besides the obvious difference in chemical composition?

5. Large quantities of hydrogen are required for ammonia synthesis. One large scale process treats CO with steam according to the following equation:

$$CO + H_2O \rightleftharpoons CO_2 + H_2 + heat \ (9.8 \ kcal)$$

How would you get this reaction to go further right, favoring hydrogen formation? Why won't a pressure increase do much good here?

6. What general conditions would you suggest for the preparation of ammonia by the Haber Process:

$$N_2(g) + 3H_2(g) \rightleftharpoons 2NH_3(g) + heat \ 946 \ kcal)$$

Explain why you chose the conditions you chose.

7. What role does the catalyst play in the Haber process?

8. Offer a brief explanation of the need for
   (a) crop rotation.
   (b) the Haber process.
   (c) the Ostwald process.
   (d) Rhizobium.

9. How come the halogens aren't found free in nature, but always combined (Na_2AlF_6, NaCl, NaBr, $NaIO_3$).

10. Isoelectronic means . . . having the same electronic structure. What noble gas element is isoelectronic with chloride ion? With iodide ion?

11. Do you believe it easier or harder for cesium to be oxidized than sodium? Why do you believe that?

12. Make a similar comparison and justification for the oxidizing behavior of iodine.

13. What happens to this relative capacity for gaining or losing electrons as you move from family to family across the periodic table, say from sodium to chlorine?

14. A certain drying agent, used to remove traces of moisture from gas samples, is coated with an indicator, anhydrous cobalt chloride. It's blue, but turns pink when the effectiveness of the drying agent is all used up. How do you think the indicator works? Why?

15. It's very embarrassing to look at an old textbook and read about the "inert" and "unreactive" noble gas elements. Why is it embarrassing? And what very important lesson about science does that experience teach? In what principal way is it difficult to study these elements?

16. The human environment is controlled by a collection of factors, social, biological, physical, and chemical. Draw up an outline for a discussion of air pollution based on these factors.

17. Photochemical smog often has a creamy hue to it. Offer a simple explanation. Why is smog often more prominantly colored on a sunny day?

18. One of the steps in the commercial synthesis of sulfuric acid is the difficult conversion of SO_2 to SO_3. Comment on the fact that the same process can occur with some facility in polluted airs.

19. Formation of ozone is generally an upper atmosphere phenomenon. But it does play a significant role in the pollution of airs in local urban environments. Comment briefly about that.

20. As a member of your local chemistry society debate team, you've been given the task of defending the position that the internal combustion engine has produced a greater social, political, and cultural impact on our society than has the atom bomb.

21. Now place yourself on the otherside and defend the opposite position.

Chapter 13

☐ **Perceptions and Deceptions**

1 On the whole, carbon compounds show the typical characteristics of covalent substances. The reverse is not true.

2 Organic chemistry has a lot to do with multiple bonds, long chains, and life.

3 There is only one "methane"; one "ethane"; one "propane." But there are two butanes, and three pentanes, and five hexanes, and nine heptanes, and . . .

4 If a hydrocarbon molecule is too big to be used in gasoline, it can be "cracked" down to size.

5 Nitration of glycerine can produce shocking results.

6 Rubber isn't "useable" for tires until the long strands are bridged through a process called *vulcanization.*

7 The multiple bonds in benzene aren't at all like the multiple bonds you find in ethylene.

8 Giant molecules have been feeding, clothing, and housing human beings since we began to manipulate nature.

☐ **The Compounds of Carbon Are Special**

The preceding chapter provided a brief impression of the chemistry of the more important elements but with one major exception: the element carbon. Altogether, the number of known compounds of carbon far exceeds the total number of compounds of all the other elements. It is for this reason that we have reserved the two closing chapters of *Chemistry Decoded* for the chemistry of carbon and its compounds. That being the case, we'll want to do a little bit more than just "talk" carbon chemistry. We'll want to take some time to collect and review our pedagogy, the furrows we've been channeling through the fields of chemistry, while trying to point out as many connections between furrows and fields as we can. Perhaps we can highlight most of the central themes developed through previous chapters: states of matter, chemical bonding, energy flow and forces in nature, stoichiometry, the nucleus, acids and bases, solutions, and the ways in which we aid the senses in perceiving nature. At the same time, we'll be looking at the very special chemistry of carbon and its compounds, and the vital field of human knowledge where biology and chemistry come together as one discipline.

There are many illustrations we might use to begin a discussion of carbon's compounds. For example, we could certainly say that all carbon compounds are typically covalent. By achieving an octet of electrons through sharing four valence electrons with atoms such as hydrogen, the halogens, or more carbon atoms, the

Polymers are giant molecules—cellophane, rubber, albumin, leather, rayon, starch, silk, cotton, nylon, DNA, orlon, dacron, crestlan, fortrel, mylar, bakelite, neoprene, polyethylene, saran, teflon, lyrca, acrilan, silicone, styrofoam, urethanes, lexan . . .

**The Catalog's
Organic Supplement**

Figure 13-1
It was the nylon stocking in the 1940s that made synthetic fibers as great an innovation as the horseless carriage (top left). Slender monofilament strands of man-made fibers (lower left). Electron photomicrograph of a single fiber strand (magnification 1000X) (right).

stable electron configuration characteristic of the noble gas, neon, is approached. On the other hand, one thing we definitely could *not* say is that *conversely* all covalent compounds show the typical characteristics of carbon compounds. No, that would definitely be false. No other element shows such structural diversity in its compounds. Carbon's uniqueness stems from the fact that each carbon atom participates in sharing four pairs of electrons, that is, in forming four electron-pair bonds with other atoms. By comparison, hydrogen and the halogens participate in forming only one such bond. Carbon's unique, bond-forming ability also leads to a number of interesting and unusual possibilities such as formation of chain and ring structures. Still other possibilities arise when more than one pair of electrons connect either consecutive carbon atoms or carbon atoms to atoms of oxygen, nitrogen, or sulfur—multiple bond formation.

Early chapters introduced us to physical ideas and fundamental laws governing the behavior of matter. Subsequent discussion led us through the microscopic, subatomic world, and brought to light the molecular construction of matter. In this chapter we will introduce a new level of association—a *macromolecular* level of association—resulting in large and often complex molecules such as proteins and polysaccharides, nylons and acrylics, rubber, and teflon (Fig. 13-1). Wood, meat, and silk are among our oldest and most familiar forms of such *polymeric* materials, housing, feeding, and clothing man since his first efforts at matching wits with his environment. By forming direct links with other carbon atoms, carbon participates in formation of the chain-like molecules that polymeric materials are made of. Hydrocarbon molecules are built of carbon-to-carbon links. Although hydrocarbons are generally regarded as "too small" to be called polymers, they are very useful polymer models. The butane gas in a lighter has 4 linked carbon atoms; gasolines have about 8; kerosenes run to perhaps 15; paraffin waxes to 20. Polyethylene, a true polymer, has approximately 1,600. Because of their unique properties and special significance these giant polymer molecules have become part of a scientific specialty, a discipline called *macromolecular,* or **polymer chemistry,** often studied quite apart from the rest of the chemistry of carbon.

There is another organizing theme concerning the chemistry of carbon and its compounds that perhaps has still greater significance. Almost all of the compounds of carbon are associated with what we think of as living matter and matter that has once lived (now dead). Here then is the "chemistry of life." We don't necessarily understand it all, but great strides have been made over the past 150 years. We now have some pretty good ideas about the chemical uniqueness of complex living organisms. A *bio*chemist will tell you that the giant, high molecular mass substances are the really exciting molecules to study in this regard. Living cells are composed of literally tens of hundreds of different proteins, each acting out some complex, programed sequence of events that bring about the breath of life. These proteins and other large biomolecules make up skin, muscles, and hair; tree barks and plant stems; DNA, hemoglobin, insulin, and chlorophyll.

In short, the chemistry of carbon is twice special. No other element is so uniquely capable of multiple-compound formation, and no other element is so uniquely associated with the fabric of life. The chemistry of the compounds of carbon is also a world of extremes in size: the small world of low molecular mass molecules, coexisting with a molecular world of giants. The general name given to this branch of chemistry is *organic* chemistry. There are also names given to the important specialties within that field of knowledge: biochemistry is the brand of organic chemistry that deals with reactions in living systems; macromolecular chemistry deals with the giant carbon-containing molecules. Biochemistry and polymer chemistry: they have a lot in common. The unifying feature of all of organic chemistry is the carbon atom.

One last introductory comment. The concepts to be dealt with in this chapter need to be extensively illustrated with formulas and structures. It is important at the outset that you realize you're not expected to remember *all* the details and *all* the structures. The idea is to perceive the principles which these illustrations depict. Don't try to memorize structures. Many of the simpler ones you already know; others you'll become familiar with through the study of the material in this chapter. The more complicated structures are presented only to help you understand the rudiments of molecular architecture and the relationship between structure and reactivity. Let's begin.

☐ In the Neighborhood of Carbon

We've already gotten a hint at the uniqueness of carbon. Certainly none of its nearest neighbors in the periodic table can duplicate its very special activities: chain-building; forming multiple bonds; entering into a mind-boggling complex of literally millions of discrete, stable, chemical combinations; and being the principal participant in constructing the matter that makes up living systems (Fig. 13-2). From a chemical point of view it's instructive to look at the properties of boron, nitrogen, and silicon to see just why these neighbors have no "organic-like" chemistry. Boron, carbon, and nitrogen fall in the second row of the

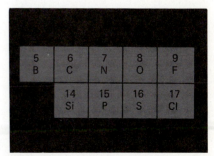

Figure 13-2
In the neighborhood of carbon.

periodic table; they're of similar size, and have a principal quantum number of $n = 2$, making available four possible L shell atomic orbitals or bonding sites into which eight electrons can be placed and paired. Boron has three valence electrons available for bonding in four orbitals; carbon has four in four; and nitrogen, five in four. Those differences in valence electrons account for a big part of our story here: boron has too few electrons; nitrogen has too many electrons; carbon, just the right number.

Silicon Chemistry

A look at the periodic table suggests immediately that silicon should bear closest resemblance to carbon, being in the same periodic family (the IVA family). Silicon, too, has four valence electrons in four bonding atomic orbitals. The key difference between silicon and carbon lies in silicon's being not an $n = 2$ (L shell) element but an $n = 3$ (M shell) element, one row under carbon. This means that inside the outer, bonding shell, silicon has ten electrons—two in the innermost $n = 1$ (K shell), eight in the inner $n = 2$ (L shell)—not simply two electrons as in carbon. The extra, inner shell of electrons prevents silicon atoms from getting close enough for easy bond formation. Remember, there are two competing electrostatic interactions, the positive nucleus of one atom attracting the negative electron cloud of another, and the repulsion of two close electron clouds. With ten electrons in two inner shells, the positive nucleus is effectively shielded, minimizing its influence, and the extra electrons increase the inherent repulsiveness between atoms. Consequently, there is no easy silicon-to-silicon bond formation as there is carbon-to-carbon bonding.

Boron Has Too Few Electrons

The effect of boron's electron deficiency can be illustrated with an example. Consider the simplest possible boron hydride (BH_3) which would be analogous to methane (CH_4) and ammonia (NH_3). Well, BH_3 doesn't exist. The simplest known boron hydride is instead an eight atom molecule called diborane (B_2H_6). There are twelve valence, or bonding electrons available: three each on two boron atoms, and one each on six hydrogens. If a chain structure similar to carbon were to begin to form, an ethane-like structure would be required.

Such a structure would require seven bonds: six H—B bonds and one B—B bond; therefore, seven pairs of electrons, fourteen electrons in all. But in fact there are only twelve valence electrons. That would appear to make diborane an electron-deficient molecule. The true structure is quite different, a circular kind of affair that hardly lends itself to forming chains and being carbon-like. There are four regular H—B bonds, making use of eight of the twelve electrons, and two strange-looking B—H—B bridges in which the remaining four electrons are somehow spread out. Unusual, to say the very least, and a situation that defied the chemist's understanding until recent years.

H—CH$_2$CH$_2$—H

C_2H_6
or

H H
| |
H—C—C—H
| |
H H

H—BH$_2$BH$_2$—H

B_2H_6
or

H H
| |
H—B—B—H
| |
H H

H   H   H
 \   / \   /
  B   B
 /   \ /   \
H   H   H

Nitrogen Is a Reactive Element

Nitrogen has the opposite affliction, too many electrons. That situation results in electrostatic repulsions between atoms. Whenever chains of nitrogen get started, molecules of a highly reactive, often explosive nature result. Hydrazine is a rocket fuel; hydrazoic acid is extremely shock- and heat-sensitive; and the triazanes and tetrazines are all equally treacherous.

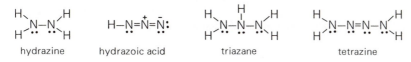

hydrazine   hydrazoic acid   triazane   tetrazine

One relevant association to note here is the obvious stability of the nitrogen molecule (N_2). It has a very strong *triple* bond connection; in fact, the nitrogen-to-nitrogen triple bond is six times stronger than the nitrogen-to-nitrogen single bond. Comparing nitrogen with carbon shows the carbon-to-carbon triple bond in the acetylene molecule is only about 2½ times as strong as a carbon-to-carbon single bond. The implication is clear: a much more stable state of affairs results if a chain of nitrogen atoms becomes pairs of nitrogen molecules. That might be one explanation for 80 percent of the atmosphere in the vicinity of the earth's surface being nitrogen molecules. Interestingly, when carbon bonds to nitrogen, this excessive quantity of energy is spread between the two in a compromise of sorts. Indeed, throughout the natural world many carbon chains contain nitrogen and they play important parts in a variety of processes.

Carbon and silicon both have a valence of four. Silicon bonds to itself, to oxygen, and to hydrogen, much as carbon does, but with an energy difference worth mentioning. The Si—Si bond is much weaker than the C—C bond, but the Si—O bond is stronger than the C—O bond. Therefore, carbon forms long chains linked carbon-to-carbon, while silicon tends to form long chains linked silicon-to-oxygen. Further, the C—H bond is much stronger than the Si—H bond. Consequently, Si—H compounds such as silane (SiH_4) undergo rapid reaction with oxygen, forming stable Si—O bonds; C—H compounds as methane (CH_4) are much more stable.

You have to heat this reaction to get it to go in any reasonable time.

$$CH_4 + 2\,O_2 \longrightarrow CO_2 + 2\,H_2O$$

This reaction happens all by itself: easily, rapidly.

$$SiH_4 + 2\,O_2 \longrightarrow SiO_2 + 2\,H_2O$$

Thinking about the strength of the Si—O bond in terms of the earth's crust, composed mainly of oxygen and silicon, it shouldn't come as a surprise that virtually all rocks, soils, and sands are basically substances of the Si—O type. Silicon polymers of the Si—O variety do exist, are quite stable as you might expect, and are used commercially for a variety of applications, for example,

silicon rubber

where *n* = 10,000 to 40,000

Hydrocarbons
compounds of only
carbon and hydrogen

Aliphatic
hydrocarbons

Alkanes   Alkenes   Alkynes

Aromatic
hydrocarbons

water-repellant silicones, heat-resistant silicones, and silicone films and membranes.

However, no multiple silicon-to-carbon type bonds similar to those found in carbon are yet known. A number of chemists have tried very hard to make Si=Si or Si=C types but so far, without success. Boron, nitrogen and silicon, then, are quite incapable of doing what carbon does, and we again conclude that carbon is unique among the elements.

□ Large and Small Hydrocarbon Molecules

The largest single subclass of organic compounds is the group of molecules referred to as *hydrocarbons,* molecules consisting of hydrogen and carbon atoms. There are two principal hydrocarbon categories, based on structural differences: *aliphatic* and *aromatic* hydrocarbons. Aliphatic hydrocarbons are further differentiated according to structure into three families: alkanes, alkenes, and alkynes. The aliphatic hydrocarbons and their functional derivatives, in which we find atoms other than hydrogen (such as nitrogen, oxygen, phosphorous, and sulfur) attached to carbon, will occupy our interest in this section. Aromatic hydrocarbons will follow in a later section of this chapter. Let's begin with the alkane family in particular. We'll see that a great deal of our present understanding has to do with carbon's amazing ability to form chains; in the case of the alkanes, the defining adjective is *saturated*: alkanes are "saturated" hydrocarbons; in other words, all of the bonds to carbon are single bonds. (See Table 13-1.)

Nature's Alkane Series Begins With Methane

Methane (CH_4) is the smallest (five atoms: one carbon; four hydrogens) and lightest (*M* = 16) of the hydrocarbons. A gas at room temperature (boiling point $-161.7°C$), it is the dreaded, explosive, "fire damp," the gas miners still fear. We can write methane's structure to show a methylene ($-CH_2-$) unit, with two end bonds to hydrogen. Writing methane in this fashion as $H-CH_2-H$ provides a model for understanding the succeeding members of the alkane family of aliphatic hydrocarbons: ethane, propane, and butane. Ethane, then, would be $H-CH_2CH_2-H$. Together, methane (CH_4) and ethane (C_2H_6) make up 95 percent of natural gas. Propane is next, the carbon chain growing to three. Using the $-CH_2-$ or methylene repeating unit device, we now find ourselves with $H-CH_2CH_2CH_2-H$ or C_3H_8. Propane gas is bottled and sold for a variety of heating purposes, from home use and camping to light industry and agriculture. The largest of the gaseous hydrocarbon molecules is butane (boiling point $-0.5°C$), the four-carbon cigarette lighter gas, $H-CH_2CH_2CH_2CH_2-H$ or C_4H_{10}.

Straight chain hydrocarbons become liquids in the vicinity of room temperature when there are five or more carbons in a straight chain. Moving on through to eight carbons, we find the gasoline range hydrocarbons pentane (C-5), hexane (C-6), heptane (C-7), and octane (C-8). By about 18 the hydrocarbons have turned from semisolid lube oils and greases to petroleum waxes. Applications range

Table 13-1
Structural representations for the *n*-alkanes

Name	Condensed formula	Poly(methylene) formula	Structural formulas
Methane	CH_4	$H(CH_2)_1H$	CH_4
Ethane	C_2H_6	$H(CH_2)_2H$	CH_3-CH_3
Propane	C_3H_8	$H(CH_2)_3H$	$CH_3-CH_2-CH_3$
n-butane	C_4H_{10}	$H(CH_2)_4H$	$CH_3-CH_2-CH_2-CH_3$
n-pentane	C_5H_{12}	$H(CH_2)_5H$	
n-hexane	C_6H_{14}	$H(CH_2)_6H$	
n-heptane	C_7H_{16}	$H(CH_2)_7H$	
n-octane	C_8H_{18}		
n-decane	$C_{10}H_{22}$		
n-heptadecane	$C_{17}H_{36}$		
n-triacontane	$C_{30}H_{62}$		
General formula	C_nH_{2n+2}		

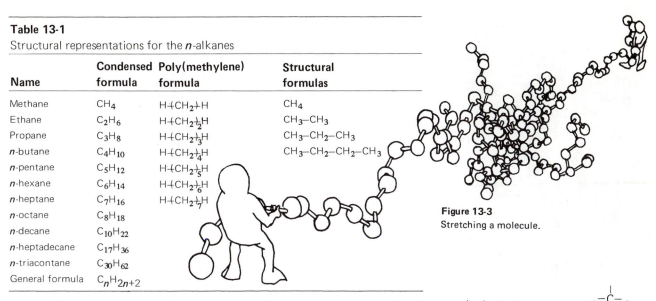

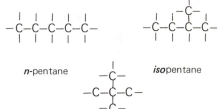

Figure 13-3
Stretching a molecule.

from processes such as candlemaking and weather-proofing (remember: oil and water don't mix—we say why in Chap. 11) to products like petroleum jelly (vaseline) and shoe polish.

The small *n*- prefixed to most of the alkanes named in Table 13-1 is a shorthand notation for ***normal*-butane** or ***normal*-octane**. It means that the carbons are linked in a head-to-tail chain arrangement with no branching. Branching, which can occur with four or more carbon atoms, is very important. When branching does take place, compounds with the same composition but different structures or arrangements for those atoms arise. The result is molecules with the same composition but different physical and chemical properties arise. Such molecules are called **isomers.** Isomeric forms of many molecular collections of atoms are known. The two structural isomers of the C-4 butanes are shown (right) along with their common names; only the bonds to hydrogen atoms are shown, the symbol for the hydrogen atom being left off for clarity.

Naming Hydrocarbons Systematically

At this point there is obviously going to be some confusion and ambiguity about names. A helpful numbering system has been introduced to clear things up. In its simplest form, the longest consecutive chain of carbon atoms that can be followed through the molecule is chosen. The molecule is then stretched, *figuratively*, by grabbing the ends of this longest chain (Fig. 13-3). (It's okay to do that; remember, pencil structures on paper are only models or representations.) Then number the carbons beginning at the end closest to where branching first appears. Therefore, propane can only be propane: no isomeric forms, no matter how you choose

n-butane   *iso*butane

For the 5-carbon pentanes, we can do the same; three isomers turn up.

n-pentane   *iso*pentane

neo-pentane

For the 6-carbon hexanes, five isomers are possible:

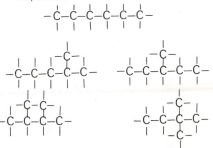

to write the formula on paper, because when properly stretched there are always three carbons in a row, without branches.

The longest chain is four in *n*-butane, but three in isobutane which can then be named methylpropane or better, 2-methylpropane. Hydrocarbons with side chains such as methane are named by dropping the *ane* in the alkane title and adding *yl*. Consequently, methane becomes *methyl* when CH_4 becomes CH_3; hence, 2-methylpropane.

n-butane   2-methylpropane

Isopentane is correctly known as 2-methylbutane. With the hexanes and beyond, the only useful naming system is this systematic method. Note isooctane, the standard used by the gasoline industry for comparing the combustion characteristics of automotive fuels: those that are smooth-burning without pre-ignition versus those in which combustion occurs too early, resulting in a "pinging" or "knock" during the engine cycle.

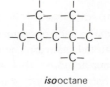

n-heptane

*iso*octane
(2,2,4-trimethylpentane)

Isooctane is systematically named 2,2,4-trimethylpentane. It has been given an engine knock rating of 100, spontaneously detonating only at very high compression. When the octane rating system was introduced in 1927, isooctane was a better fuel than any gasoline known for smooth burning. *n*-Heptane on the other hand was especially poor and therefore given a zero octane rating; it cannot be burned for long in any modern internal combustion engine without doing irreparable damage. The traditional **octane number** rating of any particular gasoline is the percent isooctane blended with *n*-heptane: 92 octane means 92 percent isooctane. Most engines will audibly ping due to pre-ignition at octane levels much below that.

We have seen, then, two isomeric butanes, three isomeric pentanes, five hexanes, and nine heptanes. Looking at the table of isomers for the *normal*-alkanes (Table 13-2) through 40 carbon atoms, you begin to gain some appreciation for how chain formation and branching rapidly multiply the possible numbers of molecules. By the way, the calculation for the higher alkanes was done by mathematical

Table 13-2
Numbers of isomeric alkanes

Number of carbon atoms in the hydrocarbons	Number of possible isomers
C_1	—
C_2	—
C_3	—
C_4	2
C_5	3
C_6	5
C_7	9
C_8	18
C_9	35
C_{10}	75
C_{11}	159
C_{12}	355
C_{13}	802
C_{14}	1,858
C_{15}	4,347
C_{20}	366,319
C_{30}	4,111,846,763
C_{40}	62,491,178,805,831

computation; nobody sat down and drew all the possible structures, and then counted them up. However, try your hand at C_7 or even C_8, and name them systematically as well.

The Larger and Largest Hydrocarbons

Large, straight-chained hydrocarbons such as *n*-triacontane ($C_{30}H_{62}$) or hexacontane ($C_{60}H_{122}$) are nothing more than stretched out collections of regularly repeating $-CH_2-$ groups: a polymethylene arrangement. These are the largest of nature's hydrocarbon polymers. The research scientist and the industrial chemist can do better. Repeating $-CH_2-$'s can be put together into chains of not 30 to 60 carbon atoms, but a couple of hundred thousand in number, end-to-end. These small, methane-derived units can be snapped into long chains, in effect, copying and bettering nature's own process. The petroleum hydrocarbons are all believed to have been formed through the action of high pressure and temperature on trapped, decaying organic matter. Nature's hydrocarbons allow us the opportunity to view and study the entire range of the states of matter, from the gaseous, to the liquid and solid states. It's interesting to note that a decade ago almost all disposable paper containers for milk cartons were coated with wax, the natural hydrocarbon polymer, while today, all are coated with polyethylene, a synthetic hydrocarbon polymer. Actually, by polymer standards we shouldn't call waxes polymers. The idea is right even though the molecular weights are too low. Both natural wax and polyethylene provide the paper container with the same **hydrophobic** surface properties, making it moisture-proof inside and out, hardly the usual properties for cardboard.

During the synthesis of giant molecules such as polyethylene, branching often occurs. The effect of such a structural modification is quite pronounced. Compare the boiling and melting points of the *linear n*-octane to the *branched* iso-octane (see Table 13-3). A more graphic example is illustrated by the pair of plastic cups (see Fig. 13-4), both made of polyethylene molecules, one the straight-chained variety, the other branched. The effects of branching are very pronounced; equal quantities of heat melted the branched polyethylene cup. In the straight-chained material, the molecules lay close to each other like so many neatly aligned strands. This close crowding results in a form of polyethylene that is rigid and tough, making it ideal for bottles and other applications where stiffness is desirable. The cup that melted was also polyethylene; the chemical composition was exactly the same; however, branching prevented the molecules from neatly packing together. That resulted in a less rigid, softer, more flexible material, best used in all sorts of *squeeze* bottles from catsup at the hamburger stand to the water bottle in the chemistry laboratory. Perhaps higher boiling points for straight-chained hydrocarbons (*n*-octane or *n*-butane) is easier to understand now; there is a greater opportunity for making the most of what weak interactions exist between hydrogen atoms; branching breaks up these interactions because the molecules can no longer get close enough to each other. The result is that *less*

Table 13-3

Aliphatic hydrocarbons (straight versus branched)

Hydrocarbon	Melting point	Boiling point
n-butane	−138.3	−0.5
Isobutane	−159.6	−11.7
n-octane	−56.5	125.6
Isooctane	−107.4	99.2

NOTE: In each case the branched molecules require less energy to reach the respective phase transitions, melting and boiling both taking place at lower temperatures. What do you think about that?

Figure 13-4
The two plastic cups were made of the same type of polymeric material and exposed to the same oven heating procedure. The cup that melted had a branched chain structure, the other was unbranched.

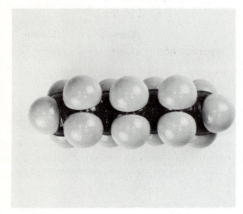

Figure 13-5
Space-filling and zig-zag backbone structure typical of hydrocarbon-type structures.

energy is needed to get the branched, liquid aggregates torn apart and boosted into the higher energy gaseous state.

Before going on let's review a few features of alkane structure while adding a couple of hints of what's ahead. That will blow some life and realism into what you must have felt was a lesson in language—all these chemical nouns and adjectives: hydrocarbons and alkanes; branched and linear; rigid and pliable. The emphasis needed is on the ***three***-dimensional nature of these molecules, an aspect easily overlooked on paper and blackboards, as well as on the interwoven relationships between structure and bonding, and between geometry and reactivity. For example, when we talk about linear versus branched hydrocarbons, either the petroleum or the polymer kind, what is really meant by linear or branched? Because of the tetrahedral arrangement characteristic of atoms bonded to carbon, the three-dimensional structure is never truly linear. After all, that could only happen if the bond angles between connected carbons were 180°, which is not the case. The angles are really about 109°, resulting in a zigzag arrangement (Fig. 13-5). Nevertheless, linear is all right if we are describing the overall interlocking chain arrangement of many connected carbon atoms. We'll find the same type of zigzagging, in a family of biologically important compounds known as lipids. Branched, on the other hand, refers to carbons hanging off the main carbon chain. It is very important to note that branched molecules are often globular in shape; but a linear molecule that is folded about itself can also give rise to an overall globular geometry, a structural feature commonly found in proteins. Molecules existing in a real, three-dimensional context, are never quite the same as what any textbook can adequately describe. The limitation is ours, not the molecules.

☐ Getting Hydrocarbons to React

Alkanes are saturated hydrocarbons containing no multiple carbon-to-carbon bonds and virtually inert to most kinds of chemical reactions. They are often referred to as paraffins because of the waxy nature of the higher members of the family in the C_{20}-C_{30} range. For example, saturated hydrocarbons are essentially inert to concentrated sulfuric acid and sodium hydroxide; you can boil them in nitric acid as well, to no avail. They're stubborn molecules. But they do burn, making them useful as fuels (Fig. 13-6). Halogens such as chlorine or bromine can be substituted for hydrogen, or hydrogen can be catalytically removed to form carbon-to-carbon double bonds, both processes producing new reaction sites (halogen atoms and double bonds) not present earlier.

COMBUSTION (burning) degrades hydrocarbons to carbon dioxide and water.

$$2 C_8H_{18} + 25 O_2 \longrightarrow 16 CO_2 + 18 H_2O$$

octane range hydrocarbon fuel

HALOGENATION (chlorination-bromination) substitutes hydrogen for chlorine or the other halogen elements.

$$CH_4 + Cl_2 \longrightarrow CH_3Cl + HCl$$

Catalytic cracking degrades large hydrocarbons to smaller fragments.

$$\underset{\text{ethane}}{C_2H_6} \xrightarrow[\underset{\text{catalyst}}{Cr_2O_3}]{500°C} \underset{\text{ethylene}}{C_2H_4} + H_2$$

Many higher alkanes crack, or rupture, at elevated temperatures in the presence of a catalyst. Carbon-to-carbon bonds are broken and the smaller fragments are often more useful for other chemical syntheses or applications. For example, petroleum distillation fractions of higher molar mass can be cut down to suitable gasoline range size by "cat" cracking (Fig. 13-7).

CATALYTIC CRACKING degrades large hydrocarbons to smaller fragments.

$$\underset{\substack{\text{higher} \\ \text{alkanes}}}{C_{12}H_{26}} \longrightarrow \underset{\substack{\text{motor fuel} \\ \text{range alkane} \\ \text{fragments}}}{C_8H_{18}} + \underset{\substack{\text{reactive unsaturated} \\ \text{alkene fragments}}}{C_4H_8}$$

In a typical halogenation reaction such as the chlorination of methane, it is possible to replace one, or all four hydrogen atoms, producing a mixture of

Figure 13-6
Hydrocarbons do burn. Advertising poster from the turn of the century for lamp oil (top, right). Gasoline engulfs a racing car, hollywood style (bottom).

Figure 13-7
Plant for separation of liquid components from the crude produced during high temperature pyrolysis.

substitution products. Careful control of reaction conditions such as temperature, pressure, and stoichiometry (ratios of reacting materials) allows one to isolate each of four products: methyl chloride (substitution of one hydrogen atom), methylene chloride (substitution of a second hydrogen atom), chloroform (substitution of a third hydrogen atom), and carbon tetrachloride (substitution of the last hydrogen atom).

$$CH_4 + Cl_2 \longrightarrow CH_3Cl + HCl$$
$$CH_3Cl + Cl_2 \longrightarrow CH_2Cl_2 + HCl$$
$$CH_2Cl_2 + Cl_2 \longrightarrow CHCl_3 + HCl$$
$$CHCl_3 + Cl_2 \longrightarrow CCl_4 + HCl$$

One equation summing the individual steps can be written for chlorination proceeding all the way to carbon tetrachloride.

$$CH_4 + 4\,Cl_2 \longrightarrow CCl_4 + 4\,HCl$$
$$CH_3-CH_3 + Cl_2 \longrightarrow CH_3CH_2-Cl + HCl$$

Halogenated Hydrocarbons Are Especially Important Industrially

Hydrocarbons are end products in themselves and chemical intermediates in the synthesis of more complex substances. Methyl chloride (CH_3Cl), particularly toxic to the central nervous system and internal organs, is manufactured by direct chlorination of methane at 400°C. Formation of higher chlorination products is minimized by having about a 10-to-1 excess of methane around throughout the process. Preparation of the gasoline antiknock compound, tetramethyllead (TML), is methyl chloride's main use. Methyl bromide is an important grain fumigating agent. Methylene chloride (CH_2Cl_2) is a key component in paint removers and is used for other solvent applications in textile processing, cosmetics, and paper sizing. Chloroform ($CHCl_3$) still has some minor uses as a solvent and medicinal agent, but its principal role is as a raw material for preparation of Teflon, (poly-tetrafluoroethylene) (see Fig. 13-8). Teflon is prepared in the following manner:

$$CHCl_3 + 2\,HF \longrightarrow CHClF_2 + 2\,HCl$$
$$2\,CHClF_2 \xrightarrow{\text{heat}} CF_2=CF_2 + 2\,HCl$$
$$n\,(CF_2=CF_2) \xrightarrow[\substack{\text{pressure} \\ \text{catalyst}}]{\text{heat}} (\!-CF_2CF_2\!)_n$$

Figure 13-8
The steel reactor in which teflon (polytetra-fluoroethylene) was first accidentally prepared.

Carbon tetrachloride (CCl_4) is usually prepared from carbon disulfide, which is prepared from methane.

$$CH_4 + 4\,S \xrightarrow[\text{heat}]{\text{catalyst}} CS_2 + 2\,H_2S$$

$$CS_2 + 3\,Cl_2 \xrightarrow[\text{temperature}]{\text{catalyst}} CCl_4 + S_2Cl_2$$

Its largest use is in preparation of a class of small fluorinated molecules called **freons.** Long used as a refrigerant, dichlorodifluoromethane (CCl_2F_2), is now widely used as a freon propellant for a wide variety of aerosol sprays:

$$CCl_4 + 2\,HF \xrightarrow{\text{catalyst}} CCl_2F_2 + 2\,HCl$$

Ethyl chloride is manufactured at the millions-of-pounds per annum level, mostly for use in tetraethyl lead (TEL) manufacture. Ethylbromide is used for preparation of barbiturates such as *Barbital* (5, 5-diethyl barbituric acid) and other related hypnotic drugs. Ethylene dihalides are also components of automotive antiknock fluids.

☐ Alcohols and Ethers, Aldehydes and Ketones

A little time should be spent describing several of the more important functional groups listed on page 368. We'll begin with alcohols and ethers, then aldehydes and ketones, and go on from there.

Something About Alcohols

Alcohols are widely used as raw materials and reaction media for a host of synthetic processes. Ethyl alcohol (grain alcohol) is perhaps the best known of all organic chemicals, being one of the two ubiquitous legal drugs in Western culture (Fig. 13-9) (tobacco is the other). But besides being used in the cocktail hour martini, vin rouge at dinner, or sacramental wine, ethyl alcohol is extensively used as an industrial solvent and reactant. Its medical uses make it important as a topical antiseptic and solvent for many other drugs; its cosmetic uses range from lotions and tonics to colognes and perfumes. Ethyl alcohol is prepared by fermentation of glucose (sugars) or by catalytic addition of water to the carbon-to-carbon double bond in ethylene, obtained from gas and oil wells.

Figure 13-9
William Hogarth's engraving "Gin Lane" bespoke the moral question of alcohol 250 years ago.

$$\underset{\text{glucose}}{C_6H_{12}O_6} \xrightarrow[\text{enzymes}]{\text{yeast}} 2\,C_2H_5OH + 2\,CO_2$$

$$\underset{\text{ethylene}}{CH_2{=}CH_2} + H_2O \xrightarrow[\text{catalyst}]{\text{acid}} C_2H_5OH$$

Methyl alcohol is prepared by the destructive distillation of the polymeric lignins in wood (hence, the pseudonym *wood* alcohol). It is much more toxic to humans than ethyl alcohol when taken internally since it attacks the central nervous system through its solvent action, causing progressive blindness and eventual death. Methyl alcohol is presently manufactured by reduction of carbon monoxide in a hydrogen atmosphere using a metal oxide catalyst at about 350°C. As you can see from the equation, the process would be favored by an increase in pressure but adversely affected by higher temperatures: Le Chatelier's principle in action again.

$$2\,H_2 + CO \rightleftharpoons CH_3OH + \text{heat}$$

For example, at 350°C and moderate pressures, only about 5 percent methanol forms; however, at the same temperature but higher pressure the equilibrium shifts, forming about 20 percent methanol. The unreacted carbon monoxide-hydrogen mixture can be continually recycled, increasing the overall yield of alcohol produced.

Along with the rising costs of hydrocarbon fuels for automobile transport due to the world energy crisis and the politics of oil in the Middle East, possible alternative fuels such as ethyl alcohol and mixtures of methyl alcohol and hydrocarbons have been studied. Although engine modification would be required, it may well prove to be economically and technically acceptable to use alcohols in cars. The difunctional alcohol, ethylene glycol, is a coolant in automobile radiators; a trifunctional alcohol, glycerol, is best known to you as its nitration product, nitroglycerin (Fig. 13-10).

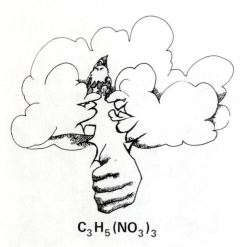

$$CH_2OH$$
$$CHOH \quad + \quad 3\,HONO_2 \xrightarrow[H_2SO_4]{conc.} \quad CH_2O{-}NO_2$$
$$CH_2OH \qquad\qquad\qquad\qquad CHO{-}NO_2 \quad + \quad 3\,H_2O \xrightarrow{shock}$$
$$CH_2O{-}NO_2$$

glycerol   nitric acid

$$\left\{ \begin{array}{l} 1\frac{1}{2}\,N_2 \\ + \\ 3\,CO_2 \\ + \\ 3\,H_2O \end{array} \right.$$

$C_3H_5(NO_3)_3$

Figure 13-10
"Shocking" nitroglycerin. Explosive business.

This oily liquid with its sweet, burning taste detonates violently on the slightest shock. There is sufficient oxygen in the molecule to convert all the carbon and hydrogen present into carbon dioxide and water, liberating molecular nitrogen. The instantaneous release of such a large number of moles of gas ($7\frac{1}{2}$ moles) into the space initially occupied by a small volume of liquid at a relatively high temperature results in an explosion and shock wave of enormous proportions. In marked contrast, nitroglycerine has had an interesting pharmaceutical history in the treatment of angina pectoris; it functions as a coronary vasodilator when taken in tablet form or as a dilute alcohol solution.

Some Things About Ethers

Ethers are condensation products of alcohols. A good solvent for many other organic substances, diethylether, is widely known for its anesthetic properties.

$$CH_3CH_2OH \; + \; HOCH_2CH_3 \xrightarrow[\substack{causes\ loss\ of \\ water\ molecule}]{H_2SO_4} CH_3CH_2{-}O{-}CH_2CH_3 \; + \; H_2O$$

Sulfuric acid brings about condensation by removal of water between two alcohol molecules. Diethylether is a very hazardous substance because of its highly flammable nature and its density, which is greater than air. Fumes have been known to roll out of containers and flow long distances to sources of sparks and flames, leading to flash vapor explosions and fires. The possibilities of explosion of the anesthetic during surgery and the hazard of fire have lessened its use in the operating room (Fig. 13-11).

Aldehydes and Ketones

In a sense, alcohols can be looked upon as oxidation products of hydrocarbons,

Functional groups

R—X where X = F, Cl, Br, I	Halide
R—OH	Alcohol
R—O—R′	Ether
R—C̈—H (=O)	Aldehyde
R—C̈—OH (=O)	Acid
R—C̈—R (=O)	Ketone
R—C̈—OR (=O)	Ester
R—C̈—NH₂ (=O)	Amide
R—NH₂	Amine

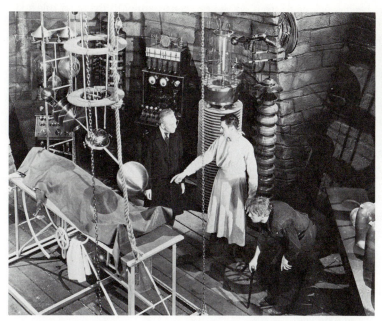

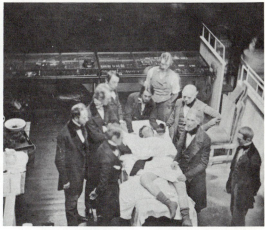

Figure 13-11
Just over a century ago, this photograph was made of one of the very first surgical procedures in which general anesthesia was used. The patient's leg was to be amputated (top). Dr. Frankenstein apparently had little need for anesthesia for his patient (left).

an oxygen atom being introduced into one of the carbon-to-hydrogen bonds.

$$
\underset{H}{\overset{H}{H-C-H}} + \tfrac{1}{2}O_2 \longrightarrow \underset{H}{\overset{H}{H-C-O-H}}
$$

The second stage along such an oxidation pathway leads to two new functional groups, aldehydes and ketones. Methanol can be carefully oxidized to formaldehyde, ethanol to acetaldehyde.

$$
CH_3OH + \tfrac{1}{2}O_2 \longrightarrow \underset{OH}{\overset{H}{H-C-OH}} \xrightarrow{-H_2O} \overset{H}{H-C=O}
$$

formaldehyde

$$
CH_3CH_2OH + \tfrac{1}{2}O_2 \longrightarrow \underset{OH}{\overset{H}{CH_3-C-OH}} \xrightarrow{-H_2O} \overset{H}{CH_3-C=O}
$$

acetaldehyde

unstable

The manner in which both reactions have been structurally represented shows two things: first, the aldehyde functional group, —CHO; second having two OH groups on the same carbon atom tends to be a relatively unstable arrangement, leading to loss of a molecule of water. The principal structural difference between aldehydes and ketones is the aldehyde hydrogen atom. Replace it with a bond to carbon and the $>$C=O or ketone structure is what you have. Here's the oxidation of isopropyl alcohol:

$$
\underset{CH_3}{\overset{CH_3}{C}}\!\!\overset{H}{\underset{OH}{}} + \tfrac{1}{2}O_2 \longrightarrow \underset{CH_3}{\overset{CH_3}{C}}\!\!\overset{OH}{\underset{OH}{}} \xrightarrow{-H_2O} \underset{CH_3}{\overset{CH_3}{C}}\!\!=O
$$

Figure 13-12
"Untitled, 1968." The use of plastics (lucite) as art media.

If you've been checking to see if we've been consistent with the octet rule and electron sharing in all these covalent hydrocarbons and functional derivatives, unless there's been a printing error, you'll find we have. Check and see for yourself. Recognize formaldehyde? Its many uses range from embalming fluids, germicides, and fungicides to waterproofing and photography; if your dinnerware is Melmac or your plumbing, Delrin, formaldehyde was one of the key raw materials. Acetone is widely used as a solvent in the textile, fiber, and paint industries; its the principal ingredient in the familiar airplane glue. The characteristic acetone odor can under some circumstances be detected on the breath of a diabetic person; having accumulated in the blood, it is expired through the lungs. Acetone is also a basic raw material in the synthesis of the biologically important alpha-amino acids, and the Lucite-Plexiglas glass-like polymers (Fig. 13-12). More about most of these biological and polymeric substances shortly. One particularly interesting cosmetic chemical is the *poly*functional compound, dihydroxyacetone: it is used in commercial suntan oils and lotions to help darken skin gradually.

$$HO-CH_2\overset{\displaystyle O}{\overset{\|}{C}}CH_2-OH$$
dihydroxyacetone

Adding Water to Aldehydes

It is a curious fact that the hydrated form of the simplest aldehyde, formaldehyde, happens to be quite stable. We drew the structure in brackets, indicating that it has an independent existence only as part of a favorable chemical equilibrium. Add water to an aldehyde; two hydroxides end up on what was the carbonyl carbon atom.

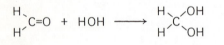

Try to think of it like the formation of carbonic acid in aqueous solutions of carbon dioxide (remember that from our discussions of blood equilibria in Chap.12).

$$CO_2 + H_2O \rightleftharpoons H_2CO_3$$

$$O=C=O + H_2O \rightleftharpoons \overset{HO}{\underset{HO}{\diagdown}}C=O$$

In the case of formaldehyde, the equilibrium favors the hydrated form. That leads to stable trimers and polymers in much the same way as ethers form from alcohols via dehydration and elimination of water molecules. The trimer is called trioxane $(CH_2O)_3$ and the polymer, paraldehyde $(CH_2O)_x$; both are poly(ethers). Under proper reaction conditions, thermally stable forms of the formaldehyde polymer, polyoxymethylene, have been successfully fabricated into a wide variety of products.

$$-CH_2OCH_2OCH_2OCH_2O-$$

polyoxymethylene

trioxane

Stiffness, light weight, dimensional stability, resistance to corrosion, wear, and abrasion, but especially their lower unit cost (about 0.75 cents per pound on average in 1973) have led to use of this type of polymer, replacing brass, cast iron, and zinc in many applications: auto parts such as instrument panels; door hardware; pump housing mechanisms; piping for oil fields and municipal water systems. Du Pont markets the raw material for fabrication under the trade name "Delrin."

Another stable hydrated carbonyl group is trichloroacetaldehyde, better known as chloral hydrate. It is of interest in medicine, particularly because of its hypnotic action.

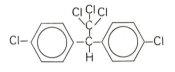

Apparently the presence of three chlorine atoms favor the equilibrium to the right, in the hydrated form. It is very water-soluble and is used as a sedative as well as surgical anesthetic. As you can see from the structure, it is also a principal ingredient in the synthesis of the insecticide, DDT, about which we'll have more to say shortly.

For now, remember this: by and large, equilibria involving addition of water to carbonyl groups lie far left, not right. These were simply a couple of the interesting exceptions. Acetaldehyde, acetone, and most other aldehydes and ketones normally show little tendency toward stable hydrate formation.

☐ Organic Acids and Esters

If the oxidation of methane to formaldehyde continues a step further, the carboxylic acid functional group —COOH is produced:

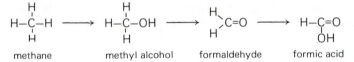

| methane | methyl alcohol | formaldehyde | formic acid |

Formic acid is the principal component of the juices of bees and certain ants, responsible for the blistering evident after a sting or bite. Oxidize acetaldehyde and you get acetic acid, or good old vinegar.

$$CH_3\text{--}\overset{H}{\underset{}{C}}=O \ + \ \tfrac{1}{2}O_2 \ \longrightarrow \ CH_3\text{--}\overset{O}{\overset{\|}{C}}\text{--}OH$$

Oxidize acetone? But there are no more hydrogens remaining on acetone's central carbon atom. Consequently, oxidation stops here unless you begin to operate on a new carbon atom and its hydrogens, or take the more drastic step of breaking of carbon-to-carbon bonds.

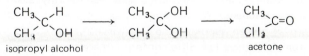

isopropyl alcohol   acetone

Any further oxidation requires action either (1) at a new C—H bond or (2) at a C—C bond.

You end up with either a ketone or carboxylic acid, or if you persist, oxidation continues all the way to carbon dioxide and water. Try that with formic acid; there's still one hydrogen to burn.

$$H-\overset{\overset{\displaystyle O}{\|}}{C}-OH + \tfrac{1}{2} O_2 \longrightarrow HO-\overset{\overset{\displaystyle O}{\|}}{C}-OH \xrightarrow{-H_2O} O{=}C{=}O + H_2O$$

The result is two hydroxyl groups on the same carbon: unstable; loss of water. Carbon dioxide is all that's left; it's the ultimate oxidation product.

Organic Acids Are Relatively Weak

Generally, organic acids are poorer proton donors than most of the common inorganic acids, dissociating only to a limited extent in aqueous solutions. That means the equilibrium lies farther left for carboxylic acids such as acetic acid, compared to the likes of hydrochloric acid.

$$CH_3-\overset{\overset{\displaystyle O}{\|}}{C}-OH + H_2O \rightleftharpoons CH_3-\overset{\overset{\displaystyle O}{\|}}{C}-O^- + H_3O^+$$

$$H-Cl + H_2O \rightleftharpoons H_3O^+ + Cl^-$$

A 0.10 *M* solution of acetic acid is only about 1.3 percent dissociated: about 13 molecules in 1,000 have given up their hydroxyl hydrogen atom as a proton. By comparison, a 0.10 *M* solution of hydrogen chloride in water is completely dissociated, forming 1,000 hydronium ions for every 1,000 hydrochloric acid molecules introduced. That means a pH of about 1 for the hydrochloric acid solution and about 5 for acetic acid solution. Still, acetic acid is clearly more acidic than water (5 versus 7), but not in the same league as hydrochloric acid (5 versus 1).

$$\overset{\overset{\displaystyle O}{\|}}{CH_3COH}$$
acetic acid

$$CH_3CH_2OH$$
ethyl alcohol

It's useful to compare acetic acid and ethyl alcohol. You might expect ethyl alcohol to have an ionizable hydroxyl hydrogen atom, much as acetic acid. Perhaps ethyl alcohol is also acidic to some extent. But it hardly turns out that way. The ethyl alcohol equilibrium sits much further left than the water equilibrium. Water is a better proton donor than alcohol, and remember, in plain water, only about one molecule in ten million (on average) donates a proton.

$$H_2O + H_2O \rightleftharpoons H_3O^+ + OH^-$$

$$CH_3CH_2OH + H_2O \rightleftharpoons H_3O^+ + CH_3CH_2O^-$$

Nagging question: why do acetic acid molecules donate protons so much better? Why does the acetic acid equilibrium sit more to the right than the ethyl alcohol equilibrium? The answer is **resonance.** When acetic acid ionizes, the extra electrons remaining on the hydroxyl oxygen, supplying the negative charge, are spread across both oxygen atoms. Are there two different forms of acetate ion, then? Well, perhaps that's one way of looking at it: two forms are better than one as far as resonance stabilization and lower energy are concerned. Of course, there's really just one, lower energy form; our writing two structures is again only a useful device. Resonance favors a shift of the equilibrium to the right, compared to ethyl alcohol where the electrons on oxygen have no other place to go. Only one form can be written for ethyl alcohol; no resonance; no help toward a favorable equilibrium shift. Acetic acid is more acidic than water, which in turn is more acidic than ethyl alcohol. Actually, aqueous ethyl alcohol solutions are so *un*-acidic, it's probably best not to even speak of the *acidity* of ethyl alcohol. Essentially it has no acid properties in aqueous solutions.

$$CH_3-C{\overset{O}{\underset{OH}{}}} + H_2O \rightleftharpoons CH_3-C{\overset{O}{\underset{O^-}{}}} + H_3O^+$$

$$CH_3-C{\overset{O^-}{\underset{O}{}}} \quad \text{perhaps best represented as} \quad CH_3-C{\overset{O}{\underset{O}{}}}^-$$

two equivalent forms

$$CH_3CH_2-\ddot{O}H + H_2O \rightleftharpoons CH_3CH_2-\ddot{O}{:}^- + H_3O^+$$

When an alkali metal hydroxide such as sodium hydroxide reacts with a carboxylic acid, the corresponding sodium salt forms as expected in acid-base reactions. Propionic acid and sodium hydroxide *neutralize* each other, forming sodium propionate.

$$CH_3CH_2C{\overset{O}{\underset{OH}{}}} + NaOH \longrightarrow CH_3CH_2C{\overset{O}{\underset{O^-}{}}} + Na^+ + H_2O$$

As the arrow indicates, the reaction is entirely to the right, sodium propionate being entirely ionized into sodium ions and propionate ions (resonance stabilized, of course) in aqueous solution. The solid sodium propionate salt, recovered on evaporation of solvent, is widely used as a fungicidal agent and mold preventative in the food industry. It's virtually impossible to find any commercially prepared, packaged bread that doesn't list sodium propionate among the added ingredients (Fig. 13-13).

Acids React With Alcohols, Forming Esters

Carboxylic acids react with alcohols forming the *ester* functional group. Ethyl acetate, the industrial solvent with a pleasing odor, is formed from acetic acid and ethyl alcohol.

$$CH_3C{\overset{O}{\underset{OH}{}}} + CH_3CH_2OH \rightleftharpoons CH_3C{\overset{O}{\underset{OCH_2CH_3}{}}} + H_2O$$

This is also an acid-base reaction of sorts, but the ester product is not ionized or salt-like at all. Many of the more common esters are sweet-smelling, fruity liquids: amyl acetate is the characteristic odor-causing agent in bananas, and is known as "oil of banana"; ethyl butyrate is the essence of pineapples; amyl butyrate,

A TREATISE
ON
ADULTERATIONS OF FOOD,
AND
Culinary Poisons,
EXHIBITING
THE FRAUDULENT SOPHISTICATIONS
OF
BREAD, BEER, WINE, SPIRITUOUS LIQUORS, TEA, COFFEE,
Cream, Confectionery, Vinegar, Mustard, Pepper, Cheese, Olive Oil, Pickles,
AND OTHER ARTICLES EMPLOYED IN DOMESTIC ECONOMY.
AND
Methods of detecting them.

BY FREDRICK ACCUM,
Operative Chemist, Lecturer on Practical Chemistry, Mineralogy, and on Chemistry
applied to the Arts and Manufactures; Member of the Royal Irish Academy;
Fellow of the Linnean Society; Member of the Royal Academy of
Sciences, and of the Royal Society of Arts of Berlin, &c. &c.

London:
Printed by J. Mallett, 59, Wardour Street, Soho.
SOLD BY LONGMAN, HURST, REES, ORME, AND BROWN,
PATERNOSTER ROW.
1820

Figure 13-13
Frederick Accum was one of the first to be concerned with the public interest and adulteration of foods. Note the ominous title of his famous treatise.

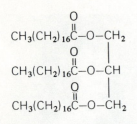

glycerol stearate, the glyceride from stearic acid and glycerol found in animals

apricots; isoamyl acetate, pears; and octyl acetate, oranges.

Fats are a very special group of esters derived from a number of long-chained carboxylic acids esterified to one particular alcohol, glycerol. One of the main constituents of fat cells in higher plants and animals, these esters function as food reserves. If you were to try and isolate these animal and vegetable fats you'd come up with corn and coconut oil, cottonseed and palm oil, not to mention butter, bacon grease, and tallow.

Soap-making and Saponification

Something must be said about one of the oldest chemical syntheses, soap-making. Soluble soaps are generally sodium salts of fatty acids such as stearic acid, produced by reacting a glyceride ester with a metal hydroxide. The process is called *saponification.*

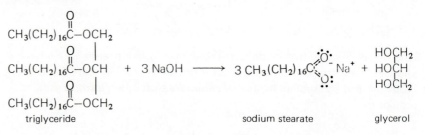

Tallow is the *depot* fat of cattle and sheep and the principal soap stock; it has good cleansing and water-softening characteristics. Soap made from olive oil is referred to as Castile soap. Ivory soap is $99\,^{44}/_{100}$ percent pure, and floats because air has been whipped through it in the processing. If soap smells good, is colored, or disinfects, it's got perfumed, dyes, or germicidal agents in the formulation. Potassium hydroxide, used instead of sodium hydroxide imparts "softness." Forgotten about soaps and detergent action and water softness, have you? Go back to Chap. 11 for a quick review.

Acetic, Citric, and Tartaric Acids

If the number of tons manufactured annually is our yardstick, acetic acid is perhaps the most important of the carboxylic acids. Its uses range from dyestuffs and vinegar to chemical intermediates and raw materials for a variety of polymeric substances and industrial solvents. More than half is used in manufacture of a highly reactive organic molecule, acetic anhydride. Two molecules of acetic acid are put together with loss of a molecule of water between them. Reactivity results from interaction with water-like hydroxyl groups to restore the original structure.

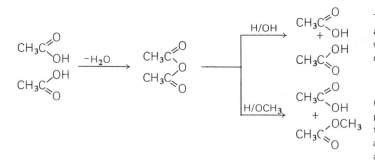

Two molecules of acetic acid are produced by reaction with water, reversing the original synthesis.

One molecule of an ester is produced by reaction with the alcoholic OH group, along with one molecule of acetic acid.

An interesting polyfunctional acid is citric acid which is obtained by fermentation of aqueous solutions of beet molasses with a particular mold culture, *Aspergillus niger.*

It is the most important acid used by the huge soft drink manufacturing industry in North America; several other applications are found in food products. Tartaric acid, a byproduct of wine production, is historically important because of Louis Pasteur's researches in the mid-nineteenth century (Fig. 13-14).

$$C_{12}H_{22}O_{11} + 3 O_2$$

citric acid

tartaric acid

Figure 13-14
The movie duplication of this famous Pasteur work is accurate in almost every detail.

☐ Organic Bases and the Peptide Bond

Amines Are Organic Bases

Organic amines are proton acceptors derived from the ammonia molecule by progressive substitution of bonds to carbon, in place of hydrogen atoms bonded to nitrogen. Basicity is related to how available the pair of electrons on nitrogen is as a landing site for an electron-deficient hydrogen atom, or proton. Keeping in mind earlier definitions of acids and bases as proton sources and proton receptors, let's look at the simplest of these basic organic derivatives of ammonia:

ammonia	$NH_3 + H_2O \rightleftharpoons NH_4^+ + OH^-$
methylamine	$CH_3NH_2 + H_2O \rightleftharpoons CH_3NH_3^+ + OH^-$
dimethylamine	$(CH_3)_2NH + H_2O \rightleftharpoons (CH_3)_2NH_2^+ + OH^-$
trimethylamine	$(CH_3)_3N + H_2O \rightleftharpoons (CH_3)_3NH^+ + OH^-$

Methylamine is a *primary* amine, having but one amine hydrogen replaced; dimethylamine is a *secondary* amine; trimethylamine, a *tertiary* amine. All are approximately as basic as ammonia: about pH 10 for an 0.10 *M* aqueous solution as compared to pH 13 for an equivalent solution of sodium hydroxide. The extent of proton transfer to nitrogen's available electron pair, or in other words where the equilibrium position lies, is about 13 molecules per thousand, about 1.3 percent to the right. (That makes ammonia comparable in strength as a base to acetic acid as an acid.)

Methylamine and ethylamine have ammonia-like odors. Many other amines are characteristically foul-smelling and toxic. Both dimethylamine and trimethylamine have odors associated with rotting fish and can be found in herring brines. The decomposition of animal flesh produces two *di*amines, putrescine and cadaverine.

In sharp contrast is the water-soluble, polyfunctional tertiary amine, triethanolamine included in many shaving creams, hair shampoos, and other cosmetic formulations.

Two polyfunctional amines that are particularly interesting for their physical and biological action are choline and ethylenediaminetetracetic acid (EDTA). Choline is structurally derived from trimethylamine and ethylene glycol; EDTA is structurally derived from ethylenediamine and acetic acid. As shown, both amines are ionic.

Choline salts are regularly added to poultry and animal feeds to stimulate growth. A much more active form of choline, acetylcholine, is obtained if you react the alcoholic OH group in the free choline base with acetic anhydride; it is also found naturally in certain plants (shepherd's-purse, for one) and in active muscle in many animals. Acetylcholine produces a powerful muscle-contracting drug effect, and causes considerable lowering of blood pressure. It is also the hormone

$NH_2CH_2CH_2CH_2CH_2NH_2$

putrescine

$NH_2CH_2CH_2CH_2CH_2CH_2NH_2$

cadaverine

triethanolamine

$[HOCH_2CH_2\overset{+}{N}(CH_3)_3]\,OH^-$

free choline base

ethylenediaminetetracetic acid
(EDTA)

of the peristaltic intestine (Fig. 13-15).

EDTA and Chelating Action

The sodium salt of EDTA is a sequestering, or complexing, agent for a variety of metal ions. It quantitatively removes a number of ions such as Fe^{+++} from aqueous solutions. This may be desirable for analytical purposes, or simply because it is chemically or biologically undesirable. By complexing, the sequestered ion can be maintained in the presence of ions (such as hydroxide ions) that would otherwise cause its precipitation (for example, the insoluble, hydrated iron oxides). The metal chelate with the metal ion in water-soluble form is readily available for later use. Chelating action comes about through donation of electron pairs to the metal ion, forming coordinate bonds with the chelating agent. Remember the hemoglobin molecule we looked at in Chap. 12? Well, heme is a chelating agent in exactly the same sense. In the case of EDTA, available electron pairs on nitrogen and oxygen are involved. One way of treating heavy metal poisoning is to administer EDTA or a similar chelate as an antidote. The metal ions in question will be preferentially sequestered by the chelate and excreted from the body. Iron, lead, mercury, and copper poisoning have been treated in this fashion. Unfortunately, this treatment has a deleterious side effect: EDTA also removes calcium ions from body tissue (for example, from bones).

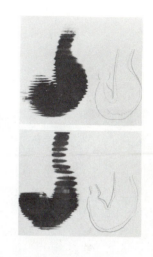

Figure 13-15
An anticholinergic drug inhibits the peristaltic spasms in the stomach and intestine.

Amides and Peptides

Hydroxide ions react with hydronium ions; similarly, amines react with carboxylic acids. However, in the reaction of carboxylic acids with amines, just as in the case of reaction of alcohols and carboxylic acids (forming esters), the reaction product is not a dissociable salt. Instead, organic acids and the ammonia-derived amines form a new functional group, the amides. Looking at a simple case, acetic acid and ammonia shows that salt formation occurs first. That's what you'd expect, but if you now heat the product, a molecule of water pops out. The acet*amide* molecule formed has a characteristic "essence of mouse" odor.

With *methyl*amine, the organic product is *methyl*acetamide.

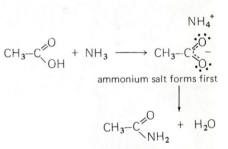

ammonium salt forms first

amide molecule forms

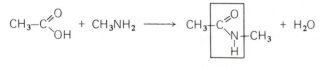

peptide bond

We have another name for the amide functional group when it shows up in giant molecules: a *peptide* bond. It shows up in important places ranging from nylon to DNA. In much the same way as many cola-type soft drinks are called "coke," the word "nylon" has become an accepted proper name for synthetic polyamides. The most famous is 66 nylon, the two numbers representing the 6-carbon diamine (hexamethylenediamine) and the 6-carbon dicarboxylic acid (adipic acid) from which the polymer is prepared. The polymer chemist in the laboratory and the chemical engineer in the plant assemble the nylon polymer in much the same way as we just described for the preparation of acetamide. Blending the difunctional acid molecule and the difunctional amine molecule produces the "nylon salt." Heating the salt in a vacuum oven at about 250°C produces the condensed amide molecule, containing all the original atoms less one molecule of water. About 45 to 50 of these amide units then link head-to-tail, releasing water molecules at each connecting site, and forming an elongated nylon polymer strand of molecular weight about 15,000 or so. Nylon is a polyamide.

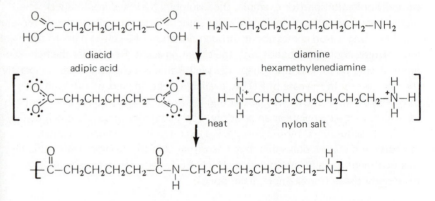

Production of nylon fiber in the United States in 1973 was about 1.5 billion pounds, 100 million of which were earmarked for plastics use, the rest going into nylon tire cord and industrial fibers. At current price levels of about one dollar per pound, these synthetics have tremendous cost advantages over many other materials. Furthermore, their unique physical properties make them desirable. As a plastic and as a fiber, 66 nylon is characterized by high strength, elasticity, toughness, abrasive resistance, and low temperature flexibility. 66 Nylon is also generally resistant to most solvents, acids and bases, hydrolysis, and outdoor weathering. Fiber applications include tire cord, rope, thread, belting, and cloths where resistance to abrasive and chemical attack are required. Apparel uses for fibers include stockings of all kinds and fabrics for products ranging from underwear to suits, coats, dresses, you name it. One key characteristic is the "permanent press" given nylon fibers by an annealing process at about 100°C, allowing permanent pleating and preshaping of garments. 66 Nylon plastics are important engineering materials as substitutes for metals in bearings, gears, cams, rollers, slides, and door latches; electrical wire can be jacketed with nylon; textile machinery makes use of nylon bearings, bushings, and read-guides because no lubricant is needed that could damage yarn or cloth.

DuPont, Nylon and Wallace Carothers

If there is a thread of history in all of this polymer, fiber, and plastic business it's right here. 66 Nylon was squeezed out of a hypodermic syringe in 1934 by a

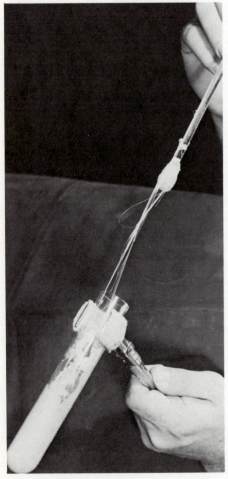

Nylon, the synthetic fiber.

chemical genius named Wallace Carothers at DuPont's laboratories in Wilmington, Delaware (Fig. 13-16). It became the first practical synthetic fiber. A few short years later, in May, 1940, 400 million pairs of nylon stockings sold out in four days as women stood in long lines to buy the new stockings made of "coal, air, and water." (See Fig. 13-17.) In 1941 nylon went to war in the form of fibers for nylon parachutes and cord for just about every airplane, truck, and jeep tire. After the war ended, the plastics revolution really began. It is one of the ironies of modern science and technology that Wallace Carothers, the genius whose researches revolutionized our way of life, never lived to taste the completeness of his success. This brilliant chemist who changed our whole view of what a molecule is, had been spirited away from Harvard and the confines of academia in 1928. In a few short years he emerged as father and prime builder of the macromolecular science of plastics and fibers. Tragically, Carothers committed suicide

Figure 13-16
Wallace Carothers in his laboratory, early in his career at DuPont, where his fundamental researches into neoprene and nylon were underway.

Figure 13-17
Nylon comes home as World War II ends. Oblivious to on-lookers in a "nylon line" the stockings are tried on immediately (left). The caricature of Wallace Carothers is by Philip Burke (below).

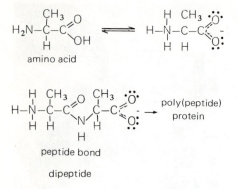

amino acid

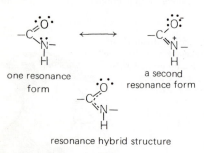

peptide bond

dipeptide

→ poly(peptide) protein

one resonance form

a second resonance form

resonance hybrid structure

in the spring of 1937, a twisted counterpoint to the glamorous career of his scientific progeny, the synthetic macromolecules, especially nylon.

Poly(amides) and Amino Acids

The building blocks of nature's poly(amides) are amino acids, molecules in which both functional groups required for condensation, amine and carboxylic acid, are contained within the *same* molecule. The initial condensation product is called a *dipeptide,* the connecting—CONH—peptide bond being present; the polymer is referred to as a *polypeptide* or more familiarly perhaps as a **protein.**

The amino acid used in illustrating this example is alanine, one of the *essential* amino acids found in nature, required by our life processes but not synthesized by the human organism. The dipeptide would be called alanylalanine, the polymer, polyalanyl. Nature's proteins are usually not very simple, as we'll see shortly. Generally, several different amino acids are put together in a programmed sequence. For example, the complex protein, myoglobin, consists of 21 different amino acids arranged into a single polypeptide strand of 153 units. Myoglobin's ability to function in oxygen storage is directly related to (1) the sequence of these 153 units, (2) the coiling of the long, spaghetti-like strands into a helical or spring-like arrangement, and (3) the way the resulting helix is folded into a compact globular structure. (See Chap. 12.)

Whether it's a synthetic polyamide or a natural protein, once the peptide bond is formed, it takes on two characteristics of special importance due to resonance. First, the peptide bond is unusually stable; second, the peptide bond is planar, or, in other words, the four atoms making up the bond all lie in the same plane—it's flat. This structure is the cornerstone of all polyamide-protein structures, and resonance is particularly important here. The partial double bond character of the carbon-to-nitrogen bond makes use of the free (or not involved in bonding) pair of electrons on nitrogen, coupled to the now less than double bond character of the carbon-to-oxygen bond.

Electron mobility, or delocalization, has produced a *resonance hybrid* structure in which the four atoms of the peptide bond are locked into a planar (flat) arrangement. In turn, that has a lot to do with the spatial orientation of these macromolecules, and therefore their ultimate physical and biological properties and functions. More about that later.

☐ **Unsaturated Hydrocarbons Have Very Reactive Carbon-to-Carbon Bonds**

One thing hydrocarbons can be made to do is dehydrogenate. When petroleum is cracked into gasoline range hydrocarbons, **unsaturated** molecules form, molecules with carbon-to-carbon double bonds. The **alkene** series of unsaturated hydrocarbons begins with ethylene and propylene (eth*ene* and prop*ene*, when named systematically).

$$CH_3-CH_3 \xrightarrow[\text{catalyst}]{\text{heat}} CH_2{=}CH_2 \ + \ H_2$$

$$CH_3-CH_2-CH_3 \xrightarrow[\text{catalyst}]{\text{heat}} CH_3-CH{=}CH_2 \ + \ H_2$$

Triple bonds can be introduced in hydrocarbons, too, but they are of lesser importance, All we'll say about them is that they are called alk*ynes,* and representative molecules such as acetylene ($H{-}C{\equiv}C{-}H$) do a lot of things alkenes do. That's because unsaturation, be it the double or triple bond variety, is characterized by a common property, the presence of the *pi bond.* In making a comparison of saturation versus unsaturation (of alkanes versus alkenes and alkynes; ethane versus ethylene and acetylene), the comparison should be in terms of chemical reactivity and the ability to build long polymer chains. Sigma bonds in ethane can be broken only with difficulty, for example, by burning; ethane makes a good fuel, releasing considerable energy, but the molecule completely disintegrates in the process. Consequently, there is also no easy route to chain formation. On the other hand, the pi bond in ethylene can be broken in a controlled fashion for it is a center of reactivity. Many molecules add to double bonds. In polymer formation, ethylene units link to ethylene units. The triple bond, however, is too easily broken. When acetylene reacts, the energy released is so great and the manner of release often so violent, that its uses must be restricted. There are some general raw material uses for alkynes that will be mentioned in passing, but by and large, we'll stick with the much more useful double bonds.

The presence of double bonds in hydrocarbon molecules introduces new possibilities for the existence of geometric isomers. There is no longer free rotation about the carbon-to-carbon bond. For example, 2-butene can exist as either of the isomeric cis- or trans-2-butenes. The presence of the double bond fixes the two middle carbon atoms in a plane, along with any other attached atoms. Cis means similar groups adjacent; trans means similar groups opposed to each other.

Check the properties given for the pairs of isomers in Tables 13-4 and 13-5. Note the small but significant differences between the two. Trans-2-butene is a more stable, lower energy molecule because the two bulky methyl groups are spaced far apart. The possibility that adjacent methyls (or chlorines) in the cis-isomer might interfere with each other has deep significance. When hindrance arises due to bulky groups getting in the way of each other, thus upsetting the geometry of the molecule, the function of the molecule is altered whether it is biologically important as in enzyme action or physically significant as in the properties of a polymer.

Table 13-4
Contrasting properties of maleic and fumaric acid

Structure	Name	Melting point, °C	Comments
H, $COOH$ / C / C / H, $COOH$	Maleic acid (cis-isomer)	137-138	Maleic acid is about 100 times as soluble in water as fumaric acid. Maleic acid is about 10 times as strong an acid as fumaric acid. Maleic acid loses water vapor on heating, producing a new, reactive substance, maleic anhydride.
H, $COOH$ / C / C / $HOOC$, H	Fumaric acid (trans-isomer)	286-287	

Geometric Isomers Also Exist Simply Because of the Location of Double Bonds

There is a correct structure possible with two double bonds present in the molecule. 1,3-Butadiene turns out to be very unusual in its chemistry, particularly in its polymer-forming reactions. The butadiene structure has alternating double bonds which means that at least to some extent, the available pi electrons are spread across all four carbon atoms.

Electrons in double bonds are more loosely bound than those in single bonds. This looseness, or *polarizability* becomes magnified when double bonds alternate with single bonds, a phenomenon called **conjugation.** When one molecule of chlorine reacts with one molecule of butadiene, one of the two double bonds is

both are C_4H_8

$CH_3CH_2CH=CH_2$
1-butene

$CH_3CH=CHCH_3$
2-butene

$C=C-C=C$
is better represented as

$C \cdots C \cdots C \cdots C$

Table 13-5
Geometric isomerism

Structure	Name		Boiling point, °C
H, H / $C=C$ / CH_3, CH_3	2-butenes	(cis-isomer)	3.7
H, CH_3 / $C=C$ / CH_3, H		(trans-isomer)	0.9
H, H / $C=C$ / Cl, Cl	1,2-dichloroethylenes	(cis-isomer)	40.3
Cl, H / $C=C$ / H, Cl		(trans-isomer)	47.5
$CH_3CH_2CH=CH_2$	1-butene		−6.3
$CH_3CH=CHCH_3$	2-butenes		3.7 (cis) 0.9 (trans)

Note: There are *no* geometric isomers for the following. Switching atoms about the double bond only produces the original molecule again. If you can't readily see that, draw the other *possible* structures out and prove it for yourself.

"added to" or saturated, normal enough behavior for double bonds. But the other double bond shifts to the center of the molecule in the process. Thus, 1-butene does the expected thing; 1,3-butadiene does not.

$$CH_2=CH-CH_2-CH_3 \;+\; Cl_2 \longrightarrow \underset{\underset{Cl}{|}}{\overset{\overset{Cl}{|}}{CH_2}}-CH-CH_2CH_3$$ addition across the double bond

$$CH_2=CH-CH=CH_2 \;+\; Cl_2 \longrightarrow \underset{\underset{Cl}{|}}{\overset{\overset{Cl}{|}}{CH_2}}-CH=CH-CH_2$$ addition to ends with shifting of double bond

Only 1-2 addition can take place when 1-butene reacts with chlorine. However, when a molecule of chlorine adds to 1,3-butadiene, addition is mostly 1-4, or head-to-tail, accompanied by what amounts to a shift of the remaining double bond to the center of the molecule. That shift of the double bond is significant in nature. Consider the preparation and properties of natural and synthetic rubber as an illustration of the importance of such a double bond shift. Both rubbers are butadiene structures. Natural rubber is made up of anywhere from 1,000 to 5,000 units, added end-to-end; the structure about the remaining double bond is the cis-arrangement.

$$CH_2=C\overset{\displaystyle CH_3}{\underset{\displaystyle CH=CH_2}{<}}$$ basic rubber or isoprene unit

(C_5H_8 monomer)

$$\cdot CH_2-C\overset{\displaystyle CH_3}{\underset{\displaystyle CH-CH_2 \cdot}{<}}$$ drawn to show the electrons in from one of the cis-pi-double bonds placed for end-to-end addition

$$\cdot \underset{CH_2}{\overset{CH_3}{}}C=C\overset{H}{\underset{CH_2-CH_2}{}} \;\; \underset{CH_2-CH_2}{\overset{CH_3}{}}C=C\overset{H}{\underset{}{}} \;\; \underset{CH_2-CH_2}{\overset{CH_3}{}}C=C\overset{H}{\underset{CH_2 \cdot}{}}$$ note cis arrangement in each of the linked C_5H_8 groups

(C_5H_8 polymer)

Natural rubber as obtained from the rubber tree is a soft, elastic, relatively low-melting, sticky substance in which the main structure is the 1-4, head-to-tail, sequence, cis about the double bond. Another closely related natural product, Guttapercha, has a similar polyisoprene structure. However, the orientation about the double bond is all trans, a change which results in loss of the characteristic elastic properties of the cis-structured natural rubber.

Natural rubber is not directly usable in tires or most other products because it would soften or melt on warm days or during long rides. That problem is solved by taking advantage of the available double bond. In a process called *vulcanization,* long strands of polyisoprene units are linked together through sulfur bridges or bonds. The cross-linked polymer now finds it cannot do much wiggling or flowing, hot or cold. Heating natural rubber with sulfur changes its nature from a *thermoplastic* material to one which cannot be altered when molded or formed

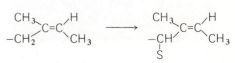

without destroying the chemical properties of the product.

Apparently, the presence of the double bond makes the hydrogens on the next carbon atom very reactive. The sulfur "bridge" is a *sulfide* bond, and the rubber is now harder, stronger, and no longer tacky to the touch; in short, it is no longer thermoplastic.

The vulcanization process has been the focal point of nearly 150 years of rubber technology. Although much-researched, developed, and improved, the essential chemistry is unchanged since the pioneering experiments of Charles Goodyear with elemental sulfur in 1839. For natural rubber, vulcanization provides poly-sulfide-type bridges, or cross-links, giving the thermal stability required for such products as automobile tires. These bridges eventually degrade, however, reducing the number of cross-links, and resulting in eventual deterioration of the product. Furthermore, sulfur bridges are subject to oxidative degradation; the obvious streaking caused by brittle windshield wipers is due to this kind of reaction.

$$CH_2=\overset{\overset{\displaystyle Cl}{|}}{C}-CH=CH_2 \longrightarrow \underset{\cdot CH_2}{\overset{Cl}{\diagdown}}C=C\underset{CH_2\cdot}{\overset{H}{\diagup}}$$

Schematic of Vulcanized Natural Rubber

Rubber strands · · · Different types of sulfur bridges connecting rubber strands.

Nonbridging sulfide links are also present.

Today, natural rubber supplies less than 40 percent of the world's needs for rubber-like materials. That's a reflection of increased demand on the one hand, and the progressive development of synthetic rubber substitutes from petroleum feed stocks on the other (Fig. 13-18). The first commercially successful synthetic rubber was prepared in 1938 using a chlorobutadiene repeating unit. Polychloro-prene is somewhat inferior to rubber in its elastic properties, but is less susceptible to the decomposing effects of oils, gasolines, and other organic solvents that rubber often comes in contact with.

☐ Aromatic Hydrocarbons and Their Derivatives

Hydrocarbon molecules containing a pair of double bonds are especially interesting when these polarizable double bonds are coupled to each other, as in the

Figure 13-18
Looking much like popcorn is polybutadiene rubber (left). At the right a viscous sample of synthetic rubber is taken.

conjugated butadiene molecule. The altered behavior of the double bonds results in a substantial difference in chemical reactivity. That was clear in our discussions of chlorination: 1-2 versus 1-4 addition to the pi bonds. More evidence can be gotten by measuring the amount of thermal energy (heat) released when hydrogen is added, converting double bonds to singles. When 1 mole of hydrogen molecules adds to a mole of 1-butene molecules, 29.5 kilocalories are released. Therefore, 2 moles of hydrogen added to 2 moles of 1-butene produce 59.0 kilocalories. But 2 moles of hydrogen will also add to the two double bonds in 1 mole of 1,3-butadiene molecules; still, the heat given off is only 55.4 kilocalories, not the 59.0 kilocalories you'd expect from the 1-butene addition experiment for a pair of double bonds.

$$CH_2=CH-CH_2CH_3$$
$$CH_2=CH-CH_2CH_3 \quad + \; 2\,H_2 \longrightarrow \quad \begin{array}{l} CH_3-CH_2CH_2CH_3 \\ CH_3-CH_2CH_2CH_3 \end{array} \quad + \; 59.0 \; kcal$$

$$CH_2=CH-CH=CH_2 + 2\,H_2 \longrightarrow CH_3-CH_2-CH_2-CH_3 \; + \; 55.4 \; kcal$$
$$\text{difference} \; = \quad 3.6 \; kcal$$

Adding the same quantity of hydrogen (2 moles) to the same number of double bonds (two) in butadiene produce 3.6 kilocalories less heat. A pair of butadiene double bonds are more stable than a pair of 1-butene double bonds by that amount of energy. The reason is the altered behavior introduced by coupling between alternating double bonds. Data obtained from X-ray crystallographic studies (see Chap. 5) confirm the *altered* character of butadiene's carbon skeleton. The usual carbon-to-carbon single bond distance as found in ethane is 1.54 angstrom units; the usual carbon-to-carbon double bond distance as found in ethylene is 1.33 angstrom units. Compare those to the *altered* carbon-to-carbon distance of 1.47 angstrom units found for the C_2-C_3 bond in butadiene. Reading the structure as written, something closer to the 1.54 single bond distance was expected; something closer to the double bond distance is found. At the same time, the C_1-C_2 and C_3-C_4 double bonds have more single bond character than the written formula would imply. Again, the fault is not the molecules. Butadiene is real. It is only our inability to accurately represent the way in which the electrons are distributed that complicates matters for us.

Benzene-like Hydrocarbons

To begin a study of benzene-like, aromatic hydrocarbons, look at a *homo*logue of butadiene, 1,3,5-hexatriene.

$$CH_2-CH-CH=CH_2 \qquad\qquad CH_2=CH-CH-CH-CH=CH_2$$
1,3-butadiene   1,3,5-hexatriene

The carbon chain has been extended from four to six, while maintaining the

$CH_2{=}CH{-}CH{=}CH{-}CH{=}CH_2$

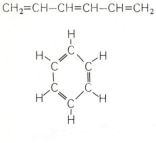

representation indicating the
delocalized state of the pi bond electron-pairs

alternating pattern of double bonds. As you might anticipate from our discussion of butadiene, the reactive pi bond electrons spread themselves across the length of the hexatriene chain.

Now, instead of a *linear* hexatriene structure, consider the same alternating double bond arrangement in a ring, the aromatic benzene molecule.

In marked contrast to aliphatic hydrocarbons, aromatic hydrocarbons have special properties that are a direct result of delocalization of the pi bond electrons. Here is the preferred notation for representing the benzene structure according to resonance ideas:

the two possible resonance forms

An interesting feature of these aromatic hydrocarbons is their relationship to the graphite structure for elemental carbon. The larger the aromatic hydrocarbon, the smaller the relative number of hydrogen atoms, until you reach the limiting case of graphite, in which you have sheets of these tiled-floor arrangements of aromatic carbon rings with virtually no hydrogen present. By the way, the *"aromatic"* title given these hydrocarbons has to do with the sometimes pleasant odor these molecules have, compared to aliphatic hydrocarbons.

There are six idential carbon-to-carbon bond lengths in benzene of about $1\frac{1}{3}$ bond character. Our resonance model suggests a bond length between single and double. The energy in the benzene molecule can be compared to that in cyclohex*ene*, a comparison of a single ring-type carbon-to-carbon double bond in cyclohexene versus the three ring-type carbon-to-carbon double bonds in benzene. There is much less energy than expected from multiplying cyclohexene by three. For example, when the heat of reaction for hydrogenation is measured, the following results are obtained:

One might be led to expect benzene to have a heat of reaction three times cyclohexene: 3(28.6) = 85.8 kilocalories. However, the observed value is only 49.8 kilocalories. The heat of reaction falls short by some 36 kilocalories per mole (85.8 − 49.8 = 36), a measure of the stabilization of the benzene molecule due to resonance.

Considerable interest and research is currently being expended on the carcino-
genic, or cancer-producing, properties of these condensed aromatic substances.
Some of the most potent carcinogens are derivatives of 1,2-benzanthracene.

☐ Color

When one small segment of the electromagnetic spectrum strikes the retina of
the eye, a complex series of physiological responses occur and we perceive color
(see Chap. 8). The visible region of the spectrum, the region in which the human
eye is sensitive, ranges roughly from 4000 to 8000 angstrom units in wavelength.
Visible light is composed of a continuous series of wavelengths ranging from the
short, higher energy *blue* region (the 4000 end) to the longer, lower energy *red*
region (the 8000 end). When you see red, your eye is absorbing all visible wavelengths except red; when you observe blue, your eye is absorbing all visible
wavelengths except blue. When you look through red or blue stained glass, the
glass is absorbing all visible wavelengths except for the color you see. When
light is absorbed, the complementary color is transmitted or reflected (Table 13-6).

Question: Can we identify the molecular features of a colored substance that
are responsible for the absorption and transmission of visible light? Can we perceive the structural difference between colored and noncolored collections of
molecules?
Answer: Yes, and it has a lot to do with particular groups of atoms associated
with the presence of color called **chromophores**:

$$-N=N- \qquad -C=C- \qquad -\overset{O}{\underset{\|}{C}}- \qquad -\overset{NH}{\underset{\|}{C}}-$$

We can learn a lot about chromophores and colors from the carotenoid family
of molecules. They're old friends, with a few new connections. Carotenoids
are built of the same repeating units found in natural rubber—the methyl substituted 1,3-butadiene or isoprene units. The orange color in carrots, beta carotene, is made up of 18 conjugated carbons connecting two 6-carbon rings, a
grand total of 40 carbon atoms. That's the equivalent of eight isoprene units.
The arrangement is all trans, a very important geometric feature:

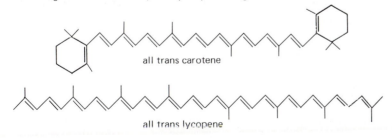

all trans carotene

all trans lycopene

The usual kind of red tomatoes contain the second carotenoid shown, all trans
lycopene. Note that the only difference between beta carotene and lycopene is

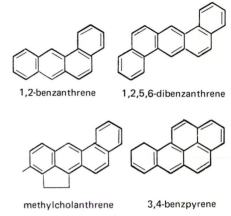

1,2-benzanthrene   1,2,5,6-dibenzanthrene

methylcholanthrene   3,4-benzpyrene

Table 13-6
Relationship between the color you see
and the wavelength of light absorbed

| Light absorbed | | Color |
Wavelength	Color	you see
4000-4400	violet	green-yellow
4400-4800	blue	yellow
4800-4900	green-blue	orange
4900-5000	blue-green	red
5000-5600	green	purple
5600-5800	yellow-green	violet
5800-6000	yellow	blue
6000-6100	orange	green-blue
6100-7500	red	blue-green

Note: Green light, for example, has no complementary spectral color (5000-5600 region);
the optical stimulus recognized as purple, green's
apparent complement, is a result of mixing red
and violet from the extreme ends of the visible
spectrum.

It is also interesting to note that the term
"white light" has no exact meaning since many
spectral combinations produce a visual stimulus
corresponding to white:
red (6560) + green-blue (4920) = white
orange (6080) + blue (4900) = white
green-yellow (5640) + violet (4330) = white

that the two 6-carbon rings at the ends of lycopene are open. Both molecules contain 40 carbon atoms, 8 isoprene units, with perfect symmetry around the carbon-to-carbon double bond in the middle. There is also an unusual kind of tomato, a yellow mutant known as the tangerine tomato. Instead of lycopene, the tangerine tomato contains the cis isomer, prolycopene. The relationship between the two can be domonstrated in a visual experiment: a yellow solution of the cis isomer, freshly extracted, can be dramatically converted to a red-orange solution of the trans isomer by exposing the solution to light in the presence of a a trace of iodine as a catalyst. The real significance of understanding how human vision works is illustrated by the cis-trans conversion in this experiment. Some near relatives of the carotenoids—vitamin A and retinene (vitamin A aldehyde), the all trans and the 11-cis retinene— are the isomers involved in vision.

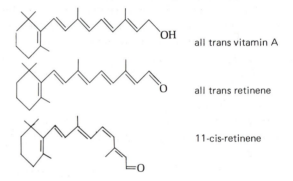

all trans vitamin A

all trans retinene

11-cis-retinene

Dyeing and Dyes. Indigo and Mauve

In order to successfully dye a fabric to another color, it is necessary that the dye, or coloring agent, be strongly bound to the fabric. The natural blue dye, indigo, and the natural orange-red dye, alizarin, were articles of commerce long before anything was known of their structure (Fig. 13-19).

Since wool fibers are made of polypeptide molecules, structures literally covered with polar groups, what's needed to dye wool is a polar dye capable of bonding to the polar surface of the wool fiber. Naphthol yellow is a polar dye which can interact via hydrogen bonding through the OH and NO_2 groups with the —NH— and —CO— groups of the wool fiber:

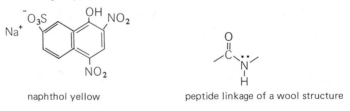

naphthol yellow

peptide linkage of a wool structure

Contrast that with the problem of dyeing polypropylene, a synthetic fiber with no polar groups at all. Solving that problem required introduction of polarity onto the woven fabric during the manufacturing process or spreading the dye

Figure 13-19
Pieter Brueghel's Dyemakers—sixteenth century Dutch.

through the polymer before the spinning and weaving steps.

A century ago there were no synthetic dyes. Articles of clothing, ornamentation, or whatever had to be colored with naturally available material mostly taken from plants. With few exceptions, these tended to be green, or reddish-brown. Things weren't very colorful. But all that has changed since mauvine was artificially produced in 1856 by an Englishman, William Henry Perkin (Fig. 13-20).

A Color Called White

Before continuing, something should be said about the color called "white." It is a matter of common experience that white fabrics tend to yellow long before they begin to show serious signs of wear. The world of advertising has decided that "yellowing" is undesirable, and the chemist has come up with a couple of interesting ways to get around the problem. One way to make white "white" is to apply a small quantity of a blue coloring agent; yellow light is absorbed, causing the yellowed fabric to appear white (actually, more nearly a very pale grey). A second technique utilizes a fluorescent substance which absorbs ultraviolet light converting the acquired energy into visible light of longer wavelength. In this way, yellowness (due to absorption of blue-violet light) is corrected by emission of a corresponding amount of blue-violet light from the fluorescent substance The fluorescent effect often produces fabrics that are bright white with a bluish cast. Since the end of World War II, such *optical brighteners* have been widely used by the soap and detergent industry.

Figure 13-20
William Perkin, the discoverer of Mauve.

☐ "Plastics"

Macromolecules are high molecular weight chemical entities. The word *polymer* means "something of many parts." Water (H_2O) has a molecular weight of 18 and benzene (C_6H_6), 78. That means 6×10^{23} molecules weigh 18 and 78 grams respectively. However, a single molecule of poly(isoprene), natural rubber, has a molecular weight of about 1 million; that means a mole of rubber molecules weighs about 10^6 grams, or more than a ton. Want to compare equal piles, or moles, of molecules, as we did in our earlier discussion of the mole concept? Eighteen grams of water versus 10^6 grams of rubber: an ounce versus a ton. Quite a striking comparison.

Polymer science and the plastics industry, both of which continue to exert an incredibly large impact on Western culture, trace their beginnings to natural rubber. Erasers and rubberized fabrics were in use just before the introduction of Goodyear's vulcanization process in 1839. That discovery pushed the rubber industry into its first period of rapid growth. The oldest synthetic plastic material is *Bakelite,* made from phenol and formaldehyde; it was first produced at the turn of the century as a synthetic shellac. Chemists had been plagued for years by numerous varieties of plastic goops accidently prepared in their reaction flasks. Bakelite was a first, a made-on-purpose, synthetic resin that had no twin in nature. Alive and well today, Bakelite is the prototype of a phenomenally comprehensive

Figure 13-21
His master's voice (top). On Bakelite of course (bottom).

family of synthetic polymers we call **plastics** and **resins.** The background is worth a few words.

Shellac is found in lacquers, varnishes, waxes, and other protective agents used for coating a variety of surface materials. It is a natural product made from the resinous secretions of the tiny "lac" bugs common to India and Southeast Asia. Lac bugs pierce the bark of a tree and feed on the sap, discharging a quantity of *lac* as a protective agent. This sticky resin accumulates about the bug until it is all but completely encapsulated, leaving only an opening or two for breathing and for the worm-like larvae of the next generation to exit. The females die after breeding, leaving colonies of bodies to be collected and processed to make shellac. A few hundred thousand of these little bugs are needed for each pound of shellac produced, and as this century began, more than 7 million pounds of shellac were being imported into the United States alone each year.

Leo Baekeland, an extraordinarily gifted young chemist and entrepreneur began a search for a synthetic substitute for shellac. First, he looked back through the recent scientific literature for hints and guidelines in the works of others. Some earlier studies of the German chemist, Adolph von Baeyer pointed Baekeland down the right road to his discovery. Baeyer had mixed phenol, the commonly used disinfectant, with formaldehyde, the preservative liquid, and obtained a hard, porous, insoluble mass. For Baeyer and most of his chemist colleagues, such reaction products were a nuisance, uselessly gunking up all the glassware and equipment, most of which then had to be thrown away because the mess was so insoluble.

Baekeland realized that these very properties might make this material better able to withstand weathering and chemical action. Here might be a better coating material than shellac. Baekeland began purposely preparing phenol-formaldehyde condensation products. It soon became evident that this new material, Bakelite, would have wide applications. It was very hard, but it could be molded and machined; in spite of its relatively light weight, it was unusually strong; it was inert to acids and bases, unaffected by heat, and effective as an electrical insulator; it could be colored or dyed to suit consumer tastes. One of the most versatile man-made materials, Bakelite has found its way into everything from buttons to automobiles (Fig. 13-21). Baekeland sold his invention to George Eastman, inventor of the Kodak camera. Before the historic sale of his invention, Baekeland had determined not to give it up for a penny less than 25,000 dollars; he secretly hoped to get 50,000 dollars; and he ultimately sold it for a million dollars which in those days was really worth a million (no income tax either).

What Baekeland started in 1907 is still going on to an extent that even he could not have anticipated. By the time of his death in 1944, nylon had been synthesized and the wide dimensions of its wartime use offered some indication of what was just ahead. The best we can do here is summarize a few of the more important synthetic polymers, their properties, and uses. Nylon and polyethylene you know; chloroprene you've seen, too. Polystyrene is one of the most important synthetic hydrocarbon polymers.

Addition of monomer units via the double bond produces a polymer whose uses range from molded objects to electrical insulators. Because of its excellent optical properties (color and clarity) it makes useful optical components. One of polystyrene's special features has to do with the arrangement of the benzene rings along the length of the polymer chain. Three kinds of polystyrene are possible: an amorphous form in which the arrangement is random; and two crystalline forms, one in which the benzene rings are all on one side, another in which they alternate down the chain.

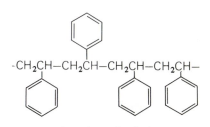

amorphous form of polystyrene

Polyvinyl chloride and polyvinylidene chloride are used, sometimes separately, sometimes together, in films such as the Saran type of wrapping product, phonograph records, and latex paints, to mention a few (Fig. 13-22).

$CH_2=CHCl$ vinyl chloride

$CH_2=CCl_2$ vinylidene chloride

$-CH_2CH-CH_2CH-CH_2CH-CH_2CH-CH_2CH-CH_2C-CH_2C-CH_2CH-CH_2CH-$
vinyl chloride/vinylidene chloride copolymer

Teflon, one of the most resistant of all polymers to chemical attack, has a peculiarly low surface energy; few things stick to it. It is used in molded objects, lubricants, chemically resistant films, insulation, and as the surfacing material for "nonstick" kitchen cookery.

Acrylic fibers go into orlon type fabrics for sweaters as well as carpeting materials; Lucite and Plexiglass are useful in sheet form as glass substitutes, and in many situations offer superior optical properties (Fig. 13-23). Epoxy resins have excellent adhesive properties; urethane foams insulate houses and make pleasure boats unsinkable. The list is virtually endless.

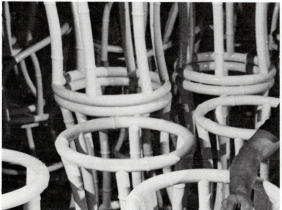

Figure 13-22
Polyvinyl chloride for deck furniture.

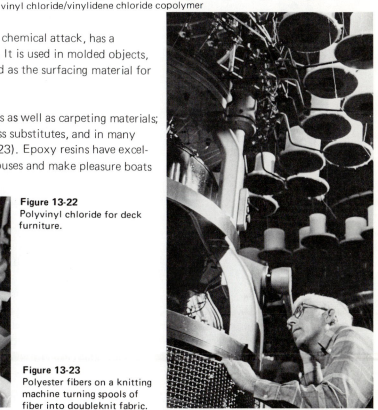

Figure 13-23
Polyester fibers on a knitting machine turning spools of fiber into doubleknit fabric.

☐ **Questions to Answer . . . Problems to Solve**

Note: Better go back and review the appropriate sections of Chapters 13 and 14 to be sure you have it clear in your mind just what covalent bonding is about, and how it differs from ionic bonding . . . and while you're at it, take another brief look at the discussion of hydrogen bonding in Chapter 12.

1. Why are there so many compounds of carbon?

2. What makes the chemistry of carbon compounds so different from that of boron and nitrogen? Why so different from silicon?

3. Why does carbon form long chains, and no other element does?

4. Contrast carbon, boron and nitrogen with respect to forming hydrides (BH_3, NH_3, CH_4).

5. Contrast carbon and silicon with respect to forming stable chains.

6. The two pairs of molecules drawn below are said to be isomeric:

$$CH_3CHCH_3 \quad \text{and} \quad CH_3CH_2CH_2CH_3;$$
$$\quad\ \ |$$
$$\quad\ \ CH_3$$

$$CH_3CH_2CH=CH_2 \quad \text{and} \quad CH_3CH=CHCH_3$$

   (a) What does that statement mean and what does it imply about their physical and chemical properties? Would you expect them to be the same or different? Why?
   (b) Without looking back through the chapter, see if you can draw all the possible isomeric monobromopentanes, $C_5H_{11}Br$. The first is drawn for you, leaving off the hydrogens for simplicity:

$$-C-C-C-C-C-Br$$

7. Ethane, ethyl alcohol, acetaldehyde, acetic acid: Show how all four are related in terms of intermediate stages of oxidation along the ultimate road to carbon dioxide.

8. Briefly distinguish between the following pairs of terms, and illustrate with examples where possible:
   (a) alkane and alkene
   (b) aliphatic and aromatic
   (c) cis and trans isomers
   (d) aldehyde and ketone
   (e) aliphatic and aromatic —OH
   (f) a purple and an orange dye

9. Here are some important types of chemical processes. What kinds of reaction products would you expect in each case?

    (a) Combustion

    $$C_8H_{18} + O_2 \longrightarrow$$

    (b) Addition

    $$CH_2=CH_2 + Br_2 \longrightarrow$$

    $$CH_2=CH_2 + HBr \longrightarrow$$

    (c) Dehydration

    $$CH_3CH_2OH \xrightarrow{H_2SO_4}$$

    (d) Substitution

    $$CH_4 + Br_2 \xrightarrow{h\nu}$$

    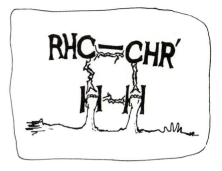 + $Br_2 \xrightarrow{Fe}$

    (e) Dehydrogenation

    $$CH_3CH_3 \xrightarrow{T, \text{ cat.}}$$

    (f) Elimination

    $$CH_3CH_2CH_2Cl \xrightarrow{KOH} CH_3CH=CH_2$$

    (g) Cracking

    $$C_{14}H_{30} \xrightarrow{T, \text{ cat.}}$$

    (h) Coupling

    $$CH_3CH_2Cl + Zn \text{ metal} \longrightarrow$$

    (i) Polymerization

    $$CH_3CH=CH_2 \xrightarrow{\text{cat.}}$$

    $$H_2NCH_2COOH \longrightarrow$$

10. How many correct structures for the formula $C_4H_{10}O$ can you come up with? Identify each particular functional group you come up with.

11. Which of the following do you perceive to be isomeric:

    (a) iso-octane and 2,2,4-trimethylpentane

    (b) isoprene and 2-methyl-1,3-butadiene

    (c) 2-chloro-1,3-butadiene and chloroprene

    (d) ethyl chloride and 1-chloroethane

    (e) ethylene chloride and vinyl chloride

12. Which of these represent pairs of structural isomers?

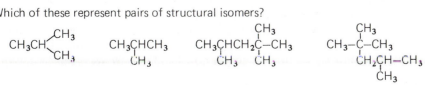

$$CH_2$$
$$CH_2 \quad CH_2$$
$$CH_2 \quad CH_2$$
$$CH_2$$

$$CH_3CH_2CH_2CH_2CH{=}CH_2$$

13. What is the maximum number of chlorinated propanes possible from the direct chlorination of propane in the presence of sunlight? Assume chlorination to be sufficiently reactive so that no single product is favored, and some of every one possible if found between the monochloropropane, C_3H_7Cl and the perchloropropane C_3Cl_8. (*Hint*: if you haven't found 23 unique structures, you missed some).

14. Distinguish between a sigma and a pi bond. Which is stronger? Which is more easily altered?

15. What's meant by the terms polarity, polarizability, conjugation, and resonance in the context of this chapter. Illustrate your answer.

16. What's wrong with the idea of trying to polymerize 1-butene (CH ($CH_3CH_2CH{=}CH_2$)? Why can't you make a polypeptide from acetic acid and methylamine?

17. Draw the carbon skeleton for 1,3-butadiene. Now draw in the dumbell-shaped pi bonds above and below the plane of the carbon skeleton. Does that picture help explain why the electrons in the two double bonds are delocalized, and the system is said to be conjugated?

18. Carboxylic acids react with amines, forming amides, as in the overall synthesis of the amide shown below:

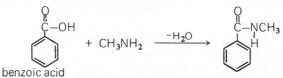

benzoic acid

(a) What is the first product formed in the reaction? Between benzoic acid and methylamine?
(b) How is that product converted to the final amide product, methylaniline?
(c) Using the same basic chemistry, write the equation illustrating the[synthesis of a polyamide (*Hint*: you'll need *di*functional monomers.)
(d) Illustrate polypeptide formation using the naturally occurring amino acid, valine,

$$\begin{array}{c} CH_3 \\ {\searrow} \\ CH_3 \end{array} CHCHCOOH \\ \quad\quad\quad\;\; NH_2$$

19. What monomer would allow you to prepare each of the following:
    (a) Dacron (polyester)
    (b) Delrin (polyether)
    (c) nylon-66 (polypeptide)
    (d) Bakelite (phenolic)
    (e) orlon (acrylate)
    (f) Teflon (fluorocarbon)

20. Now that you've acquired a better understanding of the structure of natural rubber, briefly interpret the warming and cooling that takes place when an elastic band is stretched and snaps back to its normal condition.

21. Explain why "white light" can only be regarded as a qualitative or figurative idea.

22. How much "plastic" material can you identify in your house, car, and among your personal possessions?

23. Go to your chest of drawers and check the labels on all your sweaters. How many different natural and synthetic polymeric fibers can you identify from the labels. Do the same for the jackets and coats hanging in your closet. Now check out the carpets and the curtains.

24. Offer a few words of comment that will provide a distinction between the following pairs of terms:
    (a) monomer and polymer
    (b) Saran and Teflon
    (c) poly(peptide) and poly(ester)
    (d) thermoplastic and thermosetting properties
    (e) vulcanized and natural rubber
    (f) lycopene and prolycopene
    (g) Plexiglas and Lucite
    (h) polymethylene and polyoxymethylene
    (i) polypropylene and polyethylene
    (j) polyethylene and polystyrene

25. In twenty-five words or less, give one of your curious classmates not taking this course a satisfactory explanation of
    (a) molecule
    (b) plastic material
    (c) aromatic substance
    (d) sequestering agent
    (e) gasoline

26. In addition to color, what key requirement must a dye meet? Explain what polarity has to do with dying wool fibers. Why can't naphthol yellow be successfully used to dye polypropylene? How do you think a man-made fiber such as polypropylene could be dyed?

27. The relative acidities of acetic acid, ethyl alcohol, and phenol is acetic acid > phenol >> ethyl alcohol. Write out the proton transfer reaction that takes place between each, and the solvent, water. Then write the resonance forms for acetate, phenoxide and ethoxide formed, and briefly discuss the role of resonance in acidity in terms of the equilibrium involved.

April 25, 1953, *Nature*, "Molecular Structure of Nucleic Acids, A Structure for Deoxyribose Nucleic Acid," by J. D. Watson and F. H. C. Crick.
"We wish to suggest a structure for the salt of deoxyribose nucleic acid (DNA). This structure has novel features which are of considerable biological interest . . . It has not escaped our notice that the specific pairing we have postulated immediately suggests a possible copying mechanism for the genetic material."

The Chemical Logic of Life

☐ **Perceptions and Deceptions**

1 "Handedness is one of the consequences of life in a three-dimensional world."

2 Sometimes the very weakest interactions make the very strongest contributions to biochemical behavior.

3 DNA does not participate directly in the synthesis of protein. Instead, it produces disposable copies of specific parts of its information in the form of messenger molecules.

4 Protein polymers get vulcanized, too . . . in a manner of speaking.

5 An enzyme is a protein with catalytic properties.

6 *Carbo*hydrates aren't really hydrates of carbon, as the name might imply.

7 Drugs are *selectively* toxic agents.

☐ **Merging of Two Sciences**

There is no clear line of demarcation separating what is obviously living from that which is obviously nonliving or inanimate. In fact, all living systems can ultimately be defined in terms of (1) the characteristic properties of ordinary chemical substances that make up nonliving systems and (2) by the nature of the usual physical laws responsible for action in the nonliving systems. The ultimate truth is that there is no unique chemical way to tell whether a compound has been synthesized by a cell or by a chemist. But how is it that living matter is so radically different from nonliving matter? Why does a living thing seem to be more than just the sum of its chemical parts? For example, until the first half of the nineteenth century it was believed that living matter (all plants and animals) was inscribed with an inexplicable life force, perhaps of divine origin. *Vitalism* was the name given this mystical, half-scientific doctrine. Many scientists spent the better part of the nineteenth century arguing against and finally winning rejection of that point of view. Nevertheless, the vitalism question has been rephrased in the twentieth century: how is it that nonliving, inanimate collections of atoms and molecules interact with each other so as to sustain life? Further, if you're inclined to toy with such fundamental thoughts, you probably also wonder about how it all began. There must have been a beginning, a time in earth history at which we could say "life begins here . . . in this simple way."

Traditionally, biology and chemistry are thought of as separate subjects: two distinct disciplines; each with its own collection of rules and regulations, operating procedures, and governing principles. Yet, as we noted at the very beginning of this course, although the laws of physics govern the behavior of matter from the macroscopic to the microscopic, chemistry is not a branch of physics. Still, chemistry obeys all the rules of physics. Perhaps the clearest statements of the unique, defining, chemical principles lie in our perception of chemical equilibrium, atomic structure, molecular structure, and chemical bonding.

Chapter 14-1
Louis Pasteur, from the Vanity Fair caricature series.

The same point of view connects chemistry and biology. Since every living bit of matter is a collection of uniquely interacting atoms and molecules, one's first impression might suggest that biology is simply a branch of chemistry. Not so. As was true for chemistry and physics, biology has its unique set of rules and regulations, its governing principles. Not only do the molecules of life have to follow the defining laws of physics and chemistry, but they also interact with each other according to a new collection of ground rules that define the "logic of life." (See Chapter opening.)

If the laws of physics and chemistry seem to be more exact than those laws governing life forces, that's no more than a reflection of the limits to which we have been able to approach those more complicated truths. However, when we do get still closer to the truth, we're not likely to uncover any new physical laws or chemical principles operational only in unique biological systems such as living organisms. The features that are unique to biology and life turn out to be sets of operational rules and regulations, specifying interactions among living collections of atoms and molecules, providing them with the capacity to *organize* and *repeat.*

☐ The Logic of Life Has Had a Long Historical Tradition

The early Greek natural philosophers supplied the first rational theories of life. Six hundred years before the birth of Christ, they offered the view that heat, air, and sunlight produced living organisms in sea slimes. Not a bad theory, life apparently beginning in the warm soupy primordial seas of early earth history. However, these early Greeks believed that *everything* in the universe was alive, and sea slime was about as good a choice for a beginning as any other. Their *seeds of life* were everywhere, floating like so much dust in the air. The early Greek natural philosophers were almost right . . . but for all the wrong reasons.

A few hundred years later, Aristotle complicated the picture by adding the suggestion that it was the action of the four elements, earth, water, air, and fire in supplying a soil that created animal life from inanimate matter. Good thinking, perhaps, but no supporting experiments. Aristotle's view led him and his disciples to some fanciful conclusions: for example, it was well-known to them that fireflies were spawned by the morning dew, and mice are born of moist soil. So it went, nonsense begat nonsense. Some of the nonsense was fairly sophisticated, and held true by the great Newton who believed in *spontaneous generation,* life springing spontaneously from the lifeless.

The nonsense theories of the origins of life gradually began to show signs of coming apart. In 1668 a Florentine physician, Francesco Redi, found that decaying meat which was inaccessible to flies produced no maggots. He placed meat in two separate jars, covered and uncovered, and watched as flies laid eggs in the open one. Eventually meat in both jars putrefied, but only in the open one were maggots, then flies, produced. Clearly, life did not just happen spontaneously in decaying matter as had been so long supposed. Still, another 200 years were to pass before everyone "believed," based on Louis Pasteur's experiments with microorganisms and pasteurization (Fig. 14-1).

Other features of life processes began to clear up. In 1783 an Italian cleric, Lazzarro Spallanzani, fed pieces of meat trapped in tiny cages to uniquely trained hawks who vomited back the cages after certain time intervals. The action of the bird's gastric juices progressively liquified the meat. Spallanzani concluded that liquefaction was due to certain chemicals present in the gastric juices attacking the meat. Here were the first suggestions of enzymatic action.

Friedrich Wöhler synthesized urea without the aid of a kidney in 1828 (Fig. 14-2). By reacting cyanic acid and ammonia he heralded the end of the time-honored debate over whether the chemical components of living matter require a vital force for their synthesis in nature. After 1897, *enzymes* were known to act as catalysts, causing biochemical processes. An enzyme called zymase affected the fermentation of glucose solutions, producing alcohol and carbon dioxide exactly as Pasteur's bugs did with wine grapes. In the 1920s, the first pure crystalline enzyme was prepared (urease, the one related to Wöhler's urea). During the 1930s, the metabolic pathways were mapped out for biosynthesis and biodegradation of sugars, fats, and proteins. By the 1940s, the chemical nature of energy storage and transfer in living cellular systems became known. The period between the end of World War II and the present has provided what may turn out to be the greatest scientific story every told, the molecular biology of the gene and how the transfer of hereditary information to new generations takes place (Fig. 14-3).

☐ **A New Word: Biochemistry**

The word *biochemistry* implies combination of biology and chemistry. It's a twentieth-century word. As this century began, a "biochemical" journal devoted to the new science of biochemistry appeared and at about the same time the American Chemical Society established a subdivision devoted solely to work in "biological" chemistry. There was already a department of biological chemistry at the Pasteur Institute in Paris and the active agent responsible for alcoholic fermentation had been discussed in London at the Lister Institute by scientists who now classified themselves as "biochemists."

Some 60 years before, in 1839 to be exact, two Germans, Schleiden and Schwann, first proposed the *cell theory* which stated that all living things are composites of varying complexity, put together from some small basic unit called a cell. Each cell is surrounded by a cell membrane inside of which would usually be found an inner, nuclear body. The cell theory suggested that new cells arose from existing cells by their dividing into equal daughter cells. All growing cells contain *chromosomes* which carry every bit of information that will ever be needed by the new

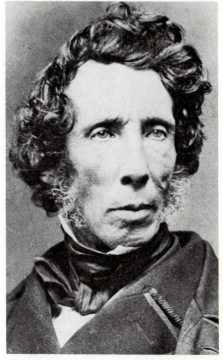

Figure 14-2
"I must tell you that I can make urea without requiring a kidney or an animal, either man or dog." So wrote Friedrich Wöhler. He had mixed solutions of silver cyanate and ammonium chloride, producing ammonium cyanate which, when warmed, gave crystals of urea identical to those obtained as a waste product in urine.

Figure 14-3
James Watson awaits his turn to receive the Nobel prize. In the background are the other participants in the historic DNA discovery. (L. to r.) Max perutz, John Kendrew, Maurice Wilkens, Missing was Roselind Franklin who had died of cancer. (Nobel prizes have not been awarded posthumously.)

Figure 14-4
Charles Darwin, as he appeared in an 1882 *Punch* cartoon. There was considerable opposition to his views on evolution in the Victorian atmosphere in which he lived.

cells, and that gets divided up equally as well. The cell theory has an aspect of universality about it; for example, the single fertilized egg is sufficient to produce the 10^{12} cells of the complex adult human organism.

The theory of evolution is also universal. By the year 1900, the scientific controversy that Darwin and Wallace seeded 50 years earlier (when they proposed their theories of evolution) finally subsided. It was now accepted that man and all other life forms evolved; the same basic principles of life guided all living things (Fig. 14-4).

The beginning of this century also brought with it profound changes in the way chemical activation of living cells was explained. For every vital chemical reaction, biochemists were learning to anticipate the presence of a unique, intracellular chemical catalyst, an enzyme. This belief was the turning point into today's dynamic understanding of the chemical logic of life processes, the hallmark of the new biochemistry. The old protoplasm theory of cell structure that dominated nineteenth-century biological science was predicated on the ability of the single cells themselves to carry out all the complex chemistry of digestion, respiration, assimilation, and growth. The elaborate, organized structure and specialized organs of the higher life forms were not directly concerned.

Replacement of this protoplasm theory began in 1897, the year J. J. Thomson announced the discovery of the electron. By the time Einstein published his three famous papers on quanta and relativity (eight years later), the radically new theory of life processes had become established. The new theory ascribed each chemical change occurring in the living cell to a specific intracellular enzyme, not the entire protoplasm. These special protein catalysts enabled the chemical reactions related to digestion, metabolism, respiration, and assimilation to take place. Life was characterized as a self-regulating, dynamic equilibrium made up of complex systems of enzyme-catalyzed reactions.

The most important single biochemical event in the establishment of the new theory may well have been the discovery of *cell-free* fermentation. Intracellular juices and proteins of yeast could be extracted from ground-up yeast cells. This juice caused the fermentation of glucose to alcohol and carbon dioxide in the complete absence of whole, living, yeast cells. This was the first time a complex physiological reaction involving the breaking and making of chemical bonds was made to happen in the presence of a cell-free intracellular enzyme. It was only the beginning.

☐ The Living Cell

One of the biological ground rules is that all true living systems are organized around a single basic unit, the cell. Since the cell theory was first put forward more than 150 years ago, our ideas of what a cell is like have markedly changed.

However, it is well-established that the cell is the basic unit of life. The proto-plasmic substance of cells once seemed to be very simple, nothing more than a homogeneous, jelly-like mass. We now know otherwise, cellular matter being extremely complex and heterogeneous, containing many chemical substances in solution and suspension. Nature's rich and unusual variety, evident even to the casual observer, can be understood as the current state-of-the-art of the evolutionary process, acting upon some prototype primordial cell.

All living cells seem to exhibit certain universal similarities as far as their chemistry is concerned. They contain two kinds of giant molecules intimately associated with life processes: **proteins** provide structure to the cell, and as enzymes, bring about large numbers of cellular chemical processes; **nucleic acids** are the cellular banks for genetic information needed in protein synthesis and determination of ultimate cell function and structure (Fig. 14-5).

☐ Biomolecules

The same laws of chemistry that determine the way in which molecules behave outside the cell are in operation as cells grow and divide. There aren't any atoms we know of that are unique to the living state. Furthermore, living cells can't synthesize any molecules of a type that the chemist hasn't already prepared. In short, cellular biochemistry is just chemistry with a special twist to it, but plain old chemistry nonetheless. Let's take a closer look at four classes of biomolecules —lipids, carbohydrates, proteins, and nucleic acids. You'll recognize some from the last chapter; a few will be familiar from what you've read so far here; none will be entirely strange to you.

The Biochemist Calls Them Lipids

The first of four main classes of biomolecules we'll discuss is the *fats,* or **lipids.** They are commonly found to be insoluble in water, but soluble in organic solvents such as chloroform. Highly unsaturated fats such as corn and olive oil tend to be liquids at body temperature; highly saturated fats such as animal fats tend to be solids. **Triglycerides** constitute one of the body's main reserves of energy-rich nutrients. When one of the three triglyceride acid groups is replaced by phosphoric acid, then connected to a nitrogen base such as choline, the fatty substance is referred to as a **phospholipid.** Important components of nerve tissue, phospho-lipids are also found in all cell membranes. A third group of fatty substances is the **steroids,** related to the aromatic hydrocarbon, phenanthrene. Cholesterol, a hydroxysteroid thought to be related to the high incidence of hardening of the arteries, is perhaps the most familiar member of the group.

Carbohydrates Make Up a Very Large Group of Biomolecules

The name carbohydrates originated in the belief that these molecules were hydrates of carbon. For example, the formula for glucose ($C_6H_{12}O_6$) could be

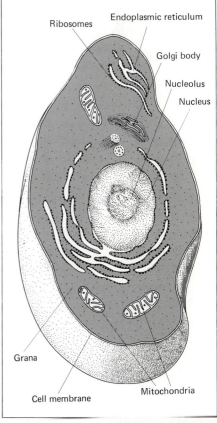

Figure 14-5
A generalized cell diagram showing the principal elements of the complex internal organization.

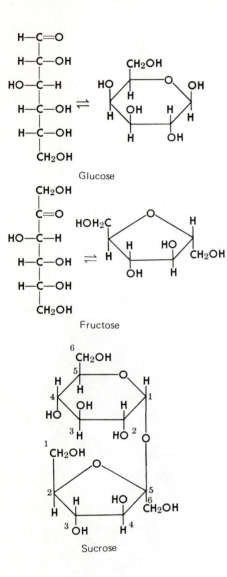

Glucose

Fructose

Sucrose

written as a carbon hydrate $C_6(H_2O)_6$. Quite a wrong view, but the name lingers on. Carbohydrates include simple sugars or **monosaccharides** such as ribose, glucose, and fructose, **disaccharides** such as maltose, sucrose, and lactose, and polymerized forms such as cellulose, pectin, starch, and glycogen, commonly referred to as **polysaccharides.** All are polyhydroxy aldehydes and ketones.

In plants, glucose molecules are put together into long-chain, polymeric cellulose molecules or, in slightly modified form, starch molecules. Living organisms degrade glucose, reversing the plant process while releasing needed energy. Starch, however, is the principal source of carbohydrate food energy. We directly consume starch stored in cereal grain, milled into flour products such as bread, or we feed the grain to animals who in turn biosynthetically convert it to protein which we then eat. Either way, it begins with starch, photosynthetically produced in the green leaves of plants. Fructose, found naturally in fruits (as you might suspect from the name), in chemical combination with glucose, shows up in the kitchen as sucrose—table sugar.

Cellulose shows up naturally as fibers in cotton; synthetic products such as carboxymethylcellulose (CMC) are used widely as extenders in foods such as ice cream. Rayon fibers are also cellulose. Wood is cellulose, too. Even our money, as one scientist-author has glibly noted, is nothing more than "notarized cellulose." But although cellulose is a carbohydrate, as is starch, don't try to get any nourishment out of cellulose. Most organisms, including man, do not have the right enzymes to catalyze its breakdown, releasing its energy. Again, the subtleties of nature: cellulose and starch differ in one small structural modification that makes all the difference in the world. We can use starch for food and energy, having the enzyme needed for its digestion. Fermentation takes place via the initial degradation of starch to glucose: polymers degraded to monomers. That occurs in the stomach (or the vats in the wine cellar). Next time you find yourself eating a piece of bread, keep it in your mouth a bit longer than usual; you'll witness the characteristic sweetness produced by saliva enzymes beginning to digest bread starch to sugar. In the human body, any excess glucose ends up in the liver where it is converted into the animal starch known as *glycogen,* the carbohydrate reserve of animals. When needed by the body, glycogen is re-issued on demand as glucose.

Proteins and Amino Acids

The third class of biomolecules we'll mention is **proteins.** They are long-chain molecules made up of polymerized alpha-amino acids linked through a particular

Figure 14-6
Cellulose is a polysaccharide of 2,000-3,000 glucose units.

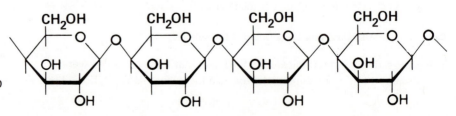

type of bond called a **peptide** bond. **Enzymes** are the glamour molecules of the protein set. In appearance, enzyme proteins are generally globular, having molecular weights ranging from 10^3 to 10^9 and are present in cells in very large numbers. Hemoglobin is a globular protein, functioning as an oxygen carrier for the blood. Gamma-globulin, with a molecular weight of about 10^5, acts as an **antibody,** attaching to foreign particles such as bacteria, thereby protecting the parent organism by causing the intruders to precipitate out from the body fluids. Keratin is a fibrous protein found in wool, hair, and nails; collagen is a fibrous protein found in silks and other insect fibers, and in tendons. Glycoproteins are proteins bonded to carbohydrates; lipoproteins are lipid-containing proteins.

Of the hundreds of amino acids in nature, most are nonprotein. Only 20 are found in living organisms. Listing the 20 as we have in Table 14-1 allows you to perceive the structural features common to all of them.

Nucleic Acids Enable Organisms to Reproduce

The fourth and last group of biomolecules we'll describe here is the **nucleic acids.** Together with the proteins, they are inseparably connected to life as it has evolved. There are two important kinds of nucleic acid, DNA and RNA. Both are polymeric strands made from nucleotide units. Nucleotides are prominent components of all cells, functioning as intermediates in metabolic, energy-transfer processes. Their most dramatic role is as nucleic acid building blocks where they are actively involved in storing, replicating, and transcribing genetic information. Each nucleo-

Table 14-1

Twenty amino acids commonly found in proteins

General formula for 19 of the 20 where R = _____

#	Amino acid	R =
1.	Glycine	H—
2.	Alanine	CH_3—
3.	Valine	$(CH_3)_2CH$—
4.	Isoleucine	CH_3CH_2CH— with CH_3
5.	Leucine	$(CH_3)_2CHCH_2$—
6.	Serine	$HOCH_2$—
7.	Threonine	CH_3CH— with OH
8.	Aspartic acid	$HOOCCH_2$—
9.	Glutamic acid	$HOOCCH_2CH_2$—
10.	Lysine	$H_2NCH_2CH_2CH_2CH_2$—
11.	Arginine	$H_2N-\overset{NH}{C}-NH-(CH_2)_3$—
12.	Asparagine	$H_2N-\overset{O}{C}-CH_2$—
13.	Glutamine	$H_2N-\overset{O}{C}CH_2CH_2$—
14.	Cysteine	$HSCH_2$—
15.	Methionine	$CH_3SCH_2CH_2$—
16.	Tryptophan	(indole ring)—CH_2—
17.	Phenylalanine	(phenyl ring)—CH_2—
18.	Tyrosine	HO—(phenyl ring)—CH_2—
19.	Histidine	(imidazole ring)—CH_2—
20.	Proline	(pyrrolidine ring with)—COOH

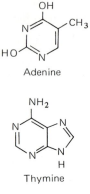

Adenine

Thymine

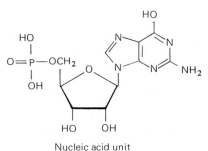

Nucleic acid unit

tide unit consists of a nitrogen-containing ring called a base, a 5-carbon sugar attached to the base, and a phosphoric acid group tacked on to the sugar. The common bases are of two types called **pyrimidines** and **purines**: the pyrimidine bases are uracil, thymine, and cytosine; adenine and guanine are the purine bases. Polymerization of the nucleotide units occurs through condensation of an —OH in the sugar of one nucleotide and in the phosphoric acid of a second nucleotide.

☐ Weak Chemical Bonds; Unique Molecular Shapes; Biological Specificity

All the organic molecules we've introduced in these last two chapters have been notably characterized by covalent bonds. It is also true that when organic molecules appear in a biochemical situation (amino acids, lipids, sugars) they still react as all organic molecules do. We now need an understanding of how cell reactions differ from traditional chemical reactions.

The cell is a well-mapped place, not simply a fluid, random arrangement. We're dealing with intermolecular forces, attractions between adjacent molecules, so we must forget about the strong, covalent bonds that connect atoms within molecules and look at the weaker types of chemical interactions. Actually, you have already been introduced to weak interactions in our discussion of hydrogen bonding and polar molecules. Again, there are no new physical or chemical forces here, just old friends in a new situation, a living cell. The important forces are of three kinds: **van der Waals forces, hydrogen bond interactions,** and **ionic bond formation.** These weaker-than-covalent interactions are responsible for the high degree of specificity we see in cell design and molecular interaction. These forces are important in establishing which molecules can sit next to, on top of, or below other molecules, producing unique bonding characteristics (Fig. 14-8).

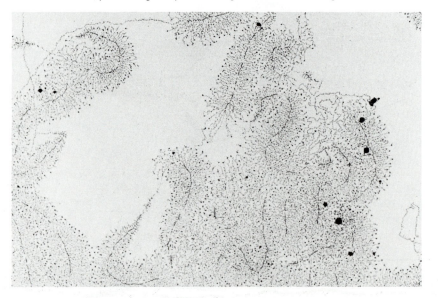

Figure 14-7
Historic electron micrograph of functioning genes magnified 25,000X. The genes are the spines of the carrot-shaped structures linked like beads along a necklace. Each gene (DNA) is shown producing about 100 molecules of RNA.

When a chemical bond is formed between two atoms, energy is usually released as heat, measured in kilocalories per mole. According to the First Law of Thermodynamics (which unequivocally states that energy is conserved) putting that same amount of energy back into the molecule can result in breaking the bond. Covalent bond-breaking normally requires thermal energy on the order of 100 kilocalories per mole. A typical example, would be the O—H bonds in the water molecule. The principal *weak* interactions that are important in biological systems have energies of only 1 to 10 kilocalories per mole. Van der Waals forces are weakest, with energies of 1 to 2 kilocalories per mole; that's not much greater than the kinetic energy of thermal motion itself (approximately 0.5 kilocalories per mole at room temperature). For hydrogen bonds and ionic bonds, energies of 3 to 8 kilocalories per mole are common. What that means is that for physiological processes occurring at body temperature (about 37°C), one can expect quite a few of these weak bonds to break, re-form, and break again (Table 14-2).

Disulfide Bonds Have Real Covalent Strength

There is one notable exception to this collection of important weak bonds (Fig. 14-9). Disulfide bonds can form between amino acid units containing sulfhydro (SH) groups in proximity to each other. Such —S—S— connections form full-fledged covalent bonds, tying together different parts of the same macromolecule or building bridges between protein polymers that are close by. You may recognize the similarity to the covalent bridges we described in the vulcanization process. As we'll see shortly, these bonds do break under certain conditions.

□ Protein Structure and the Alpha-Helix

Biochemists explain their understanding of the relationship between protein structure and biological specificity in terms of four distinct structure levels. The **primary protein structure** describes the sequence in which the various essential alpha-amino acids present in biologically-important macromolecules are joined. That was done for the first time by the British chemist, Frederick Sanger, in the early 1950s, for the insulin molecule. Since then, the primary structures of several other proteins have also been worked out. Remember that although the essential amino acids number only 20, they can appear many times in a given protein sequence.

The **secondary protein structure** refers to how neighboring atoms in the protein find themselves arranged in space. Almost simultaneously with Sanger's work in England, two chemists at the California Institute of Technology, Pauling and Corey, recorded a monumental discovery when they were able to establish an alpha-helical configuration for polypeptide chains. Pauling and Corey suggested a single strand twisted about a helical axis, stabilized by hydrogen bonds between carbonyl and amine groups that were arranged roughly parallel to the axis. The alpha-helix provides a polypeptide chain having a linear structure but with a spatial "twist" to it. Atoms in the repeating peptide bond all lie flat in a plane.

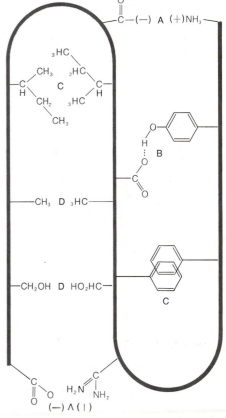

Figure 14-8
Stabilization of protein structures through chemical interactions: (A) electrostatic (ionic); (B) hydrogen bonds; (C-D) Van der Waals forces.

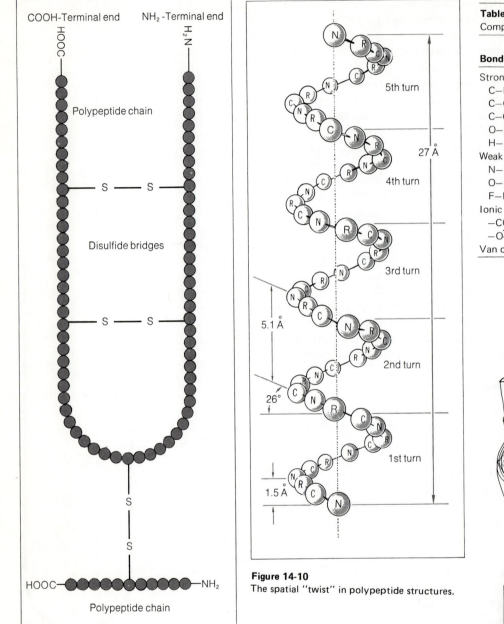

COOH-Terminal end   NH₂-Terminal end

HOOC

H₂N

Polypeptide chain

Disulfide bridges

S — S

S — S

S

S

HOOC—●●●●●●●●●●●—NH₂

Polypeptide chain

Figure 14-9
The disulfide bond.

27 Å

5th turn

4th turn

3rd turn

5.1 Å

26°

2nd turn

1st turn

1.5 Å

Figure 14-10
The spatial "twist" in polypeptide structures.

Figure 14-11
The ordered arrangement found in fibrous proteins (top). Detail of a macrofibril is shown at the bottom.

Table 14-2
Comparing bond energies

Bond	Energy average (Kcal/mole)
Strong covalent	
C–H (as in methane)	~99
C–O (as in carbon dioxide)	~85
C–C (as in ethane)	~82
O–H (as in water)	~110
H–H (as in hydrogen)	~103
Weak hydrogen	
N–H---N	
O–H---O	2-10
F–H---F	
Ionic (electrostatic)	
$-COO^-$----Na^+	
$-O^-$----K^+	
Van der Waals	

Microfibril

Macrofibril

Cuticle

Cortical cells

The angular change that takes place between amino acid units, producing the twisted, helical arrangement, occurs at the carbon next to the peptide bond, one with side groups. Hydrogen bonds hold the whole structure together, connecting amines in one peptide unit to carbonyls three units further along (Fig. 14-10).

The **tertiary protein structure** refers to the way these helical segments are folded. This folding provides the molecules with a very stable configuration.

And finally, the way in which two or more polypeptides combine into one large particle is referred to as the **quaternary protein structure.** Structure determination of myoglobin shows a delicately coiled molecule that contains a number of straight sections, each with alpha-helix configuration. Chemical bonds act as clamps to hold the giant molecule in shape. Those clamps are generally the weak interactions we just finished talking about.

Fibrous and Globular Proteins

Proteins are commonly divided into two groups: fibrous and globular. **Fibrous proteins** are best described as having a highly ordered and rigidly oriented spatial arrangement of polypeptide chains. Other kinds of proteins are found in a **globular** shape; this is characteristic of many enzymes.

Among the more complicated fibrous proteins are the collagens and keratins. Collagens are the proteins of connective tissue, tendons, and hide in higher animals; keratins provide protective cover: skin and scales; fur, hair, and feathers; horns and nails. Wool fibers and human hair are alpha-keratins whose characteristic, structural unit is the alpha-helix twisted into an unusually detailed and orderly arrangement of chains. There are three right-handed alpha-helixes in alpha-keratins coiled into a single left-handed rod called a protofibril. Exactly 11 protofibrils are bundled together into a microfibril, many hundreds of which make up a macrofibril. These major components are shown in Figs. 14-11).

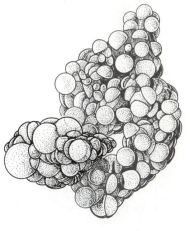

Inside the protofibrils, individual helical protein strands are cross-linked to each other through thiol (—SH) containing amino acid units (cysteine). Disulfide bridges form as two thiols become one —S—S—. Irreversible dimensional changes such as the shrinkage of woolen fabrics results when these —S—S— cross-links are broken by certain treatments such as laundering in hot water. Permanent hair waving is based on chemical treatment of cross-linked chains; preliminary treatment breaks the disulfide bonds, giving the hair additional elasticity so that it can be shaped or curled as desired; post-treatment re-forms the —S—S— bonds, giving the hair a *permanent,* thus fixing the shape.

Whereas fibrous proteins are highly structured, globular ones are not. Yet they too have been uniquely designed to carry out their specific function. In many ways, globular proteins remind one of the micelle structures in our discussion of

Figure 14-12
Unique structure of a globular enzyme, the protein lysozyme (right).

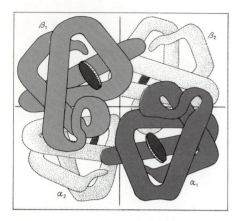

Figure 14-13
Oxygen-binding, hemoglobin molecule.

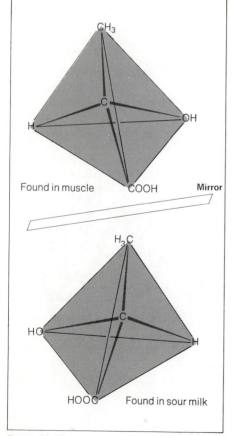

Figure 14-14
Mirror images.

soap and detergent action (Chap. 11). Globular proteins have polar surfaces, due to water-like segments on the exterior of the protein molecule; interior protein segments are usually nonpolar. That turns out to be a happy arrangement, providing water solubility. Lysozyme is an example of a globular protein. It is an enzyme which was discovered by the man who also discovered penicillin, Alexander Fleming. Lysozyme attacks a number of different bacteria by dissolving (lysing) their cell membranes. Figure 14-12 represents the amino acid chain sequence and the three-dimensional shape of the enzyme. Lysozyme is an egg-shaped molecule with a peculiar depression that runs right across it. In nature's master plan, the depression is so structured that a unique portion of the cell membrane exactly fits inside.

The best-known globular protein is the oxygen-binding, hemoglobin molecule. A representation of the structure is a portrait in complexity (Fig. 14-13). Even very small changes (for example, the subtle alteration of a single amino acid unit in this unique molecular maze) make incredible differences in hemoglobin's biological activity. In *normal* hemoglobin (Fig. 12-26), the sixth amino acid from the end one of four interwoven protein chains is glutamic acid. There are 574 amino acid units in all. Victims of sickle-cell anemia, a hereditary disease among Blacks, have a different amino acid, valine, at that sixth position (Fig. 12-27). A quarter-million Americans have this genetic aberration; most die before age 40. On the other hand, if still another amino acid, lysine, is found, only a mild form of hemolytic anemia occurs. What the hemoglobin molecule clearly portrays is that there is a *molecular* basis for disease. Small changes severely affect normal biological function.

☐ Ambidextrous Molecules

Mirror Images and Models

A subtle specificity governs the logic of life. Its basis lies in the four levels of protein structure (primary, secondary, tertiary, quaternary) and the unique, geometric folding patterns (alpha-helix) seen in many essential proteins. Another aspect of nature's geometric cleverness arises when tetrahedral carbon finds itself with four different kinds of atoms or groups of atoms attached, a rather common occurrence among collections of *living* molecules. Look at the list of essential amino acids in Table 14-1 or the natural carbohydrate sugars on page 402. Pick one carbon atom. See if it fits the description: four different atoms or groups of atoms appended. You'll find most every member has at least one such carbon atom. The presence of such carbon atoms leads to a universal geometric property we'll call "handedness." Many of nature's molecules are *isomeric pairs,* differing only in the same sense as your two hands differ from each other; they're mirror images. This phenomenon has important implications (Fig. 14-14).

Using a marshmallow or perhaps a cube cut from a potato for a carbon atom, four toothpicks for chemical bonds, and olives, cherries, grapes, or whatever else you happen to have around the kitchen, construct the glycine molecule: two hydrogens, one amino, and one carboxyl, all tetrahedrally arranged about the carbon. Construct a second model that is an exact mirror image of the first. Take the two models and try to superimpose one exactly on the other: group-to-group. It can be done.

The reason it can be done for glycine is that the mirror images *are* superimposable; the molecule does not exhibit the geometric property of "handedness." That's because there are not the specified *four* different groups about carbon; two are the same, the two hydrogen atoms. Try it with your marshmallow model.

Now remove one of the two duplicate hydrogen atoms, replacing it with a fourth group, say the methyl (CH_3) group in the amino acid alanine: CH_3, H, NH_2, COOH. The central carbon atom is **asymmetric,** that is, it has four *different* groups attached and you can no longer exactly superimpose the two mirror image models.

"Handedness"

You should be able to convince yourself that glucose has not one, but four asymmetric carbon atoms. Therefore, the existence of a pair of mirror image isomers, left-handed and right-handed forms, is to be expected for glucose. As we'll see in a moment, the organic and biochemical implications of this property called *handedness,* is profound indeed. Life, as we know it, is a consequence of the spatial geometry of atoms in molecules (Fig. 14-15).

Some of the earliest, and certainly the most famous, studies of such molecules were carried out by Louis Pasteur in the middle of the last century. Pasteur was concerned with one of France's principal preoccupations: wine-making from grapes. Working with a salt of tartaric acid, he was able to visually distinguish and physically isolate two different crystalline mirror image forms. One was exactly identical to tartaric acid obtained from the sludge found at the bottom of a wine barrel. The two different crystalline modifications were identical, physically and chemically, with one exception. Both caused the plane of a certain special kind of light (*polarized* light) to be rotated from its normal path equally but in opposite directions.

Only right-rotating tartaric acid is found in the wine sludges remaining at the bottom of the barrel. Pasteur had been examining the 50-50 mixture. In one of those fortunate scientific accidents that happen from time to time, Pasteur found that a certain penicillin mold selectively destroyed the right-handed tartaric acid but would not touch the left. Furthermore, he was able to recognize the subtle logic at work here, due to the presence of optical isomers.

Left-handed nicotine derived from tobacco is significantly more toxic than its mirror image, the right-handed form, prepared synthetically. Left-handed mono-

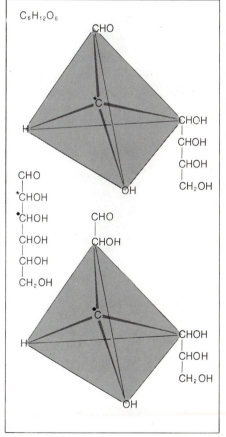

Figure 14-15
How many asymmetric carbons are there?

Figure 14-16
Direction and orientation.

sodium glutamate (MSG) is a flavoring stimulant, but the tastebuds of the human tongue do not respond to the right-handed optical isomer. The natural adrenalin, the body hormone, is left-handed; the right-handed form produces no physiological response. Only one form of chloramphenicol is active against certain bacterial strains. Phenylalanine is harmless in the left-handed configuration, but its mirror image, the right-handed configuration produces insanity when ingested. Proteins, carbohydrates, lipids, nucleic acids, and all the life-bearing macromolecules are "keyed" according to the optical similarities introduced by their ambidextrous nature. The all-important proteins are made up exclusively of left-handed amino acids bound into nature's choice of symmetry, the right-handed alpha-helix.

It's interesting to note that the difference in molecular structure that gives rise to the property of handedness is solely one of orientation. As you stand facing your image in the mirror with arms outstretched, thumbs up, right hand pointing north, you'll note that's apparently also true of your optical duplicate in the mirror (Fig. 14-16).

Well, not quite. Your outstretched, north-pointing right hand is the mirror image's outstretched, north-pointing left hand. *Up* and *north* are the same because they are directions; but right and left are *orientations,* and mirrors reverse orientations. In the case of asymmetric alanine and its mirror image, the up-and-down atoms are still up and down, but the right-and-left atoms are reversed. Place a clock in front of a mirror and you'll see the reflection running backwards (orientations again). Clockwise and counterclockwise are reverse orientations.

☐ Protein Biosynthesis

The DNA molecule is the master cutter's pattern, containing all the instructions needed for producing a fair-skinned Nordic or a dark-skinned African, a great dane or a beagle, an oyster or a clam, an oak or an elm. All the information required to put together properly the life-sustaining proteins needed by a living organism is present in the DNA molecule. It has been estimated that the instructions for replicating a human, coded into the DNA pattern, would fill several encyclopedia volumes when translated into the English language. DNA is the **template.** The RNA molecule *transfers* the information, bringing about protein synthesis in the cell.

Cellular protein synthesis cannot be carried out in the absence of certain nucleic acids; in fact, as we noted earlier, some of the simplest living things such as viruses and bacteria consist of essentially nothing but protein and nucleic acid. The biological function of the nucleic acids has to do directly with storage of coded genetic information required by the cells for synthesizing enzymes and other proteins. Furthermore, the nucleic acids direct the translation of coded information into actual amino acid sequences used in making up these proteins. As we've noted in the case of sickle cell anemia, even the slightest modification in genetic information can have a tremendous impact on the organism. Many physical and chemical agents (mutagenic agents) are capable of altering the DNA structure changing the genetic message.

Briefly, the DNA-RNA-directed synthesis of cellular protein can be summarized as follows: (Fig. 14-17)

Step 1. Needed genetic information is stored as the sequence of nucleotide units in the DNA molecule. In computer-like fashion, DNA prints out exact specifications at the precise moment of cellular protein synthesis.

Step 2. In most cases, DNA never leaves the protection of the cell's nucleus, whereas protein synthesis usually takes place in the surrounding cytoplasmic matter. DNA delegates its authority, directing formation of single-stranded RNA molecules called **messenger-RNA** to carry the original genetic information to the site of protein synthesis. These messengers are blueprints of a kind, being almost perfect copies of parts of the DNA molecule. DNA also synthesizes smaller units, referred to as **transfer-RNA,** that bring together the required raw materials. At no stage in the protein synthesis process does DNA become *directly* involved.

Step 3. Choosing from the pool of 20 amino acids, RNA (messenger and transfer) supervises and guides the collecting, ordering, and snapping together operations that produce polypeptides. Certain cytoplasmic cellular components, notably the ribosomes, assist in this procedure. With the exception of an occasional garbled message that results in a **mutation,** the correct transcription is always produced in spite of the astronomical number of possible combinations.

The secret lies in the unique structure of the DNA molecule with its two intertwining, complementary helices. Connecting the helices, as so many rungs on a ladder, are pairs of nucleic acid bases. For any unique individual, the sequence of base pairs (the ordering of the rungs of the ladder) spells out the complex coded message. Perhaps as many as 10,000 rungs make up the typical DNA ladder (Fig. 14-18).

Double Strands, Base Pairs and Replication

The miracle of reproduction is the DNA molecule's ability to replicate itself. The Watson-Crick model, proposed in 1953, provides two antiparallel, nucleic acid strands wound into the double-stranded helix. The double helix splits, much as a zipper coming undone, snapping apart the nucleic acid base pairs that make up the rungs of the ladder. As the two complementary spirals unzip, free nucleotide units hitch into the correct place, repairing the ladder according to the code. The key word here is *complementary,* not identical. Only certain base pairings

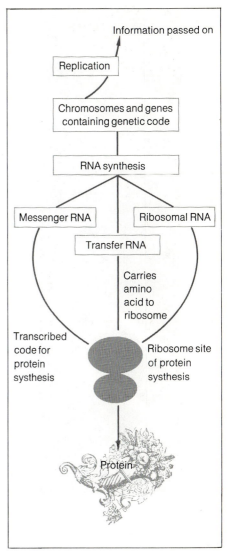

Information passed on

Replication

Chromosomes and genes containing genetic code

RNA synthesis

Messenger RNA

Ribosomal RNA

Transfer RNA

Carries amino acid to ribosome

Transcribed code for protein systhesis

Ribosome site of protein systhesis

Protein

Figure 14-17
Schematic diagram of DNA-RNA-directed synthesis of cellular protein.

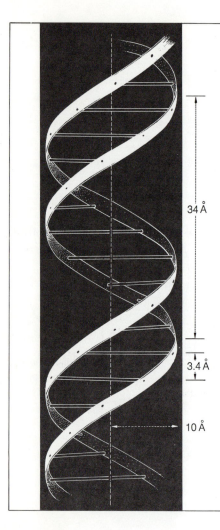

are permitted because of the molecular dimensions of the bases and their ability to hydrogen bond. Adenine commonly pairs with thymine; guanine can only pair with cytosine. The base pairs are linked by N—H---N and N—H---O type hydrogen bonds. Adenine and thymine have two groups, each exactly placed for strong hydrogen bond attraction; cytosine and guanine have three. Also, each base pair is made of one purine ring and one pyrimidine ring system. Proper combination of these particular aromatic rings establishes just the optimum distance between the sugar groups, not too close, not too distant. Pairing two pyrimidines gives rungs that are too short; pairing two purines gives rungs that are too long. One purine and one pyrimidine are just about right (Fig. 14-19).

At the end of the repair job, the original DNA molecule has split in two (Fig. 14-20). DNA has exactly replicated itself into a pair of perfect duplicates. Each strand has formed its own complement. Finally, when cell division takes place, each new daughter cell comes away with its own complete set of DNA, exactly coded to instruct in the synthesis of all its particular proteins. It's important to note the role played by the weak, hydrogen bonds in making up the rungs of the ladder connecting the complementary strands. Unzipping the rungs occurs before any coming apart of the covalent bonds holding the components of the strands takes place. Thus, the sequence of the strand is maintained; the template is preserved. Since only one particular base can be linked to any other, one strand determines what the other will be like.

Figure 14-18
Schematic of the ladder-like arrangement for the base pairs (rungs) making up the double helix structure.

Figure 14-19
Legitimate base pairing (purine/pyrimidine). Illegitimate base pairing (arbitrary arrangement of base pairs).

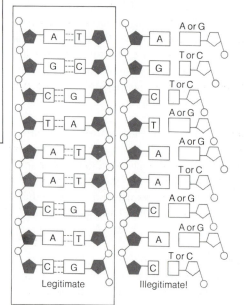

RNA is produced on a DNA template. The DNA helix partly unzips, produces the somewhat different but complementary RNA strand, and then zips itself back together again. That's called **transcription.** The coded message has been passed along. Remember that the sugars in the RNA backbone are slightly different (ribose versus deoxyribose) and in RNA uracil replaces thymine (Fig. 14-21). Here, then, is the overall route to cellular protein synthesis: replication (DNA), transcription (DNA to RNA); translation (RNA).

About 10 percent of the RNA in a cell is the messenger kind. Its function is to get the code from the DNA of the genes in the nucleus, and take the word to a ribosome region in the cytoplasmic matter of the cell where proteins will be

Figure 14-20
DNA comes apart—each separate strand serving as a template (set of instructions) for producing the missing half, resulting in replication.

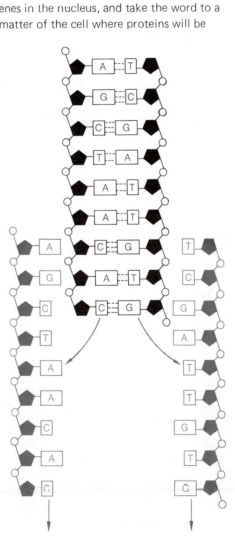

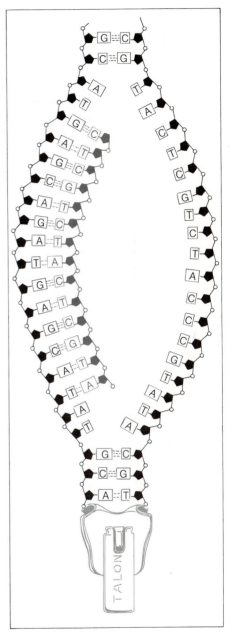

Figure 14-21
By coming partially *unzipped,* transcription of DNA-coded information into RNA-coded information is possible. The synthesized RNA strand *matches* the DNA strand.

assembled. Messenger-RNA provides information concerning the DNA base sequence. The coding for any single amino acid unit is a three-letter word, standing for three successive bases on the RNA polynucleotide chain. That's called a **codon.** The role of the transfer-RNA is to recognize and attach to certain amino acid molecules which in turn rearrange and attach to the triplet codons of the messenger-RNA at the protein building site (Fig. 14-22). After the amino acid units are properly in place, in sequence, the transfer-RNA detaches. Polymerization continues until the programmed STOP message appears. For the 20 essential amino acids, one or more codons signal their respective appearance in the growing polypeptide chain.

Biochemists believe that the entire cellular protein synthesis process takes place on the ribosomal surface. The ribosome is a template of sorts, too, orienting the transfer-RNA and it's amino acid baggage with respect to the messenger-RNA so all the codons are read correctly. Ribosomes provide properly oriented binding sites that bring together transfer-RNA, messenger-RNA, and the growing polypeptide chain. At the signal of the STOP codon, the ribosomes release the completed chain. Time required to do a job like this? It has been estimated that polypeptide chains in proteins can be put together at a rate of perhaps 25 units per second (Fig. 4-23).

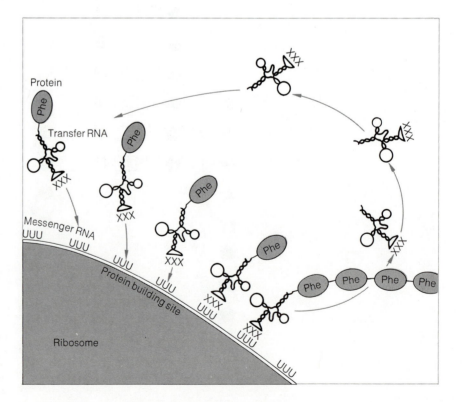

Figure 14-22
Schematic representation of polypeptide synthesis taking place on a messenger-RNA template.

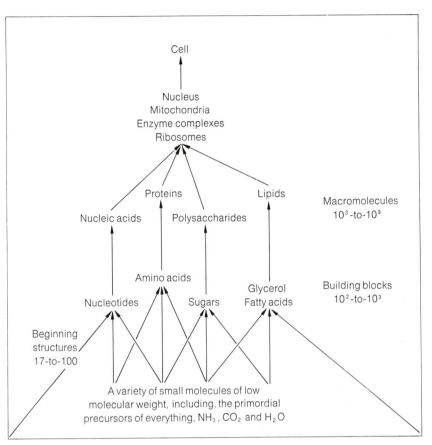

Cell

Nucleus
Mitochondria
Enzyme complexes
Ribosomes

Proteins   Lipids

Nucleic acids   Polysaccharides

Macromolecules
10^3-to-10^9

Amino acids

Nucleotides   Sugars   Glycerol
Fatty acids

Building blocks
10^2-to-10^3

Beginning
structures
17-to-100

A variety of small molecules of low
molecular weight, including, the primordial
precursors of everything, NH_3, CO_2 and H_2O

Figure 14-23
The dimension of molecular biochemistry.

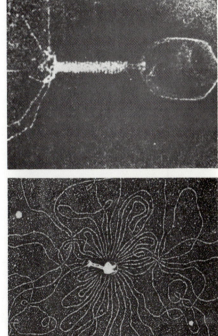

Figure 14-24
The parasitic virus known as T_2 infects the
bacterium *E. coli*, producing its own kind of
protein and DNA at the expense of the host
(top). The *E. coli* cell breaks open after it is
infected (bottom), spilling its contents out.

□ Lowly Viruses and Lawless Cells

As a model for understanding reactions taking place in more complicated environments, biochemists have looked at what may be one of the simplest demonstrations of cellular protein synthesis in the organic world. The bacterium *E. coli* is
attacked by a parasitic virus living inside bacterial cells called **bacteriophage,** or
just *phage* for short. Looking as you might imagine a lunar lander, the image of
the T-even phage, has been produced under the electron microscope (Fig. 14-24).

T-even phage consists of one huge DNA molecule with a molecular mass in the
millions, along with several kinds of protein, all contained within a distinct head-
and-tail construction. The DNA is inside the head. When an *E. coli* cell becomes
infected by a T-even virus, viral DNA is actually injected through the parasite's
tail into the host cell. The injected DNA strand assumes control of the bacteria's

metabolic system, using it solely to prepare more *viral* protein and *viral* DNA. Within 20 minutes of infection, the host cell bursts, spilling out perhaps 100 new T-even particles, and the cycle starts again. *E. coli* has used its own enzymes under the coded direction of the T-even DNA strand to put together the proper sequence of amino acids to make T-even protein and DNA. The T-even DNA has thus introduced different messages. Sounds like science fiction, doesn't it?

The Gene Is DNA

Our understanding of DNA structure and behavior may well prove to be the most important discovery of the twentieth century. Perhaps the most prominent implication of that discovery has to do with research into the causes of cancer. For example, viruses are known to produce some kinds of cancers in laboratory animals. The routine is not at all unlike the infection of *E. coli* by phage-even viruses: attachment to the host cell; injection of genetic material, usually DNA; subversion of normal host cell function to synthesis of more virus. In some laboratory animals, certain viral nucleic acids have successfully induced malignant cell regeneration, better known as cancer.

Nobody is making any kind of sweeping generalizations about imminent cures for cancers, least of all the cancer researchers. The word cancer covers a wide variety of different diseases, but all are characterized by the same, often fatal, property: cells grow and multiply as they should not. What tells the cell to divide as it does? One cannot help but to look for answers from the gene. The essential details of the cause of molecular diseases such as sickle-cell anemia are now known. One feels with that kind of knowledge at hand, nonsurgical cures will eventually be possible for cancer, too.

☐ Biochemical Energetics and Dynamics

An earlier definition of energy that we suggested was the capacity to do useful work of different kinds. There are different kinds of energy (kinetic, potential, radiant) and there are different kinds of work (mechanical, electrical, chemical). Energy transformations from the chemical potential lying dormant in hydrocarbon fuels are important to us. We should also be very much concerned with the efficiency with which one kind of energy is converted into another. Biological energy conversions are no exception. We said earlier that there is no mysterious life force. Living systems are energy converters like any machine. Cell dynamics can be understood in terms of chemistry and physics, only the viewpoint has changed because biological ground rules now take precedence.

Living cells are complex, highly organized particles of matter. Cellular demands for energy are of primary importance in order to sustain the cell's existing organization and to allow for increased organization as new proteins, new cells, and new organisms are produced. It takes place while the cell is burning fuel. There's quite an energetic hustle and bustle at the cellular level. A description of how all that happens conveniently breaks into two general categories: *plant cells* pull in their energy from the sun, using some for their normal function, while storing the rest after converting it into chemical fuels; *animal cells* depend on the energy stored in plants (Fig. 14-25). There are three major steps in the flow of energy in the biosphere: **photosynthesis, respiration,** and **biochemical** work. It all begins with a middle-aged star called the sun and a tiny fraction of the energy radiating away from its thermonuclear furnace, hitting the earth's surface.

Sunlight and Photosynthesis

Sunlight, the source of all biochemical energy, is electromagnetic radiation arising from fusion reactions taking place in the sun. The overall process by which plants absorb, use, and store radiant energy is called *photosynthesis.* Radiant energy is absorbed by certain plant pigments, mainly chlorophyll. Absorbed electromagnetic energy (all those $h\nu$'s) is converted into chemical energy; finally, chemical energy is used to reduce atmospheric carbon dioxide to glucose. Here is the overall chemical equation:

$$686 \text{ kcal of energy} + 6\,CO_2 + 6\,H_2O \longrightarrow \underset{\text{glucose}}{C_6H_{12}O_6} + 6\,O_2$$

In higher plants, glucose and oxygen form from carbon dioxide and water in the presence of a large amount of energy supplied by the radiant energy-absorbing

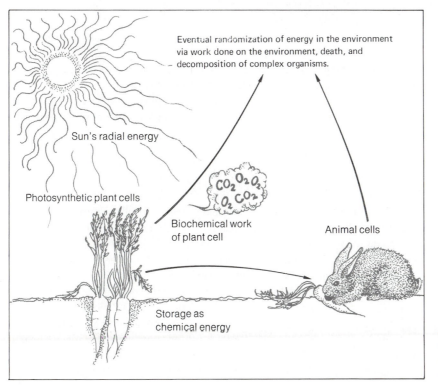

Figure 14-25
Energy flow through the biosphere: beginning with the sun's radiant energy; ending with randomization of energy within the environment.

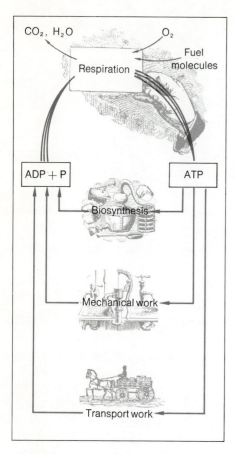

Figure 14-26
Moving energy via the ATP-ADP system.

chlorophyll in the leaves. That's a very general statement which glosses over the complexity of what is perhaps a 100-step molecular sequence; each step probably requires the action of specific catalytic enzymes, with monosaccharides, proteins, and fats (lipids) also being produced along the way.

Glucose Is an Energy-Rich Molecule

According to our photosynthetic equation, glucose is energy-rich to the extent of 686 kilocalories for every mole of molecules. Utilization of the chemical energy stored in glucose or any other carbohydrate, protein, and fat synthesized along the way, takes place through cellular oxidation.

$$C_6H_{12}O_6 \ + \ 6\,O_2 \ \longrightarrow \ 6\,CO_2 \ + \ 6\,H_2O \ + \ 686\ \text{kcal of energy released}$$

You may recognize this process as animal respiration: oxygen taken in; carbon dioxide given off (photosynthesis in reverse). However, the overall process is complex and the 686 kcal are the *maximum* supply of thermal energy available from a mole of glucose molecules. But cellular enzymes aren't perfect and 100 percent efficiency isn't ever achieved (Fig. 14-26).

On first impression, there seems to be an obvious *combustion* character to the oxidative degradation of glucose. We've certainly talked about burning, or oxidizing organic molecules to the ultimate oxidation products, carbon dioxide and water. But keep in mind the fact that biological ground rules are different. The one-step release of 686 kilocalories of energy wouldn't allow the cell to do much work at all, in fact, the cell would disintegrate. A series of intermediate transformations involving release of small amounts of energy in closely controlled events is the biochemical way oxidations proceed. That turns out to be a much more efficient way of proceeding as well. Furthermore, oxidation isn't quite the word we want to use since oxygen is rarely *directly* involved. What's really meant, biochemically, is transfer of hydrogen atoms. In addition, there is one molecule that serves as an energy carrier called adenosine triphosphate (ATP), upon which all biological function depends.

Biochemical Oxidation

Take a closer look at oxidative degradation. Here is the process whereby organic chemical nutrients such as glucose are able to yield useful chemical energy. The seat of this cellular activity seems to be the mitochondrion, a pod-shaped particle (as many as 1,000 per cell in humans) whose job is much the same as the coal burner in a power station for generating electricity (energy). The mitochondrion's raw material is food taken into the cell to be broken down by the cytoplasm. The raw material is burned, freeing up stored energy. It is then banked for future use in an easily accessible form, the high-energy ATP molecule. The power station and the mitochondrion both burn fuel and release energy, carbon dioxide, and water. The power station is an inefficient, one-step converter mainly producing heat and eventually electricity via turbines; the mitochondrion brings about an efficient, enzyme-catalyzed, multi-step transformation into a variety of more useful energy forms via ATP.

Since oxygen is absolutely essential for all animals, you'd naturally anticipate its direct and active participation in the oxidation processes. As it turns out, most biological oxidations are better described as *dehydrogenations,* processes in which a compound is oxidized by the *removal* of two hydrogen atoms. Oxygen's role is indirect. For example, lactic acid can be oxidized to pyruvic acid in an important metabolic process. Writing the process as the organic chemist might, produces the following balanced equation:

$$CH_3-\underset{\underset{\textstyle OH}{|}}{\overset{\overset{\textstyle H}{|}}{C}}-COOH \ + \ \tfrac{1}{2}\,O_2 \ \longrightarrow \ CH_3-\underset{\underset{\textstyle O}{\|}}{C}-COOH \ + \ H_2O$$

Remember what we said in our discussion of organic chemistry in Chapter 13. On paper, oxidations can be viewed as progressive insertions of oxygen atoms into C—H bonds. Look at the reaction as C—H going to C—OH:

$$CH_3-\underset{\underset{\textstyle OH}{|}}{\overset{\overset{\textstyle H}{|}}{C}}-COOH \ + \ \tfrac{1}{2}\,O_2 \ \longrightarrow \ CH_3-\underset{\underset{\textstyle OH}{|}}{\overset{\overset{\textstyle OH}{|}}{C}}-COOH$$

unstable intermediate

The unstable intermediate first formed has two OH groups on one carbon atom, a situation that often leads to loss of a water molecule, giving the oxidized product, pyruvic acid. Think about the chemistry; the net effect is removal of two hydrogens: but it is an *oxidation* that has taken place.

$$CH_3-\underset{\underset{\textstyle OH}{|}}{\overset{\overset{\textstyle H}{|}}{C}}-COOH \ \longrightarrow \ CH_3-\underset{\underset{\textstyle O}{\|}}{C}-COOH \ + \ 2\,H.$$

Oxidation, then, using biochemical ground rules, means removal of hydrogen. But you can't just *remove* hydrogen atoms. They must be transferred to another molecule that we say has been *reduced.* Oxidation and reduction are complementary processes. Several different molecules are hydrogen atom receivers. All are associated with some particular protein, forming *active* enzymes. Such assistant molecules are called **coenzymes.** One important example is the dinucleotide called nicotinamide adenine dinucleotide (NAD). Remember that nucleotides, the nucleic acid building blocks, are made of a sugar, a phosphoric acid, and an organic base. One of NAD's biochemical precursors in the body is nicotinic acid, a B complex vitamin required in nutrition.

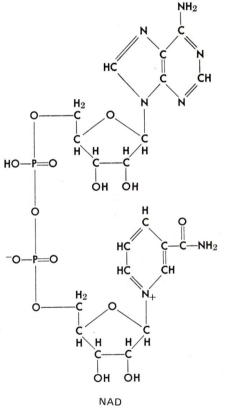

NAD

Here is the biochemical oxidation with only the main characters present:

$$CH_3-\underset{\underset{\textstyle OH}{|}}{\overset{\overset{\textstyle H}{|}}{C}}-COOH \ + \ NAD \ \longrightarrow \ CH_3-\underset{\underset{\textstyle O}{\|}}{C}-COOH \ + \ NADH_2$$

Perhaps a more familiar example of the *indirect* role of oxygen is the oxidation of glucose. The process involves glucose breaking into two fragments which then react with each other as oxidizing and reducing agents. No molecular oxygen is needed. Oxidative processes that take place in the absence of oxygen (*anaerobic* conditions) are called **fermentation.** It has been known since the time of Pasteur that glucose ferments, or oxidizes to alcohol in the absence of air.

ATP and ADP

Any outline for the flow of energy in the biosphere would be woefully lacking without mention of ATP and ADP. Cells need energy to keep all of their highly organized processes going. Glucose oxidations release energy that must be channeled directly to where it is needed in a form that's readily usable on demand. There is a coupled, universal energy transfer system built around the supercharged, high-energy adenosine triphosphate (ATP) molecule and its energy discharge partner, adenosine diphosphate (ADP). The discharged acceptor molecule forms a high-energy phosphate with absorption of energy; the supercharged ATP with its high-energy, third phosphate bond, is nature's energy exchanger. When any cell process picks energy up from ATP, the process reverses.

Of the 686 kilocalories per mole of potential energy available in a mole of glucose molecules, some 60 percent eventually reaches various compounds and cell processes via ADP-ATP transfer. Compare that to the 15 to 20 percent efficiency you might get, if you're lucky, inside an automobile's internal combustion engine. The universality of the ADP-ATP energy transfer mechanism is unchallenged: no exceptions are known, from the most complex organisms to the lowliest viruses and bacteria. In all likelihood nature must have conceived these energy messengers very early in the evolutionary process.

To illustrate complexity while demonstrating unity and coherence in biochemistry and the logic in life processes, the stepwise degradation of glucose to pyruvic acid has been drawn out for you. This was worked out in the 1920s and 1930s, along with a significant generalization that these established oxidation pathways were not unique to alcohol fermentation. For example, when muscles contract (in the absence of oxygen) glycogen breaks down to lactic acid via glucose. Exactly the same kinds of pathways as in muscle contraction supply the bugs that cause wine to ferment with their energy (yeast, microorganisms) (Fig. 14-27).

We noted that the overall efficiency realized in the burning of glucose is about 60 percent. The greatest part of that energy transfer occurs beyond the first big step, the glucose-to-pyruvate (or lactate) conversion. Most of the energy is transferred by what has come to be known as the **Krebs citric acid cycle** or Krebs cycle. Here, oxygen *is* used directly. In the presence of oxygen, ATP production continues beyond the pyruvate-lactate stage. Pyruvate is transformed into an important acetic acid coenzyme complex called *acetyl-CoA.* A cyclic series of

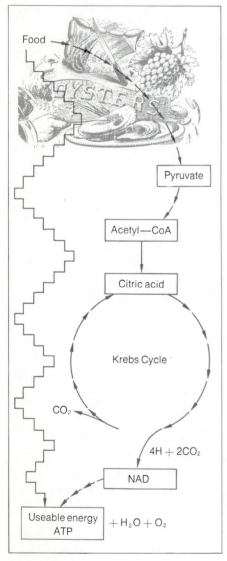

Figure 14-27
The many steps of the Citric Acid Cycle beats an open flame any time for efficient use of energy.

reactions follows in which four hydrogen atoms are produced through transfer to specific coenzyme molecules, along with two molecules of carbon dioxide. The reduced coenzyme molecules (they've picked up hydrogen atoms) can be re-oxidized directly with oxygen, yielding most of the energy used by organisms that grow in the presence of air (aerobic).

Note the way nature operates. As the reduced nicotinamide adenine dinucleotide ($NADH_2$) comes off the citric acid cycle, it is the key energy repository. At the end of the respiratory chain, all the energy has passed to three ATPs by reoxidation, using oxygen directly in the last step. If oxidation had taken place in a single step, some 53 kilocalories of energy would have been released, and that would have been too hot for the cell to handle..Instead, the cell machinery supplies a gradual series of several steps across which an average energy drop of 12 kilocalories per mole occurs.

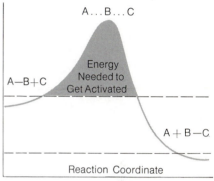

Figure 14-28
Crossing the energy barrier: reactants $\rightleftharpoons$ activated (transition) state $\rightarrow$ products.

☐ Enzymes Are Specific Biochemical Activators

When a chemical or biochemical reaction takes place, there are two principal reasons. First, the overall process is said to be energetically favorable; in other words, the total energy of the reactants is greater than the total energy of the probable products, therefore, leading to a more stable state; nature prefers that kind of lower energy situation. Second, a significant percentage of the reacting molecules are said to have an average energy greater than the rest; they've become activated, and can now cross over some invisible barrier. Think about it for a moment, the idea that an obstacle, a barrier to reaction, exists; and the need for an extra effort to get over that barrier. Sounds almost nonsensical at first; yet the explanation turns out to be quite reasonable on closer inspection. If there weren't an energy barrier, every reaction that could happen, would happen. We'd end up sliding down the slippery slope of the energy mountain, out of control. Even a casual look around you suggests that there is control, selectivity, specificity. There are energy barriers to be bridged; there is a measureable *energy of activation* needed to bring reactants to the top of the barrier after which they can then spontaneously slide downhill to products, without any further assistance.

$$A{-}B \ + \ C \quad \longrightarrow \quad A \ + \ B{-}C$$

Consider a reaction in which substance A-B reacts with substance C, producing new reaction products. One such example that we've already discussed is the reoxidation of the reduced form of nicotinamide adenine dinucleotide ($NADH_2$) by pyruvate in muscle cell.

$$NADH_2 \ + \ CH_3{-}\overset{\displaystyle O}{\underset{\displaystyle \|}{C}}{-}COOH \quad \longrightarrow \quad NAD \ + \ CH_3{-}\overset{\displaystyle H}{\underset{\displaystyle OH}{\underset{\displaystyle |}{\overset{\displaystyle |}{C}}}}{-}COOH$$

The energy diagram for the chemical reaction shows reactants to have, on average, an overall higher energy than products (Fig. 14-28). Therefore, the reaction is possible. The **probability** of reaction taking place, however, is a different matter. That is related to the concentration of reacting molecules "activated,"

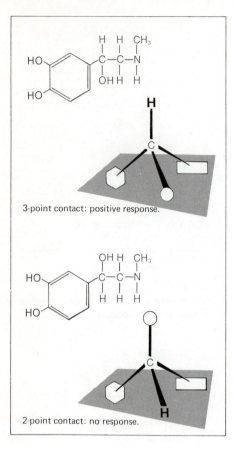

3-point contact: positive response.

2-point contact: no response.

now capable of breaking old chemical bonds and forming new ones. For this, as well as for every other chemical reaction, there is some *transition state* that describes the condition of the reacting molecules at the top of the energy barrier, at the summit, or maximum in the curve. Our model reaction would involve a complex of A—B and C molecules.

$$A–B + C \rightleftharpoons [A\text{---}B\text{---}C] \longrightarrow A + B–C$$

unstable, higher energy, transition
state complex

The transition state complex, sitting precariously at the highest point of the energy diagram, can fall apart in two ways. It can reverse itself, sliding back down the slope into a mixture of reactants, or it can zip down the other side of the energy barrier to products.

The success of the reaction in reaching the product stage has to do with the population of active molecules in the transition state. Raise the temperature of a chemical reaction; thermal energy increases, and higher energy transition state molecules show up at the summit. On average, an increase in temperature of 10°C about doubles the rate of the reaction. Catalysts can also accelerate chemical reactions. They do so by making it easier for reacting molecules to "get activated." Catalysts lower the energy barrier, thereby making it possible for greater numbers of molecules to get up to the top of the transition state and then over to the other side.

Enzymes Uniquely Catalyze Specific Biochemical Reactions

Most of the usual covalent bonds in biomolecules are very stable, decomposing in the absence of a catalyst only at temperatures much higher than the 37°C, which is normal body temperature. If you're going to burn up glucose with oxygen without the necessary enzymes, you'll have to literally burn it up, losing all specificity and control along the way. However, the presence of an enzyme catalyst lowers the activation energy barrier, and now the same reaction works quite nicely at physiological temperatures. Not only are enzyme catalysts specific, but they are speedy and efficient. It is not uncommon for the typical enzyme to catalyze a million reactions per minute, a time period in which no reaction would be likely to take place if the catalyst were absent. Some enzyme catalysts are single proteins; others are very complicated structures involving metal ions and other smaller proteins called coenzymes.

Let's take a closer look at one cellular biochemical process and its specific enzyme catalyst. Enzymes *E* react through combination with the moleucles involved. If we call the reactant molecules the substrate *S*, then our transition state for reaction might look just like our general A—B and C model reaction.

$$E + S \rightleftharpoons [E\text{---}S] \longrightarrow E + \text{products}$$

| enzyme | reactant molecules | transition state complex | enzyme catalyst regenerated for continued use |

Glucose reacts with the enzyme-rich ATP molecule in the very first stage in glycolysis, resulting in *phosphorylation.* The reaction is catalyzed by the enzyme hexokinase and takes place on the surface of this specific protein catalyst. Further, there's a three-dimensional fit of all the pieces in a puzzle. Molecular shapes and bonding sites allow only the right pieces to be correctly oriented, and reaction takes place (Fig. 14-29).

$$E \;+\; \substack{\text{glucose} \\ \text{and} \\ \text{ATP}} \;\rightleftharpoons\; [E\text{-}\text{-}\text{-}S] \;\longrightarrow\; E \;+\; \substack{\text{glucose-6-} \\ \text{phosphate and} \\ \text{ADP}}$$

☐ **Biochemical Regulation**

It has been said that the human aspects of man's nature that differentiate him from all other animals is the perception of his own mortality. Man alone among animal perceives that life is not a forever thing. By the same token, man has been very successful at making the best of the situation, delaying as long as is humanly possible that ultimate appointment. Biochemical agents called **drugs** have played an important role in this success story. Through their selective toxicity, drugs regulate a whole variety of bioprocesses from controlling the growth of grains and livestock for food to the destruction of harmful pests and parasites and the elimination or moderation of disease and pain. Much has been accomplished, especially in the last 100 years; much more remain to be done. The prospects seem good.

Drugs are chemical agents that exhibit *selective toxicity* toward living organisms. That means selectively damaging one kind of living matter without hurting another, for example, a parasite and its host; two tissues in one organism, or perhaps simply two cells. Damage may be reversible or irreversible, depending on the situation: a general anesthetic (reversible) versus an antimalarial (irreversible). In one case, the intention is to deaden the central nervous system temporarily; in the other, the death of the parasite without impairment of the host is what's wanted. In the year 1919, more than 8,000 people died in Italy of malaria. A program of chemotherapy and chemical spraying has since eliminated the disease, no such deaths have been recorded since 1948 (Fig. 14-30).

The grape and the poppy are among the oldest sources of drugs in man's pharmacopia, dating back at least as long as we have written records. Somehow most people don't think of alcohol (from the grape) as a drug, even though it is a strong depressant to the central nervous system. Morphine (from the poppy) isn't widely used as a pain killer in the same sense that aspirin is widely used, because of its habit-forming side effects. Aspirin, the most ubiquitous and perhaps best-known medicinal drug, has been known for about 65 years as an effective analgesic and antirheumatic agent. Chemotherapy and selective toxicity really began in earnest as the German chemical industry produced a profusion of synthetic analgesics, antipyretics, and anesthetics between 1885 and 1910. In the year aspirin was first introduced (1907), a curious organic molecule containing arsenic was shown to be

Figure 14-29
The enzyme serves as a specific reaction surface binding together two species allowing transfer from one to the other.

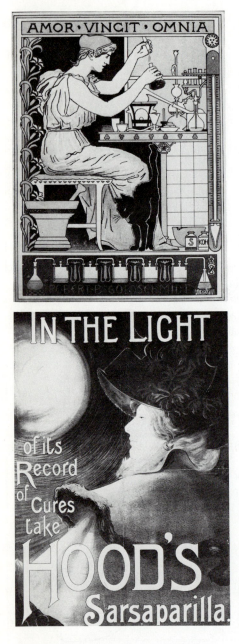

Advertising "legal" drugs: in the 1930s (top) and at the turn of the century (bottom).

effective against certain parasitic trypanosomes that caused sleeping sickness. It was also extremely effective against another protozoan-like disease, syphilis. This was the drug Salvarsan, a major scientific discovery at that time, and for many years the treatment of choice for syphilis. At about the same time the first synthetic sympathetic nervous system stimulants (sympathomimetics), adrenaline and amphetamine, were introduced into the pharmacopia. You may recognize amphetamine as the prototype of a family of abused "street" drugs, variously called speed, bennies, reds, and uppers. Heroin was synthesized in the 1880s as the search for nonaddictive analgesic substitutes for morphine began. Literally hundreds of new compounds have been prepared since that time. The deep emotional interest in drug abuse created by these addictive analgesics has generated a lot of research at many levels (chemical, biological, pharmacological, psychological, sociological, cultural) into the morphine alkaloids and related drugs.

Figure 14-30
Dusting children with DDT in an effort to control typhus.

Just before the beginning of World War II (about 1935), **prontosil,** the first of the sulfa, or *sulfonamide* drugs, was introduced. These sulfonamide drugs were very potent bacteriocidal agents. Prior to that time, streptococci infections were often fatal. That's rarely been the case since prontosil's introduction. Related members of this family of drugs are commonly used today for treatment of pneumonia and puerperal fever, strep and staph infections, meningeal infections, and dysentery. The sulfa drugs were enormously important in World War II. The period between 1942 and 1965 has been dubbed the era of **antibiotics** research. Several years after prontosil was introduced, penicillin, the first antibiotic, began to be used clinically in treating local and systemic bacterial infections. An entire family of broad-spectrum antibiotics evolved, many are likely to be familiar to you: aureomycin, streptomycin, neomycin. The age we live in has been called the age of anxiety. Chlorpromazine is the prototype of a host of **tranquilizing** substances and anti-depressants. Two of these anti-anxiety drugs, librium and valium, stand second only to aspirin in terms of annual consumption.

Insect control is one of the most important yet delicate areas to which the principles of selective toxicity and biochemical regulation have been successfully applied. No insect poison is more famous than DDT. Millions of tons have been synthesized and used annually for insect control, hygiene, and protection of plants in spite of recent restrictions in the United States. Because of DDT's immense economic value in maximizing crop yields, the drug has been of monumental importance to the developing nations of Africa and Asia in their continuing fight for food and survival. DDT exerted a profound influence on the re-emergence of Europe after World War II due to its dramatic triumph against the threat of typhus. In 1944 use of the chemical prevented a typhus outbreak in Naples from becoming an epidemic. At that time, conditions were so bad that had an epidemic developed among the millions of refugees, it is likely that the death toll would have exceeded those killed in the war itself. DDT and its chlorinated hydrocarbon relatives, dieldrin and aldrin,

Aerial spraying of insecticides to control pest infiltrations in our hardwood forest (left).

are also potential hazards to the environment, and of late, concerned people have come to question their unlimited use.

One promising alternative to the use of chemical insecticides and pesticides, with their environmental backlash, is the use of insect sex attractants to lure unsuspecting pests into deadly traps. Instead of widespread spraying of open fields with insecticides such as DDT, unwary insects are attracted to places where they come into contact with the toxic drugs that kill them. Chemical substances secreted by any insect or animal that evoke a specific behavioral response in other members of the same species are called pheromones. In many cases they are sex attractants.

☐ **Questions to Answer . . . Problems to Solve**

1. In terms of our discussions of cellular biochemistry in this chapter, comment on the proposition that all living things, past, present, and future, evolved from a ful of rare, living systems which arose spontaneously perhaps two billion years ago.

2. Based on the *apparent* logic of the *visible* univers, see if you can understand why people of a not-so-distant past supported each of the following wrong notions: (1) vitalism and (2) spontaneous generation. Explain the significance of Spallanzani and Wohler's experiments.

3. Without looking back into the chapter, see if you can recall the key functional group characteristics of each of the following biomolecules. Then go back and check yourself out in the chapter or glossary.
   (a) carbohydrates (c) proteins (e) amino acids
   (b) lipids (d) nucleic acids (f) sugars

4. Amino acid, zwitterion, peptide bond, enzyme . . . What are they?

5. Distinguish between fibrous and globular proteins. Why is a helix structure seemingly inconsistent for globular proteins? How do you justify the existence of so many different globular proteins?

6. Briefly comment on the structure levels in protein. What types of chemical interactions influence formation of secondary protein structure?

7. What is it about the twenty essential amino acids that makes them "essential"? But essential nucleotides for nucleic acid synthesis aren't essential. Comment.

8 Contrast the "usual" type of covalent bonding that holds atoms in molecules together with the weak interactions such as hydrogen bonding, ionic bonding,

and van der waals forces. What role do the "weak interactions" play in cellular biochemistry? And where does the sulfide bond in proteins fit into this discussion of covalent and weak interactions?

9. In what general way is glucose different from sucrose? Sucrose from starch? Starch from cellulose? Why is it that starch is a human nutrient but isn't?

10. Are all of the following considered to be drugs according to the interpretation of this chapter? Comment briefly on each.

(a) morphine   (e) MSG   (i) Enovid
(b) alcohol   (f) amphetamine   (j) Valium
(c) tobacco   (g) aspirin   (k) 2,4-D
(d) coffee   (h) sunlight

11. Make a simple drawing that clearly shows that lactic acid has two mirror images. Why can't you do the same for pyruvic acid?

12. Briefly state your general understanding of each of the following terms. Illustrate your answer with an example, and an explanation of how it is implicated in life processes.

(a) covalent bonds   (d) van der Waals bonds   (f) disulfide bonds
(b) hydrogen bonds   (e) peptide bonds   (g) coordinate bonds
(c) ionic bonds

13. What do catalysts do for chemical reactions?

14. Comment briefly on each of the following statements:
(a) Fresh apple cider, sealed in bottles without refrigeration may explode.
(b) If you are going to try and make alcohol by fermentation, you'll want a supply of sugar.
(c) You could try to make alcohol by fermentation using a breakfast cereal such as Quaker Oats.
(d) Yeast is needed to make alcohol.

15. There are a number of parallels that can be drawn between the flow of energy in the biosphere and some of the other chemical processes you studied in the earlier chapters. The figure at the right relates the processes taking place in the biosphere—photosynthesis, respiration, biochemical work. Think about this.

16. Prepare a concise statement (1 minute) on one of the following:
(a) Biochemistry   (c) Cell Theory
(b) Theory of Evolution   (d) Cell-Free Fermentation

17. Without looking back into the chapter, see if you can recall the key

functional groups characteristic of each of the following biomolecules. Then check your answers.

(a) sugars

(b) lipids

(c) proteins

(d) nucleic acids

(e) amino acids

18. Can you support the statement that ATP/ADP must have been nominated for their role as cellular energy transfer agents very early in the evolutionary process.

19. Comment on the statement that the essential nucleotides for nucleic acid synthesis aren't **essential.**

20. How is it that certain of nature's molecules can be described as **ambidextrous**?

21. What does each of the following terms have to do with the phenomenon of optical isomerism?

(a) tetrahedral carbon

(b) mirror images

(c) Louis Pasteur

(d) "handedness"

(e) tartaric acid

(f) polarized light

22. Here are some terms that have to do with protein biosynthesis. Making use of them, put together a brief outline that you can use in leading a discussion of the topic.

template	nucleic acid	codon
transcription	hydrogen bonds	replication
information	mutagen	Watson/Crick
polypeptide	base pairs	complementary strands
translation	double helix	ribosome
DNA/RNA		

23. In what way can the variety of cellular diseases variously referred to as *cancer* be connected to DNA and protein biosynthesis?

24. How is the DNA molecule implicated in the genetic disease called sickle cell anemia?

25. Outline the steps involved in the successful transfer of genetic information needed for protein synthesis.

26. Taking any of the twenty essential amino acids (Table 14-2) snap together a tetrapeptide.

27. What role do the weak interactions play in cellular biochemistry?

28. Explain how and why oxidations may be considered as dehydrogenations.

29. A friend has come to you for advice about setting up a moonshine still in your backyard. Advise him on raw materials, the chemistry of fermentation, and the possible hazards (other than the law).

The great book o'er the border went
And, good folk, that was the end.
But we hope you'll keep in mind
You and I were left behind.

      ...

      ...

      ...

May you now guard science' light
Kindle it and use it right
Lest it be a flame to fall
Downward to consume us all.

The first and the last paragraphs from **Galileo**
by Bertolt Brecht seem particularly appropriate
for ending our text!

A

Acceleration—Time rate of change of velocity.

Accuracy—The degree to which you have approached the true value. In other words, how correct you are.

Acid—A substance that is a proton donor; one that yields hydrogen ions in aqueous solutions. pH less than 7.

Activation Energy—The energy barrier that has to be overcome for a chemical reaction to take place. Often accompanied by formation of an activated complex.

Adhesion—Molecular forces between unlike particles, acting to hold them together. Adhesives.

Adsorption—The "sticking" of a thin layer of molecules to the surface of a solid substance.

ADP/ATP—ATP(adenosine triphosphate) hydrolyzes in water, releasing ADP (adenosine diphosphate), phosphate, and energy. The process is a principal source of cellular energy transfer in physiological systems.

Air Pollution—Fouling the atmospheric environment by introduction of natural and artificial contaminants.

Alchemy—A complex of magic, monkey business, and early scientific principles where the modern practice of chemistry began. Transmutation of base metals into gold was a favorite.

Alcohol—An organic molecule, generally consisting of a hydrocarbon portion and a hydroxyl (OH) group.

Aldehyde—An organic molecule containing the aldehyde, or —CHO functional group with its carbonyl (—CO—) carbon atom.

Alkali Metals—The IA family of elements. Extremely reactive, metallic species.

Alkaline Earth Metals—They follow the alkali metals in IIA and are generally "metallic."

Allotrope (allotropy)—Element substances that occur in more than one crystalline form: diamond and graphite.

Alloys—Homogeneous solutions of metals.

Alpha Helix—The folded, spiral chain pattern characteristic of polypeptides. Held together by hydrogen bonds.

Alpha Particle—The double positively charged nucleus of the helium atom. He^{++} Rutherford's bullet.

Amides—Organic molecules containing the $-CONH_2$ functional group.

Amines—Organic molecules derived from ammonia in which one or more hydrogens have been replaced by hydrocarbon groups.

Amphetamine—A class of organic substances that stimulate the central nervous system. One of the group of "abused" drugs.

Anode/Anions—The anode is the positive electrode in an electrochemical cell. Negatively charged anions migrate to it.

Antibiotic—Chemical substances with the ability to inhibit the action of bacteria. Many antibiotics are produced from microorganisms.

Atom—The smallest particle of an element substance retaining the characteristic physical and chemical properties of that element.

Atomic Mass (mass number)—The sum of the protons and neutrons in the nucleus. The number of nucleons.

Atomic Number—The number of protons in the nucleus, which is also equal to the number of electrons in a neutral atom.

Atomic Pile—A controlled, self-sustaining fission reactor, releasing a lot of resistance.

Autoprotolysis—An acid-base interaction between solvent molecules involving proton-transfer. In the case of water, hydronium and hydroxide ions are produced.

Autotrophic Organisms—Use external sources of energy to synthesize nutrients from simpler chemical substances.

Avogadro's Number of Particles (N)—The number of carbon atoms in 12.0000 grams of the C-12 isotope of carbon. That's about 6.023×10^{23}. The number of molecules in a mole of molecules.

B

Bacteriophage—Bacteria-infecting type of virus.

Barbiturates—A class of organic substances related to barbituric acid that act as sedatives, depressing the central nervous system. One of the group of "abused" drugs.

Base—A source of hydroxide ions in aqueous solutions or more generally, a proton acceptor.

Beta Particles—Electrons emitted during spontaneous decay of radioactive elements and cathode ray tube emanations.

Glossary

Black Body Radiation—The theoretical radiation energy limit attainable from a hot body at any given temperature. A *black body* is a perfect radiation emitter.

Boiling—Occurs when the pressure due to the atmosphere becomes equal to the vapor pressure of the liquid at that temperature.

Boyle's Law—The volume of a gas is inversely proportional to its pressure at constant temperature.

Buffers—Substances that have the chemical capacity to protect fluid systems from drastic changes in acidity and basicity. Generally salts of weak acid.

C

Calorie—A commonly used unit of heat: the amount needed to raise the temperature of one gram of water one degree centigrade.

Cancer—A disease caused by the abnormal growth of cells. Carcinogens are cancer-producing substances.

Cannabis Sativa—The hemp plant, source of marijuana and hashish.

Carbohydrates—The simple sugars and the more complex polysaccharides such as cellulose, starch, and glycogen.

Catalyst—Substances that generally promote and facilitate chemical reactions without being consumed in the process.

Cathode/Cations—The cathode is the negative electrode in an electrochemical cell. Positively charged cations migrate to it.

Cell—The simplest unit of living systems capable of independent existence.

Cell Theory (Schleiden & Schwann)—Stated that all living things are composites of varying complexity, put together from some small basic unit called a cell.

Charles Law—At constant pressure, the volume of a gas varies directly as its absolute temperature.

Chemical Equilibrium—For a chemical reaction capable of reversing itself, the state of affairs that arises when the forward and reverse processes occur at the same speed.

Chemical Properties—Those characteristic properties of an element or compound substance that have to do with the way in which they enter into chemical transformations called chemical reactions.

Chlorophyll—The several components of plants responsible for their green pigmentation. Essential to photosynthesis. The *a*-form is the yellowish-green pigment in all plants; the *b*-form is the blue-green pigment in green plants and algae.

Chromatography—A technique for physical separation and purification of substances based on the principle of selective adsorption on a solid support as the components are carried across it.

Chromosomes—The thread-like bodies in the cell nucleus containing the hereditary material, the genes.

Cloud Chamber—A device for detecting nuclear particles based on the fact that their passage through an atmosphere saturated with water vapor leaves a trail.

Compound—A homogeneous chemical combination of different elements in some definite chemical combination.

Condensation—Liquefaction of the vapors of a gaseous substance by cooling to below its normal boiling point. In distillation, the vapors pass through a "condensor."

Constant Composition (proportions)—The percent-mass composition of any pure compound substance will always have definite, fixed values, no matter the source of the substance.

Codon—The triplet sets of nucleic acid bases that code the specific amino acids in a growing protein chain.

Cohesion—Molecular forces between particles within a substance that act to unite them. Why falling water droplets are spherical.

Color—The visual appearance of an object due to the nature of light reflected from its surface.

Complementarity—Refers to situations where two different and conflicting descriptions of nature can both be made to partially fit the facts: classical and quantum mechanical descriptions of the atom.

Conductivity—The effectiveness of a substance at transferring heat (thermal conductivity) or electricity (electrical conductivity).

Conservation of Matter—Matter (mass) can neither be created nor destroyed; only transformed. The more general statement includes matter (mass) and energy conservation.

Coordination Compounds (complexes)—A central metal atom or ion that serves as a host to a number of other atoms, ions, or molecules. Usually the transition metal atoms.

Correspondence Principle (Bohr)—New theory must reduce to old theory at its boundary where the new conditions aren't important.

Coulomb—The basic unit of electric charge.

Covalence—Theory of chemical combination based on sharing of electrons.

Covalent Bond—Chemical bond between atoms sharing electrons.

Crystal—Systematically repeating, three-dimensional collection of atoms periodically extended through space.

Crystallization—A commonly employed physical method of separation that takes advantage of differences in solubility, one component of a mixture separating (crystallizing) first from a solvent as the solvent is cooled.

Crystal Structure—The orderly arrangement of atoms in the three-dimensional units or building blocks of which crystalline solids are built.

D

Decay Series (radioactive)—For all nuclei higher than 83, decay will take place until an atom of an element with stable nuclei is produced.

Dehydration—The removal or elimination of water.

Density—Mass per unit volume.

Distillation—A physical method of separation in which advantage is taken of the relative differences in volatility of a mixture of components.

DNA—Deoxyribonucleic acid. The genetic transfer agent in cellular protein synthesis. Transfer genetic traits and characteristics.

Double Helix—The parallel, spiral-stranded structures in nucleic acids as the polymeric nucleotide chains in DNA.

Ductility—The ease with which a substance can be drawn into wires or threads.

E

Electrode—The material that conducts electrons into and out of an electrolyte in an electrochemical system. Electrodes are sometimes reactive, sometimes inert.

Electrolysis—Decomposing a pure substance by passage of an electric current.

Electrolyte—A conducting medium for the passage of electricity by movement of ions.

Electron—A subatomic particle carrying a unit negative electric charge; electrons make up the non-nuclear particles within the atoms and play a principal role in chemical interactions.

Electron Affinity—Energy associated with one atom acquiring an electron from another.

Electron Shells—The principal energy levels in the electronic structure model for the atom.

Electron Spin—The intrinsic angular momentum, or spin-orientation of an electron.

Electronegativity—The relative ability of one kind of atom to attract electrons with respect to another.

Electrovalence—Theory of chemical combination based on transfer of electrons.

Element—Atoms of pure substances that cannot be decomposed to any other pure substance by any ordinary chemical processes.

Elementary Particles—The growing list of sub-atomic particles referred to as "fundamental"; lifetimes range from 10^{-6} to 10^{-11}: positron; neutrino; mesons . . .

Emission Spectra—Loss in energy in the form of light resulting from a change from a high energy state to a low energy state (excited state to ground state).

Endothermic Process—One that absorbs energy from its surroundings.

Energy—The ability to do useful work.

Enthropy—The component of a system's energy that is unavailable for doing useful work; the randomness of a system.

Enzyme—Biochemical catalysts and activators. Generally complex protein structures.

Equilibrium Vapor Pressure—Partial pressure due to vapor in equilibrium with its liquid phase at any temperature.

Equivalent Proportion—An equivalent relationship between relative quantities of two elements when combined with each other.

Escherichia coli (E. coli)—A rod-shaped bacterium commonly found in higher plants and animals.

Ester—An organic molecule containing the —COO— functional group as in ethyl acetate: $CH_3COOCH_2CH_3$. Pleasant-smelling substances.

Ether—Organic molecules in which hydrocarbon groups are bonded to oxygen as in the classic anesthetic, diethylether: $CH_3CH_2-O-CH_2CH_3$.

Eutrophication—Decay of organic matter that has accumulated in a body of water due to the presence of excessive amounts of dissolved nutrients; results in oxygen depletion from the water.

Evaporation—The process whereby the liquid state of a substance passes into the gaseous state at any temperature below the boiling point.

Exothermic Process—One that gives up energy to its surroundings.

Extraction—A physical method of separation and purification that, in the case of liquid-liquid extractions, takes advantage of differences in solubilities of a substance between two solvents.

F

Faraday of Electricity—The electric charge of one mole of electrons: 96,500 coulombs.

Fermentation—Formation of alcohol (or lactic acid) due to anaerobic decomposition of organic substances such as carbohydrates.

Filtration—Physical method for separating solids from liquids by allowing the liquid to pass through a semi-permeable membrane (filter paper), the solid phase remaining behind. Cigarette filters separate solids from gases.

Fission—Splitting heavy nuclei into fragments of smaller mass, accompanied by release in energy.

Friction—The resistance to the flow or motion of an object or substance over or through another.

Fusion—Joining light nuclei together forming heavier nuclei and releasing energy.

G

Gene—DNA. The hereditary unit of the chromosomes that control the development of inherital traits and characteristics.

Ground State Energy—The energy of an atom associated with electrons occupy-ing their lowest allowed energy levels.

H

Halogens—The family of chemical elements classified as VIIA, from fluorine to iodine (including astatine).

Harmonic Motion—That kind of motion described by the behavior of a "plucked" violin string, a swinging pendulum, or the oscillations of a diving board or a "slinky" type spring toy . . . in other words, regular motion describing a sine curve.

Heat—Energy associated with the random motion of a collection of molecules.

Hemoglobin—The iron-protein complex of red blood cells responsible for oxygen transport.

Heterogeneous—A heterogeneous material has portions that exhibit different properties.

Heterotroph—Organisms that depend on external food/energy sources: animals (man), certain types of plants, bacteria.

Homogeneous—A homogeneous material exhibits continous or identical properties throughout.

Humidity—The moisture content of the air, usually expressed as grams/cm^3

Hybridization—Equalization of energies to explain equivalency of chemical bonds formed by combination of orbitals of apparently different energies: i.e., hybridization of the *s*- and *p*-type carbon orbitals in methane.

Hydration—Binding of water molecules to a substance by weak hydrogen bonds.

Hydrocarbon—Organic molecules containing only carbon and hydrogen atoms. The four main subclasses are alkanes, alkenes, alkynes, aromatic hydrocarbons.

Hydrogen Bond—The *external* bond connecting two molecules via a hydrogen atom in one and an electronegative atom (usually O, N, F, Cl, . . .) in another. Water molecules hydrogen bond through oxygen.

Hydronium Ions—Hydrated protons.

Hypothesis—A generalization made from observations but based on as yet incomplete evidence.

I

Ideal Gas—Obeys the ideal gas law, $PV = nRT$.

Indeterminacy Principle—The position or

the velocity of a particle can be identified, but not simultaneously.

Inertia—The extent to which a body in motion or at rest offers resistance to any attempts to change that state of affairs.

Interference Phenomena—Constructive interference occurs when two wave trains impinge on each other exactly in phase, crest-to-crest, doubling the amplitude. Destructive interference occurs when waves are out-of-phase, and results in partial or complete cancellation.

Ion—Charged atom, positive or negative.

Ionic Bond—Chemical bonding due to electrostatic interaction between oppositely charged particles.

Ionization Potential—Energy required to remove an electron from an atom.

Isomers—Two chemical compounds with the same chemical composition but different spatial geometry, and therefore different properties.

Isotopes—Atoms of the same element (same Z values) but different mass numbers (different N values).

K

K_W—The ion product for water.

Ketones—Organic molecules containing the carbonyl (—CO—) group.

Kilometer—One thousand meters.

Kinetic Energy—Energy of motion; measured as half the product of mass and velocity-squared.

Kinetic-Molecular Theory—Gases, liquids, and solids are all composed of minute particles in constant motion.

L

Lanthanides (and actinides)—The group of 14 similar inner transition metallic elements positioned above slot 57 of the periodic table (lanthanides). A second such inner transition series that includes the transuranium elements positioned above slot 89.

Le Chatelier's Principle—Changes in a system at equilibrium tend to be compensated for by changes in the position of the equilibrium.

Lipids—More commonly known as fats, they are characteristically triglycerides, esters of glycerol and fatty acids.

M

Malleability—The ease with which a substance can be hammered or rolled into sheets.

Mass—The amount or quantity of matter in any body. Also a measure of the inertia of a body.

Materials—The different kinds of matter in their various forms.

Matter—Anything occupying space that has mass.

Melting Point (freezing point)—The temperature at which liquefaction usually occurs for any substance. A characteristic property of pure solids; about the same as the freezing point of pure liquids.

Micelles (in detergency)—Spherical structures in which a polar group is oriented toward the aqueous medium and a non-polar group toward the non-aqueous medium.

Micron—One-thousandth of a millimeter; one millionth of a meter.

Millimeter—One-thousandth of a meter.

Mitochondrion—One of the cytoplasmic cell bodies functioning in cell metabolism and protein synthesis.

Molecular Orbitals Models—Descriptive approximations of quantum mechanical bonding modes to supply qualitative models for simple molecules. Based on combinations of atomic orbitals (see orbital).

Momentum—For any moving body, the product of its mass and its velocity.

Multiple Proportions—The simple, small whole-number relationship that exists between the same elements when differently combined (i.e., H_2O and H_2O_2).

N

NAD/NADH$_2$—The coenzyme system that affects hydrogen transfer in biological oxidation-reduction reactions: nicotinamide adenine dinucleotide.

Nanometer—One-thousandth of a micron; often referred to as a millimicron.

Narcotic Drug—Chemical substances capable of producing *narcosis,* or stupor and insensibility: morphine, codeine, . . .

Neutralization—Acids react with bases, forming salts and water.

Neutron—One of the two principal subatomic particles found in the nucleus of all atoms except hydrogen. It is an electrically neutral particle whose mass is about the same as the proton.

Nitrogen Fixation—The "fixing" or formation of nitrogen compounds from free (molecular) nitrogen: synthetically by the Haber process; biologically in the roots of certain plants.

Nucleic Acids—Polymeric strands made from *nucleotide* units. Prominent components of all cells, they function in metabolism and energy-transfer.

O

Octet Rule—Atoms tend toward stable bonds by electron-sharing or electron-transfer until the eight-electron configuration has been achieved.

Orbital (electron)—The qualitative picture for the mathematical description supplied by quantum mechanics of the region in space where an electron is most likely to be found. A probability pattern: i.e., *s*-type electron orbital; *p*-type electron orbital.

Osmosis—Dilution of a solute by passage of solvent molecules through a semipermeable membrane.

Oxidation—Chemical reaction resulting in an increase in oxidation number. Often, oxygen serves as the oxidizing agent.

P

Pauli Exclusion Principle—No two electrons in any atom may have the same set of four quantum numbers.

Peptide—Two or more amino acid molecules linked together through peptide bonds between nitrogen in an amine group on one and carbon in the carboxyl group of the other.

Periodic Table—An ordering device for the elements according to increasing atomic number, horizontally; vertical order defines elements with family properties.

pH—Scale of measure for the relative acidity of aqueous solutions: 7 is neutral; less than 7 is acidic; greater than 7 is basic.

Phase—A visibly distinct part of a heterogeneous collection of matter.

Pheromone—Chemical substance secreted by an organism that causes specific behavioral responses in a second organism of the same species.

Photochemical Smog—Interaction of a

variety of noxious pollutants (mostly from the automobile) with ultraviolet light and a weather condition known as an *inversion,* producing the ingredients of atmospheric smog.

Photoelectric Effect—Various materials such as smooth metal surfaces emit free electrons when irradiated by light of certain wavelengths, especially visible and ultraviolet light.

Photons—Whenever one wishes to discuss radiant energy in terms of its particle aspects we speak of "photons," traveling at the speed of light, having mass, momentum and energy equal to *hv.*

Photosynthesis—Green plants affect conversion of carbon dioxide and water to carbohydrates and oxygen in the presence of sunlight.

Pigment—A chemical substance that absorbs certain wavelengths of visible light while reflecting others.

pi-type Chemical Bonds—Model for multiple bonds in which combination of *p*-type atomic orbitals takes place laterally, not linearly, i.e., the second or third bonds in the double and triple bonds in O_2 and N_2.

Polar Molecule—One characterized by an unequal distribution of electric charge within a molecule.

Polymers—Giant molecules, usually constructed from one or two basic units called monomiers that repeat at regular intervals in chains. The process in polymerization.

Precision—The degree to which you are able to rely on your result. In other words, how reproducible your result is.

Pressure of the Atmosphere—The pressure due to gas molecules colliding at any point in the atmosphere, but usually measured at sea level.

Proteins—Long-chained molecules made of polymerized alpha-amino acids linked through peptide bonds.

Proton—One of the two principal subatomic particles in the nucleus of all atoms; it is the nucleus of a hydrogen atom and carries a unit positive electric charge.

Q

Quantization of Energy—The packaging of energy into discrete energy levels according to the distribution of electrons in an atom: no electrons with between-level energies.

Quantum Mechanical Model—Atom model based on wave nature description of the behavior of matter.

R

Radical—An available energy sublevel with a free, or unpaired, bonding electron present: like molecular oxygen.

Radioactive Decay—Spontaneous transmutation of atomic nuclei.

Resonance—Representation of the electron-distribution in an ion or molecule as a composite of two or more forms in those cases where a single formula is inadequate: benzene; carbonate ion.

Rydberg Constant—The proportionality constant *R* in the empirical, spectroscopist's equation that Bohr was able to derive from theory: $\nu = R\left(\dfrac{1}{n_1{}^2} - \dfrac{1}{n_2{}^2}\right)$

S

Salt—The non-aqueous products of neutralization reactions.

Sigma-type Chemical Bonds—Model for single bonds in which linear combination of *s*- and *p*-type atomic orbitals takes place, i.e., (H_2 and F_2) or combinations thereof (H_2O and HF).

Significant Figures—The digits in an accurate measurement, plus the first doubtful digit.

Solubility—The maximum amount of a pure substance that will dissolve in 100 grams of solvent at a given temperature.

Spectral Lines—Single wavelengths of light arising from electronic transitions in atoms and molecules.

STP—Standard temperature and pressure. Defined as $0°C$ and 1 atmosphere, or $273°K$ and 760 torr.

Sub-atomic Particles—Principally, the electrons, protons, and neutrons which make up the atoms of all the known elements.

Sublimation—The ability to pass from the solid state directly to the vapor state without going through the liquid state.

Substance—A homogeneous form of matter of definite chemical composition.

Surface Tension—The tension of membrane-like structure due to the forces at the surface.

Synergist—Substance or combination of substances that cause an enhanced effect, beyond the expected, for one or more properties.

System—That sample or limited segment of the universe under investigation.

T

Temperature—A measureable quantity that is proportional to the average kinetic energy for a perfect gas.

Template—A pattern or model that supplies needed information: DNA/RNA transcription/replication, for example.

Transition Elements (metals)—Metallic elements from the block of elements in the middle of the periodic table: the B group elements and group VIII.

V

Valence—A number description of the general combining capacity of an element in its combinations.

van der Waals Forces—Weak attractive forces between atoms due to the presence of momentary electron-charge distributions.

Vapor Pressure—The partial pressure due to the vapor component in a mixture of gases.

Viscosity—The internal resistance of fluids to flow.

Vitalism—A false view, popular for a long time, that suggested the properties of the living organism to be due to a *vital* principle not based in the usual physical and chemical laws.

W

Work—The product of force and the distance through which that force operated.

X

X-radiations—High energy electromagnetic radiations of very short wavelengths.